Heinemann·Harrap

FRENCH
School Dictionary

Heinemann Educational Publishers,
Halley Court,
Jordan Hill,
Oxford OX2 8EJ

A division of Reed Educational & Professional Publishing Limited

OXFORD MELBOURNE AUCKLAND
JOHANNESBURG BLANTYRE GABORONE
IBADAN PORTSMOUTH (NH) USA CHICAGO

First Published in 1997
by Heinemann Educational Publishers
by arrangement with Chambers Harrap Publishers Ltd,
7 Hopetoun Crescent, Edinburgh EH7 4AY

00
10 9 8 7 6 5 4

A catalogue record is available for this book from
the British Library on request.

ISBN 0435 10862 X

Produced by Chambers Harrap Publishers Ltd
Cover design by Miller Craig & Cocking
Printed and bound in England at Clays Ltd, St Ives plc

Preface

The *Heinemann-Harrap French School Dictionary* is the result of
a unique collaboration between two famous publishing houses.
Combining the dictionary expertise of Harrap with Heinemann's
excellence in producing language courses, this volume is the
ideal learning tool for students up to GCSE level.

The editors have ensured that it contains a wide range of helpful,
up-to-date vocabulary, including all words required at GCSE. These
words are presented in a clear way with all part of speech labels
written in full. Indeed, the only abbreviations used are *m, f* and *mpl*
and *fpl* to mark masculine and feminine nouns.

In the middle of the book, there is a handy reference section
to help you with your studying. This includes lists of numbers,
months, days and countries, and a section on French verbs.
A * next to a French verb in the dictionary means that it is irregular
and that you can look it up in the reference section.

This dictionary conforms in all respects to the type of dictionary
allowed for examination use.

Preface

This Heinemann French 3 Pocket Dictionary is the result of a unique collaboration between two famous publishing houses. Combining the dictionary expertise of Harrap with Heinemann's excellence in producing language courses, this volume is the ideal learning tool for students up to GCSE level.

The editors have ensured that it contains a wide range of helpful, up-to-date vocabulary, including all words required at GCSE. These words are presented in a clear way, with all parts of speech labels given in full. Indeed, the only abbreviations used are m. and f. to mark masculine and feminine nouns.

In the middle of the book, there is a handy reference section to help you with your studies. This includes lists of numbers, months, days and countries, and a section on French verbs. A * next to a French verb in the dictionary means that it is irregular and that you can look it up in the reference section.

This dictionary conforms in all respects to the type of dictionary allowed for examination use.

Contents

French – English .... 1 – 242

Reference Section .... *i*

- Verbs .... *ii*

- Useful Word Groups .... *xxiv*

English – French .... 243 – 539

French-English

a *see* **avoir**.

à *preposition* (à + le = **au**, à + les = **aux**) (*direction: lieu*) to; (*temps*) till, to; **aller à Paris** to go to Paris; **de 3 à 4 h** from 3 till *or* to 4 (o'clock).

▮ (*position: lieu*) at, in; (*surface*) on; (*temps*) at; **être au bureau/à la ferme/au jardin/à Paris** to be at *or* in the office/on *or* at the farm/in the garden/in Paris; **à 8 h** at 8 (o'clock); **à mon arrivée** on (my) arrival; **à lundi!** see you (on) Monday!

▮ **à 10 kilomètres de …** 10 kilometres from … ; **le village est à 10 kilomètres** the village is 10 kilometres away; **à 5 minutes de …** 5 minutes from …

▮ (*description*) **l'homme à la barbe** the man with the beard; **verre à liqueur** liqueur glass.

▮ (*attribution*) **donner quelque chose à quelqu'un** to give something to somebody, give somebody something.

▮ (*devant infinitif*) **apprendre à lire** to learn to read; **travail à faire** work to do; **maison à vendre** house for sale.

▮ (*appartenance*) **c'est (son livre) à lui** it's his (book); **c'est à vous de** (*décider, protester etc*) it's up to you to; (*lire, jouer etc*) it's your turn to.

▮ (*prix*) for; **pain à 2F** loaf for 2F.

▮ (*poids*) by; **vendre au kilo** to sell by the kilo.

▮ (*moyen, manière*) **à bicyclette** by bicycle; **à la main** by hand; **à pied** on foot; **au crayon** with a pencil, in pencil; **au galop** at a gallop; **deux à deux** two by two.

abaisser *verb* (*levier*) to lower; (*store*) to pull down.

abaisser (s') *reflexive verb* (*barrière*) to lower; (*température*) to drop.

abandon *m noun* (*de sportif*) withdrawal; **à l'a.** in a neglected state.

abandonner *verb*
1 (*travail, combat*) to give up; (*endroit*) to desert; (*chien*) to abandon; **a. ses études** to drop out (of school/university).
2 (*renoncer*) to give up; (*sportif*) to withdraw.

abat-jour *invariable m noun* lampshade.

abattoir *m noun* slaughterhouse.

abattre * *verb* (*mur*) to knock down; (*arbre*) to cut down; (*animal*) to slaughter; (*avion*) to shoot down; (*personne*) to shoot.

abattre (s') *reflexive verb* **s'a. sur** (*pluie*) to come down on; (*foudre*) to strike.

abbaye *f noun* abbey.

abbé *m noun* (*prêtre*) priest.

abcès *m noun* abscess.

abdomen *m noun* stomach, abdomen.

abeille *f noun* bee.

abîmer *verb* to spoil.

abîmer (s') *reflexive verb* to get spoilt.

aboiement *m noun* bark; **aboiements** barking.

abominable *adjective* terrible.

abondance *f noun* une a. de plenty of.

abondant , -ante *adjective* plentiful.

abonné , -ée *m or f noun* (*à un journal, au téléphone*) subscriber.

abonnement *m noun* subscription; (**carte d'**)a. (*de train*) season ticket.

abonner (s') *reflexive verb* to subscribe, take out a subscription (à to).

abord (d') *adverb* first.

abordable *adjective* (*prix, marchandises*) affordable.

abordage *m noun* (*assaut*) boarding.

aborder *verb*
1 (*arriver au rivage*) to land.
2 (*personne*) to approach; (*problème*) to tackle; (*attaquer*) (*navire*) to board.

aboutir *verb* to succeed; a. à lead to; n'a. à rien to come to nothing.

aboyer *verb* to bark.

abréger *verb* (*récit*) to shorten.

abreuvoir *m noun* watering place; (*récipient*) drinking trough.

abréviation *f noun* abbreviation.

abri *m noun* shelter; a. (de jardin) (garden) shed; à l'a. de (*vent*) sheltered from; (*besoin*) safe from; sans a. homeless.

abricot *m noun* apricot.

abricotier *m noun* apricot tree.

abriter *verb* to shelter.

abriter (s') *reflexive verb* to (take) shelter.

abrupt , -e *adjective* (*pente etc*) steep.

abrutir *verb* a. quelqu'un (*travail, télévision*) to turn somebody into a vegetable.

absence *f noun* absence.

absent , -ente
1 *adjective* absent, away.
2 *m or f noun* absentee.

absenter (s') *reflexive verb* to go away (de from).

absolu , -ue *adjective* absolute.

absolument *adverb* absolutely.

absorbant , -ante *adjective* (*papier*) absorbent; (*travail, lecture*) absorbing.

absorber *verb* (*liquide*) to absorb; (*manger*) to eat.

abstenir * (s') *reflexive verb* to refrain (de faire from doing).

absurde *adjective* absurd.

abus *m noun* (*habituel*) abuse; (*passager*) over-indulgence (de in).

abuser *verb* (*exagérer*) to go too far; a. de (*situation, personne*) to take unfair advantage of; (*sucreries*) to over-indulge in.

acajou *m noun* mahogany.

accabler *verb* to overwhelm (de with).

accéder *verb* a. à (*lieu*) to reach.

accélérateur *m noun* accelerator.

accélérer *verb* to accelerate.

accélérer (s') *reflexive verb* to speed up.

accent *m noun* accent; a. tonique stress.

accepter *verb* to accept; a. de faire to agree to do.

accès *m noun* access (à to); (*de folie, colère, toux*) fit; (*de fièvre*) bout; 'a. interdit' 'no entry'; 'a. aux quais' 'to the trains'.

accessoires *mpl noun* (*de voiture etc*) accessories; (*de théâtre*) props.

accident *m noun* accident; a. d'avion/de train plane/train crash.

accidentel , -elle *adjective* accidental.

acclamations *fpl noun* cheers.

acclamer *verb* to cheer.

accommoder *verb* (*assaisonner*) to prepare.

accompagnateur , -trice *m or f noun* (*musical*) accompanist; (*de touristes*) guide.

accompagnement *m noun* (*musical*) accompaniment.

accompagner *verb* (*personne*) to go *or* come with; (*chose, musique*) to accompany.

accomplir *verb* (*tâche*) to carry out; (*exploit*) to accomplish; (*souhait*) to fulfil.

accord *m noun* agreement; (*musical*) chord; **être d'a.** to agree (**avec** with); **d'a.!** all right!

accordéon *m noun* accordion.

accorder *verb* (*donner*) to grant; (*instrument*) to tune; (*verbe*) to make agree; **s'a. quelque chose** to allow *or* give oneself something.

accorder (s') *reflexive verb* (*couleurs*) to go together; (*verbe, adjectif*) to agree.

accotement *m noun* verge (*of road*), shoulder.

accouchement *m noun* delivery.

accoucher *verb* to give birth (**de** to).

accouder (s') *reflexive verb* **s'a. à** *or* **sur** to lean on (*with one's elbows*).

accourir * *verb* to come running.

accroc *m noun* tear (**à** in).

accrochage *m noun* (*de voitures*) minor collision.

accrocher *verb* (*déchirer*) to catch; (*fixer*) to hook; (*suspendre*) to hang up (*on a hook*); **un titre qui accroche** an eye-catching title.

accrocher (s') *reflexive verb* (*se cramponner*) to cling (**à** to); (*ne pas céder*) *Familiar* to persevere.

accroupi , -ie *adjective* squatting.

accroupir (s') *reflexive verb* to squat (down).

accueil *m noun* welcome.

accueillant , -ante *adjective* welcoming.

accueillir * *verb* to welcome.

accumuler *verb* to pile up.

accumuler (s') *reflexive verb* to pile up.

accusation *f noun* accusation; (*au tribunal*) charge.

accusé , -ée *m or f noun* accused; (*cour d'assises*) defendant.

accuser *verb* to accuse (**de** of); (*rendre responsable*) to blame (**de** for).

acharnement *m noun* (stubborn) determination.

acharner (s') *reflexive verb* **s'a. sur** (*attaquer*) to lay into; **s'a. à faire** to struggle to do.

achat *m noun* purchase; **achats** shopping.

acheter *verb* to buy; **a. à quelqu'un** to buy from somebody; (*pour une personne*) to buy for somebody.

acheteur , -euse *m or f noun* buyer; (*dans un magasin*) shopper.

achever *verb* (*finir*) to finish (off); (*tuer*) (*personne*) to finish off; (*animal*) to put out of its misery; **a. de faire quelque chose** (*personne*) to finish doing something.

achever (s') *reflexive verb* (*finir*) to end.

acide
  1 *adjective* sour.
  2 *m noun* acid.

acier *m noun* steel.

acompte *m noun* deposit.

acquérir * *verb* (*acheter*) to purchase; (*obtenir*) to acquire.

acquis , -ise
  1 *past participle of* **acquérir**.
  2 *adjective* acquired.

acquisition *f noun* (*achat*) purchase.

acquittement *m noun* (*d'un accusé*) acquittal.

acquitter *verb* (*dette*) to pay; (*accusé*) to acquit; **s'a. envers quelqu'un** to repay somebody.

acrobate *m or f noun* acrobat.

acrobatie(s) *f(pl) noun* acrobatics.

acrobatique *adjective* acrobatic.

acte *m noun* (*action, de pièce de théâtre*) act.

acteur , -trice *m or f noun* actor, actress.

actif , -ive
  1 *adjective* active.
  2 *m noun* Grammaire active.

action *f noun* action; (*en Bourse*) share.

actionnaire *m or f noun* shareholder.

activer *verb* (*feu*) to boost.

activer (s') *reflexive verb* (*se dépêcher*) Familiar to get a move on.

activité *f noun* activity.

actualité *f noun* (*événements*) current events; **actualités** (*à la télévision etc*) news.

actuel , -elle *adjective* (*présent*) present; (*contemporain*) topical.

actuellement *adverb* at the present time.

adaptation *f noun* adjustment; (*de roman*) adaptation.

adapter *verb* to adapt; (*ajuster*) to fit (à to); **s'a. à** (*s'habituer*) to adapt to, adjust to; (*tuyau*) to fit.

additif *m noun* additive.

addition *f noun* addition; (*au restaurant*) bill.

additionner *verb* to add (à to); (*nombres*) to add up.

adhérent , -ente *m or f noun* member.

adhérer *verb* **a. à** (*coller*) to stick to; (*s'inscrire*) to join.

adhésif , -ive *adjective & m noun* adhesive.

adieu , -x *interjection & m noun* farewell.

adjectif *m noun* adjective.

adjoint , -ointe *m or f noun* assistant; **a. au maire** deputy mayor.

admettre * *verb* (*laisser entrer, accueillir, reconnaître*) to admit; (*autoriser, tolérer*) to allow; (*candidat*) to pass; **être admis à** (*examen*) to have passed.

administratif , -ive *adjective* administrative.

administration *f noun* administration; **l'A.** (*service public*) the Civil Service.

administrer *verb* (*gérer, donner*) to administer.

admirable *adjective* admirable.

admirateur , -trice *m or f noun* admirer.

admiratif , -ive *adjective* admiring.

admiration *f noun* admiration.

admirer *verb* to admire.

adolescent , -ente *m or f noun* adolescent, teenager.

adopter *verb* to adopt.

adoptif , -ive *adjective* (*fils, patrie*) adopted.

adoption *f noun* adoption.

adorable *adjective* adorable.

adoration *f noun* worship.

adorer *verb* to love, adore (**faire** doing); (*dieu*) to worship.

adosser (s') *reflexive verb* to lean back (**à** against).

adoucir *verb* (*peau etc*) to soften.

adoucir (s') *reflexive verb* (*temps*) to turn milder.

adresse *f noun* (*domicile*) address; (*habileté*) skill.

adresser *verb* (*lettre*) to send; (*compliment, remarque*) to address; **a. la parole à** to speak to; **s'a. à** to speak to; (*personne*) to go and see; (*bureau*) to inquire at; (*remarque*) to be aimed at.

adroit , -oite *adjective* skilful.

adulte *m or f noun* adult, grown-up.

adverbe *m noun* adverb.

adversaire *m or f noun* opponent.

aération *f noun* ventilation.

aérer *verb* to air (out).

aérien , -ienne *adjective* (*photo*) aerial; **attaque aérienne** air attack; **transports aériens** air transport.

aérobic *m noun* aerobics.

aérogare *f noun* air terminal.

aéroglisseur *m noun* hovercraft.

aéroport *m noun* airport.

aérosol *m noun* aerosol.

affaiblir *verb* to weaken.

affaiblir (s') *reflexive verb* to weaken.

affaire *f noun* (*question*) matter; **affaires** business; (*effets*) things; **avoir a. à** to have to deal with; **c'est mon a.** that's my business;

faire une bonne a. to get a bargain.

affamé , -ée *adjective* starving.

affection *f noun* (*attachement*) affection.

affectueusement *adverb* affectionately.

affectueux , -euse *adjective* affectionate, loving.

affichage *m noun* **panneau d'a.** hoarding.

affiche *f noun* poster.

afficher *verb* (*affiche*) to stick up.

affirmatif , -ive *adjective* (*ton, réponse*) positive, affirmative.

affirmation *f noun* assertion.

affirmer *verb* to assert.

affliger *verb* to distress.

affluence *f noun* crowd; **heure(s) d'a.** rush hour(s).

affluent *m noun* tributary.

affolement *m noun* panic.

affoler *verb* to drive crazy.

affoler (s') *reflexive verb* to panic.

affranchir *verb* (*lettre*) to stamp.

affreux , -euse *adjective* horrible.

affront *m noun* insult; **faire un a. à** to insult.

affronter *verb* to confront; (*mauvais temps, difficultés etc*) to brave.

affûter *verb* to sharpen.

afin

  1 *preposition* **a. de** (+ *infinitive*) in order to.

  2 *conjunction* **a. que** (+ *subjunctive*) so that.

africain , -aine *adjective & m or f noun* African; **nord-/sud- a.** North/South African.

Afrique (l') *f noun* Africa; **l'A. du**

Nord North Africa; **l'A. du Sud** South Africa.

agacer *verb* to irritate.

âge *m noun* age; **quel â. as-tu?** how old are you?; **d'un certain â.** middle-aged; **le moyen â.** the Middle Ages.

âgé , -ée *adjective* elderly; **â. de six ans** six years old; **enfant â. de six ans** six-year-old child.

agence *f noun* agency; (*succursale*) branch office; **a. immobilière** estate agent's office.

agenda *m noun* diary.

agenouiller (s') *reflexive verb* to kneel (down); **être agenouillé** to be kneeling (down).

agent *m noun* agent; **a. de change** stockbroker; **a. (de police)** policeman; **a. immobilier** estate agent; **a. secret** secret agent.

agglomération *f noun* built-up area; (*ville*) town.

aggloméré *m noun* chipboard.

aggraver *verb* to worsen.

aggraver (s') *reflexive verb* to worsen.

agile *adjective* agile.

agilité *f noun* agility.

agir *verb* to act.

agir (s') *impersonal verb* **il s'agit d'argent/etc** it's a question *or* matter of money/*etc*; **de quoi s'agit-il?** what is it?, what's it about?

agitation *f noun* (*de la mer*) roughness; (*d'une personne*) restlessness.

agité , -ée *adjective* (*mer*) rough; (*personne*) restless.

agiter *verb* (*remuer*) to stir; (*secouer*) to shake; (*brandir*) to wave.

agiter (s') *reflexive verb* (*enfant*) to fidget.

agneau , -x *m noun* lamb.

agrafe *f noun* hook; (*pour papiers*) staple.

agrafer *verb* (*robe*) to do up; (*papiers*) to staple.

agrafeuse *f noun* stapler.

agrandir *verb* to enlarge.

agrandir (s') *reflexive verb* to expand.

agrandissement *m noun* (*de ville*) expansion; (*de maison*) extension; (*de photo*) enlargement.

agréable *adjective* pleasant.

agréer *verb* **veuillez a. (l'expression de) mes salutations distinguées** (*dans une lettre*) yours faithfully.

agrès *mpl noun* (*de gymnastique*) apparatus.

agresser *verb* to attack.

agresseur *m noun* attacker; (*dans la rue*) mugger.

agressif , -ive *adjective* aggressive.

agression *f noun* (*dans la rue*) mugging.

agressivité *f noun* aggressiveness.

agricole *adjective* **ouvrier/machine a.** farm worker/machine; **travaux agricoles** farm work.

agriculteur , -trice *m or f noun* farmer.

agriculture *f noun* farming.

aguets (aux) *adverb* on the look-out.

ah! *interjection* ah!, oh!

ai *see* **avoir.**

aide
  1 *f noun* help; **à l'a. de** with the aid of.
  2 *m or f noun* (*personne*) assistant.

aider *verb* to help (**à faire** to do); **s'a. de** to make use of.

aïe! *interjection* ouch!

aie(s) , aient *see* avoir.

aigle *m noun* eagle.

aigre *adjective* sour.

aigu, -uë *adjective* (*douleur*) acute; (*voix*) shrill; (*lame*) sharp.

aiguillage *m noun* (*pour train*) points.

aiguille *f noun* (*à coudre, de pin*) needle; (*de montre*) hand.

aiguiller *verb* (*train*) to shunt.

aiguilleur *m noun* signalman; **a. du ciel** air-traffic controller.

aiguiser *verb* (*couteau*) to sharpen.

ail *m noun* garlic.

aile *f noun* wing; (*de moulin à vent*) sail; (*d'automobile*) wing.

ailier *m noun* Football wing(er).

aille(s) , aillent *see* aller [1].

ailleurs *adverb* somewhere else; **d'a.** (*du reste*) anyway; (*au fait*) by the way.

aimable *adjective* (*gentil*) kind; (*sympathique*) likeable.

aimant *m noun* magnet.

aimanter *verb* to magnetize.

aimer *verb* to love; **a. (bien)** (*apprécier*) to like, be fond of; **a. faire** to like doing *or* to do; **a. mieux** to prefer; **ils s'aiment** they're in love.

aîné, -ée
1 *adjective* (*de deux frères etc*) elder, older; (*de plus de deux*) eldest, oldest.
2 *m or f noun* elder *or* older (child); eldest *or* oldest (child).

ainsi *adverb* (*comme ça*) (in) this *or* that way; **a. que** as well as; **et a. de suite** and so on.

air [1] *m noun* (*gaz*) air; (*mélodie*) tune; (*paroles*) empty; **ficher en l'a.** *Familiar* (*jeter*) to chuck away; (*gâcher*) to mess up.

air [2] *m noun* (*expression*) look; **avoir l'a. fatigué/de s'ennuyer** to look tired/bored; **avoir l'a. d'un clochard** to look like a tramp.

aire *f noun* area; **a. de stationnement** parking area; **a. de repos** (*sur autoroute*) rest area.

aise *f noun* **à l'a.** (*dans un vêtement etc*) comfortable; (*dans une situation*) at ease; **mal à l'a.** uncomfortable.

aisé, -ée *adjective* (*riche*) comfortably off; (*facile*) easy.

ait *see* avoir.

ajouter *verb* to add (**à** to).

ajuster *verb* (*pièce, salaires*) to adjust; **a. à** (*adapter*) to fit to.

alaise *f noun* (waterproof) undersheet.

alarme *f noun* (*signal*) alarm; **a. antivol/d'incendie** burglar/fire alarm.

alarmer *verb* to alarm.

albanais, -aise *adjective & m or f noun* Albanian.

Albanie (l') *f noun* Albania.

album *m noun* album; **a. de timbres/photos** stamp/photo album.

alcool *m noun* alcohol; (*spiritueux*) spirits; **a. à 90°** surgical spirit.

alcoolique *adjective & m or f noun* alcoholic.

alcoolisé, -ée *adjective* alcoholic.

alcotest ® *m noun* breath test;

(*appareil*) breathalyzer.

alentours *mpl noun* surroundings.

alerte *f noun* alarm; **en état d'a.** on the alert.

alerter *verb* to warn.

algèbre *f noun* algebra.

Algérie (l') *f noun* Algeria.

algérien , -ienne *adjective & m or f noun* Algerian.

algue(s) *f(pl) noun* seaweed.

alibi *m noun* alibi.

aliéné , -ée *m or f noun* insane person.

alignement *m noun* alignment.

aligner *verb* to line up.

aligner (s') *reflexive verb* to line up.

aliment *m noun* food.

alimentaire *adjective* **ration/etc a.** food rations/etc; **produits alimentaires** foods.

alimentation *f noun* (*action*) feeding; (*régime*) diet; (*nourriture*) food; **magasin d'a.** grocer's shop.

alimenter *verb* (*nourrir*) to feed.

allaiter *verb* to breastfeed.

allécher *verb* to tempt.

allée *f noun* (*de parc etc*) path; (*de cinéma, supermarché etc*) aisle.

allégé , -ée *adjective* (*fromage etc*) low-fat.

alléger *verb* to make lighter.

Allemagne (l') *f noun* Germany; *Formerly* **l'A. de l'Est/Ouest** East/West Germany.

allemand , -ande
1 *adjective & m or f noun* German.
2 *m noun* (*langue*) German.

aller *¹ verb* (*auxiliary* **être**) to go; **pour a. à la gare, s'il vous plaît?** excuse me, how can I get to the station?; **a. à** (*convenir à*) to suit; **a. avec** (*vêtement*) to go with; **a. bien/mieux** (*personne*) to be well/better; **a. mal** not to be well; **il va le faire** he's going to do it; **il va partir** he's about to leave, he's going to leave; **va voir!** go and see!; **comment vas-tu?, (comment) ça va?** how are you?; **ça va!** all right!, fine!; **allez-y!** go on!, go ahead!; **allez! au lit!** come on *or* go on, (to) bed!

aller *² m noun* outward journey; **a. (simple)** single (ticket); **a. (et) retour** return (ticket).

aller (s'en) *reflexive verb* to go away; (*tache*) to come out.

allergie *f noun* allergy.

allergique *adjective* allergic (**à** to).

alliance *f noun* (*anneau*) wedding ring; (*de pays*) alliance.

allié , -ée *m or f noun* ally.

allier *verb* to combine (**à** with); (*pays*) to ally (**à** with).

allier (s') *reflexive verb* (*pays*) to become allied (**à** with, to).

allô! *interjection* hello!

allocation *f noun* allowance, benefit; **a. (de) chômage** unemployment benefit; **allocations familiales** child benefit.

allongé , -ée *adjective* (*étiré*) elongated.

allonger *verb*
1 (*bras*) to stretch out; (*jupe*) to lengthen.
2 (*jours*) to get longer.

allonger (s') *reflexive verb* to lie down.

allumage *m noun* (*de voiture*) ignition.

allumer *verb* (*feu, cigarette, gaz*) to light; (*électricité*) to turn *or* switch on.

allumer (s') *reflexive verb* (*lumière*) to come on.

allumette *f noun* match.

allure *f noun* (*vitesse*) pace; (*de véhicule*) speed; (*air*) look.

allusion *f noun* allusion; **faire a. à** to refer to.

alors *adverb* (*en ce cas-là*) so; **a. que** (*tandis que*) whereas.

alouette *f noun* (sky)lark.

alourdir *verb* to weigh down.

alourdir (s') *reflexive verb* to become heavy *or* heavier.

Alpes (les) *fpl noun* the Alps.

alphabet *m noun* alphabet.

alphabétique *adjective* alphabetical.

alpinisme *m noun* mountaineering.

alpiniste *m or f noun* mountaineer.

alterner *verb* to alternate.

altitude *f noun* height.

alu *m noun Familiar* **papier (d')a.** tinfoil.

aluminium *m noun* aluminium; **papier a.** tinfoil.

amabilité *f noun* kindness.

amaigri , -ie *adjective* thinner.

amaigrissant *adjective* **régime a.** slimming diet.

amande *f noun* almond.

amarrer *verb* to moor.

amarres *fpl noun* moorings.

amas *m noun* heap, pile.

amasser *verb* to pile up.

amasser (s') *reflexive verb* to pile up.

amateur *m noun* (*d'art etc*) lover; (*sportif*) amateur; **une équipe a.** an amateur team.

ambassade *f noun* embassy.

ambassadeur , -drice *m or f noun* ambassador.

ambiance *f noun* atmosphere.

ambitieux , -euse *adjective* ambitious.

ambition *f noun* ambition.

ambulance *f noun* ambulance.

ambulant , -ante *adjective* travelling.

âme *f noun* soul.

amélioration *f noun* improvement.

améliorer *verb* to improve.

améliorer (s') *reflexive verb* to improve.

aménagement *m noun* fitting out; conversion.

aménager *verb* (*arranger*) to fit out (**en** as); (*transformer*) to convert (**en** into).

amende *f noun* fine.

amener *verb* to bring.

amer , -ère *adjective* bitter.

américain , -aine *adjective & m or f noun* American; **nord-/sud-a.** North/South American.

Amérique (l') *f noun* America; **l'A. du Nord/Sud** North/South America.

amertume *f noun* bitterness.

ameublement *m noun* furniture.

ami , -ie *m or f noun* friend; (*de la nature etc*) lover (**de** of); **petit a.** boyfriend; **petite amie** girlfriend.

amical , -e, -aux *adjective* friendly.

amicalement *adverb* in a friendly way.

amiral , -aux *m noun* admiral.

amitié *f noun* friendship; **faire ses amitiés à quelqu'un** to send one's best wishes to somebody; **amitiés** (*sur une lettre*) love.

amonceler (s') *reflexive verb* to pile up.

amont (en) *adverb* upstream.

amorce *f noun* (*de pêcheur*) bait; (*de pistolet d'enfant*) cap.

amortir *verb* (*coup*) to cushion; (*bruit*) to deaden.

amortisseur *m noun* shock absorber.

amour *m noun* love; **pour l'a. de** for the sake of.

amoureux , -euse
1 *m or f noun* lover.
2 *adjective* **a. de quelqu'un** in love with somebody.

amour-propre *m noun* self-respect.

amovible *adjective* removable.

amphithéâtre *m noun* (*romain*) amphitheatre; (*à l'université*) lecture hall.

ample *adjective* (*vêtement*) full, ample.

ampleur *f noun* (*de robe*) fullness.

amplificateur *m noun* amplifier.

amplifier *verb* (*son*) to amplify; (*tendance*) to intensify.

ampoule *f noun* (*électrique*) (light) bulb; (*aux pieds etc*) blister; (*de médicament*) phial.

amputer *verb* to amputate.

amusant , -ante *adjective* amusing.

amusement *m noun* amusement.

amuser *verb* to entertain.

amuser (s') *reflexive verb* to enjoy oneself, have fun; **s'a. avec** to play with; **s'a. à faire** to amuse oneself doing.

amygdales *fpl noun* tonsils.

an *m noun* year; **il a dix ans** he's ten (years old); **Nouvel A.** New Year.

analogue *adjective* similar.

analyse *f noun* analysis.

analyser *verb* to analyse.

ananas *m noun* pineapple.

anarchie *f noun* anarchy.

anatomie *f noun* anatomy.

ancêtre *m noun* ancestor.

anchois *m noun* anchovy.

ancien , -ienne *adjective* old; (*meuble*) antique; (*qui n'est plus*) former; (*antique*) ancient; (*dans une fonction*) senior.

ancre *f noun* anchor.

ancrer *verb* to anchor.

andouille *f noun* = type of sausage; **espèce d'a.!** *Familiar* (you) nitwit!

âne *m noun* (*animal*) donkey; (*personne*) *Familiar* ass.

anéantir *verb* to wipe out.

anecdote *f noun* anecdote.

ânesse *f noun* she-ass.

anesthésie *f noun* an(a)esthesia; **a. générale** general an(a)esthetic.

anesthésier *verb* to an(a)esthetize.

ange *m noun* angel.

angine *f noun* sore throat.

anglais , -aise
1 *adjective* English.
2 *m or f noun* Englishman, Englishwoman; **les A.** the English.
3 *m noun* (*langue*) English.

angle *m noun* angle; (*de rue*) corner.

Angleterre (l') *f noun* England.

angoissant , -ante *adjective* distressing.

angoisse *f noun* (great) anxiety, anguish.

anguille *f noun* eel.

animal , -e, -aux *m noun* & *adjective* animal.

animateur , -trice *m or f noun* (*de télévision*) compere; (*de club*) leader, organizer.

animation *f noun* (*des rues*) activity; (*de réunion*) liveliness.

animé , -ée *adjective* lively.

animer *verb* (*débat*) to lead; (*soirée*) to liven up; (*mécanisme*) to drive.

animer (s') *reflexive verb* (*rue etc*) to come to life.

ankylosé , -ée *adjective* stiff.

anneau , -x *m noun* ring.

année *f noun* year; **bonne a.!** Happy New Year!

annexe *f noun* (*bâtiment*) annexe.

anniversaire *m noun* (*d'événement*) anniversary; (*de naissance*) birthday.

annonce *f noun* (*publicitaire*) advertisement; **petite a.** small ad; **les petites annonces** the classified advertisements.

annoncer *verb* to announce; (*vente*) to advertise; **a. la nouvelle à quelqu'un** to tell somebody the news; **s'a. pluvieux/difficile**/*etc* to look (like being) rainy/difficult/*etc*.

annuaire *m noun* (*téléphonique*) directory, phone book.

annuel , -elle *adjective* yearly.

annulaire *m noun* ring finger.

annuler *verb* to cancel.

ânonner *verb* to stumble through.

anonyme *adjective & m or f noun* anonymous (person).

anorak *m noun* anorak.

anormal , -e, -aux *adjective* abnormal.

anse *f noun* (*de tasse etc*) handle.

Antarctique (l') *m noun* the Antarctic.

antenne *f noun* (*de radio etc*) aerial; (*d'insecte*) antenna.

antérieur , -eure *adjective* (*précédent*) former; (*placé devant*) front.

antibiotique *m noun* antibiotic.

antibrouillard *adjective & m noun* (phare) a. fog lamp.

antichoc *invariable adjective* shockproof.

anticorps *m noun* antibody.

antillais , -aise *adjective & m or f noun* West Indian.

Antilles (les) *fpl noun* the West Indies.

antilope *f noun* antelope.

antipathique *adjective* disagreeable.

antiquaire *m or f noun* antique dealer.

antique *adjective* ancient.

antiquité *f noun* (*temps, ancienneté*) antiquity; (*objet ancien*) antique.

antiseptique *adjective & m noun* antiseptic.

antivol *m noun* anti-theft device.

anxiété *f noun* anxiety.

anxieux , -euse *adjective* anxious.

août *m noun* August.

apaiser *verb* to calm.

apercevoir * *verb* to see; (*brièvement*) to catch a glimpse of; **s'a. de** to realize.

apéritif *m noun* aperitif.

aplanir *verb* (*terrain*) to level; (*difficulté*) to iron out, smooth out.

aplati , -ie *adjective* flat.

aplatir *verb* to flatten (out).

aplomb (d') *adverb* (*meuble etc*) level, straight.

apostrophe *f noun* (*signe*) apostrophe.

apparaître * *verb* to appear.

appareil *m noun* (*électrique*) appliance; (*téléphone*) telephone; (*avion*) aircraft; (*dentaire*) brace; (*digestif*) system; **a. photo** camera; **qui est à l'a.?** (*au téléphone*) who's speaking?

apparemment *adverb* apparently.

apparence *f noun* appearance.

apparent , -ente *adjective* apparent; (*visible*) conspicuous, noticeable.

apparition *f noun* appearance; (*spectre*) apparition.

appartement *m noun* flat.

appartenir * *verb* to belong (**à** to).

appât *m noun* bait.

appâter *verb* to lure.

appauvrir (s') *reflexive verb* (*personne*) to get poorer; (*sol*) to become impoverished.

appel *m noun* (*cri*) call; (*en justice*) appeal; **faire l'a.** to take the register; **faire a. à** to call upon.

appeler *verb* (*personne, nom*) to call; (*en criant*) to call out to; **a. à l'aide** to call for help.

appeler (s') *reflexive verb* to be called; **il s'appelle Paul** his name is Paul.

appendicite *f noun* appendicitis.

appétissant , -ante *adjective* appetizing.

appétit *m noun* appetite (**de** for); **manger de bon a.** to tuck in; **bon a.!** enjoy your meal!

applaudir *verb* to applaud.

applaudissements *mpl noun* applause.

application *f noun* application.

applique *f noun* wall lamp.

appliqué , -ée *adjective* painstaking.

appliquer (s') *reflexive verb* **s'a. à** (*un travail*) to apply oneself to; (*concerner*) to apply to; **s'a. à faire** to take pains to do.

apporter *verb* to bring.

appréciation *f noun* (*de professeur*) comment (**sur** on).

apprécier *verb* (*aimer, percevoir*) to appreciate.

appréhender *verb* (*craindre*) to dread (**de faire** doing).

apprendre * *verb* (*étudier*) to learn; (*événement, fait*) to hear of; (*nouvelle*) to hear; **a. à faire** to learn to do; **a. quelque chose à quelqu'un** to teach somebody something; (*informer*) to tell somebody something; **a. à quelqu'un à faire** to teach somebody to do; **a. que** to learn that; (*être informé*) to hear that.

apprenti , -ie *m or f noun* apprentice.

apprentissage *m noun* apprenticeship; (*d'une langue*) learning (**de** of).

apprêter (s') *reflexive verb* to get ready (**à faire** to do).

apprivoisé , -ée *adjective* tame.

apprivoiser *verb* to tame.

approcher *verb*
1 (*mettre plus près*) to bring nearer (**de** to); (*venir plus près*) to come nearer (**de** to); **nous approchons de Lyon** we're getting near Lyons.
2 (*fin, hiver*) to draw nearer.

approcher (s') *reflexive verb* to come *or* get near(er) (**de** to); **il s'est approché de moi** he came up to me.

approfondir *verb* (*trou*) to dig

deeper; (*question*) to go into thoroughly.

approprié *adjective* appropriate (à for).

approprier (s') *reflexive verb* to take, help oneself to.

approuver *verb* (*décision*) to approve of; (*contrat*) to approve; **je t'approuve** I think you're right.

approvisionner (s') *reflexive verb* to get one's supplies (**de** of).

appui *m noun* support; **prendre a. sur quelque chose** to lean on something.

appui-tête *m noun* (*plural* appuis-tête) headrest.

appuyer *verb*
1 (*poser*) to lean, rest (**contre** against); **a. le doigt sur** to press one's finger on; **s'a. sur** to lean on, rest on.
2 a. sur quelque chose to rest on something; **a. sur un bouton** to press a button.

après
1 *preposition* (*temps*) after; (*espace*) beyond; **a. un an** after a year; **a. le pont** beyond the bridge; **a. avoir mangé** after eating.
2 *adverb* after(wards); **l'année d'a.** the following year.

après (d') *preposition* according to.

après-demain *adverb* the day after tomorrow.

après-midi *invariable m or f noun* afternoon.

apte *adjective* capable (à of).

aptitude *f noun* aptitude (à *or* pour for).

aquarelle *f noun* watercolour.

aquarium *m noun* aquarium.

aquatique *adjective* aquatic.

arabe
1 *adjective & m or f noun* (*personne*) Arab.
2 *adjective & m noun* (*langue*) Arabic; **chiffres arabes** Arabic numerals.

Arabie saoudite (l') *f noun* Saudi Arabia.

arachide *f noun* peanut.

araignée *f noun* spider.

arbitre *m noun Football, Boxe* referee; *Tennis* umpire.

arbitrer *verb* to referee; to umpire.

arbre *m noun* tree.

arbuste *m noun* (small) shrub.

arc *m noun* (*arme*) bow; (*voûte*) arch; (*de cercle*) arc; **en a. de cercle** in a semicircle.

arcades *fpl noun* arcade, arches.

arc-en-ciel *m noun* (*plural* arcs-en-ciel) rainbow.

arche *f noun* (*voûte*) arch.

archer *m noun* archer.

archiplein , -pleine *adjective Familiar* chock-a-block.

architecte *m noun* architect.

architecture *f noun* architecture.

archives *fpl noun* records.

Arctique (l') *m noun* the Arctic.

ardent , -ente *adjective* (*passionné*) ardent.

ardeur *f noun* (*énergie*) enthusiasm.

ardoise *f noun* slate.

are *m noun* = 100 square metres.

arène *f noun* (*pour taureaux*) bullring; **arènes** (*romaines*) amphitheatre.

arête *f noun* (*de poisson*) bone; (*de cube*) edge, ridge.

argent *m noun* (*métal*) silver; (*monnaie*) money; **collier en a.**

silver necklace; **a. de poche** pocket money; **a. liquide** cash.

argenterie *f noun* silverware.

argentin, -ine *adjective & m or f noun* Argentinian.

Argentine (l') *f noun* Argentina.

argile *f noun* clay.

argot *m noun* slang.

argument *m noun* argument.

arithmétique *f noun* arithmetic.

armature *f noun* (*de lunettes, tente*) frame.

arme *f noun* arm, weapon; **a. à feu** firearm.

armée *f noun* army; **a. de l'air** air force.

armement(s) *m(pl) noun* arms.

armer *verb* (*personne*) to arm (**de** with); (*fusil*) to cock; **s'a.** to arm oneself (**de** with).

armoire *f noun* (*penderie*) wardrobe; **a. à pharmacie** medicine chest *or* cabinet.

armure *f noun* armour.

arôme *m noun* (*goût*) flavour; (*odeur*) (pleasant) smell.

arracher *verb* (*clou, dent, cheveux, page*) to pull out; (*plante*) to pull up; **a. quelque chose à quelqu'un** to snatch something from somebody.

arranger *verb* (*rendre beau*) to fix up; (*réparer*) to fix; (*organiser*) to arrange; **ça m'arrange** that suits me.

arranger (s') *reflexive verb* to come to an agreement; (*finir bien*) to turn out fine; **s'a. pour faire** to manage to do.

arrestation *f noun* arrest; **en état d'a.** under arrest.

arrêt *m noun* (*halte, endroit*) stop; (*action*) stopping; **a. d'autobus/ de bus** bus stop; **temps d'a.**

pause; **sans a.** constantly.

arrêté *m noun* order.

arrêter *verb*
1 (*personne, animal, véhicule*) to stop; (*criminel*) to arrest.
2 (*cesser*) to stop; **il n'arrête pas de critiquer**/*etc* he's always criticizing/*etc*.

arrêter (s') *reflexive verb* to stop (**de faire** doing).

arrhes *f pl noun* deposit.

arrière
1 *adverb* **en a.** (*marcher*) backwards; (*rester*) behind.
2 *m noun & invariable adjective* rear, back; **faire marche a.** to reverse, back.
3 *m noun Football* (full) back.

arrière-boutique *f noun* back room (*of a shop*).

arrière-goût *m noun* aftertaste.

arrière-grand-mère *f noun* great-grandmother.

arrière-grand-père *m noun* great-grandfather.

arrivage *m noun* consignment.

arrivée *f noun* arrival; (*ligne, poteau*) (winning) post.

arriver *verb* (*auxiliary* être) (*personne*) to arrive; (*événement*) to happen; **a. à** to reach; **a. à faire** to manage to do; **a. à quelqu'un** to happen to somebody; **il m'arrive d'oublier**/*etc* I (sometimes) forget/*etc*.

arrondir *verb* (*chiffre, angle*) to round off.

arrondissement *m noun* (*d'une ville*) district.

arrosage *m noun* watering.

arroser *verb* (*terre*) to water.

arrosoir *m noun* watering can.

art *m noun* art.

artère *f noun* artery; (*rue*) main

road.

artichaut *m noun* artichoke.

article *m noun* (*de presse, de commerce, en grammaire*) article; **articles de toilette** toiletries.

articulation *f noun* (*de membre*) joint.

articuler *verb* (*mot*) to articulate; **articule!** speak clearly!

artifice *m noun* **feu d'a.** firework display.

artificiel , -elle *adjective* artificial.

artisan *m noun* craftsman.

artiste *m or f noun* artist.

artistique *adjective* artistic.

as [1] *see* **avoir**.

as [2] *m noun* (*carte, champion*) ace.

ascenseur *m noun* lift.

ascension *f noun* ascent; **l'A.** Ascension Day.

asiatique *adjective & m or f noun* Asian.

Asie (l') *f noun* Asia.

asile *m noun* (*abri*) shelter.

aspect *m noun* (*air*) appearance.

asperge *f noun* asparagus.

asperger *verb* to spray (**de** with).

asphyxie *f noun* suffocation.

asphyxier *verb* to suffocate.

aspirateur *m noun* vacuum cleaner, hoover ®; **passer l'a.** (*dans la maison*) to vacuum *or* hoover (the house).

aspirer *verb* (*liquide*) to suck up.

aspirine *f noun* aspirin.

assaisonnement *m noun* seasoning.

assaisonner *verb* to season.

assassin *m noun* murderer.

assassinat *m noun* murder.

assassiner *verb* to murder.

assaut *m noun* onslaught; **prendre d'a.** to (take by) storm.

assemblée *f noun* (*personnes réunies*) gathering; (*parlement*) assembly.

assembler *verb* to put together.

assembler (s') *reflexive verb* to gather.

asseoir * **(s')** *reflexive verb* to sit (down).

assez *adverb* enough; **a. de pain/ gens** enough bread/people; **j'en ai a.** I've had enough; **a. grand/ etc** (*suffisamment*) big/*etc* enough (**pour faire** to do); **a. fatigué**/*etc* (*plutôt*) fairly *or* quite tired/*etc*.

assiéger *verb* (*magasin, vedette*) to mob.

assiette *f noun* plate; **a. anglaise** (assorted) cold meats.

assis , -ise
1 *past participle of* **asseoir**.
2 *adjective* sitting (down).

assises *fpl noun* (**cour d'**)**a.** court of assizes.

assistance *f noun* (*assemblée*) audience; (*aide*) assistance.

assistant , -ante *m or f noun* assistant; **assistant(e) social(e)** social worker; **assistante maternelle** child minder.

assister *verb*
1 (*aider*) to help.
2 **a. à** (*réunion, cours etc*) to attend; (*accident*) to witness.

association *f noun* association.

associé , -ée *m or f noun* partner.

associer (s') *reflexive verb* to associate (**à** with).

assoiffé , -ée *adjective* thirsty.

assombrir (s') *reflexive verb* (*ciel*) to cloud over.

assommer *verb* (*personne*) to

knock unconscious.

assortiment *m noun* assortment.

assortir *verb* to match.

assoupir (s') *reflexive verb* to doze off.

assouplir *verb* (*personne*) to make supple; (*chaussure*) to soften up; **s'a.** (*personne*) to get supple; (*chaussure*) to soften up.

assouplissement *m noun* exercices d'a. limbering up exercises.

assourdir *verb* to deafen.

assourdissant , -ante *adjective* deafening.

assurance *f noun* (*confiance*) self-assurance; (*contrat*) insurance.

assurer *verb* (*par un contrat*) to insure; (*travail*) to carry out; **s'a.** to insure oneself (**contre** against); **a. à quelqu'un que** to assure somebody that; **a. quelqu'un de quelque chose** to assure somebody of something; **s'a. que/de** to make sure that/of.

astérisque *m noun* asterisk.

asthmatique *adjective & m or f noun* asthmatic.

asthme *m noun* asthma.

asticot *m noun* maggot.

astiquer *verb* to polish.

astre *m noun* star.

astrologie *f noun* astrology.

astronaute *m or f noun* astronaut.

astronomie *f noun* astronomy.

astuce *f noun* (*procédé*) knack, trick.

astucieux , -euse *adjective* clever.

atelier *m noun* (*d'ouvrier etc*) workshop; (*de peintre*) studio.

athlète *m or f noun* athlete.

athlétique *adjective* athletic.

athlétisme *m noun* athletics.

atlantique
1 *adjective* Atlantic.
2 *m noun* l'A. the Atlantic.

atlas *m noun* atlas.

atmosphère *f noun* atmosphere.

atome *m noun* atom.

atomique *adjective* (*bombe etc*) atomic.

atout *m noun* trump (card).

atroce *adjective* atrocious.

atrocités *fpl noun* atrocities.

attabler (s') *reflexive verb* to sit down at the/a table.

attachant , -ante *adjective* (*enfant etc*) likeable.

attaché-case *m noun* attaché case.

attacher *verb* (*lier*) to tie (up) (à to); (*boucler, fixer*) to fasten (à to); **s'a. à quelqu'un** to become attached to somebody.

attaquant , -ante *m or f noun* attacker.

attaque *f noun* attack.

attaquer *verb* to attack; **s'a. à** to attack.

attarder (s') *reflexive verb* to dawdle.

atteindre * *verb* to reach; être atteint de (*maladie*) to be suffering from.

attelage *m noun* (*animaux*) team.

atteler *verb* (*bêtes*) to harness; (*remorque*) to hook up.

attendre *verb*
1 (*ami, taxi*) to wait for; elle attend un bébé she's expecting a baby; **a. que quelqu'un vienne** to wait for somebody to come; en attendant que ... (+ *subjunctive*) until ...
2 (*patienter*) to wait; **a. une heure** to wait for an hour; **s'a. à** to ex-

pect; **faire a. quelqu'un** to keep somebody waiting; **en attendant** meanwhile.

attendrir (s') *reflexive verb* to be moved (**sur** by).

attentat *m noun* attempt on somebody's life; **a. (à la bombe)** (bomb) attack.

attente *f noun* wait(ing); **salle d'a.** waiting room.

attentif , -ive *adjective (personne)* attentive; *(examen)* careful.

attention *f noun* attention; **faire a. à** to pay attention to; **il a fait a. de ne pas la blesser** he took care not to hurt her; **a.!** watch out!, be careful!; **a. à la voiture!** watch out for the car!; **a. au départ!** mind the doors!

attentivement *adverb* attentively.

atterrir *verb* to land.

atterrissage *m noun* landing.

attirer *verb* to attract; *(attention)* to draw (**sur** on).

attitude *f noun* attitude.

attraction *f noun* attraction.

attraper *verb (ballon, maladie, voleur, train etc)* to catch; *(accent)* to pick up; **se laisser a.** *(duper)* to get taken in.

attrayant , -ante *adjective* attractive.

attribuer *verb (donner)* to assign (**à** to); *(décerner)* to award (**à** to).

attribut *m noun* attribute.

attrister *verb* to sadden.

attroupement *m noun (disorderly)* crowd.

attrouper (s') *reflexive verb* to gather.

au *see* **à, le.**

aube *f noun* dawn.

auberge *f noun* inn; **a. de jeunesse** youth hostel.

aubergine *f noun* aubergine.

aucun , -une

1 *adjective* no, not any; **il n'a a. talent** he has no talent, he doesn't have any talent; **a. professeur n'est venu** no teacher has come.

2 *pronoun* none, not any; **il n'en a a.** he has none (at all), he doesn't have any (at all).

audace *f noun (courage)* daring.

audacieux , -euse *adjective* daring.

au-dessous de *preposition* under, below.

au-dessus

1 *adverb* above; over; *(à l'étage supérieur)* upstairs.

2 *preposition* **au-d. de** above; *(âge, température, prix)* over.

audio *invariable adjective* audio.

auditeur , -trice *m or f noun* listener.

auditoire *m noun* audience.

auge *f noun (feeding)* trough.

augmentation *f noun* increase (**de** in, of); **a. de salaire** (pay) rise; **être en a.** to be on the increase.

augmenter *verb* to increase (**de** by).

aujourd'hui *adverb* today.

auprès de *preposition* by, close to.

auquel *see* **lequel.**

aura , aurai(t) *etc see* **avoir.**

aurore *f noun* dawn.

ausculter *verb* to examine (*with a stethoscope*).

aussi

1 *adverb (comparaison)* as; **a. sage que** as wise as.

I *(également)* too, also, as well; **moi a.** so do, can, am *etc* I.

▮ (*tellement*) so; **un repas a. dé-licieux** so delicious a meal, such a delicious meal.
2 *conjunction* therefore, so.

aussitôt
1 *adverb* immediately; **a. que** as soon as; **a. levé, il s'est habillé** as soon as he was up, he got dressed.
2 *conjunction* **a. que** as soon as.

Australie (l') *f noun* Australia.

australien , -ienne *adjective &
m or f noun* Australian.

autant *adverb* **a. de … que** (*quantité*) as much … as; (*nombre*) as many … as.
▮ **a. de** (*tant de*) so much; (*nombre*) so many.
▮ **a. (que)** (*souffrir, lire etc*) as much (as); **en faire a.** to do the same; **j'aimerais a. aller au ciné-ma** I'd just as soon go to the cinema.

autel *m noun* altar.

auteur *m noun* (*de livre*) author; (*de chanson*) composer.

authentique *adjective* genuine.

auto *f noun* car; **autos tampon-neuses** bumper cars.

autobus *m noun* bus.

autocar *m noun* bus, coach.

autocollant *m noun* sticker.

auto-école *f noun* driving school.

autographe *m noun* autograph.

automatique *adjective* auto-matic.

automatiquement *adverb* automatically.

automne *m noun* autumn.

automobile *f noun & adjective* car.

automobiliste *m or f noun* motorist, driver.

autoradio *m noun* car radio.

autorisation *f noun* permission.

autoriser *verb* to permit (**à faire** to do).

autoritaire *adjective* authoritar-ian.

autorité *f noun* authority.

autoroute *f noun* motorway.

auto-stop *m noun* hitchhiking; **faire de l'a.** to hitchhike.

auto-stoppeur , -euse *m or f noun* hitchhiker.

autour
1 *adverb* around.
2 *preposition* **a. de** around.

autre *adjective & pronoun* other; **un a. livre** another book; **un a.** another (one); **l'a. jour** the other day; **d'autres** others; **d'autres médecins** other doctors; **d'au-tres questions?** any other ques-tions?; **quelqu'un/personne/rien d'a.** somebody/no one/nothing else; **a. chose/part** something/somewhere else; **qui/quoi d'a.?** who/what else?; **l'un l'a., les uns les autres** each other; **l'un et l'a.** both (of them); **l'un ou l'a.** either (of them); **ni l'un ni l'a.** neither (of them); **les uns…. les autres** some … others; **d'un mo-ment à l'a.** any moment.

autrefois *adverb* in the past.

autrement *adverb* differently; (*sinon*) otherwise; **a. dit** in other words.

Autriche (l') *f noun* Austria.

autrichien , -ienne *adjective & m or f noun* Austrian.

autruche *f noun* ostrich.

aux *see* **à, le.**

auxiliaire *adjective & m noun* (*verbe*) **a.** auxiliary (verb).

auxquel(le)s *see* **lequel.**

aval (en) *adverb* downstream.

avalanche *f noun* avalanche.

avaler *verb* to swallow.

avance *f noun* à l'a., d'a. in advance; **en a.** (*arriver, partir*) early; (*avant l'horaire prévu*) ahead (of time); **en a. sur** ahead of; **avoir une heure d'a.** (*train etc*) to be an hour early.

avancement *m noun* (*de personne*) promotion.

avancer *verb*
1 (*date*) to bring forward; (*main, chaise*) to move forward; **a. de l'argent à quelqu'un** to advance somebody money.
2 (*personne*) to move forward; (*armée*) to advance; (*montre*) to be fast.

avancer (s') *reflexive verb* to move forward.

avant
1 *preposition* before; **a. de voir** before seeing; **a. qu'il (ne) parte** before he leaves; **a. tout** above all.
2 *adverb* before; **en a.** (*mouvement*) forward; (*en tête*) ahead; **la nuit d'a.** the night before.
3 *m noun & invariable adjective* front.
4 *noun* (*d'un véhicule*) front; (*joueur*) forward.

avantage *m noun* advantage.

avantager *verb* to favour.

avantageux , -euse *adjective* (*prix*) reasonable; (*produit*) good value; (*conditions*) favourable.

avant-bras *invariable m noun* forearm.

avant-dernier , -ière *adjective & m or f noun* last but one.

avant-hier *adverb* the day before yesterday.

avant-veille *f noun* l'a. (de) two days before.

avare
1 *adjective* miserly.
2 *m or f noun* miser.

avarice *f noun* meanness.

avarié , -ée *adjective* (*aliment*) rotting, rotten.

avec *preposition* with; (*envers*) to(wards); **et a. ça?** (*dans un magasin*) anything else?

avenir *m noun* future; **à l'a.** in future.

aventure *f noun* adventure.

aventurer (s') *reflexive verb* to venture.

aventurier , -ière *m or f noun* adventurer.

avenue *f noun* avenue.

averse *f noun* shower.

avertir *verb* (*mettre en garde*) to warn; (*informer*) to notify.

avertissement *m noun* warning; notification.

avertisseur *m noun* (*klaxon®*) horn; **a. d'incendie** fire alarm.

aveu , -x *m noun* confession.

aveugle
1 *adjective* blind.
2 *m or f noun* blind man, blind woman; **les aveugles** the blind.

aveugler *verb* to blind.

aveuglette (à l') *adverb* **chercher quelque chose à l'a.** to grope around for something.

aviateur , -trice *m or f noun* airman, airwoman.

aviation *f noun* (*armée de l'air*) air force; (*avions*) aircraft; **l'a.** (*activité*) flying; **faire de l'a.** to go flying.

avion *m noun* aircraft, (aero)-plane; **a. à réaction** jet; **a. de ligne** airliner; **par a.** (*sur lettre*) airmail; **en a., par a.** (*voyager*) by plane, by air.

aviron *m noun* oar; **l'a.** (*sport*) rowing; **faire de l'a.** to row.

avis *m noun* opinion; (*communiqué*) notice; **à mon a.** in my opinion; **à ton a., ils vont se marier?** do you think they'll get married?; **changer d'a.** to change one's mind.

avocat , -ate

1 *m or f noun* barrister.

2 *m noun* (*fruit*) avocado (pear).

avoine *f noun* oats.

avoir *

1 *auxiliary verb* to have; **je l'ai vu** I've seen him.

2 *verb* (*posséder*) to have; (*obtenir*) to get; **qu'est-ce que tu as?** what's the matter with you?; **il n'a qu'à essayer** he only has to try; **a. faim/chaud/etc** to be *or* feel hungry/hot/etc; **a. cinq ans** to be five (years old); **j'en ai pour dix minutes** this will take me ten minutes.

3 (*locution*) **il y a** there is, *plural* there are; **il y avait** there was, *plural* there were; **il y a six ans** six years ago.

avortement *m noun* abortion.

avorter *verb* (*médecin*) to abort; (*femme*) to have an abortion; **se faire a.** to have an abortion.

avouer *verb* to confess (**que** that).

avril *m noun* April; **le premier** April Fools' Day.

axe *m noun* (*ligne*) axis; (*essieu*) axle; **grands axes** (*routes*) main roads.

ayant , ayez , ayons *see* **avoir**.

azote *m noun* nitrogen.

azur *m noun* (sky) blue; **la Côte d'A.** the (French) Riviera.

B

baby-foot *invariable m noun* table football.

baby-sitting *m noun* baby-sitting; **faire du b.** to baby-sit.

bac
1 *m noun* (*bateau*) ferry(boat); (*cuve*) tank.
2 *abbreviation* = **baccalauréat**.

baccalauréat *m noun* school leaving certificate.

bâche *f noun* tarpaulin.

bachelier , -ière *m or f noun* holder of the *baccalauréat*.

bâcher *verb* to cover over (*with a tarpaulin*).

badaud *m noun* onlooker.

badigeonner *verb* (*mur*) to whitewash; (*écorchure*) to coat, paint.

bafouiller *verb* to stammer.

bagage *m noun* piece of luggage *or* baggage; **bagages** luggage, baggage; **faire ses bagages** to pack one's cases.

bagarre *f noun* fight(ing).

bagarrer (se) *reflexive verb* Familiar to fight.

bagnole *f noun* Familiar car.

bague *f noun* (*anneau*) ring.

baguette *f noun* stick; (*de chef d'orchestre*) baton; (*pain*) baguette (*French stick*); **baguettes** (*de tambour*) drumsticks; (*pour manger*) chopsticks; **b. (magique)** (magic) wand.

baie *f noun* (*de côte*) bay.

baignade *f noun* (*bain*) bathe, bathing; (*endroit*) bathing place.

baigner *verb*
1 (*œil, blessure*) to bathe; (*enfant*) to bath.
2 **b. dans** (*aliment*) to be steeped in.

baigner (se) *reflexive verb* to go swimming *or* bathing.

baigneur , -euse
1 *m or f noun* bather.
2 *m noun* (*poupée*) baby doll.

baignoire *f noun* bath (tub).

bâillement *m noun* yawn.

bâiller *verb* to yawn.

bâillon *m noun* gag.

bâillonner *verb* to gag.

bain *m noun* bath; **salle de bain(s)** bathroom; **b. moussant** bubble bath; **prendre un b. de soleil** to sunbathe; **être dans le b.** *Familiar* to have got into the swing of things; **b. de bouche** mouthwash.

baiser *m noun* kiss.

baisse *f noun* fall, drop (**de** in); **en b.** falling.

baisser *verb*
1 (*rideau, vitre de voiture*) to lower; (*radio, chauffage*) to turn down; **b. la tête** to duck; **b. les yeux** to look down.
2 (*température, prix*) to fall; **le jour baisse** night is falling.

baisser (se) *reflexive verb* to bend down.

bal *m noun* (*plural* **bals**) ball; (*populaire*) dance.

balade *f noun* Familiar walk; (*en auto*) drive.

balader (se) *reflexive verb* Familiar (*à pied*) to (go for a) walk; (*en voiture*) to go for a drive.

baladeur *m noun* Walkman®.

balai *m noun* broom; **manche à b.** broomstick.

balance *f noun* (pair of) scales.

balancer *verb* (*bras, jambe*) to swing; (*lancer*) *Familiar* to chuck; (*se débarrasser de*) *Familiar* to chuck out.

balancer (se) *reflexive verb* to sway (from side to side).

balançoire *f noun* (*suspendue*) swing.

balayer *verb* to sweep (up); (*enlever*) to sweep away.

balayette *f noun* (hand) brush.

balayeur , -euse
 1 *m or f noun* roadsweeper.
 2 *f noun* (*véhicule*) roadsweeper.

balbutier *verb* to stammer.

balcon *m noun* balcony.

baleine *f noun* whale.

balisage *m noun* beacons.

balise *f noun* (*pour naviguer*) beacon.

baliser *verb* to mark with beacons.

ballast *m noun* (*pierres*) ballast.

balle *f noun* (*de tennis, golf etc*) ball; (*d'arme*) bullet.

ballerine *f noun* ballerina.

ballet *m noun* ballet.

ballon *m noun* (*jouet d'enfant, appareil*) balloon; (*sport*) ball; **b. de football** football.

ballot *m noun* bundle.

ballottage *m noun* (*scrutin*) second ballot.

balnéaire *adjective* **station b.** seaside resort.

balustrade *f noun* (hand)rail.

bambin *m noun* tiny tot.

bambou *m noun* bamboo.

ban *m noun* (*applaudissements*) round of applause; **un (triple) b. pour …** three cheers for …

banane *f noun* banana.

banc *m noun* (*siège*) bench; **b. de sable** sandbank.

bancaire *adjective* **compte b.** bank account.

bandage *m noun* bandage.

bande [1] *f noun* (*de terrain, papier etc*) strip; (*de film*) reel; (*rayure*) stripe; (*pansement*) bandage; (*sur la chaussée*) line; **b. (magnétique)** tape; **b. vidéo** videotape; **b. dessinée** comic strip.

bande [2] *f noun* (*groupe*) gang.

bandeau , -x *m noun* (*sur les yeux*) blindfold; (*pour la tête*) headband.

bander *verb* (*blessure*) to bandage; (*yeux*) to blindfold.

banderole *f noun* (*sur montants*) banner.

bandit *m noun* robber.

bangladais, -aise *adjective & m or f noun* Bangladeshi.

Bangladesh (le) *m noun* Bangladesh.

banlieue *f noun* **la b.** the suburbs; **une b.** a suburb; **maison/etc de b.** suburban house/etc.

banque *f noun* bank; (*activité*) banking.

banquette *f noun* (*de véhicule, train*) seat.

banquier *m noun* banker.

banquise *f noun* ice floe.

baptême *m noun* christening, baptism.

baptiser *verb* (*enfant*) to christen, baptize.

baquet *m noun* tub, basin.

bar *m noun* (*lieu, comptoir*) bar.

baraque *f noun* hut, shack.

baraquement *m noun* (make-shift) huts.

barbare *adjective* (*cruel*) barbaric.

barbe *f noun* beard.

barbecue *m noun* barbecue.

barbelé *adjective* **fil de fer b.** barbed wire.

barboter *verb* to splash about.

barbouillage *m noun* smear (ing); (*gribouillage*) scribble, scribbling.

barbouiller *verb* (*salir*) to smear; (*gribouiller*) to scribble.

barbu , -ue *adjective* bearded.

baril *m noun* barrel; **b. de poudre** powder keg.

barman *m noun* (*plural* **barmans** *ou* **barmen**) barman.

baromètre *m noun* barometer.

baron *m noun* baron.

baronne *f noun* baroness.

barque *f noun* (small) boat.

barrage *m noun* (*sur une route*) roadblock; (*sur un fleuve*) dam.

barre *f noun* bar; (*de bateau*) helm; (*trait*) stroke.

barreau , -x *m noun* (*de fenêtre*) bar; (*d'échelle*) rung.

barrer *verb* (*route etc*) to block off; (*mot, phrase*) to cross out.

barrette *f noun* (hair)slide.

barricade *f noun* barricade.

barricader *verb* to barricade; **se b.** to barricade oneself (in).

barrière *f noun* (*porte*) gate; (*clôture*) fence; (*obstacle*) barrier.

barrique *f noun* (large) barrel.

bas , basse
  1 *adjective* low.
  2 *adverb* low; (*parler*) in a whisper; **plus b.** further *or* lower down.
  3 *m noun* (*de côte, page, mur etc*) bottom; **tiroir/etc du b.** bottom drawer/*etc*; **en b.** down (below);

(*par l'escalier*) downstairs; **en** *or* **au b. de** at the bottom of.

bas *m noun* (*chaussette*) stocking.

bas-côté *m noun* roadside, verge, shoulder.

bascule *f noun* weighing machine; (*jeu d'enfant*) seesaw.

basculer *verb* to topple over.

base *f noun* base; **bases** (*d'un argument, accord etc*) basis; **salaire de b.** basic pay; **à b. de lait/citron** milk-/lemon-based; **b. navale/aérienne** naval/air base.

baser *verb* to base (**sur**, on).

basket(-ball) *m noun* basketball.

baskets *mpl or fpl noun* baseball boots.

basque *adjective & m or f noun* Basque.

basse *see* bas.

basse-cour *f noun* (*plural* **basses-cours**) farmyard.

bassin *m noun* pond; (*rade*) dock; (*du corps*) pelvis; **b. houiller** coalfield.

bassine *f noun* bowl.

bataille *f noun* battle.

batailleur , -euse
  1 *m or f noun* fighter.
  2 *adjective* fond of fighting, belligerent.

bateau , -x *m noun* boat; (*grand*) ship; **b. -mouche** river boat (*on the Seine*).

bâtiment *m noun* building; (*navire*) vessel; **le b.** (*industrie*) the building trade.

bâtir *verb* to build; **bien bâti** well-built.

bâton *m noun* stick; (*d'agent*) baton; **b. de rouge** lipstick; **donner des coups de b. à quelqu'un** to beat somebody (with a stick).

battante *adjective* **pluie b.** driving rain.

battement *m noun* beat(ing); (*de paupières*) blink(ing); (*délai*) interval; **b. de cœur** heartbeat.

batterie *f noun* battery; **la b.** (*d'un orchestre*) the drums.

batteur *m noun* (*d'orchestre*) drummer.

battre **verb*
1 (*personne, adversaire*) to beat; (*record*) to break.
2 (*cœur*) to beat; (*porte, volet*) to bang; **b. des mains** to clap (one's hands); **b. des paupières** to blink; **b. des ailes** to flap its wings.

battre (se) *reflexive verb* to fight.

battu , -ue
1 *past participle of* **battre**.
2 *adjectif* (*femme, enfant*) battered.

bavard , -arde *adjective* talkative.

bavardage *m noun* chatting.

bavarder *verb* to chat.

baver *verb* to dribble; **en b.** *Familiar* to have a rough time of it.

bavoir *m noun* bib.

bavure *f noun* (*tache*) smudge.

bazar *m noun* (*magasin*) bazaar; (*désordre*) mess.

beau (*or* **bel** *before vowel or mute h*), **belle** *adjective* (*plural* **beaux, belles**) beautiful, attractive; (*voyage, temps etc*) fine, lovely; **au b. milieu** right in the middle; **j'ai b. crier**/*etc* it's no use (my) shouting/*etc.*

beaucoup *adverb* (*lire etc*) a lot; **aimer b.** to like very much *or* a lot; **b. de** (*livres etc*) many, a lot of; (*courage etc*) a lot of; **pas b. d'argent**/*etc* not much money/ *etc*; **j'en ai b.** (*quantité*) I have a lot; (*nombre*) I have lots; **b. plus** much more; many more (**que** than).

beau-fils *m noun* (*plural* **beaux-fils**) (*gendre*) son-in-law; (*après remariage*) stepson.

beau-frère *m noun* (*plural* **beaux-frères**) brother-in-law.

beau-père *m noun* (*plural* **beaux-pères**) father-in-law.

beauté *f noun* beauty.

beaux-parents *mpl noun* parents-in-law.

bébé *m noun* baby.

bec *m noun* (*d'oiseau*) beak; (*de cruche*) spout; **coup de b.** peck.

bécane *f noun Familiar* bike.

bêche *f noun* spade.

bêcher *verb* (*cultiver*) to dig.

becquée *f noun* **donner la b. à** (*oiseau*) to feed.

bedonnant , -ante *adjective* potbellied.

bégayer *verb* to stutter.

bègue
1 *m or f noun* stutterer.
2 *adjective* **être b.** to stutter.

beige *adjective* & *m noun* beige.

beignet *m noun* (*pâtisserie*) fritter.

bel *see* **beau**.

bêler *verb* to bleat.

belette *f noun* weasel.

belge *adjective* & *m or f noun* Belgian.

Belgique (la) *f noun* Belgium.

belle *see* **beau**.

belle-fille *f noun* (*plural* **belles-filles**) (*épouse d'un fils*) daughter-in-law.

belle-mère *f noun* (*plural* **belles-mères**) mother-in-law.

belle-sœur *f noun* (*plural* **belles-sœurs**) sister-in-law.

belliqueux , -euse *adjective*

(*agressif*) aggressive.

bénédiction *f noun* blessing.

bénéfice *m noun* (*gain*) profit; (*avantage*) benefit.

bénéficier *verb* to benefit (**de** from).

bénéfique *adjective* beneficial.

bénévole *adjective & m or f noun* voluntary (worker).

bénir *verb* to bless.

bénit , -ite *adjective* (*pain*) consecrated; **eau bénite** holy water.

benjamin , -ine *m or f noun* youngest child; (*sportif*) young junior.

benne *f noun* (*de camion*) (movable) container; **b. à ordures** bin lorry.

béquille *f noun* (*canne*) crutch; (*de moto*) stand.

berceau , -x *m noun* cradle.

bercer *verb* (*balancer*) to rock; (*apaiser*) to soothe, lull.

berceuse *f noun* lullaby.

béret *m noun* beret.

berge *m noun* (*rive*) (raised) bank.

berger *m noun* shepherd; **b. allemand** Alsatian (dog).

bergère *f noun* shepherdess.

bergerie *f noun* sheepfold.

besogne *f noun* job, task.

besoin *m noun* need; **avoir b. de** to need.

bestiole *f noun* (*insecte*) bug.

bétail *m noun* livestock.

bête [1] *f noun* animal; (*insecte*) bug; **b. noire** pet hate.

bête [2] *adjective* stupid.

bêtement *adverb* stupidly; **tout b.** quite simply.

bêtise *f noun* stupidity; (*action, parole*) stupid thing.

béton *m noun* concrete; **mur/etc en b.** concrete wall/*etc*.

betterave *f noun* beetroot.

beurre *m noun* butter.

beurrer *verb* to butter.

beurrier *m noun* butter dish.

bibelot *m noun* (small) ornament, trinket.

biberon *m noun* (feeding) bottle.

bible *f noun* bible; **la B.** the Bible.

bibliothécaire *m or f noun* librarian.

bibliothèque *f noun* library; (*meuble*) bookcase.

bic ® *m noun* biro ®, ballpoint.

biceps *m noun* (*muscle*) biceps.

biche *f noun* doe.

bicyclette *f noun* bicycle.

bidet *m noun* bidet.

bidon
1 *m noun* can.
2 *invariable adjective* Familiar phoney.

bidonville *f noun* shantytown.

bidule *m noun* (*chose*) Familiar whatsit.

bien
1 *adverb* well; **b. fatigué/souvent**/*etc* (*très*) very tired/often/*etc*; **un travail b. payé** a well-paid job; **merci b.!** thanks very much!; **b.!** fine!, right!; **b. des fois/des gens/***etc* lots of *or* many times/people/*etc*; **je l'ai b. dit** (*intensif*) I DID say so; **tu as b. fait** you did right; **c'est b. fait (pour lui)** it serves him right.
2 *invariable adjective* (*convenable, compétent etc*) fine.
3 *m noun* (*avantage*) good; (*chose*) possession; **ça te fera du b.** it will do you good; **pour ton b.** for your own good; **le b. et le mal** good and evil.

bien-être *m noun* wellbeing.

bienfaisant , -ante *adjective* beneficial.

bien que *conjunction* (+ *subjunctive*) although.

bientôt *adverb* soon; **à b.!** see you soon!; **il est b. midi**/*etc* it's nearly twelve/*etc*.

bienvenu , -ue
1 *adjective* welcome.
2 *f noun* welcome; **souhaiter la bienvenue à** to welcome.

bière *f noun* beer; **b. pression** draught beer.

bifteck *m noun* steak.

bifurcation *f noun* (*route etc*) fork.

bifurquer *verb* to fork.

bigoudi *m noun* (hair) roller.

bijou , -x *m noun* jewel.

bijouterie *f noun* (*commerce*) jeweller's shop.

bijoutier , -ière *m or f noun* jeweller.

bilan *m noun* (*financier*) balance sheet; (*résultat*) outcome; (*d'un accident*) (casualty) toll; **b. de santé** checkup.

bile *f noun* bile; **se faire de la b.** *Familiar* to worry.

bilingue *adjective* bilingual.

billard *m noun* (*jeu*) billiards; (*table*) billiard table.

bille *f noun* (*d'enfant*) marble; **stylo à b.** ballpoint (pen).

billet *m noun* ticket; **b.** (**de banque**) (bank)note; **un b. de 100 francs** a 100-franc note; **b. aller, b. simple** single ticket; **b.** (**d'**)**aller retour** return ticket.

biologie *f noun* biology.

biologique *adjective* biological; (*légumes etc*) organic.

bip(-bip) *m noun* bleeper.

biscotte *f noun* rusk, Melba toast.

biscuit *m noun* biscuit.

bise *f noun Familiar* kiss; **faire une b. à quelqu'un** to give somebody a kiss; **faire la b. à quelqu'un** to kiss somebody on both cheeks; **grosses bises** (*sur une lettre*) love and kisses.

bison *m noun* (American) buffalo.

bissextile *adjective* **année b.** leap year.

bistouri *m noun* scalpel.

bistro(t) *m noun* bar.

bitume *m noun* (*revêtement*) asphalt.

bizarre *adjective* peculiar, odd.

blague *f noun Familiar* (*plaisanterie, farce*) joke; **raconter des blagues** (*mensonges*) to lie.

blaguer *verb Familiar* to be joking.

blâmer *verb* to criticize, blame.

blanc , blanche
1 *adjective* white; (*page*) blank.
2 *m or f noun* (*personne*) white man *or* woman.
3 *m noun* (*couleur*) white; (*de poulet*) breast; (*espace*) blank; **b. cassé** off-white; **b. d'œuf** egg white; **laisser en b.** to leave blank; **chèque en b.** blank cheque.

blancheur *f noun* whiteness.

blanchir *verb* to turn white.

blanchisserie *f noun* (*lieu*) laundry.

blé *m noun* wheat.

blessant , -ante *adjective* hurtful.

blessé , -ée *m or f noun* casualty.

blesser *verb* to injure, hurt; (*avec un couteau, une balle etc*) to wound; (*offenser*) to hurt; **se b. au bras**/*etc* to hurt one's arm/*etc*.

blessure *f noun* injury; wound.

bleu , -e
1 *adjective* blue.
2 *m noun* (*plural* **bleus**) (*couleur*) blue; (*contusion*) bruise; **b. ciel** sky blue; **b. marine** navy (blue); **b. de travail** overalls.

blindé , -ée *adjective* (*voiture etc*) armoured; **porte blindée** reinforced steel door; **une vitre blindée** bulletproof glass.

bloc *m noun* block; (*de papier*) pad; **à b.** (*visser etc*) tight.

bloc-notes *m noun* (*plural* **blocs-notes**) writing pad.

blond , -onde
1 *adjective* fair(-haired).
2 *m or f noun* fair-haired man *or* woman; (**bière**) **blonde** lager.

bloquer *verb* (*obstruer*) to block; (*coincer*) to jam; (*roue*) to lock; (*prix*) to freeze.

bloquer (se) *reflexive verb* to jam; (*roue*) to lock.

blottir (se) *reflexive verb* to crouch; (*dans son lit*) to snuggle down; **se b. contre** to snuggle up to.

blouse *f noun* (*tablier*) smock.

blouson *m noun* windcheater.

blue-jean *m noun* (*plural* **blue-jeans**) jeans.

bobine *f noun* reel, spool.

bocal , -aux *m noun* glass jar; (*à poissons*) bowl.

bœuf *m noun* ox; (*viande*) beef.

bof *interjection* Familiar **ça te plaît?–b., pas tellement** do you like it?–not really, no; **il est chouette, hein, ce pull? – b.** this sweater's great, isn't it? – I suppose not.

boire * *verb* to drink; **offrir à b. à quelqu'un** to offer somebody a drink.

bois *m noun* wood; (*de construction*) timber; **en** *or* **de b.** wooden; **b. de chauffage** firewood.

boisé , -ée *adjective* wooded.

boisson *f noun* drink.

boîte *f noun* box; **b. de conserve** tin; **des haricots en b.** tinned beans; **b. d'allumettes** box of matches; **b. aux** *or* **à lettres** letterbox; **b. (de nuit)** nightclub; **aller en b.** to go to a nightclub.

boiter *verb* to limp.

boîtier *m noun* (*de montre*) case.

bol *m noun* bowl; **un b. d'air** a breath of fresh air.

bombardement *m noun* bombing; shelling.

bombarder *verb* to bomb; (*avec des obus*) to shell.

bombe *f noun* bomb; (*de laque etc*) spray.

bon , bonne *adjective* good; (*qui convient*) right; (*apte*) fit; **b. anniversaire!** happy birthday!; **b. week-end!** have a nice weekend!; **le b. choix/moment** the right choice/time; **b. à manger** fit to eat; **c'est b. à savoir** it's worth knowing; **croire b. de** to think it wise to; **b. en français/etc** good at French/etc; **un b. moment** (*intensif*) a good while; **pour de b.** really (and truly); **ah b.?** is that so?

bon *m noun* (*billet*) coupon, voucher.

bonbon *m noun* sweet.

bond *m noun* leap.

bondé , -ée *adjective* packed.

bondir *verb* to leap.

bonheur *m noun* happiness; (*chance*) good luck; **par b.** luckily.

bonhomme *m noun* (*plural*

bonshommes) fellow; **b. de neige** snowman.

bonjour *m noun & interjection* good morning; (*après-midi*) good afternoon; **donner le b. à, dire b. à** to say hello to.

bonne [1] *see* bon.

bonne [2] *f noun* maid.

bonnet *m noun* (*de ski etc*) cap; (*de femme, d'enfant*) bonnet, hat.

bonsoir *m noun & interjection* (*en arrivant*) good evening; (*en partant*) goodbye; (*au coucher*) good night.

bonté *f noun* kindness.

bord *m noun* (*rebord*) edge; (*rive*) bank; **au b. de la mer/route** at *or* by the seaside/roadside; **b. du trottoir** kerb; **à bord (de)** (*avion, bateau*) on board.

Bordeaux *m or f noun* Bordeaux.

border *verb* (*vêtement*) to edge; (*lit, personne*) to tuck in; **b. la rue**/*etc* (*maisons, arbres*) to line the street/*etc*.

bordure *f noun* border.

borne *f noun* boundary mark; **b. kilométrique** = milestone.

bosniaque *adjective & m or f noun* Bosnian.

Bosnie (la) *f noun* Bosnia.

bosse *f noun* (*dans le dos*) hump; (*enflure, de terrain*) bump.

bosser *verb Familiar* to work (hard).

bossu , -ue
  1 *adjective* hunchbacked.
  2 *m or f noun* hunchback.

botte *f noun* (*chaussure*) boot; (*de fleurs etc*) bunch.

bottine *f noun* (ankle) boot.

bouc *m noun* billy goat; (*barbe*) goatee.

bouche *f noun* mouth; **b. de mé-** tro métro entrance; **b. d'égout** drain opening.

bouchée *f noun* mouthful.

boucher [1] *verb* (*évier, nez etc*) to stop up; (*bouteille*) to cork; (*vue, rue etc*) to block; **se b. le nez** to hold one's nose.

boucher [2] *m noun* butcher.

bouchère *f noun* butcher; (*femme du boucher*) butcher's wife.

boucherie *f noun* butcher's (shop).

bouchon *m noun* stopper; (*de liège*) cork; (*de tube, bidon*) cap; (*embouteillage*) traffic jam.

boucle *f noun* (*de ceinture*) buckle; **b. d'oreille** earring; **b. (de cheveux)** curl.

bouclé , -ée *adjective* (*cheveux*) curly.

boucler *verb*
  1 (*ceinture, valise*) to fasten; (*cheveux*) to curl.
  2 (*friser*) to be curly.

bouclier *m noun* shield.

bouder *verb* to sulk.

boudin *m noun* black pudding.

boue *f noun* mud.

bouée *f noun* buoy; **b. de sauvetage** lifebelt.

boueux , -euse *adjective* muddy.

bouffée *f noun* (*de fumée*) puff.

bougeoir *m noun* candlestick.

bouger *verb* to move.

bougie *f noun* candle; (*d'automobile*) spark(ing) plug.

bouillie *f noun* mush; (*pour bébé*) baby food.

bouillir * *verb* to boil.

bouilloire *f noun* kettle.

bouillon *m noun* (*aliment*) broth; (*bulles*) bubbles.

bouillonner *verb* to bubble.

boulanger *m noun* baker.

boulangère *f noun* baker; (*femme du boulanger*) baker's wife.

boulangerie *f noun* baker's (shop).

boule *f noun* ball; **boules** (*jeu*) bowls; **b. de neige** snowball.

bouleau , -x *m noun* (silver) birch.

bouledogue *m noun* bulldog.

boulet *m noun* **b. de canon** cannonball.

boulette *f noun* (*de papier*) ball; (*de viande*) meatball.

boulevard *m noun* boulevard.

bouleversement *m noun* upheaval.

bouleverser *verb* (*déranger*) to turn upside down; (*émouvoir*) to upset (greatly).

Boulogne-sur-Mer *m or f noun* Boulogne.

boulon *m noun* bolt.

boulot *m noun* Familiar (*travail, lieu de travail*) work; (*emploi*) job.

boum *f noun* Familiar party (*for young people*).

bouquet *m noun* (*de fleurs*) bunch.

bouquin *m noun* Familiar book.

bourdon *m noun* (*insecte*) bumblebee.

bourdonnement *m noun* buzzing.

bourdonner *verb* to buzz.

bourg *m noun* (small) market town.

bourgeois , -oise *adjective & m or f noun* middle-class (person).

bourgeon *m noun* bud.

bourgeonner *verb* to bud.

bourrasque *f noun* squall, gust of wind.

bourrer *verb* to stuff, cram (**de** with); (*pipe*) to fill.

bourse *f noun* (*sac*) purse; (*d'études*) grant; **la B.** the Stock Exchange.

bousculade *f noun* jostling.

bousculer *verb* (*heurter, pousser*) to jostle.

boussole *f noun* compass.

bout *m noun* end; (*de langue, canne, doigt*) tip; (*de papier, pain, ficelle*) bit; **un b. de temps** a little while; **au b. d'un moment** after a moment; **au b. de la rue** at the end of the street; **à b.** exhausted; **à b. de souffle** out of breath.

bouteille *f noun* bottle; (*de gaz*) cylinder.

boutique *f noun* shop.

bouton *m noun* (*bourgeon*) bud; (*au visage etc*) pimple; (*de vêtement*) button; (*qu'on pousse*) (push-)button; (*de porte, télévision*) knob.

bouton-d'or *m noun* (*plural* **boutons-d'or**) buttercup.

boutonner *verb* to button (up).

boutonner (se) *reflexive verb* to button (up).

boutonnière *f noun* buttonhole.

bouton-pression *m noun* (*plural* **boutons-pression**) snap (fastener), press-stud.

box *m noun* (*garage*) (lockup) garage.

boxe *f noun* boxing.

boxer *verb* to box.

boxeur *m noun* boxer.

boycotter *verb* to boycott.

bracelet *m noun* bracelet; (*de montre*) strap.

braconner *verb* to poach.

braconnier *m noun* poacher.

braguette *f noun* (*de pantalon*) fly, flies.

brailler *verb* to bawl.

braise(s) *f(pl) noun* embers.

brancard *m noun* (*civière*) stretcher.

branchages *mpl noun* (cut) branches.

branche *f noun* (*d'arbre*) branch; (*de compas*) arm, leg.

branchement *m noun* connection.

brancher *verb* to plug in.

brandir *verb* to flourish.

branlant , -ante *adjective* (*table etc*) wobbly, shaky.

braquer *verb*
1 (*arme etc*) to point (**sur** at).
2 (*en voiture*) to turn the steering wheel, steer.

bras *m noun* arm; **b. dessus b. dessous** arm in arm; **à b. ouverts** with open arms.

brasier *m noun* blaze.

brassard *m noun* armband.

brasse *f noun* (*nage*) breaststroke.

brasserie *f noun* (*usine*) brewery; (*café*) brasserie.

brassière *f noun* (*de bébé*) vest.

brave *adjective & m noun* brave (man).

bravement *adverb* bravely.

bravo
1 *interjection* well done.
2 *m noun* cheer.

bravoure *f noun* bravery.

brebis *f noun* ewe.

brèche *f noun* gap.

bredouille *adjective* **rentrer b.** to come back empty-handed.

bref , brève
1 *adjective* brief, short.

2 *adverb* (**enfin**) b. in a word.

Brésil (le) *m noun* Brazil.

brésilien , -ienne *adjective & m or f noun* Brazilian.

Bretagne (la) *f noun* Brittany.

bretelle *f noun* strap; (*d'accès*) access road; **bretelles** (*pour pantalon*) braces.

breton , -onne *adjective & m or f noun* Breton.

brevet *m noun* diploma; **b. (des collèges)** = general exam taken at 15; **b. (d'invention)** patent.

bricolage *m noun* (*passe-temps*) do-it-yourself; **faire du b.** to do some DIY.

bricoler *verb*
1 (*faire de petits travaux*) to do odd jobs.
2 (*fabriquer*) to put together.

bricoleur , -euse *m or f noun* handyman, handywoman.

bride *f noun* bridle.

bridé *adjective* **avoir les yeux bridés** to have slit eyes.

brièvement *adverb* briefly.

brièveté *f noun* shortness, brevity.

brigand *m noun* robber; (*enfant*) rascal.

brillamment *adverb* brilliantly.

brillant , -ante
1 *adjective* (*luisant*) shining; (*astiqué*) shiny; (*couleur*) bright; (*doué*) brilliant.
2 *m noun* shine; (*couleur*) brightness.

briller *verb* to shine; **faire b.** (*meuble*) to polish (up).

brin *m noun* (*d'herbe*) blade; (*de corde, fil*) strand; (*de muguet*) spray.

brindille *f noun* twig.

brioche *f noun* brioche (*light*

sweet bun).

brique *f noun* brick; (*de lait, jus de fruit*) carton.

briquet *m noun* (*cigarette*) lighter.

brise *f noun* breeze.

briser *verb* to break.

briser (se) *reflexive verb* to break.

britannique
1 *adjective* British.
2 *m or f noun* Briton; **les Britanniques** the British.

broc *m noun* pitcher, jug.

brocanteur , -euse *m or f noun* secondhand dealer (*in furniture etc*).

broche *f noun* (*pour rôtir*) spit; (*bijou*) brooch.

brochet *m noun* pike.

brochette *f noun* (*tige*) skewer; (*plat*) kebab.

brochure *f noun* brochure, booklet.

broder *verb* to embroider (**de** with).

broderie *f noun* embroidery.

bronchite *f noun* bronchitis.

bronzage *m noun* (sun)tan.

bronze *m noun* bronze.

bronzer *verb* to go brown, to tan; **se (faire) b.** to sunbathe, get a (sun)tan.

brosse *f noun* brush; **b. à dents** toothbrush.

brosser *verb* to brush; **se b. les dents/cheveux** to brush one's teeth/hair.

brouette *f noun* wheelbarrow.

brouhaha *m noun* hubbub.

brouillard *m noun* fog; **il y a du b.** it's foggy.

brouiller *verb* (*idées*) to muddle up; **b. la vue à quelqu'un** to blur somebody's vision.

brouiller (se) *reflexive verb* (*temps*) to cloud over; (*vue*) to get blurred; (*amis*) to fall out (**avec** with).

brouillon *m noun* rough draft.

broussailles *fpl noun* bushes.

brousse *f noun* **la b.** the bush.

brouter *verb* to graze.

broyer *verb* to grind.

bruit *m noun* noise, sound; (*nouvelle*) rumour; **faire du b.** to make a noise.

brûlant , -ante *adjective* (*objet, soleil*) burning (hot).

brûlé *m noun* **odeur de b.** smell of burning.

brûler *verb* to burn; **se b.** to burn oneself; **b. un feu (rouge)** to go through the lights.

brûlure *f noun* burn.

brume *f noun* mist, haze.

brumeux , -euse *adjective* misty, hazy.

brun , brune
1 *adjective* brown; (*cheveux*) dark, brown; (*personne*) dark-haired.
2 *m noun* (*couleur*) brown.
3 *m or f noun* dark-haired person.

brunir *verb* (*peau, personne*) to tan; (*cheveux*) to go darker.

brushing *m noun* blow-dry.

brusque *adjective* (*manière, personne*) abrupt; (*subit*) sudden.

brusquement *adverb* suddenly.

brusquerie *f noun* abruptness.

brut *adjective* (*pétrole*) crude; (*poids*) gross.

brutal , -e, -aux *adjective* (*violent*) brutal; (*enfant*) rough.

brutaliser *verb* to ill-treat.

brutalité *f noun* brutality.

brute *f noun* brute.
Bruxelles *m or f noun* Brussels.
bruyamment *adverb* noisily.
bruyant , -ante *adjective* noisy.
bu , bue *past participle of* **boire**.
bûche *f noun* log; **b. de Noël** Yule log.
bûcheron *m noun* lumberjack.
budget *m noun* budget.
buée *f noun* mist.
buffet *m noun* (*armoire*) sideboard; (*table, repas*) buffet.
buisson *m noun* bush.
bulgare *adjective & m or f noun* Bulgarian.
Bulgarie (la) *f noun* Bulgaria.
bulldozer *m noun* bulldozer.
bulle *f noun* bubble; (*de bande dessinée*) balloon.
bulletin *m noun* (*météo*) report;

(*scolaire*) report; **b. de paie** pay slip *or* stub; **b. de vote** ballot paper.
bureau , -x *m noun* (*table*) desk; (*lieu*) office; **b. de change** foreign exchange office, bureau de change; **b. de tabac** tobacconist's (shop).
burette *f noun* oilcan.
bus *m noun* bus.
but *m noun* (*objectif*) aim, goal; *Football* goal.
buter *verb* **b. contre** to stumble over.
butoir *m noun* (*de porte*) stopper.
butte *f noun* mound.
buvard *m noun* blotting paper.
buvette *f noun* refreshment bar.
buveur , -euse *m or f noun* drinker.

chevaline *adjective* **boucherie c.** horse butcher's (shop).

chevelure *f noun* (head of) hair.

chevet *m noun* **table/livre de c.** bedside table/book; **au c. de** at the bedside of.

cheveu , -x *m noun* **un c.** a hair; **cheveux** hair; **tiré par les cheveux** far-fetched.

cheville *f noun* ankle; (*pour vis*) (wall) plug.

chèvre *f noun* goat.

chevreau , -x *m noun* (*petit de la chèvre*) kid.

chez *preposition* **c. quelqu'un** at somebody's house, flat *etc*; **il est c. Jean/c. l'épicier** he's at John's (place)/at the grocer's; **il va c. Jean/c. l'épicier** he's going to John's (place)/to the grocer's; **c. moi, c. nous** at home; **je vais c. moi** I'm going home; **c'est une habitude c. elle** it's a habit with her; **c. Mme Dupont** (*adresse*) care of Mme Dupont.

chic
1 *invariable adjective* smart; (*gentil*) *Familiar* nice.
2 *interjection* **c. (alors)!** great!
3 *m noun* style.

chicorée *f noun* (*à café*) chicory; (*pour salade*) endive.

chien *m noun* dog; **c. d'aveugle** guide dog; **c. de chasse** retriever; **c. policier** police dog; **c. de race** pedigree dog; **se donner un mal de c. pour faire** *Familiar* to take great pains to do; **temps de c.** *Familiar* rotten *or* filthy weather.

chien-loup *m noun* (*plural* **chiens-loups**) wolfhound.

chienne *f noun* dog, bitch.

chiffon *m noun* rag; **c. (à poussière)** duster.

chiffonner *verb* to crumple.

chiffre *m noun* figure, number; (*romain, arabe*) numeral; **c. d'affaires** (sales) turnover.

chimie *f noun* chemistry.

chimique *adjective* chemical.

chimpanzé *m noun* chimpanzee.

Chine (la) *f noun* China.

chinois , -oise
1 *adjective* Chinese.
2 *m or f noun* Chinese man *or* woman, Chinese; **les C.** the Chinese.
3 *m noun* (*langue*) Chinese.

chiot *m noun* pup(py).

chips *fpl noun* (potato) crisps.

chirurgical , -e, -aux *adjective* surgical.

chirurgie *f noun* surgery.

chirurgien *m noun* surgeon.

choc *m noun* (*d'objets, émotion*) shock.

chocolat *m noun* chocolate; **c. à croquer** *or* **noir** plain chocolate; **c. au lait** milk chocolate; **c. chaud** hot chocolate.

chocolaté , -ée *adjective* chocolate-flavoured.

chœur *m noun* (*chanteurs, nef*) choir; **en c.** (all) together.

choisir *verb* to choose, pick.

choix *m noun* choice; (*assortiment*) selection.

cholestérol *m noun* cholesterol.

chômage *m noun* unemployment; **au c.** unemployed.

chômer *verb* to be unemployed.

chômeur , -euse *m or f noun* unemployed person; **les chômeurs** the unemployed.

choquant , -ante *adjective* shocking.

choquer *verb* to shock.

chorale *f noun* choral society.

chose *f noun* thing; **monsieur C.**

Mr What's-his-name.

chou , -x *m noun* cabbage; **choux de Bruxelles** Brussels sprouts.

choucroute *f noun* sauerkraut.

chouette
1 *f noun* owl.
2 *adjective Familiar* super, great.

chou-fleur *m noun* (*plural* **choux-fleurs**) cauliflower.

choyer *verb* to pamper.

chrétien , -ienne *adjective & m or f noun* Christian.

chrome *m noun* chrome.

chromé , -ée *adjective* chrome-plated.

chronique *f noun* (*à la radio*) report; (*dans le journal*) column.

chronomètre *m noun* stopwatch.

chronométrer *verb* to time.

chrysanthème *m noun* chrysanthemum.

chuchotement *m noun* whisper(-ing).

chuchoter *verb* to whisper.

chut! *interjection* sh!, shush!

chute *f noun* fall; **c. d'eau** waterfall; **c. de neige** snowfall; **c. de pluie** rainfall.

Chypre *m or f noun* Cyprus.

chypriote *adjective & m or f noun* Cypriot.

ci
1 *adverb* **par-ci par-là** here and there.
2 *demonstrative pronoun* **comme ci comme ça** so so.

cible *f noun* target.

cicatrice *f noun* scar.

cicatrisation *f noun* healing (up).

cicatriser *verb* to heal up.

cicatriser (se) *reflexive verb* to heal up.

cidre *m noun* cider.

Cie *abbreviation* (*compagnie*) Co.

ciel *m noun* (*plural* **cieux**) sky; (*paradis*) heaven.

cierge *m noun* candle.

cigale *f noun* (*insecte*) cicada.

cigare *m noun* cigar.

cigarette *f noun* cigarette.

cigogne *f noun* stork.

cil *m noun* (eye)lash.

cime *f noun* (*d'un arbre*) top; (*d'une montagne*) peak.

ciment *m noun* cement.

cimenter *verb* to cement.

cimetière *m noun* cemetery.

ciné *m noun Familiar* cinema.

ciné-club *m noun* film society.

cinéma *m noun* cinema; **faire du c.** to make films.

cinglé , -ée *adjective Familiar* crazy.

cinq *adjective & m noun* five.

cinquantaine *f noun* about fifty.

cinquante *adjective & m noun* fifty.

cinquantième *adjective & m or f noun* fiftieth.

cinquième *adjective & m or f noun* fifth.

cintre *m noun* coathanger.

cirage *m noun* (shoe) polish.

circonférence *f noun* circumference.

circonflexe *adjective Grammaire* circumflex.

circonstance *f noun* circumstance; **pour la c.** for this occasion.

circonstanciel , -ielle *adjective Grammaire* adverbial.

circuit *m noun* (*électrique, sportif etc*) circuit; (*voyage*) tour.

circulaire
1 *adjective* circular.
2 *f noun* (*lettre*) circular.

circulation *f noun* circulation; (*automobile*) traffic.

circuler *verb* to circulate; (*véhicule, train*) to travel; (*passant*) to walk about; (*rumeur*) to go round; **faire c.** (*piétons etc*) to move on.

cire *f noun* wax.

cirer *verb* to polish.

cirque *m noun* circus.

ciseau , -x *m noun* chisel; (**une paire de**) **ciseaux** (a pair of) scissors.

citadin , -ine *m or f noun* city dweller.

citation *f noun* quotation.

cité *f noun* city; **c. universitaire** (students') halls of residence.

citer *verb* to quote.

citerne *f noun* (*réservoir*) tank.

citoyen , -enne *m or f noun* citizen.

citron *m noun* lemon; **c. pressé** (fresh) lemon juice.

citronnade *f noun* lemon drink.

citrouille *f noun* pumpkin.

civière *f noun* stretcher.

civil , -e
1 *adjective* civil; (*non militaire*) civilian; **année civile** calendar year.
2 *m noun* civilian; **en c.** (*policier*) in plain clothes.

civilisation *f noun* civilization.

civilisé , -ée *adjective* civilized.

civique *adjective* civic; **instruction c.** civics.

clair , -e
1 *adjective* (*distinct, limpide, évident*) clear; (*éclairé*) light; (*pâle*) light(-coloured); **bleu/vert c.** light blue/green.

2 *adverb* (*voir*) clearly.
3 *m noun* **c. de lune** moonlight.

clairement *adverb* clearly.

clairière *f noun* clearing.

clairon *m noun* bugle.

clairsemé , -ée *adjective* sparse.

clandestin , -ine *adjective* (*journal, mouvement*) underground; **passager c.** stowaway.

claque *f noun* smack, slap.

claquement *m noun* (*de porte*) slam(ming).

claquer *verb*
1 (*fermer*) (*porte*) to slam, bang; **se c. un muscle** to tear a muscle.
2 (*faire du bruit*) (*porte*) to slam, bang; (*coup de feu*) to ring out; **c. des mains** to clap one's hands; **elle claque des dents** her teeth are chattering.

clarinette *f noun* clarinet.

clarté *f noun* light; (*précision*) clarity.

classe *f noun* class; **aller en c.** to go to school.

classement *m noun* classification; filing; grading; (*rang*) place; (*en sport*) placing.

classer *verb* to classify; (*papiers*) to file; (*candidats*) to grade; **se c. premier** to come first.

classeur *m noun* (*meuble*) filing cabinet; (*dossier*) (loose leaf) file.

classique *adjective* classical.

clavicule *f noun* collarbone.

clavier *m noun* keyboard.

clé , clef *f noun* key; (*outil*) spanner, wrench; **fermer à c.** to lock; **sous c.** under lock and key; **c. de contact**, ignition key.

clémentine *f noun* clementine.

clergé *m noun* clergy.

cliché *m noun* (*de photo*) negative.

client , -ente *m or f noun* customer; (*d'un avocat*) client; (*d'un médecin*) patient; (*d'hôtel*) guest.

clientèle *f noun* customers; (*d'un avocat, d'un médecin*) practice.

cligner *verb* c. des yeux to blink; (*fermer à demi*) to screw up one's eyes; c. de l'œil to wink.

clignotant *m noun* indicator.

clignoter *verb* to blink; (*lumière*) to flicker.

climat *m noun* climate.

climatisation *f noun* air-conditioning.

climatiser *verb* to air-condition.

clin d'œil *m noun* wink; en un c. d'œil in no time (at all).

clinique *f noun* (private) clinic.

clochard , -arde *m or f noun* down-and-out, tramp.

cloche *f noun* bell.

cloche-pied (à) *adverb* sauter à c. to hop on one foot.

clocher *m noun* bell tower; (*en pointe*) steeple.

clochette *f noun* (small) bell.

cloison *f noun* partition.

clope *m or f noun Familiar* fag, smoke, cigarette.

clopin-clopant *adverb* aller c. to hobble.

cloque *f noun* blister.

clos , close *adjective* closed.

clôture *f noun* (*barrière*) fence.

clôturer *verb* to enclose.

clou *m noun* nail; les clous (*passage*) pedestrian crossing.

clouer *verb* to nail; **cloué au lit** confined to bed.

clouté , -ée *adjective* (*pneus*) studded; **passage c.** pedestrian crossing.

clown *m noun* clown.

club *m noun* (*association*) club.

cm *abbreviation* (*centimètre*) cm.

coaguler *verb* to clot.

coaguler (se) *reflexive verb* to clot.

coalition *f noun* coalition.

cobaye *m noun* guinea pig.

coca *m noun* (*boisson*) *Familiar* coke ®.

Coca-Cola ® *invariable m noun* Coca-Cola ®.

cocaïne *f noun* cocaine.

coccinelle *f noun* ladybird.

cocher [1] *verb* to tick (off).

cocher [2] *m noun* coachman.

cochon , -onne

1 *m noun* pig; c. d'Inde guinea pig.

2 *m or f noun* (*personne sale*) pig.

cocorico *interjection & m noun* cock-a-doodle-doo.

cocotier *m noun* coconut palm.

cocotte *f noun* casserole; c. minute ® pressure cooker.

code *m noun* code; codes (*de voiture*) dipped headlights; C. de la route Highway Code.

cœur *m noun* heart; (*couleur*) *Cartes* hearts; au c. de (*ville, hiver etc*) in the middle *or* heart of; par c. (off) by heart; avoir mal au c. to feel sick; avoir le c. gros to have a heavy heart; avoir bon c. to be kind-hearted; de bon c. (*offrir*) willingly; (*rire*) heartily.

coffre *m noun* chest; (*de banque*) safe; (*de voiture*) boot.

coffre-fort *m noun* (*plural* coffres-forts) safe.

coffret *m noun* (*à bijoux etc*) box.

cogner *verb* to knock, bang; se c. la tête/*etc* to knock *or* bang one's head/*etc*; se c. à quelque chose to knock *or* bang into something.

cohue *f noun* crowd.

coiffer *verb* c. quelqu'un to do somebody's hair; se c. to do one's hair.

coiffeur , -euse *m or f noun* hairdresser.

coiffure *f noun* hat; (*arrangement*) hairstyle.

coin *m noun* (*angle*) corner; (*endroit*) spot; du c. (*magasin etc*) local; dans le c. in the (local) area.

coincé , -ée *adjective* stuck.

coincer *verb* (*mécanisme etc*) to jam; se c. to get stuck *or* jammed; se c. le doigt to get one's finger stuck.

coïncidence *f noun* coincidence.

coing *m noun* quince.

col *m noun* collar; (*de montagne*) pass; c. roulé polo neck.

colère *f noun* anger; une c. a fit of anger; en c. angry (contre with); se mettre en c. to lose one's temper.

coléreux , -euse *adjective* quick-tempered.

colique *f noun* diarrh(o)ea.

colis *m noun* parcel.

collaboration *f noun* collaboration.

collaborer *verb* collaborate (à on).

collant , -ante
1 *adjective* (*papier*) sticky; (*vêtement*) skin-tight.
2 *m noun* (pair of) tights; c. de danse dance tights.

colle *f noun* glue; (*blanche*) paste.

collecte *f noun* (*quête*) collection.

collectif , -ive *adjective* collective; billet c. group ticket.

collection *f noun* collection.

collectionner *verb* to collect.

collectionneur , -euse *m or f noun* collector.

collège *m noun* (secondary) school.

collégien *m noun* schoolboy.

collégienne *f noun* schoolgirl.

collègue *m or f noun* colleague.

coller *verb* to stick; (à la colle transparente) to glue; (à la colle blanche) to paste; (*affiche*) to stick up; (*papier peint*) to hang; (*mettre*) *Familiar* to stick; c. contre (*nez, oreille etc*) to press against.

collier *m noun* (*bijou*) necklace; (*de chien*) collar.

colline *f noun* hill.

collision *f noun* collision; entrer en c. avec to collide with.

colombe *f noun* dove.

colonel *m noun* colonel.

colonie *f noun* colony; c. de vacances (children's) holiday camp.

colonne *f noun* column; c. vertébrale spine.

coloré , -ée *adjective* colourful; (*verre, liquide*) coloured.

colorer *verb* to colour.

coloriage *m noun* album de coloriages colouring book.

colorier *verb* to colour (in).

coloris *m noun* (*nuance*) shade.

colosse *m noun* giant.

coma *m noun* coma; dans le c. in a coma.

combat *m noun* fight.

combatif , -ive *adjective* eager to fight; (*instinct, esprit*) fighting.

combattant *m noun* fighter, brawler.

combattre * *verb* to fight.

combien
1 *adverb* (*quantité*) how much;

(*nombre*) how many; **c. de** (*argent etc*) how much; (*gens, livres etc*) how many; **c. de temps** how long; **c'est c.?** *Familiar* how much is it? ▌ (*à quel point*) how; **c. y a-t-il d'ici à … ?** how far is it to … ? **2** *invariable m noun* **le c. sommes-nous?** *Familiar* what date is it?; **tous les c.?** *Familiar* how often?

combinaison *f noun* combination; (*vêtement de femme*) slip; (*de mécanicien*) boiler suit; **c. de vol/plongée/ski** flying/diving/ski suit.

combiné *m noun* (*de téléphone*) receiver.

combiner *verb* (*assembler*) to combine.

comble
1 *m noun* **le c. de** (*la joie etc*) the height of; **c'est un** *or* **le c.!** that's the limit!
2 *adjective* (*bondé*) packed.

combler *verb* (*trou etc*) to fill; **c. son retard** to make up lost time.

combustible *m noun* fuel.

comédie *f noun* comedy; **c. musicale** musical; **jouer la c.** to put on an act, pretend.

comédien *m noun* actor.

comédienne *f noun* actress.

comestible *adjective* edible.

comique *adjective* (*amusant*) funny; (*acteur etc*) comic.

comité *m noun* committee.

commandant *m noun* (*d'un navire*) captain; **c. de bord** (*d'un avion*) captain.

commande *f noun* (*achat*) order; **sur c.** to order; **les commandes** (*d'un avion etc*) the controls.

commandement *m noun* (*autorité*) command.

commander *verb*
1 (*marchandises, repas*) to order.
2 **c. à quelqu'un de faire** to command somebody to do.

comme
1 *adverb* (*with nouns and pronouns*) like; **c. moi** like me; **c. cela** like that; **qu'as-tu c. diplômes?** what do you have in the way of certificates?
▌ (*followed by a clause*) as; **c. si** as if; **c. pour faire** as if to do; **c. par hasard** as if by chance; **blanc c. neige** (as) white as snow.
▌ (*dans une exclamation*) **regarde c. il pleut!** look how it's raining!; **c. c'est petit!** isn't it small!
2 *conjunction* (*temps, cause*) as; **c. elle entrait** as she was coming in.

commencement *m noun* beginning, start.

commencer *verb* to begin, start (**à faire** to do, doing; **par** with; **par faire** by doing); **pour c.** to begin with.

comment
1 *adverb* how; **c. le sais-tu?** how do you know?; **c.?** (*répétition, surprise*) what?; **c. est-il?** what is he like?; **c. faire?** what can we do?; **c. t'appelles-tu?** what's your name?; **c. allez-vous?** how are you?
2 *interjection* what!

commerçant , -ante *m or f noun* shopkeeper; **rue commerçante** shopping street.

commerce *m noun* trade, commerce; (*magasin*) shop, business; **dans le c.** (*objet*) (on sale) in the shops.

commercial , -e, -aux *adjective* commercial.

commettre * *verb* (*délit etc*) to commit; (*erreur*) to make.

commissaire *m noun* c. (de police) police superintendent.

commissariat *m noun* c. (de police) (central) police station.

commission *f noun* (*course*) errand; (*pourcentage*) commission (sur on); **faire les commissions** to do the shopping.

commode
1 *adjective* (*pratique*) handy.
2 *f noun* chest of drawers.

commun , -une *adjective* (*collectif, habituel etc*) common; (*frais, cuisine*) shared; **ami c.** mutual friend; **en c.** in common; **avoir** *or* **mettre en c.** to share.

commune *f noun* commune.

communication *f noun* communication; **c. (téléphonique)** (telephone) call.

communier *verb* to receive Holy Communion.

communion *f noun* (Holy) Communion.

communiqué *m noun* (official) statement; (*publicitaire*) message; **c. de presse** press release.

communiquer *verb* to communicate.

communiste *adjective & m or f noun* communist.

compact , -e *adjective* dense.

compagne *f noun* friend; (*épouse*) companion.

compagnie *f noun* (*présence, société*) company; **tenir c. à quelqu'un** to keep somebody company.

compagnon *m noun* companion; **c. de jeu** playmate; **c. de travail** fellow worker, workmate.

comparable *adjective* comparable.

comparaison *f noun* comparison

(avec with).

comparer *verb* to compare (à, to, with).

compartiment *m noun* compartment.

compas *m noun* (pair of) compasses; (*boussole*) compass.

compatriote *m or f noun* compatriot.

compenser *verb* to compensate for.

compétence *f noun* competence.

compétent , -ente *adjective* competent.

compétition *f noun* competition; (*épreuve sportive*) event; **de c.** (*esprit, sport*) competitive.

complaisance *f noun* kindness.

complaisant , -ante *adjective* kind.

complément *m noun* Grammaire complement.

complet , -ète
1 *adjective* complete; (*train, hôtel etc*) full; (*aliment*) whole.
2 *m noun* suit.

complètement *adverb* completely.

compléter *verb* to complete; (*somme*) to make up.

complexe
1 *adjective* complex.
2 *m noun* (*sentiment, construction*) complex.

complication *f noun* complication.

complice *m noun* accomplice.

compliment *m noun* compliment; **mes compliments!** congratulations!

complimenter *verb* to compliment (**sur, pour** on).

compliqué , -ée *adjective* complicated.

compliquer *verb* to complicate; **se c.** to get complicated.

complot *m noun* plot.

comploter *verb* to plot (**de faire** to do).

comporter (se) *reflexive verb* to behave; (*joueur, voiture*) to perform.

composé , -ée *adjective* & *m noun* (*mot, en chimie etc*) compound; **temps c.** compound tense; **passé c.** perfect (tense).

composer *verb* to make up, compose; (*numéro*) to dial; **se c. de, être composé de** to be made up *or* composed of.

compositeur , -trice *m or f noun* composer.

composter *verb* (*billet*) to cancel.

compote *f noun* stewed fruit; **c. de pommes** stewed apples.

compréhensible *adjective* understandable.

compréhensif , -ive *adjective* (*personne*) understanding.

comprendre * *verb* to understand; (*comporter*) to include; **je n'y comprends rien** I don't understand anything about it; **ça se comprend** that's understandable.

comprimé *m noun* tablet.

comprimer *verb* to compress.

compris , -ise
1 *past participle of* **comprendre**.
2 *adjective* (*inclus*) included (**dans in**); **tout c.** (all) inclusive; **y c.** including.

comptable *m or f noun* bookkeeper; (*expert*) accountant.

comptant *adverb* **payer c.** to pay (in) cash.

compte *m noun* account; (*calcul*) calculation; **avoir un c. en ban-** que to have a bank account; **c. chèque** cheque account; **c. à rebours** countdown; **le c. y est** (*somme*) it's the right amount; (*objets*) they're all there; **tenir c. de** to take into account; **c. tenu de** considering; **se rendre c. de** to realize; **à son c.** (*travailler*) for oneself; (*s'installer*) on one's own; **en fin de c.** all things considered.

compte-gouttes *invariable m noun* dropper.

compter *verb* to count; **c. faire** to expect to do; (*avoir l'intention de*) to intend to do; **c. sur** to rely on; **c. quelque chose à quelqu'un** (*facturer*) to charge somebody for something.

compte rendu *m noun* (*plural* **comptes rendus**) report; (*de livre, film*) review.

compteur *m noun* meter; **c. (de vitesse)** speedometer; **c. (kilométrique)** milometer.

comptoir *m noun* (*de magasin*) counter; (*de café*) bar; (*de bureau*) (reception) desk.

comte *m noun* count; (*en Grande-Bretagne*) earl.

comtesse *f noun* countess.

concentré , -ée
1 *adjective* (*lait*) condensed; (*attentif*) concentrating (hard).
2 *m noun* **c. de tomates** tomato purée.

concentrer *verb* to concentrate.

concentrer (se) *reflexive verb* to concentrate.

concerner *verb* to concern.

concert *m noun* concert.

concessionnaire *m or f noun* (authorized) dealer.

concierge *m or f noun* caretaker.

concitoyen , -enne *m or f noun* fellow citizen.

conclure * *verb* to conclude (que that).

conclusion *f noun* conclusion.

concombre *m noun* cucumber.

concordant , -ante *adjective* in agreement.

concorder *verb* to agree; **c. avec** to match.

concours *m noun* (*examen*) competitive examination; (*jeu*) competition; **c. hippique** horse show.

concret , -ète *adjective* concrete.

conçu , -ue *adjective* **c. pour faire/pour quelqu'un** designed to do/for somebody; **bien c.** (*maison etc*) well designed.

concurrence *f noun* competition; **faire c. à** to compete with.

concurrencer *verb* to compete with.

concurrent , -ente *m or f noun* competitor.

condamnation *f noun* (*peine*) sentence; (*critique*) condemnation.

condamné , -ée *m or f noun* condemned man *or* woman.

condamner *verb* to condemn; (*accusé*) to sentence (à to); (*porte*) to block up; **c. à une amende** to fine.

condition *f noun* condition; **conditions** (*clauses, tarifs*) terms; **à c. de faire, à c. que l'on fasse** providing *or* provided (that) one does.

conditionné *adjective* **à air c.** (*pièce etc*) air-conditioned.

conditionnel *m noun* Grammaire conditional.

condoléances *fpl noun* sympathy.

conducteur , -trice *m or f noun* driver.

conduire * *verb* to lead; (*voiture*) to drive; (*eau*) to carry; **c. quelqu'un à** (*accompagner*) to take somebody to.

conduire (se) *reflexive verb* to behave.

conduite *f noun* behaviour; (*de voiture*) driving (de of); (*d'eau, de gaz*) main; **c. à gauche** (*volant*) left-hand drive.

cône *m noun* cone.

confection *f noun* making (de of); **vêtements de c.** ready-made clothes.

confectionner *verb* to make.

conférence *f noun* conference.

confesser *verb* to confess.

confesser (se) *reflexive verb* to confess.

confession *f noun* confession.

confettis *mpl noun* confetti.

confiance *f noun* trust; **faire c. à quelqu'un, avoir c. en quelqu'un** to trust somebody; **c. en soi** (self-)confidence.

confiant , -ante *adjective* trusting; (*sûr de soi*) confident.

confidence *f noun* (*secret*) confidence; **faire une c. à quelqu'un** to confide in somebody

confidentiel , -ielle *adjective* confidential.

confier *verb* **c. à quelqu'un** (*enfant, objet*) to give somebody to look after; **c. un secret/etc à quelqu'un** to confide a secret/etc to somebody; **se c. à quelqu'un** to confide in somebody

confirmation *f noun* confirmation.

confirmer *verb* to confirm (que that).

confiserie *f noun* sweet shop; **confiseries** (*produits*) sweets.

confiseur , -euse *m or f noun* confectioner.

confisquer *verb* to confiscate (à quelqu'un from somebody).

confit *adjective* fruits confits candied fruit.

confiture *f noun* jam.

conflit *m noun* conflict.

confondre *verb* (*choses, personnes*) to mix up, confuse; c. avec to mistake for.

confort *m noun* comfort.

confortable *adjective* comfortable.

confrère *m noun* colleague.

confus , -fuse *adjective* confused; (*gêné*) embarrassed; je suis c.! (*désolé*) I'm terribly sorry!

confusion *f noun* confusion; (*gêne, honte*) embarrassment.

congé *m noun* (*vacances*) holiday; c. de maladie sick leave; congés payés paid holidays.

congélateur *m noun* freezer, deep-freeze.

congeler *verb* to freeze.

congère *f noun* snowdrift.

congrès *m noun* congress.

conjoint *m noun* spouse.

conjonction *f noun* Grammaire conjunction.

conjugaison *f noun* conjugation.

conjuguer *verb* to conjugate.

connaissance *f noun* knowledge; (*personne*) acquaintance; connaissances knowledge (en of); faire la c. de quelqu'un, faire c. avec quelqu'un to meet somebody; perdre c. to lose consciousness; sans c. unconscious.

connaître * *verb* to know; (*rencontrer*) to meet; nous nous connaissons déjà we've met before; s'y c. en quelque chose to know

(all) about something.

connu , -ue
1 *past participle of* connaître.
2 *adjective* (*célèbre*) well-known.

conquérant , -ante *m or f noun* conqueror.

conquérir * *verb* to conquer.

conquête *f noun* conquest; faire la c. de to conquer.

consacrer *verb* (*temps, vie etc*) to devote (à to); se c. à to devote oneself to.

conscience *f noun* (*psychologique*) consciousness; (*morale*) conscience; avoir/prendre c. de to be/become conscious or aware of; c. professionnelle conscientiousness.

consciencieux , -euse *adjective* conscientious.

conscient , -ente *adjective* c. de aware of.

conseil [1] *m noun* un c. a piece of advice; des conseils advice.

conseil [2] *m noun* (*assemblée*) council; c. d'administration board of directors; c. des ministres (*réunion*) cabinet meeting.

conseiller *verb* to advise; c. quelque chose à quelqu'un to recommend something to somebody; c. à quelqu'un de faire to advise somebody to do.

conseiller , -ère *m or f noun* (*expert*) consultant, adviser; (*d'un conseil*) councillor; c. municipal town councillor.

consentement *m noun* consent.

consentir * *verb* c. à to consent to.

conséquence *f noun* consequence.

conséquent (par) *adverb* consequently.

conservation f noun preservation.

conservatoire m noun school (of music, drama).

conserve f noun conserves tinned or canned food; **en c.** tinned, canned; **mettre en c.** to tin, can; **boîte de c.** tin, can.

conserver verb to keep; (fruits, vie, tradition etc) to preserve; **se c.** (aliment) to keep.

considérable adjective considerable.

considérer verb to consider (que that, comme to be).

consigne f noun (instruction) orders; (de gare) left-luggage office; (somme) deposit; **c. automatique** luggage lockers.

consigner verb (bouteille etc) to charge a deposit on.

consistant , -ante adjective (sauce etc) thick; (repas) solid.

consister verb **c. en/dans** to consist of/in; **c. à faire** to consist in doing.

consolation f noun comfort.

console f noun console.

consoler verb to comfort, console (de for); **se c. d'un échec** to get over a failure.

consolider verb to strengthen.

consommateur , -trice m or f noun consumer; (au café) customer.

consommation f noun consumption; (boisson) drink.

consommer verb
1 (aliment etc) to consume.
2 (au café) to drink; **c. beaucoup/peu** (véhicule) to be heavy/light on petrol.

consonne f noun consonant.

conspirateur , -trice m or f noun plotter.

conspiration f noun plot.

conspirer verb to plot (contre against).

constamment adverb constantly.

constat m noun (official) report.

constatation f noun observation.

constater verb to note, observe (que that); (enregistrer) to record.

consternation f noun distress.

consterner verb to distress.

constipé , -ée adjective constipated.

constituer verb (composer) to make up; (représenter) to represent; **constitué de** made up of; **se c. prisonnier** to give oneself up.

constitution f noun constitution; (composition) composition.

construction f noun building; **matériaux/jeu de c.** building materials/set.

construire * verb to build.

consul m noun consul.

consulat m noun consulate.

consultation f noun consultation; **cabinet de c.** surgery.

consulter verb to consult.

consulter (se) reflexive verb to consult.

contact m noun contact; (toucher) touch; (de voiture) ignition; **être en c. avec** to be in touch or contact with; **entrer en c. avec** to come into contact with; **mettre/couper le c.** (dans une voiture) to switch on/off the ignition; **lentilles** or **verres de c.** contact lenses.

contacter verb to contact.

contagieux , -euse adjective

contagious, infectious.

contagion *f noun* infection.

conte *m noun* tale; **c. de fée** fairy tale.

contempler *verb* to gaze at.

contemporain , -aine *adjective* & *m or f noun* contemporary.

contenance *f noun* (*d'un récipient*) capacity.

contenir * *verb* to contain; (*avoir comme capacité*) to hold.

content , -ente *adjective* pleased, happy (**de faire** to do, **de quelqu'un/quelque chose** with somebody/something); **c. de soi** self-satisfied.

contenter *verb* to satisfy, please; **se c. de** to be content *or* happy with.

contenu *m noun* (*de récipient*) contents.

conter *verb* (*histoire etc*) to tell.

contestataire *m or f noun* protester.

contestation *f noun* protest.

contester *verb*
  1 (*étudiants etc*) to protest.
  2 (*décision*) to protest against.

conteur , -euse *m or f noun* storyteller.

contexte *m noun* context.

continent *m noun* continent; (*opposé à une île*) mainland.

continu , -ue *adjective* continuous.

continuel , -elle *adjective* continual.

continuellement *adverb* continually.

continuer *verb*
  1 (*ne pas cesser*) to continue, carry on (**à** *or* **de faire** doing).
  2 (*études, préparations etc*) to continue with, to carry on with.

contour *m noun* outline.

contourner *verb* (*colline etc*) to go round.

contraceptif , -ive *adjective* & *m noun* contraceptive.

contracter *verb* (*dette*) to contract; (*assurance*) to take out.

contracter (se) *reflexive verb* to contract.

contractuel , -elle *m or f noun* traffic warden.

contradiction *f noun* contradiction.

contradictoire *adjective* contradictory; (*théories*) conflicting.

contraindre * *verb* to compel (**à faire** to do).

contrainte *f noun* compulsion.

contraire
  1 *adjective* opposite; **c. à** contrary to.
  2 *m noun* opposite; **au c.** on the contrary.

contrairement *adverb* **c. à** contrary to.

contrariant , -ante *adjective* (*action etc*) annoying; (*personne*) difficult.

contrarier *verb* (*projet etc*) to spoil; (*personne*) to annoy.

contrariété *f noun* annoyance.

contraste *m noun* contrast.

contrat *m noun* contract.

contravention *f noun* (*pour stationnement interdit*) (parking) ticket.

contre *preposition* & *adverb* against; (*en échange de*) (in exchange) for; **fâché c.** angry with; **six voix c. deux** six votes to two; **Nîmes c. Arras** (*match*) Nîmes versus Arras; **par c.** *Familiar* on the other hand; **tout c. quelque chose/quelqu'un** close to something/somebody

contre - *préfixe* counter-.

contre-attaque *f noun (plural* contre-attaques) counterattack.

contrebande *f noun (fraude)* smuggling; **de c.** *(tabac etc)* smuggled; **passer quelque chose en c.** to smuggle something.

contrebandier , -ière *m or f noun* smuggler.

contrecœur (à) *adverb* reluctantly.

contredire * *verb* to contradict; **se c.** to contradict oneself.

contre-jour (à) *adverb* against the (sun)light.

contremaître *m noun* foreman.

contre-plaqué *m noun* plywood.

contretemps *m noun* hitch.

contribuable *m or f noun* taxpayer.

contribuer *verb* to contribute (**à** to).

contribution *f noun* contribution; *(impôt)* tax.

contrôle *m noun* inspection, check(ing) *(de of)*; *(des prix, de la qualité)* control; *(maîtrise)* control; **un c.** *(examen)* a check (**sur** on); *(à l'école)* a test (**sur** on).

contrôler *verb (examiner)* to inspect, check; *(maîtriser, surveiller)* to control.

contrôleur , -euse *m or f noun* (ticket) inspector.

contrordre *m noun* change of orders.

contusion *f noun* bruise.

convaincant , -ante *adjective* convincing.

convaincre * *verb* to convince (**de** of); **c. quelqu'un de faire** to persuade somebody to do.

convaincu , -ue *adjective (certain)* convinced (**de** of).

convalescence *f noun* convalescence; **être en c.** to convalesce.

convalescent , -ente
1 *m or f noun* convalescent.
2 *adjective* **être c.** to convalesce.

convenable *adjective* suitable; *(correct)* decent.

convenablement *adverb* suitably; decently.

convenir * *verb* **c. à** *(être fait pour)* to be suitable for; *(plaire à, aller à)* to suit.

convenu , -ue *adjective (prix etc)* agreed.

conversation *f noun* conversation.

convertir *verb* to convert (**à** to, **en** into).

conviction *f noun (certitude)* conviction.

convive *m or f noun* guest (*at table*).

convocation *f noun (lettre)* (written) notice to attend.

convoi *m noun (véhicules)* convoy.

convoquer *verb* to summon (**à** to).

coopération *f noun* co-operation.

coopérer *verb* to co-operate (**à** in, **avec** with).

coordonnées *fpl noun (adresse, téléphone) Familiar* contact address and phone number, particulars.

copain *m noun Familiar (camarade)* pal; *(petit ami)* boyfriend; **être c. avec** to be pals with.

copeau , -x *m noun (de bois)* shaving.

copie *f noun* copy; *(devoir, examen)* paper.

copier *verb* to copy (**sur** from).

copieux , -euse *adjective* plentiful.

copine *f noun* Familiar (*camarade*) pal; (*petite amie*) girlfriend; **être c. avec** to be pals with.

copropriété *f noun* (**immeuble en**) **c.** block of flats in joint ownership.

coq *m noun* rooster, cock; **c. au vin** coq au vin (*chicken cooked in red wine*).

coque *f noun* (*de navire*) hull; (*de noix*) shell; (*fruit de mer*) cockle; **œuf à la c.** boiled egg.

coquelicot *m noun* poppy.

coqueluche *f noun* whooping cough.

coquet , -ette *adjective* (*chic*) smart.

coquetier *m noun* egg cup.

coquetterie *f noun* (*élégance*) smartness.

coquillage *m noun* (*mollusque*) shellfish; (*coquille*) shell.

coquille *f noun* shell; **c. Saint-Jacques** scallop.

coquin , -ine *adjective* mischievous.

cor *m noun* (*instrument*) horn; **c. (au pied)** corn.

corail , -aux *m noun* coral.

Coran *m noun* **le C.** the Koran.

corbeau , -x *m noun* crow.

corbeille *f noun* basket; **c. à papier** waste paper basket.

corbillard *m noun* hearse.

corde *f noun* rope; (*plus mince*) cord; (*de raquette, violon etc*) string; **c. à linge** (washing- *or* clothes-)line; **c. à sauter** skipping rope; **les cordes** (*d'un orchestre*) the strings.

cordial , -e, -aux *adjective* warm.

cordon *m noun* (*de tablier, sac etc*) string; (*de rideau*) cord.

cordon-bleu *m noun* (*plural* **cordons-bleus**) first-class cook.

cordonnerie *f noun* shoe repair *or* repairer's shop.

cordonnier *m noun* shoe repairer.

Corée *f noun* **la C. du Nord/Sud** North/South Korea.

coréen , -enne *adjective & m or f noun* Korean.

coriace *adjective* tough.

corne *f noun* (*de chèvre etc*) horn; (*de cerf*) antler; (*matière, instrument*) horn.

corneille *f noun* crow.

cornet *m noun* (*de glace*) cornet, cone; **c. (de papier)** (paper) cone.

cornichon *m noun* gherkin.

corps *m noun* body; **lutter c. à c.** to fight hand-to-hand; **prendre c.** (*projet*) to take shape.

correct , -e *adjective* (*exact, décent*) correct.

correctement *adverb* correctly.

correction *f noun* correction; (*punition*) thrashing; (*exactitude, décence*) correctness; **la c. de** (*devoirs, examen*) the marking of.

correspondance *f noun* correspondence; (*de train, d'autocar*) connection.

correspondant , -ante **1** *adjective* corresponding. **2** *m or f noun* (*d'un adolescent etc*) pen friend; (*au téléphone*) caller.

correspondre *verb* to correspond (**à** to, with); (*écrire*) to correspond (**avec** with).

corrida *f noun* bullfight.

corriger *verb* to correct; (*devoir*) to mark; **c. quelqu'un de** (*défaut*) to cure somebody of.

corriger (se) *reflexive verb* (*soi-même*) (*ses erreurs*) to correct one's work; (*ses défauts*) to mend one's ways; (*l'un l'autre*) to correct each other's works.

corrompu , -ue *adjective* corrupt.

corsage *m noun* (*chemisier*) blouse.

Corse (la) *f noun* Corsica.

corse *adjective & m or f noun* Corsican.

cortège *m noun* procession; **c. officiel** (*automobiles*) motorcade.

corvée *f noun* chore.

cosmonaute *m or f noun* cosmonaut.

cosmos *m noun* (*univers*) cosmos; (*espace*) outer space.

cosse *f noun* (*de pois etc*) pod.

costaud , -aude *adjective* Familiar brawny.

costume *m noun* (*déguisement*) costume; (*complet*) suit.

costumé *adjective* **bal c.** fancy-dress *or* costume ball.

côte *f noun* rib; (*de mouton*) chop; (*de veau*) cutlet; (*montée*) hill; (*littoral*) coast; **c. à c.** side by side.

côté *m noun* side; (*direction*) way; **d'un c. ... de l'autre c.** on one side ... on the other side (**de** of); **partir de l'autre c.** to go the other way; **du c. de** (*vers, près de*) towards; **de c.** (*mettre de l'argent etc*) to one side; (*regarder*) sideways; **à c.** nearby; (*pièce*) in the other room; (*maison*) next door; **à c. de** next to, beside; (*comparaison*) compared to; **à mes côtés** by my side.

coteau , -x *m noun* (small) hill.

côtelette *f noun* (*d'agneau, de porc*) chop; (*de veau*) cutlet.

côtier , -ière *adjective* coastal.

cotisation *f noun* (*de club*) dues.

cotiser (se) *reflexive verb* to club together (**pour acheter** to buy).

coton *m noun* cotton; **c. (hydrophile)** cotton wool; **un drap en c.** a cotton sheet.

cou *m noun* neck.

couchage *m noun* **sac de c.** sleeping bag.

couchant *adjective* (*soleil*) setting.

couche *f noun* (*épaisseur*) layer; (*de peinture*) coat; (*linge de bébé*) nappy.

couché , -ée *adjective* **être c.** (*au lit*) to be in bed; (*étendu*) to be lying (down).

coucher *verb*
1 (*mettre au lit*) to put to bed; (*allonger*) to lay (down *or* out).
2 (*dormir*) to sleep.

coucher (se) *reflexive verb* to go to bed; (*s'allonger*) to lie flat *or* down; (*soleil*) to set.

couchette *f noun* (*de train*) sleeper, sleeping berth; (*de bateau*) bunk.

coucou *m noun* (*oiseau*) cuckoo; (*fleur*) cowslip.

coude *m noun* elbow; **se serrer les coudes** to help one another; **c. à c.** side by side; **coup de c.** nudge; **pousser du c.** to nudge.

coudre * *verb* to sew.

couette *f noun* duvet, continental quilt.

couler ¹ *verb* (*eau etc*) to flow; (*robinet, nez, sueur*) to run; (*fuir*) to leak.

couler ² *verb* (*bateau, nageur*) to sink.

couleur *f noun* colour; *Cartes* suit; **couleurs** (*teint*) colour; **de c. col-**

oured; **photo**/*etc* **en couleurs**
colour photo/*etc*; **téléviseur c.** *or*
en couleurs colour TV set; **de
quelle couleur est-il?** what colour is it?

couleuvre *f noun* (grass) snake.

coulisses *fpl noun* **dans les c.** in
the wings, backstage.

couloir *m noun* corridor; (*de circulation, d'une piste*) lane.

coup *m noun* blow, knock; (*léger*)
tap; (*choc moral*) blow; (*de fusil
etc*) shot; (*de crayon, d'horloge*)
stroke; (*aux échecs etc*) move;
(*fois*) *Familiar* time; **donner des
coups à** to hit; **donner un c. de
dents à quelqu'un** to bite somebody; **donner un c. de chiffon à
quelque chose** to give something
a wipe; **c. de chance** stroke of
luck; **tenter le c.** *Familiar* to have
a go; **tenir le c.** *Familiar* to hold
out; **sous le c. de** (*émotion*) under
the influence of; **après c.** afterwards; **tué sur le c.** killed outright; **à c. sûr** for sure; **tout à c.,
tout d'un c.** suddenly; **d'un seul
c.** in one go; **du c.** (*de ce fait*) as a
result.

coupable
1 *adjective* guilty (**de** of).
2 *m or f noun* guilty person,
culprit.

coupant , -ante *adjective* sharp.

coupe *f noun* (*trophée*) cup; (*à
boire*) goblet; (*de vêtement etc*)
cut; **c. de cheveux** haircut.

coupe-ongles *invariable m noun*
(finger nail) clippers.

coupe-papier *invariable m noun*
paper knife.

couper *verb* to cut; (*arbre*) to cut
down; (*téléphone*) to cut off;
(*courant etc*) to switch off; (*mor-
celer*) to cut up; (*traverser*) to cut

across; **c. la parole à quelqu'un**
to cut somebody short; **ne coupez
pas!** (*au téléphone*) hold the line!

couper (se) *reflexive verb*
(*routes*) to intersect; **se c. au
doigt** to cut one's finger.

couple *m noun* pair, couple.

couplet *m noun* verse.

coupure *f noun* cut; (*de journal*)
cutting; **c. d'électricité** blackout,
power cut.

cour *f noun* court(yard); (*de roi*)
court; **c. (de récréation)** playground.

courage *m noun* courage; **bon c.!**
good luck!

courageux , -euse *adjective*
courageous.

couramment *adverb* (*parler*)
fluently; (*souvent*) frequently.

courant , -ante
1 *adjective* (*fréquent*) common;
(*eau*) running; (*modèle*) standard.
2 *m noun* (*de l'eau, électrique*)
current; **c. d'air** draught; **coupure de c.** blackout, power cut;
être/mettre au c. to know/tell
(**de** about).

courbaturé , -ée *adjective*
aching (all over).

courbe
1 *adjective* curved.
2 *f noun* curve.

courber *verb* to bend.

coureur *m noun* runner; (*cycliste*)
cyclist; (*automobile*) racing
driver.

courgette *f noun* courgette.

courir * *verb*
1 (*enfant, sportif*) to run; (*se hâter*) to rush; (*participer à une
course*) to race; **le bruit court
que...** there's a rumour going
around that ...
2 (*risque*) to run; (*épreuve spor-*

tive) to run (in); (*danger*) to face.

couronne *f noun* crown; (*pour enterrement*) wreath.

couronnement *m noun* (*de roi etc*) coronation.

couronner *verb* to crown.

courrier *m noun* post, mail; **c. électronique** electronic mail, e-mail.

courroie *f noun* strap; (*de transmission*) belt.

cours *m noun* course; (*d'une monnaie etc*) rate; (*leçon*) class; (*série de leçons*) course; **c. d'eau** river, stream; **c. du change** exchange rate; **en c.** (*travail*) in progress; (*année*) current; **en c. de route** on the way; **au c. de** during.

course [1] *f noun* (*action*) run(ning); (*épreuve de vitesse*) race; **courses** (*de chevaux*) races; **cheval de c.** racehorse; **voiture de c.** racing car.

course [2] *f noun* (*commission*) errand; **courses** (*achats*) shopping; **faire une c.** to run an errand; **faire les courses** to do the shopping.

coursier , -ière *m or f noun* messenger.

court , courte
  1 *adjective* short.
  2 *adverb* (*couper, s'arrêter*) short; **à c. de** (*argent etc*) short of.
  3 *m noun Tennis* court.

couru , -ue
  1 *past participle of* **courir**.
  2 *adjective* (*spectacle*) popular.

couscous *m noun* couscous.

cousin , -ine *m or f noun* cousin.

coussin *m noun* cushion.

cousu, -ue *past participle of* **coudre**.

couteau , -x *m noun* knife.

coûter *verb* to cost; **ça coûte combien?** how much does it cost?; **coûte que coûte** at all costs.

coûteux , -euse *adjective* costly, expensive.

coutume *f noun* custom; **avoir c. de faire** to be accustomed to doing.

couture *f noun* sewing; (*métier*) dressmaking; (*raccord*) seam.

couturier *m noun* fashion designer.

couturière *f noun* dressmaker.

couvée *f noun* (*oiseaux*) brood.

couvent *m noun* convent.

couver *verb*
  1 (*œufs*) to sit on.
  2 (*poule*) to brood.

couvercle *m noun* lid, cover.

couvert *m noun* des **couverts** cutlery; **mettre le c.** to set *or* lay the table.

couvert , -erte *adjective* covered (**de** with, in); (*ciel*) overcast.

couverture *f noun* (*de lit*) blanket; (*de livre etc*) cover.

couveuse *f noun* incubator.

couvrir * *verb* to cover (**de** with).

couvrir (se) *reflexive verb* (*s'habiller*) to wrap up; (*ciel*) to cloud over.

cow-boy *m noun* cowboy.

crabe *m noun* crab.

crachat *m noun* spit, spittle.

cracher *verb*
  1 (*personne*) to spit.
  2 (*nourriture etc*) to spit (out).

craie *f noun* chalk.

craindre * *verb* to be afraid of, fear; (*chaleur, froid*) to be sensitive to; **c. de faire** to be afraid of doing; **ne craignez rien** don't be afraid.

craint , -ainte *past participle of* craindre.

crainte *f noun* fear.

craintif , -ive *adjective* timid.

crampe *f noun* cramp.

cramponner (se) *reflexive verb* se c. à to hold on to, cling to.

crampons *mpl noun* (*de chaussures*) studs.

cran *m noun* (*entaille*) notch; (*de ceinture*) hole; **couteau à c. d'arrêt** flick-knife; **c. de sûreté** safety catch.

crâne *m noun* skull.

crapaud *m noun* toad.

craquement *m noun* snapping *or* cracking (sound).

craquer *verb* (*branche*) to snap; (*bois sec*) to crack; (*sous la dent*) to crunch; (*se déchirer*) to split, rip; (*personne*) to break down.

crasse *f noun* filth.

crasseux , -euse *adjective* filthy.

cratère *m noun* crater.

cravate *f noun* tie.

crawl *m noun* (*nage*) crawl.

crayon *m noun* pencil; **c. de couleur** coloured pencil; (*en cire*) crayon; **c. à bille** ballpoint (pen).

crayonner *verb* to pencil.

création *f noun* creation.

créature *f noun* creature.

crèche *f noun* (*de Noël*) manger; (*pour bébé*) (day) nursery, crèche.

crédit *m noun* credit; **à c.** on credit; **faire c.** (*prêter*) to give credit (à to).

créditeur *adjective* **compte c.** account in credit.

créer *verb* to create.

crémaillère *f noun* **pendre la c.** to have a house-warming (party).

crématorium *m noun* crematorium.

crème *f noun* cream; (*dessert*) cream dessert; **c. Chantilly** whipped cream; **c. glacée** ice cream; **c. à raser** shaving cream; **c. anglaise** custard.

crémerie *f noun* dairy.

créneau , -x *m noun* **faire un c.** to reverse into a parking space.

crêpe *f noun* pancake.

crêperie *f noun* pancake house.

crépiter *verb* to crackle.

crépu , -ue *adjective* frizzy.

crépuscule *m noun* twilight, dusk.

cresson *m noun* (water)cress.

crête *f noun* (*de montagne etc*) crest.

creuser *verb* to dig; **se c. la tête** to rack one's brains.

creux , -euse
1 *adjective* hollow; (*estomac*) empty; **assiette creuse** soup plate.
2 *m noun* hollow; (*de l'estomac*) pit.

crevaison *f noun* (*de pneu*) puncture, flat.

crevasse *f noun* (*trou*) crevice.

crevé , -ée *adjective* (*fatigué*) Familiar worn out; (*mort*) Familiar dead.

crever *verb*
1 (*éclater*) (*bulle etc*) to burst; (*pneu*) to puncture, burst; (*mourir*) Familiar to die.
2 (*sac, ballon, pneu*) to burst; (*œil*) to put out.

crevette *f noun* (*grise*) shrimp; (*rose*) prawn.

cri *m noun* (*de joie, surprise*) cry, shout; (*de peur*) scream; (*de douleur*) cry; (*appel*) call, cry.

cric *m noun* (*de voiture*) jack.

crier verb to shout (out); (de peur) to scream; **c. après quelqu'un** Familiar to shout at somebody.

crime m noun crime; (assassinat) murder.

criminel , -elle
1 adjective criminal.
2 m or f noun criminal; (assassin) murderer.

crinière f noun mane.

crise f noun crisis; (accès) attack; (de colère etc) fit.

crisper verb (visage) to make tense; (poing) to clench.

cristal , -aux m noun crystal.

critique
1 adjective critical.
2 f noun (reproche) criticism.

critiquer verb to criticize.

croate adjective & m or f noun Croat(ian).

Croatie (la) f noun Croatia.

croc m noun (dent) fang.

croche-pied m noun **faire un c. à quelqu'un** to trip somebody up.

crochet m noun hook; (aiguille) crochet hook; (travail) crochet; **faire quelque chose au c.** to crochet something; **faire un c.** (personne) to make a detour.

crochu , -ue adjective (nez) hooked.

crocodile m noun crocodile.

croire * verb to believe (à, en in); (estimer) to think, believe (que that); **j'ai cru la voir** I thought I saw her.

croisement m noun (de routes) crossroads.

croiser verb (jambes, ligne etc) to cross; **c. quelqu'un** to pass or meet somebody.

croiser (se) reflexive verb (voitures etc) to pass (each other); (routes) to cross.

croisière f noun cruise.

croissant m noun crescent; (pâtisserie) croissant.

croix f noun cross.

croque-madame invariable m noun = toasted cheese and ham sandwich topped with fried egg.

croque-monsieur invariable m noun toasted cheese and ham sandwich.

croquer verb to crunch.

croquis m noun sketch.

crosse f noun (de fusil) butt.

crotte f noun (de lapin etc) droppings, mess.

crottin m noun (horse) dung.

croustillant , -ante adjective (pain) crusty.

croustiller verb to be crusty.

croûte f noun (de pain etc) crust; (de fromage) rind; (de plaie) scab.

croûton m noun crust (at end of loaf).

croyant , -ante
1 adjective **être c.** to be a believer.
2 m or f noun believer.

CRS mpl abbreviation (Compagnies républicaines de sécurité) riot police.

cru [1], **crue** past participle of croire.

cru [2], **crue** adjective (aliment etc) raw.

cruauté f noun cruelty (envers to).

cruche f noun pitcher, jug.

crudités fpl noun assorted raw vegetables.

cruel , -elle adjective cruel (envers, avec to).

Cuba m or f noun Cuba.

cubain , -aine adjective & m or f

noun Cuban.

cube
1 *m noun* cube; **cubes** (*jeu*) building blocks.
2 *adjective* (*mètre etc*) cubic.

cueillette *f noun* picking; (*fruits cueillis*) harvest.

cueillir * *verb* to pick.

cuiller , cuillère *f noun* spoon; petite c., c. à café teaspoon; c. à soupe soup spoon, tablespoon.

cuillerée *f noun* spoonful; c. à café teaspoonful; c. à soupe tablespoonful.

cuir *m noun* leather.

cuire * *verb* to cook; c. (au four) to bake; (*viande*) to roast; faire c. to cook.

cuisine *f noun* (*pièce*) kitchen; (*article, aliments*) cooking; faire la c. to cook, do the cooking; livre de c. cook(ery) book.

cuisiner *verb* to cook.

cuisinier , -ière
1 *m or f noun* cook.
2 *f noun* (*appareil*) cooker, stove; c. électrique/à gaz electric/gas cooker.

cuisse *f noun* thigh; (*de poulet*) leg.

cuisson *f noun* cooking.

cuit , cuite
1 *past participle of* **cuire**.
2 *adjective* cooked; bien c. well done.

cuivre *m noun* (*rouge*) copper; (*jaune*) brass; les cuivres (*d'un orchestre*) the brass (section).

culbute *f noun* (*saut*) somersault; (*chute*) (backward) tumble.

culbuter *verb* to tumble over (backwards).

culotte *f noun* (*de sportif*) (pair of) shorts; (*de femme*) (pair of) knickers; **culottes (courtes)** short trousers.

culte *m noun* (*de dieu*) worship; (*religion*) form of worship.

cultivateur , -trice *m or f noun* farmer.

cultivé , -ée *adjective* (*personne*) cultivated.

cultiver *verb* (*terre*) to farm; (*plantes*) to grow.

cultiver (se) *reflexive verb* to improve one's mind.

culture *f noun* culture; (*agriculture*) farming; (*de légumes*) growing.

culturel , -elle *adjective* cultural.

cure *f noun* (course of) treatment, cure.

curé *m noun* (parish) priest.

cure-dents *invariable m noun* toothpick.

curer *verb* to clean out.

curieux , -euse
1 *adjective* (*bizarre*) curious; (*indiscret*) inquisitive, curious (de about).
2 *m or f noun* inquisitive person; (*badaud*) onlooker.

curiosité *f noun* curiosity.

curriculum (vitæ) *invariable m noun* cv.

curseur *m noun* (*d'ordinateur*) cursor.

cuve *f noun* (*réservoir*) tank.

cuvette *f noun* (*récipient*) basin, bowl; (*des toilettes*) bowl.

cycle *m noun* (*série*) cycle.

cyclisme *m noun* cycling.

cycliste *m or f noun* cyclist; course c. cycle *or* bicycle race; champion c. cycling champion.

cyclomoteur *m noun* moped.

cyclone *m noun* cyclone.

cygne *m noun* swan.

cylindre *m noun* cylinder.

cylindrée *f noun* (engine) capacity.

cylindrique *adjective* cylindrical.

cymbale *f noun* cymbal.

cyprès *m noun* (*arbre*) cypress.

cypriote *adjective & m or f noun* Cypriot.

D

dactylo *f noun* (*personne*) typist; (*action*) typing.

dactylographier *verb* to type.

daim *m noun* fallow deer; (*cuir*) suede.

dallage *m noun* paving.

dalle *f noun* paving stone.

dallé , -ée *adjective* paved.

dame *f noun* lady; (*mariée*) married lady; *Échecs Cartes* queen; (*au jeu de dames*) king; **(jeu de) dames** draughts.

damier *m noun* draughtboard.

dandiner (se) *reflexive verb* to waddle.

Danemark (le) *m noun* Denmark.

danger *m noun* danger; **en d.** in danger; **mettre en d.** to endanger; **en cas de d.** in an emergency; **en d. de mort** in peril of death; **'d. de mort'** (*panneau*) 'danger'; **être sans d.** to be safe.

dangereusement *adverb* dangerously.

dangereux , -euse *adjective* dangerous (**pour** to).

danois , -oise
1 *adjective* Danish.
2 *m or f noun* Dane.
3 *m noun* (*langue*) Danish.

dans *preposition* in; (*changement de lieu*) into; (*à l'intérieur de*) inside; **entrer d.** to go in(to); **boire/ prendre**/*etc* **d.** to drink/take/*etc* from *or* out of; **d. deux jours**/*etc* (*temps futur*) in two days/*etc*; **d. les dix francs**/*etc* about ten francs/*etc*.

danse *f noun* dance; **la d.** (*art*) dancing.

danser *verb* to dance.

danseur , -euse *m or f noun* dancer.

date *f noun* date; **en d. du ...** dated the ... ; **d. d'expiration** expiry date; **d. limite** deadline.

dater *verb* to date (**de** from); **à d. de** as from.

datte *f noun* (*fruit*) date.

dauphin *m noun* dolphin.

davantage *adverb* (*quantité*) more; (*temps*) longer; **d. de temps**/*etc* more time/*etc*; **d. que** more than; longer than.

de ¹ (**d'** *before a vowel or mute h*; **de + le = du, de + les = des**) *preposition* (*complément d'un nom*) of; **les rayons du soleil** the rays of the sun; **le livre de Paul** Paul's book; **un pont de fer** an iron bridge; **une augmentation d'impôts**/*etc* an increase in taxes/*etc*.

▪ (*complément d'un adjectif*) **digne de** worthy of; **heureux de** happy to; **content de quelque chose/quelqu'un** pleased with something/somebody.

▪ (*complément d'un verbe*) **parler de** to speak of *or* about; **décider de faire** to decide to do.

▪ (*provenance: lieu & temps*) from; **mes amis du village** my friends from the village.

▪ (*agent*) **accompagné de** accompanied by.

▪ (*moyen*) **armé de** armed with; **se nourrir de** to live on.

▪ (*manière*) **d'une voix douce** in *or* with a gentle voice.

▪ (*cause*) **mourir de faim** to die of hunger.

▪ (*temps*) **travailler de nuit** to

work by night; **six heures du matin** six o'clock in the morning.
▮ (*mesure*) **avoir** or **faire six mètres de haut** to be six metres high; **homme de trente ans** thirty-year-old man; **gagner cent francs de l'heure** to earn a hundred francs an hour.

de[2] *article* some; **elle boit du vin** she drinks (some) wine; **il ne boit pas de vin** (*négation*) he doesn't drink (any) wine; **des fleurs** (some) flowers; **de jolies fleurs** (some) pretty flowers; **il y en a six de tués** (*avec un nombre*) there are six killed.

dé *m noun* (*à jouer*) dice; (*à coudre*) thimble; **jouer aux dés** to play dice.

déballer *verb* to unpack.

débarbouiller (se) *reflexive verb* to wash one's face.

débarcadère *m noun* quay, wharf.

débarquement *m noun* landing; unloading.

débarquer *verb* (*passagers*) to land; (*marchandises*) to unload.

débarras *m noun* lumber room; **bon d.!** *Familiar* good riddance!

débarrasser *verb* (*table etc*) to clear (**de** of); **d. quelqu'un de** (*ennemi, soucis etc*) to rid somebody of; (*manteau etc*) to relieve somebody of; **se d. de** to get rid of.

débat *m noun* discussion, debate.

débattre * *verb* to discuss, debate.

débattre (se) *reflexive verb* to struggle (to get free).

débile
  1 *adjective* (*esprit, enfant etc*) weak; *Familiar* idiotic.
  2 *m or f noun Familiar* idiot.

débit *m noun* (*vente*) turnover;

(*compte*) debit; (*de fleuve*) flow; **d. de boissons** bar, café.

débiter *verb* (*découper*) to cut up (**en** into); (*vendre*) to sell; (*compte*) to debit.

débiteur , -trice
  1 *m or f noun* debtor.
  2 *adjective* **compte d.** account in debit.

déblayer *verb* (*terrain, décombres*) to clear.

débloquer *verb* (*mécanisme*) to unjam; (*crédits*) to release.

déboîter *verb*
  1 (*tuyau*) to disconnect; (*os*) to dislocate.
  2 (*sortir d'une file*) to pull out, change lanes.

déborder *verb*
  1 (*fleuve, liquide*) to overflow; **l'eau déborde du vase** the vase is overflowing.
  2 (*dépasser*) to go beyond; **débordé de travail** snowed under with work.

débouché *m noun* (*carrière*) opening; (*marché pour produit*) outlet.

déboucher *verb* (*bouteille*) to open, uncork; (*lavabo, tuyau*) to unblock.

débourser *verb* to pay out.

debout *adverb* standing (up); **mettre d.** (*planche etc*) to stand up, put upright; **se mettre d.** to stand or get up; **rester d.** to remain standing; **être d.** (*levé*) to be up; **d.!** get up!

déboutonner *verb* to unbutton, undo.

débraillé , -ée *adjective* (*tenue etc*) slovenly, sloppy.

débrancher *verb* to unplug, disconnect.

débrayer *verb* (*conducteur*) to

press the clutch.

débris *mpl noun* fragments; (*restes*) remains; (*détritus*) rubbish.

débrouillard , -arde *adjective* smart, resourceful.

débrouiller (se) *reflexive verb* to manage (**pour faire** to do).

début *m noun* start, beginning; **au d.** at the beginning.

débutant , -ante *m or f noun* beginner.

débuter *verb* to start, begin.

décaféiné , -ée *adjective* decaffeinated.

décalage *m noun* (*écart*) gap; **d. horaire** time difference.

décalcomanie *f noun* (*image*) transfer.

décaler *verb* to shift.

décalquer *verb* (*dessin*) to trace.

décapant *m noun* cleaning agent; (*pour enlever la peinture*) paint stripper.

décaper *verb* (*métal*) to clean; (*surface peinte*) to strip.

décapiter *verb* to behead.

décapotable *adjective* (*voiture*) convertible.

décapsuler *verb* **d. une bouteille** to take the top off a bottle.

décapsuleur *m noun* bottle-opener.

décéder *verb* to die.

déceler *verb* (*trouver*) to detect.

décembre *m noun* December.

décemment *adverb* decently.

décent , -ente *adjective* (*convenable*) decent.

déception *f noun* disappointment.

décerner *verb* (*prix*) to award.

décès *m noun* death.

décevant , -ante *adjective* disappointing.

décevoir * *verb* to disappoint.

déchaîné , -ée *adjective* (*foule*) wild.

déchaîner *verb* **d. l'enthousiasme/les rires** to set off wild enthusiasm/a storm of laughter.

déchaîner (se) *reflexive verb* (*tempête, rires*) to break out; (*foule*) to run riot; (*personne*) to fly into a rage.

décharge *f noun* **d. (publique)** (rubbish) dump; **d. (électrique)** (electric) shock.

déchargement *m noun* unloading.

décharger *verb* to unload; (*batterie*) to discharge.

décharger (se) *reflexive verb* (*batterie*) to go flat.

déchausser (se) *reflexive verb* to take one's shoes off.

déchet *m noun* **déchets** (*restes*) waste; **il y a du d.** there's some waste.

déchiffrer *verb* to decipher.

déchiqueter *verb* to tear to shreds.

déchirer *verb* (*page etc*) to tear (up); (*vêtement*) to tear; (*ouvrir*) to tear open.

déchirer (se) *reflexive verb* (*robe etc*) to tear.

déchirure *f noun* tear.

décidé , -ée *adjective* (*air, ton*) determined; **d. à faire** determined to do.

décidément *adverb* undoubtedly.

décider *verb*
1 (*opération*) to decide on; **d. que** to decide that.
2 d. de faire to decide to do.

décider (se) *reflexive verb* **se d. à faire** to make up one's mind to do.

décimal , -e, -aux *adjective* decimal.

décimètre *m noun* decimetre; **double d.** ruler.

décisif , -ive *adjective* decisive.

décision *f noun* decision; *(fermeté)* determination.

déclaration *f noun* declaration; *(de vol etc)* notification; *(commentaire)* statement; **d. de revenus** tax return.

déclarer *verb* to declare **(que** that); *(vol etc)* to notify; **'rien à d.'** *(à la douane)* nothing to declare.

déclarer (se) *reflexive verb* *(incendie)* to break out.

déclencher *verb* *(mécanisme, réaction)* to trigger off, start (off); *(attaque)* to launch.

déclencher (se) *reflexive verb* *(alarme etc)* to go off.

déclic *m noun* *(bruit)* click.

décoiffer *verb* **d. quelqu'un** to mess up somebody's hair.

décollage *m noun* *(d'avion)* take-off.

décoller *verb*
1 *(avion)* to take off.
2 *(timbre)* to unstick; **se d.** to come unstuck.

décolorer (se) *reflexive verb* to fade.

décombres *mpl noun* rubble.

décongeler *verb*
1 (faire) d. *(aliment)* to thaw.
2 *(fondre)* to thaw.

déconseiller *verb* **d. quelque chose à quelqu'un** to advise somebody against something; **d. à quelqu'un de faire** to advise somebody against doing.

décontracter (se) *reflexive verb* to relax.

décor *m noun* *(théâtre, paysage)* scenery; *(d'intérieur)* decoration.

décorateur , -trice *m or f noun* (interior) decorator.

décoratif , -ive *adjective* decorative.

décoration *f noun* decoration.

décorer *verb* *(maison, soldat)* to decorate **(de** with).

découdre *verb* to unstitch; **se d.** to come unstitched.

découpage *m noun* *(image)* cut-out.

découper *verb* *(viande)* to carve; *(article)* to cut out.

découragement *m noun* discouragement.

décourager *verb* to discourage; **se d.** to get discouraged.

découvert *m noun* *(d'un compte)* overdraft.

découverte *f noun* discovery.

découvrir * *verb* to discover **(que** that).

découvrir (se) *reflexive verb* *(dans son lit)* to push to bedcovers off; *(ciel)* to clear (up).

décrasser *verb* *(nettoyer)* to clean.

décrire * *verb* to describe.

décroché *adjective* *(téléphone)* off the hook.

décrocher *verb* *(détacher)* to unhook; *(tableau)* to take down; **se d.** *(tableau)* to fall down; **d. (le téléphone)** to pick up the phone.

décrotter *verb* to clean (the mud off).

déçu , -ue
1 *past participle of* **décevoir**.
2 *adjective* disappointed.

déculotter (se) *reflexive verb* to take off one's trousers.

dédaigner *verb* to scorn, despise.

dédaigneux , -euse *adjective* scornful.

dédain *m noun* scorn.

dedans
1 *adverb* inside; **en d.** on the inside; **tomber d.** (*trou*) to fall in (it); **je me suis fait rentrer d.** (*accident de voiture*) someone crashed into me.
2 *m noun* **le d.** the inside.

dédommagement *m noun* compensation.

dédommager *verb* to compensate (**de** for).

déduction *f noun* deduction.

déduire * *verb* (*soustraire*) to deduct (**de** from).

déesse *f noun* goddess.

défaire * *verb* (*nœud etc*) to undo; (*valise*) to unpack; **se d.** to come undone.

défait *adjective* (*lit*) unmade.

défaite *f noun* defeat.

défaut *m noun* (*faiblesse*) fault; (*de fabrication*) defect.

défavorable *adjective* unfavourable (**à** to).

défavoriser *verb* to put at a disadvantage.

défectueux , -euse *adjective* faulty, defective.

défendre [1] *verb* (*protéger*) to defend; **se d.** to defend oneself.

défendre [2] *verb* (*interdire*) **d. à quelqu'un de faire** to forbid somebody to do; **d. quelque chose à quelqu'un** to forbid somebody something.

défendu , -ue
1 *past participle of* **défendre**.
2 *adjective* forbidden.

défense [1] *f noun* (*protection*) defence; (*d'éléphant*) tusk.

défense [2] *f noun* (*interdiction*) **'d. de fumer'** 'no smoking'; **'d. (absolue) d'entrer'** '(strictly) no entry'.

défenseur *m noun* defender.

défi *m noun* challenge; **lancer un d. à quelqu'un** to challenge somebody.

défier *verb* to challenge (**à** to); **d. quelqu'un de faire** to challenge somebody to do.

défiguré , -ée *adjective* disfigured.

défilé *m noun* (*militaire*) parade; (*gorge*) pass.

défiler *verb* (*soldats*) to march.

défini, -ie
1 *past participle of* **définir**.
2 *adjective* definite.

définir *verb* to define.

définitif , -ive *adjective* final, definitive.

définition *f noun* definition; (*de mots croisés*) clue.

défoncé , -ée *adjective* (*route*) bumpy; (*drogué*) Familiar high.

défoncer *verb* (*porte, mur*) to smash in *or* down; (*trottoir, route*) to dig up.

déformé , -ée *adjective* misshapen; **chaussée déformée** uneven road surface, bumpy road.

déformer *verb* to put out of shape; **se d.** to lose its shape.

défouler (se) *reflexive verb* to let off steam.

défricher *verb* (*terrain*) to clear.

défroisser *verb* to smooth out.

dégagé , -ée *adjective* (*ciel*) clear.

dégagement *m noun* (*action*) clearing; *Football* kick (down the pitch); **itinéraire de d.** relief road, alternative road (*to ease* traffic congestion).

dégager *verb*
1 (*table etc*) to clear (de of); (*odeur*) to give off; **d. quelqu'un de** (*décombres etc*) to pull somebody out of.
2 *Football* to clear the ball (down the pitch); **dégagez!** *Familiar* clear the way!

dégager (se) *reflexive verb* (*ciel*) to clear; **se d. de** (*personne*) to pull oneself free from; (*odeur*) to come out of.

dégainer *verb* (*arme*) to draw.

dégarni , -ie *adjective* bare; **front d.** receding hairline.

dégarnir *verb* (*arbre de Noël*) to take down the decorations from.

dégarnir (se) *reflexive verb* (*crâne*) to go bald.

dégâts *mpl noun* damage.

dégel *m noun* thaw.

dégeler *verb* to thaw (out).

dégivrer *verb* (*réfrigérateur*) to defrost.

déglingué , -ée *adjective* falling to bits.

dégonflé , -ée
1 *adjective* (*pneu*) flat; (*lâche*) *Familiar* yellow.
2 *m or f noun Familiar* yellow belly.

dégonfler *verb* (*pneu*) to let down.

dégonfler (se) *reflexive verb* (*pneu*) to go down; (*se montrer lâche*) *Familiar* to chicken out.

dégouliner *verb* to trickle.

dégourdi , -ie
1 *adjective* (*malin*) smart.
2 *m or f noun* smart boy *or* girl.

dégourdir (se) *reflexive verb* **se d. les jambes** to stretch one's legs.

dégoût *m noun* disgust; **avoir du**

d. pour quelque chose to have a (strong) dislike for something.

dégoûtant , -ante *adjective* disgusting.

dégoûté , -ée *adjective* disgusted (de, with, by); **il n'est pas d.** (*difficile*) he's not fussy.

dégoûter *verb* to disgust; **d. quelqu'un de quelque chose** to put somebody off something.

degré *m noun* (*angle, température*) degree.

dégringolade *f noun* tumble.

dégringoler *verb* to tumble (down).

déguerpir *verb* to clear off *or* out, make tracks.

dégueulasse *adjective Familiar* disgusting.

déguisement *m noun* disguise; (*de bal costumé*) fancy dress, costume.

déguiser *verb* to disguise; **d. quelqu'un (en)** (*costumer*) to dress somebody up (as); **se d. (en)** to dress oneself up (as).

déguster *verb* (*goûter*) to taste.

dehors
1 *adverb* out(side); **en d.** on the outside; **en d. de la maison** outside the house; **en d. de la ville** out of town; **au-d. (de), au d. (de)** outside.
2 *m noun* (*extérieur*) outside.

déjà *adverb* already; **elle l'a d. vu** she's seen it before, she's already seen it; **quand partez-vous, d.?** when did you say you are leaving?

déjeuner
1 *verb* (*à midi*) to have lunch; (*le matin*) to have breakfast.
2 *m noun* lunch; **petit d.** breakfast.

delà *adverb* **au-d. (de), au d. (de),** beyond.

délabré , -ée *adjective* dilapidated.

délacer *verb* (*chaussures*) to undo.

délai *m noun* time limit; **sans d.** without delay; **dernier d.** final date.

délasser (se) *reflexive verb* to relax.

délayer *verb* (*mélanger*) to mix (with liquid).

délégation *f noun* delegation.

délégué , -ée *m or f noun* delegate.

délibérer *verb* (*se consulter*) to deliberate (**de** about).

délicat , -ate *adjective* (*santé, travail*) delicate; (*geste*) tactful; (*exigeant*) particular.

délicatement *adverb* (*doucement*) delicately.

délice *m noun* delight.

délicieux , -euse *adjective* (*plat*) delicious.

délier *verb* to undo; **se d.** (*paquet*) to come undone.

délimiter *verb* (*terrain*) to mark off.

délinquant , -ante *m or f noun* delinquent.

délirer *verb* (*dire n'importe quoi*) to rave.

délit *m noun* offence.

délivrer *verb* (*prisonnier*) to release, (set) free; (*billet*) to issue.

déloger *verb* to drive out.

deltaplane ® *m noun* hang-glider.

déluge *m noun* flood; (*de pluie*) downpour.

demain *adverb* tomorrow; **à d.!** see you tomorrow!

demande *f noun* request (de

quelque chose for something); **demandes d'emploi** situations *or* jobs wanted.

demander *verb* to ask for; (*nécessiter*) to require; **d. le chemin/ l'heure** to ask the way/the time; **d. quelque chose à quelqu'un** to ask somebody for something; **d. à quelqu'un de faire** to ask somebody to do; **ça demande du temps** it takes time; **être très demandé** to be in great demand.

demander (se) *reflexive verb* to wonder (**pourquoi** why, **si** if).

démangeaison *f noun* itch; **avoir des démangeaisons** to be itching.

démanger *verb* to itch; **son bras le démange** his arm itches.

démaquiller (se) *reflexive verb* to take off one's make-up.

démarche *f noun* walk; **faire des démarches** to go through the process (**pour faire** of doing).

démarrage *m noun* start.

démarrer *verb* (*moteur*) to start (up); (*voiture*) to move off.

démarreur *m noun* starter.

démasquer *verb* to expose.

démêler *verb* (*cheveux*) to untangle.

déménagement *m noun* move, moving (house); **camion de d.** removal van.

déménager *verb* to move (house).

déménageur *m noun* removal man.

démettre *verb* **se d. le pied**/*etc* to dislocate one's foot/*etc*.

demeure *f noun* (*belle maison*) mansion.

demeurer *verb* (*auxiliary* être) (*rester*) to remain; (*auxiliary*

avoir) (*habiter*) to live.

demi , -ie
1 *adjective* half; **d.-journée** half-day; **une heure et demie** an hour and a half; (*à l'horloge*) half past one.
2 *adverb* (à) **d. plein**/*etc* half-full/*etc*.
3 *m noun* (*verre*) (half-pint) glass of beer.

demi-cercle *m noun* (*plural* **demi-cercles**) semicircle.

demi-douzaine *f noun* (*plural* **demi-douzaines**) **une d. (de)** half a dozen.

demi-finale *f noun* (*plural* **demi-finales**) semifinal.

demi-frère *m noun* (*plural* **demi-frères**) stepbrother.

demi-heure *f noun* (*plural* **demi-heures**) **une d.** a half-hour, half an hour.

demi-pension *f noun* (*plural* **demi-pensions**) half-board.

demi-pensionnaire *m or f noun* (*plural* **demi-pensionnaires**) day boarder.

démission *f noun* resignation.

démissionner *verb* to resign.

demi-sœur *f noun* (*plural* **demi-sœurs**) stepsister.

demi-tarif *invariable adjective* (*billet*) half-price.

demi-tour *m noun* (*plural* **demi-tours**) (*en voiture*) U-turn; **faire d.** (*à pied*) to turn back; (*en voiture*) to make a U-turn.

démocratie *f noun* democracy.

démocratique *adjective* democratic.

démodé , -ée *adjective* old-fashioned.

demoiselle *f noun* (*célibataire*) single woman; **d. d'honneur** (*à un mariage*) bridesmaid.

démolir *verb* (*maison*) to demolish, knock or pull down.

démolition *f noun* demolition.

démonstratif , -ive *adjective & m noun Grammaire* demonstrative.

démonstration *f noun* demonstration.

démonter *verb* (*mécanisme*) to take apart; (*tente*) to take down; **se d.** to come apart; to come down.

démontrer *verb* to show.

démoraliser *verb* to demoralize; **se d.** to become demoralized.

déneiger *verb* to clear of snow.

dénicher *verb* (*trouver*) *Familiar* to dig up.

dénoncer *verb* **d. quelqu'un** (*au professeur*) to tell on somebody (à to); **se d.** to own up (à to).

dénouer *verb* (*corde*) to undo, untie; **se d.** (*nœud*) to come undone or untied.

denrées *fpl noun* **d. alimentaires** foods.

dense *adjective* dense.

dent *f noun* tooth; (*de fourchette*) prong; **faire ses dents** (*enfant*) to be teething; **coup de d.** bite.

dentaire *adjective* dental.

dentelle *f noun* lace.

dentier *m noun* (set of) false teeth.

dentifrice *m noun* toothpaste.

dentiste *m or f noun* dentist.

déodorant *m noun* deodorant.

dépannage *m noun* (emergency) repair.

dépanner *verb* (*voiture*) to repair.

dépanneur *m noun* (*de télévision*) repairman; (*de voiture*) breakdown mechanic, emergency car mechanic.

dépanneuse *f noun* (*voiture*) breakdown lorry.

départ *m noun* departure; (*d'une course*) start; **ligne de d.** starting post; **au d.** at the start.

département *m noun* department (*subdivision administered by a prefect*).

départementale *adjective* **route d.** secondary road.

dépasser *verb*
1 (*véhicule*) to overtake; **d. quelqu'un** (*en hauteur*) to be taller than somebody; (*surclasser*) to be ahead of somebody.
2 (*se voir*) to stick out (**de** of); (*jupon etc*) to show.

dépêcher (se) *reflexive verb* to hurry (up).

dépeigné , -ée *adjective* **être d.** to have untidy hair.

dépendre *verb* to depend (**de** on, upon); **ça dépend** it depends; **ça ne dépend pas de moi** it's not up to me.

dépense *f noun* (*frais*) expense.

dépenser *verb* (*argent*) to spend.

dépenser (se) *reflexive verb* to exert oneself.

dépensier , -ière *adjective* wasteful.

dépister *verb* (*criminel*) to track down; (*maladie*) to detect.

dépit *m noun* **en d. de** in spite of; **en d. du bon sens** (*mal*) atrociously.

déplacement *m noun* (*voyage*) (business) trip.

déplacer *verb* to shift, move.

déplacer (se) *reflexive verb* (*voyager*) to travel (about).

déplaire * *verb* **ça me déplaît** I

don't like it.

dépliant *m noun* (*prospectus*) leaflet.

déplier *verb* to unfold.

déplier (se) *reflexive verb* to unfold.

déplorable *adjective* regrettable, deplorable.

déplorer *verb* (*regretter*) to deplore; **d. que** (+ *subjunctive*) to regret that.

déployer *verb* (*ailes*) to spread.

déporter *verb* (*dévier*) to carry (off course).

déposer *verb* (*poser*) to put down; (*laisser*) to leave; (*plainte*) to lodge; (*ordures*) to dump; **d. quelqu'un** (*en voiture*) to drop somebody (off).

déposer (se) *reflexive verb* (*poussière*) to settle.

dépôt *m noun* (*d'ordures*) dump; (*dans une bouteille*) deposit.

dépotoir *m noun* rubbish dump.

dépouillé , -ée *adjective* (*arbre*) bare.

dépression *f noun* depression; **d. nerveuse** nervous breakdown.

déprimé , -ée *adjective* depressed.

déprimer *verb* to depress.

depuis
1 *preposition* since; **d. lundi** since Monday; **d. qu'elle est partie** since she left; **j'habite ici d. un mois** I've been living here for a month; **d. quand êtes-vous là?** how long have you been here?; **d. Paris** from Paris.
2 *adverb* since (then).

député *m noun* (*au Parlement*) deputy, = MP.

déraciner *verb* (*arbre*) to uproot.

déraillement *m noun* derailment.

dérailler *verb* (*train*) to jump the rails.

dérangement *m noun* en d. (*téléphone*) out of order.

déranger *verb* (*affaires*) to disturb, upset; d. quelqu'un to disturb *or* bother somebody; ça vous dérange si je fume? do you mind if I smoke?

déranger (se) *reflexive verb* (*se déplacer*) to bother to come *or* go; ne te dérange pas! don't bother!

dérapage *m noun* skid.

déraper *verb* to skid.

déréglé , -ée *adjective* out of order.

dérégler *verb* (*télévision etc*) to put out of order; se d. (*montre etc*) to go wrong.

dériver *verb* (*bateau*) to drift.

dernier , -ière
1 *adjective* last; (*mode*) latest; (*étage*) top; en d. last.
2 *m or f noun* last (person *or* one); ce d. the latter; être le d. de la classe to be (at the) bottom of the class.

dernièrement *adverb* recently.

dérober *verb* (*voler*) to steal (à from).

dérouiller *verb* se d. les jambes to stretch one's legs.

dérouler *verb* (*tapis*) to unroll; (*fil*) to unwind.

dérouler (se) *reflexive verb* (*événement*) to take place.

derrick *m noun* oil rig.

derrière
1 *preposition & adverb* behind; assis d. (*dans une voiture*) sitting in the back; par d. (*attaquer*) from behind.
2 *m noun* back; (*fesses*) behind;

pattes de d. hind legs.

des *see* de [1,2], le.

dès *preposition* from; d. le début (right) from the start; d. qu'elle viendra as soon as she comes.

désaccord *m noun* disagreement.

désaccordé , -ée *adjective* (*violon etc*) out of tune.

désaffecté , -ée *adjective* (*gare etc*) disused.

désagréable *adjective* unpleasant.

désaltérer *verb* d. quelqu'un to quench somebody's thirst; se d. to quench one's thirst.

désapprouver *verb* to disapprove of.

désarmer *verb* to disarm.

désastre *m noun* disaster.

désastreux , -euse *adjective* disastrous.

désavantage *m noun* disadvantage.

désavantager *verb* to handicap.

desceller (se) *reflexive verb* to come loose.

descendre *verb*
1 (*auxiliary* être) to come *or* go down (de from); (*d'un arbre etc*) to climb down (de from); (*marée*) to go out; d. d'un train to get off a train; d. de cheval to dismount; d. en courant to run down.
2 (*auxiliary* avoir) (*escalier*) to come *or* go down; (*objet*) to bring *or* take down.

descente *f noun* (*d'avion etc*) descent; (*pente*) slope; d. de lit (*tapis*) bedside rug.

description *f noun* description.

désenfler *verb* to go down.

déséquilibre (en) *adverb* (*meuble*) unsteady.

déséquilibrer *verb* to throw off

balance.

désert , -erte *adjective* deserted;
île déserte desert island.

désert *m noun* desert.

désespérant , -ante *adjective*
(*enfant*) hopeless.

désespéré , -ée *adjective* (*personne*) in despair; (*situation*)
hopeless; (*efforts*) desperate.

désespérer *verb*
1 (*causer du désespoir à*) to drive
to despair.
2 (*éprouver du désespoir*) to despair.

désespérer (se) *reflexive verb*
to despair.

désespoir *m noun* despair.

déshabiller *verb* to undress.

déshabiller (se) *vpr* to get undressed.

désherbant *m noun* weed killer.

désherber *verb* to weed.

désigner *verb* (*montrer*) to point
to; (*élire*) to appoint; (*signifier*) to
indicate.

désinfectant *m noun* disinfectant.

désinfecter *verb* to disinfect.

désirer *verb* to want; **je désire
que tu viennes** I want you to
come.

désobéir *verb* to disobey; **d. à
quelqu'un** to disobey somebody.

désobéissant , -ante *adjective*
disobedient.

désodorisant *m noun* air
freshener.

désolé , -ée *adjective* **être d.**
(*navré*) to be sorry (**que** (+ *subjunctive*) that, **de faire** to do).

désoler *verb* to upset (very much).

désordonné , -ée *adjective*
(*personne*) messy, untidy.

désordre *m noun* (*dans une
chambre*) mess; (*dans une classe*)
disturbance; **en d.** messy, untidy.

désorganisé , -ée *adjective*
disorganized.

désormais *adverb* from now on.

desquel(le)s *see* **lequel**.

dessécher *verb* (*bouche*) to
parch.

déssécher (se) *reflexive verb*
(*plante*) to wither; (*peau*) to get
dry.

desserrer *verb* (*ceinture*) to loosen; (*poing*) to open; (*frein*) to release; **se d.** to come loose.

dessert *m noun* dessert, sweet.

desservir *verb* (*table*) to clear
(away); **le car dessert ce village**
the bus stops at this village.

dessin *m noun* drawing; **d. (humoristique)** cartoon; **d. animé**
(*film*) cartoon; **école de d.** art
school.

dessinateur , -trice *m or f noun*
drawer; **d. humoristique** cartoonist.

dessiner *verb* to draw.

dessous
1 *adverb* under(neath), below; **en
d.** under(neath); **par-d.** (*passer*)
under(neath).
2 *m noun* underside, underneath;
drap de d. bottom sheet; **les gens
du d.** the people downstairs.

dessous-de-plat *invariable m
noun* tablemat.

dessus
1 *adverb* (*marcher, monter*) on it;
(*passer*) over it; **par-d.** (*sauter*)
over (it).
2 *m noun* top; **drap de d.** top
sheet; **les gens du d.** the people
upstairs.

dessus-de-lit *invariable m noun*
bedspread.

destin *m noun* fate.

destination *f noun* (*lieu*) destination; **à d. de** (*train*) to, for.

destiner *verb* **d. quelque chose à quelqu'un** to intend something for somebody

destruction *f noun* destruction.

détachant *m noun* stain remover.

détacher [1] *verb* (*ceinture*) to undo; (*personne*) to untie; (*ôter*) to take off; **se d.** (*chien*) to break loose; (*se dénouer*) to come undone; **se d. (de quelque chose)** (*fragment*) to come off (something).

détacher [2] *verb* (*linge*) to remove the stains from.

détail [1] *m noun* detail; **en d.** in detail.

détail [2] *m noun* **de d.** (*magasin, prix*) retail; **vendre au d.** to sell retail.

détaillant , -ante *m or f noun* retailer.

détaillé , -ée *adjective* (*récit etc*) detailed.

détaler *verb* to run off.

détecteur *m noun* detector.

détective *m noun* **d. (privé)** (private) detective.

déteindre * *verb* (*couleur*) to run; **ton tablier bleu a déteint sur ma chemise** the blue of your apron has come off on my shirt.

détendre *verb* **d. quelqu'un** to relax somebody.

détendre (se) *reflexive verb* (*se reposer*) to relax; (*corde etc*) to slacken.

détendu , -ue *adjective* relaxed; (*ressort etc*) slack.

détente *f noun* (*repos*) relaxation.

détenu , -ue *m or f noun* prisoner.

détergent *m noun* detergent.

détérioration *f noun* deterioration (**de** in).

détériorer (se) *reflexive verb* to deteriorate.

déterminer *verb* (*préciser*) to determine.

déterrer *verb* to dig up.

détester *verb* to hate (**faire** doing, to do).

détonation *f noun* explosion.

détour *m noun* (*crochet*) detour.

détourné , -ée *adjective* (*chemin*) roundabout.

détournement *m noun* (*d'avion*) hijack(ing).

détourner *verb* (*dévier*) to divert; (*tête*) to turn (away); (*avion*) to hijack; **d. les yeux** to look away.

détourner (se) *reflexive verb* to turn away; **se d. de** (*chemin*) to stray from.

détraqué , -ée *adjective* out of order.

détraquer *verb* (*mécanisme*) to put out of order.

détraquer (se) *reflexive verb* (*machine*) to go wrong.

détresse *f noun* distress; **en d.** (*navire*) in distress.

détritus *mpl noun* rubbish.

détroit *m noun* strait(s).

détruire * *verb* to destroy.

dette *f noun* debt; **avoir des dettes** to be in debt.

deuil *m noun* (*vêtements*) mourning; **en d.** in mourning.

deux *adjective & m noun* two; **d. fois** twice; **tous (les) d.** both.

deuxième *adjective & m or f noun* second.

deuxièmement *adverb* secondly.

deux-pièces *invariable m noun*

(*maillot de bain*) bikini.

deux-points *invariable m noun* Grammaire colon.

deux-roues *invariable m noun* two-wheeled vehicle.

dévaler *verb*
1 (*escalier*) to race down.
2 (*tomber*) to tumble down.

dévaliser *verb* to rob.

devancer *verb* to get *or* be ahead of.

devant
1 *preposition & adverb* in front (of); d. (l'hôtel/*etc*) in front (of the hotel/*etc*); passer d. (l'église/*etc*) to go past (the church/*etc*); assis d. (*dans une voiture*) sitting in the front.
2 *m noun* front; roue de d. front wheel; patte de d. foreleg.

devanture *f noun* (*vitrine*) shop window.

dévaster *verb* to ruin, devastate.

développer *verb* (*muscles, photos etc*) to develop; se d. to develop.

devenir * *verb* (*auxiliary* être) to become; qu'est-il devenu? what's become of him?

déverser *verb* (*liquide*) to pour out (dans into).

déverser (se) *reflexive verb* (*liquide*) to pour out (dans into).

déviation *f noun* (*itinéraire provisoire*) diversion.

dévier *verb*
1 (*circulation*) to divert; (*balle*) to deflect.
2 (*de sa route*) to veer (off course).

deviner *verb* to guess.

devinette *f noun* riddle.

devis *m noun* estimate (*of cost of work to be done*).

devise *f noun* (*légende*) motto;

devises (*argent*) (foreign) currency.

dévisser *verb* to unscrew.

dévisser (se) *reflexive verb* (*bouchon*) to unscrew; (*se desserrer*) to come loose.

dévoiler *verb* (*secret*) to disclose.

devoir * 1 *auxiliary verb* (*nécessité*) je dois refuser I must refuse, I have (got) to refuse; j'ai dû refuser I had to refuse.
▮ (*probabilité*) il doit être tard it must be late; elle a dû oublier she must have forgotten; il ne doit pas être bête he can't be stupid.
▮ (*obligation*) tu dois apprendre tes leçons you must learn your lessons; il aurait dû venir he should have come; vous devriez rester you should stay.
▮ (*événement prévu*) elle doit venir she's supposed to be coming, she's due to come.

devoir * 2
1 *verb* (*argent etc*) to owe (à to).
2 *m noun* (*obligation*) duty; (*exercice*) exercise; devoirs (*à faire à la maison*) homework; d. sur table class exam(ination).

dévorer *verb* (*manger*) to eat up.

dévoué , -ée *adjective* (*soldat etc*) dedicated.

dévouement *m noun* dedication.

dévouer (se) *reflexive verb* se d. (pour quelqu'un) to sacrifice oneself (for somebody).

diabète *m noun* diabetes.

diabétique *m or f noun* diabetic.

diable *m noun* devil; habiter au d. to live miles from anywhere.

diagnostic *m noun* diagnosis.

diagonale *f noun* diagonal (line); en d. diagonally.

dialecte *m noun* dialect.

dialogue *m noun* conversation; (*de film*) dialogue.

diamant *m noun* diamond.

diamètre *m noun* diameter.

diapositive , *Familiar* **diapo** *f noun* (colour) slide.

diarrhée *f noun* diarrh(o)ea.

dictée *f noun* dictation.

dicter *verb* to dictate (à to).

dictionnaire *m noun* dictionary.

dicton *m noun* saying.

Dieppe *m or f noun* Dieppe.

diesel *adjective & m noun* (**moteur**) **d.** diesel (engine).

diète *f noun* à la d. (*au régime*) on a diet.

diététique *adjective* **produit d.** health food.

dieu , **-x** *m noun* god; **D.** God; **mon D.!** *Familiar* (good) God!

différé *m noun* **en d.** (*émission*) recorded.

différence *f noun* difference (de in).

différent , **-ente** *adjective* different (de from, to).

difficile *adjective* difficult; (*exigeant*) fussy; **d. à faire** difficult to do; **il nous est d. de** it's difficult for us to.

difficulté *f noun* difficulty; **en d.** in a difficult situation.

diffuser *verb* (*émission*) to broadcast.

digérer *verb* to digest.

digestif , **-ive**
1 *adjective* digestive.
2 *m noun* after-dinner liqueur.

digestion *f noun* digestion.

digne *adjective* **d. de** worthy of.

digue *f noun* dike; (*en bord de mer*) sea wall.

dilater *verb* (*pupille*) to dilate; (*gaz*) to expand.

dilater (se) *reflexive verb* (*pupille*) to dilate; (*gaz*) to expand.

diligence *f noun* (*véhicule*) stagecoach.

dimanche *m noun* Sunday.

dimension *f noun* dimension.

diminuer *verb*
1 (*réduire*) to reduce.
2 (*se réduire*) (*réserves*) to decrease; (*jours*) to get shorter; (*prix*) to drop.

diminutif *m noun* (*prénom*) nickname.

dinde *f noun* turkey.

dindon *m noun* turkey (cock).

dîner
1 *verb* to have dinner; (*au Canada, en Belgique*) to have lunch.
2 *m noun* dinner.

dînette *f noun* (*jouet*) doll's dinner service *or* set.

dinosaure *m noun* dinosaur.

diphtongue *f noun* diphthong.

diplôme *m noun* certificate, diploma.

dire * *verb* (*mot*) to say; (*vérité, secret, heure*) to tell; **d. des bêtises** to talk nonsense; **d. quelque chose à quelqu'un** to tell somebody something, say something to somebody; **d. à quelqu'un que** to tell somebody that, say to somebody that; **d. à quelqu'un de faire** to tell somebody to do; **on dirait un château/du Mozart** it looks like a castle/sounds like Mozart; **ça ne me dit rien** (*envie*) I don't feel like it; (*souvenir*) it doesn't ring a bell; **ça ne se dit pas** that's not said.

direct , **-e**
1 *adjective* direct; **train d.** fast train.
2 *m noun* **en d.** (*émission*) live.

directement *adverb* directly.

directeur , -trice *m or f noun* director; (*d'école*) headmaster, headmistress.

direction *f noun* (*sens*) direction; **en d. de** (*train*) to, for; **toutes directions** (*sur panneau*) all directions; **sous la d. de** (*orchestre*) conducted by; **la d.** (*équipe dirigeante*) the management.

dirigeable *adjective & m noun* (*ballon*) **d.** airship, dirigible.

dirigeant *m noun* (*de parti etc*) leader; (*d'entreprise, club*) manager.

diriger *verb* (*société*) to run; (*parti, groupe*) to lead; (*véhicule*) to steer; (*orchestre*) to conduct; (*arme etc*) to point (**vers** towards); **se d. vers** (*lieu*) to make one's way towards.

dis , disant *see* **dire**.

discipline *f noun* (*règle*) discipline.

discipliné , -ée *adjective* welldisciplined.

discipliner (se) *reflexive verb* to discipline oneself.

disco *f noun* disco.

discothèque *f noun* (*club*) discotheque.

discours *m noun* speech.

discret , -ète *adjective* (*personne*) discreet.

discrètement *adverb* discreetly.

discrétion *f noun* discretion.

discrimination *f noun* discrimination.

discussion *f noun* discussion; (*conversation*) talk; **pas de d.!** no argument!

discuter *verb* (*parler*) to talk (**de** about); (*répliquer*) to argue; **d. sur quelque chose** to discuss something.

dise(nt) *etc see* **dire**.

disloquer (se) *reflexive verb* (*meuble*) to fall apart.

disparaître * *verb* to disappear; (*être porté manquant*) to go missing.

disparition *f noun* disappearance.

disparu , -ue
1 *past participle of* **disparaître**.
2 *adjective* (*soldat*) missing.

dispense *f noun* exemption.

dispenser *verb* **d. quelqu'un de** (*obligation*) to exempt somebody from.

disperser *verb* (*objets*) to scatter.

disperser (se) *reflexive verb* (*foule*) to disperse.

disponible *adjective* (*article, place etc*) available.

disposé , -ée *adjective* **bien d.** in a good mood; **d. à faire** prepared to do.

disposer *verb*
1 (*objets*) to arrange; **se d. à faire** to prepare to do.
2 d. de quelque chose to make use of something.

dispositif *m noun* (*mécanisme*) device.

disposition *f noun* arrangement; **à la d. de quelqu'un** at somebody's disposal; **prendre ses dispositions** to make arrangements.

dispute *f noun* quarrel.

disputer *verb* (*match*) to play; (*rallye*) to compete in; **d. quelqu'un** (*gronder*) *Familiar* to tell somebody off.

disputer (se) *reflexive verb* to quarrel (**avec** with).

disqualifier *verb* (*équipe*) to disqualify.

disque *m noun* (*de musique*) record; (*cercle*) disc; (*d'ordinateur*) disk; **d. compact** compact disc; **d. vidéo** video disc.

disquette *f noun* (*d'ordinateur*) floppy (disk).

dissertation *f noun* (*au lycée etc*) essay.

dissimuler *verb* (*cacher*) to hide (**à** from); **se d.** to hide (oneself).

dissipé , -ée *adjective* (*élève*) unruly.

dissiper *verb* (*brouillard*) to dispel; **d. quelqu'un** to distract somebody.

dissiper (se) *reflexive verb* (*brume*) to lift; (*élève*) to misbehave.

dissoudre * *verb* to dissolve.

dissoudre (se) *reflexive verb* to dissolve.

distance *f noun* distance; **à deux mètres de d.** two metres apart.

distancer *verb* to leave behind.

distinct , -incte *adjective* distinct.

distinctement *adverb* clearly.

distinguer *verb* to distinguish; (*voir*) to make out; **se d. de** to be distinguishable from.

distraction *f noun* amusement; (*étourderie*) absent-mindedness.

distraire * *verb* (*divertir*) to entertain; **se d.** to amuse oneself.

distrait , -aite *adjective* absent-minded.

distribuer *verb* (*donner*) to hand out; (*courrier*) to deliver; (*cartes*) to deal.

distributeur *m noun* **d.** (**automatique**) vending machine; **d. de billets** ticket machine; (*de banque*) cash dispenser *or* machine.

distribution *f noun* distribution; (*du courrier*) delivery.

dit , dite , dites *see* **dire.**

divan *m noun* couch.

divers , -erses *adjective* (*distincts*) varied; (*plusieurs*) various.

divertir *verb* to entertain.

divertir (se) *reflexive verb* to enjoy oneself.

divertissement *m noun* entertainment.

diviser *verb* to divide (**en** into).

diviser (se) *reflexive verb* to divide (**en** into).

division *f noun* division.

divorce *m noun* divorce.

divorcé , -ée *adjective* divorced.

divorcer *verb* to get divorced.

dix *adjective & m noun* ten.

dix-huit *adjective & m noun* eighteen.

dixième *adjective & m or f noun* tenth.

dix-neuf *adjective & m noun* nineteen.

dix-sept *adjective & m noun* seventeen.

dizaine *f noun* **une d.** (**de**) about ten.

docile *adjective* docile.

docker *m noun* docker.

docteur *m noun* doctor.

doctorat *m noun* doctorate, = PhD.

document *m noun* document.

documentaire *m noun* (*film*) documentary.

documentaliste *m or f noun* (*à l'école*) (school) librarian.

documentation *f noun* (*documents*) documentation.

documenter (se) *reflexive verb* to collect information.

dodo *m noun* (*langage enfantin*) faire d. to sleep.

doigt *m noun* finger; **d. de pied** toe; **petit d.** little finger.

dois , doit , doive(nt) *see* devoir [1, 2].

dollar *m noun* dollar.

domaine *m noun* (*terres*) estate.

dôme *m noun* dome.

domestique
1 *adjective* (*animal*) domestic; **travaux domestiques** housework.
2 *m or f noun* servant.

domicile *m noun* home; **livrer à d.** to deliver (to the house).

domination *f noun* domination.

dominer *verb* to dominate.

domino *m noun* domino; **dominos** (*jeu*) dominoes.

dommage *m noun* (**c'est**) **d.!** it's a pity *or* a shame! (**que** + *subjunctive* that); **dommages** (*dégâts*) damage.

dompter *verb* (*animal*) to tame.

dompteur , -euse *m or f noun* (*de lions*) lion tamer.

don *m noun* (*cadeau, aptitude*) gift; (*charité*) donation.

donc *conjunction* (*par conséquent*) so; **asseyez-vous d.!** will you sit down!

données *fpl noun* (*information*) data.

donner *verb*
1 (*objet, cadeau etc*) to give; (*récolte*) to produce; (*sa place*) to give up; (*cartes*) to deal; **d. un coup à** to hit; **d. à réparer** to take (in) to be repaired; **ça donne soif/faim** it makes you thirsty/hungry; **se d. du mal** to go to a lot of trouble (**pour faire** to do).
2 **d. sur** (*fenêtre*) to overlook;

(*porte*) to open onto.

dont *relative pronoun* (= **de qui, duquel, de quoi** *etc*) (*personne*) of whom; (*chose*) of which; (*appartenance: personne, chose*) whose; **une mère d. le fils est malade** a mother whose son is ill; **la fille d. il est fier** the daughter he is proud of *or* of whom he is proud; **la façon d.** the way in which.

Dordogne (la) *f noun* the Dordogne.

doré , -ée *adjective* (*objet*) gilt, gold; (*couleur*) golden.

dorer *verb* (*objet*) to gild; **se d. au soleil** to sunbathe.

dormir * *verb* to sleep.

dortoir *m noun* dormitory.

dos *m noun* (*de personne, d'animal*) back; **avoir mal au d.** to have a sore back; **à d. d'âne** (riding) on a donkey; **'voir au d.'** (*verso*) 'see over'.

dose *f noun* dose.

dossier *m noun* (*de siège*) back; (*papiers*) file.

douane *f noun* customs.

douanier *m noun* customs officer.

double
1 *adjective* & *adverb* double.
2 *m noun* **le d. (de)** (*quantité*) twice as much (as), double; **je l'ai en d.** I have two of them.

doubler *verb*
1 (*vêtement*) to line; (*film*) to dub.
2 (*augmenter*) to double; (*en voiture*) to overtake.

doublure *f noun* (*étoffe*) lining.

douce *see* doux.

doucement *adverb* (*délicatement*) gently; (*à voix basse*) softly; (*lentement*) slowly.

douceur *f noun* (*de miel*) sweetness; (de peau) softness; (de temps) mildness.

douche f noun shower.

doucher verb d. quelqu'un to give somebody a shower; se d. to take or have a shower.

doué , -ée adjective gifted (en at); (intelligent) clever.

douillet , -ette adjective (lit) soft, cosy; tu es d. (délicat) you're such baby.

douleur f noun (mal) pain; (chagrin) sorrow.

douloureux , -euse adjective painful.

doute m noun doubt; sans d. probably, no doubt.

douter verb to doubt; se d. de quelque chose to suspect something; je m'en doute I would think so.

Douvres m or f noun Dover.

doux , douce adjective (miel etc) sweet; (peau) soft; (temps) mild.

douzaine f noun dozen; (environ) about twelve; une d. d'œufs/etc a dozen eggs/etc.

douze adjective & m noun twelve.

douzième adjective & m or f noun twelfth.

dragée f noun sugared almond.

dragon m noun (animal) dragon.

draguer verb (rivière) to dredge; (personne) Familiar to chat up.

dramatique adjective dramatic; film d. drama.

drame m noun drama; (catastrophe) tragedy.

drap m noun (de lit) sheet; d. housse fitted sheet; d. de bain bath towel.

drapeau , -x m noun flag.

dressage m noun training.

dresser verb (échelle) to put up; (animal) to train.

dresser (se) reflexive verb (personne) to stand up; (montagne) to stand.

dribbler verb Football to dribble.

drogue f noun une d. (stupéfiant) a drug; la d. drugs.

drogué , -ée m or f noun drug addict.

droguer (se) reflexive verb to take drugs.

droguerie f noun hardware shop.

droit [1] m noun (privilège) right (de faire to do); (d'inscription etc) fee(s); le d. (science) law; avoir d. à to be entitled to.

droit [2], **droite**
1 adjective (route etc) straight; (vertical) upright; (angle) right.
2 adverb straight; tout d. straight ahead.

droit [3], **droite** adjective (côté etc) right.

droite f noun la d. (côté) the right (side); à d. (tourner) (to the) right; (rouler etc) on the right; à votre d. to or on your right; de d. (fenêtre etc) right-hand; à d. de on or to the right of.

droitier , -ière adjective & m or f noun right-handed (person).

drôle adjective funny; d. d'air/de type funny look/fellow.

drôlement adverb (extrêmement) terribly.

du see de [1], [2], le.

dû , due
1 past participle of devoir [1], [2].
2 adjective d. à due to.

duc m noun duke.

duchesse f noun duchess.

duel m noun duel.

dune f noun (sand) dune.

duplex *m noun* split-level flat.

duquel *see* lequel.

dur , -e
 1 *adjective* (*substance*) hard; (*difficile*) hard, tough; (*hiver, personne, ton*) harsh; (*œuf*) hard-boiled.
 2 *adverb* (*travailler*) hard.

durant *preposition* during.

durcir *verb* to harden.

durcir (se) *reflexive verb* to harden.

durée *f noun* (*de film etc*) length.

durer *verb* to last; **ça dure depuis** it's been going on for.

dureté *f noun* hardness; (*de ton etc*) harshness.

duvet *m noun* (*d'oiseau*) down; (*sac*) sleeping bag.

dynamique *adjective* dynamic.

dynamite *f noun* dynamite.

dynamo *f noun* dynamo.

dyslexique *adjective & m or f noun* dyslexic.

eau , -x *f noun* water; **e. minérale** mineral water; **e. douce/salée** fresh/salt water; **e. de Cologne** eau de Cologne; **tomber à l'e.** (*projet*) to fall through.

eau-de-vie *f noun* (*plural* **eaux-de-vie**) brandy.

ébattre (s') *reflexive verb* to run about, play about.

ébéniste *m noun* cabinet-maker.

éblouir *verb* to dazzle.

éboueur *m noun* dustman.

ébouillanter (s') *reflexive verb* to scald oneself.

éboulement *m noun* landslide.

ébouler (s') *reflexive verb* (*falaise*) to crumble; (*roches*) to fall.

ébouriffé , -ée *adjective* (*cheveux*) dishevelled.

ébranler *verb* to shake; (*santé*) to weaken.

ébranler (s') *reflexive verb* (*train etc*) to move off.

ébrécher *verb* (*assiette*) to chip.

ébullition *f noun* **être en é.** (*eau*) to be boiling.

écaille *f noun* (*de poisson*) scale; (*de tortue*) shell; (*pour lunettes*) tortoiseshell; (*de peinture*) flake.

écailler *verb* (*poisson*) to scale; (*huître*) to shell.

écailler (s') *reflexive verb* (*peinture*) to flake (off), peel.

écarlate *adjective* scarlet.

écarquiller *verb* **é. les yeux** to open one's eyes wide.

écart *m noun* (*intervalle*) gap; (*embardée*) swerve; (*différence*) difference (de in, **entre** between); **à l'é.** out of the way; **à l'é. de** away from.

écarté , -ée *adjective* (*endroit*) remote; **les jambes écartées** with legs apart.

écarter *verb* (*objets*) to move apart; (*jambes, rideaux*) to open; **é. quelque chose de quelque chose** to move something away from something; **é. quelqu'un de** (*exclure*) to keep somebody out of.

écarter (s') *reflexive verb* (*s'éloigner*) to move away (**de** from).

échafaud *m noun* scaffold.

échafaudage *m noun* (*de peintre etc*) scaffold(ing).

échalote *f noun* shallot.

échange *m noun* exchange; **en é.** in exchange (**de** for).

échanger *verb* to exchange (**contre** for).

échangeur *m noun* (*intersection*) interchange.

échantillon *m noun* sample.

échapper *verb* **é. à quelqu'un** to escape from somebody; **é. à la mort** to escape death; **son nom m'échappe** his name escapes me.

échapper (s') *reflexive verb* to escape (**de** from).

écharde *f noun* splinter.

écharpe *f noun* scarf; (*de maire*) sash; **en é.** (*bras*) in a sling.

échauffer (s') *reflexive verb* (*sportif*) to warm up.

échec *m noun* failure; **les échecs** (*jeu*) chess; **é.!** check!; **é. et mat!** checkmate!

échelle *f noun* (*marches*) ladder; (*dimension*) scale; **faire la courte**

é. à quelqu'un to give somebody a leg up.

échelon *m noun* (*d'échelle*) rung; (*de fonctionnaire*) grade.

échiquier *m noun* chessboard.

écho *m noun* (*d'un son*) echo.

échouer *verb* to fail; **é. à** (*examen*) to fail.

échouer (s') *reflexive verb* (*navire*) to run aground.

éclabousser *verb* to splash (**de** with).

éclaboussure *f noun* splash.

éclair *m noun* (*lumière*) flash; (*d'orage*) flash of lightning.

éclairage *m noun* (*de pièce etc*) lighting.

éclaircie *f noun* (*durée*) sunny spell.

éclaircir *verb* (*couleur etc*) to make lighter; (*mystère*) to clear up.

éclaircir (s') *reflexive verb* (*ciel*) to clear (up); (*situation*) to become clear.

éclaircissement *m noun* explanation.

éclairé , -ée *adjective* **bien/mal é.** well/badly lit.

éclairer *verb* (*pièce etc*) to light (up); **é. quelqu'un** (*avec une lampe*) to give somebody some light.

éclairer (s') *reflexive verb* (*visage*) to brighten up; (*situation*) to become clear; **s'é. à la bougie** to use candlelight.

éclaireur , -euse *m or f noun* (boy) scout, (girl) guide.

éclat [1] *m noun* (*de la lumière*) brightness; (*de phare*) glare.

éclat [2] *m noun* (*de verre ou de bois*) splinter; **é. de rire** burst of laughter.

éclatant , -ante *adjective* (*lumière, succès*) brilliant.

éclatement *m noun* (*de pneu etc*) bursting.

éclater *verb* (*pneu etc*) to burst; (*bombe*) to go off; (*verre*) to shatter; (*guerre, incendie*) to break out; (*orage*) to break; **é. de rire** to burst out laughing; **é. en sanglots** to burst into tears.

éclore * *verb* (*œuf*) to hatch.

éclosion *f noun* hatching.

écluse *f noun* (*de canal*) lock.

écœurer *verb* **é. quelqu'un** to make somebody feel sick.

école *f noun* school; **à l'é.** in or at school; **aller à l'é.** to go to school; **é. primaire** (*bâtiment*) primary school; (*enseignement*) primary education.

écolier , -ière *m or f noun* schoolboy, schoolgirl.

écologiste *m or f noun* environmentalist.

économe *adjective* thrifty.

économie *f noun* economy; **économies** (*argent*) savings; **une é. de** a saving of; **faire des économies** to save (up).

économique *adjective* (*bon marché*) economical.

économiser *verb* to economize (**sur** on).

écorce *f noun* (*d'arbre*) bark; (*de fruit*) peel, skin.

écorcher *verb* (*érafler*) to graze; **s'é.** to graze oneself; **é. les oreilles à quelqu'un** to grate on somebody's ears.

écorchure *f noun* graze.

écossais , -aise
1 *adjective* Scottish; (*tissu*) tartan; (*whisky*) Scotch.
2 *m or f noun* Scot.

Écosse (l') *f noun* Scotland.

écosser *verb* (*pois*) to shell.

écoulement *m noun* (*de liquide*) flow; (*de temps*) passage.

écouler (s') *reflexive verb* (*eau*) to flow out; (*temps*) to pass.

écouter *verb*
1 to listen to.
2 to listen.

écouteur *m noun* (*de téléphone*) earpiece; **écouteurs** (*casque*) earphones.

écran *m noun* screen; **le petit é.** television.

écrasant , -ante *adjective* overwhelming.

écraser *verb* to crush; (*cigarette*) to put *or* stub out; (*piéton*) to run over; **se faire é.** to get run over.

écraser (s') *reflexive verb* to crash (**contre** into).

écrémé *adjective* (*lait*) skimmed.

écrier (s') *reflexive verb* to exclaim (**que** that).

écrire * *verb* to write; (*en toutes lettres*) to spell; **é. à la machine** to type.

écrire (s') *reflexive verb* (*mot*) to be spelled *or* spelt; **comment ça s'écrit?** how do you spell it?

écrit
1 *past participle of* **écrire**.
2 *m noun* **par é.** in writing.

écriteau , -x *m noun* notice, sign.

écriture *f noun* writing.

écrivain *m noun* author, writer.

écrou *m noun* (*de boulon*) nut.

écrouler (s') *reflexive verb* to collapse.

écueil *m noun* reef; (*obstacle*) pitfall.

écuelle *f noun* bowl.

écume *f noun* (*de mer etc*) foam.

écureuil *m noun* squirrel.

écurie *f noun* stable.

écusson *m noun* (*en étoffe*) badge.

EDF *f abbreviation* (*Électricité de France*) (French) Electricity Company.

édifice *m noun* building.

édifier *verb* to erect.

Édimbourg *m or f noun* Edinburgh.

éditer *verb* to publish.

éditeur , -trice *m or f noun* publisher.

édition *f noun* (*livre, journal*) edition; (*métier*) publishing.

édredon *m noun* eiderdown.

éducatif , -ive *adjective* educational.

éducation *f noun* education; **avoir de l'é.** to have good manners; **é. physique** physical training *or* education.

éduquer *verb* to educate.

effacer *verb* to rub out, erase; (*en lavant*) to wash out; (*avec un chiffon*) to wipe away.

effectivement *adverb* actually.

effectuer *verb* (*expérience etc*) to carry out; (*trajet etc*) to make.

effet *m noun* effect (**sur** on); **faire de l'e.** (*remède*) to be effective; **en e.** indeed, in fact; **sous l'e. de la colère** in anger.

efficace *adjective* (*mesure etc*) effective; (*personne*) efficient.

efficacité *f noun* effectiveness; efficiency.

effilocher (s') *reflexive verb* to fray.

effleurer *verb* to skim, touch (lightly).

effondrer (s') *reflexive verb* to collapse.

efforcer (s') *reflexive verb* **s'e. de faire** to try (hard) to do.

effort *m noun* effort; **sans e.** (*réussir etc*) effortlessly.

effrayant , -ante *adjective* frightening.

effrayer *verb* to frighten, scare.

effroyable *adjective* dreadful.

égal , -e, -aux
1 *adjective* equal (à to); (*uniforme, régulier*) even; **ça m'est é.** I don't care.
2 *m or f noun* (*personne*) equal.

également *adverb* (*aussi*) also, as well.

égaler *verb* to equal.

égaliser *verb* to equalize.

égalité *f noun* equality; (*régularité*) evenness; **à é.** (*de score*) even, equal (in points).

égard *m noun* **à l'é. de** (*envers*) towards.

égarer *verb* (*objet*) to mislay.

égarer (s') *reflexive verb* to lose one's way.

égayer *verb* (*pièce*) to brighten up; **é. quelqu'un** to cheer somebody up.

église *f noun* church.

égoïste *adjective & m or f noun* selfish (person).

égorger *verb* to cut the throat of.

égout *m noun* sewer; **eaux d'é.** sewage.

égoutter *verb*
1 (*vaisselle, légumes etc*) to drain.
2 **laisser é. quelque chose** to leave something to drain.

égoutter (s') *reflexive verb* to drain.

égouttoir *m noun* (dish) drainer.

égratigner *verb* to scratch.

égratignure *f noun* scratch.

Égypte (l') *f noun* Egypt.

égyptien, -ienne *adjective & m or f noun* Egyptian.

eh! *interjection* hey!; **eh bien!** well!

élan *m noun* (*vitesse*) momentum; (*impulsion*) impulse; **prendre son é.** to take a run (up).

élancer (s') *reflexive verb* (*bondir*) to leap *or* rush (forward).

élargir *verb* (*route etc*) to widen; (*vêtement*) to let out.

élargir (s') *reflexive verb* (*route etc*) to widen; (*vêtement*) to stretch.

élastique
1 *adjective* (*objet*) elastic.
2 *m noun* (*lien*) elastic *or* rubber band.

électeur , -trice *m or f noun* voter.

élection *f noun* election.

électoral , -e, -aux *adjective* **campagne électorale** election campaign.

électricien , -ienne *m or f noun* electrician.

électricité *f noun* electricity.

électrique *adjective* electric.

électrocuter *verb* to electrocute.

électronique *adjective* electronic.

électrophone *m noun* record player.

élégance *f noun* elegance; **avec é.** elegantly; (*s'habiller*) smartly.

élégant , -ante *adjective* elegant; (*bien habillé*) smart.

élément *m noun* element; (*de meuble*) unit; **éléments** (*notions*) rudiments.

élémentaire *adjective* basic;

(*cours, école etc*) elementary.

éléphant *m noun* elephant.

élevage *m noun* breeding, rearing.

élève *m or f noun* pupil.

élevé , -ée *adjective* (*haut*) high; **bien/mal é.** well-/bad-mannered.

élever *verb* (*prix, voix etc*) to raise; (*enfant*) to bring up, raise; (*animal*) to breed, rear.

élever (s') *reflexive verb* (*prix, ton etc*) to rise; **s'é. à** (*prix*) to amount to.

éleveur , -euse *m or f noun* breeder.

éliminatoire *adjective & f noun* (*épreuve*) é. heat.

éliminer *verb* to eliminate.

élire * *verb* to elect (à to).

elle *pronoun* (*sujet*) she; (*chose, animal*) it; **elles** they.
∎ (*complément*) her; (*chose, animal*) it; **elles** them.

elle-même *pronoun* herself; (*chose, animal*) itself; **ellesmêmes** themselves.

éloigné , -ée *adjective* (*lieu*) far away; (*date*) distant; **é. de** (*village etc*) far (away) from.

éloigner *verb* (*chose, personne*) to move *or* take away (de from).

éloigner (s') *reflexive verb* (*partir*) to move *or* go away (de from).

émail , -aux *m noun* enamel.

emballage *m noun* (*action*) packing; wrapping; (*caisse*) packaging; (*papier*) wrapping (paper).

emballer *verb* (*dans une caisse etc*) to pack; (*dans du papier*) to wrap (up); **e. quelqu'un** (*passionner*) Familiar to thrill somebody.

emballer (s') *reflexive verb* (*personne*) Familiar to get carried away; (*cheval*) to bolt.

embarcadère *m noun* quay, wharf.

embarcation *f noun* (small) boat.

embardée *f noun* (sudden) swerve.

embarquement *m noun* (*de passagers*) boarding.

embarquer *verb*
1 (*passagers*) to take on board; (*marchandises*) to load (up).
2 (*monter à bord*) to (go on) board.

embarquer (s') *reflexive verb* to (go on) board.

embarras *m noun* (*gêne*) embarrassment.

embarrassant , -ante *adjective* (*paquet*) cumbersome; (*question*) embarrassing.

embarrasser *verb* **e. quelqu'un** to be in somebody's way; (*question etc*) to embarrass somebody; **s'e. de** to burden oneself with.

embaucher *verb* (*ouvrier*) to hire.

embêtant , -ante *adjective* annoying; boring.

embêtement *m noun* trouble.

embêter *verb* Familiar (*agacer*) to bother; (*ennuyer*) to bore.

embêter (s') *reflexive verb* Familiar to get bored.

emboîter *verb* to fit together.

emboîter (s') *reflexive verb* to fit together.

embouchure *f noun* (*de fleuve*) mouth.

embourber (s') *reflexive verb* to get bogged down.

embouteillage *m noun* traffic jam.

embouteillé , -ée *adjective* (*rue*) congested.

emboutir *verb* (*voiture*) to crash into.

embranchement *m noun* (*de voie*) junction.

embrasser *verb* (*donner un baiser à*) to kiss; **s'e.** to kiss (each other).

embrayage *m noun* (*de véhicule*) clutch.

embrocher *verb* to skewer.

embrouiller *verb* (*fils*) to tangle (up); (*papiers etc*) to mix up; **e. quelqu'un** to confuse somebody.

embrouiller (s') *reflexive verb* to get confused (**dans** in, with).

embuscade *f noun* ambush.

émerger *verb* to emerge (**de** from).

émerveiller *verb* to amaze, fill with wonder.

émetteur *m noun* (*poste*) **é. transmitter.**

émettre * *verb* (*lumière, son etc*) to give out; (*message radio*) to broadcast; (*timbre, monnaie*) to issue.

émeute *f noun* riot.

émietter *verb* to crumble.

émietter (s') *reflexive verb* to crumble.

émigrer *verb* to emigrate.

émission *f noun* (*de radio etc*) broadcast; (*diffusion*) transmission; (*de timbre, monnaie*) issue.

emmanchure *f noun* arm hole.

emmêler *verb* to tangle (up).

emménager *verb* (*dans un logement*) to move in; **e. dans** to move into.

emmener *verb* to take (**à** to); **e. quelqu'un en promenade** to take somebody for a walk.

emmitoufler (s') *reflexive verb* to wrap (oneself) up.

émotion *f noun* emotion; (*trouble*) excitement; **une é.** (*peur*) a scare.

émouvant , -ante *adjective* moving.

émouvoir * *verb* to move, touch.

empailler *verb* to stuff.

emparer (s') *reflexive verb* **s'e. de** to take, grab.

empêchement *m noun* **avoir un e.** to have something come up at the last minute (*to prevent or delay an action*).

empêcher *verb* to prevent, stop (**de faire** (from) doing); **elle ne peut pas s'e. de rire** she can't help laughing.

empereur *m noun* emperor.

empester *verb*
1 (*tabac etc*) to stink of; **e. quelqu'un** to stink somebody out. **2** (*sentir mauvais*) to stink.

empiler *verb* to pile up (**sur** on).

empiler (s') *reflexive verb* to pile up (**sur** on).

empire *m noun* empire.

emplacement *m noun* site; (*de stationnement*) place.

emplir *verb* to fill (**de** with).

emplir (s') *reflexive verb* to fill (**de** with).

emploi *m noun* (*usage*) use; (*travail*) job, employment; **e. du temps** timetable; **sans e.** (*au chômage*) unemployed.

employé , -ée *m or f noun* employee; (*de bureau, banque*) clerk, employee.

employer *verb* (*utiliser*) to use; **e. quelqu'un** to employ somebody.

employer (s') *reflexive verb* (*expression*) to be used.

employeur , -euse *m or f noun* employer.

empoigner *verb* to grab.

empoisonner *verb* to poison; **s'e.** to poison oneself; (*par accident*) to be poisoned.

emporter *verb* (*prendre*) to take (away) (**avec soi** with one); (*entraîner*) to carry away; (*par le vent*) to blow off *or* away.

emporter (s') *reflexive verb* to lose one's temper (**contre** with).

empreinte *f noun* mark; **e. (digitale)** fingerprint; **e. (de pas)** footprint.

empresser (s') *reflexive verb* **s'e. de faire** to hasten to do.

emprisonner *verb* to jail.

emprunt *m noun* (*argent etc*) loan.

emprunter *verb* (*argent*) to borrow (**à** from); (*route*) to use.

EMT *f abbreviation* (*éducation manuelle et technique*) = school subject comprising home economics, woodwork, metalwork *etc*.

ému , -ue *adjective* moved; (*attristé*) upset.

en [1] *preposition* (*lieu*) in; (*direction*) to; **être/aller en France** to be in/go to France.

▪ (*temps*) in; **en février** in February; **d'heure en heure** from hour to hour.

▪ (*moyen, état etc*) by; in; on; **en avion** by plane; **en groupe** in a group; **en congé** on leave.

▪ (*matière*) in; **une table en bois** a wooden table; **elle est en bois** it's made of wood; **chemise en nylon** nylon shirt; **c'est en or** it's (made of) gold.

▪ (*comme*) **en cadeau** as a present.

▪ (+ *present participle*) **en mangeant**/*etc* while eating/*etc*; **en apprenant que** on hearing that; **en souriant** smiling, with a smile.

▪ (*transformation*) into; **traduire en** to translate into.

en [2] *pronoun & adverb* (= *de là*) from there; **j'en viens** I've just come from there.

▪ (= *de ça, lui etc*) **il en est content** he's pleased with it *or* him *or* them; **en parler** to talk about it; **en mourir** to die of *or* from it.

▪ (*partitif*) some; **j'en ai** I have some.

encadrer *verb* (*tableau*) to frame; (*entourer d'un trait*) to circle.

encaisser *verb* (*argent, loyer etc*) to collect.

enceinte *adjective* (*femme*) pregnant; **e. de six mois** six months pregnant.

encens *m noun* incense.

encercler *verb* to surround.

enchaîner *verb* to chain (up); (*idées etc*) to link (up).

enchaîner (s') *reflexive verb* (*idées etc*) to be linked (up).

enchanté , -ée *adjective* (*ravi*) delighted (**de** with, **que** (+ *subjunctive*) that); **e. de faire votre connaissance!** pleased to meet you!

enchantement *m noun* delight; **comme par e.** as if by magic.

enchanter *verb* (*ravir*) to delight.

enchanteur *m noun* magician.

enclos *m noun* enclosure.

encoche *f noun* nick (**à** in).

encolure *f noun* neck; (*tour du cou*) collar (size).

encombrant , -ante *adjective* (*paquet*) bulky.

encombrement *m noun* (*d'ob-

jets) clutter; (*de rue*) traffic jam.

encombrer *verb* (*pièce etc*) to clutter up (**de** with); (*rue*) to congest (**de** with); **e. quelqu'un** to hamper somebody.

encore *adverb* (*toujours*) still; **e. là** still here.

◾ (*avec négation*) yet; **pas e.** not yet.

◾ (*de nouveau*) again; **essaie e.** try again.

◾ (*de plus*) **e. un café** another coffee, one more coffee; **e. une fois** (once) again, once more; **e. un** another (one), one more; **e. du pain** (some) more bread; **e. quelque chose** something else; **qui/quoi e.?** who/what else?

◾ (*avec comparatif*) even, still; **e. mieux** even better, better still.

encourageant , -ante *adjective* encouraging.

encouragement *m noun* encouragement.

encourager *verb* to encourage (**à faire** to do).

encrasser *verb* to clog up (with dirt).

encre *f noun* ink; **e. de Chine** Indian ink.

encrier *m noun* inkpot.

encyclopédie *f noun* encyclopaedia.

endetter (s') *reflexive verb* to get into debt.

endive *f noun* chicory, endive.

endommager *verb* to damage.

endormi , -ie *adjective* asleep, sleeping.

endormir * *verb* to put to sleep.

endormir (s') *reflexive verb* to fall asleep, go to sleep.

endroit *m noun* (*lieu*) place; **à l'e.** (*vêtement*) right side out.

endurant , -ante *adjective* tough.

endurcir *verb* **e. quelqu'un** to harden somebody; **s'e. à** to become hardened to.

endurer *verb* to endure.

énergie *f noun* energy.

énergique *adjective* energetic; (*remède*) powerful; (*mesure, ton*) forceful.

énergiquement *adverb* energetically.

énervé , -ée *adjective* on edge.

énerver *verb* **é. quelqu'un** (*irriter*) to get on somebody's nerves; (*inquiéter*) to make somebody nervous.

énerver (s') *reflexive verb* to get worked up.

enfance *f noun* childhood.

enfant *m or f noun* child; **e. en bas âge** infant; **e. de chœur** altar boy.

enfantin , -ine *adjective* (*voix, joie*) childlike; (*simple*) easy.

enfer *m noun* hell; **d'e.** (*bruit etc*) infernal; **à un train d'e.** at breakneck speed.

enfermer *verb* to lock up; **s'e. dans** (*chambre etc*) to lock oneself (up) in.

enfiler *verb* (*aiguille*) to thread; (*perles etc*) to string; (*vêtement*) to pull on.

enfin *adverb* (*à la fin*) finally, at last; (*en dernier lieu*) lastly; **e. bref** in a word; **(mais) e.!** for heaven's sake!

enflammer *verb* to set fire to; (*allumette*) to light; (*irriter*) to inflame.

enflammer (s') *reflexive verb* to catch fire.

enfler *verb* to swell.

enflure *f noun* swelling.

enfoncer *verb* (*clou*) to knock in, bang in; (*porte, voiture*) to smash in; **e. dans quelque chose** (*couteau, mains etc*) to plunge into something.

enfoncer (s') *reflexive verb* (*s'enliser*) to sink (**dans** into).

enfouir *verb* to bury.

enfuir * (s') *reflexive verb* to run away *or* off (**de** from).

enfumer *verb* (*pièce*) to fill with smoke.

engagement *m noun* (*promesse*) commitment; (*dans une compétition*) entry; **prendre l'e. de** to undertake to.

engager *verb* (*discussion, combat*) to start; **e. quelqu'un** (*embaucher*) to hire somebody

engager (s') *reflexive verb* (*dans l'armée*) to enlist; (*sportif*) to enter (**pour** for); (*action, jeu*) to start; **s'e. à faire** to undertake to do.

engelure *f noun* chilblain.

engin *m noun* machine; **e. spatial** spaceship.

engloutir *verb* (*nourriture*) to wolf down; (*faire disparaître*) to swallow up.

engouffrer (s') *reflexive verb* **s'e. dans** to sweep *or* rush into.

engourdir (s') *reflexive verb* to go numb.

engrais *m noun* fertilizer; (*naturel*) manure.

engraisser *verb*
1 (*animal*) to fatten (up).
2 (*grossir*) to get fat.

engrenage *m noun* gears.

engueuler *verb* **e. quelqu'un** *Familiar* to give somebody hell, bawl somebody out.

énigme *f noun* riddle.

enivrer (s') *reflexive verb* to get drunk (**de** on).

enjambée *f noun* stride.

enjamber *verb* to step over; (*pont etc*) to span (*river etc*).

enjoliveur *m noun* hubcap.

enlèvement *m noun* (*d'enfant*) kidnapping.

enlever *verb* to take away (**à quelqu'un** from somebody); (*vêtement*) to take off; (*tache*) to take out; (*enfant etc*) to kidnap.

enlever (s') *reflexive verb* (*tache*) to come out.

enliser (s') *reflexive verb* to get bogged down (**dans** in).

enneigé , -ée *adjective* snow-covered.

enneigement *m noun* **bulletin d'e.** snow report.

ennemi , -ie
1 *m or f noun* enemy.
2 *adjective* **pays/soldat e.** enemy country/soldier.

ennui *m noun* boredom; **un e.** (*tracas*) trouble; **l'e., c'est que** the annoying thing is that.

ennuyé , -ée *adjective* (*las*) bored; (*contrarié*) annoyed (**de** about).

ennuyer *verb* (*agacer, préoccuper*) to bother; (*fatiguer*) to bore.

ennuyer (s') *reflexive verb* to get bored.

ennuyeux , -euse *adjective* (*lassant*) boring; (*contrariant*) annoying.

énorme *adjective* enormous, huge.

énormément *adverb* enormously; **e. de** an enormous amount of.

enquête *f noun* (*de police*) investigation; (*judiciaire*) inquiry;

(*sondage*) survey.

enquêter *verb* to investigate; e. sur to investigate.

enquêteur , -euse *m or f noun* investigator.

enragé , -ée *adjective* (*chien*) rabid; (*furieux*) furious.

enregistrement *m noun* (*des bagages*) registration; (*sur bande etc*) recording.

enregistrer *verb* to record; (faire) e. (*bagages*) to register.

enrhumé, -ée *adjective* être e. to have a cold.

enrhumer (s') *reflexive verb* to catch a cold.

enrichir (s') *reflexive verb* to get rich.

enrobé , -ée *adjective* e. de chocolat chocolate-coated.

enroué , -ée *adjective* hoarse.

enrouler *verb* to wind; (*tapis*) to roll up; s'e. dans (*couvertures*) to wrap oneself up in.

enseignant , -ante *m or f noun* teacher.

enseigne *f noun* sign; e. lumineuse neon sign.

enseignement *m noun* education; (*action, métier*) teaching.

enseigner *verb* to teach; e. quelque chose à quelqu'un to teach somebody something.

ensemble
   1 *adverb* together.
   2 *m noun* (*d'objets*) set; (*vêtement féminin*) outfit; l'e. du personnel the whole of the staff; l'e. des enseignants all of the teachers; dans l'e. on the whole; d'e. (*vue etc*) general.

ensevelir *verb* to bury.

ensoleillé , -ée *adjective* sunny.

ensuite *adverb* (*puis*) next; (*plus tard*) afterwards.

entaille *f noun* (*fente*) notch; (*blessure*) gash.

entailler *verb* to notch; to gash.

entamer *verb* (*pain, peau etc*) to cut (into); (*bouteille, pain etc*) to start (on).

entasser *verb* (*objets*) to pile up.

entasser (s') *reflexive verb* (*objets*) to pile up; (s')e. dans (*passagers etc*) to crowd *or* pile into.

entendre *verb* to hear; e. parler de to hear of; e. dire que to hear (it said) that.

entendre (s') *reflexive verb* (*être d'accord*) to agree (sur on); s'e. (avec quelqu'un) to get on (with somebody).

entendu , -ue *adjective* (*convenu*) agreed; e.! all right!; bien e. of course.

entente *f noun* (*accord*) agreement; (bonne) e. (*amitié*) good relationship.

enterrement *m noun* burial; (*funérailles*) funeral.

enterrer *verb* to bury.

entêtement *m noun* stubbornness.

entêter (s') *reflexive verb* to persist (à faire in doing).

enthousiasme *m noun* enthusiasm.

enthousiasmer *verb* to fill with enthusiasm; s'e. pour to be *or* get enthusiastic about.

enthousiaste *adjective* enthusiastic.

entier , -ière
   1 *adjective* (*total*) whole; (*intact*) intact; le pays tout e. the whole country.
   2 *m noun* en e. completely.

entièrement *adverb* entirely.

entonnoir *m noun* (*ustensile*) funnel.

entorse *f noun* sprain.

entortiller *verb* e. quelque chose autour de quelque chose to wrap something around something.

entourage *m noun* circle of family and friends.

entouré, -ée *adjective* surrounded (de with *or* by).

entourer *verb* to surround (de with); entouré de surrounded by.

entracte *m noun* (*au théâtre*) interval.

entraider (s') *reflexive verb* to help each other.

entrain *m noun* plein d'e. lively.

entraînant , -ante *adjective* (*musique*) lively.

entraînement *m noun* (*sportif*) training.

entraîner *verb* to carry away; (*causer*) to bring about; (*emmener de force*) to drag (away); (*athlète etc*) to train (à for).

entraîner (s') *reflexive verb* (*sportif*) to train.

entraîneur *m noun* (*d'athlète*) coach.

entre *preposition* between; l'un d'e. vous one of you.

entrebâillé , -ée *adjective* slightly open.

entrebâiller *verb* to open slightly.

entrechoquer (s') *reflexive verb* to chink.

entrecôte *f noun* (boned) rib steak.

entrée *f noun* (*action*) entry; (*porte*) entrance; (*accès*) admission (de to); (*vestibule*) entrance hall; (*billet*) ticket (for admis-

sion); (*plat*) first course; (*en informatique*) input; à son e. as he *or* she came in; e. principale main entrance; 'e. interdite' 'no entry'; 'e. libre' 'admission free'.

entreposer *verb* to store.

entrepôt *m noun* warehouse.

entreprendre * *verb* to undertake (de faire to do).

entrepreneur *m noun* (*en bâtiment*) contractor.

entreprise *f noun* company, firm.

entrer *verb* (*auxiliary* être) to go in; (*venir*) to come in; e. dans (*pièce*) to come *or* go into; (*arbre etc*) to crash into; faire/laisser e. quelqu'un to show/let somebody in.

entre-temps *adverb* meanwhile.

entretenir * *verb* to maintain; e. sa forme to keep fit.

entretenir (s') *reflexive verb* s'e. de to talk about (avec with).

entretien *m noun* maintenance; (*dialogue*) conversation; (*entrevue*) interview.

entrevue *f noun* interview.

entrouvert , -erte *adjective* half-open.

énumération *f noun* list(ing).

énumérer *verb* to list.

envahir *verb* to invade; (*herbe etc*) to overrun (*garden*).

envahisseur *m noun* invader.

enveloppe *f noun* (*pour lettre*) envelope; e. timbrée à votre adresse stamped addressed envelope.

envelopper *verb* to wrap (up) (dans in).

envers
1 *preposition* toward(s), to.
2 *m noun* à l'e. (*chaussette*) inside out; (*pantalon*) back to front; (*la*

tête en bas) upside down.

envie *f noun* (*jalousie*) envy; (*désir*) desire; **avoir e. de quelque chose** to want something; **j'ai e. de faire** I feel like doing.

envier *verb* to envy (**quelque chose à quelqu'un** somebody something).

environ *adverb* (*à peu près*) about.

environnant , -ante *adjective* surrounding.

environnement *m noun* environment.

environner *verb* to surround.

environs *mpl noun* surroundings; **aux environs de** around.

envisager *verb* to consider (**de faire** doing).

envoi *m noun* sending; (*paquet*) package; **coup d'e.** *Football* kick-off.

envoler (s') *reflexive verb* (*oiseau*) to fly away; (*avion*) to take off; (*chapeau etc*) to blow away.

envoyé , -ée *m or f noun* (*reporter*) correspondent.

envoyer * *verb* to send; (*lancer*) to throw.

épais , -aisse *adjective* thick.

épaisseur *f noun* thickness.

épaissir *verb* to thicken.

épaissir (s') *reflexive verb* to thicken.

épanoui , -ie *adjective* in full bloom; (*visage*) beaming.

épanouir (s') *reflexive verb* to blossom; (*visage*) to beam.

épargner *verb* (*argent*) to save; (*ennemi etc*) to spare; **e. quelque chose à quelqu'un** (*ennuis etc*) to spare somebody something.

éparpiller *verb* to scatter.

éparpiller (s') *reflexive verb* to scatter.

épatant , -ante *adjective* marvellous.

épaule *f noun* shoulder.

épave *f noun* wreck.

épée *f noun* sword.

épeler *verb* (*mot*) to spell.

éperon *m noun* spur.

épi *m noun* (*de blé etc*) ear.

épice *f noun* spice.

épicé , -ée *adjective* spicy.

épicer *verb* to spice.

épicerie *f noun* grocer's (shop); (*produits*) groceries.

épicier , -ière *m or f noun* grocer.

épidémie *f noun* epidemic.

épinards *mpl noun* spinach.

épine *f noun* (*de plante*) thorn.

épineux , -euse *adjective* thorny.

épingle *f noun* pin; **é. à nourrice** safety pin; **é. à linge** clothes peg; **é. à cheveux** hairpin.

épisode *m noun* episode.

épithète *f noun* (*adjectif*) attribute.

éplucher *verb* (*carotte, pomme etc*) to peel; (*salade*) to clean.

épluchure *f noun* peeling.

éponge *f noun* sponge.

éponger *verb* to sponge up.

époque *f noun* (*date*) time; (*historique*) age.

épouse *f noun* wife.

épouser *verb* **é. quelqu'un** to marry somebody.

épousseter *verb* to dust.

épouvantable *adjective* terrifying; (*mauvais*) appalling.

épouvantail *m noun* scarecrow.

épouvante *f noun* terror; **film d'é.** horror film.

épouvanter verb to terrify.

époux m noun husband; **les é. Thomas** Mr and Mrs Thomas.

épreuve f noun (examen) test; (sportive) event; (malheur) ordeal.

éprouver verb to test; (sentiment etc) to feel.

éprouvette f noun test tube.

EPS f abbreviation (éducation physique et sportive) PE.

épuisant , -ante adjective exhausting.

épuisé , -ée adjective exhausted; (marchandise) out of stock.

épuiser verb to exhaust; **s'é. à faire** to exhaust oneself doing.

épuiser (s') reflexive verb (réserves) to run out.

équateur m noun equator.

équation f noun equation.

équerre f noun setsquare.

équilibre m noun balance; **tenir or mettre en é.** to balance (**sur** on); **perdre l'é.** to lose one's balance.

équilibrer verb (budget) to balance.

équipage m noun crew.

équipe f noun team; (d'ouvriers) gang; **é. de secours** search party.

équipement m noun equipment; (de camping, ski) gear.

équiper verb to equip (**de** with).

équipier , -ière m or f noun team member.

équitable adjective fair.

équitation f noun (horse) riding; **faire de l'é.** to go riding.

équivalent , -ente adjective & m noun equivalent.

érafler verb to graze.

éraflure f noun graze.

errer verb to wander.

erreur f noun mistake.

éruption f noun (de boutons) rash.

es see être.

escabeau , -x m noun stepladder.

escadrille f noun (groupe d'avions) flight.

escalade f noun climbing.

escalader verb to climb.

escale f noun **faire e. à** (avion) to stop (over) at; (navire) to put in at.

escalier m noun stairs; **e. roulant** escalator.

escalope f noun escalope.

escargot m noun snail.

escarpé , -ée adjective steep.

esclave m or f noun slave.

escorte f noun escort.

escorter verb to escort.

escrime f noun fencing.

escrimeur , -euse m or f noun fencer.

escroc m noun crook.

espace m noun space; **e. vert** garden, park.

espacer verb to space out.

Espagne (l') f noun Spain.

espagnol , -ole
1 adjective Spanish.
2 m or f noun Spaniard.
3 m noun (langue) Spanish.

espèce f noun (race) species; (genre) kind, sort; **e. d'idiot!** (you) silly fool!

espérance f noun hope.

espérer verb
1 (résultat, amélioration etc) to hope for; **e. que** to hope that; **e. faire** to hope to do.
2 **j'espère bien!** I hope so!

espiègle adjective mischievous.

espion , -onne m or f noun spy.

espionnage *m noun* spying.

espionner *verb* to spy on.

espoir *m noun* hope; **sans e.** (*cas etc*) hopeless.

esprit *m noun* spirit; (*intellect*) mind; (*humour*) wit; **venir à l'e. de quelqu'un** to cross somebody's mind.

Esquimau , -de , -aux *m or f noun* Eskimo.

esquiver *verb* to dodge.

essai *m noun* (*épreuve*) test; (*tentative*) try, attempt; *Rugby* try.

essaim *m noun* swarm (*of bees etc*).

essayage *m noun* (*de costume*) fitting.

essayer *verb* to try (**de faire** to do); (*vêtement*) to try on.

essence *f noun* petrol.

essentiel , -ielle
1 *adjective* essential.
2 *m noun* **l'e.** the main thing.

essentiellement *adverb* essentially.

essieu , -x *m noun* axle.

essoufflé , -ée *adjective* out of breath.

essuie-glace *m noun* windscreen wiper.

essuie-mains *invariable m noun* (hand) towel.

essuyer *verb* to wipe.

est [1] *see* être.

est [2] *m noun & invariable adjective* east; **d'e.** (*vent*) east(erly); **de l'e.** eastern.

est-ce que *adverb* **e. je peux entrer?** can I come in?; **est-ce qu'il est là?** is he here?; **e. tu la connais?** do you know her?

estime *f noun* regard.

estimer *verb* (*objet*) to value; (*juger*) to consider (**que** that); **e. quelqu'un** to have a high regard for somebody; **s'e. heureux**/*etc* to consider oneself happy/*etc*.

estomac *m noun* stomach.

Estonie (l') *f noun* Estonia.

estonien , -ienne *adjective & m or f noun* Estonian.

estrade *f noun* platform.

estropier *verb* to cripple.

estuaire *m noun* estuary.

et *conjunction* and; **vingt et un**/*etc* twenty-one/*etc*.

étable *f noun* cowshed.

établi *m noun* (work)bench.

établir *verb* (*installer*) to set up; (*plan, liste*) to draw up.

établir (s') *reflexive verb* (*habiter*) to settle.

établissement *m noun* establishment; **é. scolaire** school.

étage *m noun* (*d'immeuble*) floor; **à l'é.** upstairs; **au premier é.** on the first floor.

étagère *f noun* shelf.

étais , était *etc see* être.

étalage *m noun* (*vitrine*) display window.

étaler *verb* to lay out; (*en vitrine*) to display; (*beurre etc*) to spread.

étanche *adjective* watertight; (*montre*) waterproof.

étang *m noun* pond.

étant *see* être.

étape *f noun* stage; (*lieu*) stop (-over).

État *m noun* (*nation*) State; **homme d'É.** statesman.

état *m noun* (*condition*) state; **en bon/mauvais é.** in good/bad condition; **en é. de faire** in a position to do.

États-Unis (les) *mpl noun* les É.

(d'Amérique) the United States (of America).

étau , -x *m noun* vice.

été [1] *past participle of* être.

été [2] *m noun* summer; **en é.** in (the) summer.

éteindre * *verb*
1 (*feu etc*) to put out; (*lampe, lumière etc*) to turn *or* switch off.
2 (*appuyer sur le bouton*) to switch off.

éteindre (s') *reflexive verb* (*feu*) to go out.

éteint , -einte *adjective* (*feu, bougie*) out; (*lampe*) off.

étendre *verb* (*nappe*) to spread (out); (*linge*) to hang out; **é. le bras**/*etc* to stretch out one's arm/*etc*.

étendre (s') *reflexive verb* (*personne*) to stretch out; (*plaine*) to stretch; (*feu*) to spread.

étendu , -ue *adjective* (*forêt etc*) extensive; (*personne*) stretched out.

étendue *f noun* (*importance*) extent; (*surface*) area.

éternité *f noun* eternity.

éternuement *m noun* sneeze.

éternuer *verb* to sneeze.

êtes *see* être.

étinceler *verb* to sparkle.

étincelle *f noun* spark.

étiqueter *verb* to label.

étiquette *f noun* label.

étirer (s') *reflexive verb* to stretch (oneself).

étoffe *f noun* material.

étoile *f noun* star; **à la belle é.** in the open.

étoilé , -ée *adjective* (*ciel*) starry.

étonnant , -ante *adjective* surprising.

étonnement *m noun* surprise.

étonner *verb* to surprise.

étonner (s') *reflexive verb* to be surprised (**de quelque chose** at something, **que** (+ *subjunctive*) that).

étouffant , -ante *adjective* (*air*) stifling.

étouffer *verb*
1 (*tuer*) to suffocate, smother; (*bruit*) to muffle; (*feu*) to smother; **é. quelqu'un** (*chaleur*) to stifle somebody.
2 **on étouffe!** it's stifling!

étouffer (s') *reflexive verb* (*en mangeant*) to choke (**sur, avec** on).

étourderie *f noun* thoughtlessness; **une é.** a thoughtless blunder.

étourdi , -ie *adjective* thoughtless.

étourdir *verb* to stun; (*vertige*) to make dizzy.

étourdissant , -ante *adjective* (*bruit*) deafening.

étourdissement *m noun* (*malaise*) dizzy spell.

étrange *adjective* strange, odd.

étranger , -ère
1 *adjective* (*d'un autre pays*) foreign; (*inconnu*) strange (**à** to).
2 *m or f noun* foreigner; stranger; **à l'é.** abroad; **de l'é.** from abroad.

étrangler *verb* (*tuer*) to strangle.

étrangler (s') *reflexive verb* to choke.

être *
1 *verb* to be; **il est tailleur** he's a tailor; **est-ce qu'elle vient?** is she coming?; **il vient, n'est-ce pas?** he's coming, isn't he?; **est-ce qu'il aime le thé?** does he like tea?; **nous sommes dix** there are ten of us; **nous sommes le dix** today is

the tenth (of the month); **il a été à Paris** he has been to Paris.
2 *auxiliary verb* (*avec venir, partir etc*) to have; **elle est arrivée** she has arrived.
3 *m noun* ê. **humain** human being.

étrennes *fpl noun* New Year gift.

étrier *m noun* stirrup.

étroit , -oite *adjective* narrow; (*vêtement*) tight; **être à l'é.** to be cramped.

étroitement *adverb* (*surveiller etc*) closely.

étude *f noun* study; (*salle*) study room; **à l'é.** (*projet*) under consideration; **faire des études de** (*médecine etc*) to study.

étudiant , -ante *m or f noun & adjective* student.

étudier *verb* to study.

étui *m noun* (*à lunettes etc*) case.

eu , eue *past participle of* **avoir**.

euh! *interjection* hem!, er!

euro- *préfixe* Euro-.

euro *m noun* (*monnaie*) Euro.

Europe (l') *f noun* Europe.

européen , -enne *adjective & m or f noun* European.

eux *pronoun* (*sujet*) they; (*complément*) them; (*réfléchi, emphase*) themselves.

eux-mêmes *pronoun* themselves.

évacuer *verb* to evacuate.

évadé , -ée *m or f noun* escaped prisoner.

évader (s') *reflexive verb* to escape (**de** from).

évaluer *verb* to estimate.

Évangile *m noun* Gospel.

évanouir (s') *reflexive verb* to faint, pass *or* black out.

évanouissement *m noun* black-out.

évasion *f noun* escape (**de** from).

éveiller *verb* (*susciter*) to arouse.

événement *m noun* event.

éventail *m noun* fan; (*choix*) range.

éventrer *verb* (*sac, oreiller*) to rip open; (*animal*) to open up.

éventuellement *adverb* possibly.

évêque *m noun* bishop.

évidemment *adverb* obviously.

évident *adjective* obvious (**que** that); (*facile*) *Familiar* easy.

évier *m noun* (kitchen) sink.

éviter *verb* to avoid (**de faire** doing); **é. quelque chose à quelqu'un** to spare somebody something.

ex- *préfixe* ex-; **ex-mari** ex-husband.

exact , -e *adjective* (*précis*) exact, accurate; (*juste, vrai*) correct.

exactement *adverb* exactly.

exactitude *f noun* accuracy; correctness.

ex æquo *adverb* **être classés e.** to tie.

exagération *f noun* exaggeration.

exagéré , -ée *adjective* excessive.

exagérer *verb* to exaggerate.

examen *m noun* examination; (*bac etc*) exam(ination).

examinateur , -trice *m or f noun* examiner.

examiner *verb* to examine.

excédent *m noun* **e. de bagages** excess luggage.

excellent , -ente *adjective* excellent.

excepté *preposition* except.

exception *f noun* exception; **à l'e.**

de except (for).

exceptionnel , -elle *adjective* exceptional.

exceptionnellement *adverb* exceptionally.

excès *m noun* excess; **e. de vitesse** speeding.

excessif , -ive *adjective* excessive.

excitant , -ante *adjective Familiar* exciting.

excitation *f noun* excitement.

excité , -ée *adjective* excited.

exciter *verb* **e. quelqu'un** (*mettre en colère*) to provoke somebody.

exclamation *f noun* exclamation.

exclamer (s') *reflexive verb* to exclaim.

exclure * *verb* to exclude (**de** from).

excursion *f noun* trip, outing; (*à pied*) hike.

excuse *f noun* (*prétexte*) excuse; **excuses** (*regrets*) apology; **faire des excuses** to apologize (**à** to).

excuser *verb* to excuse (**quelqu'un d'avoir fait, quelqu'un de faire** somebody for doing).

excuser (s') *reflexive verb* to apologize (**de** for, **auprès de** to); **excusez-moi** (*j'ai fait une faute*) I'm sorry; (*pour attirer l'attention*) excuse me.

exécuter *verb* (*travail etc*) to carry out; (*jouer*) to perform; **e. quelqu'un** (*tuer*) to execute somebody.

exécution *f noun* (*mise à mort*) execution.

exemplaire *m noun* copy.

exemple *m noun* example; **par e.** for example; **donner l'e.** to set an example (**à** to).

exercer *verb* (*muscles, droits*) to exercise.

exercer (s') *reflexive verb* to practise (**à quelque chose** something, **à faire** doing).

exercice *m noun* exercise; **faire de l'e.** to (take) exercise.

exigeant , -eante *adjective* demanding.

exigence *f noun* demand.

exiger *verb* to demand (**de** from, **que** (+ *subjunctive*) that).

existence *f noun* existence.

exister *verb* to exist; **il existe** there is; (*plural*) there are.

exorbitant , -ante *adjective* exorbitant.

expédier *verb* (*envoyer*) to send off.

expéditeur , -trice *m or f noun* sender.

expédition *f noun* (*envoi*) dispatch; (*voyage*) expedition.

expérience *f noun* (*connaissance*) experience; (*scientifique*) experiment; **faire l'e. de quelque chose** to experience something.

expérimenté , -ée *adjective* experienced.

expert *m noun* expert (**en** on, in).

expirer *verb* to breathe out; (*mourir*) to pass away.

explication *f noun* explanation; (*mise au point*) discussion.

expliquer *verb* to explain (**à** to, **que** that).

expliquer (s') *reflexive verb* (*discuter*) to talk things over (**avec** with).

exploit *m noun* feat, exploit.

exploitation *f noun* (*agricole*) farm.

exploiter *verb* (*champs*) to farm; (*profiter de*) to exploit.

explorateur , -trice *m or f noun* explorer.

exploration *f noun* exploration.

explorer *verb* to explore.

exploser *verb* to explode.

explosif *m noun* explosive.

explosion *f noun* explosion.

exportation *f noun* export.

exporter *verb* to export (**vers** to, **de** from).

exposé , -ée *adjective* **e. au sud/ etc** facing south/*etc*.

exposer *verb* to expose (**à** to); (*tableau etc*) to exhibit; (*vie*) to risk; **s'e. à** to expose oneself to.

exposition *f noun* (*salon*) exhibition.

exprès *adverb* on purpose; (*spécialement*) specially.

express *invariable m noun* (*train*) express; (*café*) espresso.

expression *f noun* (*phrase, mine*) expression.

exprimer *verb* to express; **s'e.** to express oneself.

exquis , -ise *adjective* (*nourriture*) delicious.

exténué , -ée *adjective* exhausted.

extérieur , -e
1 *adjective* outside; (*surface*) outer, external; (*signe*) outward.
2 *m noun* outside; **à l'e. (de)** outside.

externe *m or f noun* (*élève*) day pupil.

extincteur *m noun* fire extinguisher.

extra- *préfixe* extra-.

extraire * *verb* to extract (**de** from).

extrait *m noun* extract.

extraordinaire *adjective* extraordinary.

extrême *adjective & m noun* extreme.

extrêmement *adverb* extremely.

extrémité *f noun* end.

F

fable *f noun* fable.

fabricant , -ante *m or f noun* manufacturer.

fabrication *f noun* manufacture.

fabrique *f noun* factory.

fabriquer *verb* to make; (*en usine*) to manufacture; **qu'est-ce qu'il fabrique?** *Familiar* what's he up to?

fabuleux , -euse *adjective* fabulous.

fac *f noun Familiar* university.

façade *f noun* (*de bâtiment*) front.

face *f noun* face; (*de cube etc*) side; **en f.** opposite; **en f. de** opposite, facing; (*en présence de*) in front of, face to face with; **f. à un problème** faced with a problem; **regarder quelqu'un en f.** to look somebody in the face; **f. à f.** face to face.

fâché , -ée *adjective* (*air*) angry; (*amis*) on bad terms.

fâcher *verb* to anger.

fâcher (se) *reflexive verb* to get angry (**contre** with); **se f. avec quelqu'un** to fall out with somebody.

facile *adjective* easy; **c'est f. à faire** it's easy to do; **il nous est f. de** it's easy for us to.

facilement *adverb* easily.

facilité *f noun* (*simplicité*) easiness; (*aisance*) ease.

faciliter *verb* to make easier.

façon *f noun* way; **la f. dont elle parle** the way (in which) she talks; **f. (d'agir)** behaviour; **façons** (*manières*) manners; **de toute f.** anyway; **à ma f.** my way.

facteur *m noun* postman.

factrice *f noun* postwoman.

facture *f noun* bill, invoice.

facultatif , -ive *adjective* optional.

faculté *f noun* university; **à la f.** at university.

fade *adjective* (*nourriture*) bland.

faible
1 *adjective* weak; (*bruit*) faint; (*vent*) slight; **f. en anglais**/*etc* poor at English/*etc*.
2 *m noun* **avoir un f. pour** to have a soft spot for.

faiblement *adverb* weakly; (*légèrement*) slightly; (*éclairer*) faintly.

faiblesse *f noun* weakness; faintness; slightness.

faiblir *verb* (*forces*) to weaken.

faillir * *verb* **il a failli tomber** he almost fell.

faillite *f noun* **faire f.** to go bankrupt.

faim *f noun* hunger; **avoir f.** to be hungry; **donner f. à quelqu'un** to make somebody hungry.

fainéant , -ante *m or f noun* idler.

faire *
1 *verb* (*bruit, faute, gâteau etc*) to make; (*devoir, ménage etc*) to do; (*rêve, chute*) to have; (*sourire*) to give; (*promenade*) to have, take; **ça fait dix mètres/francs** (*mesure, prix*) it's *or* that's ten metres/francs; **qu'a-t-il fait (de)?** what's he done (with)?; **que f.?** what's to be done?; **f. du tennis**/*etc* to play tennis/*etc*; **f. l'idiot** to play the fool; **ça ne fait rien** that doesn't matter.

2 verb (agir) to do; (paraître) to look; **il fait vieux** he looks old; **elle ferait bien de partir** she'd do well to leave; **il fait beau/froid/** etc it's fine/cold/etc; **ça fait deux ans que je ne l'ai pas vu** I haven't seen him for two years; **ça fait un an que je suis là** I've been here for a year.

3 auxiliary verb (+ infinitive); **f. construire une maison** to have or get a house built; **f. crier/**etc **quelqu'un** to make somebody shout/etc; **se f. obéir/**etc to make oneself obeyed/etc; **se f. tuer/**etc to get or be killed/etc.

faire (se) reflexive verb **se f. des amis** to make friends; **se f. vieux** to get old; **se f. beau** to do oneself up; **se f. mal** to hurt oneself; **il se fait tard** it's getting late; **se f. à** to get used to; **ne t'en fais pas!** don't worry!

faire-part invariable m noun announcement.

fais , **fait** , **faites** see faire.

faisan m noun pheasant.

faisceau , **-x** m noun (rayons) beam.

fait , **faite** (past participle of faire)
1 adjective (fromage) ripe; (yeux) made up; **tout f.** ready made; **c'est bien f.!** it serves you right!
2 m noun event; (réalité) fact; **prendre sur le f.** to catch red-handed; **f. divers** news item; **au f.** by the way; **en f.** in fact.

falaise f noun cliff.

falloir * verb **il faut quelque chose/quelqu'un** I, you, we etc need something/somebody; **il lui faut un stylo** he or she needs a pen; **il faut partir** I, you, we etc have to go; **il faut que je parte** I have to go; **il faudrait qu'elle**

reste she ought to stay; **il faut un jour** it takes a day (**pour faire** to do).

fameux , **-euse** adjective famous; (excellent) first-class.

familiarité f noun familiarity (**avec** with).

familier , **-ière** adjective familiar (**à** to); **f. avec quelqu'un** (over-)familiar with somebody; **animal f.** pet.

familièrement adverb (parler) informally.

famille f noun family; **en f.** with one's family.

fan m noun Familiar fan.

fana m or f noun Familiar **être f. de** to be crazy about.

fané , **-ée** adjective faded.

faner (se) reflexive verb to fade.

fantaisie f noun (caprice) whim; **(de) f.** (bouton etc) novelty, fancy.

fantastique adjective fantastic.

fantôme m noun ghost.

farce [1] f noun practical joke.

farce [2] f noun (viande) stuffing.

farceur , **-euse** m or f noun practical joker.

farcir verb to stuff.

fardeau , **-x** m noun burden.

farine f noun flour.

farouche adjective (animal) easily scared; (violent) fierce.

fascination f noun fascination.

fasciner verb to fascinate.

fasse(s) , **fassent** etc see faire.

fatal , **-e** adjective (plural fatals) fatal; (inévitable) inevitable.

fatalement adverb inevitably.

fatigant , **-ante** adjective tiring; (ennuyeux) tiresome.

fatigue f noun tiredness.

fatigué , **-ée** adjective tired (de

of).

fatiguer *verb* to tire.

fatiguer (se) *reflexive verb* to get tired (**de** of).

faubourg *m noun* suburb.

faucher *verb* (*herbe*) to mow; (*blé*) to reap.

faucon *m noun* hawk.

faufiler (se) *reflexive verb* to edge one's way (**dans** through, into).

fausse *see* faux.

faut *see* falloir.

faute *f noun* mistake; (*responsabilité*) fault; (*péché*) sin; **c'est ta f.** it's your fault.

fauteuil *m noun* armchair; **f. roulant** wheelchair.

fauve *m noun* wild animal, big cat.

faux , fausse
  1 *adjective* false; (*pas exact*) wrong; (*monnaie*) forged.
  2 *adverb* (*chanter*) out of tune.

faux *f noun* scythe.

faux-filet *m noun* sirloin.

faveur *f noun* **en f. de** in aid *or* favour of.

favorable *adjective* favourable (**à** to).

favori , -ite *adjective & m or f noun* favourite.

favoriser *verb* to favour.

fax *m noun* (*appareil*, *message*) fax.

faxer *verb* (*message*) to fax.

fée *f noun* fairy.

féerique *adjective* fairy(-like).

fêler *verb* to crack.

fêler (se) *reflexive verb* to crack.

félicitations *fpl noun* congratulations (**pour** on).

féliciter *verb* to congratulate (**quelqu'un de** *or* **sur** somebody

fêlure *f noun* crack.

femelle *adjective & f noun* (*animal*) female.

féminin , -ine *adjective* (*prénom etc*) female; (*trait, pronom etc*) feminine; (*mode, revue etc*) women's.

femme *f noun* woman; (*épouse*) wife; **f. médecin** woman doctor; **f. de ménage** cleaning woman.

fendre *verb* (*bois etc*) to split.

fendre (se) *reflexive verb* to crack.

fenêtre *f noun* window.

fente *f noun* slit.

fer *m noun* iron; **barre de f.** iron bar; **f. forgé** wrought iron; **f. à cheval** horseshoe; **santé de f.** cast-iron health.

fer (à repasser) *m noun* iron (*for clothes*).

fera , ferai(t) *etc see* faire.

fer-blanc *m noun* (*plural* fers-blancs*) tin.

férié *adjective* **jour f.** (public) holiday.

ferme [1] *f noun* farm.

ferme [2]
  1 *adjective* firm; (*pas, voix*) steady.
  2 *adverb* (*travailler, boire*) hard.

fermé , -ée *adjective* (*porte etc*) closed, shut; (*route etc*) closed; (*gaz etc*) off.

fermement *adverb* firmly.

fermer *verb* to close, shut; (*gaz etc*) to turn *or* switch off; (*vêtement*) to do up; **f. (à clef)** to lock.

fermer (se) *reflexive verb* (*porte, boîte*) to close, shut.

fermeture *f noun* closing; (*heure*) closing time; **f. éclair** ® zip (fastener).

fermier , -ière *m or f noun* farmer.

féroce *adjective* fierce, savage.

feront *see* faire.

ferraille *f noun* scrap metal, old iron; **mettre à la f.** to scrap.

ferrée *adjective* **voie ferrée** railway; (*rails*) track.

ferroviaire *adjective* **compagnie f.** railway company.

fertile *adjective* fertile.

fesse *f noun* buttock; **les fesses** one's behind.

fessée *f noun* spanking.

festin *m noun* (*banquet*) feast.

festival *m noun* (*plural* **festivals**) festival.

festivités *fpl noun* festivities.

fête *f noun* (*civile*) holiday; (*religieuse*) festival; (*entre amis*) party; **f. foraine** (fun)fair; **f. de famille** family celebration; **f. des Mères** Mother's Day; **jour de f.** (public) holiday; **faire la f.** to have a good time; **c'est sa f.** it's his *or* her saint's day; **Bonnes Fêtes!** Have a good holiday!

fêter *verb* to celebrate.

feu , -x *m noun* fire; (*de réchaud*) burner; **feux (tricolores)** traffic lights; **feux de détresse** (hazard) warning lights; **f. rouge** red light; (*objet*) traffic lights; **mettre le f. à** to set fire to; **en f.** on fire; **faire du f.** to light *or* make a fire; **avez-vous du f.?** have you got a light?; **à f. doux** on a low light; **au f.!** fire!; **coup de f.** (*bruit*) gunshot.

feuillage *m noun* leaves.

feuille *f noun* leaf; (*de papier etc*) sheet; **f. d'impôt** tax form; **f. de paye** pay slip.

feuilleter *verb* to flip through; **pâte feuilletée** puff pastry.

feuilleton *m noun* serial.

feutre *m noun* **crayon f.** felt-tip (pen).

février *m noun* February.

fiançailles *fpl noun* engagement.

fiancé *m noun* fiancé.

fiancée *f noun* fiancée.

fiancer (se) *reflexive verb* to become engaged (**avec** to).

ficeler *verb* to tie up.

ficelle *f noun* string.

fiche *f noun* (*carte*) index card; (*papier*) form.

fiche(r) *verb* (*past participle* **fichu**) *Familiar* **f. le camp** to shove off; **fiche-moi la paix!** leave me alone!; **se f. de quelqu'un** to make fun of somebody; **je m'en fiche!** I don't give a damn!

fichier *m noun* card index.

fichu , -ue *adjective* **c'est f.** (*abîmé*) *Familiar* it's had it.

fidèle *adjective* faithful (**à** to); (*client*) regular.

fier (se) *reflexive verb* **se f. à** to trust.

fier , fière *adjective* proud (**de** of).

fièrement *adverb* proudly.

fierté *f noun* pride.

fièvre *f noun* fever; **avoir de la f.** to have a temperature *or* a fever.

fiévreux , -euse *adjective* feverish.

figer *verb* to congeal.

figer (se) *reflexive verb* to congeal.

figue *f noun* fig.

figure *f noun* (*visage*) face; (*géométrique*) figure.

figurer *verb* to appear.

figurer (se) *reflexive verb* to imagine.

fil[1] *m noun* thread; **f. dentaire** dental floss.

fil[2] *m noun* (*métallique*) wire; **f. de fer** wire; **passer un coup de f. à quelqu'un** to give somebody a ring, call somebody up; **au bout du f.** *Familiar* on the line.

file *f noun* line; (*couloir*) lane; **f. d'attente** queue; **en f. (indienne)** in single file.

filer *verb*
1 f. quelqu'un (*suivre*) to shadow somebody
2 *Familiar* (*partir*) to rush off; (*aller vite*) to speed along.

filet *m noun* (*à bagages*) rack; (*d'eau*) trickle; (*de poisson*) fillet; **f. (à provisions)** net bag.

fille *f noun* girl; (*parenté*) daughter; **petite f.** (*fillette*) little girl; **jeune f.** girl, young lady.

fillette *f noun* little girl.

filleul *m noun* godson.

filleule *f noun* goddaughter.

film *m noun* film, movie; (*pellicule*) film; **f. d'aventures** adventure film; **f. comique** comedy; **f. d'horreur** horror film; **f. policier** detective film; **f. plastique** cling-film.

filmer *verb* to film.

fils *m noun* son.

filtre *m noun* filter; **(à bout) f.** (*cigarette*) (filter-)tipped; **(bout) f.** filter tip.

filtrer *verb* to filter.

fin *f noun* end; **mettre f. à** to put an end to; **prendre f.** to come to an end; **sans f.** endless; **à la f.** in the end; **f. mai** at the end of May.

fin , fine
1 *adjective* (*pointe etc*) fine; (*peu épais*) thin; (*esprit, oreille*) sharp.
2 *adverb* (*couper etc*) finely.

final , -e, -aux *or* **-als** *adjective* final.

finale *f noun* final.

finalement *adverb* finally.

finance *f noun* finance.

financer *verb* to finance.

financier , -ière *adjective* financial.

finir *verb* to finish; **f. de faire** to finish doing; (*cesser*) to stop doing; **f. par faire** to end up doing; **c'est fini** it's over.

finlandais , -aise
1 *adjective* Finnish.
2 *m or f noun* Finn.

Finlande (la) *f noun* Finland.

fissure *f noun* crack.

fissurer (se) *reflexive verb* to crack.

fixe *adjective* fixed; **idée f.** obsession; **regard f.** stare.

fixement *adverb* **regarder f.** to stare at.

fixer *verb* (*attacher*) to fix (**à** to); (*date etc*) to fix; **f. (du regard)** to stare at; **être fixé** (*décidé*) to be decided.

flacon *m noun* (small) bottle.

flair *m noun* (*d'un chien etc*) (sense of) smell; (*intuition*) insight.

flairer *verb* to smell.

flamand , -ande
1 *adjective* Flemish.
2 *m noun* (*langue*) Flemish.

flamber *verb* to burn.

flamme *f noun* flame; **en flammes** on fire.

flan *m noun* (*dessert*) custard tart, baked custard.

flanc *m noun* side.

flâner *verb* to stroll.

flaque *f noun* puddle.

flash *m noun* (*plural* **flashes**) (*de*

photographie) flash(light); (*dispositif*) flash(gun); (*d'informations*) (news) flash.

flatter *verb* to flatter.

flatterie *f noun* flattery.

fléau , -x *m noun* (*catastrophe*) scourge.

flèche *f noun* arrow; (*d'église*) spire; **monter en f.** (*prix*) to shoot up.

flécher *verb* to signpost (with arrows).

fléchette *f noun* dart; **fléchettes** (*jeu*) darts.

fléchir *verb*
1 (*membre*) to flex.
2 (*poutre*) to sag.

flétrir *verb* to wither.

flétrir (se) *reflexive verb* to wither.

fleur *f noun* flower; (*d'arbre*) blossom; **en fleur(s)** in flower; **à fleurs** (*tissu*) flowered, flowery.

fleuri , -ie *adjective* in bloom; (*tissu*) flowered, flowery.

fleurir *verb* to flower; (*arbre*) to blossom.

fleuriste *m or f noun* florist.

fleuve *m noun* river.

flexible *adjective* pliable.

flic *m noun Familiar* cop.

flipper *m noun* (*jeu*) pinball; (*appareil*) pinball machine.

flocon *m noun* (*de neige*) flake.

flot *m noun* (*de souvenirs etc*) flood; **à f.** afloat.

flotte *f noun* (*de bateaux*) fleet; (*pluie*) *Familiar* rain; (*eau*) *Familiar* water.

flotter *verb* to float; (*drapeau*) to fly.

flotteur *m noun Pêche* float.

flou , -e *adjective* fuzzy, blurred.

fluide *adjective & m noun* fluid.

fluo *invariable adjective* (*couleur etc*) luminous, fluorescent.

fluorescent , -ente *adjective* fluorescent.

flûte
1 *f noun* flute; (*verre*) champagne glass; **f. à bec** recorder; **f. de Pan** panpipes.
2 *interjection* heck!

foi *f noun* faith; **être de bonne/ mauvaise f.** to be/not to be (completely) sincere.

foie *m noun* liver.

foin *m noun* hay.

foire *f noun* fair.

fois *f noun* time; **une f.** once; **deux f.** twice; **chaque f. que** whenever; **une f. qu'il sera arrivé** once he has arrived; **à la f.** at the same time; **des f.** sometimes; **une f. pour toutes** once and for all.

fol *see* fou.

folie *f noun* madness.

folklore *m noun* folklore.

folklorique *adjective* **musique f.** folk music.

folle *see* fou.

foncé , -ée *adjective* (*couleur*) dark.

foncer *verb* (*aller vite*) to tear along; **f. sur quelqu'un** to charge at somebody.

fonction *f noun* function; **la f. publique** the public *or* civil service.

fonctionnaire *m or f noun* civil servant.

fonctionnement *m noun* working.

fonctionner *verb* (*machine etc*) to work; **faire f.** to operate.

fond *m noun* (*de boîte, jardin etc*) bottom; (*de salle etc*) back;

(*arrière-plan*) background; **au f. de** at the bottom of; at the back of; **f. de teint** foundation cream; **à f.** (*connaître etc*) thoroughly.

fonder *verb* (*ville etc*) to found.

fondre *verb* to melt; (*métal*) to melt down; **faire f.** to melt; **f. en larmes** to dissolve into tears.

fonds *mpl noun* (*argent*) funds.

font *see* **faire**.

fontaine *f noun* fountain.

fonte *f noun* (*des neiges*) melting; (*fer*) cast iron.

football *m noun* football, soccer.

footballeur , -euse *m or f noun* footballer.

footing *m noun* jogging.

force *f noun* force; (*physique, morale*) strength; **ses forces** one's strength; **de f.** by force; **à f. de lire**/*etc* through reading/*etc*, after much reading/*etc*.

forcément *adverb* obviously; **pas f.** not necessarily.

forcer *verb* (*porte etc*) to force; **f. quelqu'un à faire** to force somebody to do; **se f.** to force oneself (**à faire** to do).

forêt *f noun* forest.

forfait *m noun* **déclarer f.** to withdraw from the game.

formalité *f noun* formality.

format *m noun* size.

formation *f noun* education, training.

forme *f noun* (*contour*) shape, form; **en f. de poire**/*etc* pear/*etc* -shaped; **en (pleine) f.** in good shape *or* form.

formel , -elle *adjective* (*absolu*) formal.

former *verb* to form; (*apprenti etc*) to train.

former (se) *reflexive verb* (*appa-*

raître) to form.

formidable *adjective* terrific, tremendous.

formulaire *m noun* (*feuille*) form.

formule *f noun* formula; (*phrase*) (set) expression; **f. de politesse** polite form of address.

fort , forte
1 *adjective* strong; (*pluie, mer*) heavy; (*voix, radio*) loud; (*fièvre*) high; (*élève*) bright; **f. en** (*maths etc*) good at; **c'est plus f. qu'elle** she can't help it.
2 *adverb* (*frapper, pleuvoir*) hard; (*parler*) loud(ly); (*serrer*) tight; **sentir f.** to have a strong smell.

fort *m noun* fort.

forteresse *f noun* fortress.

fortifiant *m noun* tonic.

fortune *f noun* fortune; **faire f.** to make one's fortune.

fosse *f noun* (*trou*) pit; (*tombe*) grave.

fossé *m noun* ditch.

fou (*or* **fol** *before vowel or mute h*), **folle**
1 *adjective* mad; (*succès, temps*) tremendous; **f. de** (*musique etc*) mad about; **f. de joie** wildly happy.
2 *m or f noun* madman, madwoman.
3 *m* Échecs bishop; **faire le f.** to play the fool.

foudre *f noun* **la f.** lightning.

foudroyant , -ante *adjective* (*succès etc*) staggering.

foudroyer *verb* (*tuer*) to electrocute.

fouet *m noun* whip; (*de cuisine*) (egg) whisk.

fouetter *verb* to whip; (*œufs*) to whisk.

fougère *f noun* fern.

fouiller *verb*
1 (*personne, maison etc*) to search.
2 **f. dans** (*tiroir etc*) to search through.

fouillis *m noun* jumble, mess.

foulard *m noun* (head) scarf.

foule *f noun* crowd; **une f. de** (*objets etc*) a mass of.

fouler *verb* **se f. la cheville**/*etc* to sprain one's ankle/*etc*.

foulure *f noun* sprain.

four *m noun* oven.

fourche *f noun* fork.

fourchette *f noun* fork (*used for eating or cooking*).

fourgon *m noun* van; (*mortuaire*) hearse.

fourgonnette *f noun* (small) van.

fourmi *f noun* ant; **avoir des fourmis** to have pins and needles (**dans** in).

fourneau , -x *m noun* (*poêle*) stove.

fournée *f noun* batch.

fournir *verb* to supply; (*effort*) to make; **f. quelque chose à quelqu'un** to supply somebody with something.

fourré , -ée *adjective* (*gant etc*) fur-lined; **un gâteau f. à la confiture** a cake filled with jam.

fourrer *verb* Familiar (*mettre*) to stick.

fourre-tout *invariable m noun* (*sac*) holdall.

fourrière *f noun* (*lieu*) pound.

fourrure *f noun* fur.

foyer *m noun* (*maison, famille*) home; (*résidence de jeunes etc*) hostel.

fracas *m noun* din.

fracasser *verb* to smash.

fracasser (se) *reflexive verb* to smash.

fraction *f noun* fraction.

fracture *f noun* fracture; **se faire une f. au bras**/*etc* to fracture one's arm/*etc*.

fracturer *verb* (*porte etc*) to break (open); **se f. la jambe**/*etc* to fracture one's leg/*etc*.

fragile *adjective* fragile.

fragment *m noun* fragment.

fraîcheur *f noun* freshness; coolness.

frais , fraîche
1 *adjective* fresh; (*temps*) cool; (*boisson*) cold; **servir f.** (*vin etc*) to serve chilled.
2 *m noun* **il fait f.** it's cool; **mettre au f.** to put in a cool place; (*au frigidaire*) to refrigerate.

frais *mpl noun* expenses; **à mes f.** at my (own) expense.

fraise *f noun* strawberry.

framboise *f noun* raspberry.

franc , franche *adjective* (*personne etc*) frank; **coup f.** *Football* free kick.

franc *m noun* (*monnaie*) franc.

français , -aise
1 *adjective* French.
2 *m or f noun* Frenchman, Frenchwoman; **les F.** the French.
3 *m noun* (*langue*) French.

France (la) *f noun* France.

France 2/3 *f noun* = French second/third TV channel (*state-owned*).

franchement *adverb* frankly; (*vraiment*) really.

franchir *verb* (*fossé*) to jump (over), clear; (*frontière etc*) to cross; (*porte*) to go through; (*distance*) to cover.

franchise *f noun* frankness.

francophone *m or f noun* French speaker.

frange *f noun* (*de cheveux*) fringe.

frappant , -ante *adjective* striking.

frapper *verb*
1 (*donner un coup à*) to hit; (*étonner*) to strike.
2 (*à la porte etc*) to knock (à at); **f. du pied** to stamp (one's foot).

fraude *f noun* (*à un examen*) cheating; (*crime*) fraud; **passer quelque chose en f.** to smuggle something.

frauder *verb* (*à un examen*) to cheat (à in).

frayer *verb* **se f. un passage** to clear a way (à travers, dans through).

frayeur *f noun* fright.

fredonner *verb* to hum.

freezer *m noun* freezer.

frein *m noun* brake; **donner un coup de f.** to brake.

freinage *m noun* braking.

freiner *verb* to brake.

frémir *verb* (*trembler*) to shudder (de with).

fréquemment *adverb* frequently.

fréquent , -ente *adjective* frequent.

fréquenter *verb* (*école, église*) to attend; **f. quelqu'un** to see somebody; **se f.** to see each other.

frère *m noun* brother.

friandises *fpl noun* sweets.

fric *m noun* (*argent*) *Familiar* cash.

frictionner *verb* to rub (down).

frigidaire ® *m noun* fridge.

frigo *m noun Familiar* fridge.

frileux , -euse *adjective* sensitive to cold.

frire * *verb* to fry; **faire f.** to fry.

frise *f noun* frieze.

frisé , -ée *adjective* curly.

friser *verb* (*cheveux*) to curl.

frisson *m noun* shiver; shudder.

frissonner *verb* (*de froid*) to shiver; (*de peur etc*) to shudder (de with).

frit , frite (*past participle of* **frire**) *adjective* fried.

frites *fpl noun* chips.

friteuse *f noun* (deep) fryer.

froid , froide
1 *adjective* cold.
2 *m noun* cold; **avoir/prendre f.** to be/catch cold; **il fait f.** it's cold.

froisser *verb* (*tissu*) to crumple; (*personne*) to offend.

froisser (se) *reflexive verb* (*tissu*) to crumple; (*personne*) to take offence (de at).

frôler *verb* (*toucher*) to brush against.

fromage *m noun* cheese; **f. blanc** soft white cheese.

fromagerie *f noun* (*magasin*) cheese shop.

froncer *verb* **f. les sourcils** to frown.

front *m noun* forehead, brow; (*de bataille*) front.

frontière *f noun* border.

frotter *verb* to rub; (*pour nettoyer*) to scrub.

frousse *f noun Familiar* fear; **avoir la f.** to be scared.

fruit *m noun* fruit; **des fruits, les fruits** fruit; **fruits de mer** seafood.

fruitier *adjective* **arbre f.** fruit tree.

fuel *m noun* (fuel) oil.

fugitif , -ive *m or f noun* fugitive.

fuir * *verb* to run away; (*gaz, robinet etc*) to leak.

fuite *f noun* flight (**de** from); (*de gaz etc*) leak; **en f.** on the run; **prendre la f.** to run away *or* off.

fumé , -ée *adjective* smoked.

fumée *f noun* smoke; (*vapeur*) fumes.

fumer *verb* to smoke; (*liquide brûlant*) to steam.

fumeur , -euse *m or f noun* smoker; **compartiment fumeurs** smoking compartment.

fumier *m noun* manure.

funérailles *fpl noun* funeral.

fur et à mesure (au) *adverb* as one goes along; **au f. et à m. que** as.

fureur *f noun* fury; **faire f.** (*mode etc*) to be all the rage.

furie *f noun* fury.

furieux , -euse *adjective* furious (**contre** with, at); (*vent*) raging.

furoncle *m noun* boil.

fuseau , -x *m noun* (*pantalon*) ski pants; **f. horaire** time zone.

fusée *f noun* rocket.

fusible *m noun* fuse.

fusil *m noun* rifle, gun; (*de chasse*) shotgun; **coup de f.** gunshot.

fusillade *f noun* (*tirs*) gunfire.

fusiller *verb* (*exécuter*) to shoot; **f. quelqu'un du regard** to glare at somebody.

fût *m noun* (*tonneau*) barrel, cask.

futé , -ée *adjective* cunning.

futur , -ure *adjective & m noun* future.

gâcher verb to spoil; (argent etc) to waste.

gâchette f noun trigger.

gâchis m noun (gaspillage) waste.

gadget m noun gadget.

gag m noun gag.

gage m noun (garantie) security; **mettre en g.** to pawn.

gagnant , -ante
1 adjective winning.
2 m or f noun winner.

gagner verb (argent, objet) to earn; (par le jeu) to win; (atteindre) to reach; **g. une heure**/etc to save an hour/etc.

gai , gaie adjective cheerful.

gaiement adverb cheerfully.

gaieté f noun cheerfulness.

gain m noun **un g. de temps** a saving of time; **gains** (salaire) earnings; (au jeu) winnings.

gaine f noun (sous-vêtement) girdle; (étui) sheath.

gala m noun gala.

galant , -ante adjective gallant.

galerie f noun gallery; (porte-bagages) roof rack.

galet m noun pebble.

gallois , -oise
1 adjective Welsh.
2 m noun (langue) Welsh.
3 m or f noun Welshman, Welshwoman.

galon m noun (ruban) braid; (de soldat) stripe.

galop m noun gallop; **aller au g.** to gallop.

galoper verb to gallop.

gambade f noun leap.

gambader verb to leap about.

gamelle f Familiar pan; (de chien) bowl; (d'ouvrier) lunch tin or box.

gamin , -ine m or f noun (enfant) kid.

gamme f noun (de notes) scale; (série) range.

gangster m noun gangster.

gant m noun glove; **g. de toilette** facecloth; **boîte à gants** glove compartment.

ganté , -ée adjective (main) gloved; (personne) wearing gloves.

garage m noun garage.

garagiste m or f noun garage mechanic.

garantie f noun guarantee; **garantie(s)** (d'assurance) cover.

garantir verb to guarantee (contre against); **g. à quelqu'un que** to assure or guarantee somebody that.

garçon m noun boy; (jeune homme) young man; **petit g.** little boy; **g. (de café)** waiter.

garde
1 m noun guard; **g. du corps** bodyguard.
2 f noun (d'enfants, de bagages etc) care (de of); **avoir la g. de** to be in charge of; **prendre g.** to pay attention (à quelque chose to something); **prendre g. de ne pas faire** to be careful not to do; **mettre en g.** to warn (contre against); **mise en g.** warning; **de g.** on duty; **monter la g.** to stand guard; **sur ses gardes** on one's guard; **chien de g.** watchdog.

garde-chasse m noun (plural **gardes-chasses**) gamekeeper.

garder *verb* to keep; (*vêtement*) to keep on; (*surveiller*) to watch (over); (*enfant*) to look after; **g. la chambre** to stay in one's room; **g. le lit** to stay in bed.

garder (se) *reflexive verb* (*aliment*) to keep.

garderie *f noun* crèche, nursery.

gardien , -ienne *m or f noun* (*d'immeuble etc*) caretaker; (*de prison*) (prison) guard; (*de zoo, parc*) keeper; (*de musée*) attendant; **g. de but** goalkeeper.

gare *f noun* station; **g. maritime** harbour station; **g. de marchandises** goods station; **g. routière** bus *or* coach station.

garer *verb* to park; (*au garage*) to put in the garage.

garer (se) *reflexive verb* to park.

garnement *m noun* rascal.

garnir *verb* (*équiper*) to fit out (**de** with); (*magasin*) to stock; (*orner*) to trim (**de** with).

garniture *f noun* (*de légumes*) garnish.

Garonne (la) *f noun* the Garonne.

gars *m noun* fellow, guy.

gas-oil *m noun* diesel (oil).

gaspillage *m noun* waste.

gaspiller *verb* to waste.

gâté , -ée *adjective* (*dent etc*) bad.

gâteau , -x *m noun* cake; **g. de riz** rice pudding; **g. sec** (sweet) biscuit.

gâter *verb* to spoil.

gâter (se) *reflexive verb* (*aliment, dent*) to go bad; (*temps, situation*) to get worse.

gauche
1 *adjective* left.
2 *f noun* **la g.** (*côté*) the left (side); **à g.** (*tourner*) (to the) left;

(*marcher etc*) on the left; **de g.** (*fenêtre etc*) left-hand; **à g. de** on *or* to the left of; **à votre g.** to *or* on your left.

gaucher , -ère *adjective & m or f noun* left-handed (person).

gaufre *f noun* waffle.

gaufrette *f noun* wafer (biscuit).

Gaulois (les) *mpl noun* the Gauls.

gaver (se) *reflexive verb* to stuff oneself (**de** with).

gaz *invariable m noun* gas; **réchaud à g.** gas stove.

gaze *f noun* gauze.

gazeux , -euse *adjective* (*boisson, eau*) fizzy, carbonated.

gazinière *f noun* gas cooker.

gazole *m noun* diesel (oil).

gazon *m noun* grass, lawn.

GDF *m abbreviation* (*Gaz de France*) = French gas company.

géant , -ante *adjective & m or f noun* giant.

gel *m noun* frost; (*pour cheveux etc*) gel.

gelé , -ée *adjective* frozen.

gelée *f noun* frost; (*de fruits*) jelly.

geler *verb* to freeze; **il gèle** it's freezing.

gémir *verb* to groan.

gémissement *m noun* groan.

gênant , -ante *adjective* (*objet*) cumbersome; (*situation*) awkward; (*bruit*) annoying.

gencive *f noun* gum.

gendarme *m noun* gendarme.

gendarmerie *f noun* (*local*) police headquarters.

gendre *m noun* son-in-law.

gêne *f noun* (*trouble physique*) discomfort; (*confusion*) embarrassment.

gêné , -ée *adjective* (*mal à l'aise*)

awkward.

gêner verb to bother; (troubler) to embarrass; (mouvement) to hamper; (circulation) to hold up; **g. quelqu'un** (par sa présence) to be in somebody's way.

général , -e, -aux
1 adjective general; **en g.** in general.
2 m noun (officier) general.

généralement adverb generally.

génération f noun generation.

généreusement adverb generously.

généreux , -euse adjective generous (de with).

générosité f noun generosity.

génial , -e, -aux adjective brilliant.

génie m noun genius.

genou , -x m noun knee; **à genoux** kneeling (down); **se mettre à genoux** to kneel (down); **sur ses genoux** on one's lap.

genre m noun (espèce) kind, sort; (d'un nom) gender.

gens mpl noun people; **jeunes g.** young people; (hommes) young men.

gentil , -ille adjective nice; **g. avec quelqu'un** nice or kind to somebody; **sois g.** (sage) be good.

gentillesse f noun kindness.

gentiment adverb kindly; (sagement) nicely.

géographie f noun geography.

géographique adjective geographical.

géomètre m noun surveyor.

géométrie f noun geometry.

géométrique adjective geometric(al).

gerbe f noun (de blé) sheaf; (de fleurs) bunch.

gercer verb to chap.

gercer (se) reflexive verb to chap.

gerçure f noun **avoir des gerçures aux mains/lèvres** to have chapped hands/lips.

germe m noun (microbe) germ; (de plante) shoot.

germer verb (graine) to start to grow; (pomme de terre) to sprout.

geste m noun gesture; **ne pas faire un g.** not to make a move.

gesticuler verb to gesticulate.

gibier m noun (animaux etc) game.

giboulée f noun shower.

gicler verb (liquide) to spurt; **faire g.** to spurt.

gifle f noun slap (in the face).

gifler verb **g. quelqu'un** to slap somebody.

gigantesque adjective gigantic.

gigot m noun leg of mutton or lamb.

gigoter verb to wriggle, fidget.

gilet m noun cardigan; (de costume) waistcoat; **g. de sauvetage** life jacket.

girafe f noun giraffe.

giratoire adjective **sens g.** roundabout.

girouette f noun weathercock.

gitan , -ane m or f noun (Spanish) gipsy.

gîte m noun **g. d'étape** = transit accommodation for hikers, cyclists etc; **g. rural** gîte, self-catering holiday cottage/apartment.

givre m noun frost.

givré , -ée adjective frost-covered.

glace f noun (eau gelée) ice; (crème glacée) ice cream; (vitre) window; (miroir) mirror.

glacé , -ée *adjective* (*eau, main etc*) icy.

glacer *verb* to chill.

glacial , -e, -aux *adjective* icy.

glacier *m noun* (*vendeur*) ice-cream man.

glacière *f noun* icebox.

glaçon *m noun* ice cube.

gland *m noun* acorn.

glande *f noun* gland.

glissant , -ante *adjective* slippery.

glisser *verb*
1 (*déraper*) (*involontairement*) to slip; (*volontairement*) (*sur la glace etc*) to slide; (*coulisser*) (*tiroir etc*) to slide; **ça glisse** it's slippery.
2 (*objet*) to slip (**dans** into).

glissière *f noun* **porte à g.** sliding door.

globe *m noun* globe.

gloire *f noun* glory.

glorieux , -euse *adjective* glorious.

gloussement *m noun* cluck(ing).

glousser *verb* to cluck.

glouton , -onne
1 *adjective* greedy.
2 *m or f noun* glutton.

gluant , -ante *adjective* sticky.

goal *m noun* goalkeeper.

gobelet *m noun* (*de plastique, papier*) cup.

godet *m noun* pot.

golf *m noun* golf; (*terrain*) golf course.

golfe *m noun* gulf, bay.

golfeur , -euse *m or f noun* golfer.

gomme *f noun* (*à effacer*) rubber.

gommer *verb* (*effacer*) to rub out, erase.

gond *m noun* hinge.

gonflable *adjective* inflatable.

gonflé , -ée *adjective* swollen.

gonfler *verb*
1 (*pneu*) to pump up; (*en soufflant*) to blow up.
2 (*enfler*) to swell.

gonfler (se) *reflexive verb* to swell.

gonfleur *m noun* (air) pump.

gorge *f noun* throat; (*vallée*) gorge.

gorgée *f noun* mouthful; **petite g.** sip.

gorille *m noun* gorilla.

gosier *m noun* throat.

gosse *m or f noun* (*enfant*) *Familiar* kid.

gouache *f noun* gouache.

goudron *m noun* tar.

goudronner *verb* to tar.

goulot *m noun* (*de bouteille*) neck; **boire au g.** to drink from the bottle.

gourde *f noun* water bottle.

gourdin *m noun* club, cudgel.

gourmand , -ande
1 *adjective* (over)fond of food; **g. de fond of.**
2 *m or f noun* hearty eater.

gourmandise *f noun* (over)-fondness for food.

gourmet *m noun* gourmet.

gourmette *f noun* identity bracelet.

gousse *f noun* **g. d'ail** clove of garlic.

goût *m noun* taste; **de bon g.** in good taste; **sans g.** tasteless.

goûter *verb*
1 (*nourriture*) to taste; **g. à quelque chose** to taste (a little of) something.
2 (*prendre un goûter*) to have an

afternoon snack.

3 *m noun* afternoon snack, tea.

goutte *f noun* drop; **une g. de pluie** a raindrop.

gouttelette *f noun* droplet.

goutter *verb* to drip (**de** from).

gouttière *f noun* (*d'un toit*) gutter.

gouvernail *m noun* rudder; (*barre*) helm.

gouvernement *m noun* government.

gouverner *verb* to govern.

grâce

  1 *f noun* grace; (*avantage*) favour.

  2 *preposition* **g. à** thanks to.

gracieux , -euse *adjective* (*élégant*) graceful.

grade *m noun* rank.

gradin *m noun* tier (of seats).

graffiti *mpl noun* graffiti.

grain *m noun* grain; (*de café*) bean; (*de poussière*) speck; **g. de beauté** mole; (*sur le visage*) beauty spot.

graine *f noun* seed.

graisse *f noun* fat; (*pour machine*) grease.

graisser *verb* to grease.

graisseux , -euse *adjective* (*vêtement etc*) greasy.

grammaire *f noun* grammar; **livre de g.** grammar (book).

gramme *m noun* gram(me).

grand , grande

  1 *adjective* big, large; (*en hauteur*) tall; (*chaleur, découverte etc*) great; (*bruit*) loud; (*différence*) big, great; **g. frère/etc** (*plus âgé*) big brother/*etc*; **il est g. temps** it's high time (**que** that).

  2 *adverb* **g. ouvert** wide-open; **ouvrir g.** to open wide.

grand-chose *pronoun* **pas g.** not much.

Grande-Bretagne (la) *f noun* Great Britain.

grandeur *f noun* (*importance*) greatness; (*dimension*) size; **g. nature** life-size.

grandir *verb* to grow.

grand-mère *f noun* (*plural* **grands-mères**) grandmother.

grand-père *m noun* (*plural* **grands-pères**) grandfather.

grand-route *f noun* main road.

grands-parents *mpl noun* grandparents.

grange *f noun* barn.

graphique *m noun* graph.

grappe *f noun* cluster; **g. de raisin** bunch of grapes.

gras , grasse

  1 *adjective* fat; (*aliment*) fatty; (*graisseux*) greasy; **matières grasses** fat.

  2 *m noun* (*de viande*) fat.

gratin *m noun* **chou-fleur au g.** cauliflower cheese.

gratitude *f noun* gratitude.

gratte-ciel *invariable m noun* skyscraper.

gratter *verb* to scrape; (*avec les ongles etc*) to scratch; **se g.** to scratch oneself; **ça me gratte** it itches.

gratuit , -uite *adjective* free.

gratuitement *adverb* free (of charge).

gravats *mpl noun* rubble.

grave *adjective* serious; (*voix*) deep; **ce n'est pas g.!** it's not important!; **accent g.** grave accent.

gravement *adverb* seriously.

graver *verb* (*sur métal etc*) to engrave; (*sur bois*) to carve.

graveur *m noun* engraver.

gravier *m noun* gravel.

gravillons *mpl noun* gravel, (loose) chippings.

gravir *verb* to climb.

gravité *f noun* (*de situation etc*) seriousness.

gravure *f noun* (*image*) print.

grec , grecque
  1 *adjective & m or f noun* Greek.
  2 *m noun* (*langue*) Greek.

Grèce (la) *f noun* Greece.

greffe *f noun* (*de peau, d'arbre*) graft; (*d'organe*) transplant.

greffer *verb* (*peau etc*) to graft (à on to); (*organe*) to transplant.

grêle *f noun* hail.

grêler *impersonal verb* to hail.

grêlon *m noun* hailstone.

grelot *m noun* (small round) bell.

grelotter *verb* to shiver (**de** with).

grenade *f noun* (*fruit*) pomegranate; (*projectile*) grenade.

grenadine *f noun* pomegranate syrup, grenadine.

grenier *m noun* attic.

grenouille *f noun* frog.

grève *f noun* strike; **g. de la faim** hunger strike; **se mettre en g.** to go (out) on strike.

gréviste *m or f noun* striker.

gribouiller *verb* to scribble.

gribouillis *m noun* scribble.

grièvement *adverb* **g. blessé** seriously injured.

griffe *f noun* (*ongle*) claw; (*de couturier*) (designer) label.

griffer *verb* to scratch.

griffonner *verb* to scribble.

grignoter *verb* to nibble.

gril *m noun* grill.

grillade *f noun* (*viande*) grill.

grillage *m noun* wire mesh *or* netting.

grille *f noun* (*clôture*) railings.

grille-pain *invariable m noun* toaster.

grillé, -ée *adjective* (*viande, poisson*) grilled; **pain g.** toast.

griller *verb*
  1 (*viande*) to grill; (*pain*) to toast; **g. un feu rouge** *Familiar* to jump a red light.
  2 mettre à g. to put on the grill.

grillon *m noun* (*insecte*) cricket.

grimace *f noun* **faire des grimaces/la g.** to make faces/a face.

grimacer *verb* to make faces *or* a face.

grimpant , -ante *adjective* climbing.

grimper *verb*
  1 g. à quelque chose to climb up something.
  2 (*escalier etc*) to climb.

grincement *m noun* creaking; grinding.

grincer *verb* to creak; **g. des dents** to grind one's teeth.

grincheux , -euse *adjective* grumpy.

grippe *f noun* flu.

grippé , -ée *adjective* **être g.** to have (the) flu.

gris , grise
  1 *adjective* grey.
  2 *m noun* grey.

grisaille *f noun* greyness.

grisâtre *adjective* greyish.

grognement *m noun* growl; grunt.

grogner *verb* to growl (**contre** at); (*cochon*) to grunt.

grognon , -onne *adjective* grumpy.

grondement *m noun* growl; rumble.

gronder *verb*
 1 (*chien*) to growl; (*tonnerre*) to rumble.
 2 (*enfant*) to scold, tell off.

groom *m noun* page (boy).

gros , grosse
 1 *adjective* big; (*gras*) fat; (*épais*) thick; (*effort, progrès*) great; (*somme*) large; (*averse, rhume*) heavy; **g. mot** swear word.
 2 *adverb* **en g.** roughly; (*écrire*) in big letters; (*vendre*) wholesale.

groseille *f noun* (white *or* red) currant.

grossesse *f noun* pregnancy.

grosseur *f noun* size; (*tumeur*) lump.

grossier , -ière *adjective* rough; (*personne*) rude (**envers** to).

grossièrement *adverb* roughly; (*répondre*) rudely.

grossièreté *f noun* roughness; (*insolence*) rudeness; (*mot*) rude word.

grossir *verb* to put on weight.

grotte *f noun* cave, grotto.

grouiller *verb* to be swarming (**de** with).

groupe *m noun* group.

grouper *verb* to group (together).

grouper (se) *reflexive verb* to group (together).

grue *f noun* crane.

grumeau , -x *m noun* lump.

gruyère *m noun* gruyère (cheese).

guenilles *fpl noun* rags (and tatters).

guêpe *f noun* wasp.

guère *adverb* **(ne) ... g.** hardly; **il ne sort g.** he hardly goes out.

guéri , -ie *adjective* cured, better.

guérir *verb*
 1 (*personne, maladie*) to cure (**de** of).
 2 (*malade*) to recover (**de** from).

guérison *f noun* recovery.

guerre *f noun* war; **en g.** at war (**avec** with).

guerrier , -ière *m or f noun* warrior.

guet *m noun* **faire le g.** to be on the lookout.

guetter *verb* to be on the lookout for.

gueule *f noun* mouth.

guichet *m noun* ticket office; (*de banque etc*) window.

guichetier , -ière *m or f noun* (*de banque etc*) counter clerk; (*à la gare*) ticket office clerk.

guide *m noun* (*personne, livre*) guide.

guider *verb* to guide; **se g. sur un manuel**/*etc* to use a handbook/ *etc* as a guide.

guidon *m noun* handlebar(s).

guignol *m noun* (*spectacle*) = Punch and Judy show.

guillemets *mpl noun* inverted commas; **entre g.** in inverted commas.

guirlande *f noun* garland.

guitare *f noun* guitar.

guitariste *m or f noun* guitarist.

gymnase *m noun* gymnasium.

gymnastique *f noun* gymnastics.

gynécologue *m or f noun* gynaecologist.

H

habile *adjective* skilful (**à quelque chose** at something, **à faire** at doing).

habileté *f noun* skill.

habillé , -ée *adjective* dressed (**de** in, **en** as a).

habiller *verb* to dress (**de** in).

habiller (s') *reflexive verb* to dress, get dressed; (*avec élégance*) to dress up.

habit *m noun* **h. de soirée** evening dress, tails; **habits** clothes.

habitable *adjective* (*maison*) fit to live in.

habitant , -ante *m or f noun* (*de pays etc*) inhabitant; (*de maison*) occupant.

habitation *f noun* house.

habité , -ée *adjective* (*région*) inhabited; (*maison*) occupied.

habiter *verb*
1 (*vivre*) to live (**à, en, dans** in).
2 (*maison etc*) to live in.

habitude *f noun* habit; **avoir l'h. de quelque chose/faire** to be used to something/doing; **d'h.** usually; **comme d'h.** as usual.

habituel , -elle *adjective* usual.

habituellement *adverb* usually.

habituer *verb* **h. quelqu'un à** to accustom somebody to.

habituer (s') *reflexive verb* to get accustomed (**à** to).

hache *f noun* axe.

hacher *verb* to chop (up); (*avec un appareil*) to mince.

hachis *m noun* mince(meat).

haie *f noun* (*clôture*) hedge; **course de haies** (*coureurs*) hurdle race.

haine *f noun* hatred.

haïr * *verb* to hate.

haleine *f noun* breath; **hors d'h.** out of breath.

haleter *verb* to pant.

hall *m noun* (*de gare*) main hall; (*de maison*) hall(way).

halte
1 *f noun* (*arrêt*) stop.
2 *interjection* stop!

haltères *mpl noun* weights.

hamac *m noun* hammock.

hamburger *m noun* hamburger.

hameçon *m noun* (fish) hook.

hamster *m noun* hamster.

hanche *f noun* hip.

handball *m noun* handball.

handicapé , -ée *adjective & m or f noun* handicapped (person).

hangar *m noun* shed; (*pour avions*) hangar.

hanté , -ée *adjective* haunted.

harassé , -ée *adjective* (*fatigué*) exhausted.

hardi , -ie *adjective* bold.

hareng *m noun* herring.

hargneux , -euse *adjective* bad-tempered.

haricot *m noun* (*blanc*) (haricot) bean; **h. vert** green bean.

harmonica *m noun* harmonica.

harmonie *f noun* harmony.

harmonieux , -euse *adjective* harmonious.

harnais *m noun* harness.

harpe *f noun* harp.

hasard *m noun* **le h.** chance; **un h.** a coincidence; **par h.** by chance; **au h.** at random; **à tout h.** just in case.

hasardeux , -euse *adjective* risky.

hâte *f noun* haste; **à la h.** in a hurry; **avoir h. de faire** to be eager to do.

hâter (se) *reflexive verb* to hurry (**de faire** to do).

hausse *f noun* rise (**de** in); **en h.** rising.

haut , haute
1 *adjective* high; **à haute voix** aloud; **h. de 5 mètres** 5 metres high *or* tall; **une femme de haute taille** a tall woman.
2 *adverb* (*voler etc*) high (up); (*parler*) loud; **tout h.** (*lire etc*) aloud; **h. placé** (*personne*) in a high position.
3 *m noun* top; **en h. de** at the top of; **en h.** (*loger*) upstairs; (*regarder*) up; (*mettre*) on (the) top; **avoir 5 mètres de h.** to be 5 metres high *or* tall.

hauteur *f noun* height.

haut-parleur *m noun* (*plural* **haut-parleurs**) loudspeaker.

Havre (le) *m or f noun* Le Havre.

hayon *m noun* (*porte*) hatchback.

hé! *interjection* (*appel*) hey!

hebdo *m noun Familiar* weekly.

hebdomadaire *adjective & m noun* weekly.

hébergement *m noun* (*d'amis*) putting up.

héberger *verb* to put up.

hectare *m noun* hectare (= *2.47 acres*).

hein! *interjection Familiar* eh!

hélas! *interjection* unfortunately.

hélice *f noun* propeller.

hélicoptère *m noun* helicopter.

hémorragie *f noun* h(a)emor-rhage; **h. cérébrale** stroke.

hennir *verb* to neigh.

hépatite *f noun* hepatitis.

herbe *f noun* grass; (*pour soigner etc*) herb; **mauvaise h.** weed; **fines herbes** herbs.

hérisser (se) *reflexive verb* (*poils*) to bristle (up).

hérisson *m noun* hedgehog.

héritage *m noun* (*biens*) inher-itance.

hériter *verb* to inherit (**quelque chose de quelqu'un** something from somebody); **h. de quelque chose** to inherit something.

héritier *m noun* heir.

héritière *f noun* heiress.

hermétique *adjective* airtight.

héroïne *f noun* (*femme*) heroine; (*drogue*) heroin.

héroïque *adjective* heroic.

héros *m noun* hero.

hésitant , -ante *adjective* hes-itant; (*pas, voix*) unsteady.

hésitation *f noun* hesitation; **avec h.** hesitantly.

hésiter *verb* to hesitate (**sur** over, about; **à faire** to do).

hêtre *m noun* (*arbre, bois*) beech.

heu! *interjection* er!

heure *f noun* hour; (*moment*) time; **quelle h. est-il?** what time is it?; **à quelle h. … ?** what time … ?; **il est six heures** it's six (o'clock); **six heures moins cinq** five to six; **six heures cinq** five past six; **à l'h.** (*arriver*) on time; **dix kilo-mètres à l'h.** ten kilometres an hour; **de bonne h.** early; **tout à l'h.** (*futur*) later; (*passé*) a mo-ment ago; **à tout à l'h.!** see you later!; **heures supplémentaires** overtime; **l'h. de pointe** (*circula-tion etc*) rush hour.

heureusement *adverb* (*par chance*) fortunately (**pour** for).

heureux , -euse
  1 *adjective* happy; (*chanceux*)
  lucky; **h. de quelque chose/de
  voir quelqu'un** happy *or* glad
  about something/to see somebody.
  2 *adverb* (*vivre etc*) happily.

heurter *verb* to hit; **se h. à** to
  bump into, hit.

hibou , -x *m noun* owl.

hier *adverb & m noun* yesterday; **h.
  soir** last *or* yesterday night.

hi-fi *invariable adjective & invariable f noun Familiar* hi-fi.

hippique *adjective* **concours h.**
  horse show.

hippopotame *m noun* hippopotamus.

hirondelle *f noun* swallow.

histoire *f noun* history; (*récit,
  mensonge*) story; **des histoires**
  (*ennuis*) trouble; **sans histoires**
  (*voyage etc*) uneventful.

historique *adjective* historical;
  (*lieu, événement*) historic.

hiver *m noun* winter.

HLM *f abbreviation* (*habitation à
  loyer modéré*) = council flats.

hocher *verb* **h. la tête** (*pour dire
  oui*) to nod one's head; (*pour dire
  non*) to shake one's head.

hochet *m noun* (*jouet*) rattle.

hockey *m noun* hockey; **h. sur
  glace** ice hockey.

hold-up *invariable m noun*
  (*attaque*) holdup.

hollandais , -aise
  1 *adjective* Dutch.
  2 *m or f noun* Dutchman, Dutch-
  woman; **les H.** the Dutch.
  3 *m noun* (*langue*) Dutch.

Hollande (la) *f noun* Holland.

homard *m noun* lobster.

homme *m noun* man; **l'h.** (*espèce*)

man(kind); **des vêtements d'h.**
  men's clothes; **h. d'affaires** businessman; **jeune h.** young man.

homosexuel , -elle *adjective &
  m or f noun* homosexual.

Hong Kong *m or f noun* Hong
  Kong.

Hongrie (la) *f noun* Hungary.

hongrois , -oise *adjective & m or
  f noun* Hungarian.

honnête *adjective* honest;
  (*satisfaisant*) decent.

honnêtement *adverb* honestly;
  decently.

honnêteté *f noun* honesty.

honneur *m noun* honour; **en l'h.
  de** in honour of; **faire h. à** (*sa
  famille etc*) to be a credit to;
  (*repas*) to do justice to.

honorable *adjective* honourable;
  (*convenable*) respectable.

honte *f noun* shame; **avoir h.** to be
  or feel ashamed (**de quelque
  chose/de faire** of something/to
  do, of doing).

honteux , -euse *adjective*
  ashamed; (*scandaleux*) shameful.

hôpital , -aux *m noun* hospital; **à
  l'h.** in hospital.

hoquet *m noun* **avoir le h.** to have
  (the) hiccups.

horaire *m noun* timetable.

horizon *m noun* horizon; **à l'h.** on
  the horizon.

horizontal , -e, -aux *adjective*
  horizontal.

horloge *f noun* clock.

horreur *f noun* horror; **faire h. à**
  to disgust; **avoir h. de** to hate.

horrible *adjective* horrible.

horriblement *adverb* horribly.

horrifiant , -ante *adjective*
  horrifying.

horrifié , -ée *adjective* horrified.

hors *preposition* h. de out of.

hors-bord *invariable m noun* speedboat.

hors-d'œuvre *invariable m noun* (*à table*) hors d'oeuvre, starter.

hors-taxe *invariable adjective* duty-free.

hospitaliser *verb* to hospitalize.

hospitalité *f noun* hospitality.

hostile *adjective* hostile (à to, towards).

hostilité *f noun* hostility (**envers** to, towards).

hôte
1 *m noun* (*qui reçoit*) host.
2 *m or f noun* (*invité*) guest.

hôtel *m noun* hotel; h. de ville town hall.

hôtesse *f noun* hostess; h. (de l'air) (air) hostess.

hotte *f noun* basket (*carried on back*).

hourra! *interjection* hurray!

housse *f noun* (protective) cover.

hovercraft *m noun* hovercraft.

hublot *m noun* porthole.

huile *f noun* oil.

huit *adjective & m noun* eight; h. jours a week.

huitième *adjective & m or f noun* eighth.

huître *f noun* oyster.

humain , -aine *adjective* human.

humanité *f noun* humanity.

humble *adjective* humble.

humblement *adverb* humbly.

humecter *verb* to moisten.

humeur *f noun* mood; (*caractère*) temperament; **bonne h.** (*gaieté*) good humour; de bonne/mauvaise h. in a good/bad mood.

humide *adjective* damp.

humidité *f noun* humidity; (*plutôt froide*) damp(ness).

humiliation *f noun* humiliation.

humilier *verb* to humiliate.

humoristique *adjective* humorous.

humour *m noun* humour; **avoir de l'h.** to have a sense of humour.

hurlement *m noun* howl; scream.

hurler *verb*
1 (*loup, vent*) to howl; (*personne*) to scream.
2 (*slogan, injures etc*) to scream.

hygiène *f noun* hygiene.

hygiénique *adjective* hygienic; **papier h.** toilet paper.

hymne *m noun* h. national national anthem.

hypermarché *m noun* hypermarket.

hypocrisie *f noun* hypocrisy.

hypocrite
1 *adjective* hypocritical.
2 *m or f noun* hypocrite.

hypothèse *f noun* (*supposition*) assumption.

I

iceberg *m noun* iceberg.

ici *adverb* here; **par i.** (*passer*) this way; (*habiter*) around here; **jusqu'i.** (*temps*) up to now; (*lieu*) as far as this *or* here; **d'i. peu** before long.

idéal , -e, -aux *or* **-als** *adjective &* *m noun* ideal.

idée *f noun* idea; **changer d'i.** to change one's mind.

identifier *verb* to identify; **s'i. à** *or* **avec** to identify (oneself) with.

identique *adjective* identical (**à** to, with).

identité *f noun* identity; **carte d'i.** identity card.

idiot , -ote
1 *adjective* silly.
2 *m or f noun* idiot.

idiotie *f noun* **une i.** a silly thing.

idole *f noun* idol.

igloo *m noun* igloo.

ignifugé , -ée *adjective* fire-proof(ed).

ignorance *f noun* ignorance.

ignorant , -ante *adjective* ignorant (**de** of).

ignorer *verb* not to know; **i. quel-qu'un** to ignore somebody.

il *pronoun* (*personne*) he; (*chose, animal*) it; **il pleut** it's raining; **il y a** there is; *plural* there are; **il y a six ans** six years ago; **il y a une heure qu'il travaille** he's been working for an hour; **qu'est-ce qu'il y a?** what's the matter?

île *f noun* island.

illégal , -e, -aux *adjective* illegal.

illettré , -ée *adjective* illiterate.

illisible *adjective* illegible.

illuminer *verb* to light up.

illuminer (s') *reflexive verb* to light up.

illusion *f noun* illusion; **se faire des illusions** to delude oneself (**sur** about).

illustration *f noun* illustration.

illustré *m noun* comic.

illustrer *verb* to illustrate (**de** with).

ils *pronoun* they.

image *f noun* picture; (*dans une glace*) reflection.

imaginaire *adjective* imaginary.

imagination *f noun* imagination.

imaginer *verb* to imagine (**que** that).

imaginer (s') *reflexive verb* to imagine (**que** that).

imbattable *adjective* unbeat-able.

imbécile *m or f noun* idiot.

imitateur , -trice *m or f noun* (*artiste*) impersonator.

imitation *f noun* imitation.

imiter *verb* to imitate; **i. quel-qu'un** (*pour rire*) to mimic some-body; (*faire comme*) to do the same as somebody.

immangeable *adjective* inedible.

immatriculation *f noun* registration.

immédiat , -ate *adjective* immediate.

immédiatement *adverb* immediately.

immense *adjective* immense.

immeuble *m noun* building; (*d'habitation*) block of flats; (*de* *bureaux*) office building *or* block.

immigration *f noun* immigration.

immigré , -ée *adjective & m or f noun* immigrant.

immobile *adjective* still.

immobiliser *verb* to bring to a stop.

immobiliser (s') *reflexive verb* to come to a stop.

immortel , -elle *adjective* immortal.

impair , -e *adjective* odd.

impardonnable *adjective* unforgivable.

imparfait *m noun* (*temps*) *Grammaire* imperfect.

impartial , -e, -aux *adjective* fair, unbiased.

impasse *f noun* dead end.

impatience *f noun* impatience.

impatient , -ente *adjective* impatient (*de faire* to do).

impatienter (s') *reflexive verb* to get impatient.

impeccable *adjective* (*propre*) immaculate.

impératif *m noun Grammaire* imperative.

imperméable
1 *adjective* (*tissu*) waterproof.
2 *m noun* raincoat.

impitoyable *adjective* ruthless.

impoli , -ie *adjective* rude.

impolitesse *f noun* rudeness.

importance *f noun* importance; **ça n'a pas d'i.** it doesn't matter.

important , -ante
1 *adjective* important; (*quantité etc*) big.
2 *m noun* **l'i., c'est de** the important thing is to.

importation *f noun* import; **d'i.**

(*article*) imported.

importer
1 *impersonal verb* to matter, be important; **peu m'importe** it doesn't matter to me; **n'importe qui/quoi/où/quand/comment** anyone/anything/anywhere/any time/anyhow.
2 *verb* (*marchandises*) to import (*de* from).

imposer *verb* to impose (*à* on).

impossibilité *f noun* impossibility.

impossible *adjective* impossible (*à faire* to do); **il (nous) est i. de le faire** it is impossible (for us) to do it.

impôt *m noun* tax; **i. sur le revenu** income tax; (**service des**) **impôts** tax authorities.

impression *f noun* impression.

impressionnant , -ante *adjective* impressive.

impressionner *verb* (*émouvoir*) to make a strong impression on.

imprévisible *adjective* unforeseeable.

imprévu , -ue *adjective* unexpected.

imprimante *f noun* printer.

imprimé *m noun* printed form.

imprimer *verb* (*livre etc*) to print.

imprimerie *f noun* printing works.

improviser *verb* to improvise.

improviste (à l') *adverb* unexpectedly.

imprudence *f noun* carelessness, foolishness; **commettre une i.** to do something foolish.

imprudent , -ente *adjective* careless, foolish.

impuissant , -ante *adjective* helpless.

impulsif , -ive *adjective* impulsive.

inabordable *adjective* (*prix*) prohibitive.

inacceptable *adjective* unacceptable.

inachevé , -ée *adjective* unfinished.

inadmissible *adjective* unacceptable, inadmissible.

inanimé , -ée *adjective* (*mort*) lifeless; (*évanoui*) unconscious.

inaperçu , -ue *adjective* passer i. to go unnoticed.

inattendu , -ue *adjective* unexpected.

inattention *f noun* lack of attention; **un moment d'i.** a moment of distraction.

inauguration *f noun* inauguration.

inaugurer *verb* to inaugurate.

incapable *adjective* i. de faire unable to do.

incassable *adjective* unbreakable.

incendie *m noun* fire.

incendier *verb* to set fire to.

incertain , -aine *adjective* uncertain; (*temps*) unsettled.

incertitude *f noun* uncertainty.

incessant , -ante *adjective* continual.

inchangé , -ée *adjective* unchanged.

incident *m noun* incident.

incisive *f noun* incisor (tooth).

incliner *verb* (*courber*) to bend; (*pencher*) to tilt.

incliner (s') *reflexive verb* (*se courber*) to bow (down).

inclus , -use *adjective* inclusive; **jusqu'à lundi i.** up to and inclu-ding Monday.

incolore *adjective* colourless; (*vernis*) clear.

incommoder *verb* to bother.

incompatible *adjective* incompatible.

incompétent , -ente *adjective* incompetent.

incomplet , -ète *adjective* incomplete.

incompréhensible *adjective* incomprehensible.

inconnu , -ue
  1 *adjective* unknown (**à** to).
  2 *m or f noun* (*étranger*) stranger.

inconscient , -ente *adjective* unconscious (**de** of); (*imprudent*) thoughtless.

inconsolable *adjective* heartbroken, cut up.

incontestable *adjective* undeniable.

inconvénient *m noun* drawback.

incorrect , -e *adjective* (*grossier*) impolite.

incroyable *adjective* incredible.

inculpé , -ée *m or f noun* l'i. the accused.

inculper *verb* to charge (**de** with).

incurable *adjective* incurable.

Inde (l') *f noun* India.

indécis , -ise *adjective* (*hésitant*) undecided.

indéfini , -ie *adjective* indefinite.

indéfiniment *adverb* indefinitely.

indemne *adjective* unhurt.

indemnité *f noun* compensation; (*allocation*) allowance.

indépendance *f noun* independence.

indépendant , -ante *adjective* independent (**de** of).

indescriptible *adjective* indescribable.

index *m noun* (*doigt*) index finger, forefinger.

indicatif *m noun* (*à la radio*) signature tune; (*téléphonique*) dialling code; *Grammaire* indicative.

indication *f noun* (piece of) information; **indications** (*pour aller quelque part*) directions.

indice *m noun* (*dans une enquête*) clue.

indien , -ienne *adjective & m or f noun* Indian.

indifférence *f noun* indifference (à to).

indifférent , -ente *adjective* indifferent (à to).

indigestion *f noun* (attack of) indigestion.

indignation *f noun* indignation.

indigner (s') *reflexive verb* to be *or* become indignant (de at).

indiquer *verb* (*montrer*) to show; (*dire*) to tell; **i. du doigt** to point to *or* at.

indirect , -e *adjective* indirect.

indirectement *adverb* indirectly.

indiscipliné , -ée *adjective* unruly.

indiscret , -ète *adjective* inquisitive.

indiscrétion *f noun* indiscretion.

indispensable *adjective* essential.

indistinct , -incte *adjective* unclear.

individu *m noun* individual.

individuel , -elle *adjective* individual.

indolore *adjective* painless.

Indonésie (l') *f noun* Indonesia.

indonésien , -ienne *adjective & m or f noun* Indonesian.

indulgent , -ente *adjective* indulgent (**envers** to).

industrialisé , -ée *adjective* industrialized.

industrie *f noun* industry.

industriel , -elle *adjective* industrial.

inefficace *adjective* (*mesure etc*) ineffective; (*personne*) inefficient.

inépuisable *adjective* inexhaustible

inestimable *adjective* priceless.

inévitable *adjective* inevitable, unavoidable.

inexact , -e *adjective* inaccurate.

inexcusable *adjective* inexcusable.

inexplicable *adjective* inexplicable.

inexpliqué , -ée *adjective* unexplained.

infaillible *adjective* infallible.

infarctus *m noun* **un i.** a coronary.

infatigable *adjective* tireless.

infect , -e *adjective* (*odeur*) foul; (*café etc*) vile.

infecter (s') *reflexive verb* to get infected.

infection *f noun* infection; (*odeur*) stench.

inférieur , -e *adjective* lower; (*qualité etc*) inferior (à to); **l'étage i.** the floor below.

infériorité *f noun* inferiority.

infernal , -e, -aux *adjective* infernal.

infesté , -ée *adjective* **i. de requins**/*etc* shark/*etc*-infested.

infiltrer (s') *reflexive verb* (*liquide*) to seep (through) (**dans**

into).

infini , -ie
1 *adjective* infinite.
2 *m noun* infinity.

infiniment *adverb* (*regretter, remercier*) very much.

infinitif *m noun Grammaire* infinitive.

infirme *adjective & m or f noun* disabled (person).

infirmerie *f noun* sick room, sickbay.

infirmier *m noun* male nurse.

infirmière *f noun* nurse.

inflammable *adjective* (in)flammable.

inflammation *f noun* inflammation.

inflation *f noun* inflation.

inflexible *adjective* inflexible.

influence *f noun* influence.

influencer *verb* to influence.

informaticien, -ienne *m or f noun* computer scientist.

information *f noun* information; (*nouvelle*) piece of news; **les informations** the news.

informatique *f noun* (*science*) computer science; (*technique*) data processing.

informatisé , -ée *adjective* computerized.

informer *verb* to inform (**de** of, about; **que** that).

informer (s') *reflexive verb* to inquire (**de** about; **si** if, whether).

infraction *f noun* offence.

infusion *f noun* herbal *or* herb tea.

ingénieur *m noun* engineer; **femme i.** woman engineer.

ingénieux , -euse *adjective* ingenious.

ingrat , -ate *adjective* ungrateful

(**envers** to).

ingratitude *f noun* ingratitude.

ingrédient *m noun* ingredient.

inhabité , -ée *adjective* uninhabited.

inhabituel , -elle *adjective* unusual.

inhumain , -aine *adjective* inhuman.

inimaginable *adjective* unimaginable.

ininflammable *adjective* non-flammable.

ininterrompu , -ue *adjective* continuous.

initiale *f noun* (*lettre*) initial.

injecter *verb* to inject.

injection *f noun* injection.

injure *f noun* insult.

injurier *verb* to insult.

injuste *adjective* (*contraire à la justice*) unjust; (*non équitable*) unfair.

injustice *f noun* injustice.

innocence *f noun* innocence.

innocent , -ente
1 *adjective* innocent (**de** of).
2 *m or f noun* innocent person.

innombrable *adjective* countless.

inoccupé , -ée *adjective* unoccupied.

inoffensif , -ive *adjective* harmless.

inondation *f noun* flood.

inonder *verb* to flood.

inoubliable *adjective* unforgettable.

inox *m noun* stainless steel.

inoxydable *adjective* **acier i.** stainless steel.

inquiet , -iète *adjective* worried (**de** about).

inquiétant , -ante *adjective* worrying.

inquiéter *verb* to worry; **s'i. (de)** to worry (about).

inquiétude *f noun* worry.

inscription *f noun* enrolment, registration; (*sur écriteau etc*) inscription; **frais d'i.** (*à l'université*) tuition fees.

inscrire * *verb* to write *or* put down; **i. quelqu'un** to enrol somebody.

inscrire (s') *reflexive verb* to put one's name down; **s'i. à** (*club*) to join; (*examen*) to enrol for, register for.

insecte *m noun* insect.

insecticide *m noun* insecticide.

insensible *adjective* insensitive (**à** to).

inséparable *adjective* inseparable (**de** from).

insigne *m noun* badge.

insignifiant , -ante *adjective* insignificant.

insistance *f noun* insistence.

insister *verb* to insist (**pour faire** on doing); **i. sur** (*détail etc*) to stress.

insolation *f noun* sunstroke.

insolence *f noun* insolence.

insolent , -ente *adjective* insolent.

insomnie *f noun* insomnia.

insonoriser *verb* to soundproof.

insouciant , -ante *adjective* carefree.

inspecter *verb* to inspect.

inspecteur , -trice *m or f noun* inspector.

inspection *f noun* inspection.

inspiration *f noun* inspiration.

inspirer *verb* to inspire (**quelque chose à quelqu'un** somebody with something).

instable *adjective* (*meuble*) shaky.

installation *f noun* putting in; moving in.

installer *verb* (*appareil etc*) to install, put in; (*étagère*) to put up.

installer (s') *reflexive verb* (*s'asseoir, s'établir*) to settle (down); **s'i. dans** (*maison*) to move into.

instant *m noun* moment; **à l'i.** a moment ago; **pour l'i.** for the moment.

instinct *m noun* instinct.

instinctif , -ive *adjective* instinctive.

instituteur , -trice *m or f noun* primary school teacher.

institution *f noun* (*organisation, structure*) institution.

instructif , -ive *adjective* instructive.

instruction *f noun* education; **instructions** (*ordres*) instructions.

instruire * *verb* to teach, educate; **s'i.** to educate oneself.

instrument *m noun* instrument; (*outil*) implement.

insuffisant , -ante *adjective* inadequate.

insulte *f noun* insult (**à** to).

insulter *verb* to insult.

insupportable *adjective* unbearable.

intact , -e *adjective* intact.

intégralement *adverb* in full.

intellectuel , -elle *adjective* & *m or f noun* intellectual.

intelligemment *adverb* intelligently.

intelligence *f noun* intelligence.

intelligent , -ente *adjective* intelligent.

intempéries *fpl noun* les i. bad weather.

intense *adjective* intense; (*circulation*) heavy.

intensifier *verb* to intensify.

intensifier (s') *reflexive verb* to intensify.

intensité *f noun* intensity.

intention *f noun* intention; avoir l'i. de faire to intend to do.

interchangeable *adjective* interchangeable.

interdiction *f noun* ban (de on); 'i. de fumer' 'no smoking'.

interdire * *verb* to forbid, not to allow (quelque chose à quelqu'un somebody something); i. à quelqu'un de faire not to allow somebody to do.

interdit , -ite *adjective* forbidden; 'stationnement i.' 'no parking'.

intéressant , -ante *adjective* interesting; (*prix etc*) attractive.

intéresser *verb* to interest; s'i. à to take an interest in.

intérêt *m noun* interest; intérêts (*argent*) interest; tu as i. à faire you'd do well to do.

intérieur , -e
1 *adjective* inner; (*poche*) inside; (*politique*) domestic.
2 *m noun* inside (de of); à l'i. (de) inside.

interlocuteur , -trice *m or f noun* mon i. the person I am/was *etc* speaking to.

intermédiaire *m or f noun* par l'i. de through (the medium of).

interminable *adjective* endless.

international , -e, -aux *adjective* international.

interne *m or f noun* (*élève*) boarder.

interpeller *verb* to shout at.

interphone *m noun* intercom.

interposer (s') *reflexive verb* to intervene (dans in).

interprète *m or f noun* interpreter; (*chanteur*) singer.

interpréter *verb* (*expliquer*) to interpret; (*chanter*) to sing.

interrogatif , -ive *adjective* Grammaire interrogative.

interrogation *f noun* question; (à l'école) test.

interrogatoire *m noun* interrogation.

interroger *verb* to question.

interrompre * *verb* to interrupt.

interrupteur *m noun* switch.

interruption *f noun* interruption.

intersection *f noun* intersection.

intervalle *m noun* (*écart*) gap; (*temps*) interval.

intervenir * *verb* to intervene; (*survenir*) to occur.

intervention *f noun* intervention; i. (chirurgicale) operation.

interview *f noun* interview.

interviewer *verb* to interview.

intestin *m noun* bowel.

intime *adjective* intimate; (*journal, mariage*) private.

intimider *verb* to intimidate.

intituler (s') *reflexive verb* to be entitled.

intolérable *adjective* intolerable (que (+ *subjunctive*) that).

intraduisible *adjective* difficult to translate.

intransitif , -ive *adjective* Grammaire intransitive.

intrépide *adjective* fearless.

introduction *f noun* introduction.

introduire * *verb* (*insérer*) to put in (**dans** to); (*faire entrer*) to show in; **s'i. dans** to get into.

introuvable *adjective* nowhere to be found.

inusable *adjective* hardwearing, durable.

inutile *adjective* useless.

inutilement *adverb* needlessly.

inutilisable *adjective* unusable.

invariable *adjective* invariable.

invasion *f noun* invasion.

inventer *verb* to invent; (*imaginer*) to make up.

inventeur , -trice *m or f noun* inventor.

invention *f noun* invention.

inverse *adjective* (*sens*) opposite; (*ordre*) reverse.

inverser *verb* (*ordre*) to reverse.

investir *verb* to invest (**dans** in).

investissement *m noun* investment.

invisible *adjective* invisible.

invitation *f noun* invitation.

invité , -ée *m or f noun* guest.

inviter *verb* to invite; **s'i.** (**chez quelqu'un**) to gatecrash.

involontaire *adjective* (*geste etc*) unintentional.

ira , irai(t) *see* aller [1].

Irak (l') *m noun* Iraq.

irakien , -ienne *adjective & m or f noun* Iraqi.

Iran (l') *m noun* Iran.

iranien , -ienne *adjective & m or f noun* Iranian.

iraquien , -ienne *adjective & m or f noun* Iraqi.

irlandais , -aise
1 *adjective* Irish.

2 *m or f noun* Irishman, Irish-woman; **les I.** the Irish.
3 *m noun* (*langue*) Irish.

Irlande (l') *f noun* Ireland; **l'I. du Nord** Northern Ireland.

ironie *f noun* irony.

ironique *adjective* ironic(al).

iront *see* aller [1].

irrégulier , -ière *adjective* irregular.

irremplaçable *adjective* irreplaceable.

irréparable *adjective* (*véhicule etc*) beyond repair.

irrésistible *adjective* irresistible.

irriguer *verb* to irrigate.

irritable *adjective* irritable.

irritation *f noun* irritation.

irriter *verb* to irritate.

islamique *adjective* Islamic.

isolant *m noun* insulation (material).

isolé , -ée *adjective* isolated (**de** from).

isoler *verb* to isolate (**de** from); (*du froid etc*) to insulate.

Israël *m noun* Israel.

israélien , -ienne *adjective & m or f noun* Israeli.

issue *f noun* way out; **rue** *etc* **sans i.** dead end.

Italie (l') *f noun* Italy.

italien , -ienne
1 *adjective & m or f noun* Italian.
2 *m noun* (*langue*) Italian.

italique *m noun* italics.

itinéraire *m noun* route.

ivoire *m noun* ivory.

ivre *adjective* drunk.

ivresse *f noun* drunkenness.

ivrogne *m or f noun* drunk(ard).

J

jaillir *verb* (*liquide*) to spurt (out); (*lumière*) to beam out, shine (forth).

jalousie *f noun* jealousy.

jaloux , -ouse *adjective* jealous (de of).

jamaïcain , -aine *adjective & m or f noun* Jamaican.

Jamaïque (la) *f noun* Jamaica.

jamais *adverb* never; **elle ne sort j.** she never goes out; **j. de la vie!** (absolutely) never!; **si j.** if ever.

jambe *f noun* leg.

jambon *m noun* ham.

janvier *m noun* January.

Japon (le) *m noun* Japan.

japonais , -aise
1 *adjective* Japanese.
2 *m or f noun* Japanese man *or* woman, Japanese *invariable*; **les J.** the Japanese.
3 *m noun* (*langue*) Japanese.

jardin *m noun* garden; **j. public** park.

jardinage *m noun* gardening; **faire du j.** to do some gardening.

jardinier *m noun* gardener.

jardinière *f noun* (*caisse à fleurs*) window box.

jaune
1 *adjective* yellow.
2 *m noun* yellow; **j. d'œuf** (egg) yolk.

jaunir *verb* to turn yellow.

jaunisse *f noun* jaundice.

Javel (eau de) *f noun* bleach.

jazz *m noun* jazz.

je *pronoun* (**j'** before vowel or mute *h*) I.

jean *m noun* (pair of) jeans.

jeep ® *f noun* jeep ®.

jerrycan *m noun* petrol can; (*pour l'eau*) water can.

jet *m noun* (*de vapeur*) burst; (*de tuyau d'arrosage*) nozzle; **j. d'eau** (*fontaine*) fountain.

jetable *adjective* disposable.

jetée *f noun* pier.

jeter *verb* to throw (**à** to, **dans** into); (*à la poubelle*) to throw away; **se j. sur** to pounce on; **le fleuve se jette dans** the river flows into.

jeton *m noun* (*pièce*) token; (*de jeu*) chip.

jeu , -x *m noun* game; (*amusement*) play; (*d'argent*) gambling; (*série complète*) set; (*de cartes*) deck; **j. de mots** play on words; **jeux d'arcade** arcade games; **jeux de société** parlour *or* indoor games; **j. télévisé** television quiz; **j. électronique** computer game; **j. vidéo** video games.

jeudi *m noun* Thursday.

jeun (à) *adverb* **être à j.** to have eaten no food.

jeune
1 *adjective* young.
2 *m or f noun* young person; **les jeunes** young people.

jeunesse *f noun* youth; **la j.** (*jeunes*) the young.

jockey *m noun* jockey.

jogging *m noun* jogging; **faire du j.** to jog.

joie *f noun* joy.

joindre * *verb* to join; (*envoyer avec*) to enclose (**à** with); **j. quelqu'un** to get in touch with somebody; **se j. à** (*un groupe etc*) to join.

joint , -e
1 *past participle of* **joindre**.
2 *adjective* **sauter à pieds joints**
to jump from a standing position;
les mains jointes with hands together; **pièces jointes** (*dans une
lettre*) enclosures; **vous trouve-
rez ci-j. copie de votre lettre**
please find enclosed copy of your
letter.

joker *m noun Cartes* joker.

joli , -ie *adjective* nice; (*femme,
enfant*) pretty.

jongler *verb* to juggle (**avec** with).

jongleur , -euse *m or f noun*
juggler.

jonquille *f noun* daffodil.

joue *f noun* cheek.

jouer *verb*
1 (*enfant*) to play; (*acteur*) to act;
(*au tiercé etc*) to gamble, bet; **j. au
tennis/aux cartes/etc** to play
tennis/cards/*etc*; **j. du piano/etc**
to play the piano/*etc*.
2 (*musique, jeu, rôle*) to play;
(*risquer*) to bet (**sur** on); (*pièce*) to
perform; (*film*) to show.

jouet *m noun* toy.

joueur , -euse *m or f noun* player;
(*au tiercé etc*) gambler; **bon j.**
good loser.

jour *m noun* day; (*lumière*) (day)-
light; **il fait j.** it's light; **en plein j.**
in broad daylight; **de nos jours**
nowadays; **du j. au lendemain**
overnight; **tous les jours** every
day; **le j. de l'An** New Year's
Day.

journal , -aux *m noun* (news)pa-
per; (*intime*) diary; **j. (parlé)** news
bulletin.

journaliste *m or f noun* journalist.

journée *f noun* day; **toute la j.** all

day (long).

joyeux , -euse *adjective* merry,
happy; **j. Noël!** merry *or* happy
Christmas!; **j. anniversaire!**
happy birthday!

judo *m noun* judo.

juge *m noun* judge.

jugement *m noun* judg(e)ment;
(*verdict*) sentence; **passer en j.** to
stand trial.

juger *verb* to judge; (*au tribunal*)
to try; (*estimer*) to consider (**que**
that).

juif , juive
1 *adjective* Jewish.
2 *m or f noun* Jew.

juillet *m noun* July.

juin *m noun* June.

jumeau , -elle *m or f noun & adjective* (*plural* jumeaux, **-elle**)
twin; **frère j.** twin brother; **sœur
jumelle** twin sister; **lits jumeaux**
twin beds.

jumelage *m noun* (*de villes*)
twinning.

jumelé, -ée *adjective* (*villes*)
twinned; (*maison*) semi-detached.

jumelles *fpl noun* (*pour regarder*)
binoculars.

jument *f noun* mare.

jungle *f noun* jungle.

jupe *f noun* skirt.

jupon *m noun* petticoat.

jurer *verb*
1 (*dire un gros mot*) to swear
(**contre** at).
2 (*promettre*) to swear (**que** that,
de faire to do).

juron *m noun* swearword.

jury *m noun* jury.

jus *m noun* juice; (*de viande*) gravy;
j. de fruit fruit juice.

jusque
1 *preposition* **jusqu'à** (*espace*) as

far as; (*temps*) until; **jusqu'à dix francs** (*limite*) up to ten francs; **jusqu'en mai** until May; **jusqu'où?** how far?; **jusqu'ici** (*temps*) up till now.
2 *conjunction* **jusqu'à ce qu'il vienne** until he comes.

juste
  1 *adjective* (*équitable*) fair; (*légitime*) just; (*exact*) right; (*étroit*) tight.
  2 *adverb* (*deviner etc*) right; (*chanter*) in tune; (*seulement*) just.

justement *adverb* exactly.

justice *f noun* justice; (*autorités*) law.

justifier *verb* to justify.

juteux , -euse *adjective* juicy.

K

kangourou *m noun* kangaroo.
karaté *m noun* karate.
Kenya (le) *m noun* Kenya.
kenyan , -e *adjective & m or f noun* Kenyan.
képi *m noun* cap, kepi.
kermesse *f noun (fête de bienfaisance)* (charity) fête; *(d'une école)* school fête *(to raise funds).*
kidnapper *verb* to kidnap.
kilo *m noun* kilo.
kilogramme *m noun* kilogram(me).

kilométrage *m noun* = mileage.
kilomètre *m noun* kilometre.
kiosque *m noun* k. (à journaux) kiosk.
kit *m noun* meuble en k. self-assembly unit.
klaxon ® *m noun* horn.
klaxonner *verb* to hoot.
k.-o. *invariable adjective* mettre k. to knock out.
Koweït (le) *m noun* Kuwait.
koweïtien , -ienne *adjective & m or f noun* Kuwaiti.

L

l', **la** *see* **le**.

là
   1 *adverb* (*lieu*) there; (*chez soi*) in; (*temps*) then; **je reste là** I'll stay here; **c'est là que** that's where; **à cinq mètres de là** five metres away; **jusque-là** (*lieu*) as far as that; (*temps*) up till then.
   2 *interjection* **oh là là!** oh dear!

là-bas *adverb* over there.

labo *m noun Familiar* lab.

laboratoire *m noun* laboratory.

labourer *verb* to plough.

labyrinthe *m noun* maze.

lac *m noun* lake.

lacet *m noun* (shoe-)lace; (*de route*) twist.

lâche
   1 *adjective* cowardly.
   2 *m or f noun* coward.

lâcher *verb*
   1 (*main*, *objet*) to let go of; (*bombe*) to drop.
   2 (*rompre*) (*corde*) to give way.

lâcheté *f noun* cowardice.

là-dedans *adverb* in there.

là-dessous *adverb* underneath.

là-dessus *adverb* on there.

là-haut *adverb* up there; (*à l'étage*) upstairs.

laid, **laide** *adjective* ugly.

laideur *f noun* ugliness.

lainage *m noun* woollen garment.

laine *f noun* wool; **en l.** woollen.

laisse *f noun* lead, leash.

laisser *verb* to leave; **l. quelqu'un partir/***etc* to let somebody go/ *etc*; **l. quelque chose à quelqu'un** to let somebody have something.

lait *m noun* milk.

laitier *adjective* **produit l.** dairy product.

laitue *f noun* lettuce.

lambeau, **-x** *m noun* shred, bit.

lame *f noun* (*de couteau etc*) blade; (*vague*) wave.

lamentable *adjective* (*mauvais*) terrible.

lampadaire *m noun* standard lamp; (*de rue*) street lamp.

lampe *f noun* lamp; (*au néon*) light; **l. de poche** torch, flashlight.

lance *f noun* spear; (*extrémité de tuyau*) nozzle; **l. d'incendie** fire hose.

lancement *m noun* (*de fusée etc*) launch(ing).

lancer *verb* to throw (à to); (*avec force*) to hurl; (*fusée, produit etc*) to launch; (*appel etc*) to issue.

lancer (se) *reflexive verb* (*se précipiter*) to rush.

landau *m noun* (*plural* **landaus**) pram.

langage *m noun* language.

langouste *f noun* (spiny) lobster.

langue *f noun* tongue; (*langage*) language; **l. maternelle** mother tongue; **langues vivantes** modern languages.

lanière *f noun* strap.

lanterne *f noun* lantern; **lanternes** (*de véhicule*) sidelights.

lapin *m noun* rabbit.

laque *f noun* lacquer.

lard *m noun* (*fumé*) bacon; (*gras*) (pig's) fat.

large
  1 *adjective* wide, broad; (*vête-ment*) loose; **l. de six mètres** six metres wide.
  2 *m noun* breadth, width; **avoir six mètres de l.** to be six metres wide; **le l.** (*mer*) the open sea; **au l. de Cherbourg** off Cherbourg.

largement *adverb* (*ouvrir*) wide; (*au moins*) easily; **avoir l. le temps** to have plenty of time.

largeur *f noun* width, breadth.

larme *f noun* tear; **en larmes** in tears.

las, lasse *adjective* tired, weary (**de** of).

laser *m noun* laser.

lasser *verb* to tire.

lasser (se) *reflexive verb* to tire (**de** of).

latin *m noun* (*langue*) Latin.

lavabo *m noun* washbasin, sink.

laver *verb* to wash; **se l.** to wash (oneself); **se l. les mains** to wash one's hands.

laverie *f noun* (*automatique*) launderette.

lavette *f noun* dish cloth.

lave-vaisselle *m noun* dish-washer.

lave-vitre *m noun* (*plural* **lave-vitres**) windscreen washer.

layette *f noun* baby clothes.

le , la, *plural* **les** (**le & la** *become* **l'** *before a vowel or mute h*)
  1 *definite article* (**à + le = au, à + les = aux; de + le = du, de + les = des**) the.
  ▪ (*généralisation*) **la beauté** beauty; **la France** France; **les hommes** men; **aimer le café** to like coffee.
  ▪ (*possession*) **il ouvrit la bouche** he opened his mouth;

avoir les cheveux blonds to have blond hair.
  ▪ (*mesure*) **dix francs le kilo** ten francs a kilo.
  ▪ (*temps*) **elle vient le lundi** she comes on Monday(s); **l'an prochain** next year; **une fois l'an** once a year.
  2 *pronoun* (*homme*) him; (*femme*) her; (*chose, animal*) it; *plural* them; **es-tu fatigué? je le suis** are you tired? I am; **je le crois** I think so.

lécher *verb* to lick; **se l. les doigts** to lick one's fingers.

lèche-vitrine *m noun Familiar* **faire du l.** to go window-shopping.

leçon *f noun* lesson.

lecteur , -trice *m or f noun* reader; **l. de cassettes/CD** cassette/CD player.

lecture *f noun* reading; **lectures** (*livres*) books.

légal , -e, -aux *adjective* legal.

légende *f noun* (*histoire*) legend; (*de plan*) key; (*de photo*) caption.

léger , -ère *adjective* light; (*bruit, fièvre etc*) slight; (*café, thé*) weak; (*bière, tabac*) mild.

légèrement *adverb* (*un peu*) slightly.

légèreté *f noun* lightness.

légitime *adjective* **être en état de l. défense** to act in self-defence.

légume *m noun* vegetable.

lendemain *m noun* **le l.** the next day; **le l. de** the day after; **le l. matin** the next morning.

lent , lente *adjective* slow.

lentement *adverb* slowly.

lenteur *f noun* slowness.

lentille *f noun* (*graine*) lentil.

léopard *m noun* leopard.

lequel , laquelle , *plural* **les-quels, lesquelles** (+ à = au-quel, à laquelle, auxquel(le)s; + de = duquel, de laquelle, des-quel(le)s) *pronoun* (*chose, ani-mal*) which; (*personne*) who, (*indirect*) whom; (*interrogatif*) which (one); **dans l.** in which; **parmi lesquels** (*choses, ani-maux*) among which; (*personnes*) among whom.

les *see* **le.**

lessive *f noun* washing powder; (*linge*) washing; **faire la l.** to do the wash(ing).

lettre *f noun* letter; **en toutes lettres** (*mot*) in full.

leur
1 *possessive adjective* their.
2 *possessive pronoun* **le l., la l., les leurs** theirs.
3 *pronoun* (*indirect*) (to) them; **il l. est facile de** it's easy for them to.

levé , -ée *adjective* **être l.** (*debout*) to be up.

levée *f noun* (*de sanctions*) lifting; (*d'une séance*) close; (*du courrier*) collection.

lever
1 *verb* to lift (up); **l. les yeux** to look up.
2 *m noun* **le l. du soleil** sunrise.

lever (se) *reflexive verb* to get up; (*soleil, rideau*) to rise; (*jour*) to break.

levier *m noun* lever; (*pour soulever*) crowbar.

lèvre *f noun* lip.

lézard *m noun* lizard.

liaison *f noun* (*routière etc*) link; (*entre mots*) liaison.

liasse *f noun* bundle.

Liban (le) *m noun* the Lebanon.

libanais , -aise *adjective & m or f noun* Lebanese.

libération *f noun* freeing, release.

libérer *verb* to (set) free, release (de from); **se l.** to free oneself (*de* from).

liberté *f noun* freedom; **en l. provisoire** on bail; **mettre en l.** to free.

libraire *m or f noun* bookseller.

librairie *f noun* bookshop.

libre *adjective* free (*de quelque chose* from something, *de faire* to do); (*voie*) clear; **auriez-vous une chambre (de) l.?** do you have any vacancies?

librement *adverb* freely.

libre-service *m noun* (*plural* **libres-services**) self-service.

Libye (la) *f noun* Libya.

libyen , -enne *adjective & m or f noun* Libyan.

licence *f noun* (*diplôme*) (Bach-elor's) degree; (*sportive*) licence.

licencié , -ée *adjective & m or f noun* graduate; **l. ès lettres/sciences** Bachelor of Arts/Science.

licenciement *m noun* dismissal.

licencier *verb* (*ouvrier*) to lay off, dismiss.

liège *m noun* (*matériau*) cork.

lien *m noun* (*rapport*) link; (*ficelle*) tie; **l. de parenté** family tie.

lier *verb* (*attacher*) to tie (up); (*relier*) to link (up).

lieu , -x *m noun* place; (*d'un acci-dent*) scene; **les lieux** (*locaux*) the premises; **avoir l.** to take place; **au l. de** instead of.

lièvre *m noun* hare.

ligne *f noun* line; (*belle silhouette*) figure; **(se) mettre en l.** to line up; **en l.** (*au téléphone*) connected; **grandes lignes** (*de train*) main line (services); **à la l.** new paragraph.

ligoter *verb* to tie up.

lilas *m noun* lilac.

lime *f noun* file.

limer *verb* to file.

limitation *f noun* (*de vitesse, poids*) limit.

limite
  1 *f noun* limit (à to); (*frontière*) boundary.
  2 *adjective* (*cas*) extreme; (*vitesse etc*) maximum; **date l.** latest date; **date l. de vente** sell-by date.

limiter *verb* to limit (à to).

limonade *f noun* (fizzy) lemonade.

limpide *adjective* (crystal) clear.

linge *m noun* linen; (à laver) washing.

lingerie *f noun* underwear.

lion *m noun* lion.

lionne *f noun* lioness.

liqueur *f noun* liqueur.

liquide
  1 *adjective* liquid; **argent l.** ready cash.
  2 *m noun* liquid; **du l.** (*argent*) ready cash.

lire * *verb* to read.

lis *m noun* lily.

lis , lisant , lise(nt) *etc see* **lire**.

lisible *adjective* (*écriture*) legible.

lisse *adjective* smooth.

lisser *verb* to smooth.

liste *f noun* list; **sur la l. rouge** (*numéro de téléphone*) ex-directory.

lit [1] *m noun* bed; **l. d'enfant** cot; **lits superposés** bunk beds; **faire le lit** to make the bed.

lit [2] *see* **lire**.

literie *f noun* bedding.

litre *m noun* litre.

littéraire *adjective* literary.

littérature *f noun* literature.

littoral *m noun* coast(line).

livraison *f noun* delivery; **l. à domicile** home delivery.

livre [1] *m noun* book; **l. de poche** paperback (book).

livre [2] *f noun* (*monnaie, poids*) pound; **l. sterling** pound (sterling).

livrer *verb* to deliver (à to); **l. quelqu'un à** (*la police etc*) to give somebody over to.

livret *m noun* **l. scolaire** school report book; **l. de caisse d'épargne** bankbook.

livreur , -euse *m or f noun* delivery man, delivery woman.

local , -ale, -aux *adjective* local.

local , -aux *m noun* room; **locaux** premises.

locataire *m or f noun* tenant.

location *f noun* (*de maison etc*) renting; (*de voiture*) hiring; (*par propriétaire*) renting (out), letting; hiring (out); (*loyer*) rental.

locomotive *f noun* (*de train*) engine.

locution *f noun* phrase.

loge *f noun* (*de concierge*) lodge; (*d'acteur*) dressing room; (*de spectateur*) box.

logement *m noun* accommodation; (*appartement*) flat; (*maison*) house; **le l.** housing.

loger *verb*
  1 (*recevoir*) to accommodate; (*héberger*) to put up.
  2 (à l'hôtel etc) to put up; (*habiter*) to live.

logiciel *m noun* software *invariable*.

logique *adjective* logical.

logiquement *adverb* logically.

loi *f noun* law; (*du Parlement*) act; **projet de l.** bill.

loin *adverb* far (away) (**de** from); **Boston est l. (de Paris)** Boston is a long way away (from Paris); **c'est l. d'ici?** is it far from here?; **plus l.** further, farther; **de l.** from a distance.

lointain , -aine *adjective* distant.

Loire (la) *f noun* the Loire.

loisirs *mpl noun* spare time, leisure (time); (*distractions*) leisure activities.

Londres *m or f noun* London.

long , longue
 1 *adjective* long; **être l. (à faire)** to be a long time *or* slow (in doing); **l. de deux mètres** two metres long. **2** *m noun* **avoir deux mètres de l.** to be two metres long; (*tout*) **le l. de** (*espace*) (all) along; **de l. en large** (*marcher*) up and down; **à la longue** in the long run.

longer *verb* to go along; (*forêt, mer*) to skirt; (*mur*) to hug.

longtemps *adverb* (for) a long time; **trop l.** too long.

longueur *f noun* length; **à l. de journée** all day long; **l. d'ondes** wavelength.

lors *adverb* **l. de** at the time of.

lorsque *conjunction* when.

losange *m noun* (*forme*) diamond.

lot *m noun* (*de loterie*) prize; **gros l.** top prize.

loterie *f noun* lottery.

lotion *f noun* lotion.

lotissement *m noun* (*habitations*) housing estate.

loto *m noun* (*jeu national*) national lottery; **jouer au l.** to do the lottery.

louche *f noun* ladle.

loucher *verb* to squint.

louer *verb* (*prendre en location*) to rent (*house etc*); (*voiture*) to hire, rent; (*donner en location*) to rent (out), let; to hire (out); **maison à l.** house to let.

loup *m noun* wolf; **avoir une faim de l.** to be ravenous.

loupe *f noun* magnifying glass.

lourd , lourde
 1 *adjective* heavy; (*temps*) close; (*faute*) gross. **2** *adverb* **peser l.** to be heavy.

loyal , -e, -aux *adjective* (*honnête*) fair (**envers** to).

loyauté *f noun* fairness.

loyer *m noun* rent.

lu , lue *past participle of* lire.

lucarne *f noun* (*fenêtre*) skylight.

lueur *f noun* glimmer.

lui
 1 *pronoun m or f* (*complément indirect*) (to) him; (*femme*) (to) her; (*chose, animal*) (to) it; **il lui est facile de** it's easy for him *or* her to. **2** *m pronoun* (*complément direct*) him; (*chose, animal*) it; (*sujet emphatique*) he.

lui-même *pronoun* himself; (*chose, animal*) itself.

luisant , -ante *adjective* shiny.

lumière *f noun* light.

lumineux , -euse *adjective* (*idée, ciel etc*) bright.

lundi *m noun* Monday.

lune *f noun* moon; **l. de miel** honeymoon.

lunettes *fpl noun* glasses, spectacles; (*de protection, de plongée*) goggles; **l. de soleil** sunglasses.

lustre *m noun* (*éclairage*) chandelier.

lutte *f noun* fight, struggle; (*sport*)

wrestling.

lutter *verb* to fight, struggle.

luxe *m noun* luxury; **article de l.** luxury article.

Luxembourg (le) *m noun* Luxembourg.

luxembourgeois , -oise
1 *adjective* of Luxembourg.
2 *m or f noun* Luxembourger.

luxueux , -euse *adjective* luxurious.

lycée *m noun* (secondary) school (*for pupils aged fifteen to eighteen*).

lycéen , -enne *m or f noun* pupil.

Lyon *m or f noun* Lyons.

M

M6 *noun* = French cable television channel.

ma *see* mon.

macaroni(s) *m(pl) noun* macaroni.

macédoine *f noun* m. (de légumes) mixed vegetables.

mâcher *verb* to chew.

machin *m noun Familiar* (*chose*) what's-it.

machinal , -e, -aux *adjective* instinctive.

machinalement *adverb* instinctively.

machine *f noun* machine; **m. à coudre** sewing machine; **m. à écrire** typewriter; **m. à laver** washing machine.

mâchoire *f noun* jaw.

maçon *m noun* bricklayer.

madame *f noun* (*plural* mesdames) madam; **bonjour mesdames** good morning (ladies); **Madame** *or* **Mme Legras** Mrs Legras; **Madame** (*dans une lettre*) Dear Madam.

madeleine *f noun* (small) sponge cake.

mademoiselle *f noun* (*plural* mesdemoiselles) miss; **bonjour mesdemoiselles** good morning (ladies); **Mademoiselle** *or* **Mlle Legras** Miss Legras; **Mademoiselle** (*dans une lettre*) Dear Madam.

magasin *m noun* shop; **grand m.** department store; **en m.** in stock.

magazine *m noun* magazine.

magicien , -ienne *m or f noun* magician.

magie *f noun* magic.

magique *adjective* (*baguette etc*) magic; (*mystérieux*) magical.

magnéto *m noun Familiar* tape recorder.

magnétophone *m noun* tape recorder; **m. à cassettes** cassette recorder.

magnétoscope *m noun* video (recorder), VCR.

magnifique *adjective* magnificent.

mai *m noun* May.

maigre *adjective* (*personne*) thin; (*viande*) lean.

maigrir *verb* to get thin(ner).

maille *f noun* (*de tricot*) stitch; (*de filet*) mesh.

maillon *m noun* (*de chaîne*) link.

maillot *m noun* (*de sportif*) jersey, shirt; **m. (de corps)** vest; **m. (de bain)** (*de femme*) swimsuit; (*d'homme*) (swimming) trunks.

main *f noun* hand; **tenir à la m.** to hold in one's hand; **à la m.** (*faire, coudre etc*) by hand; **haut les mains!** hands up!; **donner un coup de m. à quelqu'un** to lend somebody a (helping) hand; **sous la m.** handy.

maintenant *adverb* now; **m. que** now that.

maintenir * *verb* (*conserver*) to keep; (*retenir*) to hold.

maire *m noun* mayor.

mairie *f noun* town hall.

mais *conjunction* but; **m. oui, m. si** yes of course; **m. non** definitely not.

maïs *m noun* (*céréale*) maize; (*légume*) sweetcorn.

maison
1 *f noun* (*bâtiment*) house; (*chez-soi*) home; (*entreprise*) firm; **à la m.** at home; **aller à la m.** to go home; **m. de la culture** arts centre; **m. des jeunes** youth club.
2 *invariable adjective* home-made.

maître *m noun* (*d'un chien etc*) master; **m. d'école** teacher; **m. d'hôtel** (*restaurant*) head waiter; **m. nageur** swimming instructor (and lifeguard).

maîtresse *f noun* mistress; **m. d'école** teacher.

maîtrise *f noun* (*diplôme*) Master's degree (**de** in).

maîtriser *verb* (*incendie*) to (bring under) control; **m. quel-qu'un** to overpower somebody.

majesté *f noun* **Votre M.** (*titre*) Your Majesty.

majeur , -e
1 *adjective* **être m.** to be of age.
2 *m noun* (*doigt*) middle finger.

majorette *f noun* majorette.

majorité *f noun* majority (**de** of); (*âge*) coming of age.

majuscule *f noun* capital letter.

mal
1 *m noun* (*plural* **maux**) (*douleur*) pain; **dire du m. de quelqu'un** to say bad things about somebody; **m. de dents** toothache; **m. de gorge** sore throat; **m. de tête** headache; **m. de ventre** stomach-ache; **avoir le m. de mer** to be seasick; **avoir m. à la tête/gorge/** *etc* to have a headache/sore throat/*etc*; **ça (me) fait m., j'ai m.** it hurts (me); **faire du m. à** to hurt; **avoir du m. à faire** to have trouble doing; **le bien et le m.** good and evil.
2 *adverb* (*travailler etc*) badly;

(*entendre, comprendre*) not too well; **être m. payé** to be badly paid; **pas m.!** not bad!; **c'est m. de mentir** it's wrong to lie.

malade
1 *adjective* ill, sick; **être m. du cœur** to have a bad heart.
2 *m or f noun* sick person; (*d'un médecin*) patient.

maladie *f noun* illness.

maladresse *f noun* clumsiness.

maladroit , -droite *adjective* clumsy.

malais , -aise *adjective & m or f noun* Malaysian.

malaise *m noun* **avoir un m.** to feel dizzy.

Malaisie (la) *f noun* Malaysia.

malaria *f noun* malaria.

malchance *f noun* bad luck.

mâle *adjective & m noun* male.

malentendu *m noun* misunderstanding.

malfaiteur *m noun* criminal.

malgré *preposition* in spite of; **m. tout** after all.

malheur *m noun* (*événement, malchance*) misfortune.

malheureusement *adverb* unfortunately.

malheureux , -euse
1 *adjective* (*triste*) miserable.
2 *m or f noun* (*pauvre*) poor man *or* woman.

malhonnête *adjective* dishonest.

malice *f noun* mischievousness.

malicieux , -euse *adjective* mischievous.

malin , -igne *adjective* (*astucieux*) clever.

malle *f noun* (*coffre*) trunk; (*de véhicule*) boot.

mallette *f noun* small suitcase;

(*pour documents*) attaché case.

malpoli , -ie *adjective* rude.

malsain , -saine *adjective* unhealthy.

maltraiter *verb* to ill-treat.

maman *f noun* mum(my).

mamie *f noun Familiar* grandma.

mammifère *m noun* mammal.

Manche (la) *f noun* the (English) Channel.

manche [1] *f noun* (*de vêtement*) sleeve; (*d'un match*) round.

manche [2] *m noun* (*d'outil*) handle; **m. à balai** broomstick; (*d'avion etc*) joystick.

manchette *f noun* (*de chemise*) cuff.

manchot *m noun* (*oiseau*) penguin.

mandarine *f noun* tangerine.

mandat *m noun* (*postal*) money order.

manège *m noun* merry-go-round.

manette *f noun* lever.

mangeoire *f noun* (feeding) trough.

manger *verb* to eat; **donner à m. à** to feed.

maniable *adjective* easy to handle.

maniaque
1 *adjective* fussy.
2 *m or f noun* fusspot.

manie *f noun* craze.

manier *verb* to handle.

manière *f noun* way; **de toute m.** anyway; **à ma m.** (in) my own way; **la m. dont elle parle** the way (in which) she talks; **faire des manières** to make a fuss.

manifestant , -ante *m or f noun* demonstrator.

manifestation *f noun* (*défilé*) demonstration.

manifester *verb*
1 (*sa colère etc*) to show; **se m.** (*maladie*) to show itself.
2 (*dans la rue*) to demonstrate.

manipuler *verb* (*manier*) to handle.

mannequin *m noun* (*personne*) (fashion) model; (*statue*) dummy.

manœuvre
1 *m noun* (*ouvrier*) labourer.
2 *f noun* (*action*) manoeuvre.

manœuvrer *verb* (*véhicule*) to manoeuvre.

manque *m noun* lack (**de** of).

manquer *verb*
1 (*cible, train etc*) to miss.
2 (*faire défaut*) to be short; (*être absent*) to be absent (**à** from); **m. de** (*pain, argent etc*) to be short of; (*patience etc*) to lack; **ça manque de sel** there isn't enough salt; **elle lui manque** he misses her; **elle a manqué (de) tomber** she nearly fell; **il manque/il nous manque dix tasses** there are/we are ten cups short.

mansarde *f noun* attic.

manteau , -x *m noun* coat.

manuel , -elle
1 *adjective* (*travail*) manual.
2 *m noun* handbook, manual; (*scolaire*) textbook.

mappemonde *f noun* map of the world; (*sphère*) globe.

maquereau , -x *m noun* mackerel.

maquette *f noun* (scale) model.

maquillage *m noun* (*fard*) make-up.

maquiller *verb* (*visage*) to make up; **se m.** to make (oneself) up.

marais *m noun* marsh.

marathon *m noun* marathon.

marbre *m noun* marble.

marchand , -ande *m or f noun* shopkeeper; (*de voitures, meubles*) dealer; **m. de journaux** (*dans un magasin*) newsagent; **m. de légumes** greengrocer.

marchander *verb* to haggle.

marchandise(s) *f(pl) noun* goods.

marche *f noun* (*d'escalier*) step; (*trajet*) walk; **la m.** (*sport*) walking; **faire m. arrière** (*en voiture*) to reverse; **un train en m.** a moving train; **mettre quelque chose en m.** to start something (up).

marché *m noun* (*lieu*) market; **faire son** *or* **le m.** to do one's shopping; **bon m.** cheap.

marcher *verb* (*à pied*) to walk; (*poser le pied*) to step (**dans** in); (*fonctionner*) to work; **faire m.** (*machine*) to work; **ça marche?** *Familiar* how's it going?

mardi *m noun* Tuesday; **M. gras** Shrove Tuesday.

mare *f noun* (*étang*) pond.

marécage *m noun* swamp.

marécageux , -euse *adjective* swampy.

marée *f noun* tide; **m. noire** oil slick; **à m. haute/basse** at high/low tide.

marelle *f noun* hopscotch.

margarine *f noun* margarine.

marge *f noun* (*de page*) margin.

marguerite *f noun* daisy.

mari *m noun* husband.

mariage *m noun* marriage; (*cérémonie*) wedding.

marié , -ée
1 *adjective* married.
2 *m noun* (bride)groom; **les mariés** the bride and (bride)groom.
3 *f noun* bride.

marier *verb* **m. quelqu'un** (*prêtre etc*) to marry somebody.

marier (se) *reflexive verb* to get married (**avec quelqu'un** to somebody).

marin , -ine
1 *adjective* **air**/*etc* **m.** sea air/*etc.*
2 *m noun* sailor.

marine
1 *f noun* **m. (de guerre)** navy.
2 *m noun & invariable adjective* (*couleur*) **(bleu) m.** (*couleur*) navy (blue).

marionnette *f noun* puppet.

marmelade *f noun* **m. (de fruits)** stewed fruit.

marmite *f noun* (cooking) pot.

marmonner *verb* to mutter.

Maroc (le) *m noun* Morocco.

marocain , -aine *adjective & m or f noun* Moroccan.

maroquinerie *f noun* (*magasin*) leather goods shop.

marque *f noun* (*trace*) mark; (*de produit*) make, brand; (*points*) score; **m. de fabrique** trademark; **m. déposée** (registered) trademark.

marquer *verb*
1 (*par une marque*) to mark; (*écrire*) to note down; (*but*) to score; **m. les points** to keep (the) score.
2 (*laisser une trace*) to leave a mark; (*joueur*) to score.

marqueur *m noun* (*crayon*) marker.

marraine *f noun* godmother.

marrant , -ante *adjective Familiar* funny.

marre *f noun* **en avoir m.** *Familiar* to be fed up (**de** with).

marron
1 *m noun* chestnut.

2 *m noun & invariable adjective* (*couleur*) brown.

mars *m noun* March.

Marseille *m or f noun* Marseilles.

marteau , -x *m noun* hammer; m. piqueur pneumatic drill.

martien , -ienne *m or f noun & adjective* Martian.

martyriser *verb* (*enfant*) to batter.

mascara *m noun* mascara.

mascotte *f noun* mascot.

masculin , -ine
  1 *adjective* male.
  2 *adjective & m noun Grammaire* masculine.

masque *m noun* mask.

massacre *m noun* slaughter.

massacrer *verb* to slaughter.

massage *m noun* massage.

masse *f noun* (*volume*) mass; en m. in large numbers.

masser *verb* (*frotter*) to massage.

masser (se) *reflexive verb* (*gens*) to (form a) crowd.

masseur *m noun* masseur.

masseuse *f noun* masseuse.

massif , -ive
  1 *adjective* (*or, bois etc*) solid.
  2 *m noun* (*de fleurs*) clump; (*de montagnes*) massif; le M. central the Massif Central (*mountains in central France*).

mastic *m noun* (*pour vitres*) putty.

mastiquer *verb* (*vitre*) to putty; (*mâcher*) to chew.

mat , mate *adjective* (*papier, couleur*) mat(t).

mât *m noun* (*de navire*) mast; (*poteau*) pole.

match *m noun* match.

matelas *m noun* mattress; m. pneumatique air bed.

matelot *m noun* sailor.

matériaux *mpl noun* (building) materials.

matériel , -ielle
  1 *adjective* (*dégâts*) material.
  2 *m noun* equipment; (*pour ordinateur*) hardware *invariable*; m. de camping camping equipment.

maternel , -elle
  1 *adjective* (*amour etc*) maternal; (*langue*) native.
  2 *f noun* (*école*) maternelle nursery school.

maternité *f noun* (*hôpital*) maternity hospital.

mathématiques *fpl noun* mathematics.

maths *fpl noun* maths.

matière *f noun* (*à l'école*) subject; (*substance*) material; m. première raw material.

matin *m noun* morning; le m. (*chaque matin*) in the morning; à sept heures du m. at seven in the morning.

matinal , -e, -aux *adjective* être m. to be an early riser.

matinée *f noun* morning; faire la grasse m. to sleep late.

matraque *f noun* (*de policier*) truncheon; (*de malfaiteur*) cosh.

maussade *adjective* (*personne*) bad-tempered, moody; (*temps*) gloomy.

mauvais , -aise *adjective* bad (en at); (*méchant*) wicked; (*mal choisi*) wrong; (*mer*) rough; plus m. worse; le plus m. the worst; il fait m. the weather's bad.

mauve *adjective & m noun* (*couleur*) mauve.

maximal , -e *adjective* maximum.

maximum *m noun* maximum; le

m. de (*force etc*) the maximum (amount of); **au m.** (*tout au plus*) at most.

mayonnaise *f noun* mayonnaise.

mazout *m noun* (fuel) oil.

me (**m'** *before vowel or mute h*) *pronoun* (*complément direct*) me; (*indirect*) (to) me; (*réfléchi*) myself.

mécanicien , -ienne *m or f noun* mechanic; (*de train*) train driver.

mécanique *adjective* mechanical; **jouet m.** wind-up toy.

mécanisme *m noun* mechanism.

méchanceté *f noun* malice; **une m.** (*parole*) a malicious word.

méchant , -ante *adjective* (*cruel*) wicked; (*enfant*) naughty.

mèche *f noun* (*de cheveux*) lock; (*de bougie*) wick; (*de pétard*) fuse.

méconnaissable *adjective* unrecognizable.

mécontent , -ente *adjective* dissatisfied (de with).

mécontentement *m noun* dissatisfaction.

mécontenter *verb* to displease.

médaille *f noun* (*décoration*) medal; (*bijou*) medallion; **être m. d'or** to be a gold medallist.

médecin *m noun* doctor.

médecine *f noun* medicine; **étudiant en m.** medical student.

médias *mpl noun* (mass) media.

médical , -e, -aux *adjective* medical.

médicament *m noun* medicine.

médiéval , -e, -aux *adjective* medi(a)eval.

médiocre *adjective* second-rate.

médisance(s) *f(pl) noun* malicious gossip.

Méditerranée *f noun* **la M.** the Mediterranean.

méditerranéen , -enne *adjective* Mediterranean.

meeting *m noun* meeting.

méfiance *f noun* distrust.

méfiant , -ante *adjective* suspicious.

méfier (se) *reflexive verb* **se m. de** to distrust; (*faire attention à*) to watch out for; **méfie-toi!** watch out!; **je me méfie** I'm suspicious.

mégot *m noun* cigarette butt.

meilleur , -e
  1 *adjective* better (**que** than); **le m. résultat**/*etc* the best result/ *etc*.
  2 *m or f noun* **le m., la meilleure** the best (one).

mélange *m noun* mixture.

mélanger *verb* (*mêler*) to mix.

mélanger (se) *reflexive verb* (*mêler*) to mix.

mêlée *f noun Rugby* scrum.

mêler *verb* to mix (**à** with).

mêler (se) *reflexive verb* to mix (**à** with); **se m. à** (*la foule*) to join; **mêle-toi de ce qui te regarde!** mind your own business!

mélodie *f noun* melody.

melon *m noun* (*fruit*) melon; (*chapeau*) m. bowler (hat).

membre *m noun* (*bras, jambe*) limb; (*d'un groupe*) member; **m. de la famille** family member, member of the family.

même
  1 *adjective* same; **en m. temps** at the same time (**que** as).
  2 *pronoun* **le m., la m.** the same (one); **les mêmes** the same (ones).
  3 *adverb* even; **m. si** even if; **ici m.** in this very place.

mémoire *f noun* memory; **à la m.**

de in memory of.

mémorable *adjective* memorable.

menaçant , -ante *adjective* threatening.

menace *f noun* threat.

menacer *verb* to threaten (**de faire** to do).

ménage *m noun* housekeeping; (*couple*) couple; **faire le m.** to do the housework.

ménager , -ère *adjective* (*appareil*) domestic; **travaux ménagers** housework.

ménagère *f noun* housewife.

mendiant , -ante *m or f noun* beggar.

mendier *verb*
1 (*demander, l'aumône*) to beg.
2 (*argent, nourriture*) to beg for.

mener *verb* to lead; (*enquête etc*) to carry out; **m. quelqu'un à** to take somebody to.

menottes *fpl noun* handcuffs.

mensonge *m noun* lie.

mensuel , -elle *adjective* monthly.

mental , -e, -aux *adjective* mental.

menteur , -euse *m or f noun* liar.

menthe *f noun* mint.

mention *f noun* (*à un examen*) distinction.

mentir * *verb* to lie (**à** to).

menton *m noun* chin.

menu *m noun* menu; **m. touristique** cheap fixed-price, three-course meal.

menuiserie *f noun* carpentry.

menuisier *m noun* carpenter.

mépris *m noun* contempt (**pour** for).

méprisant , -ante *adjective* contemptuous.

mépriser *verb* to despise.

mer *f noun* sea; **en m.** at sea; **aller à la m.** to go to the seaside; **la m. d'Irlande** the Irish Sea; **la m. du Nord** the North Sea.

mercerie *f noun* haberdasher's.

merci *interjection & m noun* thank you (**de, pour** for); **m. bien, m. beaucoup** thanks very much.

mercredi *m noun* Wednesday.

merde! *interjection Familiar* hell!

mère *f noun* mother; **m. de famille** wife and mother.

merguez *f noun* merguez (*spicy North African sausage*).

mériter *verb* (*être digne de*) to deserve.

merle *m noun* blackbird.

merveille *f noun* wonder.

merveilleux , -euse *adjective* wonderful.

mes *see* mon.

mésaventure *f noun* slight mishap.

mesdames *see* madame.

mesdemoiselles *see* mademoiselle.

message *m noun* message.

messager *m noun* messenger.

messe *f noun* mass (*church service*).

messieurs *see* monsieur.

mesure *f noun* (*dimension*) measurement; (*action*) measure; (*cadence*) time.

mesurer *verb* to measure; **m. 1 mètre 83** (*personne*) to be six feet tall; (*objet*) to measure six feet.

métal , -aux *m noun* metal; **chaise en m.** metal chair.

métallique *adjective* **échelle/etc m.** metal ladder/etc.

métallurgie *f noun* (*industrie*) steel industry.

météo *f noun* (*bulletin*) weather forecast.

météorologie *f noun* meteorology.

météorologique *adjective* **bulletin/etc** m. weather report/*etc*.

méthode *f noun* method.

méthodique *adjective* methodical.

métier *m noun* (*travail*) job.

mètre *m noun* (*mesure*) metre; (*règle*) (metre) rule; **m. carré** square metre.

métrique *adjective* metric.

métro *m noun* underground.

metteur *m noun* **m. en scène** (*de cinéma*) director.

mettre * *verb* to put; (*vêtement*) to put on; (*chauffage etc*) to put on, switch on; (*réveil*) to set (**à** for); **j'ai mis une heure** it took me an hour; **m. en colère** to make angry; **m. la table** to set *or* lay the table.

mettre (se) *reflexive verb* to put oneself; (*debout*) to stand; (*assis*) to sit; (*objet*) to go; **se m. en short/etc** to get into one's shorts/*etc*; **se m. en colère** to get angry; **se m. à faire** to start doing; **se m. à table** to sit (down) at the table.

meuble *m noun* piece of furniture; **meubles** furniture.

meublé, -ée
1 *adjective* furnished..
2 *m noun* (*appartement*) furnished flat.

meubler *verb* to furnish.

meugler *verb* (*vache*) to moo.

meule *f noun* (*de foin*) haystack.

meurtre *m noun* murder.

meurtrier, -ière *m or f noun* murderer.

mexicain, -aine *adjective & m or f noun* Mexican.

Mexique (le) *m noun* Mexico.

mi - *préfixe* **la mi-mars/etc** mid March/*etc*.

miauler *verb* to miaow.

miche *f noun* round loaf.

mi-chemin (à) *adverb* halfway.

mi-côte (à) *adverb* halfway up *or* down (the hill).

micro *m noun* microphone.

microbe *m noun* germ.

micro-onde *f noun* **four à micro-ondes** microwave oven.

micro-ordinateur *m noun* (*plural* **micro-ordinateurs**) microcomputer.

microscope *m noun* microscope.

midi *m noun* (*heure*) twelve o'clock, noon; (*heure du déjeuner*) lunchtime; **le M. (de la France)** the South of France.

mie *f noun* **la m.** the soft part of the bread; **pain de m.** sandwich loaf.

miel *m noun* honey.

mien, mienne *possessive pronoun* **le m., la mienne, les miens, les miennes** mine; **les deux miens** my two.

miette *f noun* (*de pain*) crumb.

mieux *adverb & invariable adjective* better (**que** than); **le m., la m., les m.** the best; (*de deux*) the better; **tu ferais m. de partir** you had better leave.

mignon, -onne *adjective* (*joli*) cute; (*agréable*) nice.

migraine *f noun* headache.

mil *invariable m noun* (*dans les dates*) **l'an deux m.** the year two thousand.

milieu, -x *m noun* (*centre*) middle; **au m. de** in the middle of.

militaire
1 *adjective* military.
2 *m noun* soldier.

mille *adjective & invariable m noun* thousand; **m. hommes**/*etc* a *or* one thousand men/*etc*.

mille-pattes *invariable m noun* centipede.

milliard *m noun* billion, thousand million.

millième *adjective & m or f noun* thousandth.

millier *m noun* thousand; **un m. (de)** a thousand or so.

millimètre *m noun* millimetre.

million *m noun* million; **un m. de livres**/*etc* a million pounds/*etc*; **deux millions** two million.

millionnaire *m or f noun* millionaire.

mime *m or f noun* (*acteur*) mime.

mimer *verb* to mime.

minable *adjective* shabby.

mince *adjective* thin; (*élancé*) slim.

mincir *verb* to grow slim.

mine [1] *f noun* appearance; **avoir bonne m.** to look well.

mine [2] *f noun* (*de charbon etc*) mine; (*de crayon*) lead; (*bombe*) mine.

miner *verb* (*terrain*) to mine.

minerai *m noun* ore.

minéral , -e, -aux *adjective & m noun* mineral.

mineur *m noun* (*ouvrier*) miner.

miniature *invariable adjective* (*train etc*) miniature.

minimal , -e *adjective* minimum.

minimum *m noun* minimum; **le m. de** (*force etc*) the minimum (amount of); **au (grand) m.** at the

very least.

ministère *m noun* ministry.

ministre *m noun* minister.

Minitel ® *m noun* = consumer information network accessible via home computer terminal.

minorité *f noun* minority.

minou *m noun* (*chat*) puss.

minuit *m noun* midnight.

minuscule *adjective* (*petit*) tiny.

minute *f noun* minute.

minuterie *f noun* (*pour l'éclairage*) time switch.

minuteur *m noun* timer.

minutieux , -euse *adjective* meticulous.

miracle *m noun* miracle; **par m.** miraculously.

miraculeux , -euse *adjective* miraculous.

miroir *m noun* mirror.

mis , mise *past participle of* **mettre.**

mise [1] *f noun* (*action*) putting; **m. en marche** starting up; **m. en scène** (*de film*) direction.

mise [2] (*argent*) stake.

misérable *adjective* (*très pauvre*) destitute.

misère *f noun* (grinding) poverty.

missile *m noun* (*fusée*) missile.

mission *f noun* mission.

mite *f noun* (clothes) moth.

mi-temps *f noun* (*pause*) (*en sport*) half-time; (*période*) (*en sport*) half; **à m.** (*travailler*) part-time.

mitraillette *f noun* machine-gun (*portable*).

mitrailleuse *f noun* machine-gun.

mixer , mixeur *m noun* (*pour mélanger*) (food) mixer.

mixte *adjective* (*école*) co-educational, mixed.

MJC *f abbreviation* (*Maison des jeunes et de la culture*) community centre.

mobile *adjective* (*pièce*) moving; (*personne*) mobile.

mobilier *m noun* furniture.

mobylette ® *f noun* moped.

moche *adjective* (*laid*) ugly.

mode
 1 *f noun* fashion; **à la m.** fashionable.
 2 *m noun* Grammaire mood; **m. d'emploi** directions (for use).

modèle *m noun* model; **m. (réduit)** (scale) model.

modération *f noun* moderation.

modéré , -ée *adjective* moderate.

modérer *verb* (*vitesse*, *chaleur etc*) to reduce.

moderne *adjective* modern.

moderniser *verb* to modernize.

moderniser (se) *reflexive verb* to modernize.

modeste *adjective* modest.

modestie *f noun* modesty.

modification *f noun* alteration.

modifier *verb* to alter.

moelle *f noun* (*d'os*) marrow; **m. épinière** spinal cord.

moelleux , -euse *adjective* (*lit*, *tissu*) soft.

moi *pronoun* (*complément direct*) me; (*indirect*) (to) me; (*sujet emphatique*) I.

moi-même *pronoun* myself.

moindre *adjective* **la m. erreur/ etc** the slightest mistake/*etc*; **le m.** (*de mes problèmes etc*) the least (**de** of).

moine *m noun* monk.

moineau , -x *m noun* sparrow.

moins
 1 *adverb* (*before vowel*) less (**que** than); **m. de** (*temps*, *travail*) less (**que** than); (*gens*, *livres*) fewer (**que** than); (*cent francs*) less than; **m. grand** not as big (**que** as); **de m. en m.** less and less; **le m.** (*travailler*) the least; **le m. grand, la m. grande, les m. grand(e)s** the smallest; **au m.**, **du m.** at least; **de m.**, **en m.** (*qui manque*) missing; **dix ans de m.** ten years less; **en m.** (*personne*, *objet*) less; (*personnes*, *objets*) fewer; **à m. que** (+ *subjunctive*) unless.
 2 *preposition* (*en calcul*) minus; **deux heures m. cinq** five to two; **il fait m. dix (degrés)** it's minus ten (degrees).

mois *m noun* month; **au m. de juin** in (the month of) June.

moisi , -ie
 1 *adjective* mouldy.
 2 *m noun* mould; **sentir le m.** to smell musty.

moisir *verb* to go mouldy.

moisson *f noun* harvest.

moissonner *verb* to harvest.

moite *adjective* sticky.

moitié *f noun* half; **la m. de la pomme** half (of) the apple; **à m. fermé** half closed; **à m. prix** (at) half-price; **de m.** by half.

mol *see* **mou.**

molaire *f noun* back tooth.

molette *f noun* **clé à m.** adjustable wrench *or* spanner.

molle *see* **mou.**

mollet *m noun* (*de jambe*) calf.

moment *m noun* (*instant*) moment; (*période*) time; **en ce m.** at the moment; **par moments** at times; **au m. de partir** when just about to leave; **à ce m.-là** (*à cette époque*) at that time; (*à cet ins-*

tant) at that moment; **au m. où** just as; **du m. que** (*puisque*) seeing that.

mon , ma (**ma** *becomes* **mon** *before a vowel or mute h*) *possessive adjective* my; **mon père** my father; **ma mère** my mother; **mon ami(e)** my friend.

monarchie *f noun* monarchy.

monde *m noun* world; **il y avait du m.** *or* **beaucoup de m.** there were a lot of people; **le m. entier** the whole world; **tout le m.** everybody.

mondial , -e, -aux *adjective* (*crise etc*) worldwide; **guerre mondiale** world war.

moniteur , -trice *m or f noun* instructor; (*de colonie de vacances*) assistant.

monnaie *f noun* (*devise*) currency; (*pièces*) change; **faire de la m.** to get change; **faire de la m. à quelqu'un** to give somebody change (**sur un billet** for a note).

monopoliser *verb* to monopolize.

monotone *adjective* monotonous.

monotonie *f noun* monotony.

monsieur *m noun* (*plural* **messieurs**) (*homme*) man, gentleman; **oui m.** yes sir; **oui messieurs** yes gentlemen; **M. Legras** Mr Legras; **Monsieur** (*dans une lettre*) Dear Sir.

monstre *m noun* monster.

monstrueux , -euse *adjective* (*abominable*) hideous.

mont *m noun* mount.

montagne *f noun* mountain; **la m.** (*zone*) the mountains.

montagneux , -euse *adjective* mountainous.

montant *m noun* (*somme*) amount; (*de barrière*) post.

montée *f noun* (*ascension*) climb; (*chemin*) slope.

monter *verb*
1 (*auxiliary* **être**) (*aller vers le haut*) (*personne*) to go *or* come up; (*s'élever*) (*ballon, prix etc*) to go up; (*grimper*) to climb (up) (**sur** onto); (*marée*) to come in; **m. dans un véhicule** to get in(to) a vehicle; **m. dans un train** to get on(to) a train; **m. sur** *or* **à** (*échelle*) to climb up; **m. en courant**/*etc* to run/*etc* up; **m. (à cheval)** to ride (a horse).
2 (*auxiliary* **avoir**) (*côte*) to climb (up); (*objet*) to bring *or* take up; (*cheval*) to ride; (*tente*) to set up; **m. l'escalier** to go *or* come up the stairs.

montre *f noun* (wrist)watch.

Montréal *m or f noun* Montreal.

montrer *verb* to show (**à** to); **m. du doigt** to point to; **se m.** to show oneself.

monture *f noun* (*de lunettes*) frame.

monument *m noun* monument; **m. aux morts** war memorial.

moquer (se) *reflexive verb* **se m. de** to make fun of; **je m'en moque!** I couldn't care less!

moquette *f noun* fitted carpet(s).

moral *m noun* spirits, morale.

morale *f noun* (*d'histoire*) moral.

morceau , -x *m noun* piece; (*de sucre*) lump.

mordiller *verb* to nibble.

mordre *verb* to bite.

morse *m noun* (*animal*) walrus; (*code*) Morse (Code).

morsure *f noun* bite.

mort *f noun* death.

mort , morte (*past participle of* **mourir**)
1 *adjective* (*personne, plante etc*) dead.
2 *m or f noun* dead man, dead woman; **les morts** the dead; **de nombreux morts** (*victimes*) many casualties *or* dead.

mortel , -elle *adjective* (*hommes, ennemi etc*) mortal; (*accident*) fatal.

morue *f noun* cod.

mosquée *f noun* mosque.

mot *m noun* word; **envoyer un m. à** to drop a line to; **mots croisés** crossword (puzzle); **m. de passe** password.

motard *m noun* motorcyclist.

moteur *m noun* (*de véhicule etc*) engine, motor.

motif *m noun* (*raison*) reason (**de** for).

motivé , -ée *adjective* motivated.

moto *f noun* motorcycle, motor-bike.

motocyclette *f noun* motor-cycle.

motocycliste *m or f noun* motor-cyclist.

motte *f noun* (*de terre*) lump.

mou (*or* **mol** *before vowel or mute h*), **molle** *adjective* soft; (*sans énergie*) feeble.

mouche *f noun* (*insecte*) fly.

moucher (se) *reflexive verb* to blow one's nose.

mouchoir *m noun* handkerchief; (*en papier*) tissue.

moudre * *verb* (*café*) to grind.

moue *f noun* long face; **faire la m.** to pull a (long) face.

mouette *f noun* (sea)gull.

moufle *f noun* mitten.

mouillé , -ée *adjective* wet (**de** with).

mouiller *verb* to (make) wet; **se faire m.** to get wet; **se m.** to get (oneself) wet.

moule [1] *m noun* (*récipient*) mould; **m. à gâteaux** cake tin.

moule [2] *f noun* (*animal*) mussel.

mouler *verb* to mould; **m. quelqu'un** (*vêtement*) to fit somebody tightly.

moulin *m noun* mill; **m. à vent** windmill; **m. à café** coffee-grinder.

moulu (*past participle of* **moudre**) *adjective* (*café*) ground.

mourir * *verb* (*auxiliary* **être**) to die (**de** of, from); **m. de froid** to die of exposure; **je meurs de faim!** I'm starving!

mousse *f noun* (*plante*) moss; (*écume*) foam; (*de bière*) froth; (*de savon*) lather; (*dessert*) mousse.

mousser *verb* (*bière*) to froth; (*savon*) to lather; (*eau*) to foam.

moustache *f noun* moustache; **moustaches** (*de chat*) whiskers.

moustachu , -ue *adjective* wearing a moustache.

moustique *m noun* mosquito.

moutarde *f noun* mustard.

mouton *m noun* sheep; (*viande*) mutton.

mouvement *m noun* (*geste, groupe etc*) movement; (*de colère*) outburst.

mouvementé , -ée *adjective* (*vie, voyage etc*) eventful.

moyen , -enne
1 *adjective* average; (*format etc*) medium(-sized); **classe moyenne** middle class.
2 *f noun* average; (*dans un examen*) pass mark; (*dans un devoir*) half marks; **en moyenne** on

average.

moyen *m noun* (*procédé, façon*) means, way (**de faire** of doing, to do); **il n'y a pas m. de faire** it's not possible to do; **je n'ai pas les moyens** (*argent*) I can't afford it.

muer *verb* (*animal*) to moult; (*voix*) to break.

muet , -ette
1 *adjective* (*infirme*) dumb; (*film, voyelle*) silent.
2 *m or f noun* dumb person.

mufle *m noun* (*d'animal*) muzzle.

mugir *verb* (*bœuf*) to bellow.

mugissement(s) *m*(*pl*) *noun* bellow(-ing).

muguet *m noun* lily of the valley.

mule *f noun* (*pantoufle*) mule; (*animal*) (she-)mule.

multicolore *adjective* multicoloured.

multiple *m noun* multiple.

multiplication *f noun* multiplication.

multiplier *verb* to multiply.

municipal , -e, -aux *adjective* municipal; **conseil m.** town council.

munir *verb* **m. de** to equip with; **se m. de** to provide oneself with.

munitions *fpl noun* ammunition.

mur *m noun* wall; **m. du son** sound barrier.

mûr , mûre *adjective* (*fruit*) ripe.

muraille *f noun* (high) wall.

mûre *f noun* (*baie*) blackberry.

mûrir *verb* (*fruit*) to ripen.

murmure *m noun* murmur.

murmurer *verb* to murmur.

muscle *m noun* muscle.

musclé , -ée *adjective* (*bras*) muscular.

museau , -x *m noun* (*de chien, chat*) nose, muzzle.

musée *m noun* museum.

muselière *f noun* muzzle.

musical , -e, -aux *adjective* musical.

musicien , -ienne *m or f noun* musician.

musique *f noun* music; **m. classique** classical music.

musulman , -ane *adjective & m or f noun* Muslim.

mutuel , -elle *adjective* (*réciproque*) mutual.

myope *adjective & m or f noun* shortsighted (person).

mystère *m noun* mystery.

mystérieux , -euse *adjective* mysterious.

N

N *f abbreviation* (*Nationale*) N20 = A 20 (*main road*).

nage *f noun* (*swimming*) stroke; **traverser à la n.** to swim across; **en n.** sweating.

nageoire *f noun* (*de poisson*) fin.

nager *verb* to swim.

nageur , -euse *m or f noun* swimmer.

naïf , -ïve *adjective* naïve.

nain , naine *m or f noun* dwarf.

naissance *f noun* (*de personne, animal*) birth.

naître * *verb* to be born.

nappe *f noun* (*sur une table*) table cloth.

napperon *m noun* (*pour vase etc*) (cloth) mat.

narine *f noun* nostril.

naseau , -x *m noun* (*de cheval*) nostril.

natal , -e *adjective* (*plural* **natals, natales**) (*pays*) native; **sa maison natale** the house where he *or* she was born.

natation *f noun* swimming; **faire de la n.** to go swimming.

nation *f noun* nation; **les Nations unies** the United Nations.

national , -e, -aux *adjective* national; **(route) nationale** = A road.

nationalité *f noun* nationality.

natte *f noun* (*de cheveux*) plait; (*tapis*) mat.

nature
1 *f noun* (*monde naturel, caractère*) nature.
2 *invariable adjective* (*omelette, yaourt etc*) plain; (*café*) black; **thé**

n. tea without milk.

naturel , -elle *adjective* natural.

naturellement *adverb* naturally.

naufrage *m noun* (*ship*)wreck; **faire n.** to be (ship)wrecked.

naufragé , -ée *adjective & m or f noun* shipwrecked (person).

nautique *adjective* **ski**/*etc* **n.** water skiing/*etc*.

naval , -e *adjective* (*plural* **navals, navales**) naval.

navet *m noun* (*plante*) turnip.

navette *f noun* **faire la n.** to shuttle back and forth (**entre** be-tween); **n. spatiale** space shuttle.

navigation *f noun* (*trafic de bateaux*) shipping.

naviguer *verb* (*bateau*) to sail.

navire *m noun* ship.

navré , -ée *adjective* **je suis n.** I'm (terribly) sorry (**de faire** to do).

ne (**n'** *before vowel or mute h; used to form negative verb with* **pas, jamais, personne, rien** *etc*) *adverb* (+ *pas*) not; (+ *jamais*) never; **il ne boit pas** he does not *or* doesn't drink.

né , -ée *adjective* (*past participle of* **naître**) born; **elle est née** she was born; **né le 2 janvier à Paris** born on January 2nd in Paris.

nécessaire
1 *adjective* necessary.
2 *m noun* **n. de toilette** sponge bag; **faire le n.** to do what's necessary.

nécessité *f noun* necessity.

nécessiter *verb* to require.

nectarine *f noun* nectarine.

néerlandais , -aise
1 *adjective* Dutch.
2 *m or f noun* Dutchman, Dutch-woman.

négatif , -ive
1 *adjective* negative.
2 *m noun* (*de photo*) negative.

négation *f noun* Grammaire negation; (*mot*) negative.

négligence *f noun* (*défaut*) carelessness.

négligent , -ente *adjective* careless.

négliger *verb* (*personne, travail etc*) to neglect; **n. de faire** to neglect to do.

négociation *f noun* negotiation.

négocier *verb* to negotiate.

neige *f noun* snow; **n. fondue** sleet.

neiger *verb* to snow.

nénuphar *m noun* water lily.

néon *m noun* éclairage au n. neon lighting.

néo-zélandais , -aise
1 *adjective* New Zealand.
2 *m or f noun* New Zealander.

nerf *m noun* nerve; **du n.!** buck up!; **ça me tape sur les nerfs** it gets on my nerves.

nerveux , -euse *adjective* (*agité*) nervous.

nescafé ® *m noun* instant coffee.

n'est-ce pas? *adverb* isn't he?, don't you? *etc*; **il est beau, n.?** he's handsome, isn't he?; **tu le connais, n.?** you know him, don't you?; **tu viendras, n.?** you'll come, won't you?

net , nette
1 *adjective* (*image, refus*) clear; (*coupure, linge*) clean; (*soigné*) neat; (*poids, prix*) net.
2 *adverb* (*s'arrêter*) dead; (*casser, couper*) clean.

nettement *adverb* (*bien plus*) definitely.

nettoyage *m noun* cleaning; **n. à sec** dry cleaning.

nettoyer *verb* to clean (up).

neuf , neuve
1 *adjective* new; **quoi de n.?** what's new(s)?
2 *m noun* **remettre à n.** to make as good as new.

neuf *adjective* & *m noun* nine.

neutre *adjective* (*pays*) neutral.

neuvième *adjective* & *m or f noun* ninth.

neveu , -x *m noun* nephew.

nez *m noun* nose; **n. à n.** face to face (**avec** with).

ni *conjunction* **ni … ni** (+ *ne*) neither … nor; **ni Pierre ni Paul ne sont venus** neither Pierre nor Paul came; **il n'a ni faim ni soif** he's neither hungry nor thirsty; **sans manger ni boire** without eating or drinking; **ni l'un(e) ni l'autre** neither (of them).

niche *f noun* (*de chien*) kennel.

nicher *verb* (*oiseau*) to nest (**dans** in).

nicher (se) *reflexive verb* (*oiseau*) to nest.

nid *m noun* nest.

nièce *f noun* niece.

nier *verb* to deny (**que** that).

Nigeria (le) *m noun* Nigeria.

nigérian , -e *adjective* & *m or f noun* Nigerian.

niveau , -x *m noun* level; **au n. de quelqu'un** (*élève etc*) up to somebody's standard.

noble
1 *adjective* noble.
2 *m or f noun* nobleman, noble-woman.

noce(s) *f(pl) noun* wedding.

nocif , -ive *adjective* harmful.

Noël *m noun* Christmas; **le père N.** Father Christmas, Santa Claus.

nœud *m noun* knot; (*ruban*) bow; **n. coulant** slipknot, noose; **n. papillon** bow tie.

noir , noire
  1 *adjective* black; (*nuit, lunettes etc*) dark; **il fait n.** it's dark.
  2 *m noun* (*couleur*) black; (*obscurité*) dark; **N.** (*homme*) black.
  3 *f noun* **Noire** (*femme*) black.

noircir *verb*
  1 (*rendre noir*) to make black.
  2 (*devenir noir*) to turn black.

noircir (se) *reflexive verb* to turn black; **se n. le visage** to black one's face.

noisetier *m noun* hazel (tree).

noisette *f noun* hazelnut.

noix *f noun* (*du noyer*) walnut; **n. de coco** coconut.

nom *m noun* name; *Grammaire* noun; **n. de famille** surname; **n. propre** *Grammaire* proper noun; **au n. de** for the sake of; **l'appartement est au n. de sa femme** the flat is in his wife's name.

nombre *m noun* number.

nombreux , -euse *adjective* (*amis, livres*) numerous, many; (*famille*) large; **peu n.** few; **venir n.** to come in large numbers.

nombril *m noun* navel.

nommer *verb* (*appeler*) to name; **n. quelqu'un** (*désigner*) to appoint somebody (**à un poste** to a post).

nommer (se) *reflexive verb* to be called.

non *adverb & invariable m noun* no; **tu viens ou n.?** are you coming or not?; **n. seulement** not only; **je crois que n.** I don't think so; **(ni) moi n. plus** neither do, am, can *etc* I.

nonante *adjective* (*en Belgique, en Suisse*) ninety.

non-fumeur , -euse *m or f noun* non-smoker.

nord *m noun* north; **au n. de** north of; **du n.** (*vent*) northerly; (*ville*) northern.

nord-africain , -aine *adjective & m or f noun* North African.

nord-américain , -aine *adjective & m or f noun* North American.

nord-est *m noun & invariable adjective* north-east.

nord-ouest *m noun & invariable adjective* north-west.

normal , -e, -aux *adjective* normal.

normale *f noun* **au-dessus/au-dessous de la n.** above/below normal.

normalement *adverb* normally.

Normandie (la) *f noun* Normandy.

Norvège (la) *f noun* Norway.

norvégien , -ienne *adjective & m or f noun* Norwegian.

nos *see* notre.

notaire *m noun* solicitor, lawyer.

notamment *adverb* particularly.

note *f noun* (*de musique, remarque*) note; (*à l'école*) mark; (*facture*) bill; **prendre n. de** to make a note of.

noter *verb* to note; (*devoir*) to mark.

notice *f noun* (*mode d'emploi*) instructions.

notre *possessive adjective* (*plural* **nos**) our.

nôtre *possessive pronoun* **le** *or* **la**

n., les nôtres ours.

nouer *verb* (*chaussure etc*) to tie.

nouilles *fpl noun* noodles.

nounours *m noun Familiar* teddy bear.

nourrice *f noun* (*assistante maternelle*) child minder.

nourrir *verb* to feed.

nourrissant , -ante *adjective* nourishing.

nourrisson *m noun* infant.

nourriture *f noun* food.

nous *pronoun* (*sujet*) we; (*complément direct*) us; (*indirect*) (to) us; (*réfléchi*) ourselves; (*réciproque*) each other.

nous-mêmes *pronoun* ourselves.

nouveau (*or* **nouvel** *before vowel or mute h*), **nouvelle** (*plural* nouveaux, nouvelles) **1** *adjective* new. **2** *m or f noun* (*dans une classe*) new boy, new girl. **3** *m noun* de n., à n. again.

nouveau-né , -ée *m or f noun* new-born baby.

nouvelle *f noun* (*information*) nouvelle(s) news; **une n.** a piece of news.

Nouvelle-Zélande (la) *f noun* New Zealand.

novembre *m noun* November.

noyade *f noun* drowning.

noyau , -x *m noun* (*fruit*) stone.

noyé , -ée *m or f noun* drowned man *or* woman.

noyer [1] *verb* to drown.

noyer [2] *m noun* (*arbre*) walnut tree.

noyer (se) *reflexive verb* to drown.

nu , nue *adjective* (*personne*) naked; (*mains*) bare; **tout nu** (stark) naked; **tête nue, nu-tête** bare-headed; **nu-pieds** barefoot.

nuage *m noun* cloud.

nuageux , -euse *adjective* cloudy.

nuance *f noun* (*de couleurs*) shade.

nucléaire *adjective* nuclear.

nuire * *verb* n. à quelqu'un to harm somebody

nuisible *adjective* harmful.

nuit *f noun* night; (*obscurité*) dark(ness); **il fait n.** it's dark; **la n.** (*se promener etc*) at night; **cette n.** (*aujourd'hui*) tonight; (*hier*) last night; **bonne n.** (*au coucher*) good night.

nul , nulle *adjective* (*médiocre*) hopeless; **match n.** draw; **faire match n.** to draw; **nulle part** nowhere.

numéro *m noun* number; (*de journal*) issue; (*au cirque*) act; **un n. de danse** a dance number; **n. vert** (*au téléphone*) = 0-800 number.

numéroter *verb* (*page etc*) to number.

nuque *f noun* back of the neck.

nylon *m noun* nylon; **chemise/etc en n.** nylon shirt/etc.

obéir *verb* to obey; **o. à quelqu'un** to obey somebody.

obéissance *f noun* obedience.

obéissant , -ante *adjective* obedient.

objectif *m noun* (*but*) objective; (*d'appareil photo*) lens.

objet *m noun* (*chose*) object; **objets trouvés** (*bureau*) lost property.

obligation *f noun* obligation.

obligatoire *adjective* compulsory.

obliger *verb* to force, compel (**à faire** to do); **être obligé de faire** to have to do.

oblique *adjective* oblique.

obscène *adjective* obscene.

obscur , -e *adjective* (*noir*) dark.

obscurcir *verb* (*pièce*) to make dark(er).

obscurcir (s') *reflexive verb* (*ciel*) to get dark(er).

obscurité *f noun* dark(ness).

obsèques *fpl noun* funeral.

observation *f noun* (*étude*) observation; (*reproche*) (critical) remark.

observatoire *m noun* (*endroit élevé*) lookout (post).

observer *verb* (*regarder*) to watch; (*remarquer, respecter*) to observe.

obstacle *m noun* obstacle.

obstiné , -ée *adjective* stubborn, obstinate.

obstiner (s') *reflexive verb* **s'o. à faire** to persist in doing.

obtenir * *verb* to get, obtain.

obus *m noun* (*arme*) shell.

occasion *f noun* chance (**de faire** to do); (*prix avantageux*) bargain; **d'o.** second-hand, used.

occidental , -e, -aux *adjective* western.

occupation *f noun* occupation.

occupé , -ée *adjective* busy (**à faire** doing); (*place, maison etc*) occupied; (*téléphone*) engaged; (*taxi*) hired.

occuper *verb* (*maison, pays etc*) to occupy; (*place, temps*) to take up; **o. quelqu'un** (*travail, jeu*) to keep somebody busy.

occuper (s') *reflexive verb* to keep (oneself) busy (**à faire** doing); **s'o. de** (*affaire, problème*) to deal with; **s'o. de quelqu'un** (*malade etc*) to take care of somebody; **occupe-toi de tes affaires!** mind your own business!

océan *m noun* ocean.

octobre *m noun* October.

oculiste *m or f noun* eye specialist.

odeur *f noun* smell.

odieux , -euse *adjective* horrible.

odorat *m noun* sense of smell.

œil *m noun* eye; **lever/baisser les yeux** to look up/down; **coup d'o.** look; **jeter un coup d'o. sur** to (have a) look at; **o. poché, o. au beurre noir** black eye.

œillet *m noun* carnation.

œuf *m noun* egg; **o. sur le plat** fried egg; **œufs brouillés** scrambled eggs.

œuvre *f noun* (*travail, livre etc*) work.

offenser *verb* to offend.

office *m noun* (*messe*) service; **o.**

du tourisme tourist information centre.

officiel , -ielle *adjective* official.

officier *m noun* (*dans l'armée etc*) officer.

offre *f noun* offer; **l'o. et la de-mande** supply and demand; **of-fres d'emploi** job vacancies, situations vacant.

offrir * *verb* to offer (**de faire** to do); (*cadeau*) to give; **s'o. quel-que chose** to treat oneself to something.

oh! *interjection* oh!

oie *f noun* goose.

oignon *m noun* (*légume*) onion; (*de fleur*) bulb.

oiseau , -x *m noun* bird.

oisif , -ive *adjective* (*inactif*) idle.

oisiveté *f noun* idleness.

olive *f noun* olive; **huile d'o.** olive oil.

olivier *m noun* olive tree.

olympique *adjective* (*jeux*) Olympic.

ombragé , -ée *adjective* shady.

ombre *f noun* (*d'arbre etc*) shade; (*de personne, objet*) shadow; **à l'o.** in the shade.

omelette *f noun* omelet(te); **o. au fromage/etc** cheese/*etc* om-elet(te).

omnibus *adjective & m noun* (**train**) **o.** slow *or* stopping train.

omoplate *f noun* shoulder blade.

on *pronoun* (*les gens*) they, people; (*nous*) we; (*vous*) you; **on frappe** someone's knocking; **on m'a dit que** I was told that.

oncle *m noun* uncle.

onde *f noun* (*de radio*) wave; **grandes ondes** long wave; **ondes courtes** short wave.

ondulation *f noun* (*de cheveux*) wave.

onduler *verb* (*cheveux*) to be wavy.

ongle *m noun* (finger) nail.

ont *see* **avoir.**

onze *adjective & m noun* eleven.

onzième *adjective & m or f noun* eleventh.

opaque *adjective* opaque.

opéra *m noun* (*musique*) opera; (*édifice*) opera house.

opération *f noun* operation.

opérer *verb* (*en chirurgie*) to operate on (**de** for); **se faire o.** to have an operation.

opinion *f noun* opinion (**sur** about, on).

opposé , -ée
1 *adjective* (*direction, opinion etc*) opposite; (*équipe*) opposing; **o. à** opposed to.
2 *m noun* **l'o.** the opposite (**de** of); **à l'o.** (*côté*) on the opposite side (**de** from, to).

opposer *verb* (*résistance*) to put up (**à** against); (*équipes*) to bring together; **o. quelqu'un à quel-qu'un** to set somebody against somebody

opposer (s') *reflexive verb* (*équipes*) to play against each other; **s'o. à** (*mesure, personne*) to be opposed to, oppose.

opposition *f noun* opposition (**à** to).

opticien , -ienne *m or f noun* optician.

optimiste *adjective* optimistic.

or
1 *m noun* gold; **montre/etc en or** gold watch/*etc*; **d'or** (*règle*) gol-den; **mine d'or** goldmine.
2 *conjunction* (*cependant*) now,

well.

orage *m noun* (thunder)storm.

orageux , -euse *adjective* stormy.

oral , -e, -aux
1 *adjective* oral.
2 *m noun* (*examen*) oral.

orange
1 *f noun* (*fruit*) orange.
2 *adjective & invariable m noun* (*couleur*) orange.

orangeade *f noun* orangeade.

orbite *f noun* (*d'astre*) orbit; (*d'œil*) socket.

orchestre *m noun* (*classique*) orchestra; (*jazz, pop*) band; (*places*) stalls.

ordinaire *adjective* (*habituel, normal*) ordinary; (*médiocre*) ordinary; **d'o.** usually.

ordinateur *m noun* computer.

ordonnance *f noun* (*de médecin*) prescription.

ordonné , -ée *adjective* tidy.

ordonner *verb* to order (**que** (+ *subjunctive*) that); (*médicament etc*) to prescribe; **o. à quelqu'un de faire** to order somebody to do.

ordre *m noun* (*commandement, classement*) order; (*absence de désordre*) tidiness (*of room, person etc*); **en o.** (*chambre etc*) tidy; **mettre en o., mettre de l'o. dans** to tidy (up); **mettre quelque chose dans le bon o.** to put something in the right order; **jusqu'à nouvel o.** until further notice.

ordures *fpl noun* (*débris*) rubbish.

oreille *f noun* ear; **faire la sourde o.** to take no notice, refuse to listen.

oreiller *m noun* pillow.

oreillons *mpl noun* mumps.

organe *m noun* (*de corps*) organ.

organisateur , -trice *m or f noun* organiser.

organisation *f noun* organization.

organiser *verb* to organize; **s'o.** to get organized.

organisme *m noun* (*corps*) body; (*bureaux etc*) organization.

orge *f noun* barley.

orgue
1 *m noun* (*instrument*) organ.
2 *fpl noun* **grandes orgues** great organ.

orgueil *m noun* pride.

orgueilleux , -euse *adjective* proud.

oriental , -e, -aux *adjective* (*côte, pays etc*) eastern; (*du Japon, de la Chine*) far-eastern, oriental.

orientation *f noun* direction; (*de maison*) aspect; **o. professionnelle** careers' advice.

orienté , -ée *adjective* (*appartement etc*) **o. à l'ouest** facing west.

orienter *verb* (*lampe etc*) to position; (*voyageur, élève*) to direct.

orienter (s') *reflexive verb* to find one's bearings *or* direction.

originaire *adjective* **être o. de** (*personne*) to be a native of; (*plat, coutume*) to originate from.

original , -e, -aux
1 *adjective* (*idée, artiste etc*) original.
2 *m noun* (*texte*) original.

originalité *f noun* originality.

origine *f noun* origin; **à l'o.** originally; **d'o.** (*pneu etc*) original; **pays d'o.** country of origin.

ornement *m noun* ornament.

orner *verb* to decorate (**de** with).

orphelin , -ine *m or f noun*

orphan.

orphelinat *m noun* orphanage.

orteil *m noun* toe; **gros o.** big toe.

orthographe *f noun* spelling.

ortie *f noun* nettle.

os *m noun* bone; **trempé jusqu'aux os** soaked to the skin.

oser *verb* to dare; **o. faire** to dare (to) do.

osier *m noun* wicker; **panier d'o.** wicker basket.

otage *m noun* hostage; **prendre quelqu'un en o.** to take somebody hostage.

otarie *f noun* sea lion.

ôter *verb* to take away (**à quelqu'un** from somebody); (*vêtement*) to take off; (*déduire*) to take (away).

ou *conjunction* or; **ou bien** or else; **ou elle ou moi** either her or me.

où *adverb & pronoun* where; **le jour où** the day when; **la table où** the table on which; **par où?** which way?; **d'où?** where from?; **le pays d'où** the country from which.

ouate *f noun* (*pour soins*) cotton wool.

oubli *m noun* **l'o. de quelque chose** forgetting something; **un o.** (*dans une liste etc*) an oversight.

oublier *verb* to forget (**de faire** to do).

ouest *m noun & invariable adjective* west; **d'o.** (*vent*) west(erly); **de l'o.** western.

ouf! *interjection* what a relief!

oui *adverb & invariable m noun* yes; **tu viens, o. ou non?** are you coming or aren't you?; **je crois que o.** I think so.

ouïe *f noun* hearing.

ouïes *fpl noun* (*de poisson*) gills.

ouille! *interjection* ouch!

ouragan *m noun* hurricane.

ourlet *m noun* hem.

ours *m noun* bear; **o. blanc** polar bear.

outil *m noun* tool.

outillage *m noun* tools.

outre
1 *preposition* besides.
2 *adverb* **en o.** besides.

outré , -ée *adjective* (*révolté*) outraged.

ouvert , -erte (*past participle of* **ouvrir**) *adjective* open; (*robinet, gaz*) on.

ouvertement *adverb* openly.

ouverture *f noun* opening; (*trou*) hole.

ouvrage *m noun* (*travail, livre*) work; (*couture*) (needle)work; **un o.** (*travail*) a piece of work.

ouvre-boîtes *invariable m noun* tin opener.

ouvre-bouteilles *invariable m noun* bottle opener.

ouvreuse *f noun* (*de théâtre, de cinéma*) usherette.

ouvrier , -ière
1 *m or f noun* worker; **o. qualifié/ spécialisé** skilled/unskilled worker.
2 *adjective* (*quartier*) working-class; **classe ouvrière** working class.

ouvrir * *verb* to open; (*gaz, radio etc*) to turn on; **j'ai sonné, il a ouvert** I rang and he opened the door.

ouvrir (s') *reflexive verb* (*porte, boîte etc*) to open (up).

ovale *adjective & m noun* oval.

OVNI *m abbreviation* (*objet volant non identifié*) UFO.

oxygène *m noun* oxygen.

P

pacifique
1 *adjective* (*manifestation etc*) peaceful; (*côte etc*) Pacific.
2 *m noun* **le P.** the Pacific.

pagaie *f noun* paddle.

pagaïe , pagaille *f noun* (*désordre*) mess; **en p.** in a mess.

pagayer *verb* to paddle.

page *f noun* (*de livre etc*) page.

paie *f noun* pay, wages.

paiement *m noun* payment.

paillasson *m noun* (door)mat.

paille *f noun* straw; (*pour boire*) (drinking) straw; **tirer à la courte p.** to draw lots.

paillette *f noun* (*d'habit*) sequin; **paillettes** (*de savon*) flakes.

pain *m noun* bread; **un p.** a loaf (of bread); **p. grillé** toast; **p. complet** wholemeal bread; **p. d'épice** gingerbread; **p. de seigle** rye bread; **petit p.** roll.

pair , -e *adjective* (*numéro*) even.

paire *f noun* pair (**de** of).

paisible *adjective* (*vie, endroit*) peaceful.

paître * *verb* to graze.

paix *f noun* peace; (*traité*) peace treaty; **en p.** in peace; **avoir la p.** to have (some) peace and quiet.

Pakistan (le) *m noun* Pakistan.

pakistanais , -aise *adjective & m or f noun* Pakistani.

palais ¹ *m noun* (*château*) palace; **P. de justice** law courts; **p. des sports** sports stadium.

palais ² (*dans la bouche*) palate.

pâle *adjective* pale.

paletot *m noun* (knitted) cardigan.

palette *f noun* (*de peintre*) palette.

pâleur *f noun* paleness.

palier *m noun* (*d'escalier*) landing; **être voisins de p.** to live on the same floor.

pâlir *verb* to turn pale (**de** with).

palissade *f noun* wooden fence.

palme *f noun* palm (leaf); (*de nageur*) flipper.

palmier *m noun* palm (tree).

palper *verb* to feel.

palpitant , -ante *adjective* thrilling.

palpiter *verb* (*cœur*) to throb.

pamplemousse *m noun* grapefruit.

pan! *interjection* bang!

panaché *adjective & m noun* shandy.

pancarte *f noun* sign; (*de manifestant*) placard.

pané , -ée *adjective* breaded.

panier *m noun* basket; **p. à salade** (*ustensile*) salad basket.

panique *f noun* panic.

paniqué , -ée *adjective* panic-stricken.

paniquer *verb* to panic.

panne *f noun* breakdown; **tomber en p.** to break down; **être en p.** to have broken down; **p. d'électricité** blackout, power cut.

panneau , -x *m noun* (*écriteau*) sign; (*de porte etc*) panel; **p. (de signalisation)** road sign; **p. (d'affichage)** hoarding; **p. indicateur** road sign.

panoplie *f noun* (*jouet*) outfit.

panorama *m noun* view.

pansement *m noun* dressing,

bandage; **p. adhésif** sticking plaster.

panser *verb* (*blessure*) to dress.

pantalon *m noun* (pair of) trousers; **en p.** in trousers.

pantin *m noun* puppet, jumping jack.

pantoufle *f noun* slipper.

paon *m noun* peacock.

papa *m noun* dad(dy).

pape *m noun* pope.

papeterie *f noun* (*magasin*) stationer's shop.

papi *m noun Familiar* grand(d)ad.

papier *m noun* (*matière*) paper; **un p.** (*feuille*) a sheet of paper; (*formulaire*) a form; **sac/etc en p.** paper bag/*etc*; **papiers (d'identité)** (identity) papers; **p. hygiénique** toilet paper; **p. à lettres** writing paper; **du p. journal** (some) newspaper; **p. peint** wallpaper; **p. de verre** sandpaper.

papillon *m noun* butterfly; **p. (de nuit)** moth.

paquebot *m noun* (ocean) liner.

pâquerette *f noun* daisy.

Pâques *m or fpl noun* Easter.

paquet *m noun* (*de bonbons etc*) packet; (*colis*) package; (*de cigarettes*) pack(et); (*de cartes*) pack, deck.

par *preposition* (*agent, manière, moyen*) by; **choisi p.** chosen by; **p. le train** by train; **p. le travail** by *or* through work; **apprendre p. un ami** to learn from *or* through a friend; **commencer p. quelque chose** to begin with something.

▮ (*lieu*) through; **p. la porte** through *or* by the door; **jeter p. la fenêtre** to throw out (of) the window; **p. ici/là** (*aller*) this/that way; (*habiter*) around here/there.

▮ (*motif*) out of, from; **p. pitié** out of *or* from pity.

▮ (*temps*) on; **p. un jour d'hiver** on a winter's day; **p. ce froid** in this cold.

▮ (*distributif*) **dix fois p. an/jour** ten times a year/day; **100 francs p. personne** 100 francs per person; **deux p. deux** two by two.

parachute *m noun* parachute.

paradis *m noun* heaven, paradise.

paragraphe *m noun* paragraph.

paraître * *verb* (*sembler*) to seem; (*livre*) to come out; **il paraît qu'il va partir** it appears *or* seems he's leaving.

parallèle *adjective* parallel (**à** with, to).

paralyser *verb* to paralyse.

parapluie *m noun* umbrella.

parasite *m noun* parasite; **parasites** (*à la radio*) interference.

parasol *m noun* sunshade.

paravent *m noun* (folding) screen.

parc *m noun* park; (*de château*) grounds; (*de bébé*) (play)pen; **p. (de stationnement)** car park.

parce que *conjunction* because.

parcelle *f noun* fragment; (*terrain*) plot.

par-ci par-là *adverb* here, there and everywhere.

parcmètre *m noun* parking meter.

parcourir * *verb* (*région*) to travel all over; (*distance*) to cover; (*texte*) to glance through.

parcours *m noun* (*itinéraire*) route; (*distance*) distance.

par-dessous *preposition* & *adverb* under(neath).

pardessus *m noun* overcoat.

par-dessus *preposition* & *adverb*

over (the top of); **p. tout** above all.

pardon *m noun* p.! (*excusez-moi*) sorry!; **demander p.** to apologize (à to).

pardonner *verb* to forgive; **p. quelque chose à quelqu'un** to forgive somebody for something; **p. à quelqu'un d'avoir fait quelque chose** to forgive somebody for doing something.

pare-brise *invariable m noun* windscreen.

pare-chocs *invariable m noun* bumper.

pareil , -eille
  1 *adjective* similar; **p. à** the same as; **être pareils** to be the same; **un p. désordre**/*etc* such a mess/*etc*.
  2 *adverb Familiar* the same.

parent , -ente
  1 *m or f noun* relative.
  2 *mpl noun* (*père et mère*) parents.
  3 *adjective* related (**de** to).

parenthèse *f noun* bracket.

paresse *f noun* laziness.

paresseux , -euse *adjective & m or f noun* lazy (person).

parfait , -aite *adjective* perfect; **p.!** excellent!

parfaitement *adverb* perfectly; (*certainement*) certainly.

parfois *adverb* sometimes.

parfum *m noun* (*odeur*) fragrance; (*goût*) flavour; (*liquide*) perfume.

parfumé , -ée *adjective* (*savon, fleur*) scented; **p. au café**/*etc* coffee-/*etc* flavoured.

parfumer *verb* to perfume; (*glace, crème*) to flavour (**à** with).

parfumer (se) *reflexive verb* to put on perfume.

parfumerie *f noun* perfume shop.

pari *m noun* bet; **p. mutuel urbain**

= the tote.

parier *verb* to bet (**sur** on, **que** that).

Paris *m or f noun* Paris.

parisien , -ienne
  1 *adjective* Parisian; **la banlieue parisienne** the Paris suburbs.
  2 *m or f noun* Parisian.

parking *m noun* car park.

parlement *m noun* parliament.

parlementaire *m or f noun* member of parliament.

parler *verb*
  1 (*s'exprimer*) to talk, speak (**de** about, of; **à** to).
  2 (*langue*) to speak.

parler (se) *reflexive verb* (*langue*) to be spoken.

parmi *preposition* among(st).

paroi *f noun* (inside) wall; (*de rocher*) (rock) face.

paroisse *f noun* parish.

paroissial , -e, -aux *adjective* **église**/*etc* **paroissiale** parish church/*etc*.

parole *f noun* (*mot, promesse*) word; **adresser la p. à** to speak to; **prendre la p.** to speak; **demander la p.** to ask to speak.

parquet *m noun* (parquet) floor.

parrain *m noun* godfather.

parrainer *verb* (*course etc*) to sponsor.

parsemé , -ée *adjective* **p. de** (*sol*) strewn (all over) with.

part *f noun* (*portion*) share; (*de gâteau*) portion; **prendre p. à** (*activité*) to take part in; (*la joie d'une personne*) to share; **de toutes parts** from *or* on all sides; **de p. et d'autre** on both sides; **d'autre p.** (*d'ailleurs*) moreover; **de la p. de** (*provenance*) from; **c'est de la p. de qui?** (*au télé-*

phone) who's calling?; **quelque p.** somewhere; **nulle p.** nowhere; **autre p.** somewhere else; **à p.** (_mettre_) aside; (_excepté_) apart from; (_personne_) different.

partage _m noun_ (_de gâteau, trésor etc_) sharing.

partager _verb_ (_repas, joie etc_) to share (**avec** with).

partenaire _m or f noun_ partner.

parterre _m noun_ (_de jardin_) flower bed.

parti , -ie
1 _past participle of_ **partir**.
2 _m noun_ (_politique_) party.

participant , -ante _m or f noun_ participant.

participation _f noun_ participation; **p. (aux frais)** contribution (_towards expenses_).

participe _m noun_ Grammaire participle.

participer _verb_ **p. à** (_jeu etc_) to take part in; (_frais, joie_) to share (in).

particularité _f noun_ peculiarity.

particulier , -ière _adjective_ (_spécial_) particular; (_privé_) private; (_bizarre_) peculiar; **en p.** (_surtout_) in particular.

particulièrement _adverb_ particularly.

partie _f noun_ part; (_de cartes, tennis etc_) game; **en p.** partly; **faire p. de** to be a part of; (_club etc_) to belong to.

partir * _verb_ (_auxiliary_ **être**) (_aller_) to go; (_s'en aller_) to go, leave; (_coup de feu_) to go off; (_tache_) to come out; **à p. de** (_date, prix_) from.

partisan _m noun_ supporter; **être p. de quelque chose/de faire** to be in favour of something/of doing.

partition _f noun_ (_musique_) score.

partout _adverb_ everywhere; **p. où tu vas** _or_ **iras** everywhere _or_ wherever you go.

paru, -ue _past participle of_ **paraître**.

parvenir * _verb_ (_auxiliary_ **être**) **p. à** (_lieu_) to reach; **p. à faire** to manage to do.

pas [1] _adverb_ not; (**ne**) ... **p.** not; **je ne sais p.** I don't know; **p. de pain**/_etc_ no bread/_etc_; **p. encore** not yet; **p. du tout** not at all; **p. mal de gens** quite a few people.

pas [2] _m noun_ step; (_allure_) pace; (_bruit_) footstep; (_trace_) footprint; **rouler au p.** (_véhicule_) to go dead slow; **au p. (cadencé)** in step; **faire les cent p.** to walk up and down; **faux p.** (_en marchant_) stumble; **le p. de la porte** the doorstep.

passable _adjective_ (_travail, résultat_) (just) average.

passage _m noun_ passing; (_traversée en bateau_) crossing; (_extrait, couloir_) passage; (_droit_) right of way; (_chemin_) path; **p. clouté** _or_ **pour piétons** _or_ **protégé** (pedestrian) crossing; **p. souterrain** subway; **p. à niveau** level crossing; **'p. interdit'** 'no through traffic'; **'cédez le p.'** (_au carrefour_) 'give way'.

passager , -ère _m or f noun_ passenger.

passant , -ante _m or f noun_ passer-by.

passe _f noun_ Football etc pass; **mot de p.** password.

passé , -ée
1 _adjective_ (_temps_) past; (_couleur_) faded; **la semaine passée** last week; **dix heures passées** after ten (o'clock); **être passé** (_per-_

sonne) to have been; (*orage*) to be over; **avoir vingt ans passés** to be over twenty.
2 *m noun* past; *Grammaire* past (tense).

passe-passe *invariable m noun* **tour de p.** conjuring trick.

passeport *m noun* passport.

passer *verb*
1 (*auxiliary* **être**) (*se déplacer*) to pass (**à** to, **de** from); (*traverser*) to go through *or* over; (*facteur*) to come; (*temps*) to pass, go by; (*film*) to be shown, be on; (*douleur*) to pass; (*couleur*) to fade; **p. devant** (*maison etc*) to go past, pass (by); **p. à la boulangerie** *or* **chez le boulanger** to go round to the baker's; **laisser p.** (*personne, lumière*) to let through; **p. prendre** to fetch; **p. voir quelqu'un** to drop in on somebody; **p. pour** (*riche etc*) to be taken for; **p. en** (*seconde etc*) (*à l'école*) to pass up into; (*en voiture*) to change up to.
2 (*auxiliary* **avoir**) (*frontière etc*) to cross; (*donner*) to pass, hand (**à** to); (*temps*) to spend (**à faire** doing); (*disque, chemise, film*) to put on; (*examen*) to take; (*thé*) to strain; (*café*) to filter; (*limites*) to go beyond; (*visite médicale*) to have; **p. quelque chose à quelqu'un** (*caprice etc*) to grant somebody something; **p. un coup d'éponge/etc à quelque chose** to go over something with a sponge/etc.

passer (se) *reflexive verb* to take place, happen; (*douleur*) to go (away); **se p. de** to do *or* go without; **ça s'est bien passé** it went off well.

passerelle *f noun* footbridge; (*d'avion, de bateau*) gangway.

passe-temps *invariable m noun* pastime.

passif , -ive
1 *adjective* passive.
2 *m noun Grammaire* passive.

passion *f noun* passion; **avoir la p. des voitures/d'écrire** to have a passion for cars/writing.

passionnant , -ante *adjective* thrilling.

passionné , -ée *adjective* passionate; **p. de quelque chose** passionately fond of something.

passionner *verb* to thrill; **se p. pour** to have a passion for.

passoire *f noun* sieve; (*à thé*) strainer; (*à légumes*) colander.

pasteurisé , -ée pasteurized.

pastille *f noun* pastille, lozenge.

patauger *verb* to wade (*in the mud etc*); (*barboter*) to splash about.

pâte *f noun* paste; (*à pain*) dough; (*à tarte*) pastry; **pâtes (alimentaires)** pasta; **p. dentifrice** toothpaste; **p. à modeler** plasticine ®.

pâté *m noun* (*charcuterie*) pâté; **p. (en croûte)** meat pie; **p. (de sable)** sand castle; **p. de maisons** block of houses.

pâtée *f noun* (*pour chien, chat*) dog food, cat food.

paternel , -elle *adjective* paternal.

patiemment *adverb* patiently.

patience *f noun* patience.

patient , -ente
1 *adjective* patient.
2 *m or f noun* (*malade*) patient.

patin *m noun* **p. (à glace)** (ice) skate; **p. à roulettes** roller-skate.

patinage *m noun* skating.

patiner *verb* (*en sport*) to skate; (*roue*) to spin round.

patinoire *f noun* skating rink.

pâtisserie *f noun* pastry; (*magasin*) cake shop.

pâtissier , -ière *m or f noun* pastrycook.

patrie *f noun* (native) country.

patriote
1 *m or f noun* patriot.
2 *adjective* patriotic.

patriotique *adjective* (*chant etc*) patriotic.

patron , -onne
1 *m or f noun* (*chef*) boss.
2 *m noun* (*modèle de papier*) pattern.

patrouille *f noun* patrol.

patrouiller *verb* to patrol.

patte *f noun* leg; (*de chat, chien*) paw; **marcher à quatre pattes** to crawl.

pâturage *m noun* pasture.

paume *f noun* (*de main*) palm.

paupière *f noun* eyelid.

pause *f noun* (*arrêt*) break; **p. de midi** lunch break.

pauvre
1 *adjective* poor.
2 *m or f noun* poor man *or* woman; **les pauvres** the poor.

pauvreté *f noun* (*besoin*) poverty.

pavé *m noun* (*de rue*) paving stone.

paver *verb* to pave.

pavillon *m noun* (*maison*) (detached) house; (*drapeau*) flag.

payant , -ante *adjective* (*hôte, spectateur*) paying; (*place, entrée*) that one has to pay for.

paye *f noun* pay, wages.

payer *verb* to pay; (*service, objet*) to pay for; **p. quelqu'un pour faire** to pay somebody to do *or* for doing.

pays *m noun* country; **du p.** (*vin,*

gens) local; **le P. de Galles** Wales.

paysage *m noun* landscape.

paysan , -anne *m or f noun* (small) farmer.

Pays-Bas (les) *mpl noun* the Netherlands.

PCV *abbreviation* (*paiement contre vérification*) reverse-charge call; **téléphoner en PCV** to reverse the charges.

PDG *m abbreviation* = **président directeur général.**

péage *m noun* (*droit*) toll; (*lieu*) tollbooth.

peau , -x *f noun* skin; (*de fruit*) peel, skin; (*cuir*) hide.

pêche [1] *f noun* fishing; (*poissons*) catch; **p. (à la ligne)** angling; **aller à la p.** to go fishing.

pêche [2] *f noun* (*fruit*) peach.

péché *m noun* sin.

pêcher [1] *verb*
1 (*pratiquer la pêche*) to fish.
2 (*attraper*) to catch.

pêcher [2] *m noun* peach tree.

pêcheur *m noun* fisherman; (*à la ligne*) angler.

pédale *f noun* pedal; **p. de frein** footbrake (pedal).

pédaler *verb* to pedal.

pédalo *m noun* pedal boat.

pédiatre *m or f noun* children's doctor.

pédicure *m or f noun* chiropodist.

peigne *m noun* comb; **se donner un coup de p.** to give one's hair a comb.

peigner *verb* (*cheveux*) to comb; **p. quelqu'un** to comb somebody's hair.

peigner (se) *reflexive verb* to comb one's hair.

peignoir *m noun* dressing gown;

p. (de bain) bathrobe.

peindre * *verb* to paint; **p. en bleu**/*etc* to paint blue/*etc*.

peine (à) *adverb* hardly.

peine *f noun* (*châtiment*) **la p. de mort** the death penalty; **p. de prison** prison sentence.

▪ (*chagrin*) sorrow; **avoir de la p.** to be upset; **faire de la p. à** to upset.

▪ (*effort, difficulté*) trouble; **se donner de la p.** to go to a lot of trouble (**pour faire** to do); **avec p.** with difficulty; **ça vaut la p. d'attendre**/*etc* it's worth (while) waiting/*etc*; **ce n'est pas** *or* **ça ne vaut pas la p.** it's not worth it.

peint , -e *see* peindre.

peintre *m noun* painter; **p. (en bâtiment)** (house) painter.

peinture *f noun* (*tableau, activité*) painting; (*matière*) paint; **'p. fraîche'** 'wet paint'.

pelage *m noun* (*d'animal*) coat, fur.

peler *verb* to peel.

pelle *f noun* shovel; (*d'enfant*) spade; (*pour la poussière*) dustpan.

pelleteuse *f noun* mechanical digger *or* shovel.

pellicule *f noun* (*pour photos*) film; (*couche*) layer; **pellicules** (*dans les cheveux*) dandruff.

pelote *f noun* (*de laine*) ball.

peloton *m noun* (*cyclistes*) pack.

pelotonner (se) *reflexive verb* to curl up (into a ball).

pelouse *f noun* lawn.

peluche *f noun* **peluches** (*flocons*) fluff; **jouet en p.** soft toy; **chien en p.** (*jouet*) furry dog; **ours en p.** teddy bear.

penalty *m noun* Football penalty.

penché , -ée *adjective* leaning.

pencher *verb*
1 (*incliner*) (*objet*) to tilt; (*tête*) to lean.
2 (*s'incliner*) (*arbre etc*) to lean (over).

pencher (se) *reflexive verb* to lean (over *or* forward); **se p. par** (*fenêtre*) to lean out of.

pendant *preposition* during; **p. la nuit** during the night; **p. deux mois** for two months; **p. que** while.

penderie *f noun* wardrobe.

pendre *verb* to hang (**à** from); **p. quelqu'un** to hang somebody (**pour** for); **se p.** (*se suspendre*) to hang (**à** from).

pendu , -ue *adjective* (*objet*) hanging (**à** from).

pendule *f noun* clock.

pénétrer *verb* **p. dans** to enter; (*profondément*) to penetrate (into).

pénible *adjective* difficult; (*douloureux*) painful.

péniblement *adverb* with difficulty.

péniche *f noun* barge.

pénicilline *f noun* penicillin.

pensée *f noun* (*idée*) thought.

penser *verb*
1 (*songer, réfléchir*) to think (**à** of, about); **p. à quelque chose/à faire quelque chose** (*ne pas oublier*) to remember something/to do something.
2 (*estimer*) to think (**que** that); **je pensais rester** I was thinking of staying; **je pense réussir** I hope to succeed; **que pensez-vous de?** what do you think of *or* about?

pension [1] *f noun* boarding school; (*somme à payer*) board; **être en p.** to board (**chez** with); **p. com-**

plète full board.

pension [2] *f noun* (*de retraite etc*) pension.

pensionnaire *m or f noun* (*élève*) boarder; (*d'hôtel*) resident; (*de famille*) lodger.

pensionnat *m noun* boarding school.

pente *f noun* slope; **en p.** sloping.

Pentecôte *f noun* Whitsun.

pépin *m noun* (*de fruit*) pip.

perçant , -ante *adjective* (*cri, froid*) piercing; (*yeux*) sharp.

percepteur *m noun* tax collector.

percer *verb*
1 (*transpercer*) to pierce; (*avec une perceuse*) to drill (a hole in); (*ouverture*) to make.
2 (*apparaître*) to break through; (*devenir célèbre*) to make a name for oneself.

perceuse *f noun* (*outil*) drill.

perche *f noun* (*bâton*) pole.

percher (se) *reflexive verb* (*oiseau*) to perch.

perchoir *m noun* perch.

perçu , -ue *past participle of* percevoir.

percuter *verb* (*véhicule*) to crash into.

perdant , -ante *m or f noun* loser.

perdre *verb* to lose; (*gaspiller*) to waste; (*habitude*) to get rid of; **p. de vue** to lose sight of.

perdre (se) *reflexive verb* (*s'égarer*) to get lost; **je m'y perds** I'm lost *or* confused.

perdrix *f noun* partridge.

perdu , -ue *adjective* lost; (*gaspillé*) wasted; **c'est du temps p.** it's a waste of time.

père *m noun* father.

perfection *f noun* perfection; **à la**

p. perfectly.

perfectionné , -ée *adjective* (*machine*) advanced.

perfectionner *verb* to improve; **se p. en anglais/***etc* to improve one's English/*etc*.

perforeuse *f noun* (paper) punch.

performance *f noun* (*d'athlète etc*) performance.

péril *m noun* danger, peril.

périlleux , -euse *adjective* dangerous.

périmé , -ée *adjective* (*billet*) expired.

période *f noun* period.

périphérique *adjective & m noun* (**boulevard**) **p.** (motorway) ring road.

perle *f noun* (*bijou*) pearl; (*de bois, verre*) bead.

permanence *f noun* (*salle d'étude*) study room; **être de p.** to be on duty; **en p.** permanently.

permanent , -ente
1 *adjective* permanent; (*spectacle*) continuous.
2 *f noun* (*coiffure*) perm.

permettre * *verb* to allow; **p. à quelqu'un de faire** to allow somebody to do; **vous permettez?** may I?; **je ne peux pas me le p.** I can't afford it.

permis , -ise
1 *adjective* allowed.
2 *m noun* licence; **p. de conduire** driving licence; **passer son p. de conduire** to take one's driving test.

permission *f noun* permission; (*congé de soldat*) leave; **demander la p.** to ask permission (**de faire** to do).

perpendiculaire *adjective* perpendicular (à to).

perpétuel , -elle adjective (incessant) continual.

perron m noun (front) steps.

perroquet m noun parrot.

perruche f noun budgerigar.

perruque f noun wig.

persécuter verb to persecute.

persécution f noun persecution.

persévérance f noun perseverance.

persévérer verb to persevere (dans in).

persil m noun parsley.

persister verb to persist (à faire in doing, dans quelque chose in something).

personnage m noun (important) person; (de livre, film) character.

personnalité f noun personality.

personne
1 f noun person; **personnes** people; **grande p.** grown-up; **en p.** in person.
2 pronoun nobody; **je ne vois p.** I don't see anybody; **mieux que p.** better than anybody.

personnel , -elle
1 adjective personal.
2 m noun staff.

personnellement adverb personally.

perspective f noun (idée, possibilité) prospect (de of).

persuader verb to persuade (quelqu'un de faire somebody to do); **être persuadé que** to be convinced that.

persuasion f noun persuasion.

perte f noun loss; (gaspillage) waste (de temps/d'argent of time/money).

perturbation f noun disruption.

perturber verb (trafic etc) to disrupt; (personne) to disturb.

pesant , -ante adjective heavy.

pesanteur f noun (force) gravity.

pèse-personne m noun (plural **pèse-personnes**) (bathroom) scales.

peser verb to weigh; **p. lourd** to be heavy.

pessimiste adjective pessimistic.

peste f noun (maladie) plague.

pétale m noun petal.

pétanque f noun (jeu) bowls.

pétard m noun firecracker.

pétillant , -ante adjective fizzy; (vin, yeux) sparkling.

pétiller verb (champagne) to fizz; (yeux) to sparkle.

petit , -ite
1 adjective small, little; (bruit, coup) slight; (jeune) little; **tout p.** tiny; **une femme de petite taille** a short woman; **un p. Français** a French boy.
2 m or f noun little one; (personne) small person; (à l'école) junior; **petits** (d'animal) young.
3 adverb **p. à p.** little by little.

petite-fille f noun (plural **petites-filles**) granddaughter.

petit-fils m noun (plural **petits-fils**) grandson.

petits-enfants mpl noun grandchildren.

petit-suisse m noun soft cheese (for dessert).

pétrole m noun oil.

pétrolier m noun (navire) (oil) tanker.

peu adverb (manger etc) not much, little; **un p.** a little, a bit; **p. de sel/de temps**/etc not much salt/time/etc; **un p. de fromage**/etc a little cheese/etc; **p. de gens**/etc few people/etc; **un (tout) petit p.** a (tiny) little bit; **un p. plus** a little more; **p. intéressant**/etc not very interesting/etc; **p. de chose** not much; **p. à p.** little by little; **à p. près** more or less; **p. après** shortly after.

peuple m noun people.

peuplé , -ée adjective **très/peu/ etc p.** highly/sparsely/etc populated; **p. de** populated by.

peur f noun fear; **avoir p.** to be afraid or frightened (**de quelque chose/quelqu'un** of something/ somebody; **de faire** to do, of doing); **faire p. à** to frighten; **de p. que** (+ subjunctive) for fear that.

peureux , -euse adjective easily frightened.

peut , peuvent , peux see **pouvoir**.

peut-être adverb perhaps, maybe; **p. qu'il viendra** perhaps or maybe he'll come.

phare m noun (pour bateaux) lighthouse; (de véhicule) headlight; **faire un appel de phares** to flash one's lights.

pharmacie f noun chemist's shop; (armoire) medicine cabinet.

pharmacien , -ienne m or f noun chemist.

philatélie f noun stamp collecting.

philatéliste m or f noun stamp collector.

philippin , -ine adjective & m or f noun Filipino.

Philippines (les) fpl noun the Philippines.

philosophe
  1 m or f noun philosopher.
  2 adjective philosophical.

philosophie f noun philosophy.

phonétique adjective phonetic.

phoque m noun seal.

photo f noun (technique) photography; (cliché) photo; **prendre une p. de** to take a photo of; **se faire prendre en p.** to have one's photo taken.

photocopie f noun photocopy.

photocopier verb to photocopy.

photocopieuse f noun (machine) photocopier.

photographe m or f noun photographer.

photographie f noun (technique) photography; (cliché) photograph.

photographier verb to photograph.

photographique adjective photographic.

photomaton ® m noun photo booth.

phrase f noun sentence.

physique
  1 adjective physical.
  2 m noun (corps, aspect) physique; (science) physics.

physiquement adverb physically.

pianiste m or f noun pianist.

piano m noun piano.

pic m noun (cime) peak.

pic (à) adverb **couler à p.** to sink to the bottom.

pichet m noun jug.

pickpocket m noun pickpocket.

picorer verb to peck.

picoter verb (yeux) to make smart; **les yeux me picotent** my eyes are smarting.

pièce f noun (de maison etc) room; (de pantalon) patch; **p. (de monnaie)** coin; **p. (de théâtre)** play;

p. d'identité identity card; **pièces détachées** (*de véhicule etc*) spare parts; **cinq dollars p.** five dollars each.

pied *m noun* foot; (*de meuble*) leg; (*de verre, lampe*) base; **à p.** on foot; **au p. de** at the foot of; **coup de p.** kick; **donner un coup de p. (à quelqu'un)** to kick (somebody).

piège *m noun* trap.

piéger *verb* (*animal*) to trap; (*voiture*) to booby-trap.

pierre *f noun* stone; (*précieuse*) gem; **p. (à briquet)** flint.

piétiner *verb*
1 p. quelque chose (*en trépignant*) to stamp on something; (*en marchant*) to trample on something.
2 p. d'impatience to stamp (one's feet) impatiently.

piéton *m noun* pedestrian.

piétonne *adjective* **rue p.** pedestrian(ized) street.

pieu , -x *m noun* post, stake.

pieuvre *f noun* octopus.

pigeon *m noun* pigeon.

pile
1 *f noun* (*électrique*) battery; (*tas*) pile; **radio à piles** battery radio; **en p.** in a pile; **p. (ou face)?** heads (or tails)?
2 *adverb Familiar* **s'arrêter p.** to stop short; **à deux heures p.** on the dot of two.

pilier *m noun* pillar.

pillage *m noun* looting.

piller *verb* to loot.

pilotage *m noun* **poste de p.** cockpit.

pilote *m noun* (*d'avion*) pilot; (*de voiture*) driver.

piloter *verb* (*avion*) to fly;

(*voiture*) to drive.

pilule *f noun* pill; **prendre la p.** to be on the pill.

piment *m noun* pepper.

pimenté , -ée *adjective* spicy.

pin *m noun* (*arbre*) pine; **pomme de p.** pine cone.

pince *f noun* (*outil*) pliers; (*de cycliste*) clip; (*de crabe*) pincer; **p. (à linge)** (clothes) peg; **p. (à épiler)** tweezers; **p. (à sucre)** sugar tongs; **p. à cheveux** hairgrip.

pinceau , -x *m noun* (paint)brush.

pincée *f noun* (*de sel etc*) pinch (**de** of).

pincer *verb* to pinch; **se p. le doigt** to get one's finger caught (**dans** in).

pingouin *m noun* penguin.

ping-pong *m noun* table tennis.

pin's *invariable m noun* badge, lapel pin.

pioche *f noun* pick(axe).

piocher *verb* to dig (with a pick).

pion *m noun* (*au jeu de dames*) piece; *Échecs* pawn.

pipe *f noun* pipe; **fumer la p.** to smoke a pipe.

pipi *m noun* **faire p.** *Familiar* to go for a pee.

piquant , -ante *adjective* (*plante, barbe*) prickly.

pique *m noun* (*couleur*) *Cartes* spades.

pique-nique *m noun* picnic.

pique-niquer *verb* to picnic.

piquer *verb*
1 (*percer*) to prick; (*langue, yeux*) to sting; (*coudre*) to (machine-) stitch; **p. quelqu'un** (*abeille*) to sting somebody; **p. quelque chose dans** (*enfoncer*) to stick something into; **p. une colère** *Familiar* to fly into a rage.

2 (*avion*) to dive; (*moutarde etc*) to be hot.

piquet *m noun* (*pieu*) stake; (*de tente*) peg.

piqûre *f noun* (*d'abeille*) sting; (*avec une seringue*) injection.

pirate *m noun* pirate; **p. de l'air** hijacker.

pire

1 *adjective* worse (**que** than); **le p. moment**/*etc* the worst moment/ *etc*.

2 *m or f noun* **le** *or* **la p.** the worst.

piscine *f noun* swimming pool.

pissenlit *m noun* dandelion.

pistache *f noun* pistachio.

piste *f noun* (*traces*) trail; (*de course*) racetrack; (*de cirque*) ring; (*de patinage*) rink; **p. (d'envol)** runway; **p. cyclable** cycle track; **p. de danse** dance floor; **p. de ski** ski run *or* slope.

pistolet *m noun* gun; **p. à eau** water pistol.

pitié *f noun* pity; **j'ai p. de lui** I feel sorry for him.

pittoresque *adjective* picturesque.

pivoter *verb* (*personne*) to swing round; (*fauteuil*) to swivel.

pizza *f noun* pizza.

pizzeria *f noun* pizzeria.

placard *m noun* cupboard.

place *f noun* (*endroit, rang*) place; (*espace*) room; (*lieu public*) square; (*siège*) seat, place; (*emploi*) job; **p. de parking** parking place *or* space; **à la p. (de)** instead (of); **à votre p.** in your place; **sur p.** on the spot; **en p.** in place; **mettre en p.** (*installer*) to set up; **changer de p.** to change places; **changer quelque chose de p.** to move something.

placement *m noun* (*d'argent*) investment.

placer *verb* to place; (*invité, spectateur*) to seat; (*argent*) to invest (**dans** in).

placer (se) *reflexive verb* (*debout*) to stand; (*s'asseoir*) to sit; **se p. troisième**/*etc* (*en sport*) to come third/*etc*.

plafond *m noun* ceiling.

plage *f noun* beach; **p. arrière** (*de voiture*) (back) window shelf.

plaie *f noun* wound; (*coupure*) cut.

plaindre * *verb* to feel sorry for.

plaindre (se) *reflexive verb* to complain (**de** about, **que** that); **se p. de** (*douleur*) to complain of.

plaine *f noun* plain.

plainte *f noun* complaint; (*cri*) moan.

plaire * *verb* **p. à quelqu'un** to please somebody; **elle lui plaît** he likes her; **ça me plaît** I like it; **s'il vous** *or* **te plaît** please.

plaire (se) *reflexive verb* (*à Paris etc*) to like *or* enjoy it.

plaisanter *verb* to joke (**sur** about).

plaisanterie *f noun* joke; **par p.** for a joke.

plaisir *m noun* pleasure; **faire p. à** to please; **pour le p.** for fun; **avec p.!** with pleasure.

plan *m noun* (*projet, dessin*) plan; (*de ville*) map; **au premier p.** in the foreground.

planche *f noun* board; **p. à repasser** ironing board; **p. (à roulettes)** skateboard; **faire de la p. (à roulettes)** to go skateboarding; **p. (à voile)** sailboard; **faire de la p. (à voile)** to go windsurfing.

plancher *m noun* floor.

planer *verb* (*oiseau, avion*) to

glide.

planète *f noun* planet.

plante [1] *f noun* plant; **p. verte** house plant.

plante [2] *f noun* **p. des pieds** sole (of the foot).

planter *verb* (*fleur etc*) to plant; (*clou, couteau*) to drive in; **se p. devant** to come *or* go and stand in front of, plant oneself in front of.

plaque *f noun* plate; (*de verre, verglas*) sheet; (*de chocolat*) bar; **p. chauffante** hotplate; **p. d'immatriculation** number plate.

plaqué , -ée *adjective* **p. or** gold-plated.

plaquer *verb Rugby* to tackle; (*aplatir*) to flatten (**contre** against).

plastique *adjective & m noun* (*matière*) **p.** plastic; **en p.** (*bouteille etc*) plastic.

plat , plate
 1 *adjective* flat; **à p. ventre** flat on one's face; **à p.** (*pneu, batterie*) flat; **poser à p.** to put down flat; **assiette plate** dinner plate; **eau plate** still water.
 2 *m noun* (*récipient, nourriture*) dish; (*partie du repas*) course; **p. principal** main course; **p. cuisiné** ready meal; **'p. du jour'** 'today's special'.

platane *m noun* plane tree.

plateau , -x *m noun* (*pour servir*) tray; **p. à fromages** cheeseboard.

plate-forme *f noun* (*plural* **plates-formes**) platform; **p. pétrolière** oil rig.

plâtre *m noun* (*matière*) plaster; **un p.** a plaster cast; **dans le p.** in plaster.

plâtrer *verb* (*bras, jambe*) to put in plaster.

plein , pleine
 1 *adjective* full (**de** of); **en pleine mer** out at sea; **en pleine figure** right in the face.
 2 *preposition & adverb* **des billes p. les poches** pockets full of marbles; **du chocolat p. la figure** chocolate all over one's face; **p. de lettres/d'argent**/*etc Familiar* lots of letters/money/*etc*.
 3 *m noun* **faire le p. (d'essence)** to fill up (the tank).

pleurer *verb* to cry.

pleuvoir * *verb* to rain; **il pleut** it's raining.

pli *m noun* (*de papier*) fold; (*de jupe*) pleat; (*de pantalon*) crease; **(faux) p.** crease; **mise en plis** (*coiffure*) set.

pliant , -ante *adjective* (*chaise etc*) folding.

plier *verb* to bend; (*drap, vêtements*) to fold.

plier (se) *reflexive verb* (*lit, chaise etc*) to fold (up).

plissé , -ée *adjective* (*tissu, jupe*) pleated.

plisser *verb* (*front*) to wrinkle; (*yeux*) to screw up.

plomb *m noun* (*métal*) lead; (*fusible*) fuse; **plombs** (*de chasse*) lead shot; **essence sans p.** unleaded petrol.

plombage *m noun* (*de dent*) filling.

plomber *verb* (*dent*) to fill.

plomberie *f noun* plumbing.

plombier *m noun* plumber.

plongée *f noun* (*sport*) diving.

plongeoir *m noun* diving board.

plongeon *m noun* dive.

plonger *verb*
 1 (*personne*) to dive.
 2 (*mettre*) to plunge (**dans** into).

plongeur , -euse *m or f noun*
diver.

plu *see* **plaire, pleuvoir.**

pluie *f noun* rain; **sous la p.** in the
rain.

plume *f noun* (*d'oiseau*) feather;
(*de stylo*) (pen) nib; **stylo à p.**
(fountain) pen.

plumer *verb* (*volaille*) to pluck.

plupart (la) *f noun* most; **la p. des
cas** most cases; **la p. du temps**
most of the time; **la p. d'entre
eux** most of them; **pour la p.**
mostly.

pluriel , -ielle *adjective & m noun*
plural; **au p.** in the plural.

plus [1] *adverb* (*dans les comparai-
sons*) (*travailler etc*) more (**que**
than); **p. d'un kilo/de dix** more
than a kilo/ten; **p. de thé** more
tea; **p. beau** more beautiful (**que**
than); **p. tard** later; **p. petit** smaller; **de p. en p.** more and more; **p.
ou moins** more or less; **en p.** in
addition (**de** to); **de p.** more (**que**
than); (*en outre*) moreover; (*âgé*)
de p. de dix ans over ten; **j'ai dix
ans de p. qu'elle** I'm ten years
older than she is; **il est p. de cinq
heures** it's after five.

    ■ (*avec les superlatifs*) **le p.** (*tra-
vailler etc*) (the) most; **le p. beau**
the most beautiful (**de** in); **le p.
grand** the biggest (**de** in); **j'ai le p.
de livres** I have (the) most books.

plus [2] *adverb* (*exprime la négation*) **il ne l'aime p.** he doesn't
love her any more; **il n'y a p. de
pain/d'argent** there's no more
bread/money; **il n'a p. de pain** he
has no more bread, he doesn't
have any more bread; **je ne la
reverrai p.** I won't see her again.

plus [3] *preposition* plus; **deux p.
deux** two plus two; **il fait p. deux
(degrés)** it's two degrees above

freezing.

plusieurs *adjective & pronoun*
several.

plutôt *adverb* rather (**que** than).

pluvieux , -euse *adjective* rainy.

pneu *m noun* (*plural* -s) tyre.

pneumatique *adjective* **matelas
p.** air-bed; **canot p.** rubber
dinghy.

poche *f noun* pocket; (*de kangourou*) pouch.

pocher *verb* (*œufs*) to poach; **p.
l'œil à quelqu'un** to give somebody a black eye.

pochette *f noun* (*sac*) bag; (*d'allumettes*) book; (*de disque*) sleeve;
(*sac à main*) (clutch) bag.

poêle
    1 *m noun* stove.
    2 *f noun* **p. (à frire)** frying pan.

poème *m noun* poem.

poésie *f noun* poetry; (*poème*)
poem.

poète *m noun* poet.

poétique *adjective* poetic.

poids *m noun* weight; **au p.** by
weight.

poids lourd *m noun* (heavy)
lorry.

poignard *m noun* dagger.

poignarder *verb* to stab.

poignée *f noun* (*quantité*) handful
(**de** of); (*de porte etc*) handle; **p.
de main** handshake; **donner une
p. de main à** to shake hands with.

poignet *m noun* wrist; (*de chemise*) cuff.

poil *m noun* hair; (*pelage*) fur.

poilu , -ue *adjective* hairy.

poinçonner *verb* to punch.

poing *m noun* fist; **coup de p.**
punch.

point *m noun* (*lieu, score etc*)

point; (*sur i, à l'horizon*) dot; (*tache*) spot; (*note scolaire*) mark; (*de couture*) stitch; **sur le p. de faire** about to do; **p. (final)** full stop; **p. d'exclamation** exclamation mark; **p. d'interrogation** question mark; **points de suspension** suspension points; **p. de vue** (*opinion*) point of view; **à p.** (*steak*) medium rare; **au p. mort** (*véhicule*) in neutral; **p. de côté** (*douleur*) stitch (in one's side).

pointe *f noun* (*extrémité*) tip; (*clou*) nail; **sur la p. des pieds** on tiptoe; **en p.** pointed.

pointer *verb*
1 (*cocher*) to tick (off); (*braquer*) to point (**sur** at).
2 p. vers to point towards.

pointillé *m noun* dotted line.

pointu , -ue *adjective* (*en pointe*) pointed.

pointure *f noun* (*de chaussure, gant*) size.

point-virgule *m noun* (*plural* **points-virgules**) semicolon.

poire *f noun* pear.

poireau , -x *m noun* leek.

poirier *m noun* pear tree.

pois *m noun* pea; **petits p.** (garden) peas; **p. chiche** chickpea.

poison *m noun* poison.

poisseux , -euse *adjective* sticky.

poisson *m noun* fish; **p. rouge** goldfish.

poissonnerie *f noun* fish shop.

poissonnier , -ière *m or f noun* fishmonger.

poitrine *f noun* chest; (*de femme*) bust.

poivre *m noun* pepper.

poivré , -ée *adjective* (*piquant*) peppery.

poivrer *verb* to pepper.

poivrière *f noun* pepperpot.

poivron *m noun* (*légume*) pepper.

pôle *m noun* **p. Nord/Sud** North/South Pole.

poli , -ie *adjective* (*courtois*) polite (**avec** to, with); (*lisse*) polished.

police [1] *f noun* police; **p. secours** emergency services.

police [2] *f noun* **p. (d'assurance)** (insurance) policy.

policier , -ière
1 *adjective* **enquête/etc policière** police inquiry/etc; **roman p.** detective novel.
2 *m noun* policeman, detective.

poliment *adverb* politely.

polio
1 *f noun* (*maladie*) polio.
2 *m or f noun* (*personne*) polio victim.

polir *verb* to polish.

politesse *f noun* politeness.

politique
1 *adjective* political; **homme p.** politician.
2 *f noun* (*activité*) politics; **une p.** a policy.

pollen *m noun* pollen.

pollué , -ée *adjective* polluted.

polluer *verb* to pollute.

pollution *f noun* pollution.

polo *m noun* (*chemise*) sweat shirt.

polochon *m noun Familiar* bolster.

Pologne (la) *f noun* Poland.

polonais , -aise
1 *adjective* Polish.
2 *m or f noun* Pole.
3 *m noun* (*langue*) Polish.

polycopié *m noun* duplicated course notes.

polyester *m noun* polyester; **che-**

mise/*etc* en p. polyester shirt/*etc.*

pommade *f noun* ointment.

pomme *f noun* apple; **p. de terre** potato; **pommes frites** chips; **pommes chips** potato crisps.

pommier *m noun* apple tree.

pompe *f noun* pump; **p. à essence** petrol station; **pompes funèbres** undertaker's; **entrepreneur de pompes funèbres** undertaker.

pomper *verb* (*eau*) to pump out (de of).

pompier *m noun* fireman; **voiture des pompiers** fire engine.

pompiste *m or f noun* petrol station attendant.

pompon *m noun* pompon.

poncer *verb* to rub down, sand.

ponctuation *f noun* punctuation.

ponctuel , -elle *adjective* (*à l'heure*) punctual.

pondre *verb*
1 (*œuf*) to lay.
2 (*poule*) to lay (eggs *or* an egg).

poney *m noun* pony.

pont *m noun* bridge; (*de bateau*) deck.

pop *m noun & invariable adjective* (*musique*) pop.

populaire *adjective* (*qui plaît*) popular; (*quartier*) working-class; (*expression*) colloquial.

population *f noun* population.

porc *m noun* pig; (*viande*) pork.

porcelaine *f noun* china.

porche *m noun* porch.

porcherie *f noun* (pig)sty.

port *m noun* port, harbour.

portable *adjective* (*portatif*) portable.

portail *m noun* gate.

portant , -ante *adjective* **bien p.** in good health.

portatif , -ive *adjective* portable.

porte *f noun* door; (*de jardin*) gate; (*de ville*) entrance; **p. (d'embarquement)** (*d'aéroport*) (departure) gate; **p. d'entrée** front door; **p. coulissante** sliding door; **mettre quelqu'un à la p.** to throw somebody out.

porte-avions *invariable m noun* aircraft carrier.

porte-bagages *invariable m noun* luggage rack.

porte-bonheur *invariable m noun* (lucky) charm.

porte-clefs *invariable m noun* key ring.

porte-documents *invariable m noun* briefcase.

portée *f noun* (*de fusil etc*) range; (*animaux*) litter; **à p. de la main** within (easy) reach; **à p. de voix** within earshot; **hors de p.** out of reach.

porte-fenêtre *f noun* (*plural* **portes-fenêtres**) French door *or* window.

portefeuille *m noun* wallet.

portemanteau , -x *m noun* hatstand, hallstand; (*crochet*) coat peg.

porte-monnaie *invariable m noun* purse.

porte-parole *invariable m noun* spokesman; (*femme*) spokeswoman.

porter *verb* to carry; (*vêtement, lunettes, barbe etc*) to wear; **p. quelque chose à** (*apporter*) to take something to; **p. bonheur/ malheur** to bring good/bad luck.

porter (se) *reflexive verb* (*vêtement*) to be worn; **se p. bien/mal** to be well/ill; **comment te portes-tu?** how are you?

porte-revues *invariable m noun*

newspaper rack.

porte-savon *m noun* soapdish.

porte-serviettes *invariable m noun* towel rail.

porteur *m noun* (*à la gare*) porter.

porte-voix *invariable m noun* loudspeaker, megaphone.

portier *m noun* doorkeeper.

portière *f noun* (*de véhicule, train*) door.

portion *f noun* (*partie*) portion; (*de nourriture*) helping.

portique *m noun* (*de balançoire etc*) crossbar.

portrait *m noun* portrait.

portugais , -aise
  1 *adjective* Portuguese.
  2 *m or f noun* Portuguese man *or* woman, Portuguese; **les P.** the Portuguese.
  3 *m noun* (*langue*) Portuguese.

Portugal (le) *m noun* Portugal.

pose *f noun* (*installation*) putting up; laying; (*attitude de modèle*) pose.

poser *verb*
  1 (*mettre*) to put (down); (*papier peint, rideaux*) to put up; (*moquette*) to lay; (*question*) to ask (**à quelqu'un** somebody).
  2 (*modèle*) to pose (**pour** for).

poser (se) *reflexive verb* (*oiseau, avion*) to land.

positif , -ive *adjective* positive.

position *f noun* position.

posséder *verb* to possess; (*maison etc*) to own.

possessif , -ive *adjective & m noun* Grammaire possessive.

possibilité *f noun* possibility.

possible
  1 *adjective* possible (**à faire** to do); **il (nous) est p. de le faire** it is possible (for us) to do it; **il est p.**
que (+ *subjunctive*) it is possible that; **si p.** if possible; **le plus tôt p.** as soon as possible; **autant que p.** as far as possible; **le plus p.** as much *or* as many as possible.
  2 *m noun* **faire son p.** to do one's best (**pour faire** to do).

postal , -e , -aux *adjective* postal; **boîte postale** PO Box; **code p.** postcode.

poste
  1 *f noun* (*service*) post; (**bureau de**) **p.** post office; **par la p.** by post; **mettre quelque chose à la p.** to mail *or* post something; **la P.** the Post Office; **p. aérienne** airmail; **p. restante** post restante.
  2 *m noun* (*lieu, emploi*) post; (*radio, télévision*) set; **p. de secours** first-aid post; **p. de police** police station.

poster *verb* (*lettre*) to post, mail.

postier , -ière *m or f noun* postal worker.

pot *m noun* pot; (*à confiture*) jar; (*à lait*) jug; (*à bière*) mug; (*de crème, yaourt*) carton; (*de bébé*) potty; **p. de fleurs** flower pot.

potable *adjective* drinkable; '**eau p.**' 'drinking water'; '**eau non p.**' 'water not suitable for drinking'.

potage *m noun* soup.

potager *adjective & m noun* (**jardin**) **p.** vegetable garden.

pot-au-feu *invariable m noun* beef stew.

pot-de-vin *m noun* (*plural* **pots-de-vin**) bribe.

poteau , -x *m noun* post; **p. indicateur** signpost; **p. d'arrivée** winning post; **p. télégraphique** telegraph pole.

poterie *f noun* (*article*) pottery; **une p.** a piece of pottery; **des poteries** (*objets*) pottery.

potier *m noun* potter.

potiron *m noun* pumpkin.

pou , -x *m noun* louse; **poux** lice.

poubelle *f noun* dustbin.

pouce *m noun* thumb; (*mesure*) inch.

poudre *f noun* powder; (*explosif*) gunpowder; **en p.** (*lait*) powdered; (*chocolat*) drinking.

poudrer (se) *reflexive verb* (*femme*) to powder one's face.

poudrier *m noun* (powder) compact.

pouf *m noun* (*siège*) pouf(fe).

poulailler *m noun* henhouse.

poulain *m noun* (*cheval*) foal.

poule *f noun* hen.

poulet *m noun* chicken.

poulie *f noun* pulley.

pouls *m noun* pulse.

poumon *m noun* lung; **à pleins poumons** (*respirer*) deeply; (*crier*) loudly.

poupée *f noun* doll.

pour
1 *preposition* for; **p. toi**/*etc* for you/*etc*; **partir p.** (*Paris, cinq ans*) to leave for; **elle est p.** she's in favour; **p. faire** (in order) to do; **p. que tu saches** so (that) you may know; **p. quoi faire?** what for?; **trop petit**/*etc* **p. faire** too small/*etc* to do; **assez grand**/*etc* **p. faire** big/*etc* enough to do.
2 *m noun* **le p. et le contre** the pros and cons.

pourboire *m noun* (*argent*) tip.

pourcentage *m noun* percentage.

pourquoi *adverb & conjunction* why; **p. pas?** why not?

pourra , pourrai(t) *etc see* pouvoir.

pourri , -ie *adjective* (*fruit, temps etc*) rotten.

pourrir *verb* to rot.

poursuite *f noun* chase; **se mettre à la p. de** to go after, chase (after).

poursuivant , -ante *m or f noun* pursuer.

poursuivre * *verb* to chase, go after; (*lecture, voyage etc*) to carry on (with).

poursuivre (se) *reflexive verb* to continue, go on.

pourtant *adverb* yet.

pourvu, -ue *past participle of* pourvoir.

pourvu que *conjunction* (*condition*) provided *or* providing (that); (*souhait*) **p. qu'elle soit là!** I only hope (that) she's there!

pousser *verb*
1 (*personne, brouette, meuble*) to push; (*cri*) to utter; (*soupir*) to heave; **p. quelqu'un à faire** to urge somebody to do.
2 (*croître*) to grow; **faire p.** (*plante etc*) to grow.

poussette *f noun* pushchair.

poussière *f noun* dust.

poussiéreux , -euse *adjective* dusty.

poussin *m noun* (*poulet*) chick.

poutre *f noun* (*en bois*) beam; (*en acier*) girder.

pouvoir *
1 *auxiliary verb* (*capacité*) can, be able to; (*permission, éventualité*) may, can; **je peux t'expliquer** I can explain it to you; **tu peux entrer** you may *or* can come in; **il peut être sorti** he may *or* might be out; **elle pourrait/pouvait venir** she might/could come; **j'ai pu l'obtenir** I managed to get it; **j'aurais pu l'obtenir** I could have got it; **je n'en peux plus** I'm

utterly exhausted.

2 *m noun* (*capacité, autorité*) power; **les pouvoirs publics** the authorities; **au p.** in power.

pouvoir (se) *impersonal verb* **il se peut qu'elle parte** (it's possible that) she might leave.

prairie *f noun* meadow.

pratique
1 *adjective* practical.
2 *f noun* (*exercice, procédé*) practice; **la p. de la natation/du golf** swimming/golfing.

pratiquement *adverb* (*presque*) practically.

pratiquer *verb* (*sport, art etc*) to practise.

pré *m noun* meadow.

préau , -x *m noun* (*d'école*) covered playground.

précaution *f noun* precaution (**de faire** of doing); (*prudence*) caution.

précédent , -ente
1 *adjective* previous.
2 *m or f noun* previous one.

précéder *verb* to precede.

précieux , -euse *adjective* precious.

précipice *m noun* chasm, precipice.

précipitamment *adverb* hastily.

précipitation *f noun* haste.

précipiter *verb* (*hâter*) to rush.

précipiter (se) *reflexive verb* to throw oneself; (*foncer*) to rush (**à, sur** on to); (*s'accélérer*) to speed up.

précis , -ise *adjective* precise; **à deux heures précises** at two o'clock sharp.

préciser *verb* to specify (**que** that).

préciser (se) *reflexive verb* to become clear(er).

précision *f noun* precision; (*explication*) explanation.

précoce *adjective* (*fruit etc*) early; (*enfant*) precocious.

prédécesseur *m noun* predecessor.

prédiction *f noun* prediction.

prédire * *verb* to predict (**que** that).

préfabriqué , -ée *adjective* prefabricated.

préface *f noun* preface.

préféré , -ée *adjective & m or f noun* favourite.

préférence *f noun* preference (**pour** for); **de p.** preferably.

préférer *verb* to prefer (**à** to); **p. faire** to prefer to do.

préfet *m noun* prefect (*chief administrator in a department*).

préfixe *m noun* prefix.

préhistorique *adjective* prehistoric.

préjugé *m noun* prejudice; **être plein de préjugés** to be full of prejudice.

premier , -ière
1 *adjective* first; **nombre p.** prime number; **le p. rang** the front row; **P. ministre** Prime Minister.
2 *m or f noun* first (one); **arriver le p.** to arrive first; **être le p. de la classe** to be (at the) top of the class.
3 *m noun* (*date*) first; (*étage*) first floor; **le p. de l'an** New Year's Day.
4 *f noun* (*wagon, billet*) first class; (*au lycée*) = sixth form; (*de véhicule*) first (gear).

premièrement *adverb* firstly.

prendre * *verb*
   1 (*saisir*)to take (**à quelqu'un**
   from somebody); (*attraper*) to
   catch; (*voyager par*) to take;
   (*douche*, *bain*) to take, have;
   (*repas*) to have; (*photo*) to take;
   (*temps*) to take (up); **p. quelqu'un pour** (*un autre*) to mistake
   somebody for; (*considérer*) to
   take somebody for; **p. feu** to catch
   fire; **p. de la place** to take up
   room; **p. du poids** to put on
   weight.
   2 (*feu*) to catch; (*ciment*) to set;
   (*vaccin*) to take.

prendre (se) *reflexive verb* (*objet*) to be taken; (*s'accrocher*) to
   get caught; **se p. pour un génie** to
   think one is a genius; **s'y p.** to go
   about it; **s'en p. à** to attack;
   (*accuser*) to blame.

prénom *m noun* first name.

préoccupation *f noun* worry.

préoccupé , -ée *adjective*
   worried.

préoccuper *verb* (*inquiéter*) to
   worry; **se p. de** to be worried
   about.

préparatifs *mpl noun* preparations (**de** for).

préparation *f noun* preparation.

préparer *verb* to prepare (**quelque chose pour** something for,
   quelqu'un à somebody for);
   (*examen*) to prepare for; **se p.** to
   get (oneself) ready (**à** *or* **pour**
   quelque chose for something); **se
   p. à faire** to prepare to do.

préposition *f noun Grammaire*
   preposition.

près *adverb* **p. de** (*personne*, *lieu*)
   near (to); **p. d'ici** near here; **p. de
   deux ans/etc** nearly two years/
   etc; **tout p.** nearby (**de** quelqu'un/quelque chose some-

body/something); **de p.** (*lire*,
   suivre) closely.

prescrire * *verb* (*médicament*) to
   prescribe.

présence *f noun* presence; (*à
   l'école etc*) attendance (**à** at);
   feuille de p. attendance sheet; **en
   p. de** in the presence of.

présent , -ente
   1 *adjective* (*non absent*) present (**à**
   at, **dans** in); (*actuel*) present.
   2 *m noun Grammaire* present
   (tense); **à p.** at present.

présentateur , -trice *m or f
   noun* announcer.

présentation *f noun* presentation; (*d'une personne à une autre*)
   introduction.

présenter *verb* to present; **p.
   quelqu'un à quelqu'un** to introduce somebody to somebody; **je
   vous présente Catherine** this is
   Catherine.

présenter (se) *reflexive verb* to
   introduce oneself (**à** to); **se p. à**
   (*examen*) to take; (*élections*) to
   run in.

préservatif *m noun* condom.

préserver *verb* to protect (**de**,
   contre from).

présidence *f noun* (*de nation*)
   presidency; (*de firme*) chairman-
   ship.

président , -ente *m or f noun* (*de
   nation*) president; (*de réunion*,
   firme) chairman, chairwoman; **p.
   directeur général** (chairman
   and) managing director.

présidentiel , -ielle *adjective*
   presidential.

presque *adverb* almost.

presqu'île *f noun* peninsula.

presse *f noun* (*journaux*, *appareil*)
   press; **conférence/etc de p.** press
   conference/*etc*.

presse-citron *invariable m noun*
lemon squeezer.

pressé , -ée *adjective (personne)*
in a hurry; *(travail)* urgent.

pressentir * *verb* to sense **(que**
that).

presser *verb*
1 *(serrer)* to squeeze.
2 le temps presse there isn't
much time (left); **rien ne presse**
there's no hurry.

presser (se) *reflexive verb (se*
serrer) to squeeze (together); *(se*
hâter) to hurry **(de faire** to do).

pressing *m noun (magasin)* dry
cleaner's.

pression *f noun* pressure.

prestidigitateur , -trice *m or f*
noun conjurer.

prestidigitation *f noun* **tour de**
p. conjuring trick.

prêt *m noun (emprunt)* loan.

prêt , prête *adjective (préparé)*
ready **(à faire** to do, **à quelque**
chose for something).

prêt-à-porter *invariable m noun*
ready-to-wear clothes.

prétendre *verb* to claim **(que**
that); **je ne prétend pas être ar-**
tiste I don't claim *or* pretend to be
an artist; **elle se prétend riche**
she claims to be rich.

prétendu , -ue *adjective*
so-called.

prétentieux , -euse *adjective &*
m or f noun conceited (person).

prêter *verb (argent, objet)* to lend
(à to); **p. attention** to pay attention **(à** to).

prétexte *m noun* excuse; **sous p.**
de/que on the pretext of / that.

prêtre *m noun* priest.

preuve *f noun* **une p.** a piece of
evidence, some proof; **preuves**
proof, evidence; **faire p. d'intel-**
ligence to show intelligence.

prévenir * *verb (avertir)* to warn
(que that); *(aviser)* to inform
(que that).

prévention *f noun* prevention; **p.**
routière road safety.

prévision *f noun* forecast.

prévoir * *verb (anticiper)* to foresee **(que** that); *(prédire)* to forecast **(que** that); *(temps)* to
forecast; *(organiser)* to plan;
(préparer) to provide, make provision for.

prévu , -ue *adjective* **un repas est**
p. a meal is provided; **au moment**
p. at the appointed time; **comme**
p. as expected; **p. pour** *(véhicule,*
appareil) designed for.

prier *verb*
1 *(faire une prière)* to pray **(pour**
for).
2 p. quelqu'un de faire to ask
somebody to do; **je vous en prie**
(faites donc) please; *(en réponse à*
'merci') don't mention it.

prière *f noun* prayer; **p. de ré-**
pondre/etc please answer / etc.

primaire *adjective* primary.

prime *f noun (d'employé)* bonus;
en p. *(cadeau)* as a free gift; **p.**
(d'assurance) (insurance)
premium.

primevère *f noun* primrose.

primitif , -ive *adjective (société*
etc*)* primitive.

prince *m noun* prince.

princesse *f noun* princess.

principal , -e, -aux
1 *adjective* main.
2 *m noun (de collège)* principal,
headmaster; **le p.** *(essentiel)* the
main thing.

principe *m noun* principle; **en p.**
theoretically; *(normalement)* as a

rule.

printemps *m noun* (*saison*) spring.

prioritaire *adjective* être p. to have priority; (*en voiture*) to have the right of way.

priorité *f noun* priority (**sur** over); **la p.** (*sur la route*) the right of way; **la p. à droite** right of way to traffic coming from the right; **'cédez la p.'** 'give way'.

pris , prise (*past participle of* **prendre**) *adjective* (*place*) taken; (*crème, ciment*) set; (*nez*) congested; être (très) p. to be (very) busy; **p. de** (*peur, panique*) stricken with.

prise *f noun* (*de judo etc*) hold; (*objet saisi*) catch; **p. (de courant)** (*mâle*) plug; (*femelle*) socket; **p. multiple** (*électrique*) adaptor; **p. de sang** blood test.

prison *f noun* prison, jail; **en p.** in prison *or* jail.

prisonnier , -ière *m or f noun* prisoner; **faire quelqu'un p.** to take somebody prisoner.

privé , -ée *adjective* private.

priver *verb* to deprive (**de** of); **se p. de** to do without.

prix [1] *m noun* (*d'un objet etc*) price; **à tout p.** at all costs; **à aucun p.** on no account.

prix [2] *m noun* (*récompense*) prize.

probable *adjective* likely, probable (**que** that); **peu p.** unlikely.

probablement *adverb* probably.

problème *m noun* problem.

procédé *m noun* process.

procès *m noun* (*criminel*) trial; (*civil*) lawsuit; **faire un p. à** to take to court.

procès-verbal *m noun* (*plural* procès-verbaux) (*contravention*) (traffic) fine.

prochain , -aine *adjective* next.

prochainement *adverb* shortly.

proche *adjective* (*espace*) near, close; (*temps*) close (at hand); (*parent, ami*) close; **p. de** near (to), close to.

procurer *verb* p. quelque chose à quelqu'un (*personne*) to obtain something for somebody; **se p. quelque chose** to obtain something.

prodigieux , -euse *adjective* extraordinary.

producteur , -trice
1 *m or f noun* producer.
2 *adjective* pays p. de pétrole oil-producing country.

production *f noun* production.

produire * *verb* (*fabriquer, causer etc*) to produce.

produire (se) *reflexive verb* (*événement etc*) to happen.

produit , -e
1 *past participle of* **produire**.
2 *m noun* (*article etc*) product; (*pour la vaisselle*) liquid; **produits** (*de la terre*) produce; **p. (chimique)** chemical; **p. de beauté** cosmetic.

prof *m noun* Familiar = professeur.

professeur *m noun* teacher; (*à l'université*) lecturer.

profession *f noun* occupation; (*de médecin etc*) profession; (*manuelle*) trade.

professionnel , -elle
1 *adjective* professional; (*école*) vocational.
2 *m or f noun* professional.

profil *m noun* de p. (viewed) from the side, in profile.

profit *m noun* profit; **tirer p. de** to benefit from *or* by.

profitable *adjective* (*utile*) beneficial (à to).

profiter *verb* **p. de** to take advantage of; **p. à quelqu'un** to profit somebody.

profond , -onde
1 *adjective* deep; **p. de deux mètres** two metres deep.
2 *adverb* (*pénétrer etc*) deep.

profondément *adverb* deeply; (*dormir*) soundly.

profondeur *f noun* depth; **à six mètres de p.** at a depth of six metres.

progiciel *m noun* (software) package.

programmateur *m noun* (*de four etc*) timer.

programme *m noun* programme; (*scolaire*) syllabus; (*d'ordinateur*) program.

programmer *verb* (*ordinateur*) to program.

progrès *m noun & mpl noun* progress; **faire des p.** to make progress.

progresser *verb* to progress.

progressif , -ive *adjective* gradual.

progressivement *adverb* gradually.

proie *f noun* prey.

projecteur *m noun* (*de monument*) floodlight; (*de film etc*) projector.

projectile *m noun* missile.

projection *f noun* (*de film*) projection; (*séance*) showing.

projet *m noun* plan.

projeter *verb* (*lancer*) to hurl; (*film*) to project; (*voyage, fête etc*) to plan; **p. de faire** to plan to do.

prolonger *verb* to extend.

prolonger (se) *reflexive verb* (*séance, rue*) to continue.

promenade *f noun* (*à pied*) walk; (*en voiture*) drive; (*en vélo, à cheval*) ride; **faire une p.** to go for a walk *or* a ride.

promener *verb* to take for a walk *or* ride.

promener (se) *reflexive verb* to (go for a) walk; (*en voiture*) to (go for a) drive.

promeneur , -euse *m or f noun* stroller.

promesse *f noun* promise.

promettre * *verb* to promise (**quelque chose à quelqu'un** somebody something, **que** that); **p. de faire** to promise to do; **c'est promis** it's a promise.

promotion *f noun* promotion; **en p.** (*produit*) on (special) offer.

promu , -ue *past participle of* promouvoir.

pronom *m noun* pronoun.

prononcer *verb* (*articuler*) to pronounce; (*dire*) to utter; (*discours*) to deliver.

prononcer (se) *reflexive verb* (*mot*) to be pronounced.

prononciation *f noun* pronunciation.

propager *verb* to spread.

propager (se) *reflexive verb* to spread.

proportion *f noun* proportion; (*rapport*) ratio.

propos
1 *mpl noun* (*paroles*) remarks.
2 *preposition* **à p. de** about.
3 *adverb* **à p.!** by the way!

proposer *verb* to suggest, propose (**quelque chose à quelqu'un** something to somebody,

que (+ *subjunctive*) that); (*offrir*) to offer (**quelque chose à quel-qu'un** somebody something, **de faire** to do); **je te propose de rester** I suggest you stay; **se p. pour faire** to offer to do.

proposition *f noun* suggestion; *Grammaire* clause.

propre [1]
1 *adjective* clean; (*soigné*) neat.
2 *m noun* **mettre quelque chose au p.** to make a fair copy of something.

propre [2] *adjective* own; **mon p. argent** my own money.

proprement *adverb* cleanly; (*avec netteté*) neatly.

propreté *f noun* cleanliness; (*netteté*) neatness.

propriétaire *m or f noun* owner; (*qui loue*) landlord, landlady.

propriété *f noun* (*bien, maison*) property.

prose *f noun* prose.

prospectus *m noun* leaflet.

prospère *adjective* thriving.

protecteur , -trice
1 *m or f noun* protector.
2 *adjective* (*geste etc*) protective.

protection *f noun* protection; **de p.** (*écran etc*) protective.

protège-cahier *m noun* exercise book cover.

protéger *verb* to protect (**de** from, **contre** against).

protestant , -ante *adjective & m or f noun* Protestant.

protestation *f noun* protest (**contre** against).

protester *verb* to protest (**contre** against).

prouver *verb* to prove (**que** that).

provenance *f noun* origin; **le train en p. de Lyon** the train

from Lyons.

provenir * *verb* **p. de** to come from.

proverbe *m noun* proverb.

province *f noun* province; **la p.** the provinces; **en p.** in the provinces; **de p.** (*ville etc*) provincial.

provincial , -e , -aux *adjective & m or f noun* provincial.

proviseur *m noun* (*de lycée*) headmaster, headmistress.

provision *f noun* supply; **provisions** (*achats*) shopping; (*nourriture*) food; **sac à provisions** shopping bag; **chèque sans p.** dud cheque.

provisoire *adjective* temporary.

provisoirement *adverb* temporarily.

provoquer *verb* (*causer*) to bring about; (*défier*) to provoke.

proximité *f noun* closeness; **à p.** close by; **à p. de** close to.

prudemment *adverb* cautiously, carefully.

prudence *f noun* caution, care.

prudent , -ente *adjective* cautious, careful.

prune *f noun* plum.

pruneau , -x *m noun* prune.

prunier *m noun* plum tree.

psychiatre *m or f noun* psychiatrist.

psychologie *f noun* psychology.

psychologique *adjective* psychological.

psychologue *m or f noun* psychologist.

PTT *fpl noun* (*postes, Télégraphes, Téléphones*) Post Office.

pu *see* **pouvoir**.

puanteur *f noun* stink.

pub *f noun Familiar* (*secteur*)

advertising; (*message*) ad.

public , -ique
  1 *adjective* public.
  2 *m noun* public; (*de spectacle*)
  audience; **en p.** in public.

publication *f noun* publication.

publicité *f noun* (*secteur*) advertising; (*message*) ad.

publier *verb* to publish.

puce *f noun* flea; (*d'ordinateur*)
  chip; **marché aux puces** flea
  market.

puer *verb*
  1 (*sentir mauvais*) to stink.
  2 (*le tabac, l'ail*) to stink of.

puéricultrice *f noun* children's
  nurse.

puis *adverb* then.

puiser *verb* to draw (**dans** from).

puisque *conjunction* since, as.

puissance *f noun* (*force, nation*)
  power.

puissant , -ante *adjective*
  powerful.

puisse(s) , puissent *etc see*
  pouvoir.

puits *m noun* well; (*de mine*) shaft.

pull(-over) *m noun* sweater.

pulvérisateur *m noun* spray.

pulvériser *verb* (*liquide*) to spray.

punaise *f noun* (*insecte*) bug;
  (*clou*) drawing pin.

punir *verb* to punish (**de quelque
  chose** for something, **pour avoir
  fait** for doing).

punition *f noun* punishment.

pupille *f noun* (*de l'œil*) pupil.

pur , -e *adjective* pure.

purée *f noun* purée; **p. (de
  pommes de terre)** mashed potatoes.

pureté *f noun* purity.

puzzle *m noun* (jigsaw) puzzle.

p.-v. *invariable m noun* (*procès-
  verbal*) (traffic) fine.

pyjama *m noun* pyjamas; **un p.** a
  pair of pyjamas.

pylône *m noun* pylon.

pyramide *f noun* pyramid.

Pyrénées (les) *fpl noun* the
  Pyrenees.

Q

QI *m abbreviation* (*quotient intellectuel*) IQ.

quadrillé , -ée *adjective* (*papier*) squared.

quai *m noun* (*de port*) (*pour passagers*) quay; (*pour marchandises*) wharf; (*de fleuve*) embankment; (*de gare*) platform.

qualifié , -ée *adjective* (*équipe etc*) that has qualified; (*ouvrier*) skilled.

qualifier (se) *reflexive verb* (*en sport*) to qualify (**pour** for).

qualité *f noun* quality.

quand *conjunction & adverb* when; **q. je viendrai** when I come; **q. même** all the same.

quant à *preposition* as for.

quantité *f noun* quantity; **une q.** (*beaucoup*) a lot (**de** of).

quarantaine *f noun* **une q.** (**de**) about forty.

quarante *adjective & m noun* forty.

quarantième *adjective & m or f noun* fortieth.

quart *m noun* quarter; **q. (de litre)** quarter litre; **q. d'heure** quarter of an hour; **une heure et q.** an hour and a quarter; **il est une heure et q.** it's a quarter past one; **une heure moins le q.** quarter to one.

quartier [1] *m noun* (*de ville*) neighbourhood, district; (*chinois etc*) quarter; **de q.** (*cinéma etc*) local.

quartier [2] *m noun* (*de pomme*) quarter; (*d'orange*) segment.

quartz *m noun* **montre/etc à q.** quartz watch/etc.

quatorze *adjective & m noun* fourteen.

quatre *adjective & m noun* four; **q. heures** (*goûter*) afternoon snack.

quatre-vingt see quatre-vingts.

quatre-vingt-dix *adjective & m noun* ninety.

quatre-vingts *adjective & m noun* eighty; **q. ans** eighty years; **q.-vingt-un** eighty-one; **page quatre-vingt** page eighty.

quatrième *adjective & m or f noun* fourth.

que (**qu'** *before a vowel or mute h*)
 1 *conjunction* that; **je pense qu'elle restera** I think (that) she'll stay; **qu'elle vienne ou non** whether she comes or not; **qu'il s'en aille!** let him leave!
 ▪ **(ne) … q.** only; **tu n'as qu'un franc** you only have one franc.
 ▪ (*dans une comparaison*) than; (*avec aussi, même, tel, autant*) as; **plus âgé q.** older than; **aussi sage q.** as wise as; **le même q.** the same as.
 2 *adverb* (**ce**) **qu'il est bête!** how silly he is!
 3 *relative pronoun* (*chose*) that, which; (*personne*) that; (*temps*) when; **le livre q. j'ai** the book (that *or* which) I have; **l'ami q. j'ai** the friend (that) I have; **un jour q.** one day when.
 4 *pronoun* (*dans une question*) what; **q. fait-il?** what is he doing?

Québec
 1 *m noun* **le Q.** Quebec.
 2 *m or f noun* (*ville*) Quebec.

québécois , -oise
 1 *adjective* of Quebec.
 2 *m or f noun* Quebecker.

quel , quelle
1 *adjective* (*dans une question*) what, which; (*qui*) who; **q. livre/acteur?** what *or* which book/actor?; **je sais q. est ton but** I know what your aim is.
2 *pronoun* (*dans une question*) which (one); **q. est le meilleur?** which (one) is the best?
3 *adjective* (*dans une exclamation*) **q. idiot!** what a fool!; **q. dommage!** what a pity!

quelconque *adjective* any (whatever); **une raison q.** any reason (whatever).

quelque
1 *adjective* **quelques femmes/livres/etc** some *or* a few women/books/etc; **les quelques amies qu'elle a** the few friends she has.
2 *pronoun* **q. chose** something; (*dans une question*) anything, something; **il a q. chose** (*un problème*) there's something the matter with him; **q. chose d'autre/de grand/etc** something else/big/etc.
3 *adverb* **q. part** somewhere; (*dans une question*) anywhere, somewhere.

quelquefois *adverb* sometimes.

quelques-uns , -unes *pronoun* some.

quelqu'un *pronoun* someone; (*dans une question*) anyone, someone; **q. d'intelligent/etc** someone clever/etc.

qu'est-ce que *pronoun*
▪ (*marque l'interrogation*) what; **q. tu veux?** what do you want?; **q. c'est?** what is it?; **q. tu as?** what's the matter (with you)?
▪ (*marque l'exclamation*) **qu'est-ce qu'il fait chaud!** it's so hot!; **q. tu as changé!** how you've changed!

qu'est-ce qui *pronoun* (*marque l'interrogation*) what; **q. se passe?** what's happening?

question *f noun* question; (*problème*) matter; **il est q. de** there's some talk about (**faire** doing); **il a été q. de vous** we *or* they talked about you; **il n'en est pas q.** it's out of the question.

questionner *verb* to question (**sur** about).

quête *f noun* (*collecte*) collection; **faire la q.** to collect money.

quêter *verb* to collect money.

queue[1] *f noun* (*d'animal etc*) tail; (*de fleur*) stem; (*de fruit*) stalk; (*de poêle*) handle; (*de train*) rear; **q. de cheval** (*coiffure*) ponytail; **à la q. leu leu** in single file.

queue[2] *f noun* (*file*) queue; **faire la q.** to queue up.

qui *pronoun* (*personne*) who, that; (*dans une question*) who; (*chose*) which, that; **l'homme q.** the man who *or* that; **la maison q.** the house which *or* that; **q. est là?** who's there?; **q. désirez-vous voir?** who do you want to see?; **la femme de q. je parle** the woman I'm talking about; **l'ami sur l'aide de q. je compte** the friend on whose help I rely; **à q. as-tu parlé?** who did you speak to?; **à q. est ce livre?** whose book is this?

quiche *f noun* quiche.

qui est-ce que *pronoun* (*marque l'interrogation*) who; **q. tu veux voir?** who do you want to see?; **à q. tu veux parler?** who do you want to speak to?

qui est-ce qui *pronoun* (*marque l'interrogation*) who; **q. chante?** who's singing?

quille *f noun* (*de jeu*) (bowling) pin, skittle; **jouer aux quilles** to bowl, play skittles.

quincaillerie hardware shop.

quincaillier , -ière *m or f noun*
ironmonger.

quinzaine *f noun* **une q. (de)**
about fifteen; **q. (de jours)** two
weeks.

quinze *adjective & m noun* fifteen;
q. jours two weeks.

quinzième *adjective & m or f
noun* fifteenth.

quitte *adjective* even (**envers**
with).

quitter *verb*
1 (*personne, lieu*) to leave; **q.
quelqu'un des yeux** to take one's

eyes off somebody.
2 ne quittez pas! (*au téléphone*)
hold on!

quitter (se) *reflexive verb* (*se séparer*) to part, say goodbye.

quoi *pronoun* what; (*après une
préposition*) which; **à q. penses-
tu?** what are you thinking about?;
de q. manger something to eat;
de q. couper/écrire something to
cut/write with; **il n'y a pas de q.!**
(*en réponse à 'merci'*) don't mention it!

quotidien , -ienne
1 *adjective* daily.
2 *m noun* daily (paper).

R

rabattre * *verb* to pull down; (*refermer*) to close (down).

rabattre (se) *reflexive verb* (*barrière*) to come down; (*après avoir doublé un véhicule*) to cut in.

rabbin *m noun* rabbi.

rabot *m noun* (*outil*) plane.

raboter *verb* to plane.

raccommodage *m noun* mending; darning.

raccommoder *verb* to mend; (*chaussette*) to darn.

raccompagner *verb* to see back (home); **r. à la porte** to see to the door.

raccord *m noun* (*dispositif*) connection, connector; (*de papier peint*) join.

raccourci *m noun* short cut.

raccourcir *verb*
1 (*rendre court*) to shorten.
2 (*devenir court*) to get shorter.

raccrocher *verb*
1 (*objet tombé*) to hang back up; (*téléphone*) to put down.
2 (*au téléphone*) to hang up.

race *f noun* (*groupe ethnique*) race; (*animale*) breed.

racheter *verb* **r. un manteau/ une voiture/etc** to buy another coat/car/*etc*; **r. des chaussettes/ du pain/etc** to buy some more socks/bread/*etc*.

racial , -e, -aux *adjective* racial.

racine *f noun* root; **prendre r.** (*plante*) to take root.

racisme *m noun* racism.

raciste *adjective* racist.

racler *verb* to scrape; (*enlever*) to scrape off; **se r. la gorge** to clear

one's throat.

raconter *verb* (*histoire*) to tell; **r. quelque chose à quelqu'un** (*vacances etc*) to tell somebody about something; **r. à quelqu'un que** to tell somebody that.

radar *m noun* radar.

radeau , -x *m noun* raft.

radiateur *m noun* radiator; **r. électrique** electric heater.

radieux , -euse *adjective* (*personne, visage*) beaming; (*soleil*) brilliant; (*temps*) glorious.

radio [1] *f noun* radio; (*poste*) radio; **à la r.** on the radio.

radio [2] *f noun* (*photo*) X-ray; **passer une r.** to have an X-ray.

radioactif , -ive *adjective* radioactive.

radiodiffuser *verb* to broadcast (on the radio).

radiographier *verb* to X-ray.

radis *m noun* radish.

radoucir (se) *reflexive verb* (*temps*) to become milder.

radoucissement *m noun* **r. (du temps)** milder weather.

rafale *f noun* (*vent*) gust.

raffoler *verb* **r. de** (*aimer*) to be mad about.

rafistoler *verb* *Familiar* to patch up.

rafraîchir *verb* to cool (down).

rafraîchir (se) *reflexive verb* (*boire*) to refresh oneself; (*temps*) to get cooler.

rafraîchissant , -ante *adjective* refreshing.

rafraîchissement *m noun* (*de température*) cooling; (*boisson*) cold drink; **rafraîchissements** refreshments.

rage f noun (colère) rage; (maladie) rabies; **r. de dents** violent toothache.

ragoût m noun stew.

raid m noun raid.

raide adjective (rigide) stiff; (côte) steep; (cheveux) straight; (corde) tight.

raidir verb to stiffen; (corde) to tighten.

raidir (se) reflexive verb to stiffen; (corde) to tighten.

raie f noun (de tissu, zèbre) stripe; (de cheveux) parting.

rail m noun (barre) rail (for train).

rainure f noun groove.

raisin m noun (grain de) r. grape; **du r., des raisins** grapes; **r. sec** raisin.

raison f noun reason; **la r. de/ pour laquelle ...** the reason for/ why ... ; **en r. de** on account of; **avoir r.** to be right (de faire to do).

raisonnable adjective reasonable.

raisonnement m noun reasoning.

raisonner verb
  1 (penser) to reason.
  2 **r. quelqu'un** to reason with somebody.

rajeunir verb **r. quelqu'un** to make somebody (feel or look) younger.

ralenti m noun **au r.** (filmer) in slow motion; **tourner au r.** (moteur) to tick over.

ralentir verb to slow down.

rallonge f noun (de table) extension; (électrique) extension (lead).

rallonger verb to lengthen.

rallumer verb (feu, pipe) to light again; (lampe) to switch on again.

rallye m noun (automobile) rally.

ramassage m noun picking up; collection; gathering; **r. scolaire** school bus service.

ramasser verb (prendre par terre, réunir) to pick up; (ordures, copies) to collect; (fruits, coquillages) to gather.

rame f noun (aviron) oar; (de métro) train.

ramener verb **r. quelqu'un** to bring or take somebody back.

ramer verb to row.

ramollir verb to soften.

ramollir (se) reflexive verb to soften.

ramoner verb (cheminée) to sweep.

rampe f noun (d'escalier) banister(s); **r. (d'accès)** ramp; **r. de lancement** launch pad.

ramper verb to crawl.

ranch m noun ranch.

rançon f noun (argent) ransom.

rancune f noun grudge; **garder r. à quelqu'un** to bear somebody a grudge.

rancunier , -ière adjective spiteful.

randonnée f noun (à pied) hike; (en voiture) drive; (en vélo) ride; **faire une r.** to go for a hike/ drive/ride.

rang m noun (rangée) row, line; (classement) rank; **se mettre en rang(s)** to line up (par trois/etc in threes/etc).

rangé , -ée adjective (chambre etc) tidy.

rangée f noun row, line.

rangements mpl noun (placards) storage space.

ranger verb (papiers etc) to put away; (chambre etc) to tidy (up); (chiffres, mots) to arrange; (voiture) to park.

ranger (se) reflexive verb (élèves etc) to line up; (s'écarter) to stand aside; (voiture) to pull over.

ranimer verb (réanimer) to revive; (feu) to poke, stir.

rapace m noun bird of prey.

râpe f noun (à fromage etc) grater.

râpé, -ée adjective (fromage, carotte) grated.

râper verb (fromage, carottes) to grate.

rapetisser verb to get smaller.

rapide
1 adjective fast, quick.
2 m noun (train) express (train).

rapidement adverb fast, quickly.

rapidité f noun speed.

rapiécer verb to patch (up).

rappeler verb to call back; (souvenir) to recall; **r. quelque chose à quelqu'un** to remind somebody of something.

rappeler (se) reflexive verb to remember (**que** that).

rapport m noun (lien) connection; (récit) report; **rapports** (entre personnes) relations; **par r. à** compared to; **ça m'a aucun r.!** it has nothing to do with it!

rapporter verb
1 (objet) to bring or take back; (profit) to bring in; **se r. à** to relate to.
2 (dénoncer) Familiar to tell tales; (investissement) to bring in a good return.

rapporteur , -euse
1 m or f noun telltale.
2 m noun (en géométrie) protractor.

rapprocher verb to bring closer (**de** to); (chaise) to pull up (**de** to).

rapprocher (se) reflexive verb to come or get closer (**de** to).

raquette f noun (de tennis) racket; (de ping-pong) bat.

rare adjective rare; **il est r. que** (+ subjunctive) it's seldom that.

rarement adverb rarely, seldom.

ras , rase adjective (cheveux) close-cropped; (herbe, poil) short; **en rase campagne** in the open country; **à r. bord** to the brim.

rasé , -ée adjective **être bien r.** to have shaved; **mal r.** unshaven.

raser verb (menton, personne) to shave; (barbe, moustache) to shave off; (démolir) to knock down; (frôler) to skim.

raser (se) reflexive verb to (have a) shave.

rasoir m noun razor; (électrique) shaver.

rassemblement m noun gathering.

rassembler verb (gens, objets) to gather (together).

rassembler (se) reflexive verb to gather.

rassis , f rassie or **rassise** adjective (pain etc) stale.

rassurant , -ante adjective reassuring.

rassurer verb to reassure; **rassure-toi** don't worry.

rat m noun rat.

râteau , -x m noun (outil) rake.

rater verb (bus, cible etc) to miss; (travail, gâteau etc) to ruin; (examen) to fail.

ration f noun ration.

rationnement m noun rationing.

rationner verb to ration.

ratisser verb (allée etc) to rake; (feuilles etc) to rake up.

rattacher verb (lacets etc) to tie up again.

rattrapage m noun **cours de r.** remedial class.

rattraper verb to catch; (prisonnier) to recapture; (temps perdu) to make up for; **r. quelqu'un** (rejoindre) to catch up with somebody.

rature f noun crossing out.

raturer verb to cross out.

ravager verb to devastate.

ravages mpl noun havoc; **faire des r.** to cause havoc or widespread damage.

ravaler verb (façade etc) to clean (and restore).

ravi , -ie adjective delighted (de with, de faire to do).

ravin m noun ravine.

ravioli mpl noun ravioli.

ravir verb (plaire) to delight.

ravissant , -ante adjective beautiful.

ravisseur , -euse m or f noun kidnapper.

ravitaillement m noun supplying; (denrées) supplies.

ravitailler verb to supply (en with).

ravitailler (se) reflexive verb to stock up (with supplies).

rayé , -ée adjective scratched; (tissu) striped.

rayer verb (érafler) to scratch; (mot etc) to cross out.

rayon m noun (de lumière, soleil) ray; (de cercle) radius; (de roue) spoke; (planche) shelf; (de magasin) department.

rayonnant , -ante adjective (visage etc) beaming (de with).

rayure f noun scratch; (bande) stripe; **à rayures** striped.

raz-de-marée invariable m noun tidal wave.

re- , ré- préfixe re-.

réacteur m noun (d'avion) jet engine; (nucléaire) reactor.

réaction f noun reaction; **avion à r.** jet (aircraft).

réagir verb to react (contre against, à to).

réalisateur , -trice m or f noun (de film) director.

réaliser verb (projet etc) to carry out; (rêve) to fulfil; (fabriquer) to make; (film) to direct.

réaliser (se) reflexive verb (vœu) to come true; (projet) to materialize.

réaliste adjective realistic.

réalité f noun reality; **en r.** in fact.

réanimation f noun **en r.** in intensive care.

réanimer verb to revive.

rebond m noun bounce.

rebondir verb to bounce.

rebord m noun **r. de (la) fenêtre** windowsill.

reboucher verb (flacon) to put the top back on; (trou) to fill in again.

rébus invariable m noun rebus (word guessing game).

récemment adverb recently.

récent , -ente adjective recent.

récepteur m noun (de téléphone) receiver.

réception f noun (réunion, de radio etc) reception; (d'hôtel) reception (desk); **dès r. de** on receipt of.

recette f noun (de cuisine) recipe (de for); (argent, bénéfice) ta-

kings.
recevoir * *verb*
 1 (*objet, coup de téléphone*) to receive; (*person*) to welcome; être
reçu (à) (*examen*) to pass.
 2 (*avoir des amis*) to entertain.
rechange (de) *adjective* (*outil
etc*) spare; vêtements de r. a
change of clothes.
recharge *f noun* (*de stylo*) refill.
recharger *verb* (*fusil, appareil
photo*) to reload; (*briquet, stylo*)
to refill; (*batterie*) to recharge.
réchaud *m noun* (portable) stove
r. à gaz gas ring.
réchauffement *m noun* (*de température*) rise (de in).
réchauffer *verb* to warm up; se r.
to warm oneself up; (*temps*) to get
warmer.
recherche *f noun* la r., des recherches (*scientifique etc*) research (sur on, into); faire des
recherches to (do) research; (*enquêter*) to make investigations.
recherché , -ée *adjective* r. pour
meurtre wanted for murder.
rechercher *verb* (*personne, objet*)
to search for.
récif *m noun* reef.
récipient *m noun* container.
réciproque *adjective* mutual.
récit *m noun* (*histoire*) story.
récitation *f noun* (*poème*) poem
(learnt by heart and recited aloud).
réciter *verb* to recite.
réclamation *f noun* complaint.
réclame *f noun* advertising; (*annonce*) advertisement; en r. on
(special) offer.
réclamer *verb*
 1 (*demander*) r. quelque chose to
ask for something back.
 2 (*se plaindre*) to complain.

recoin *m noun* nook.
recoller *verb* (*objet cassé*) to stick
back together; (*enveloppe*) to
stick back down.
récolte *f noun* (*action*) harvest;
(*produits*) crop.
récolter *verb* to harvest.
recommandation *f noun*
recommendation.
recommander *verb* to recommend (à to, pour for); r. à quelqu'un de faire to recommend
somebody to do; lettre recommandée registered letter; en
recommandé (*envoyer*) by
registered post.
recommencer *verb* to start
again.
récompense *f noun* reward
(pour for).
récompenser *verb* to reward
(de, pour for).
réconciliation *f noun* reconcili-
ation.
réconcilier (se) *reflexive verb* to
settle one's differences, make it up
(avec with).
reconduire * *verb* r. quelqu'un
to see somebody back.
réconfortant , -ante *adjective*
comforting.
réconforter *verb* to comfort.
reconnaissance *f noun* (*gratitude*) gratitude.
reconnaissant , -ante *adjective*
grateful (à quelqu'un de quelque chose to somebody for
something).
reconnaître * *verb* to recognize
(à quelque chose by something);
(*admettre*) to admit (que that);
reconnu coupable found guilty.
reconstruire * *verb* (*ville*) to
rebuild.

recopier *verb* to copy out.

record *m noun & invariable adjective (en sport etc)* record.

recoudre * *verb (bouton)* to sew (back) on; *(vêtement)* to stitch (up).

recourbé , -ée *adjective (clou etc)* bent; *(nez)* hooked.

recouvrir * *verb (livre, meuble etc)* to cover.

récréation *f noun (à l'école)* break.

recroquevillé , -ée *adjective* huddled up.

recrue *f noun* recruit.

rectangle *m noun* rectangle.

rectangulaire *adjective* rectangular.

rectification *f noun* correction.

rectifier *verb* to correct.

recto *m noun* front (of the page).

reçu , -ue
1 *past participle of* **recevoir**.
2 *m noun (écrit)* receipt.

recueil *m noun* anthology, collection (**de** of).

recueillir * *verb* to collect; *(prendre chez soi)* to take in.

reculer *verb*
1 *(aller en arrière)* to move back; *(véhicule, automobiliste)* to reverse.
2 *(meuble)* to push back.

reculons (à) *adverb* backwards.

récupérer *verb*
1 *(objet prêté)* to get back.
2 *(reprendre des forces)* to get one's strength back.

récurer *verb* to scrub.

recycler *verb (matériaux)* to recycle.

rédacteur , -trice *m or f noun (de journal)* editor; **r. en chef** editor (-in-chief).

rédaction *f noun (devoir de français)* essay, composition.

redescendre *verb*
1 *(auxiliary* **être**) *(aller plus bas)* to come *or* go back down.
2 *(auxiliary* **avoir**) *(objet)* to bring *or* take back down.

rediffusion *f noun (de film etc)* repeat.

rédiger *verb* to write.

redire * *verb* to repeat.

redonner *verb (donner plus)* to give more *(bread etc)*; **r. un franc/** *etc* to give another franc/*etc*.

redoublant , -ante *m or f noun* pupil repeating a year.

redoublement *m noun* repeating a year.

redoubler *verb* **r. (une classe)** to repeat a year.

redoutable *adjective* formidable.

redouter *verb* to dread (**de faire** doing).

redresser *verb (objet tordu etc)* to straighten (out).

redresser (se) *reflexive verb* to sit up; *(debout)* to stand up.

réduction *f noun* reduction (**de** in); *(prix réduit)* discount; **en r.** *(copie, modèle)* small-scale.

réduire * *verb* to reduce (**à** to, **de** by); **r. en cendres** to reduce to ashes.

réduit , -uite *adjective (prix, vitesse)* reduced; *(modèle)* small-scale.

réel , -elle *adjective* real.

réellement *adverb* really.

réexpédier *verb (faire suivre)* to forward.

refaire * *verb (exercice, travail)* to do again, redo; *(chambre etc)* to do up, redo.

réfectoire *m noun* refectory.

référence *f noun* reference.

refermer *verb* to close again.

refermer (se) *reflexive verb* to close (again).

réfléchir *verb*
1 (*image*) to reflect; **se r.** to be reflected; **verbe réfléchi** reflexive verb.
2 (*penser*) to think (**à** about).

reflet *m noun* (*image*) reflection; (*couleur*) tint.

refléter *verb* (*image etc*) to reflect; **se r.** to be reflected.

réflexe *m noun* reflex.

réflexion *f noun* (*méditation*) thought; (*remarque*) remark.

réforme *f noun* (*changement*) reform.

refrain *m noun* (*de chanson*) chorus.

réfrigérateur *m noun* refrigerator.

refroidir *verb* to cool (down).

refroidir (se) *reflexive verb* (*prendre froid*) to catch cold; (*temps*) to get cold.

refroidissement *m noun* (*rhume*) chill; **r. de la température** fall in the temperature.

refuge *m noun* refuge; (*pour piétons*) (traffic) island; (*de montagne*) (mountain) hut.

réfugié , -ée *m or f noun* refugee.

réfugier (se) *reflexive verb* to take refuge.

refus *m noun* refusal.

refuser *verb* to refuse (**quelque chose à quelqu'un** somebody something, **de faire** to do); (*candidat*) to fail.

regagner *verb* to regain, get back; (*revenir à*) to get back to.

régaler (se) *reflexive verb* to have a feast.

regard *m noun* look; (*fixe*) stare; **jeter un r. sur** to glance at.

regarder [1] *verb*
1 (*personne, objet*) to look at; (*fixement*) to stare at; (*observer*) to watch; **r. quelqu'un faire** to watch somebody do.
2 (*observer*) to look; to stare; to watch.

regarder [2] *verb* (*concerner*) to concern; **ça ne te regarde pas!** it's none of your business!

régime [1] *m noun* (*politique*) (form of) government; **r. alimentaire** diet; **se mettre au r.** to go on a diet; **suivre un r.** to be on a diet.

régime [2] *m noun* (*de bananes, dattes*) bunch.

régiment *m noun* regiment.

région *f noun* region, area.

régional , -e , -aux *adjective* regional.

registre *m noun* register.

réglable *adjective* (*siège*) adjustable.

réglage *m noun* adjustment; (*de moteur*) tuning.

règle *f noun* rule; (*instrument*) ruler; **en r. générale** as a rule; **règles** (*de femme*) (monthly) period.

règlement *m noun* (*règles*) regulations; (*paiement*) payment; **contraire au r.** against the rules.

régler *verb*
1 (*problème etc*) to settle; (*mécanisme*) to adjust; (*moteur*) to tune.
2 (*payer*) to pay; **r. quelqu'un** to settle up with somebody.

réglisse *f noun* liquorice.

règne *m noun* (*de roi*) reign.

régner *verb* (*roi, silence*) to reign (**sur** over).

regret *m noun* regret; **à r.** with

regret.

regrettable *adjective* unfortunate, regrettable.

regretter *verb* to regret; **r. quelqu'un** to miss somebody; **r. que** (+ *subjunctive*) to be sorry that; **je (le) regrette** I'm sorry.

regrouper *verb* to gather together.

regrouper (se) *reflexive verb* to gather together.

régularité *f noun* regularity; steadiness.

régulier , -ière *adjective* regular; (*progrès, vitesse*) steady.

régulièrement *adverb* regularly.

rein *m noun* kidney; **les reins** (*dos*) the (small of the) back.

reine *f noun* queen.

rejeter *verb* to throw back; (*refuser*) to reject.

rejoindre * *verb* (*famille, lieu etc*) to get back to; **r. quelqu'un** (*se joindre à*) to join somebody; (*rattraper*) to catch up with somebody.

rejoindre (se) *reflexive verb* (*personnes, routes*) to meet.

réjouir (se) *reflexive verb* to be delighted (**de** at, about; **de faire** to do).

réjouissances *fpl noun* festivities.

relâcher *verb* (*corde etc*) to loosen; **r. quelqu'un** to release somebody.

relais *m noun* **prendre le r.** to take over (**de** from).

relatif , -ive *adjective* relative.

relation *f noun* relation(ship); (*ami*) acquaintance; **entrer en relations avec** to come into contact with.

relativement *adverb* (*assez*) relatively.

relayer *verb* to take over from.

relayer (se) *reflexive verb* to take (it in) turns (**pour faire** to do).

relevé *m noun* (*de compteur*) reading; **r. de compte** (bank) statement.

relever *verb* to raise; (*personne tombée*) to help up; (*col*) to turn up; (*manches*) to roll up; (*compteur*) to read.

relever (se) *reflexive verb* (*après une chute*) to get up.

relief *m noun* (*forme*) relief; **en r.** (*cinéma*) three-D.

relier *verb* to connect (**à** to); (*livre*) to bind.

religieux , -euse
1 *adjective* religious.
2 *f noun* nun.

religion *f noun* religion.

relire * *verb* to read again, reread.

reliure *f noun* (*de livre*) binding.

reluire * *verb* to shine.

remarquable *adjective* remarkable (**par** for).

remarquablement *adverb* remarkably.

remarque *f noun* remark; (*écrite*) note.

remarquer *verb* to notice (**que** that); **faire r.** to point out (**à** to, **que** that); **se faire r.** to attract attention; **remarque!** mind you!, you know!

rembobiner *verb* (*bande*) to rewind.

rembobiner (se) *reflexive verb* (*bande*) to rewind.

rembourré , -ée *adjective* (*fauteuil etc*) padded.

remboursement *m noun* repayment; refund.

rembourser *verb* to pay back, repay; (*billet*) to refund.

remède *m noun* cure; (*médicament*) medicine.

remerciements *mpl noun* thanks.

remercier *verb* to thank (de quelque chose, pour quelque chose for something); **je vous remercie d'être venu** thank you for coming.

remettre * *verb* to put back; (*vêtement*) to put back on; (*donner*) to hand over (à to); (*démission, devoir*) to hand in; (*différer*) to postpone (à until); **r. en question** to call into question; **r. en état** to repair; **se r. à** (*activité*) to go back to; **se r. à faire** to start to do again; **se r. de** (*chagrin, maladie*) to get over.

remise *f noun* (*rabais*) discount.

remonte-pente *m noun* ski lift.

remonter *verb*
1 (*auxiliary* **être**) (*aller plus haut*) to come *or* go back up; **r. dans** (*voiture*) to get back in(to); (*bus, train*) to get back on(to); **r. sur** (*cheval, vélo*) to get back on(to).
2 (*auxiliary* **avoir**) (*escalier, pente*) to come *or* go back up; (*porter*) to bring *or* take back up; (*montre*) to wind up; (*relever*) to raise; (*col*) to turn up; (*objet démonté*) to put back together.

remords *m noun & mpl noun* remorse; **avoir des r.** to feel remorse.

remorque *f noun* (*de voiture etc*) trailer; **prendre en r.** to tow; **en r.** on tow.

remorquer *verb* to tow.

remorqueur *m noun* tug(boat).

rempart *m noun* rampart; **remparts** walls.

remplaçant , -ante *m or f noun* (*personne*) replacement; (*enseignant*) substitute teacher; (*en sport*) reserve.

remplacement *m noun* replacement; **assurer le r. de quelqu'un** to stand in for somebody.

remplacer *verb* to replace (**par** with, by); (*succéder à*) to take over from.

rempli , -ie *adjective* full (**de** of).

remplir *verb* to fill (up) (**de** with); (*fiche etc*) to fill in *or* out.

remplir (se) *reflexive verb* to fill (up).

remporter *verb* (*objet*) to take back; (*prix, victoire*) to win.

remuant , -ante *adjective* (*enfant*) restless.

remuer *verb*
1 (*café etc*) to stir; (*salade*) to toss.
2 (*bouger*) to move; (*gigoter*) to fidget.

renard *m noun* fox.

rencontre *f noun* meeting; (*en sport*) match; **aller à la r. de quelqu'un** to go to meet somebody.

rencontrer *verb* to meet; (*équipe*) to play.

rencontrer (se) *reflexive verb* to meet.

rendez-vous *invariable m noun* appointment; (*d'amoureux*) date; (*lieu*) meeting place; **donner r. à quelqu'un** to make an appointment with somebody; **prendre r. avec quelqu'un** to make an appointment with somebody.

rendormir * (se) *reflexive verb* to go back to sleep.

rendre *verb*
1 (*objet*) to give back; (*monnaie*) to give; (*vomir*) to bring up; **r. célèbre/plus grand/etc** to make

famous/bigger/*etc*.
2 (*vomir*) to throw up.

rendre (se) *reflexive verb* (*se soumettre*) to surrender (**à quel-qu'un** to somebody); (*aller*) to go (**à** to); **se r. utile**/*etc* to make oneself useful/*etc*.

rendu, -ue
1 *past participle of* **rendre**.
2 *adjective* **être r.** to have arrived.

rênes *fpl noun* reins.

renfermé *m noun* **sentir le r.** (*chambre etc*) to smell stuffy.

renfermer *verb* to contain.

renflement *m noun* bulge.

renforcer *verb* to strengthen.

renforts *mpl noun* (*troupes*) rein-forcements.

renifler *verb* to sniff.

renne *m noun* reindeer.

renommé, -ée *adjective* famous (**pour** for).

renommée *f noun* fame.

renoncer *verb* **r. à quelque chose**/**à faire** to give up some-thing/doing.

renouveler *verb* to renew; (*erreur, question*) to repeat.

renouveler (se) *reflexive verb* (*incident*) to happen again.

renseignement *m noun* (piece of) information; **des renseigne-ments** information; **le bureau des renseignements** information desk; **les renseignements** (*au téléphone*) directory inquiries.

renseigner *verb* to inform, give some information to (**sur** about).

renseigner (se) *reflexive verb* to find out, inquire (**sur** about).

rentrée *f noun* return; **r. (des classes)** beginning of term *or* of the school year.

rentrer *verb*
1 (*auxiliary* **être**) (*retourner*) to go *or* come back; (*chez soi*) to go *or* come (back) home; (*entrer de nouveau*) to go *or* come back in; (*élèves*) to go back to school; **r. dans** to go *or* come back into; (*pays*) to return to; (*heurter*) to crash into; (*s'emboîter dans*) to fit into.
2 (*auxiliary* **avoir**) (*objet, linge etc*) to bring *or* take in; (*voiture*) to put away; (*chemise*) to tuck in; (*griffes*) to draw in.

renverse (à la) *adverb* (*tomber*) backwards.

renverser *verb* (*mettre à l'envers*) to turn upside down; (*faire tom-ber*) to knock over; (*piéton*) to knock down; (*liquide*) to spill.

renverser (se) *reflexive verb* (*vase etc*) to fall over; (*liquide*) to spill.

renvoi *m noun* (*d'un employé*) dismissal; (*rot*) burp.

renvoyer * *verb* to send back; (*employé*) to dismiss; (*élève*) to expel; (*balle etc*) to throw back.

réorganiser *verb* to reorganize.

repaire *m noun* den.

répandre *verb* (*liquide*) to spill; (*nouvelle*) to spread; (*odeur*) to give off; (*lumière, larmes*) to shed; (*gravillons etc*) to scatter.

répandre (se) *reflexive verb* (*nouvelle*) to spread; (*liquide*) to spill; **se r. dans** (*fumée, odeur*) to spread through.

répandu, -ue *adjective* (*opinion etc*) widespread.

reparaître *verb* to reappear.

réparateur, -trice *m or f noun* repairer.

réparation *f noun* repair; **en r.** under repair.

réparer *verb* to repair, mend; (*erreur*) to put right.

repartir * *verb* (*auxiliary* être) to set off again; (*s'en retourner*) to go back.

répartir *verb* (*partager*) to share (out).

repas *m noun* meal; **prendre un r.** to have a meal.

repassage *m noun* ironing; **faire du r.** to do some ironing.

repasser *verb*
1 (*retourner, rentrer*) to come *or* go back.
2 (*traverser*) to go back over; (*leçon*) to go over; (*film*) to show again; (*linge*) to iron.

repêcher *verb* (*objet*) to fish out.

repentir * (se) *reflexive verb* to be sorry (**de** for).

repère *m noun* (*guide*) mark; **point de r.** (*espace, temps*) landmark.

repérer *verb* to locate.

repérer (se) *reflexive verb* to get one's bearings.

répertoire *m noun* **r. d'adresses** address book.

répéter *verb* to repeat; (*pièce de théâtre*) to rehearse.

répéter (se) *reflexive verb* (*personne*) to repeat oneself; (*événement*) to happen again.

répétitif , -ive *adjective* repetitive.

répétition *f noun* repetition; (*au théâtre*) rehearsal.

replacer *verb* to put back.

repli *m noun* fold.

replier *verb* to fold (up); (*couverture*) to fold back; (*ailes, jambes*) to tuck in.

replier (se) *reflexive verb* (*siège*) to fold up; (*couverture*) to fold back.

réplique *f noun* (sharp) reply; (*au théâtre*) lines.

répliquer *verb* to reply (**que** that); (*avec impatience*) to answer back.

répondeur *m noun* **r. (téléphonique)** answering machine.

répondre *verb* to answer (**que** that); (*être impertinent*) to answer back; (*réagir*) to respond (**à** to); **r. à quelqu'un** to answer somebody; (*avec impertinence*) to answer somebody back; **r. à** (*lettre, question*) to answer.

répondu, -ue *past participle of* répondre.

réponse *f noun* answer.

reportage *m noun* (news) report; (*en direct*) commentary.

reporter [1] *verb* to take back; (*différer*) to put off (**à** until).

reporter [2] *m noun* reporter.

repos *m noun* rest; (*tranquillité*) peace (and quiet); **jour de r.** day off.

reposant , -ante *adjective* restful.

reposer *verb* (*objet*) to put back down; (*délasser*) to relax.

reposer (se) *reflexive verb* to rest.

repousser *verb*
1 (*en arrière*) to push back; (*écarter*) to push away; (*différer*) to put off.
2 (*cheveux, feuilles*) to grow again.

reprendre * *verb*
1 (*objet*) to take back; (*évadé*) to recapture; (*souffle, forces*) to get back; (*activité*) to take up again; (*refrain*) to take up; **r. de la viande/un œuf/***etc* to take (some) more meat / another egg /

etc.
2 (*recommencer*) to start (up) (again); (*affaires*) to pick up; (*dire*) to go on.

reprendre (se) *reflexive verb* to correct oneself; **s'y r. à deux fois** to have another go (at it).

représentant , -ante *m or f noun* representative; **r. de commerce** (travelling) salesman *or* saleswoman.

représentation *f noun* (*au théâtre*) performance.

représenter *verb* to represent; (*pièce de théâtre*) to perform.

reprise *f noun* (*d'émission de télévision*) repeat; (*de tissu*) mend; *Boxe* round; (*économique*) recovery; (*pour nouvel achat*) part exchange, trade-in; **à plusieurs reprises** on several occasions.

repriser *verb* (*chaussette etc*) to mend.

reproche *m noun* criticism; **faire des reproches à quelqu'un** to criticize somebody.

reprocher *verb* **r. quelque chose à quelqu'un** to criticize somebody for something.

reproduction *f noun* breeding; (*copie*) copy.

reproduire * *verb* (*modèle etc*) to copy.

reproduire (se) *reflexive verb* (*animaux*) to breed; (*incident etc*) to happen again.

reptile *m noun* reptile.

républicain , -aine *adjective & m or f noun* republican.

république *f noun* republic; **la R. Tchèque** the Czech Republic.

réputation *f noun* reputation; **avoir la r. d'être** to have a reputation for being.

requin *m noun* (*poisson*) shark.

RER *m abbreviation* (*Réseau express régional*) = express rail network serving Paris and its suburbs.

rescapé , -ée *m or f noun* survivor.

réseau , -x *m noun* network.

réservation *f noun* reservation, booking.

réserve *f noun* (*provision*) stock, reserve; (*entrepôt*) storeroom; **en r.** in reserve; **r. naturelle** nature reserve.

réservé , -ée *adjective* (*personne, place*) reserved.

réserver *verb* (*garder*) to save, reserve (**à** for); (*place, table*) to book, reserve; **se r. pour** to save oneself for.

réservoir *m noun* (*citerne*) tank; **r. d'essence** petrol tank.

résidence *f noun* residence; **r. secondaire** second home.

résidentiel , -ielle *adjective* (*quartier*) residential.

résider *verb* to be resident (**à, en, dans** in).

résigner (se) *reflexive verb* to resign oneself (**à quelque chose** to something, **à faire** to doing).

résistance *f noun* resistance (**à** to); (*électrique*) (heating) element; **plat de r.** main dish.

résistant , -ante *adjective* tough; **r. à la chaleur** heat-resistant.

résister *verb* **r. à** to resist; (*chaleur, fatigue*) to withstand.

résolu , -ue
1 *past participle of* **résoudre**.
2 *adjective* determined (**à faire** to do).

résolution *f noun* (*décision*) décision.

résonner verb (cris etc) to ring out; (salle) to echo (de with).

résoudre * verb (problème) to solve; (difficulté) to clear up.

respect m noun respect (pour, de for).

respecter verb to respect.

respectueux , -euse adjective respectful (envers to).

respiration f noun breathing; (haleine) breath.

respirer verb
1 to breathe; (reprendre haleine) to get one's breath back.
2 (inhaler) to breathe in.

resplendissant , -ante adjective (visage) glowing (de with).

responsabilité f noun responsibility.

responsable
1 adjective responsible (de quelque chose for something, devant quelqu'un to somebody).
2 m or f noun (chef) person in charge; (coupable) person responsible (de for).

ressemblance f noun likeness (avec to).

ressembler verb r. à to look or be like.

ressembler (se) reflexive verb to look or be alike.

ressentir * verb to feel.

resserrer verb (nœud) to tighten.

resserrer (se) reflexive verb (nœud etc) to tighten.

resservir * verb (outil etc) to come in useful (again); se r. du poulet to have some more chicken.

ressort m noun (objet) spring.

ressortir * verb (auxiliary être) to go or come back out; (se voir) to stand out.

ressources fpl noun (moyens, argent) resources.

restaurant m noun restaurant.

restaurer verb (réparer) to restore.

reste m noun rest (de of); restes (de repas) leftovers; un r. de fromage/etc some left-over cheese/etc.

rester verb (auxiliary être) to stay; (calme, jeune etc) to keep, stay; (subsister) to be left; il reste du pain/etc there's some bread/etc left (over); il me reste une minute I have one minute left; l'argent qui lui reste the money he or she has left.

restreindre * verb to limit (à to).

résultat m noun (score, d'examen etc) result; (conséquence) outcome, result.

résumé m noun summary.

résumer verb to summarize; (situation) to sum up.

rétablir verb to restore.

rétablir (se) reflexive verb (malade) to recover.

rétablissement m noun (de malade) recovery.

retard m noun (sur un programme etc) delay; en r. late; en r. dans quelque chose behind in something; en r. sur quelqu'un/quelque chose behind somebody/something; rattraper son r. to catch up; avoir du r. to be late; (sur un programme) to be behind; avoir une heure de r. to be an hour late.

retardataire m or f noun latecomer.

retarder verb
1 (différer) to delay; (date, montre) to put back; r. quelqu'un

(*dans une activité*) to put somebody behind.
2 (*avoir du retard*) (*montre*) to be slow; **r. de cinq minutes** to be five minutes slow.

retenir * *verb* (*empêcher d'agir*) to hold back; (*souffle*) to hold; (*réserver*) to book; (*se souvenir de*) to remember; (*fixer*) to hold (in place); (*chiffre*) to carry; (*chaleur, odeur*) to retain; **r. quelqu'un prisonnier** to keep somebody prisoner.

retenir (se) *reflexive verb* (*se contenir*) to restrain oneself; **se r. de faire** to stop oneself (from) doing; **se r. à** to cling to.

retentir *verb* to ring (out) (**de** with).

retenue *f noun* (*punition*) detention.

retirer *verb* (*sortir*) to take out; (*ôter*) to take off; (*éloigner*) to take away; **r. quelque chose à quelqu'un** (*permis etc*) to take something away from somebody.

retomber *verb* to fall (again); (*pendre*) to hang (down); (*après un saut etc*) to land.

retouche *f noun* (*de vêtement*) alteration.

retoucher *verb* (*vêtement*) to alter.

retour *m noun* return; **être de r.** to be back (**de** from); **à mon retour** when I get *or* got back.

retourner *verb*
1 (*auxiliary* **avoir**) (*matelas, steak etc*) to turn over; (*terre etc*) to turn; (*vêtement, sac etc*) to turn inside out.
2 (*auxiliary* **être**) (*aller de nouveau*) to go back, return.

retourner (se) *reflexive verb* to turn round, look round; (*sur le

dos*) to turn over; (*voiture*) to overturn.

retraite *f noun* (*d'employé*) retirement; (*pension*) (retirement) pension; **prendre sa r.** to retire; **à la r.** retired.

retraité , -ée
1 *adjective* retired.
2 *m or f noun* senior citizen, pensioner.

retransmettre *verb* to broadcast.

retransmission *f noun* broadcast.

rétrécir *verb* (*au lavage*) to shrink.

rétrécir (se) *reflexive verb* (*rue etc*) to narrow.

rétro *invariable adjective* (*personne, idée etc*) old-fashioned.

retrousser *verb* (*manches*) to roll up.

retrouver *verb* to find (again); (*rejoindre*) to meet (again); (*forces, santé*) to get back; (*se rappeler*) to recall.

retrouver (se) *reflexive verb* (*être*) to find oneself; (*se rencontrer*) to meet; **s'y r.** to find one's way around.

rétroviseur *m noun* (*de véhicule*) mirror.

réunion *f noun* (*séance*) meeting.

réunir *verb* (*objets*) to gather; (*convoquer*) to call together.

réunir (se) *reflexive verb* to meet, get together.

réussi , -ie *adjective* successful.

réussir *verb*
1 (*bien faire*) to make a success of; (*examen*) to pass; *Rugby* (*essai*) to score; **le soufflé était très réussi** the soufflé was a great success.
2 (*bien marcher*) to be successful.
3 r. à un examen to pass an exam;

r. à faire to manage to do; **r. à quelqu'un** (*climat*, *aliment*) to agree with somebody.

réussite *f noun* success.

revanche *f noun* (*en sport*) return game; **en r.** on the other hand.

rêve *m noun* dream; **faire un r.** to have a dream; **maison**/*etc* **de r.** dream house/*etc*.

réveil *m noun* (*pendule*) alarm (clock); **à son r.** when he wakes (up) *or* woke (up).

réveillé , -ée *adjective* awake.

réveiller *verb* to wake (up).

réveiller (se) *reflexive verb* to wake (up).

réveillon *m noun* midnight supper (on *Christmas Eve or New Year's Eve*).

révéler *verb* to reveal (**que** that).

revenant *m noun* ghost.

revendication *f noun* claim; demand.

revendiquer *verb* to claim; (*exiger*) to demand.

revenir * *verb* (*auxiliary* **être**) to come back; **r. à** (*activité*, *sujet*) to go back to; **r. à quelqu'un** (*forces*, *mémoire*) to come back to somebody; **r. à soi** to come round; **r. de** (*surprise*) to get over; **r. sur** (*décision*, *promesse*) to go back on; **ça m'est revenu cher** it cost me a lot of money; **ça me revient à 100 francs par jour** it costs me 100 francs a day.

revenu *m noun* income (**de** from).

rêver *verb* to dream (**de** of, **de faire** of doing, **que** that).

revers *m noun* (*de veste*) lapel; (*de pantalon*) turn-up.

revêtement *m noun* (*de route etc*) surface.

rêveur , -euse *m or f noun* dreamer.

revient *m noun* **prix de r.** cost price.

réviser *verb* (*leçon*) to revise; (*machine*, *voiture*) to service.

révision *f noun* revision; service.

revoir * *verb* to see (again); (*texte*, *leçon*) to revise; **au r.** goodbye.

révoltant , -ante *adjective* revolting.

révolte *f noun* rebellion, revolt.

révolté , -ée *m or f noun* rebel.

révolter *verb* to sicken.

révolter (se) *reflexive verb* to rebel (**contre** against).

révolution *f noun* revolution.

révolutionnaire *adjective* & *m or f noun* revolutionary.

revolver *m noun* gun.

revue *f noun* (*magazine*) magazine.

rez-de-chaussée *invariable m noun* ground floor.

rhabiller (se) *reflexive verb* to get dressed again.

rhinocéros *m noun* rhinoceros.

Rhône (le) *m noun* the Rhone.

rhubarbe *f noun* rhubarb.

rhum *m noun* rum.

rhumatisme *m noun* rheumatism; **avoir des rhumatismes** to have rheumatism.

rhume *m noun* cold; **r. des foins** hay fever.

ri , riant *past participle* & *present participle of* **rire**.

ricaner *verb* to snigger.

riche
1 *adjective* rich.
2 *m or f noun* rich person; **les riches** the rich.

richesse *f noun* wealth; **richesses** (*trésor*) riches.

ricocher *verb* to rebound.

ricochet *m noun* (*de pierre*) rebound.

ride *f noun* wrinkle.

ridé , -ée *adjective* wrinkled.

rideau , -x *m noun* curtain; (*de magasin*) shutter.

ridicule *adjective* ridiculous.

ridiculiser (se) *reflexive verb* to make a fool of oneself.

rien
1 *pronoun* nothing; **il ne sait r.** he knows nothing, he doesn't know anything; **r. du tout** nothing at all; **r. d'autre/de bon**/*etc* nothing else/good/*etc*; **de r.!** (*je vous en prie*) don't mention it!; **ça ne fait r.** it doesn't matter; **r. que** just.
2 *m noun* (*mere*) nothing.

rigide *adjective* rigid; (*carton, muscle*) stiff.

rigoler *verb Familiar* to laugh; (*s'amuser*) to have fun.

rigolo , -ote *adjective Familiar* funny.

rime *f noun* rhyme.

rimer *verb* to rhyme (**avec** with).

rinçage *m noun* rinsing.

rincer *verb* to rinse; (*verre*) to rinse (out).

ring *m noun* (*boxing*) ring.

rire *
1 *verb* to laugh (**de** at); (*s'amuser*) to have a good time; (*plaisanter*) to joke; **pour r.** for a joke.
2 *m noun* laugh; **rires** laughter; **le fou r.** the giggles.

risque *m noun* risk; **assurance tous risques** comprehensive insurance; **courir le r. de faire** to risk doing.

risqué , -ée *adjective* risky.

risquer *verb* to risk; **r. de faire** to stand a good chance of doing.

rivage *m noun* shore.

rival , -e , -aux *adjective & m or f noun* rival.

rivaliser *verb* to compete (**avec** with, **de** in).

rive *f noun* (*de fleuve*) bank; (*de lac*) shore.

rivière *f noun* river.

riz *m noun* rice; **r. au lait** rice pudding.

RN *abbreviation* = **route nationale.**

robe *f noun* (*de femme*) dress; **r. du soir/de mariée** evening/wedding dress; **r. de chambre** dressing gown.

robinet *m noun* tap; **eau du r.** tap water.

robot *m noun* robot.

robuste *adjective* sturdy.

roche *f noun* rock.

rocher *m noun* rock.

rocheux , -euse *adjective* rocky.

rock *m noun* (*musique*) rock.

roder *verb* (*moteur, voiture*) to run in.

rôder *verb* to prowl (about).

rôdeur , -euse *m or f noun* prowler.

rognon *m noun* kidney.

roi *m noun* king.

rôle *m noun* (*au théâtre*) role, part; (*d'un père etc*) job; **à tour de r.** in turn.

romain , -aine *adjective & m or f noun* Roman.

roman *m noun* novel; **r. d'aventures** adventure story; **r. d'amour** love story.

romancier , -ière *m or f noun* novelist.

romantique *adjective* romantic.

rompre * (se) *reflexive verb*

(*corde etc*) to break; (*digue*) to burst.

rompu , -ue *past participle of* se rompre.

ronces *fpl noun* brambles.

ronchonner *verb Familiar* to grumble.

rond , ronde
1 *adjective* round; **dix francs tout r.** ten francs exactly.
2 *m noun* (*cercle*) circle, ring; **en r.** (*s'asseoir etc*) in a ring *or* circle; **tourner en r.** to go round and round.

ronde *f noun* (*de soldat*) round; (*de policier*) beat, round.

rondelle *f noun* (*tranche*) slice.

rondin *m noun* log.

rond-point *m noun* (*plural* ronds-points) roundabout.

ronflement *m noun* snore; **ronflements** snoring.

ronfler *verb* to snore.

ronger *verb* to gnaw (at); (*ver, mer, rouille*) to eat into; **se r. les ongles** to bite one's nails.

ronronnement *m noun* purr(ing).

ronronner *verb* to purr.

rosbif *m noun* **du r.** roast beef; (*à rôtir*) roasting beef; **un r.** a joint of roast beef.

rose
1 *f noun* (*fleur*) rose.
2 *adjective & m noun* (*couleur*) pink.

rosé *adjective & m noun* (*vin*) rosé.

roseau , -x *m noun* reed.

rosée *f noun* dew.

rosier *m noun* rose bush.

rossignol *m noun* nightingale.

rot *m noun Familiar* burp.

roter *verb Familiar* to burp.

rôti *m noun* **du r.** roasting meat; (*cuit*) roast meat; **un r.** a joint; **r. de porc** (joint of) roast pork.

rotin *m noun* cane.

rôtir *verb* to roast; **faire r.** to roast.

rôtir (se) *reflexive verb* to roast.

roue *f noun* wheel.

rouge
1 *adjective* red; (*fer*) red-hot.
2 *m noun* (*couleur*) red; **r.** (à lèvres) lipstick; **le feu est au r.** the (traffic) lights are red.

rouge-gorge *m noun* (*plural* rouges-gorges) robin.

rougeole *f noun* measles.

rougir *verb* (*de honte*) to blush; (*de colère*) to flush (**de** with).

rouille *f noun* rust.

rouillé , -ée *adjective* rusty.

rouiller *verb* to rust.

rouiller (se) *reflexive verb* to rust.

roulant , -ante *adjective* (*escalier*) moving; (*meuble*) on wheels.

rouleau , -x *m noun* (*outil*) roller; (*de papier etc*) roll; **r. à pâtisserie** rolling pin; **r. compresseur** steamroller.

rouler *verb* to roll; (*train, voiture*) to go; (*conducteur*) to drive; (*crêpe, tapis etc*) to roll up.

rouler (se) *reflexive verb* to roll; **se r. dans** (*couverture etc*) to roll oneself (up) in.

roulette *f noun* (*de meuble*) castor; (*de dentiste*) drill.

roulotte *f noun* (*de gitan*) caravan.

roumain , -aine *adjective & m or f noun* Romanian.

Roumanie (la) *f noun* Romania.

round *m noun Boxe* round.

rouspéter *verb Familiar* to

complain.

rousse *see* roux.

rousseur *f noun* tache de r. freckle.

roussir *verb* (*brûler*) to scorch.

route *f noun* road (de to); (*itinéraire*) way; r. **nationale/départementale** main/secondary road; **en r.!** let's go!; **par la r.** by road; **mettre en r.** (*voiture etc*) to start (up); **se mettre en r.** to set out (pour for); **une heure de r.** an hour's drive *or* walk *etc*; **bonne r.!** have a good trip!

routier , -ière
1 *adjective* carte/sécurité routière road map/safety.
2 *m noun* (long-distance) lorry driver.

roux , rousse
1 *adjective* (*cheveux*) red; (*personne*) red-haired.
2 *m or f noun* redhead.

royal , -e , -aux *adjective* royal.

royaume *m noun* kingdom.

Royaume-Uni (le) *m noun* the United Kingdom.

ruban *m noun* ribbon; **r. adhésif** sticky tape.

rubéole *f noun* German measles.

rubis *m noun* ruby; (*de montre*) jewel.

ruche *f noun* (bee)hive.

rude *adjective* (*pénible*) tough; (*hiver, voix*) harsh; (*grossier*) crude; (*rêche*) rough.

rudement *adverb* (*parler, traiter*) harshly; (*très*) *Familiar* awfully.

rue *f noun* street; **à la r.** (*sans domicile*) on the streets.

ruelle *f noun* alley(way).

ruer *verb* (*cheval*) to kick (out).

ruer (se) *reflexive verb* to rush (sur at).

rugby *m noun* rugby.

rugbyman *m noun* (*plural* rugbymen) rugby player.

rugir *verb* to roar.

rugissement *m noun* roar.

rugueux , -euse *adjective* rough.

ruine *f noun* ruin; **en r.** in ruins; **tomber en r.** (*bâtiment*) to become a ruin, crumble; (*mur*) to crumble.

ruiner *verb* (*personne, santé etc*) to ruin; **se r.** to be(come) ruined, ruin oneself.

ruisseau , -x *m noun* stream.

ruisseler *verb* to stream (de with).

rural , -e, -aux *adjective* vie/école/etc rurale country life/school/etc.

ruse *f noun* (*subterfuge*) trick; **la r.** (*habileté*) cunning.

rusé , -ée *adjective* cunning.

russe
1 *adjective & m or f noun* Russian.
2 *m noun* (*langue*) Russian.

Russie (la) *f noun* Russia.

rythme *m noun* rhythm; (*de travail*) rate; **au r. de trois par jour** at a rate of three a day.

rythmé , -ée *adjective* rhythmical.

S

sa *see* **son.**

sable *m noun* sand.

sabler *verb* (*rue*) to sand.

sablier *m noun* (*de cuisine*) egg timer.

sablonneux , -euse *adjective* sandy.

sabot *m noun* (*de cheval etc*) hoof; (*chaussure*) clog; **s. (de Denver)** (wheel) clamp.

sac *m noun* bag; (*grand et en toile*) sack; **s. (à main)** handbag; **s. à dos** rucksack.

saccadé , -ée *adjective* jerky.

saccager *verb* (*détruire*) to wreck.

sachant , sache(s) , sachent *etc see* **savoir.**

sachet *m noun* (small) bag; **s. de thé** teabag.

sacoche *f noun* bag; (*de vélo*) saddlebag.

sacré , -ée *adjective* (*saint*) sacred; **un s. menteur/etc** *Familiar* a damned liar/*etc.*

sacrifice *m noun* sacrifice.

sacrifier *verb* to sacrifice (**à** to, **pour** for); **se s.** to sacrifice oneself.

sage *adjective* wise; (*enfant*) good.

sage-femme *f noun* (*plural* **sages-femmes**) midwife.

sagement *adverb* wisely; (*avec calme*) quietly.

saignant , -ante *adjective* (*viande*) rare.

saignement *m noun* bleeding; **s. de nez** nosebleed.

saigner *verb* to bleed; **je saigne du nez** my nose is bleeding, I've got a nosebleed.

sain , saine *adjective* healthy; **s. et sauf** safe and sound.

saint , sainte
1 *adjective* holy; **s. Jean** Saint John; **la Sainte Vierge** the Blessed Virgin.
2 *m or f noun* saint.

Saint-Sylvestre *f noun* New Year's Eve.

sais , sait *see* **savoir.**

saisir *verb* to grab (hold of); (*occasion*) to jump at; (*comprendre*) to understand; **se s. de** to grab (hold of).

saison *f noun* season.

salade *f noun* (*laitue*) lettuce; **s. (verte)** (green) salad; **s. de fruits/etc** fruit/*etc* salad.

saladier *m noun* salad bowl.

salaire *m noun* wage(s).

salami *m noun* salami.

salarié , -ée *m or f noun* wage earner.

sale *adjective* dirty.

salé , -ée *adjective* (*goût, plat*) salty; (*aliment*) salted.

saler *verb* to salt.

saleté *f noun* dirtiness; filthiness; (*crasse*) dirt, filth; **saletés** (*détritus*) rubbish.

salière *f noun* saltcellar.

salir *verb* to (make) dirty.

salir (se) *reflexive verb* to get dirty.

salissant , -ante *adjective* dirty; (*étoffe*) that shows the dirt.

salive *f noun* saliva.

salle *f noun* room; (*très grande*) hall; (*de théâtre*) theatre, auditorium; (*de cinéma*) cinema; (*d'hôpi-*

tal) ward; **s. à manger** dining room; **s. de bain(s)** bathroom; **s. de classe** classroom; **s. de jeux** games room; **s. de musique** music room; **s. d'opération** operating theatre; **s. des professeurs** staff room.

salon *m noun* sitting room, lounge; (*exposition*) show.

salopette *f noun* (*d'enfant, d'ouvrier*) dungarees.

saluer *verb* to greet; (*de la main*) to wave to; (*de la tête*) to nod to.

salut
  1 *m noun* greeting; wave; nod.
  2 *interjection* hello!, hi!; (*au revoir*) bye!

samedi *m noun* Saturday.

sandale *f noun* sandal.

sandwich *m noun* sandwich; **s. au fromage** cheese sandwich.

sandwicherie *f noun* sandwich bar.

sang *m noun* blood.

sang-froid *m noun* self-control; **garder son s.** to keep calm; **avec s.** calmly.

sanglant , -ante *adjective* bloody.

sanglier *m noun* wild boar.

sanglot *m noun* sob.

sangloter *verb* to sob.

sanguin *adjective* **groupe s.** blood group.

sanitaires (les) *mpl noun* (*salle de bain et toilettes*) the bathroom and toilet.

sans *preposition* without; **s. faire** without doing; **s. qu'il le sache** without him *or* his knowing; **s. cela** otherwise; **s. importance** unimportant.

sans-abri *invariable m or f noun* homeless person.

santé *f noun* health; (**à votre**) **s.!** your (good) health!, cheers!

saoudien , ienne *adjective & m or f noun* Saudi.

sapeur-pompier *m noun* (*plural* sapeurs-pompiers) fireman.

sapin *m noun* (*arbre, bois*) fir; **s. de Noël** Christmas tree.

sardine *f noun* sardine.

satellite *m noun* satellite.

satin *m noun* satin.

satisfaction *f noun* satisfaction.

satisfaire * *verb* to satisfy.

satisfaisant , -ante *adjective* satisfactory.

satisfait, -e *adjective* satisfied (**de** with); (*désir*) fulfilled; **s. ou remboursé** (*dans une publicité*) satisfaction or your money back.

sauce *f noun* sauce; (*jus de viande*) gravy; **s. tomate** tomato sauce.

saucisse *f noun* sausage.

saucisson *m noun* (cold) sausage.

sauf *preposition* except (**que** that).

saule *m noun* willow.

saumon *m noun* salmon.

sauna *m noun* sauna.

saupoudrer *verb* to sprinkle (**de** with).

saura , saurai(t) *etc see* savoir.

saut *m noun* jump, leap; **faire un s.** to jump, leap; **faire un s. chez quelqu'un** to drop in on somebody, pop round to somebody's.

sauter *verb*
  1 (*bondir*) to jump, leap; **faire s.** (*détruire*) to blow up; **s. à la corde** to skip; **ça saute aux yeux** it's obvious.
  2 (*fossé, barrière*) to jump (over); (*mot, repas*) to skip.

sauterelle *f noun* grasshopper.

sauvage *adjective* (*animal,*

plante) wild; *(tribu, homme)* primitive.

sauver *verb* to save; *(d'un danger)* to rescue (de from); **s. la vie à quelqu'un** to save somebody's life.

sauver (se) *reflexive verb* to run away *or* off.

sauvetage *m noun* rescue.

sauveteur *m noun* rescuer.

sauveur *m noun* saviour.

savant *m noun* scientist.

savate *f noun Familiar* old slipper.

saveur *f noun* flavour.

savoir * *verb* to know; **s. lire/na-ger/etc** to know how to read/swim/etc; **faire s. à quelqu'un que** to inform somebody that; **je n'en sais rien** I have no idea.

savon *m noun* soap; *(morceau)* (bar of) soap.

savonner *verb* to wash with soap.

savonnette *f noun* bar of soap.

savonneux , -euse *adjective* soapy.

savourer *verb* to enjoy.

savoureux , -euse *adjective* tasty.

saxophone *m noun* saxophone.

scandale *m noun* scandal; **faire un s.** to make a scene.

scandaleux , -euse *adjective* shocking.

scandaliser *verb* to shock.

scandinave *adjective & m or f noun* Scandinavian.

scanner *m noun (appareil)* scanner.

scarlatine *f noun* scarlet fever.

scénario *m noun (dialogues etc)* film script.

scène *f noun (plateau)* stage; *(décors, partie de pièce, dispute)*

scene; **mettre en s.** to direct.

schéma *m noun* diagram.

scie *f noun* saw.

science *f noun* science; **étudier les sciences** to study science; **sciences naturelles** biology; **sciences physiques** physics.

science-fiction *f noun* science fiction.

scientifique
1 *adjective* scientific.
2 *m or f noun* scientist.

scier *verb* to saw.

scintiller *verb* to sparkle; *(étoiles)* to twinkle.

scolaire *adjective* **année/etc s.** school year/etc.

score *m noun (de match)* score.

scotch ® *m noun (ruban)* sellotape ®.

scrutin *m noun* voting, ballot.

sculpter *verb* to carve, sculpture.

sculpteur *m noun* sculptor.

sculpture *f noun* sculpture.

se *(s' before vowel or mute h)* pronoun *(complément direct)* himself; *(féminin)* herself; *(non humain)* itself; *(indéfini)* oneself; *plural* themselves.

▪ *(indirect)* to himself; to herself; to itself; to oneself; **elle se parle** she talks to herself.

▪ *(réciproque)* each other, one another; *(indirect)* to each other, to one another; **ils s'écrivent** they write to each other.

▪ *(avec les parties du corps)* **il se lave les mains** he washes his hands.

séance *f noun (au cinéma)* show (ing).

seau , -x *m noun* bucket.

sec , sèche
1 *adjective* dry; *(légumes)* dried;

(*ton*) harsh; **coup s.** (sharp)
knock, bang; **frapper un coup s.**
to knock (sharply), bang; **bruit s.**
(*rupture*) snap.
2 *m noun* à s. (*rivière*) dried up; **au
s.** in a dry place.

sécateur *m noun* pruning shears.

sèche-cheveux *invariable m
noun* hair drier.

sèche-linge *invariable m noun*
tumble drier.

sécher *verb*
1 (*vêtement, cheveux*) to dry.
2 (*cours*) *Familiar* to skip.

sécheresse *f noun* (*période*)
drought.

séchoir *m noun* s. à linge clothes-
horse.

second , -onde
1 *adjective & m or f noun* second.
2 *m noun* (*étage*) second floor.
3 *f noun* (*de lycée*) = fifth form;
(*vitesse*) second (gear).

secondaire *adjective* secondary.

seconde *f noun* (*instant*) second.

secouer *verb* to shake.

secourir *verb* to assist.

secouriste *m or f noun* first-aid
worker.

secours *m noun* assistance, help;
(*premiers*) s. first aid; **aller au s.
de quelqu'un** to go to somebody's assistance; **au s.!** help!;
sortie de s. emergency exit; **roue
de s.** spare wheel.

secousse *f noun* jolt.

secret , -ète
1 *adjective* secret.
2 *m noun* secret; **en s.** in secret.

secrétaire
1 *m or f noun* secretary; (*de médecin etc*) receptionist.
2 *m noun* (*meuble*) writing desk.

secrétariat *m noun* (*bureau*)
secretary's office.

secteur *m noun* (*électricité*)
mains.

section *f noun* section; (*de bus*)
stage; (*de parti*) branch.

sécurité *f noun* safety; **en s.** safe;
S. sociale Social security.

séduisant , -ante *adjective*
attractive.

segment *m noun* segment.

seigneur *m noun* lord.

sein *m noun* breast.

Seine (la) *f noun* the Seine.

seize *adjective & m noun* sixteen.

seizième *adjective & m or f noun*
sixteenth.

séjour *m noun* stay; (**salle de) s.**
living room.

séjourner *verb* to stay.

sel *m noun* salt; **sels de bain** bath
salts.

sélection *f noun* selection.

sélectionner *verb* to select.

self(-service) *m noun* self-service
restaurant *or* shop.

selle *f noun* saddle.

selon *preposition* according to
(**que** whether).

semaine *f noun* week; **en s.** in the
week.

semblable *adjective* similar (**à**
to).

semblant *m noun* **faire s.** to
pretend (**de faire** to do).

sembler *verb* to seem (**à** to); **il
(me) semble vieux** he seems *or*
looks old (to me); **il me semble
que** (+ *indicative*) I think that, it
seems to me that.

semelle *f noun* (*de chaussure*)
sole.

semer *verb* (*graines*) to sow.

semestre *m noun* half-year;

(*scolaire*) semester.

semi-remorque *m noun*
articulated lorry.

semoule *f noun* semolina.

sénat *m noun* senate.

sens [1] *m noun* (*signification*)
meaning, sense; **avoir du bon s.**
to have sense, be sensible; **ça n'a
pas de s.** that doesn't make sense.

sens [2] *m noun* (*direction*) direction; **s. giratoire** roundabout; **s.
interdit** *or* **unique** (*rue*) one-way
street; **'s. interdit'** 'no entry'; **s.
dessus dessous** (*en désordre*) upside down; **dans le s./le s. inverse
des aiguilles d'une montre**
clockwise/anticlockwise.

sensation *f noun* feeling.

sensationnel , -elle *adjective*
sensational.

sensible *adjective* sensitive (**à** to);
(*douloureux*) tender; (*progrès etc*)
noticeable.

sentier *m noun* path.

sentiment *m noun* feeling.

sentir * *verb* to feel; (*odeur*) to
smell; (*goût*) to taste; **s. le parfum**/*etc* to smell of perfume/*etc*;
s. le poisson/*etc* (*avoir le goût de*)
to taste of fish/*etc*; **je ne peux pas
le s.** (*supporter*) I can't stand him;
se s. fatigué/*etc* to feel tired/*etc*.

séparé, -ée *adjective* (*chambre*)
separate; (*personnes*) separated
(**de** from).

séparément *adverb* separately.

séparer *verb* to separate (**de**
from).

séparer (se) *reflexive verb* (*se
quitter*) to part; (*couple*) to separate; **se s. de** (*chien etc*) to part
with.

sept *adjective & m noun* seven.

septante *adjective* (*en Belgique,*

Suisse) seventy.

septembre *m noun* September.

septième *adjective & m or f noun*
seventh.

sera , serai(t) *etc see* **être**.

serbe *adjective & m or f noun* Serb,
Serbian.

Serbie (la) *f noun* Serbia.

série *f noun* series; (*ensemble*) set.

sérieusement *adverb* seriously;
(*travailler*) conscientiously.

sérieux , -euse
  1 *adjective* serious.
  2 *m noun* **prendre au s.** to take
  seriously; **garder son s.** to keep a
  straight face.

seringue *f noun* syringe.

serment *m noun* oath; **faire le s.
de faire** to promise to do.

serpent *m noun* snake.

serpillière *f noun* floor cloth.

serre *f noun* greenhouse.

serré , -ée *adjective* (*nœud etc*)
tight; (*gens*) packed (together).

serrer *verb*
  1 (*tenir*) to grip; (*presser*) to
  squeeze; (*nœud, vis*) to tighten;
  (*poing*) to clench; (*frein*) to apply;
  s. la main à quelqu'un to shake
  hands with somebody; **s. quelqu'un** (*embrasser*) to hug somebody
  2 s. à droite to keep (to the) right.

serrer (se) *reflexive verb* to
squeeze up *or* together; **se s.
contre** to squeeze up against.

serrure *f noun* lock.

serveur , -euse *m or f noun* waiter, waitress; (*au bar*) barman,
barmaid.

servie, -ie
  1 *past participle of* **servir**.
  2 *adjective* served.

serviable *adjective* helpful.

service *m noun* service; (*pour-boire*) service (charge); (*dans une entreprise*) department; **un s.** (*aide*) a favour; **rendre s.** to be of service (**à quelqu'un** to some-body); **s. (non) compris** service (not) included; **s. après-vente** aftersales service; **être de s.** to be on duty.

serviette *f noun* towel; (*sac*) briefcase; **s. hygiénique** sanitary towel; **s. (de table)** napkin, serviette.

servir * *verb*
1 (*personne, nourriture*) to serve; **s. quelque chose à quelqu'un** to serve somebody something.
2 (*être utile*) to be useful; **s. à quelque chose/à faire** (*objet*) to be used for something/to do; **ça ne sert à rien** it's useless (**de faire** doing); **ça me sert à faire/de quelque chose** I use it to do/as something.

servir (se) *reflexive verb* (*à table*) to help oneself (**de** to); **se s. de** (*utiliser*) to use.

ses *see* **son**.

set *m noun* Tennis set; **s. (de table)** place mat.

seuil *m noun* doorstep.

seul¹, -e
1 *adjective* alone; **tout s.** by one-self, on one's own; **se sentir s.** to feel lonely.
2 *adverb* (**tout**) **s.** (*rentrer, vivre etc*) by oneself, on one's own, alone; (*parler*) to oneself.

seul², -e
1 *adjective* (*unique*) only; **la seule femme/etc** the only woman/etc; **un s. chat/etc** only one cat/etc; **pas un s. livre/etc** not a single book/etc.
2 *m or f noun* **le s., la seule** the only one; **un s., une seule** only

one; **pas un s.** not (a single) one.

seulement *adverb* only.

sévère *adjective* severe; (*parents etc*) strict.

sévérité *f noun* (*de parents etc*) strictness.

sexe *m noun* sex.

sexuel , -elle *adjective* sexual; **éducation/vie sexuelle** sex education/life.

shampooing *m noun* shampoo; **faire un s. à quelqu'un** to sham-poo somebody's hair.

short *m noun* (pair of) shorts.

si¹
1 (**s'** *before* **il, ils**) *conjunction* if; **je me demande si** I wonder whether *or* if; **si on restait?** what if we stayed?
2 *adverb* (*tellement*) so; **pas si riche que toi** not as rich as you; **un si bon dîner** such a good dinner; **si bien que** (+ *indicative*) with the result that.

si² *adverb* (*après une négation*) yes; **tu ne viens pas? – si!** you're not coming? – yes (I am)!

SIDA *m noun* AIDS.

siècle *m noun* century; (*époque*) age.

siège *m noun* seat; (*de parti etc*) headquarters; **s. (social)** head office.

sien , sienne *possessive pronoun* **le s., la sienne, les sien(ne)s** his; (*de femme*) hers; (*de chose*) its; **les deux siens** his *or* her two.

sieste *f noun* **faire la s.** to take a nap.

sifflement *m noun* whistling; hiss(ing).

siffler *verb*
1 (*personne, oiseau, bouilloire*) to whistle; (*avec un sifflet*) to blow

one's whistle; (*gaz, serpent*) to
hiss.
2 (*chanson*) to whistle; (*chien*) to
whistle to; (*acteur*) to boo.

sifflet *m noun* whistle; (**coup de**)
s. (*son*) whistle; **sifflets** (*des spectateurs*) boos.

signal , -aux *m noun* signal; **s.
d'alarme** (*de train*) alarm,
communication cord.

signaler *verb* to point out (**à
quelqu'un** to somebody, **que**
that); (*à la police etc*) to report (**à**
to).

signature *f noun* signature.

signe *m noun* sign; **faire s. à
quelqu'un** (*geste*) to motion (to)
somebody (**de faire** to do).

signer *verb* to sign.

signification *f noun* meaning.

signifier *verb* to mean (**que** that).

silence *m noun* silence; **en s.** in
silence; **garder le s.** to keep silent
(**sur** about).

silencieusement *adverb*
silently.

silencieux , -euse *adjective*
silent.

silhouette *f noun* outline; (*ligne
du corps*) figure.

simple *adjective* simple.

simplement *adverb* simply.

simplifier *verb* to simplify.

simultané , -ée *adjective* simultaneous.

simultanément *adverb* simultaneously.

sincère *adjective* sincere.

sincèrement *adverb* sincerely.

sincérité *f noun* sincerity.

singe *m noun* monkey, ape.

singeries *fpl noun* antics.

singulier , -ière *adjective & m*
noun Grammar singular; (*remarquable*) remarkable; (*curieux*) peculiar, odd; **au s.** in the singular.

sinistre
1 *adjective* sinister.
2 *m noun* disaster.

sinon *conjunction* (*autrement*)
otherwise, or else.

sirène *f noun* (*d'usine etc*) siren.

sirop *m noun* syrup; **s. contre la
toux** cough medicine *or* mixture
or syrup.

situation *f noun* situation.

situé , -ée *adjective* situated.

situer (se) *reflexive verb* to be
situated.

six *adjective & m noun* six.

sixième *adjective & m or f noun*
sixth.

sketch *m noun* (*plural* **sketches**)
(*de théâtre*) sketch.

ski *m noun* ski; (*sport*) skiing; **faire
du s.** to ski; **s. nautique** water
skiing; **faire du s. nautique** to go
water skiing.

skier *verb* to ski.

skieur , -euse *m or f noun* skier.

slip *m noun* (*d'homme*) briefs, (under)pants; (*de femme*) panties,
knickers; **s. de bain** (swimming)
trunks.

slogan *m noun* slogan.

SNCF *f abbreviation* (*Société nationale des chemins de fer français*) French national railway
company.

social , -e, -aux *adjective* social.

socialiste *adjective & m or f noun*
socialist.

société *f noun* society; (*compagnie*) company.

socquette *f noun* ankle sock.

sœur *f noun* sister.

soi *pronoun* oneself; **cela va de soi** it's evident (**que** that).

soie *f noun* silk.

soient *see* être.

soif *f noun* thirst; **avoir s.** to be thirsty; **donner s. à quelqu'un** to make somebody thirsty.

soigné , -ée *adjective* (*vêtement*) neat; (*travail*) careful.

soigner *verb* to look after, take care of; (*maladie*) to treat; **se faire s.** to have (medical) treatment.

soigneusement *adverb* carefully.

soigneux , -euse *adjective* careful (**de** with); (*propre*) neat.

soi-même *pronoun* oneself.

soin *m noun* care; **soins** (*à un malade*) treatment, care; **avec s.** carefully; **prendre s. de quelque chose** to take care of something; **les premiers soins** first aid.

soir *m noun* evening; **le s.** (*chaque soir*) in the evening; **à neuf heures du s.** at nine in the evening; **le repas du s.** the evening meal.

soirée *f noun* evening; (*réunion*) party.

sois , soit *see* être.

soit *conjunction* **s. ... s. ...** either ... or ...

soixantaine *f noun* **une s. (de)** about sixty.

soixante *adjective & m noun* sixty.

soixante-dix *adjective & m noun* seventy.

soixante-dixième *adjective & m or f noun* seventieth.

soixantième *adjective & m or f noun* sixtieth.

sol *m noun* ground; (*plancher*) floor.

solaire *adjective* solar; **crème/**

huile s. sun(tan) lotion/oil.

soldat *m noun* soldier.

solde *m noun* (*de compte*) balance; **en s.** (*acheter*) at sale price; **soldes** (*marchandises*) sale goods; (*vente*) (clearance) sale(s).

soldé , -ée *adjective* reduced.

solder *verb* (*articles*) to clear.

sole *f noun* (*poisson*) sole.

soleil *m noun* sun; (*chaleur, lumière*) sunshine; **au s.** in the sun; **il fait (du) s.** it's sunny; **coup de s.** sunburn.

solennel , -elle *adjective* solemn.

solidarité *f noun* (*de personnes*) solidarity.

solide *adjective & m noun* solid.

solidement *adverb* solidly.

solitaire *adjective* (*tout seul*) all alone.

solitude *f noun* **aimer la s.** to like being alone.

solution *f noun* solution (**de** to).

sombre *adjective* dark; **il fait s.** it's dark.

somme

1 *f noun* sum; **faire la s. de** to add up.

2 *m noun* (*sommeil*) nap; **faire un s.** to take a nap.

sommeil *m noun* sleep; **avoir s.** to be *or* feel sleepy.

sommes *see* être.

sommet *m noun* top.

somnifère *m noun* sleeping pill.

son *m noun* (*bruit*) sound.

son , sa (**sa** *becomes* **son** *before a vowel or mute h*) *possessive adjective* (*plural* **ses**) his; (*de femme*) her; (*de chose*) its; (*indéfini*) one's; **son père/sa mère** his *or* her *or* one's father/mother; **son ami(e)** his *or* her *or* one's friend; **sa durée**

its duration.

sondage *m noun* s. (d'opinion) opinion poll.

songer *verb* s. à quelque chose/à faire to think of something/of doing.

sonner *verb* to ring; **on a sonné** (*à la porte*) someone has rung the (door)bell.

sonnerie *f noun* (*son*) ring(ing); (*appareil*) bell; (*au téléphone*) ringing tone; **s. 'occupé'** engaged tone.

sonnette *f noun* bell; **coup de s.** ring.

sonore *adjective* (*rire*) loud; (*salle*) resonant.

sont *see* être.

sorcière *f noun* witch.

sort *m noun* (*destin, hasard*) fate; (*condition*) lot.

sorte *f noun* sort, kind (de of); **toutes sortes de** all sorts *or* kinds of; **de (telle) s. que** (+ *subjunctive*) so that; **faire en s. que** (+ *subjunctive*) to see to it that.

sorti, -ie *past participle of* sortir.

sortie *f noun* (*promenade à pied*) walk; (*en voiture*) drive; (*excursion*) outing; (*porte*) exit, way out; (*de disque, film*) release; **à la s. de l'école** when the children come out of school.

sortir * *verb*
1 (*auxiliary* être) to go out, leave; (*venir*) to come out; (*pour s'amuser, danser etc*) to go out; (*film etc*) to come out; **s. de table** to leave the table; **s'en s.** to pull *or* come through.
2 (*auxiliary* avoir) (*objet, personne, chien*) to take out (de of).

sottise *f noun* (*action, parole*) foolish thing; **faire des sottises** (*enfant*) to be naughty.

sou *m noun* **sous** (*argent*) money; **elle n'a pas un s.** she doesn't have a penny; **machine à sous** fruit machine.

souche *f noun* (*d'arbre*) stump.

souci *m noun* worry; (*préoccupation*) concern (de for); **se faire du s.** to worry; **ça lui donne du s.** it worries him *or* her.

soucier (se) *reflexive verb* **se s. de** to be worried about.

soucieux , -euse *adjective* worried (**de quelque chose** about something).

soucoupe *f noun* saucer; **s. volante** flying saucer.

soudain *adverb* suddenly.

souder *verb* to weld.

souffle *m noun* puff; (*haleine*) breath; (*respiration*) breathing; (*de bombe etc*) blast.

souffler *verb*
1 (*vent*) to blow.
2 *verb* (*bougie*) to blow out; (*chuchoter*) to whisper.

souffrance *f noun* suffering.

souffrant , -ante *adjective* unwell.

souffrir * *verb* to suffer (de from); **faire s. quelqu'un** to hurt somebody

souhait *m noun* wish; **à vos souhaits!** (*après un éternuement*) bless you!

souhaitable *adjective* desirable.

souhaiter *verb* to wish for; **s. quelque chose à quelqu'un** to wish somebody something; **s. faire** to hope to do; **s. que** (+ *subjunctive*) to hope that.

soulagement *m noun* relief.

soulager *verb* to relieve (de of).

soulever *verb* to lift (up); (*poussière, question*) to raise.

soulier *m noun* shoe.

souligner *verb* to underline; (*faire remarquer*) to emphasize.

soupçon *m noun* suspicion.

soupçonner *verb* to suspect (**de** of, **d'avoir fait** of doing, **que** that).

soupe *f noun* soup.

souper
1 *m noun* supper.
2 *verb* to have supper.

soupir *m noun* sigh.

soupirer *verb* to sigh.

souple *adjective* supple; (*tolérant*) flexible.

souplesse *f noun* suppleness; flexibility.

source *f noun* (*point d'eau*) spring; (*origine*) source; **eau de s.** spring water.

sourcil *m noun* eyebrow.

sourd , sourde
1 *adjective* deaf; (*douleur*) dull; **bruit s.** thump.
2 *m or f noun* deaf person.

sourd-muet , sourde-muette *adjective & m or f noun* (*plural* **sourds-muets, sourdes-muettes**) deaf and dumb (person).

sourire *
1 *verb* to smile (**à quelqu'un** at somebody).
2 *m noun* smile; **faire un s. à quelqu'un** to give somebody a smile.

souris *f noun* mouse.

sous *preposition* under(-neath), beneath; **s. la pluie** in the rain; **s. Charles X** under Charles X; **s. peu** (*bientôt*) shortly.

sous-entendre *verb* to imply.

sous-marin *m noun* submarine.

sous-sol *m noun* (*d'immeuble*) basement.

sous-titre *m noun* (*plural* **sous-titres**) subtitle.

sous-titré, -ée *adjective* **film s. en anglais** film with English subtitles.

soustraction *f noun* subtraction.

soustraire * *verb* (*nombre*) to take away, subtract (**de** from).

sous-vêtements *mpl noun* underwear.

soutenir * *verb* to support; **s. que** to maintain that.

soutenir (se) *reflexive verb* (*blessé etc*) to hold oneself up straight.

souterrain , -aine
1 *adjective* underground.
2 *m noun* underground passage.

soutien *m noun* support; (*personne*) supporter.

soutien-gorge *m noun* (*plural* **soutiens-gorge**) bra.

souvenir *m noun* memory; (*objet*) memento; (*cadeau*) keepsake; (*pour touristes*) souvenir.

souvenir * (se) *reflexive verb* **se s. de** to remember; **se s. que** to remember that.

souvent *adverb* often; **peu s.** seldom; **le plus s.** usually.

soyez , soyons *see* être.

spacieux , -euse *adjective* spacious.

spaghetti(s) *mpl noun* spaghetti.

sparadrap *m noun* sticking plaster.

speaker *m noun*, **speakerine** *f noun* (*à la radio etc*) announcer.

spécial , -e, -aux *adjective* special.

spécialement *adverb* specially.

spécialiste *m or f noun* specialist.

spécialité *f noun* speciality.

spécimen *m noun* specimen.

spectacle *m noun* (*vue*) sight; (*représentation*) show.

spectaculaire *adjective* spectacular.

spectateur , -trice *m or f noun* spectator; (*témoin*) onlooker; **les spectateurs** (*le public*) the audience.

sphère *f noun* sphere.

spirale *f noun* spiral.

spirituel , -elle *adjective* (*amusant*) witty.

splendide *adjective* splendid.

spontané , -ée *adjective* spontaneous.

sport *m noun* sport; **faire du s.** to play sport; **voiture/veste/terrain de s.** sports car/jacket/ground; **les sports d'hiver** winter sports; **aller aux sports d'hiver** to go skiing.

sportif, -ive
1 *adjective* (*personne*) fond of sport.
2 *m or f noun* sportsman, sportswoman.

spot *m noun* (*lampe*) spotlight; **s. (publicitaire)** commercial.

squash *m noun* (*jeu*) squash.

squelette *m noun* skeleton.

stable *adjective* stable.

stade *m noun* stadium.

stage *m noun* (*emploi*) work placement; (*cours*) (training) course; **faire un s.** (*étudiant*) to do a work placement; (*employé*) to do a training course.

stagiaire *m or f noun* trainee.

stand *m noun* (*d'exposition etc*) stand; (*de foire*) stall.

standard
1 *m noun* (*téléphonique*) switchboard.
2 *invariable adjective* (*modèle etc*) standard.

standardiste *m or f noun* (switchboard) operator.

station *f noun* station; (*de ski etc*) resort; **s. de métro** underground station; **s. de taxis** taxi rank.

stationnement *m noun* parking.

stationner *verb* (*être garé*) to be parked.

station-service *f noun* (*plural* **stations-service**) service station, petrol station.

statistique *f noun* (*donnée*) statistic.

statue *f noun* statue.

steak *m noun* steak.

sténodactylo *f noun* shorthand typist.

stéréo *invariable adjective* stereo.

stériliser *verb* to sterilize.

stock *m noun* stock (**de** of); **en s.** in stock.

stocker *verb* (*provisions etc*) to store.

stop
1 *interjection* stop.
2 *m noun* (*panneau*) stop sign; (*feu arrière*) brake light, stoplight; **faire du s.** to hitchhike.

stopper *verb* to stop.

store *m noun* blind.

Strasbourg *m or f noun* Strasbourg.

stress *invariable m noun* stress.

stressé , -ée *adjective* under stress.

strict , -e *adjective* strict.

strictement *adverb* strictly.

structure *f noun* structure.

studio *m noun* (*de cinéma etc*) studio; (*logement*) studio flat.

stupéfaction *f noun* amazement.

stupéfait , -faite *adjective* amazed (de at, by).

stupide *adjective* stupid.

stupidité *f noun* stupidity; (*action, parole*) stupid thing.

style *m noun* style.

stylo *m noun* pen; s. à bille ballpoint (pen); s.-plume fountain pen.

su , sue *past participle of* savoir.

subir *verb* to undergo; (*conséquences, défaite*) to suffer; (*influence*) to be under.

subit , -ite *adjective* sudden.

subitement *adverb* suddenly.

subjonctif *m noun* Grammaire subjunctive.

submergé , -ée *adjective* flooded (de with); s. de travail overwhelmed with work.

substance *f noun* substance.

subtil , -e *adjective* subtle.

succéder *verb* s. à quelque chose to follow something; se s. to follow one another.

succès *m noun* success; avoir du s. to be successful.

successif , -ive *adjective* successive.

succession *f noun* (*série*) sequence (de of).

sucer *verb* to suck.

sucette *f noun* lollipop; (*tétine*) dummy.

sucre *m noun* sugar; (*morceau*) sugar lump; s. cristallisé granulated sugar; s. en morceaux lump sugar; s. en poudre, s. semoule caster sugar.

sucré , -ée *adjective* sweet.

sucrer *verb* to sugar.

sucrier *m noun* sugar bowl.

sud *m noun* south; au s. de south of; du s. (*vent*) southerly; (*ville*) southern.

sud-est *m noun & invariable adjective* south-east.

sud-ouest *m noun & invariable adjective* south-west.

Suède (la) *f noun* Sweden.

suédois , -oise
1 *adjective* Swedish.
2 *m or f noun* Swede.
3 *m noun* (*langue*) Swedish.

suer *verb* to sweat.

sueur *f noun* sweat; en s. sweating.

suffire * *verb* to be enough (à for); ça suffit! that's enough!; il suffit d'une goutte/etc pour faire a drop/etc is enough to do.

suffisamment *adverb* sufficiently; s. de enough.

suffisant , -ante *adjective* sufficient.

suffocant , -ante *adjective* stifling.

suggérer *verb* to suggest (à to, de faire doing, que (+ *subjunctive*) that).

suggestion *f noun* suggestion.

suicide *m noun* suicide.

suicider (se) *reflexive verb* to commit suicide.

suis *see* être, suivre.

Suisse (la) *f noun* Switzerland.

suisse
1 *adjective* Swiss.
2 *m or f noun* Swiss; les Suisses the Swiss.

Suissesse *f noun* Swiss woman *or* girl, Swiss.

suite *f noun* (*reste*) rest; (*de film, roman*) sequel; (*nouvel épisode*) continuation; (*série*) series; faire s. (à) to follow; par la s. afterwards; à la s. one after another; à

la s. de (*événement etc*) as a result of; **de s.** (*deux jours etc*) in a row; **s. à votre lettre du 10 mars** further to your letter of March 10.

suivant , -ante
1 *adjective* next, following.
2 *m or f noun* next (one); **au s.!** next!

suivi, -ie *past participle of* **suivre.**

suivre * *verb*
1 (*aller derrière*) to follow; (*accompagner*) to go with; (*classe*) to attend, go to; **s. (des yeux** or **du regard)** to watch; **se s.** to follow each other.
2 (*venir après*) to follow; **faire s.** (*courrier*) to forward; '**à s.**' 'to be continued'.

sujet *m noun* (*question*) & *Grammaire* subject; (*d'examen*) question; **au s. de** about; **à quel s.?** about what?

super
1 *invariable adjective* (*bon*) *Familiar* great.
2 *m noun* (*essence*) four-star (petrol).

superbe *adjective* superb.

superficie *f noun* surface.

superficiel , -ielle *adjective* superficial.

supérieur , -e *adjective* upper; (*qualité etc*) superior (**à** to); (*études*) higher; **l'étage s.** the floor above.

supériorité *f noun* superiority.

supermarché *m noun* supermarket.

superposer *verb* (*objets*) to put on top of each other.

superstitieux , -euse *adjective* superstitious.

superstition *f noun* superstition.

supplément *m noun* (*argent*) extra charge; **en s.** extra.

supplémentaire *adjective* extra.

supplier *verb* **s. quelqu'un de faire** to beg somebody to do.

support *m noun* support; (*d'instrument etc*) stand.

supporter [1] *verb* to bear; (*résister à*) to withstand; (*soutenir*) to support.

supporter [2] *m noun* supporter.

supposer *verb* to suppose (**que** that).

supposition *f noun* assumption.

suppositoire *m noun* suppository.

suppression *f noun* removal; (*de train*) cancellation.

supprimer *verb* to get rid of; (*mot*) to cut out; (*train*) to cancel.

sur *preposition* over; on, upon; (*par-dessus*) over; (*au sujet de*) on, about; **six s. dix** six out of ten; **un jour s. deux** every other day; **six mètres s. dix** six metres by ten.

sûr , sûre *adjective* sure, certain (**de** of, **que** that); (*digne de confiance*) reliable; (*lieu*) safe; **c'est s. que** (+ *indicative*) it's certain that; **s. de soi** self-assured; **bien s.!** of course!

sûrement *adverb* certainly.

sûreté *f noun* safety; **être en s.** to be safe; **mettre en s.** to put in a safe place.

surexcité , -ée *adjective* overexcited.

surf *m noun* surfing; **faire du s.** to go surfing.

surface *f noun* surface; (*dimensions*) (surface) area; **grande s.** hypermarket.

surgelé , -ée *adjective* frozen.

surgelés *mpl noun* frozen foods.

surgir *verb* to appear suddenly (de from); (*problème*) to arise.

sur-le-champ *adverb* immediately.

surlendemain *m noun* le s. two days later; le s. de two days after.

surmener (se) *reflexive verb* to overwork.

surmonter *verb* (*obstacle etc*) to get over.

surnom *m noun* nickname.

surnommer *verb* to nickname.

surpasser (se) *reflexive verb* to excel oneself.

surprenant , -ante *adjective* surprising.

surprendre * *verb* (*étonner*) to surprise; (*prendre sur le fait*) to catch; (*conversation*) to overhear.

surpris , -ise *adjective* surprised (de at, que (+ *subjunctive*) that); je suis surpris de te voir I'm surprised to see you.

surprise *f noun* surprise; s.-partie party.

sursauter *verb* to jump, start.

surtout *adverb* especially; (*avant tout*) above all; s. pas certainly not; s. que especially since.

surveillant , -ante *m or f noun* (*lycée*) supervisor (in charge of discipline); (*prison*) (prison) guard.

surveiller *verb* to watch; (*contrôler*) to supervise.

survêtement *m noun* tracksuit.

survivant , -ante *m or f noun* survivor.

survivre * *verb* to survive (à quelque chose something).

survoler *verb* to fly over.

sus (en) *adverb* in addition.

susceptible *adjective* touchy.

suspect , -ecte
1 *adjective* suspicious.
2 *m or f noun* suspect.

suspendre *verb* (*accrocher*) to hang (up) (à on); se s. à to hang from.

suspendu , -ue *adjective* s. à hanging from.

suspense *m noun* suspense.

suspension *f noun* (*de véhicule*) suspension.

suture *f noun* point de s. stitch (*in wound*).

SVP *abbreviation* (*s'il vous plaît*) please.

syllabe *f noun* syllable.

symbole *m noun* symbol.

symbolique *adjective* symbolic.

sympa *invariable adjective Familiar* = **sympathique**.

sympathie *f noun* liking; avoir de la s. pour quelqu'un to be fond of somebody

sympathique *adjective* nice, pleasant.

symphonie *f noun* symphony.

symptôme *m noun* symptom.

synagogue *f noun* synagogue.

syndicat *m noun* (*d'ouvriers*) (trade) union; s. d'initiative tourist (information) office.

syndiqué , -ée *m or f noun* union member.

synonyme
1 *adjective* synonymous (de with).
2 *m noun* synonym.

Syrie (la) *f noun* Syria.

syrien , -ienne *adjective & m or f noun* Syrian.

système *m noun* system.

T

ta *see* **ton**.

tabac *m noun* tobacco; (*magasin*) tobacconist's (shop).

table *f noun* table; (*d'école*) desk; **t. de nuit** bedside table; **t. basse** coffee table; **t. à repasser** ironing board; **t. roulante** (tea) trolley; **t. des matières** table (of contents); **à t.** sitting at the table; **à t.!** food's ready!

tableau , -x *m noun* (*image*) picture; (*panneau*) board; (*liste*) list; (*graphique*) chart; **t. (noir)** (black)board; **t. d'affichage** notice board; **t. de bord** dashboard.

tablette *f noun* (*de chocolat*) bar; (*de lavabo etc*) shelf.

tablier *m noun* apron; (*d'écolier*) smock.

tabouret *m noun* stool.

tache *f noun* spot; (*salissure*) stain.

tacher *verb* to stain.

tacher (se) *reflexive verb* (*tissu*) to stain.

tâcher *verb* **t. de faire** to try to do.

tact *m noun* tact; **avoir du t.** to be tactful.

tactique *f noun* **la t.** tactics; **une t.** a tactic.

tag *m noun* tag (*spray-painted graffiti*).

taie d'oreiller *f noun* pillowcase.

taille *f noun* (*hauteur*) height; (*dimension, mesure*) size; (*ceinture*) waist; **tour de t.** waist measurement.

taille-crayon *m noun* (*plural* **taille-crayons**) pencil sharpener.

tailler *verb* to cut; (*haie, barbe*) to trim; (*arbre*) to prune; (*crayon*) to sharpen.

tailleur *m noun* (*personne*) tailor; (*vêtement*) suit.

taire * (se) *reflexive verb* (*ne rien dire*) to keep quiet (**sur quelque chose** about something); (*cesser de parler*) to stop talking; **tais-toi!** be quiet!

talent *m noun* talent; **avoir du t. pour** to have a talent for.

talon *m noun* heel; (*de chèque, carnet*) stub.

talus *m noun* slope, embankment.

tambour *m noun* drum; (*personne*) drummer.

tambourin *m noun* tambourine.

Tamise (la) *f noun* the Thames.

tamiser *verb* (*farine*) to sift.

tampon *m noun* (*marque, instrument*) stamp; (*de coton*) wad; **t. hygiénique** tampon; **t. à récurer** scrubbing pad.

tandis que *conjunction* while.

tant *adverb* (*travailler etc*) so much (**que** that); **t. de** (*temps etc*) so much (**que** that); (*gens etc*) so many (**que** that); **t. que** (*aussi longtemps que*) as long as; **t. mieux!** good!; **t. pis!** too bad!

tante *f noun* aunt.

tantôt *adverb* **t. ... t.** sometimes ... sometimes.

tapage *m noun* din, uproar.

tape *f noun* slap.

taper [1] *verb*
1 (*enfant, cuisse*) to slap.
2 t. sur quelque chose to bang on something; **t. du pied** to stamp one's foot.

taper [2] *verb* **t. (à la machine)** to type.

tapis *m noun* carpet; **t. roulant** (*pour marchandises*) conveyor belt.

tapisser *verb* (*mur*) to (wall)paper.

tapisserie *f noun* (*papier peint*) wallpaper; (*broderie*) tapestry.

tapoter *verb* to tap; (*joue*) to pat.

taquiner *verb* to tease.

tard *adverb* late; **plus t.** later (on); **au plus t.** at the latest.

tarder *verb* **t. à faire** to take one's time doing; **elle ne va pas t.** she won't be long; **sans t.** without delay.

tarif *m noun* (*prix*) rate; (*de train*) fare; (*tableau*) price list.

tarte *f noun* tart; **t. à l'abricot/ aux fraises** apricot/strawberry tart.

tartine *f noun* slice of bread; **t. de confiture** slice of bread and jam; **t. beurrée** slice of bread and butter.

tartiner *verb* (*beurre etc*) to spread.

tas *m noun* pile, heap; **un** *or* **des t. de** (*beaucoup*) *Familiar* lots of; **mettre en t.** to pile *or* heap up.

tasse *f noun* cup; **t. à café** coffee cup; **t. à thé** teacup.

tasser *verb* to pack, squeeze (**dans** into).

tasser (se) *reflexive verb* (*se serrer*) to squeeze up.

tâter *verb* to feel.

tâtonner *verb* to grope about.

tâtons (à) *adverb* **avancer à t.** to feel one's way (along); **chercher à t.** to grope for.

tatouage *m noun* (*dessin*) tattoo.

tatouer *verb* to tattoo.

taudis *m noun* slum.

taupe *f noun* mole.

taureau , -x *m noun* bull.

taux *m noun* rate; **t. d'alcool/etc** alcohol/etc level.

taxe *f noun* (*impôt*) tax; (*de douane*) duty; **t. à la valeur ajoutée** value-added tax.

taxé , -ée *adjective* taxed.

taxi *m noun* taxi.

Tchécoslovaquie (la) *f noun* Czechoslovakia.

tchèque *adjective & m or f noun* Czech.

te (**t'** *before vowel or mute h*) *pronoun* (*complément direct*) you; (*indirect*) (to) you; (*réfléchi*) yourself.

technicien , -ienne *m or f noun* technician.

technique
1 *adjective* technical.
2 *f noun* technique.

technologie *f noun* technology.

tee-shirt *m noun* tee-shirt.

teindre * *verb* to dye; **t. en rouge** to dye red.

teindre (se) *reflexive verb* to dye one's hair.

teint *m noun* complexion.

teinte *f noun* shade.

teinture *f noun* (*produit*) dye.

teinturerie *f noun* (*boutique*) (dry) cleaner's.

teinturier , -ière *m or f noun* (dry) cleaner.

tel , telle *adjective* such; **un t. livre/etc** such a book/etc; **un t. intérêt/etc** such interest/etc; **de tels mots/etc** such words/etc; **rien de t. que** (there's) nothing like.

télé *f noun* TV; **à la t.** on TV.

Télécarte ® *f noun* phone card.

télécommande *f noun* remote

control.

télécopie *f noun* fax.

télécopieur *m noun* fax (machine).

téléfilm *m noun* TV film.

télégramme *m noun* telegram.

téléphérique *m noun* cable car.

téléphone *m noun* (tele)phone; **coup de t.** (phone) call; **passer un coup de t. à quelqu'un** to give somebody a ring; **au t.** on the (tele)phone.

téléphoner *verb* to (tele)phone; **t. à quelqu'un** to (tele)phone somebody.

téléphoner (se) *reflexive verb* to phone each other.

téléphonique *adjective* **appel/ etc t.** (tele)phone call/*etc.*

télescope *m noun* telescope.

télésiège *m noun* chair lift.

téléspectateur , -trice *m or f noun* (television) viewer.

télévisé *adjective* **journal t.** television news.

téléviseur *m noun* television (set).

télévision *f noun* television; **à la t.** on (the) television.

telle *see* tel.

tellement *adverb* (*si*) so; (*tant*) so much; **t. de** (*travail etc*) so much; (*soucis etc*) so many; **pas t.!** not much!

témoignage *m noun* evidence; (*récit*) account.

témoigner *verb* to give evidence (**contre** against).

témoin *m noun* witness; **être t. de** to witness.

température *f noun* temperature; **avoir de la t.** to have a temperature.

tempête *f noun* storm; **t. de neige** snowstorm.

temple *m noun* (*romain, grec*) temple.

temporaire *adjective* temporary.

temps ¹ *m noun* time; (*de verbe*) tense; **il est t. (de faire)** it's time (to do); **ces derniers t.** lately; **de t. en t.** from time to time; **à t.** (*arriver*) in time; **à plein t.** (*travailler*) full-time; **à t. partiel** (*travailler*) part-time; **dans le t.** (*autrefois*) once.

temps ² *m noun* (*climat*) weather; **quel t. fait-il?** what's the weather like?

tenailles *fpl noun* (*outil*) pincers.

tendance *f noun* tendency; **avoir t. à faire** to tend to do.

tendeur *m noun* (*à bagages*) elastic strap.

tendre ¹ *verb* to stretch; (*main*) to hold out (**à quelqu'un** to somebody); (*bras, jambe*) to stretch out; (*piège*) to set, lay; **t. quelque chose à quelqu'un** to hold out something to somebody; **t. l'oreille** to prick up one's ears.

tendre ² *adjective* (*viande etc*) tender; (*personne*) affectionate (**avec** to).

tendrement *adverb* tenderly.

tendresse *f noun* affection.

tendu , -ue *adjective* (*corde*) tight; (*personne, situation, muscle*) tense; (*main*) held out.

tenir * *verb*
1 (*objet*) to hold; (*promesse, comptes, hôtel*) to keep; (*rôle*) to play; **t. sa droite** (*conducteur*) to keep to the right.
2 (*nœud, corde*) to hold; (*résister*) to hold out; **t. à** (*personne, jouet etc*) to be attached to; **t. à faire** to

be anxious to do; **t. dans quelque chose** (*être contenu*) to fit into something; **tenez!** (*prenez*) here (you are)!; **tiens!** (*surprise*) well!

tenir (se) *reflexive verb* (*avoir lieu*) to be held; **se t. (debout)** to stand (up); **se t. droit** to stand up *or* sit up straight; **se t. par la main** to hold hands; **se t. bien** to behave oneself.

tennis *m noun* tennis; (*terrain*) (tennis) court; (*chaussure*) plimsoll; **t. de table** table tennis.

tension *f noun* tension; **t. (artérielle)** blood pressure; **avoir de la t.** to have high blood pressure.

tentant , -ante *adjective* tempting.

tentation *f noun* temptation.

tentative *f noun* attempt.

tente *f noun* tent.

tenter ¹ *verb* to try (**de faire** to do).

tenter ² *verb* (*faire envie à*) to tempt.

tenue *f noun* (*vêtements*) clothes; (*conduite*) (good) behaviour; **t. de soirée** evening dress.

tergal ® *m noun* Terylene ®.

terme *m noun* (*mot*) term; (*fin*) end; **mettre un t. à** to put an end to; **à court/long t.** (*conséquences*) short-/long-term; **en bons/mauvais termes** on good/bad terms (**avec** with).

terminaison *f noun* (*de mot*) ending.

terminal , -e, -aux
  1 *adjective & f noun* (**classe**) **terminale** = sixth form.
  2 *m noun* **t.** (*d'ordinateur*) (computer) terminal.

terminer *verb* to end.

terminer (se) *reflexive verb* to end (**par** with, **en** in).

terne *adjective* dull.

terrain *m noun* ground; (*étendue*) land; (*à bâtir*) plot; *Football etc* pitch; **un t.** a piece of land; **t. de camping** campsite; **t. de jeux** (*pour enfants*) playground; (*stade*) playing field; **t. de sport** sports ground; **t. vague** waste ground.

terrasse *f noun* terrace; (*de café*) pavement.

terre *f noun* (*matière, monde*) earth; (*sol*) ground; (*opposé à mer*) land; **à t.** on the ground; **par t.** (*poser, tomber*) to the ground; (*assis, couché*) on the ground; **sous t.** underground.

terrestre *adjective* **la surface t.** the earth's surface; **globe t.** globe (*model*).

terreur *f noun* terror.

terrible *adjective* awful, terrible; (*formidable*) *Familiar* terrific.

terrifiant , -ante *adjective* terrifying.

terrifier *verb* to terrify.

territoire *m noun* territory.

terroriser *verb* to terrorize.

terroriste *adjective & m or f noun* terrorist.

tes *see* **ton**.

test *m noun* test.

testament *m noun* (*en droit*) will.

tester *verb* to test.

tête *f noun* head; (*visage*) face; (*d'arbre*) top; **tenir t. à** to stand up to; **faire la t.** to sulk; **à la t. de** (*entreprise*) at the head of; (*classe*) at the top of; **en t.** (*sportif*) in the lead.

tête-à-tête *noun* tête-à-tête; **en t.** in private.

téter verb
1 (lait) to suck.
2 le bébé tète the baby is feeding; donner à t. à to feed.

tétine f noun (de biberon) teat; (sucette) dummy.

têtu , -ue adjective stubborn.

texte m noun text.

textile adjective & m noun textile.

TF 1 f abbreviation (Télévision Française 1) = French commercial television channel.

TGV m abbreviation = train à grande vitesse.

thaïlandais , -aise adjective & m or f noun Thai.

Thaïlande (la) f noun Thailand.

thé m noun tea; t. au lait tea with milk.

théâtre m noun theatre; (œuvres) drama; faire du t. to act.

théière f noun teapot.

théorie f noun theory; en t. in theory.

thermomètre m noun thermometer.

thermos ® m ou f noun Thermos ® (flask).

thermostat m noun thermostat.

thon m noun tuna (fish).

tibia m noun shin (bone).

ticket m noun ticket.

tiède adjective (luke)warm.

tien , tienne possessive pronoun le t., la tienne, les tien(ne)s yours; les deux tiens your two.

tiens , tient see tenir.

tiercé m noun = forecast of the first three horses in a race; jouer/gagner au t. = to bet/win on the horses.

tiers m noun (fraction) third; le t. de a third of.

tiers-monde (le) m noun the Third World.

tige f noun (de plante) stem; (barre) rod.

tigre m noun tiger.

timbre m noun stamp.

timbre-poste m noun (plural timbres-poste) (postage) stamp.

timbrer verb (lettre) to stamp.

timide adjective shy.

timidement adverb shyly.

timidité f noun shyness.

tinter verb (cloche) to ring; (clefs) to jingle.

tir m noun shooting; Football shot; t. à l'arc archery.

tirage m noun (de journal) circulation; (de loterie) draw; t. au sort drawing of lots.

tire-bouchon m noun corkscrew.

tirelire f noun moneybox.

tirer verb
1 (porte, manette etc) to pull; (langue) to stick out; (trait, rideaux) to draw; (balle) to shoot; t. de (sortir) to pull or draw out of; (obtenir) to get from; t. quelqu'un de (danger, lit) to get somebody out of; se t. de (travail) to cope with; (situation) to get out of; se t. d'affaire to get out of trouble.
2 (faire feu) to shoot (sur at); Football to shoot; t. sur une corde to pull on a rope; t. au sort to draw lots; t. à sa fin to draw to a close.

tiret m noun (trait) dash.

tireur m noun (au fusil) gunman.

tiroir m noun drawer.

tisonnier m noun poker.

tisser verb to weave.

tissu m noun material, cloth; du t. -éponge towelling.

titre *m noun* title; **(gros) t.** (*de journal*) headline; **à t. d'exemple** as an example; **à juste t.** rightly.

toast *m noun* (*pain grillé*) piece *or* slice of toast.

toboggan *m noun* slide; (*pour voitures*) flyover.

toc *interjection* **t. t.!** knock knock!

toi *pronoun* (*complément, sujet*) you; (*réfléchi*) **assieds-t.** sit (yourself) down; **dépêche-t.** hurry up.

toile *f noun* cloth; (*à voile, sac etc*) canvas; (*tableau*) painting; **t. d'araignée** spider's web.

toilette *f noun* (*action*) wash(ing); (*vêtements*) clothes; **eau de t.** eau de toilette; **faire sa t.** to wash (and dress); **les toilettes** the toilet(s); **aller aux toilettes** to go to the toilet.

toi-même *pronoun* yourself.

toit *m noun* roof; **t. ouvrant** (*de voiture*) sunroof.

tôle *f noun* **une t.** a metal sheet; **t. ondulée** corrugated iron.

tolérant , -ante *adjective* tolerant (**à l'égard de** of).

tolérer *verb* to tolerate.

tomate *f noun* tomato.

tombe *f noun* grave.

tombeau , -x *m noun* tomb.

tombée *f noun* **t. de la nuit** nightfall.

tomber *verb* (*auxiliary* **être**) to fall; **t. malade** to fall ill; **t. (par terre)** to fall (down); **faire t.** (*personne*) to knock over; **laisser t.** to drop; **tu tombes bien/mal** you've come at the right/wrong time; **t. sur** (*trouver*) to come across.

tombola *f noun* raffle.

ton , ta (**ta** *becomes* **ton** *before a vowel or mute h*) *possessive adjective* (*plural* **tes**) your; **t. père** your father; **ta mère** your mother; **ton ami(e)** your friend.

ton *m noun* (*de voix etc*) tone.

tonalité *f noun* (*au téléphone*) dialling tone.

tondeuse *f noun* **t. (à gazon)** (lawn)mower.

tondre *verb* (*gazon*) to mow.

tonne *f noun* metric ton, tonne; **des tonnes de** (*beaucoup*) *Familiar* tons of.

tonneau , -x *m noun* barrel.

tonner *impersonal verb* **il tonne** it's thundering.

tonnerre *m noun* thunder; **coup de t.** burst of thunder.

tonton *m noun* *Familiar* uncle.

torche *f noun* (*flamme*) torch; **t. électrique** torch.

torchon *m noun* tea towel.

tordre *verb* to twist; (*linge*) to wring (out); (*barre*) to bend; **se t. la cheville** to twist *or* sprain one's ankle.

tordre (se) *reflexive verb* to twist; (*barre*) to bend; **se t. de douleur** to be doubled up with pain; **se t. (de rire)** to split one's sides (laughing).

torrent *m noun* (mountain) stream; **il pleut à torrents** it's pouring (down).

torse *m noun* chest; **t. nu** stripped to the waist.

tort *m noun* **avoir t.** to be wrong (**de faire** to do, in doing); **être dans son t.** to be in the wrong; **donner t. à quelqu'un** (*accuser*) to blame somebody; (*résultat, preuve*) to prove somebody wrong; **à t.** wrongly; **parler à t. et à travers** to talk nonsense.

torticolis *m noun* **avoir le t.** to

have a stiff neck.

tortiller *verb* to twist, twirl.

tortue *f noun* tortoise; (*de mer*) turtle.

torture *f noun* torture.

torturer *verb* to torture.

tôt *adverb* early; **le plus t. possible** as soon as possible; **t. ou tard** sooner or later; **je n'étais pas plus t. sorti que** no sooner had I gone out than.

total , -e , -aux *adjective & m noun* total.

totalement *adverb* totally.

totalité *f noun* **en t.** (*détruit etc*) entirely; (*payé*) fully.

touchant , -ante *adjective* moving, touching.

touche *f noun* (*de clavier*) key; (*de téléphone*) (push-)button; **téléphone à touches** push-button phone.

toucher
  1 *verb* (*objet, personne*) to touch; (*paie*) to draw; (*chèque*) to cash; (*cible*) to hit; (*émouvoir*) to touch, move.
  2 *verb* **t. à** to touch.
  3 *m noun* (*sens*) touch.

toucher (se) *reflexive verb* (*lignes, mains etc*) to touch.

touffe *f noun* (*de cheveux, d'herbe*) tuft.

toujours *adverb* always; (*encore*) still; **pour t.** for ever.

tour ¹ *f noun* tower; (*immeuble*) tower block, high-rise; *Échecs* castle; **la T. Eiffel** the Eiffel Tower.

tour ² *m noun* turn; (*de magie etc*) trick; **t. de poitrine**/*etc* chest/*etc* measurement; **faire le t. de** to go round; **faire un t.** to go for a walk; (*en voiture*) to go for a drive;

(*voyage*) to go on a trip; **jouer un t. à quelqu'un** to play a trick on somebody; **c'est mon t.** it's my turn; **à t. de rôle** in turn.

tourisme *m noun* tourism; **faire du t.** to go sightseeing.

touriste *m or f noun* tourist.

touristique *adjective* **guide**/*etc* **t.** tourist guide/*etc*.

tournage *m noun* (*de film*) shooting.

tournant *m noun* (*de route*) bend.

tourne-disque *m noun* record player.

tournée *f noun* (*de livreur, boissons*) round; (*de spectacle*) tour.

tourner *verb*
  1 (*page, tête, clé etc*) to turn; (*film*) to shoot.
  2 (*planète, roue etc*) to turn; (*moteur*) to run; (*lait*) to go off; **t. autour de** (*objet*) to go round; **j'ai la tête qui tourne** my head's spinning.

tourner (se) *reflexive verb* to turn (**vers** to).

tournevis *m noun* screwdriver.

tournoi *m noun* tournament.

Toussaint *f noun* All Saints' Day.

tousser *verb* to cough.

tout , toute (*plural* **tous, toutes**)
  1 *adjective* all; **tous les livres** all the books; **t. l'argent/le temps/le village** all the money/time/village; **toute la nuit** all night; **tous (les) deux** both; **tous (les) trois** all three.
  ▪ (*chaque*) every; **tous les ans** every *or* each year; **tous les cinq mois/mètres** every five months/metres.
  2 *plural pronoun* all; **ils sont tous là** they're all there.
  3 *m singular pronoun* **tout** everything; **t. ce que** everything that,

all that; **en t.** (*au total*) in all; **ce sera t.?** (*dans un magasin*) will that be all?; **c'est t.!** (*pour finir*) that's all.
4 *adverb* (*très*) quite, very; **t. simplement** quite simply; **t. petit** very small; **t. neuf** brand new; **t. seul** all alone; **t. autour** all around; **t. en chantant**/*etc* while singing/*etc*; **t. à coup** suddenly; **t. à fait** completely; **t. de même** all the same; **t. de suite** at once.
5 *m noun* **le t.** everything, the lot; **pas du t.** not at all; **rien du t.** nothing at all.

toux *f noun* cough.

toxique *adjective* poisonous.

trac *m noun* **avoir le t.** to be or become nervous.

tracasser *verb* to worry.

tracasser (se) *reflexive verb* to worry.

trace *f noun* trace (**de** of); (*marque*) mark; **traces** (*de bête, pneus*) tracks; **traces de pas** footprints.

tracer *verb* (*dessiner*) to draw.

tracteur *m noun* tractor.

tradition *f noun* tradition.

traditionnel , -elle *adjective* traditional.

traducteur , -trice *m or f noun* translator.

traduction *f noun* translation.

traduire * *verb* to translate (**de** from, **en** into).

trafic *m noun* traffic.

tragédie *f noun* tragedy.

tragique *adjective* tragic.

trahir *verb* to betray.

trahir (se) *reflexive verb* to give oneself away.

trahison *f noun* betrayal.

train [1] *m noun* train; **t. à grande vitesse** high-speed train; **t.**
couchettes sleeper.

train [2] *m noun* **être en t. de faire** to be (busy) doing.

traîneau , -x *m noun* sledge.

traînée *f noun* (*de peinture etc*) streak.

traîner *verb*
1 (*tirer*) to drag.
2 (*jouets etc*) to lie around; (*s'attarder*) to lag behind; **t. (par terre)** (*robe etc*) to trail (on the ground).

traîner (se) *reflexive verb* (*par terre*) to crawl.

train-train *m noun* routine.

traire * *verb* to milk.

trait *m noun* line; (*en dessinant*) stroke; (*caractéristique*) feature; **t. d'union** hyphen.

traitement *m noun* treatment; (*salaire*) salary; **t. de texte** word processing; **machine de t. de texte** word processor.

traiter *verb*
1 (*patient, maladie*) to treat; (*problème*) to deal with; (*matières premières*) to process; **t. quelqu'un de lâche**/*etc* to call somebody a coward/*etc*.
2 t. de (*sujet*) to deal with.

traiteur *m noun* **chez le t.** at the delicatessen.

traître *m noun* traitor.

trajectoire *f noun* path.

trajet *m noun* trip; (*distance*) distance; (*itinéraire*) route.

tramway *m noun* tram.

tranchant , -ante *adjective* (*couteau, voix*) sharp.

tranche *f noun* (*morceau*) slice; **une t. de** a slice of.

tranchée *f noun* trench.

trancher *verb* to cut.

tranquille *adjective* quiet; (*mer*)

calm; (*conscience*) clear; **laisser t.** to leave alone.

tranquillement *adverb* calmly.

tranquillisant *m noun* tranquilizer.

tranquilliser *verb* to reassure.

tranquillité *f noun* (peace and) quiet.

transférer *verb* to transfer (**à** to).

transfert *m noun* transfer.

transformation *f noun* change.

transformer *verb* to change; (*maison*) to carry out alterations to; **t. en** to turn into.

transfusion *f noun* **t.** (**sanguine**) (blood) transfusion.

transistor *m noun* transistor (radio).

transitif , -ive *adjective Grammaire* transitive.

transmettre * *verb* (*message etc*) to pass on (**à** to).

transparent , -ente *adjective* clear, transparent.

transpercer *verb* to pierce.

transpirer *verb* to sweat.

transport *m noun* transport (**de** of); **moyen de t.** means of transport; **les transports en commun** public transport.

transporter *verb* to transport; (*à la main*) to carry; **t. quelqu'un d'urgence à l'hôpital** to rush somebody to hospital.

trappe *f noun* trap door.

travail , -aux *m noun* (*activité, lieu*) work; (*à effectuer*) job, task; (*emploi*) job; **travaux** (*dans la rue*) roadworks; (*aménagement*) alterations; **le t. manuel** manual labour; **les travaux manuels** (*à l'école*) arts and crafts; **les travaux pratiques** practical work.

travailler *verb* to work (**à** quel-que chose at *or* on something).

travailleur , -euse
1 *adjective* hard-working.
2 *m or f noun* worker.

travers
1 *preposition & adverb* **à t.** through; **en t.** (**de**) across.
2 *adverb* **de t.** (*chapeau etc*) crooked; (*comprendre*) badly; **j'ai avalé de t.** it went down the wrong way.

traversée *f noun* crossing.

traverser *verb* to cross, go across; (*foule, période*) to go through.

traversin *m noun* bolster.

trébucher *verb* to stumble (**sur** over); **faire t. quelqu'un** to trip somebody (up).

trèfle *m noun* (*couleur*) *Cartes* clubs.

treize *adjective & invariable m noun* thirteen.

treizième *adjective & m or f noun* thirteenth.

tremblement *m noun* shaking, trembling; **t. de terre** earthquake.

trembler *verb* to shake, tremble (**de** with).

tremper *verb* to soak; (*plonger*) to dip (**dans** in); **faire t. quelque chose** to soak something.

tremplin *m noun* springboard.

trentaine *f noun* **une t.** (**de**) about thirty.

trente *adjective & m noun* thirty; **un t.-trois tours** an LP.

trentième *adjective & m or f noun* thirtieth.

très *adverb* very; **t. aimé**/*etc* much *or* greatly liked/*etc.*

trésor *m noun* treasure.

tresse *f noun* (*cheveux*) plait.

tresser *verb* to plait.

triangle *m noun* triangle.

triangulaire *adjective* triangular.

tribu *f noun* tribe.

tribunal , **-aux** *m noun* court.

tribune *f noun* (*de stade*) (grand)-stand.

tricher *verb* to cheat.

tricheur , **-euse** *m or f noun* cheat.

tricolore *adjective* red, white and blue; **feu t.** traffic lights.

tricot *m noun* (*activité*) knitting; (*chandail*) sweater.

tricoter *verb* to knit.

tricycle *m noun* tricycle.

trier *verb* to sort (out).

trimestre *m noun* (*période*) quarter; (*scolaire*) term.

trimestriel , **-ielle** *adjective* (*revue*) quarterly; **bulletin t.** end-of-term report *or* report card.

tringle *f noun* rail, rod.

triomphe *m noun* triumph (**sur** over).

triompher *verb* to triumph (**de** over).

triple *m noun* **le t.** three times as much (**de** as).

tripler *verb* to treble, triple.

tripoter *verb* to fiddle about *or* around with.

triste *adjective* sad; (*couleur*, *temps*) gloomy.

tristement *adverb* sadly.

tristesse *f noun* sadness; (*du temps*) gloom(iness).

trognon *m noun* (*de fruit*) core.

trois *adjective* & *m noun* three.

troisième *adjective* & *m or f noun* third.

troisièmement *adverb* thirdly.

trombone *m noun* trombone; (*agrafe*) paper clip.

trompe *f noun* (*d'éléphant*) trunk.

tromper *verb* to deceive; (*être infidèle à*) to be unfaithful to.

tromper (se) *reflexive verb* to be mistaken; **se t. de route**/*etc* to take the wrong road/*etc*; **se t. de date**/*etc* to get the date/*etc* wrong.

trompette *f noun* trumpet.

tronc *m noun* trunk.

tronçonneuse *f noun* chain saw.

trône *m noun* throne.

trop *adverb* (*avec un adjectif ou un adverbe*) too; (*avec une quantité*) too much; **t. dur**/*etc* too hard/*etc*; **t. fatigué pour jouer** too tired to play; **boire**/*etc* **t.** to drink/*etc* too much; **t. de sel**/*etc* (*quantité*) too much salt/*etc*; **t. de gens**/*etc* (*nombre*) too many people/*etc*; **un franc**/*etc* **de t.** *or* **en t.** one franc/*etc* too many.

tropical , **-e** , **-aux** *adjective* tropical.

trot *m noun* trot; **aller au t.** to trot.

trotter *verb* (*cheval*) to trot.

trottinette *f noun* (*jouet*) scooter.

trottoir *m noun* pavement.

trou *m noun* hole; **t. de (la) serrure** keyhole; **t. (de mémoire)** lapse (of memory).

trouble *adjective* (*liquide*) cloudy; (*image*) blurred; **voir t.** to see things blurred.

troubler *verb* to disturb; (*vue*) to blur.

troubles *mpl noun* (*de santé*) trouble; (*désordres*) disturbances.

trouer *verb* to make a hole *or* holes in.

troupe *f noun* (*groupe*) group; (*de théâtre*) company; **troupes** (*armée*) troops.

troupeau , -x *m noun* (*vaches*) herd; (*moutons, oies*) flock.

trousse *f noun* (*étui*) case, kit; (*d'écolier*) pencil case; **t. à outils** toolkit; **t. à pharmacie** first-aid kit; **t. de toilette** sponge *or* toilet bag.

trousseau , -x *m noun* (*de clefs*) bunch.

trouver *verb* to find; **aller/venir t. quelqu'un** to go/come and see somebody; **je trouve que** I think that.

trouver (se) *reflexive verb* to be; **se t. gros** to think one is fat; **je me trouve bien ici** I'm happy here.

truc *m noun Familiar* (*astuce*) trick; (*moyen*) way; (*chose*) thing.

truite *f noun* trout.

T-shirt *m noun* (*plural* **T-shirts**) T-shirt, tee-shirt.

TTC *abbreviation* (*toutes taxes comprises*) inclusive of tax.

tu *pronoun* you (*familiar form of address*).

tu , tue *see* taire.

tube *m noun* tube; (*chanson*) *Familiar* hit.

tuberculose *f noun* TB.

tue-tête (à) *adverb* at the top of one's voice.

tuer *verb* to kill; **se t.** to kill oneself; (*dans un accident*) to be killed.

tuile *f noun* tile.

tulipe *f noun* tulip.

Tunisie (la) *f noun* Tunisia.

tunisien , -ienne *adjective & m or f noun* Tunisian.

tunnel *m noun* tunnel.

turbulent , -ente *adjective* (*enfant*) disruptive.

turc , turque
 1 *adjective* Turkish.
 2 *m or f noun* Turk.

Turquie (la) *f noun* Turkey.

tutoyer *verb* **t. quelqu'un** to use the familiar **tu** form to somebody.

tutu *m noun* ballet skirt.

tuyau , -x *m noun* pipe; **t. d'arrosage** hose(pipe); **t. d'échappement** exhaust (pipe).

TVA *f abbreviation* (*taxe à la valeur ajoutée*) VAT.

type *m noun* type; (*individu*) *Familiar* fellow, guy.

typique *adjective* typical (**de** of).

U

ulcère *m noun* ulcer.

ultramoderne *adjective* ultra-modern.

ultra-secret , -ète *adjective* top-secret.

un , une
  1 *indefinite article* a; *(devant voyelle)* an; **une page** a page; **un ange** an angel.
  2 *adjective* one; **la page un** page one; **un kilo** one kilo.
  3 *pronoun & m or f noun* one; **l'un** one; **les uns** some; **j'en ai un** I have one; **l'un d'eux, l'une d'elles** one of them; **la une** *(de journal)* page one.

unanime *adjective* unanimous.

unanimité *f noun* **à l'u.** unanimously.

uni , -ie *adjective* united; *(famille)* close; *(surface)* smooth; *(couleur)* plain.

unième *adjective (after a number)* **trente et u.** thirty-first; **cent u.** hundred and first.

uniforme *m noun* uniform.

union *f noun* union.

unique *adjective (fille, espoir etc)* only; *(prix, marché)* single; *(exceptionnel)* unique.

uniquement *adverb* only.

unir *verb (efforts, forces)* to combine; *(deux pays etc)* to unite, join together; **u. deux personnes** *(amitié)* to unite two people.

unir (s') *reflexive verb (étudiants etc)* to unite.

unité *f noun (mesure, élément)* unit.

univers *m noun* universe.

universel , -elle *adjective* universal.

universitaire *adjective* **ville/etc u.** university town/etc.

université *f noun* university; **à l'u.** at university.

urgence *f noun (cas)* emergency; *(de décision etc)* urgency; **faire quelque chose d'u.** to do something urgently; **(service des) urgences** *(d'hôpital)* casualty (department).

urgent , -ente *adjective* urgent.

urne *f noun* ballot box; **aller aux urnes** to go to the polls, vote.

usage *m noun* use; *(habitude)* custom; **faire u. de** to make use of; **hors d'u.** broken, not in use.

usagé , -ée *adjective* worn.

usager *m noun* user.

usé , -ée *adjective* worn (out).

user *verb* to wear out.

user (s') *reflexive verb* to wear out.

usine *f noun* factory.

ustensile *m noun* utensil.

usure *f noun* wear (and tear).

utile *adjective* useful (à to).

utilisateur , -trice *m or f noun* user.

utilisation *f noun* use.

utiliser *verb* to use.

utilité *f noun* use(fulness); **d'une grande u.** very useful.

V

va *see* aller [1].

vacances *fpl noun* holiday(s); **en v.** on holiday; **être en v.** to be on holiday; **partir en v.** to go away on holiday; **les grandes v.** the summer holidays.

vacancier , -ière *m or f noun* holidaymaker.

vacarme *m noun* din, uproar.

vaccin *m noun* vaccine; **faire un v. à** to vaccinate.

vaccination *f noun* vaccination.

vacciner *verb* to vaccinate.

vache
1 *f noun* cow.
2 *adjective* (*méchant*) *Familiar* nasty.

vachement *adverb Familiar* (*très*) damned; (*beaucoup*) a hell of a lot.

vagabond , -onde *m or f noun* tramp.

vague
1 *adjective* vague; (*regard*) vacant.
2 *f noun* wave; **v. de chaleur** heat wave; **v. de froid** cold spell.

vaguement *adverb* vaguely.

vain (en) *adverb* in vain.

vaincre * *verb* to beat.

vaincu , -ue
1 *past participle of* vaincre.
2 *m or f noun* (*sportif*) loser.

vainqueur *m noun* (*sportif*) winner.

vais *see* aller [1].

vaisselle *f noun* crockery; (*à laver*) washing up, dirty dishes; **faire la v.** to do the washing up, wash the dishes.

valable *adjective* (*billet etc*) valid.

valet *m noun Cartes* jack.

valeur *f noun* value; **avoir de la v.** to be valuable; **objets de v.** valuables.

valise *f noun* (suit)case; **faire ses valises** to pack (one's bags).

vallée *f noun* valley.

valoir * *verb* to be worth; **v. cher** to be worth a lot; **un vélo vaut bien une auto** a bicycle is just as good as a car; **il vaut mieux rester à la maison** it's better to stay at home; **il vaut mieux que j'attende** I'd better wait; **ça ne vaut rien** it's no good; **ça vaut le coup** *Familiar* it's worth while (**de faire** doing).

valoir (se) *reflexive verb* to be as good as each other; **ça se vaut** it's all the same.

valse *f noun* waltz.

valu, -ue *past participle of* valoir.

vandale *m or f noun* vandal.

vanille *f noun* vanilla; **glace à la v.** vanilla ice cream.

vaniteux , -euse *adjective* conceited.

vantard , -arde *m or f noun* bighead, boaster.

vanter (se) *reflexive verb* to boast (**de** about, of).

vapeur *f noun* **v. (d'eau)** steam.

variable *adjective* (*humeur, temps*) changeable.

varicelle *f noun* chicken pox.

varié , -ée *adjective* varied; (*divers*) various.

varier *verb* to vary.

variété *f noun* variety; **spectacle**

de variétés variety show.

vas *see* aller [1].

vase *m noun* vase.

vaste *adjective* vast, huge.

vaut *see* valoir.

veau , -x *m noun* calf; (*viande*) veal; (*cuir*) calfskin, (calf) leather.

vécu , -ue (*past participle of* vivre) *adjective* (*histoire etc*) true.

vedette *f noun* (*de cinéma etc*) star.

végétarien , -ienne *adjective &* *m or f noun* vegetarian.

végétation *f noun* vegetation.

véhicule *m noun* vehicle; v. tout terrain off-road vehicle.

veille *f noun* la v. (de) the day before; la v. de Noël Christmas Eve.

veiller *verb* to stay up; (*sentinelle*) to keep watch; v. à quelque chose to see to something; v. sur quelqu'un to watch over somebody.

veilleur *m noun* v. de nuit night watchman.

veilleuse *f noun* (*de voiture*) sidelight; (*de cuisinière*) pilot light; (*lampe allumée la nuit*) night light.

veine *f noun* vein; (*chance*) Familiar luck.

vélo *m noun* bike, bicycle; (*activité*) cycling; faire du v. to cycle; v. tout terrain mountain bike.

vélomoteur *m noun* motorcycle.

velours *m noun* velvet; v. côtelé corduroy.

vendange *f noun* (*récolte*) grape harvest; les vendanges (*période*) grape-harvesting time; faire la v. *or* les vendanges to harvest *or* pick the grapes.

vendeur , -euse *m or f noun* sales *or* shop assistant; (*de voitures etc*) salesman, saleswoman.

vendre *verb* to sell (quelque chose à quelqu'un somebody something, something to somebody); à v. for sale.

vendre (se) *reflexive verb* to sell; ça se vend bien it sells well.

vendredi *m noun* Friday; V. saint Good Friday.

vendu , -ue *past participle of* vendre.

vénéneux , -euse *adjective* poisonous.

vengeance *f noun* revenge.

venger (se) *reflexive verb* to get one's revenge, get one's own back (de quelqu'un on somebody, de quelque chose for something).

venimeux , -euse *adjective* poisonous.

venin *m noun* poison.

venir * *verb* (*auxiliary* être) to come (de from); v. faire to come to do; viens me voir come and see me; je viens/venais d'arriver I've/I'd just arrived; où veux-tu en v.? what are you getting at?; faire v. to send for, get.

vent *m noun* wind; il y a du v. it's windy; coup de v. gust of wind.

vente *f noun* sale; v. (aux enchères) auction (sale); en v. on sale; prix de v. selling price.

ventilateur *m noun* fan.

ventre *m noun* stomach; avoir mal au v. to have a stomachache.

venu , -ue
1 *past participle of* venir.
2 *m or f noun* nouveau v., nouvelle venue newcomer; le premier v. anyone.

ver *m noun* worm; (*de fruits etc*) maggot; v. de terre (earth)worm.

véranda *f noun* (*en verre*) conservatory.

verbe *m noun* verb.

verdict *m noun* verdict.

verger *m noun* orchard.

verglas *m noun* (black) ice.

vérification *f noun* check(ing).

vérifier *verb* to check.

véritable *adjective* (*histoire*, *ami*) true, real; (*nom*, *or*, *cuir*) real.

véritablement *adverb* really.

vérité *f noun* truth.

vernir *verb* to varnish.

vernis *m noun* varnish; **v. à ongles** nail polish.

verra , verrai(t) *etc see* voir.

verre *m noun* glass; **boire** *or* **prendre un v.** to have a drink; **v. de bière** glass of beer; **v. à bière** beer glass.

verrou *m noun* bolt; **fermer au v.** to bolt.

verrue *f noun* wart.

vers [1] *preposition* (*direction*) toward(s).

vers [2] *m noun* (*de poème*) line.

verse (à) *adverb* **pleuvoir à v.** to pour (down).

verser *verb* to pour; (*larmes*) to shed; (*argent*) to pay.

version *f noun* (*de film, d'incident etc*) version; **en v. originale** in the original language; **en v. française** dubbed (into French).

verso *m noun* 'voir au v.' 'see overleaf'.

vert , verte
1 *adjective* green; (*pas mûr*) unripe.
2 *m noun* green.

vertical , -e, -aux *adjective* vertical.

vertige *m noun* **avoir le v.** to be *or* feel dizzy; **donner le v. à quel-**

qu'un to make somebody (feel) dizzy.

veste *f noun* jacket.

vestiaire *m noun* cloakroom.

vestibule *m noun* (entrance) hall.

veston *m noun* (suit) jacket.

vêtement *m noun* garment; **vêtements** clothes; **vêtements de sport** sportswear.

vétérinaire *m or f noun* vet.

vêtu, -ue
1 *past participle of* vêtir.
2 *adjective* dressed (de in).

veuf , veuve
1 *adjective* widowed.
2 *m noun* widower.
3 *f noun* widow.

veuille(s) , veuillent *etc see* vouloir.

veulent , veut , veux *see* vouloir.

vexant , -ante *adjective* upsetting.

vexer *verb* to upset.

viande *f noun* meat.

vibration *f noun* vibration.

vibrer *verb* to vibrate.

vice *m noun* vice.

victime *f noun* victim; (*d'un accident*) casualty; **être v. de** to be the victim of.

victoire *f noun* victory; (*en sports*) win.

victorieux , -euse *adjective* victorious; (*équipe*) winning.

vidange *f noun* (*de véhicule*) oil change.

vide
1 *adjective* empty.
2 *m noun* emptiness; (*trou*) gap.

vidéo *invariable adjective* video.

vidéocassette *f noun* video cassette.

vide-ordures *invariable m noun* (rubbish) chute.

vide-poches *invariable m noun* glove compartment.

vider *verb* to empty.

vider (se) *reflexive verb* to empty.

vie *f noun* life; (*durée*) lifetime; **le coût de la v.** the cost of living; **gagner sa v.** to earn one's living; **en v.** living.

vieil *see* **vieux**.

vieillard *m noun* old man.

vieille *see* **vieux**.

vieillesse *f noun* old age.

vieillir *verb*
  1 (*devenir vieux*) to grow old; (*changer*) to age.
  2 v. quelqu'un (*vêtement etc*) to make somebody look old(er).

Viêt Nam (le) *m noun* Vietnam.

vietnamien, -ienne *adjective & m or f noun* Vietnamese.

vieux (*or* **vieil** *before vowel or mute h*), **vieille** (*plural* **vieux, vieilles**)
  1 *adjective* old.
  2 *m noun* old man; **les vieux** old people; **mon v.** (*mon ami*) mate, pal.
  3 *f noun* old woman; **ma vieille** (*ma chère*) dear.

vif, vive *adjective* (*enfant*) lively; (*couleur, lumière*) bright; (*froid*) biting; **brûlé v.** burnt alive.

vigne *f noun* (*petit arbre*) vine; (*vignoble*) vineyard.

vigneron, -onne *m or f noun* wine grower.

vignette *f noun* (*de véhicule*) road tax sticker.

vignoble *m noun* vineyard.

vilain, -aine *adjective* (*laid*) ugly; (*enfant*) naughty; (*impoli*) rude.

villa *f noun* (detached) house.

village *m noun* village.

villageois, -oise *m or f noun* villager.

ville *f noun* town; (*grande*) city; **aller/être en v.** to go (in)to/be in town.

vin *m noun* wine.

vinaigre *m noun* vinegar.

vinaigrette *f noun* French dressing.

vingt *adjective & m noun* twenty; **v. et un** twenty-one.

vingtaine *f noun* **une v. (de)** about twenty.

vingtième *adjective & m or f noun* twentieth.

viol *m noun* rape.

violemment *adverb* violently.

violence *f noun* violence.

violent, -ente *adjective* violent.

violer *verb* to rape.

violet, -ette *adjective & m noun* purple.

violeur *m noun* rapist.

violon *m noun* violin.

vipère *f noun* adder.

virage *m noun* (*de route*) bend; (*de véhicule*) turn.

virgule *f noun* comma; (*de nombre*) (decimal) point; **2 v. 5** 2 point 5.

virus *m noun* virus.

vis [1] *see* **vivre, voir**.

vis [2] *f noun* screw.

visa *m noun* (*de passeport*) visa.

visage *m noun* face.

viser *verb* to aim at.

visibilité *f noun* visibility.

visible *adjective* visible.

visite *f noun* visit; **rendre v. à** to visit; **v. (médicale)** medical examination; **v. guidée** guided tour.

visiter *verb* to visit.

visiteur , -euse *m or f noun* visitor.

visser *verb* to screw on.

vit *see* **vivre**, **voir**.

vitamine *f noun* vitamin.

vite *adverb* quickly.

vitesse *f noun* speed; (*sur un véhicule*) gear; **boîte de vitesses** gearbox; **à toute v.** at full speed.

vitrail , -aux *m noun* stained-glass window.

vitre *f noun* (window)pane; (*de véhicule, train*) window.

vitrine *f noun* (shop) window; (*meuble*) display cabinet.

vivant , -ante *adjective* living; (*récit, rue*) lively.

vive *interjection* **v. le roi/etc!** long live the king/*etc*!; **v. les vacances!** hurray for the holidays!

vivre * *verb* to live; (*aventure*) to live through; **v. vieux** to live to be old; **v. de** (*fruits etc*) to live on; (*travail etc*) to live by.

vocabulaire *m noun* vocabulary.

vodka *f noun* vodka.

vœu , -x *m noun* (*souhait*) wish; (*promesse*) vow; **avec mes/nos meilleurs vœux** best wishes, with all good wishes.

voici *preposition* here is, this is; *plural* here are, these are; **me v.** here I am; **v. dix ans que** it's ten years since.

voie *f noun* road; (*rails*) track; (*partie de route*) lane; (*chemin*) way; (*de gare*) platform; **v. sans issue** dead end; **sur la bonne v.** on the right track.

voilà *preposition* there is, that is; *plural* there are, those are; **les v.** there they are; **v., j'arrive!** all right, I'm coming!; **v. dix ans que** it's ten years since.

voile [1] *m noun* (*tissu*) veil.

voile [2] *f noun* (*de bateau*) sail; (*sport*) sailing; **faire de la v.** to sail.

voilier *m noun* (*de plaisance*) sailing boat.

voir * *verb* to see; **faire v. quelque chose** to show something; **fais v.** let me see; **v. quelqu'un faire** to see somebody do *or* doing; **je ne peux pas la v.** Familiar I can't stand (the sight of) her; **ça n'a rien à v. avec** that's got nothing to do with.

voir (se) *reflexive verb* (*se fréquenter*) to see each other; **ça se voit** that's obvious.

voisin , -ine
1 *adjective* neighbouring; (*maison, pièce*) next (**de** to).
2 *m or f noun* neighbour.

voisinage *m noun* neighbourhood.

voiture *f noun* car; (*de train*) carriage.

voix *f noun* voice; (*d'électeur*) vote; **à v. basse** in a whisper.

vol [1] *m noun* (*d'avion, d'oiseau*) flight.

vol [2] *m noun* (*délit*) theft; (*hold-up*) robbery.

volaille *f noun* **une v.** a fowl.

volant *m noun* (steering) wheel.

volcan *m noun* volcano.

voler [1] *verb* (*oiseau, avion etc*) to fly.

voler [2] *verb* (*prendre*) to steal (**à** from).

volet *m noun* (*de fenêtre*) shutter.

voleur , -euse *m or f noun* thief; **au v.!** stop thief!

volley-ball *m noun* volleyball.

volontaire
1 *adjective* (*voulu*) (*geste etc*) deliberate.
2 *m or f noun* volunteer.

volontairement *adverb* (*exprès*) deliberately.

volonté *f noun* will; **bonne v.** goodwill; **mauvaise v.** ill will.

volontiers *adverb* gladly.

volume *m noun* (*de boîte, de son, livre*) volume.

volumineux , -euse *adjective* bulky.

vomir *verb*
1 (*aliment*) to bring up.
2 (*être malade*) to be sick.

vont *see* aller ¹.

vos *see* votre.

vote *m noun* vote; (*de loi*) passing; **bureau de v.** polling station.

voter *verb*
1 (*électeur*) to vote.
2 (*loi*) to pass.

votre *possessive adjective* (*plural* vos) your.

vôtre *possessive pronoun* le *or* la **v.**, les vôtres yours; **à la v.!** (your) good health, cheers!

voudra , voudrai(t) *etc see* vouloir.

vouloir * *verb* to want (**faire** to do); **je veux qu'il parte** I want him to go; **v. dire** to mean (**que** that); **je voudrais rester** I'd like to stay; **je voudrais un pain** I'd like a loaf of bread; **si vous voulez bien me suivre** will you follow me; **si tu veux** if you like *or* wish; **en v. à quelqu'un d'avoir fait quelque chose** to be angry with somebody for doing something; **je veux bien (attendre)** I don't mind (waiting); **sans le v.**

unintentionally.

voulu, -ue *past participle of* vouloir.

vous *pronoun* (*sujet, complément direct*) you; (*complément indirect*) (to) you; (*réfléchi*) yourself, *plural* yourselves; (*réciproque*) each other.

vous-même *pronoun* yourself.

vous-mêmes *pronoun* yourselves.

vouvoyer *verb* v. quelqu'un to use the formal *vous* form to somebody

voyage *m noun* trip, journey; **aimer les voyages** to like travelling; **faire un v., partir en v.** to go on a trip; **bon v.!** have a pleasant trip!; **v. organisé** (package) tour; **agent/agence de voyages** travel agent/agency.

voyager *verb* to travel.

voyageur , -euse *m or f noun* traveller; (*passager*) passenger.

voyelle *f noun* vowel.

voyou *m noun* hooligan.

vrac (en) *adverb* (*en désordre*) in a muddle, haphazardly.

vrai , -e *adjective* true; (*réel*) real; (*authentique*) genuine.

vraiment *adverb* really.

vraisemblable *adjective* (*probable*) likely.

VTT *m abbreviation* (*vélo tout terrain*) mountain bike.

vu , vue *past participle of* voir.

vue *f noun* (*spectacle*) sight; (*sens*) (eye)sight; (*panorama, photo*) view; **en v.** (*proche*) in sight; **de v.** (*connaître*) by sight.

vulgaire *adjective* vulgar.

W

wagon *m noun* (*de voyageurs*) carriage; (*de marchandises*) wag(g)on.

wagon-lit *m noun* (*plural* wagons-lits) sleeping car.

wagon-restaurant *m noun* (*plural* wagons-restaurants) dining car.

w-c *mpl noun* toilet.

week-end *m noun* weekend.

western *m noun* (*film*) western.

whisky *m noun* whisky.

X

xénophobe
   1 *adjective* xenophobic.
   2 *m or f noun* xenophobe.

xénophobie *f noun* xenophobia.

xylophone *m noun* xylophone.

y

1 *adverb* there; **allons-y** let's go; **j'y suis!** now I get it! **je n'y suis pour rien** I have nothing to do with it.

2 *pronoun* **j'y pense** I think of it; **je m'y attendais** I was expecting it; **ça y est!** that's it!

yacht *m noun* yacht.

yaourt *m noun* yog(h)urt.

yeux *see* œil.

yoga *m noun* yoga; **faire du y.** to do yoga.

Yougoslavie (la) *f noun* Yugoslavia; **l'ex-Y.** the former Yugoslavia.

Z

zèbre *m noun* zebra.

zéro *m noun* (*chiffre*) nought, zero; (*dans un numéro*) 0 ; (*température*) zero; **deux buts à z.** two nil.

zigzag *m noun* zigzag; **en z.** (*route etc*) zigzag(ging).

zigzaguer *verb* to zigzag.

zone *f noun* zone, area; **z. bleue** restricted parking zone; **z. industrielle** industrial estate; **z. piétonne** *or* **piétonnière** pedestrian precinct.

zoo *m noun* zoo.

zut! *interjection* oh no!; **z. alors!** blast!

Reference Section

Verbs   (ii)
  Regular Verbs   (iv)
  Spelling changes in -er verbs   (viii)
  Irregular Verbs   (ix)

Useful Word Groups   (xxiv)

Verbs

The following pages present tables of regular and irregular verbs, divided into the following sections:

▷ Regular -er verbs
▷ Regular -ir verbs
▷ Regular -re verbs
▷ Reflexive verbs
▷ Some common irregular verbs ⎫ These do not follow a standard
▷ Other irregular verbs   ⎬ pattern and need to be
                               ⎭ learned individually.

The tables show you how to form six different tenses:

THE PRESENT TENSE

Je joue   I play / I am playing

The present tense tells us about something that is happening now or usually happens. (There are two forms in English but only one in French.)

To form the present tense of regular verbs take the stem of the infinitive and add the endings. The stem is the infinitive minus the last two letters.

● donn**er**   donne, donn**es**, donne, donn**ons**, donn**ez**, donn**ent**
● fin**ir**   fin**is**, fin**is**, fin**it**, fin**issons**, fin**issez**, fin**issent**
● répond**re**   répond**s**, répond**s**, répond, répond**ons**, répond**ez**, répond**ent**

THE PERFECT TENSE

J'ai joué   I have played / I played
Je suis allé(e) I have gone / I went

The perfect tense tells us about something that has happened or happened once in the past, i.e. a completed action.

The perfect tense of regular verbs is formed with the present tense of an auxiliary verb (**avoir** or **être**) and the past participle. To make the past participle of regular verbs, take off the last two letters to find the stem of the verb and add the appropriate ending:

▷ -er verbs: stem + **é**   e.g. jouer   joué
▷ -ir verbs: stem + **i**   e.g. finir   fini
▷ -re verbs: stem + **u**   e.g. répondre répondu

Most verbs form the perfect tense with **avoir**. There are a few irregular verbs which form the perfect tense with **être** (aller, venir, arriver, partir, entrer, sortir, monter, descendre, naître, mourir, rester, tomber, retourner).

THE IMPERFECT TENSE

Je jouais   I was playing / I used to play

The imperfect tense tells us about something that used to happen, happened for a long time or was happening, i.e. a regular, long-term or interrupted action.

To form the imperfect tense of regular verbs take the stem of the infinitive and add the endings (-ais, -ais, -ait, -ions, -iez, -aient).

THE FUTURE TENSE

Je donnerai   I will give

The future tense tells us about something that will happen in the future. To form the future tense of regular verbs take the whole of the infinitive for -er and -ir verbs, and the infinitive minus the final e for -re verbs, and add the endings (-ai, -as, -a, -ons, -ez, -ont).

(The near future is used to talk about things that will happen soon. To form the near future you use the present tense of the verb **aller** plus the infinitive, e.g. Je vais aller au cinéma.)

THE CONDITIONAL

J'aimerais   I would like

The conditional tells us about something that would happen. To form the conditional take the whole of the infinitive for -er and -ir verbs, and the infinitive minus the final e for -re verbs, and add the endings (-ais, -ais, -ait, -ions, -iez, -aient).

THE PRESENT SUBJUNCTIVE

Je joue   I play

The subjunctive is used after certain expressions. These are indicated in the dictionary.

To form the present subjunctive of regular verbs take the first person plural of the present tense, take off the -ons and add the endings (-e, -es, -e, -ions, -iez, -ent).

Regular Verbs

-er verbs

donner to give

Present	**Perfect**	**Imperfect**
je donne	j'ai donné	je donnais
tu donnes	tu as donné	tu donnais
il donne	il a donné	il donnait
nous donnons	nous avons donné	nous donnions
vous donnez	vous avez donné	vous donniez
ils donnent	ils ont donné	ils donnaient

Future	**Conditional**	**Present Subjunctive**
je donnerai	je donnerais	je donne
tu donneras	tu donnerais	tu donnes
il donnera	il donnerait	il donne
nous donnerons	nous donnerions	nous donnions
vous donnerez	vous donneriez	vous donniez
ils donneront	ils donneraient	ils donnent

Imperative
donne
donnons
donnez

Present Participle
donnant

Past Participle
donné

Regular Verbs

-ir verbs

finir to finish

Present	Perfect	Imperfect
je finis	j'ai fini	je finissais
tu finis	tu as fini	tu finissais
il finit	il a fini	il finissait
nous finissons	nous avons fini	nous finissions
vous finissez	vous avez fini	vous finissiez
ils finissent	ils ont fini	ils finissaient

Future	Conditional	Present Subjunctive
je finirai	je finirais	je finisse
tu finiras	tu finirais	tu finisses
il finira	il finirait	il finisse
nous finirons	nous finirions	nous finissions
vous finirez	vous finiriez	vous finissiez
ils finiront	ils finiraient	ils finissent

Imperative
finis
finissons
finissez

Present Participle
finissant

Past Participle
fini

Regular Verbs

-re verbs

vendre to sell

Present	**Perfect**	**Imperfect**
je vends	j'ai vendu	je vendais
tu vends	tu as vendu	tu vendais
il vend	il a vendu	il vendait
nous vendons	nous avons vendu	nous vendions
vous vendez	vous avez vendu	vous vendiez
ils vendent	ils ont vendu	ils vendaient

Future	**Conditional**	**Present Subjunctive**
je vendrai	je vendrais	je vende
tu vendras	tu vendrais	tu vendes
il vendra	il vendrait	il vende
nous vendrons	nous vendrions	nous vendions
vous vendrez	vous vendriez	vous vendiez
ils vendront	ils vendraient	ils vendent

Imperative
vends
vendons
vendez

Present Participle	**Past Participle**
vendant	vendu

Regular Verbs

reflexive verbs

se lever to get up

Present	**Perfect**	**Imperfect**
je me lève	je me suis levé	je me levais
tu te lèves	tu t'es levé	tu te levais
il se lève	il/elle s'est levé(e)	il se levait
nous nous levons	nous nous sommes levés	nous nous levions
vous vous levez	vous vous êtes levé(s)	vous vous leviez
ils se lèvent	ils/elles se sont levé(e)s	ils se levaient

Future	**Conditional**	**Present Subjunctive**
je me lèverai	je me lèverais	je me lève
tu te lèveras	tu te lèverais	tu te lèves
il se lèvera	il se lèverait	il se lève
nous nous lèverons	nous nous lèverions	nous nous levions
vous vous lèverez	vous vous lèveriez	vous vous leviez
ils se lèveront	ils se lèveraient	ils se lèvent

Imperative
lève-toi
levons-nous
levez-vous

Present Participle
se levant

Past Participle
levé

Spelling changes in -er verbs

Verbs ending in **-ger** (eg **manger**) take an extra **e** before **a** or **o**:
Present je mange, nous mangeons; *Imperfect* je mangeais, nous mangions; *Present participle* mangeant.

Verbs ending in **-cer** (eg **commencer**) change **c** to **ç** before **a** or **o**:
Present je commence, nous commençons; *Imperfect* je commençais, nous commencions; *Present participle* commençant.

Verbs in **e** + consonant + **er** fall into two groups. In the first (eg **mener, peser, lever**), **e** becomes **è** before a silent **e** (in other words before the endings **-e, -es, -ent** in the present and subjunctive, and in the future and conditional tenses, eg **je mène, ils mèneront**).

The second group contains most verbs ending in **-eler** and **-eter** (eg **appeler, jeter**). These verbs change **l** to **ll** and **t** to **tt** before silent **e** (eg **j'appelle, ils appelleront; je jette, ils jetteront**). However, the verbs **geler, dégeler** and **acheter** fall into the above-mentioned first group.

Verbs containing **é** in their second from last syllable change **é** to **è** before the endings **-e, -es, -ent** in the present and subjunctive only (eg **je cède** but **je céderai**).

Verbs ending in **-yer** (eg **essuyer**) change **y** to **i** before silent **e** in the present and subjunctive, and in the future and conditional tenses (eg **j'essuie, ils essuieront**). However, in verbs ending in **-ayer** (eg **balayer**), this change is optional (eg **je balaie** or **balaye, ils balaieront** or **balayeront**).

Irregular Verbs

Many verbs in French are irregular. In the French side of the dictionary they have been marked with a star (*****). If you see this star, it means that you can look the verb up in the tables in the following pages.

First we show eight of the most common French irregular verbs with all their forms (**aller**, **avoir**, **devoir**, **dire**, **être**, **faire**, **pouvoir**, **vouloir**). Other irregular verbs are listed in a table which gives the **je** and **nous** forms, from which all their other forms can be derived. Verbs following a similar pattern are grouped together in this table, eg **abattre**, **combattre** are shown under **battre**.

aller to go

Present	**Perfect**	**Imperfect**
je vais	je suis allé	j'allais
tu vas	tu es allé	tu allais
il va	il/elle est allé(e)	il allait
nous allons	nous sommes allés	nous allions
vous allez	vous êtes allé(s)	vous alliez
ils vont	ils/elles sont allé(e)s	ils allaient

Future	**Conditional**	**Present Subjunctive**
j'irai	j'irais	j'aille
tu iras	tu irais	tu ailles
il ira	il irait	il aille
nous irons	nous irions	nous allions
vous irez	vous iriez	vous alliez
ils iront	ils iraient	ils aillent

Imperative
va
allons
allez

Present Participle
allant

Past Participle
allé

avoir to have

Present

j'ai
tu as
il a
nous avons
vous avez
ils ont

Perfect

j'ai eu
tu as eu
il a eu
nous avons eu
vous avez eu
ils ont eu

Imperfect

j'avais
tu avais
il avait
nous avions
vous aviez
ils avaient

Future

j'aurai
tu auras
il aura
nous aurons
vous aurez
ils auront

Conditional

j'aurais
tu aurais
il aurait
nous aurions
vous auriez
ils auraient

**Present
Subjunctive**

j'aie
tu aies
il ait
nous ayons
vous ayez
ils aient

Imperative

aie
ayons
ayez

Present Participle

ayant

Past Participle

eu

devoir to have to, must

Present
je dois
tu dois
il doit
nous devons
vous devez
ils doivent

Perfect
j'ai dû
tu as dû
il a dû
nous avons dû
vous avez dû
ils ont dû

Imperfect
je devais
tu devais
il devait
nous devions
vous deviez
ils devaient

Future
je devrai
tu devras
il devra
nous devrons
vous devrez
ils devront

Conditional
je devrais
tu devrais
il devrait
nous devrions
vous devriez
ils devraient

Present Subjunctive
je doive
tu doives
il doive
nous devions
vous deviez
ils doivent

Imperative
not used

Present Participle
devant

Past Participle
dû, due
(*plural* dus, dues)

dire to say

Present
je dis
tu dis
il dit
nous disons
vous dites
ils disent

Perfect
j'ai dit
tu as dit
il a dit
nous avons dit
vous avez dit
ils ont dit

Imperfect
je disais
tu disais
il disait
nous disions
vous disiez
ils disaient

Future
je dirai
tu diras
il dira
nous dirons
vous direz
ils diront

Conditional
je dirais
tu dirais
il dirait
nous dirions
vous diriez
ils diraient

Present Subjunctive
je dise
tu dises
il dise
nous disions
vous disiez
ils disent

Imperative
dis
disons
dites

Present Participle
disant

Past Participle
dit

être to be

Present
je suis
tu es
il est
nous sommes
vous êtes
ils sont

Perfect
j'ai été
tu as été
il a été
nous avons été
vous avez été
ils ont été

Imperfect
j'étais
tu étais
il était
nous étions
vous étiez
ils étaient

Future
je serai
tu seras
il sera
nous serons
vous serez
ils seront

Conditional
je serais
tu serais
il serait
nous serions
vous seriez
ils seraient

Present Subjunctive
je sois
tu sois
il soit
nous soyons
vous soyez
ils soient

Imperative
sois
soyons
soyez

Present Participle
étant

Past Participle
été

faire to do, to make

Present
je fais
tu fais
il fait
nous faisons
vous faites
ils font

Perfect
j'ai fait
tu as fait
il a fait
nous avons fait
vous avez fait
ils ont fait

Imperfect
je faisais
tu faisais
il faisait
nous faisions
vous faisiez
ils faisaient

Future
je ferai
tu feras
il fera
nous ferons
vous ferez
ils feront

Conditional
je ferais
tu ferais
il ferait
nous ferions
vous feriez
ils feraient

Present Subjunctive
je fasse
tu fasses
il fasse
nous fassions
vous fassiez
ils fassent

Imperative
fais
faisons
faites

Present Participle
faisant

Past Participle
fait

pouvoir to be able, can

Present
je peux
tu peux
il peut
nous pouvons
vous pouvez
ils peuvent

Perfect
j'ai pu
tu as pu
il a pu
nous avons pu
vous avez pu
ils ont pu

Imperfect
je pouvais
tu pouvais
il pouvait
nous pouvions
vous pouviez
ils pouvaient

Future
je pourrai
tu pourras
il pourra
nous pourrons
vous pourrez
ils pourront

Conditional
je pourrais
tu pourrais
il pourrait
nous pourrions
vous pourriez
ils pourraient

Present Subjunctive
je puisse
tu puisses
il puisse
nous puissions
vous puissiez
ils puissent

Imperative
not used

Present Participle
pouvant

Past Participle
pu

vouloir to want

Present
je veux
tu veux
il veut
nous voulons
vous voulez
ils veulent

Perfect
j'ai voulu
tu as voulu
il a voulu
nous avons voulu
vous avez voulu
ils ont voulu

Imperfect
je voulais
tu voulais
il voulait
nous voulions
vous vouliez
ils voulaient

Future
je voudrai
tu voudras
il voudra
nous voudrons
vous voudrez
ils voudront

Conditional
je voudrais
tu voudrais
il voudrait
nous voudrions
vous voudriez
ils voudraient

Present Subjunctive
je veuille
tu veuilles
il veuille
nous voulions
vous vouliez
ils veuillent

Imperative
veux/veuille
voulons/veuillons
voulez/veuillez

Present Participle
voulant

Past Participle
voulu

Infinitive	Present	Perfect	Imperfect
acquérir	j'acquiers nous acquérons	j'ai acquis	j'acquérais
s'asseoir	je m'assieds nous nous asseyons	je me suis assis	je m'asseyais
atteindre *éteindre, peindre*	j'atteins nous atteignons	j'ai atteint	j'atteignais
battre *abattre, combattre*	je bats nous battons	j'ai battu	je battais
boire	je bois nous buvons	j'ai bu	je buvais
bouillir	je bous nous bouillons	j'ai bouilli	je bouillais
conclure	je conclus nous concluons	j'ai conclu	je concluais
conduire *construire, déduire* *détruire, produire,* *réduire, reproduire, traduire*	je conduis nous conduisons	j'ai conduit	je conduisais
connaître *apparaître,* *disparaître, paraître,* *reconnaître*	je connais nous connaissons	j'ai connu	je connaissais
coudre	je couds nous cousons	j'ai cousu	je cousais
courir	je cours nous courons	j'ai couru	je courais
couvrir *découvrir, offrir* *ouvrir, recouvrir, souffrir*	je couvre nous couvrons	j'ai couvert	je couvrais
craindre *plaindre*	je crains nous craignons	j'ai craint	je craignais
croire	je crois nous croyons	j'ai cru	je croyais
cueillir *acceuillir*	je cueille nous cueillons	j'ai cueilli	je cueillais

Future	Conditional	Present Subjunctive	Present Participle
j'acquerrai	j'acquerrais	j'acquière	acquérant
je m'assiérai	je m'assiérais	je m'asseye	asseyant
j'atteindrai	j'atteindrais	j'atteigne	atteignant
je battrai	je battrais	je batte	battant
je boirai	je boirais	je boive	buvant
je bouillirai	je bouillirais	je bouille	bouillant
je conclurai	je conclurais	je conclue	concluant
je conduirai	je conduirais	je conduise	conduisant
je connaîtrai	je connaîtrais	je connaisse	connaissant
je coudrai	je coudrais	je couse	cousant
je courrai	je courrais	je coure	courant
je couvrirai	je couvrirais	je couvre	couvrant
je craindrai	je craindrais	je craigne	craignant
je croirai	je croirais	je croie	croyant
je cueillerai	je cueillerais	je cueille	cueillant

Infinitive	Present	Perfect	Imperfect
cuire	je cuis nous cuisons	j'ai cuit	je cuisais
dormir *endormir*	je dors nous dormons	j'ai dormi	je dormais
écrire *décrire, inscrire*	j'écris nous écrivons	j'ai écrit	j'écrivais
envoyer *renvoyer*	j'envoie nous envoyons	j'ai envoyé	j'envoyais
falloir	il faut	il a fallu	il fallait
fuir *s'enfuir*	je fuis nous fuyons	j'ai fui	je fuyais
lire	je lis nous lisons	j'ai lu	je lisais
mentir *consentir, sentir*	je mens nous mentons	j'ai menti	je mentais
mettre *admettre, commettre* *permettre, promettre,* *remettre*	je mets nous mettons	j'ai mis	je mettais
moudre	je mouds nous moulons	j'ai moulu	je moulais
mourir	je meurs nous mourons	je suis mort	je mourais
naître	je nais nous naissons	je suis né	je naissais
partir *repartir*	je pars nous partons	je suis parti	je partais
plaire	je plais nous plaisons	j'ai plu	je plaisais
pleuvoir	il pleut	il a plu	il pleuvait
prendre *apprendre,* *comprendre,* *reprendre, surprendre*	je prends nous prenons	j'ai pris	je prenais

Future	Conditional	Present Subjunctive	Present Participle
je cuirai	je cuirais	je cuise	cuisant
je dormirai	je dormirais	je dorme	dormant
j'écrirai	j'écrirais	j'écrive	écrivant
j'enverrai	j'enverrais	j'envoie	envoyant
il faudra	il faudrait	il faille	
je fuirai	je fuirais	je fuie	fuyant
je lirai	je lirais	je lise	lisant
je mentirai	je mentirais	je mente	mentant
je mettrai	je mettrais	je mette	mettant
je moudrai	je moudrais	je moule	moulant
je mourrai	je mourrais	je meure	mourant
je naîtrai	je naîtrais	je naisse	naissant
je partirai	je partirais	je parte	partant
je plairai	je plairais	je plaise	plaisant
il pleuvra	il pleuvrait	il pleuve	pleuvant
je prendrai	je prendrais	je prenne	prenant

Infinitive	Present	Perfect	Imperfect
recevoir *apercevoir, décevoir*	je reçois nous recevons	j'ai reçu	je recevais
rejoindre	je rejoins nous rejoignons	j'ai rejoint	je rejoignais
résoudre	je résous nous résolvons	j'ai résolu	je résolvais
rire *sourire*	je ris nous rions	j'ai ri	je riais
savoir	je sais nous savons	j'ai su	je savais
servir	je sers nous servons	j'ai servi	je servais
sortir	je sors nous sortons	je suis sorti	je sortais
suffire	je suffis nous suffisons	j'ai suffi	je suffisais
suivre *poursuivre*	je suis nous suivons	j'ai suivi	je suivais
se taire	je me tais nous nous taisons	je me suis tu	je me taisais
tenir *appartenir, contenir, convenir, devenir, entretenir, maintenir, obtenir, prévenir, revenir, soutenir, se souvenir, venir*	je tiens nous tenons	j'ai tenu	je tenais
vaincre *convaincre*	je vaincs nous vainquons	j'ai vaincu	je vainquais
valoir	je vaux nous valons	j'ai valu	je valais
vivre	je vis nous vivons	j'ai vécu	je vivais
voir *prévoir*	je vois nous voyons	j'ai vu	je voyais

Future	Conditional	Present Subjunctive	Present Participle
je recevrai	je recevrais	je reçoive	recevant
je rejoindrai	je rejoindrais	je rejoigne	rejoignant
je résoudrai	je résoudrais	je résolve	résolvant
je rirai	je rirais	je rie	riant
je saurai	je saurais	je sache	sachant
je servirai	je servirais	je serve	servant
je sortirai	je sortirais	je sorte	sortant
je suffirai	je suffirais	je suffise	suffisant
je suivrai	je suivrais	je suive	suivant
je me tairai	je me tairais	je me taise	taisant
je tiendrai	je tiendrais	je tienne	tenant
je vaincrai	je vaincrais	je vainque	vainquant
je vaudrai	je vaudrais	je vaille	valant
je vivrai	je vivrais	je vive	vivant
je verrai	je verrais	je voie	voyant

Useful Word Groups

Numbers

zéro	0	dix-neuf	19
un	1	vingt	20
deux	2	vingt et un	21
trois	3	vingt-deux	22
quatre	4	trente	30
cinq	5	quarante	40
six	6	cinquante	50
sept	7	soixante	60
huit	8	soixante-dix	70
neuf	9	quatre-vingts	80
dix	10	quatre-vingt-un	81
onze	11	quatre-vingt-dix	90
douze	12	cent	100
treize	13	cent un	101
quatorze	14	cent cinquante	150
quinze	15	deux cents	200
seize	16	deux cent un	201
dix-sept	17	mille	1,000
dix-huit	18	un million	1,000,000

Ordinal numbers to 12

premier/première	1er/ère	first
deuxième	2ème	second
troisième	3ème	third
quatrième	4ème	fourth
cinquième	5ème	fifth
sixième	6ème	sixth
septième	7ème	seventh
huitième	8ème	eighth
neuvième	9ème	ninth
dixième	10ème	tenth
onzième	11ème	eleventh
douzième	12ème	twelfth

Months

janvier	January	octobre	October
février	February	novembre	November
mars	March	décembre	December
avril	April		
mai	May	**Note:**	
juin	June	le premier mars	1st March
juillet	July	le **vingt** février	20th February
août	August	le **vingt-trois**	
septembre	September	septembre	23rd September

Days of the week

lundi	Monday	
mardi	Tuesday	**Note:**
mercredi	Wednesday	J'y suis allé mardi.
jeudi	Thursday	I went there on Tuesday.
vendredi	Friday	
samedi	Saturday	J'y vais **le** mardi.
dimanche	Sunday	I go there on Tuesdays.

Time expressions

2.00	deux heures	
2.10	deux heures dix	Il est quatre heures et demie.
2.15	deux heures et quart	It's half past four.
2.25	deux heures vingt-cinq	Il est parti à cinq heures.
2.30	deux heures et demie	He left at five o'clock.
2.35	trois heures moins vingt-cinq	
2.45	trois heures moins le quart	Note the use of the twenty-four hour clock with trains etc.
2.55	trois heures moins cinq	00.05 zéro heures cinq
12.00	midi	06.15 six heures quinze
24.00	minuit	18.30 dix-huit heures trente
		20.45 vingt heures quarante-cinq

Seasons

le printemps	spring	
l'été	summer	au printemps in spring
l'automne	autumn	en été in summer
l'hiver	winter	

(xxv)

Question words

A quelle heure?	At what time?
Ça coûte combien?	How much is it?
C'est combien?	How much is it?
Combien?	How much?/How many?
Comment...?	How...?
Est-ce que...?	Is it that...?
Lequel/Laquelle?	Which one?
Lesquels/Lesquelles?	Which ones?
Où?	Where?
Pourquoi?	Why?
Qu'est-ce que...?	What...?
Quand?	When?
Quel/Quelle...?	Which...?
Qui?	Who?
Quoi?	What?

Prepositions

à	at, to, in
après	after
au-dessus de	above
au-dessous de	under
avant	before
avec	with
chez	at the house of
à côté de	next to
dans	in, into
depuis	since
derrière	behind
devant	in front of
en	in, to, by, on
entre	between
en face de	opposite
envers	towards
pendant	during, for
pour	for
près de	near
sans	without
sur	on
sous	under

Useful adverbs

alors	then
assez	quite
beaucoup	much/many
bien	well
au début	at first
ne... jamais	never
maintenant	now
moins	less
peu	little/few
plus	more
puis	then
sans	without
soudain	suddenly
souvent	often
surtout	above all
toujours	always
très	very

Conjunctions

donc	therefore, so
et	and
mais	but
parce que	because

Countries and regions

Africa	*African*	Afrique *f*	*africain*
South/North Africa	*South/North African*	Afrique du Sud/Nord	*sud-/nord-africain*
Algeria	*Algerian*	Algérie *f*	*algérien*
America	*American*	Amérique *f*	*américain*
South/North America	*South/North American*	Amérique du Sud/Nord	*sud-/nord-américain*
Argentina	*Argentinian*	Argentine *f*	*argentin*
Asia	*Asian*	Asie *f*	*asiatique*
Australia	*Australian*	Australie *f*	*australien*
Austria	*Austrian*	Autriche *f*	*autrichien*
Bangladesh	*Bangladeshi*	Bangladesh *m*	*bangladais*
Belgium	*Belgian*	Belgique *f*	*belge*
Brazil	*Brazilian*	Brésil *m*	*brésilien*
Canada	*Canadian*	Canada *m*	*canadien*
Caribbean (the)		Caraïbe (la) *f*	
China	*Chinese*	Chine *f*	*chinois*
Cuba	*Cuban*	Cuba *m or f*	*cubain*
Cyprus	*Cypriot*	Chypre *m or f*	*cypriote*
Czech Republic (the)	*Czech*	République tchèque (la) *f*	*tchèque*
Denmark	*Danish*	Danemark *m*	*danois*
Egypt	*Egyptian*	Égypte *f*	*égyptien*
England	*English*	Angleterre *f*	*anglais*
Europe	*European*	Europe *f*	*européen*
Finland	*Finnish*	Finlande *f*	*finlandais*
France	*French*	France *f*	*français*
Germany	*German*	Allemagne *f*	*allemand*
Great Britain	*British*	Grande-Bretagne *f*	*britannique*
Greece	*Greek*	Grèce *f*	*grec*
Holland	*Dutch*	Pays-Bas (les) *mpl*	*hollandais*
Hungary	*Hungarian*	Hongrie *f*	*hongrois*
India	*Indian*	Inde *f*	*indien*
Indonesia	*Indonesian*	Indonésie *f*	*indonésien*
Iran	*Iranian*	Iran *m*	*iranien*
Iraq	*Iraqi*	Irak *m*	*irakien*
Ireland	*Irish*	Irlande *f*	*irlandais*

Israel	*Israeli*	Israël *m*	*israélien*
Italy	*Italian*	Italie *f*	*italien*
Jamaica	*Jamaican*	Jamaïque *f*	*jamaïcain*
Japan	*Japanese*	Japon *m*	*japonais*
Kenya	*Kenyan*	Kenya *m*	*kényan*
North/South Korea	*North/South Korean*	Corée *f* du Nord /Sud	*nord-/sud-coréen*
Lebanon (the)	*Lebanese*	Liban (le) *m*	*libanais*
Libya	*Libyan*	Libye *f*	*libyen*
Luxembourg		Luxembourg *m*	*luxembour-geois*
Malaysia	*Malaysian*	Malaisie *f*	*malais*
Mexico	*Mexican*	Mexique *m*	*mexicain*
Morocco	*Moroccan*	Maroc *m*	*marocain*
New Zealand		Nouvelle-Zélande *f*	*néo-zélandais*
Nigeria	*Nigerian*	Nigeria *m*	*nigérian*
Norway	*Norwegian*	Norvège *f*	*norvégien*
Pakistan	*Pakistani*	Pakistan *m*	*pakistanais*
Philippines (the)	*Filipino*	Philippines (les) *fpl*	*philippin*
Poland	*Polish*	Pologne *f*	*polonais*
Portugal	*Portuguese*	Portugal *m*	*portugais*
Romania	*Romanian*	Roumanie *f*	*roumain*
Russia	*Russian*	Russie *f*	*russe*
Saudi Arabia	*Saudi Arabian*	Arabie *f* Saoudite	*saoudien*
Scotland	*Scottish*	Écosse *f*	*écossais*
Slovakia	*Slovakian*	Slovaquie *f*	*slovaque*
Spain	*Spanish*	Espagne *f*	*espagnol*
Sweden	*Swedish*	Suède *f*	*suédois*
Switzerland	*Swiss*	Suisse *f*	*suisse*
Syria	*Syrian*	Syrie *f*	*syrien*
Thailand	*Thai*	Thaïlande *f*	*thaïlandais*
Tunisia	*Tunisian*	Tunisie *f*	*tunisien*
Turkey	*Turkish*	Turquie *f*	*turc*
United Kingdom	*British*	Royaume-Uni *m*	*britannique*
United States	*American*	États-Unis *mpl*	*américain*
Vietnam	*Vietnamese*	Viêt Nam *m*	*vietnamien*
Wales	*Welsh*	Pays *m* de Galles	*gallois*
West Indies (the)	*West Indian*	Antilles (les) *fpl*	*antillais*

English-French

A

a *indefinite article* un, une; **a man** un homme; **an apple** une pomme; **six pence a kilo** six pence le kilo; **50 km an hour** 50 km à l'heure; **he's a doctor** il est médecin; **twice a month** deux fois par mois.

abandon *verb* abandonner.

abbey *noun* abbaye *f*.

abbreviation *noun* abréviation *f*.

ability *noun* capacité *f* (**to do** pour faire); **to the best of my a.** de mon mieux.

able *adjective* capable; **to be a. to do** être capable de faire, pouvoir faire; **to be a. to swim/drive** savoir nager/conduire.

abnormal *adjective* anormal.

aboard
1 *adverb* (*on ship*) à bord; **all a.** (*on train*) en voiture.
2 *preposition* **a. the ship** à bord du navire; **a. the train** dans le train.

abolish *verb* supprimer.

abortion *noun* avortement *m*; **to have an a.** se faire avorter.

about
1 *adverb* (*approximately*) à peu près, environ; (**at**) **a. two o'clock** vers deux heures.
■ (*here and there*) çà et là; (*flu*) dans l'air; (*rumour*) en circulation; **there are lots a.** il en existe beaucoup; (*out and*) **a.** (*after illness*) sur pied; (*up and*) **a.** (*out of bed*) levé, debout.
2 *preposition* (*around*) **a. the garden** autour du jardin; **a. the** streets par les rues.
■ (*near to*) **a. here** par ici.
■ (*concerning*) au sujet de; **to talk a.** parler de; **a book a.** un livre sur; **what's it (all) a.?** de quoi s'agit-il?; **what** *or* **how a. me?** et moi?; **what** *or* **how a. a drink?** et si on prenait un verre?
■ (+ *infinitive*) **a. to do** sur le point de faire.

above
1 *adverb* au-dessus; **from a.** d'en haut; **floor a.** étage *m* supérieur.
2 *preposition* au-dessus de; **a. all** par-dessus tout; **he's a. me** (*in rank*) c'est mon supérieur.

above-mentioned *adjective* susmentionné.

abreast *adverb* **four a.** par rangs de quatre; **to keep a. of** se tenir au courant de.

abroad *adverb* à l'étranger; **from a.** de l'étranger.

abrupt *adjective* (*sudden, rude*) brusque.

abscess *noun* abcès *m*.

absence *noun* absence *f*.

absent *adjective* absent (**from** de).

absent-minded *adjective* distrait.

absolute *adjective* absolu; (*coward etc*) parfait.

absolutely *adverb* absolument.

absorb *verb* (*liquid*) absorber; **absorbed in one's work** absorbé dans *or* par son travail.

absurd *adjective* absurde.

abuse
1 *noun* abus *m* (**of** de); (*of child*

etc) mauvais traitements *mpl*; (*insults*) injures *fpl*.
2 *verb* (*use badly or wrongly*) abuser de; (*ill-treat*) maltraiter; (*insult*) injurier.

abusive *adjective* grossier.

academic
  1 *adjective* (*of school*) scolaire; (*of university*) universitaire.
  2 *noun* (*teacher*) universitaire *m or f*.

accelerate *verb* (*in vehicle*) accélérer.

accelerator *noun* accélérateur *m*.

accent *noun* accent *m*.

accept *verb* accepter.

acceptable *adjective* acceptable.

access *noun* accès *m* (to something à quelque chose, to somebody auprès de quelqu'un).

accessible *adjective* accessible.

accessories *plural noun* (*objects*) accessoires *mpl*.

accident *noun* accident *m*; by a. (*by chance*) par hasard; (*without meaning to*) accidentellement.

accidental *adjective* accidentel.

accidentally *adverb* accidentellement.

accommodation *noun* logement *m*.

accompany *verb* accompagner.

accomplish *verb* accomplir; (*aim*) réaliser.

accord *noun* of my own a. volontairement.

accordance *noun* in a. with conformément à.

according to *preposition* selon.

accordion *noun* accordéon *m*.

account *noun* (*with bank or firm*) compte *m*; (*report*) compte rendu *m*; accounts (*of firm*) comptabi-

lité *f*; to take into a. tenir compte de; on a. of à cause de.

accountant *noun* comptable *m or f*.

account for *verb* (*explain*) expliquer; (*represent*) représenter.

accumulate *verb*
  1 (*acquire*) accumuler.
  2 (*become more numerous*) s'accumuler.

accurate *adjective* exact, précis.

accurately *adverb* avec précision.

accusation *noun* accusation *f*.

accuse *verb* accuser (of de).

accustomed *adjective* habitué (to something à quelque chose, to doing à faire); to get a. to s'habituer à.

ace *noun* (*card, person*) as *m*.

ache
  1 *noun* douleur *f*; to have an a. in one's arm avoir mal au bras.
  2 *verb* faire mal; my leg's aching la jambe me fait mal; I'm aching all over j'ai mal partout.

achieve *verb* réaliser; (*result*) obtenir; (*victory*) remporter.

achievement *noun* (*success*) réussite *f*.

aching *adjective* douloureux.

acid *adjective & noun* acide (*m*).

acknowledge *verb* reconnaître (as pour); to a. (receipt of) accuser réception de.

acne *noun* acné *f*.

acorn *noun* gland *m*.

acquaint *verb* to be acquainted with somebody connaître quelqu'un; we are acquainted on se connaît.

acquaintance *noun* connaissance *f*.

acquire *verb* acquérir.

acre *noun* acre *f* (= 0,4 *hectare*).

acrobat *noun* acrobate *m or f.*

acrobatic *adjective* acrobatique.

across *adverb & preposition* (*from side to side* (*of*)) d'un côté à l'autre (de); (*on the other side* (*of*)) de l'autre côté (de); (*so as to cross, diagonally*) en travers (de); **to be a kilometre a.** (*wide*) avoir un kilomètre de large; **to walk** *or* go **a.** (*street*) traverser.

acrylic *noun* acrylique *m;* **a. socks**/*etc* chaussettes *fpl/etc* en acrylique.

act
1 *noun* (*deed, part of play*) acte *m;* (*in circus*) numéro *m;* **caught in the a.** pris sur le fait.
2 *verb* (*part in play or film*) jouer.
3 *verb* (*take action, behave*) agir; (*in play or film*) jouer; **to a. as** (*secretary etc*) faire office de; (*of object*) servir de.

act for *verb* (*lawyer*) représenter.

action *noun* action *f;* (*military*) combat *m;* **to take a.** prendre des mesures; **to put into a.** (*plan*) exécuter; **out of a.** hors d'usage; (*person*) hors (de) combat.

active
1 *adjective* actif; (*interest, dislike*) vif (*f* vive).
2 *noun Grammar* actif *m.*

activity *noun* activité *f;* (*in street*) animation *f.*

act (up)on *verb* (*affect*) agir sur; (*advice*) suivre.

actor *noun* acteur *m.*

actress *noun* actrice *f.*

actual *adjective* réel; **the a. book** le livre lui-même.

actually *adverb* (*truly*) réellement; (*in fact*) en réalité.

acute *adjective* aigu, -uë; (*emotion*) vif, vive; (*shortage*) grave.

AD *abbreviation* (*anno Domini*) après Jésus-Christ.

ad *noun Familiar* pub *f;* (*private, in newspaper*) annonce *f;* **small ad** petite annonce.

adapt *verb* adapter (**to** à); **to a. (oneself)** s'adapter.

adaptable *adjective* (*person*) souple.

adaptor *noun* (*plug*) prise *f* multiple.

add *verb* ajouter (**to** à, **that** que); (*total*) additionner.

addict *noun* **jazz**/**sport a.** fanatique *m or f* de jazz/de sport; **drug a.** drogué, -ée *m or f.*

addicted *adjective* **to be a. to** (*music, sport*) se passionner pour; **a. to drink** alcoolique; **to be a. to smoking** avoir une dépendance à la cigarette.

addiction *noun* **drug a.** toxicomanie *f.*

add in *verb* (*include*) inclure.

adding machine *noun* machine *f* à calculer.

addition *noun* addition *f;* **in a.** de plus; **in a. to** en plus de.

additional *adjective* supplémentaire.

additive *noun* additif *m.*

address
1 *noun* (*on letter etc*) adresse *f;* (*speech*) allocution *f.*
2 *verb* (*person*) s'adresser à; (*audience*) parler devant; (*letter*) mettre l'adresse sur.

add to *verb* (*increase*) augmenter.

add together *verb* (*numbers*) additionner.

add up *verb*
1 (*numbers*) additionner.
2 to a. up to (*total*) s'élever à;

(*mean*) signifier; (*represent*)
constituer.

adenoids *plural noun* végétations
fpl (adénoïdes).

adequate *adjective* (*quantity
etc*) suffisant; (*acceptable*) convenable; (*person*) compétent.

adequately *adverb* suffisamment; convenablement.

adhesive *adjective & noun*
adhésif (*m*).

adjective *noun* adjectif *m*.

adjust *verb* (*machine*) régler;
(*salaries*) ajuster; **to a. (oneself)
to** s'adapter à.

adjustable *adjective* (*seat*) réglable.

adjustment *noun* réglage *m*; (*of
person*) adaptation *f*.

administer *verb* administrer.

administration *noun* administration *f*.

administrative *adjective*
administratif.

admiral *noun* amiral *m*.

admiration *noun* admiration *f*.

admire *verb* admirer (**for** pour,
for doing de faire).

admission *noun* (*to cinema etc*)
entrée *f*; **a. charge** prix *m* d'entrée.

admit *verb* (*let in*) laisser entrer,
admettre; (*acknowledge*) reconnaître, admettre (**that** que); **to a.
to something** reconnaître quelque chose.

admittance *noun* 'no a.' 'entrée
interdite'.

adolescent *noun* adolescent,
-ente *m or f*.

adopt *verb* (*child, attitude etc*)
adopter.

adopted *adjective* (*child*) adoptif.

adoption *noun* adoption *f*.

adorable *adjective* adorable.

adore *verb* adorer (**doing** faire).

adult
1 *noun* adulte *m or f*.
2 *adjective* (*animal etc*) adulte; **a.
class/film/etc** classe *f*/film *m*/
etc pour adultes.

advance
1 *noun* (*movement, money*)
avance *f*; **advances** (*of love*)
avances *fpl*; **in a.** à l'avance,
d'avance.
2 *adjective* (*payment*) anticipé; **a.
booking** réservation *f*.
3 *verb* avancer.

advanced *adjective* avancé;
(*studies, level*) supérieur; (*course*)
de niveau supérieur.

advantage *noun* avantage *m*
(**over** sur); **to take a. of** profiter
de; (*person*) exploiter.

adventure *noun* aventure *f*; **a.
novel** roman *m* d'aventures.

adventurous *adjective* aven-
tureux.

adverb *noun* adverbe *m*.

advert *noun* publicité *f*; (*private,
in newspaper*) annonce *f*.

advertise *verb*
1 (*product*) faire de la publicité
pour; (*job*) passer une annonce
pour; (*make known*) annoncer.
2 (*to sell product*) faire de la publicité; (*for job*) passer une annonce (**for somebody** pour trouver quelqu'un).

advertisement *noun* publicité
f; (*private, in newspaper*) annonce
f; (*poster*) affiche *f*; **classified a.**
petite annonce.

advice *noun* conseil(s) *m(pl)*; **a
piece of a.** un conseil.

advisable *adjective* (*wise*) recommandé (**to do** de faire).

advise *verb* conseiller; *(recommend)* recommander; **to a. somebody to do** conseiller à quelqu'un de faire; **to a. somebody against something** déconseiller quelque chose à quelqu'un.

adviser *noun* conseiller, -ère *m or f*.

aerial *noun* antenne *f*.

aerobics *noun* aérobic *m*.

aeroplane *noun* avion *m*.

aerosol *noun* aérosol *m*.

affair *noun* affaire *f*; **(love) a.** liaison *f*.

affect *verb (concern, move)* toucher, affecter; *(harm)* nuire à.

affection *noun* affection *f* (**for** pour).

affectionate *adjective* affectueux.

affluent *adjective* riche.

afford *verb (pay for)* avoir les moyens d'acheter; *(time)* pouvoir trouver.

affordable *adjective (price etc)* abordable.

afloat *adverb (ship, swimmer, business)* à flot.

afraid *adjective* **to be a.** avoir peur (**of, to de**); **he's a. (that) she may be ill** il a peur qu'elle (ne) soit malade; **I'm a. he's out** *(I regret to say)* je regrette, il est sorti.

Africa *noun* l'Afrique *f*; **North/South A.** l'Afrique du Nord/Sud.

African *adjective & noun* africain, -aine *(m or f)*; **North/South A.** nord-/sud-africain.

after
1 *adverb* après; **the month a.** le mois suivant.

2 *preposition* après; **a. all** après tout; **a. eating** après avoir mangé; **a. you!** après vous!; **to be a. something/somebody** *(seek)* chercher quelque chose/quelqu'un.
3 *conjunction* après que.

aftereffects *plural noun* suites *fpl*.

afternoon *noun* après-midi *invariable m or f*; **in the a.** l'après-midi; **good a.!** *(hello)* bonjour!; *(goodbye)* au revoir!

aftersales service *noun* service *m* après-vente.

aftershave (lotion) *noun* lotion *f* après-rasage.

afterward(s) *adverb* après, plus tard.

again *adverb* de nouveau, encore une fois; **never a.** plus jamais; **a. and a., time and (time) a.** bien des fois, maintes fois.

against *preposition* contre; **a. the law** illégal.

age
1 *noun* âge *m*; **(old) a.** vieillesse *f*; **the Middle Ages** le moyen âge; **five years of a.** âgé de cinq ans; **under a.** trop jeune.
2 *verb* vieillir.

aged *adjective* **a. ten** âgé de dix ans.

agency *noun (office)* agence *f*.

agenda *noun* ordre *m* du jour.

agent *noun* agent *m*; *(dealer)* concessionnaire *m or f*.

aggravate *verb (make worse)* aggraver; **to a. somebody** exaspérer quelqu'un.

aggravation *noun (bother)* ennui(s) *m(pl)*.

aggression *noun* agression *f*.

aggressive *adjective* agressif.

agile *adjective* agile.

agitated *adjective* agité.

ago *adverb* a year a. il y a un an; **how long a.?** il y a combien de temps (de cela)?

agony *noun* **to be in a.** souffrir horriblement.

agree *verb*
1 (*come to an agreement*) se mettre d'accord; (*be in agreement*) être d'accord (**with** avec); (*of facts, dates*) concorder; *Grammar* s'accorder; **to a. to something/ to doing** consentir à quelque chose/à faire; **it doesn't a. with me** (*food, climate*) ça ne me réussit pas.
2 to a. to do accepter de faire; **to a. that** admettre que.

agreeable *adjective* (*pleasant*) agréable.

agreed *adjective* (*time, place*) convenu; **we are a.** nous sommes d'accord; **a.!** entendu!

agreement *noun* accord *m*; **in a. with** d'accord avec.

agree (up)on *verb* (*decide*) convenir de.

agricultural *adjective* agricole.

agriculture *noun* agriculture *f*.

ahead *adverb* (*in space*) en avant; (*leading*) en tête; (*in the future*) dans l'avenir; **a. (of time)** en avance (sur l'horaire); **to be one hour a.** avoir une heure d'avance (**of** sur); **a. of** (*space*) devant; (*time*) en avance sur; **straight a.** (*to walk*) tout droit; (*to look*) droit devant soi.

aid *noun* aide *f*; (*device*) accessoire *m*, support *m*; **with the a. of** (*stick etc*) à l'aide de; **in a. of** (*charity*) au profit de.

AIDS *noun* SIDA *m*.

aim
1 *noun* but *m*; **with the a. of** dans le but de.
2 *verb* (*gun*) braquer (**at** sur); **aimed at children/etc** (*product*) destiné aux enfants/etc.
3 *verb* (*of person*) viser; **to a. at somebody** viser quelqu'un; **to a. to do** avoir l'intention de faire.

air
1 *noun* air *m*; **in the open a.** en plein air; **by a.** (*to travel, send*) par avion; **(up) in(to) the a.** en l'air.
2 *adjective* (*raid, base*) aérien.
3 *verb* (*room*) aérer.

air-conditioned *adjective* climatisé.

aircraft *invariable noun* avion(s) *m(pl)*.

aircraft carrier *noun* porte-avions *m invariable*.

air fare *noun* prix *m* du billet d'avion.

air force *noun* armée *f* de l'air.

air freshener *noun* désodorisant *m*.

air hostess *noun* hôtesse *f* de l'air.

airing cupboard *noun* armoire *f* sèche-linge.

airline *noun* ligne *f* aérienne.

airline ticket *noun* billet *m* d'avion.

airmail *noun* poste *f* aérienne; **by a.** par avion.

airport *noun* aéroport *m*.

airsickness *noun* mal *m* de l'air.

air terminal *noun* aérogare *f*.

airtight *adjective* hermétique.

air-traffic controller *noun* aiguilleur *m* du ciel.

aisle *noun* (*in plane, supermarket, cinema etc*) allée *f*; (*in church*) nef *f* latérale.

ajar *adjective* (*door*) entrouvert.

alarm
1 *noun* (*warning, device in house or car*) alarme *f*; (*mechanism*) sonnerie *f* (d'alarme); **a. (clock)** réveil *m*.
2 *verb* alarmer.

Albania *noun* l'Albanie *f*.

Albanian *adjective & noun* albanais, -aise (*m or f*).

album *noun* (*book, record*) album *m*.

alcohol *noun* alcool *m*.

alcoholic
1 *adjective* (*drink*) alcoolisé.
2 *noun* (*person*) alcoolique *m or f*.

alert *adjective* (*watching carefully*) vigilant.

A level *abbreviation* (*exam*) = épreuve *f* de bac.

algebra *noun* algèbre *f*.

Algeria *noun* l'Algérie *f*.

Algerian *adjective & noun* algérien, -ienne (*m or f*).

alibi *noun* alibi *m*.

alien *noun* étranger, -ère *m or f*.

alight *adjective* (*fire*) allumé; **to set a.** mettre le feu à.

alike
1 *adjective* (*people, things*) semblables; **to look** *or* **be a.** se ressembler.
2 *adverb* de la même manière.

alive *adjective* vivant, en vie.

all
1 *adjective* tout, toute, *plural* tous, toutes; **a. day** toute la journée; **a. (the) men** tous les hommes.
2 *pronoun* tous *mpl*, toutes *fpl*; (*everything*) tout; **my sisters are a. here** toutes mes sœurs sont ici;

he ate it a., he ate a. of it il a tout mangé; **a. (that) he has** tout ce qu'il a; **a. of us** nous tous; **in a.**, en tout; **a. but** (*almost*) presque; **if there's any wind at a.** s'il y a le moindre vent; **not at a.** pas du tout; (*after 'thank you'*) pas de quoi.
3 *adverb* tout; **a. alone** tout seul; **six a.** *Football* six buts partout.

allergic *adjective* allergique (**to** à).

alley *noun* ruelle *f*; (*in park*) allée *f*.

alleyway *noun* ruelle *f*.

alliance *noun* alliance *f*.

alligator *noun* alligator *m*.

all-in *adjective* (*price*) global.

allocate *verb* allouer (**to** à); (*distribute*) répartir.

allotment *noun* (*land*) lopin *m* de terre (*loué pour la culture*).

all-out *adjective* (*effort*) énergique.

allow *verb* permettre; (*give*) accorder; (*time*) compter, prévoir; **to a. somebody to do** permettre à quelqu'un de faire; **you're not allowed to go** on vous interdit de partir.

allowance *noun* allocation *f*; (*for travel, housing, food*) indemnité *f*; **to make allowances for somebody** être indulgent envers quelqu'un; **the duty-free a. is …** on autorise à acheter …

allow for *verb* tenir compte de.

all-purpose *adjective* (*tool*) universel.

all right
1 *adjective* (*satisfactory*) bien *invariable*; (*unharmed*) sain et sauf (*f* saine et sauve); (*undamaged*) intact; (*without worries*) tranquille; **it's a.** ça va; **I'm a.**

(*healthy*) je vais bien.
2 *adverb* (*well*) bien; **a.!** (*agreement*) d'accord!; **I got your letter a.** (*emphatic*) j'ai bien reçu votre lettre.

all-round *adjective* complet.

ally *noun* allié, -ée *m or f*.

almond *noun* amande *f*.

almost *adverb* presque; **he a. fell**/*etc* il a failli tomber/*etc*.

alone *adjective & adverb* seul; **to leave a.** (*person*) laisser tranquille; (*thing*) ne pas toucher à.

along
1 *preposition* (**all**) **a.** (tout) le long de; **to go** *or* **walk a.** (*street*) passer par; **a. with** avec.
2 *adverb* **all a.** (*time*) dès le début.

alongside *preposition & adverb* à côté (de).

aloud *adverb* à haute voix.

alphabet *noun* alphabet *m*.

alphabetical *adjective* alphabétique.

Alps *plural noun* **the A.** les Alpes *fpl*.

already *adverb* déjà.

alright *adverb Familiar* = **all right**.

Alsatian *noun* (*dog*) berger *m* allemand.

also *adverb* aussi.

altar *noun* autel *m*.

alter *verb* changer; (*clothing*) retoucher.

alteration *noun* changement *m*; (*of clothing*) retouche *f*.

alternate
1 *adjective* alterné; **on a. days** tous les deux jours.
2 *verb* alterner (**with** avec).

alternative
1 *adjective* (*other*) autre.

2 *noun* alternative *f*.

alternatively *adverb* comme alternative.

although *adverb* bien que (+ *subjunctive*).

altogether *adverb* (*completely*) tout à fait; (*on the whole*) somme toute; **how much a.?** combien en tout?

aluminium *noun* aluminium *m*.

always *adverb* toujours.

am *see* **be**.

a.m. *adverb* du matin.

amateur
1 *noun* amateur *m*.
2 *adjective* **a. painter**/*etc* peintre/*etc* amateur.

amaze *verb* étonner.

amazed *adjective* stupéfait (**at something** de quelque chose, **at seeing** de voir); (*filled with wonder*) émerveillé.

amazing *adjective* stupéfiant; (*incredible*) extraordinaire.

ambassador *noun* ambassadeur *m*; (*woman*) ambassadrice *f*.

amber *noun* **a. (light)** (*of traffic signal*) (feu *m*) orange *m*.

ambition *noun* ambition *f*.

ambitious *adjective* ambitieux.

ambulance *noun* ambulance *f*.

ambulance driver *noun* ambulancier *m*.

America *noun* l'Amérique *f*; **North/South A.** l'Amérique du Nord/Sud.

American *adjective & noun* américain, -aine (*m or f*).

ammunition *noun* munitions *fpl*.

among(st) *preposition* parmi, entre; **a. the crowd/books** parmi la foule/les livres; **a. themselves/friends** entre eux/amis.

amount noun quantité f; (sum of money) somme f; (total of bill etc) montant m.

amount to verb s'élever à; (mean) signifier; (represent) représenter.

ample adjective (enough) largement assez de; **you have a. time** tu as largement le temps.

amplifier noun amplificateur m.

amputate verb amputer.

amuse verb amuser.

amusement noun amusement m; **amusements** (at fair etc) machines fpl à sous.

amusement arcade noun salle f de jeux.

amusing adjective amusant.

an see a.

analyse verb analyser.

analysis noun analyse f.

anarchy noun anarchie f.

anatomy noun anatomie f.

ancestor noun ancêtre m.

anchor noun ancre f.

anchored adjective ancré.

anchovy noun anchois m.

ancient adjective ancien; (pre-medieval) antique.

and conjunction et; **two hundred a. two** deux cent deux; **better a. better** de mieux en mieux; **go a. see** va voir.

an(a)esthetic noun anesthésie f; (substance) anesthésique m; **general a.** anesthésie générale.

angel noun ange m.

anger noun colère f.

angle noun angle m; **at an a.** en biais.

angler noun pêcheur, -euse m or f à la ligne.

angling noun pêche f à la ligne.

angrily adverb avec colère.

angry adjective fâché; (letter) indigné; **to get a.** se fâcher (**with** contre).

animal noun & adjective animal (m).

ankle noun cheville f.

ankle sock noun socquette f.

annexe noun annexe f.

anniversary noun (of event) anniversaire m.

announce verb annoncer; (birth, marriage) faire part de.

announcement noun (statement) annonce f; (notice) avis m.

announcer noun (on TV) speaker m, speakerine f.

annoy verb (inconvenience) ennuyer; (irritate) agacer.

annoyed adjective fâché; **to get a.** se fâcher (**with** contre).

annoying adjective ennuyeux.

annual
1 adjective annuel.
2 noun (book) annuaire m.

annually adverb annuellement.

anonymous adjective anonyme.

anorak noun anorak m.

another adjective & pronoun un(e) autre; **a. man** un autre homme; **a. month** (additional) encore un mois; **a. ten** encore dix; **one a.** l'un(e) l'autre, plural les un(e)s les autres; **they love one a.** ils s'aiment (l'un l'autre).

answer
1 noun réponse f; (to problem) solution (**to** de).
2 verb (person, question, phone) répondre à; (prayer, wish) exaucer; **to a. the bell** or **the door** ouvrir la porte.
3 verb (reply) répondre.

answer back verb **to a. some-**

body back répondre à quelqu'un.

answer for *verb* to a. for somebody/something répondre de quelqu'un/quelque chose.

answering machine *noun* répondeur *m*.

ant *noun* fourmi *f*.

antelope *noun* antilope *f*.

anthem *noun* national a. hymne *m* national.

anthology *noun* recueil *m*.

anti- *prefix* anti-.

antibiotic *noun* antibiotique *m*.

antibody *noun* anticorps *m*.

anticipate *verb* (*foresee*) prévoir; (*expect*) s'attendre à.

anticipation *noun* in a. of en prévision de.

anticlockwise *adverb* dans le sens inverse des aiguilles d'une montre.

antics *plural noun* singeries *fpl*.

antifreeze *noun* antigel *m*.

antihistamine *noun* antihistaminique *m*.

antique
1 *adjective* (*furniture etc*) ancien.
2 *noun* antiquité *f*.

antique dealer *noun* antiquaire *m or f*.

antique shop *noun* magasin *m* d'antiquités.

antiseptic *adjective & noun* antiseptique (*m*).

anxiety *noun* (*worry*) inquiétude *f*; (*fear*) anxiété *f*.

anxious *adjective* (*worried*) inquiet (**about** de, **pour**); (*afraid*) anxieux; (*eager*) impatient (**to do** de faire).

anxiously *adverb* (*to wait*) impatiemment.

any
1 *adjective* (*with question*) du, de la, des; **have you a. milk/tickets?** avez-vous du lait/des billets?
▪ (*negative*) de; **he hasn't got a. milk/tickets** il n'a pas de lait/de billets.
▪ (*no matter which*) n'importe quel.
▪ (*every*) tout; **in a. case, at a. rate** de toute façon.
2 *pronoun* (*no matter which one*) n'importe lequel; **if a. of you** si l'un d'entre vous.
▪ (*quantity*) en; **have you a.?** en as-tu?
3 *adverb* **a. (not)** a. **happier**/*etc* (pas) plus heureux/*etc*; **I don't see him a. more** je ne le vois plus; **a. more tea?** encore du thé?; **a. better?** (un peu) mieux?

anybody *pronoun* (*indeterminate*) quelqu'un; **do you see a.?** tu vois quelqu'un?
▪ (*negative*) personne; **he doesn't know a.** il ne connaît personne.
▪ (*no matter who*) n'importe qui.

anyhow *adverb* (*at any rate*) de toute façon; (*badly*) n'importe comment.

anyone = anybody.

anything *pronoun* (*indeterminate*) quelque chose.
▪ (*negative*) rien; **he doesn't do a.** il ne fait rien.
▪ (*everything*) tout; **a. you like** (tout) ce que tu veux.
▪ (*no matter what*) **a. (at all)** n'importe quoi.

anyway *adverb* (*at any rate*) de toute façon.

anywhere *adverb* (*no matter where*) n'importe où.
▪ (*everywhere*) partout; **a. you go** partout où vous allez; **a. you**

like là où tu veux.
■ (*somewhere*) quelque part.
■ (*negative*) nulle part; **he doesn't go a.** il ne va nulle part.

apart *adverb* **we kept them a.** (*separate*) on les tenait séparés; **with legs a.** les jambes écartées; **they are a metre a.** ils se trouvent à un mètre l'un de l'autre; **a. from** (*except for*) à part.

apartment *noun* appartement *m*.

ape *noun* singe *m*.

aperitif *noun* apéritif *m*.

apologetic *adjective* **to be a.** (**about**) s'excuser (de).

apologize *verb* s'excuser (**for** de); **to a. to somebody** faire ses excuses à quelqu'un (**for** pour).

apology *noun* excuses *fpl*.

apostrophe *noun* apostrophe *f*.

appal *verb* consterner.

appalling *adjective* épouvantable.

apparatus *noun* appareil *m*; (*in gym*) agrès *mpl*.

apparent *adjective* apparent; **it's a. that** il est évident que.

apparently *adverb* apparemment.

appeal [1] *noun* (*charm*) attrait *m*; (*interest*) intérêt *m*.

appeal [2]
1 *noun* (*in court*) appel *m*.
2 *verb* faire appel.

appeal to *verb* **to a. to somebody** (*attract*) plaire à quelqu'un; (*interest*) intéresser quelqu'un.

appear *verb* (*become visible*) apparaître; (*present oneself*) se présenter; (*seem, be published*) paraître; (*in court*) comparaître; **it appears that** il semble que (+

subjunctive or indicative).

appearance *noun* (*act*) apparition *f*; (*look*) apparence *f*.

appendicitis *noun* appendicite *f*.

appendix *noun* (*in book, body*) appendice *m*.

appetite *noun* appétit *m*.

appetizing *adjective* appétissant.

applaud *verb* (*clap*) applaudir.

applause *noun* applaudissements *mpl*.

apple *noun* pomme *f*; **eating/cooking a.** pomme *f* à couteau/à cuire; **a. pie** tarte *f* aux pommes.

appliance *noun* appareil *m*.

applicant *noun* candidat, -ate *m or f* (**for** à).

application *noun* (*for job*) candidature *f*; (*for membership*) demande *f* d'adhésion; **a. (form)** (*for job*) formulaire *m* de candidature.

apply *verb*
1 (*cream, paint etc*) appliquer; (*brake*) appuyer sur; **to a. oneself to** s'appliquer à.
2 (*be relevant*) s'appliquer (**to** à).

apply for *verb* (*job*) poser sa candidature à.

appoint *verb* (*person*) nommer (**to something** à quelque chose, **to do** pour faire).

appointment *noun* nomination *f*; (*meeting*) rendez-vous *invariable m*.

appreciate *verb* (*enjoy, value*) apprécier; (*understand*) comprendre; (*be grateful for*) être reconnaissant de.

appreciation *noun* (*gratitude*) reconnaissance *f*.

apprentice *noun* apprenti, -ie *m or f*.

apprenticeship *noun* apprentissage *m*.

approach
1 *verb* (*person, door etc*) s'approcher de; (*age, result, town*) approcher de; (*subject*) aborder.
2 *verb* (*of person, vehicle*) s'approcher; (*of date*) approcher.
3 *noun* (*method*) façon *f* de s'y prendre.

appropriate *adjective* convenable.

appropriately *adverb* convenablement.

approval *noun* approbation *f*; **on a.** (*goods*) à l'essai.

approve of *verb* (*conduct etc*) approuver; **I don't a. of him** il ne me plaît pas; **I a. of his going** je trouve bon qu'il y aille.

approximate *adjective* approximatif.

approximately *adverb* à peu près.

apricot *noun* abricot *m*.

April *noun* avril *m*.

apron *noun* tablier *m*.

apt *adjective* (*remark, reply*) juste, convenable; **to be a. to** avoir tendance à.

aptitude *noun* aptitude *f* (**for** à, pour).

aquarium *noun* aquarium *m*.

Arab *adjective* & *noun* arabe (*m or f*).

Arabic *adjective* & *noun* (*language*) arabe (*m*); **A. numerals** chiffres *mpl* arabes.

arc *noun* (*of circle*) arc *m*.

arcade *noun* (*market*) passage *m* couvert.

arch *noun* (*of bridge*) arche *f*; (*of building*) voûte *f*.

archer *noun* archer *m*.

archery *noun* tir *m* à l'arc.

architect *noun* architecte *m or f*.

architecture *noun* architecture *f*.

Arctic *noun* **the A.** l'Arctique *m*.

are *see* be.

area *noun* (*in geometry*) superficie *f*; (*of country*) région *f*; (*of town*) quartier *m*; **parking a.** aire *f* de stationnement.

area code *noun* (*phone number*) indicatif *m*.

Argentina *noun* l'Argentine *f*.

Argentinian *adjective* & *noun* argentin, -ine (*m or f*).

argue *verb*
1 (*quarrel*) se disputer (**with** avec, **about** au sujet de); (*reason*) raisonner (**with** avec, **about** sur).
2 **to a. that** (*maintain*) soutenir que.

argument *noun* (*quarrel*) dispute *f*; (*reasoning*) argument *m*; **to have an a.** se disputer.

arise *verb* (*of problem, opportunity*) se présenter; (*result*) résulter (**from** de).

arithmetic *noun* arithmétique *f*.

arm
1 *noun* bras *m*; (*weapon*) arme *f*.
2 *verb* armer (**with** de).

armband *noun* brassard *m*; (*for swimming*) manchon *m*.

armchair *noun* fauteuil *m*.

armour *noun* (*of knight*) armure *f*; (*of tank etc*) blindage *m*.

armoured *adjective* (*car etc*) blindé.

armpit *noun* aisselle *f*.

army
1 *noun* armée *f*.
2 *adjective* militaire.

around
1 *preposition* autour de; (*ap-*

proximately) environ.
2 *adverb* autour; **a. here** par ici;
he's still a. il est encore là;
there's a lot of flu a. il y a pas
mal de grippes dans l'air.

arrange *verb* arranger; (*time,
meeting*) fixer; **to a. to do** s'arranger pour faire.

arrangement *noun* (*layout,
agreement*) arrangement *m*; **arrangements** préparatifs *mpl*;
(*plans*) projets *mpl*.

arrears *plural noun* **in a.** en retard
dans ses paiements.

arrest
1 *verb* arrêter.
2 *noun* arrestation *f*; **under a.** en
état d'arrestation.

arrival *noun* arrivée *f*.

arrive *verb* arriver.

arrow *noun* flèche *f*.

art *noun* art *m*; **work of a.** œuvre
f d'art.

artery *noun* artère *f*.

arthritis *noun* arthrite *f*.

article *noun* (*object, in newspaper,
in grammar*) article *m*.

articulated lorry *noun* semi-
remorque *m*.

artificial *adjective* artificiel.

artist *noun* (*actor, painter etc*) artiste *m or f*.

artistic *adjective* artistique; (*person*) artiste.

as *adverb & conjunction* (*manner
etc*) comme; **as you like** comme
tu veux; **as much** *or* **as hard as I
can** (au)tant que je peux; **as it is**
comme ça, tel quel; **as if, as
though** comme si.
  ∎ (*comparison*) **as tall as you**
aussi grand que vous; **as white
as a sheet** blanc comme un linge;
as much *or* **as hard as you** au-

tant que vous; **twice as big as**
deux fois plus grand que.
  ∎ (*though*) **(as) clever as he is** si
intelligent qu'il soit.
  ∎ (*capacity*) **as a teacher** comme
professeur; **to act as a father** agir
en père.
  ∎ (*reason*) puisque; **as it's late**
puisqu'il est tard.
  ∎ (*time*) **as I was leaving** comme
je partais; **as he slept** pendant
qu'il dormait; **as from, as of**
(*time*) à partir de.
  ∎ (*concerning*) **as for that** quant
à cela.
  ∎ (+ *infinitive*) **so as to** de manière à; **so stupid as to** assez bête
pour.

asap *abbreviation* (*as soon as
possible*) le plus tôt possible.

ash *noun* cendre *f*.

ashamed *adjective* **to be a.** avoir
honte (**of** de).

ashore *adverb* **to go a.** débarquer.

ashtray *noun* cendrier *m*.

Asia *noun* l'Asie *f*.

Asian
1 *adjective* asiatique.
2 *noun* Asiatique *m or f*.

aside *adverb* de côté.

ask *verb*
1 (*time*) demander; (*question*) poser; (*invite*) inviter; **to a. somebody (for) something**
demander quelque chose à quelqu'un; **to a. somebody to do** demander à quelqu'un de faire.
2 (*inquire*) demander; **to a. for
something/somebody** deman-
der quelque chose/quelqu'un; **to
a. about something** se renseigner sur quelque chose; **to a.
after** *or* **about somebody** demander des nouvelles de quelqu'un; **to a. somebody about**

interroger quelqu'un sur.

asleep *adjective* to be a. dormir; to fall a. s'endormir.

asparagus *noun* asperges *fpl*.

aspect *noun* aspect *m*.

aspirin *noun* aspirine *f*.

assault
1 *noun* (*crime*) agression *f*.
2 *verb* (*attack*) agresser.

assemble *verb*
1 (*objects*) assembler; (*people*) rassembler; (*machine*) monter.
2 (*get together*) se rassembler.

assembly *noun* (*meeting*) assemblée *f*; (*in school*) rassemblement *m*.

assess *verb* (*estimate*) évaluer; (*decide amount of*) fixer le montant de.

asset *noun* (*advantage*) atout *m*; assets (*of business*) biens *mpl*.

assign *verb* (*give*) attribuer (to à).

assignment *noun* (*task*) mission *f*.

assist *verb* aider (in doing, to do à faire).

assistance *noun* aide *f*; to be of a. to somebody aider quelqu'un.

assistant
1 *noun* assistant, -ante *m or f*; (*in shop*) vendeur, -euse *m or f*.
2 *adjective* adjoint.

associate
1 *verb* associer; associated with something/somebody associé à quelque chose/avec quelqu'un.
2 *noun & adjective* associé, -ée (*m or f*).

association *noun* association *f*.

assorted *adjective* variés; (*foods*) assortis.

assortment *noun* assortiment *m*.

assume *verb* (*suppose*) présumer (that que); (*take on*) prendre; (*responsibility, role*) assumer.

assurance *noun* assurance *f*.

assure *verb* assurer (somebody that à quelqu'un que, somebody of quelqu'un de).

asterisk *noun* astérisque *m*.

asthma *noun* asthme *m*.

asthmatic *adjective & noun* asthmatique (*m or f*).

astonish *verb* étonner; to be astonished s'étonner (at something de quelque chose).

astonishing *adjective* étonnant.

astray *adverb* to go a. s'égarer.

astrology *noun* astrologie *f*.

astronaut *noun* astronaute *m or f*.

astronomy *noun* astronomie *f*.

at *preposition* à; at work au travail; at six (o'clock) à six heures.
▮ chez; at the doctor's chez le médecin.
▮ en; at sea en mer.
▮ contre; angry at fâché contre.
▮ sur; to shoot at tirer sur.
▮ de; to laugh at rire de.
▮ (au)près de; at the window (au)près de la fenêtre.
▮ par; to come in at the door entrer par la porte; six at a time six par six.

ate *see* eat.

athlete *noun* athlète *m or f*.

athletic *adjective* athlétique.

athletics *plural noun* athlétisme *m*.

Atlantic
1 *adjective* atlantique.
2 *noun* the A. l'Atlantique *m*.

atlas *noun* atlas *m*.

atmosphere *noun* atmosphère *f*.

atom *noun* atome *m*.

atomic *adjective* atomique.

attach *verb* attacher (**to** à); (*document*) joindre (**to** à); **attached to** (*fond of*) attaché à.

attaché case *noun* attaché-case *m*, mallette *f*.

attachment *noun* (*tool*) accessoire *m*.

attack
1 *noun* attaque *f*.
2 *verb* attaquer.

attacker *noun* agresseur *m*.

attempt
1 *noun* tentative *f*; **to make an a. to** tenter de.
2 *verb* tenter; (*task*) entreprendre; **to a. to do** tenter de faire.

attend *verb*
1 (*meeting etc*) assister à; (*course*) suivre; (*school, church*) aller à.
2 (*be present*) être présent.

attendance *noun* présence *f* (**at** à).

attendant *noun* employé, -ée *m or f*; (*in filling station*) pompiste *m or f*; (*in museum*) gardien, -ienne *m or f*.

attend to *verb* (*take care of*) s'occuper de.

attention *noun* attention *f*; **to pay a.** faire attention (**to** à).

attentive *adjective* attentif (**to** à).

attic *noun* grenier *m*.

attitude *noun* attitude *f*.

attract *verb* attirer.

attraction *noun* (*charm*) attrait *m*.

attractive *adjective* (*price, offer etc*) intéressant; (*girl*) belle; (*boy*) beau.

aubergine *noun* aubergine *f*.

auction *noun* vente *f* (aux enchères).

auction (off) *verb* vendre (aux enchères).

auctioneer *noun* commissaire-priseur *m*.

audible *adjective* perceptible.

audience *noun* (*of speaker, musician*) auditoire *m*; (*in theatre, cinema*) spectateurs *mpl*; (*of radio broadcast*) auditeurs *mpl*; **TV a.** téléspectateurs *mpl*.

audio *adjective* audio *invariable*.

audiotypist *noun* dactylo *f* au magnétophone.

audio-visual *adjective* audio-visuel.

August *noun* août *m*.

aunt *noun* tante *f*.

auntie or **aunty** *noun* Familiar tata *f*.

au pair
1 *adverb* au pair.
2 *noun* **au p. (girl)** jeune fille *f* au pair.

Australia *noun* l'Australie *f*.

Australian *adjective & noun* australien, -ienne (*m or f*).

Austria *noun* l'Autriche *f*.

Austrian *adjective & noun* autrichien, -ienne (*m or f*).

author *noun* auteur *m*.

authority *noun* autorité *f*; (*permission*) autorisation *f* (**to do** de faire).

authorize *verb* autoriser (**to do** à faire).

autobiography *noun* autobiographie *f*.

autograph
1 *noun* autographe *m*.
2 *verb* dédicacer (**for** à).

automatic *adjective* automatique.

automatically *adverb* automatiquement.

autumn *noun* automne *m*.

auxiliary *adjective & noun* a. (verb) (verbe *m*) auxiliaire *m*.

available *adjective* disponible; **a. to all** accessible à tous.

avalanche *noun* avalanche *f*.

avenue *noun* avenue *f*.

average
1 *noun* moyenne *f*; **on a.** en moyenne.
2 *adjective* moyen.

aviation *noun* aviation *f*.

avocado *noun* **a. (pear)** avocat *m*.

avoid *verb* éviter; **to a. doing** éviter de faire.

awake
1 *verb* se réveiller.
2 *adjective* éveillé; **to keep somebody a.** empêcher quelqu'un de dormir; **he's (still) a.** il ne dort pas (encore).

award
1 *verb* (*money, prize*) attribuer.
2 *noun* (*prize*) prix *m*; (*scholarship*) bourse *f*.

aware *adjective* **a. of** (*conscious*) conscient de; (*informed*) au courant de; **to become a. of** prendre conscience de.

away *adverb* (*distant*) loin; **far a.** au loin; **5 km a.** à 5 km (de distance); **to play a.** (*of team*) jouer à l'extérieur.
 ∎ (*in time*) **ten days a.** dans dix jours.
 ∎ (*absent*) parti.
 ∎ (*continuously*) **to work/talk/** *etc* **a.** travailler / parler / *etc* sans relâche.

awful *adjective* affreux; (*terrifying*) épouvantable; (*ill*) malade; **an a. lot of** *Familiar* un nombre incroyable de.

awfully *adverb* (*very*) *Familiar* affreusement.

awkward *adjective* (*clumsy*) maladroit; (*difficult*) difficile; (*tool*) peu commode; (*time*) inopportun.

awning *noun* (*of shop*) store *m*.

axe
1 *noun* hache *f*.
2 *verb* (*job etc*) supprimer.

axle *noun* essieu *m*.

B

BA *abbreviation* = Bachelor of Arts.

baby *noun* bébé *m*; **b. boy** petit garçon *m*; **b. girl** petite fille *f*.

baby clothes *noun* vêtements *mpl* de bébé.

baby-minder *noun* gardien, -ienne *m or f* d'enfants.

baby-sit *verb* garder les enfants.

baby-sitter *noun* baby-sitter *m or f*.

bachelor *noun* célibataire *m*; **B. of Arts/of Science** licencié, -ée *m or f* ès lettres/ès sciences.

back¹
1 *noun* dos *m*; (*of chair*) dossier *m*; (*of hand*) revers *m*; (*of house*) derrière *m*, arrière *m*; (*of room*) fond *m*; (*of vehicle*) arrière *m*; (*of page*) verso *m*; **at the b. of the book** à la fin du livre; **b. to front** devant derrière.
2 *adjective* arrière *invariable*, de derrière; **b. door** porte *f* de derrière; **b. number** vieux numéro *m*; **b. tooth** molaire *f*.
3 *adverb* (*behind*) en arrière; **to come b.** revenir; **he's b.** il est de retour, il est revenu.

back² *verb* (*with money*) financer; (*horse etc*) parier sur.

back (up) *verb* **to back somebody up** appuyer quelqu'un.

backache *noun* mal *m* aux reins.

backfire *verb* (*of vehicle*) pétarader.

background *noun* fond *m*; (*events*) antécédents *mpl*; (*education*) formation *f*; (*environment*) milieu *m*; **b. music** musique *f* de fond.

backing *noun* (*aid*) soutien *m*; (*material*) support *m*.

backlog *noun* retard *m*.

back out *verb* (*withdraw*) se retirer.

backside *noun* Familiar derrière *m*.

backstage *adverb* dans les coulisses.

backward *adjective* (*retarded*) arriéré; (*glance*) en arrière.

backwards *adverb* en arrière; (*to walk*) à reculons.

backyard *noun* arrière-cour *f*.

bacon *noun* lard *m*.

bad *adjective* mauvais; (*wicked*) méchant; (*accident, wound*) grave; (*arm, leg*) malade; (*pain*) violent; **to feel b.** (*ill*) se sentir mal; **things are b.** ça va mal; **not b.!** pas mal!

badge *noun* insigne *m*; (*of postman etc*) plaque *f*; (*bearing slogan*) badge *m*.

badger *noun* blaireau *m*.

badly *adverb* mal; (*hurt*) grièvement; **b. affected** très touché; **to want b.** avoir grande envie de.

bad-mannered *adjective* mal élevé.

badminton *noun* badminton *m*.

bad-tempered *adjective* grincheux.

baffle *verb* déconcerter.

bag *noun* sac *m*; **bags** (*luggage*) valises *fpl*; (*under eyes*) poches *fpl*; **bags of** Familiar beaucoup de.

baggage *noun* bagages *mpl*.

baggy *adjective* (*trousers*) faisant

des poches.

bagpipes *plural noun* cornemuse *f*.

bail *noun* (*in court*) caution *f*; **on b.** en liberté provisoire.

bait *noun* amorce *f*, appât *m*.

bake *verb*
1 (*cake etc*) (faire) cuire (au four).
2 (*of cook*) faire de la pâtisserie *or* du pain; (*of cake etc*) cuire (au four).

baked *adjective* (*potatoes*) au four.

baked beans *noun* haricots *mpl* blancs (à la tomate).

baker *noun* boulanger, -ère *m or f*.

bakery *noun* boulangerie *f*.

balance
1 *noun* équilibre *m*; (*of account*) solde *m*; (*remainder*) reste *m*; **to lose one's b.** perdre l'équilibre.
2 *verb* (*object*) tenir en équilibre (**on** sur); (*account*) équilibrer.
3 *verb* (*of person*) se tenir en équilibre; (*of accounts*) être en équilibre.

balance sheet *noun* bilan *m*.

balcony *noun* balcon *m*.

bald *adjective* chauve.

bald-headed *adjective* chauve.

baldness *noun* calvitie *f*.

ball [1] *noun* balle *f*; (*inflated*) (*for sports*) ballon *m*; (*of string, wool*) pelote *f*; (*any round shape*) boule *f*; (*of meat or fish*) boulette *f*; **on the b.** *Familiar* (*alert*) éveillé; (*efficient*) au point.

ball [2] (*dance*) bal *m* (*plural* bals).

ballerina *noun* ballerine *f*.

ballet *noun* ballet *m*.

balloon *noun* ballon *m*.

ballot *noun* (*voting*) scrutin *m*.

ballpoint *noun* stylo *m* à bille.

ballroom *noun* salle *f* de danse.

ban
1 *noun* interdiction *f*.
2 *verb* interdire (**somebody from doing** à quelqu'un de faire); (*exclude*) exclure (**from** de).

banana *noun* banane *f*.

band *noun* (*strip*) bande *f*; (*musicians*) (petit) orchestre *m*; (*pop group*) groupe *m*; **rubber** *or* **elastic b.** élastique *m*.

bandage *noun* bande *f*.

bandage (up) *verb* (*arm, wound*) bander.

bang
1 *noun* coup *m* (violent); (*of door*) claquement *m*.
2 *verb* (*objects*) cogner; (*door*) (faire) claquer.
3 *verb* (*of objects*) cogner (**contre against**); (*of door*) claquer.

bang down *verb* (*lid*) rabattre (violemment).

banger *noun* **old b.** (*car*) *Familiar* tacot *m*.

bang into *verb* **to b. into something/somebody** heurter quelque chose/quelqu'un.

Bangladesh *noun* le Bangladesh *m*.

Bangladeshi *adjective & noun* bangladais, -aise (*m or f*).

bangle *noun* bracelet *m* (rigide).

banister(s) *plural noun* rampe *f* (d'escalier).

bank *noun* (*of river*) bord *m*; (*for money*) banque *f*; **b. account** compte *m* en banque; **b. card** carte *f* d'identité bancaire.

banker *noun* banquier *m*.

bank holiday *noun* jour *m* férié.

banking *noun* (*activity*) la banque.

banknote noun billet m de banque.

bank on verb to b. on somebody/something compter sur quelqu'un/quelque chose.

bankrupt adjective to go b. faire faillite.

bankruptcy noun faillite f.

banner noun (at rallies, on two poles) banderole f.

bar
1 noun barre f; (of gold) lingot m; (of chocolate) tablette f; (on window) barreau m; (pub, counter) bar m.
2 verb (way) bloquer; (prohibit) interdire (**somebody from doing** à quelqu'un de faire); (exclude) exclure (**from** de).

barbecue noun barbecue m.

barbed adjective b. wire fil m de fer barbelé.

barber noun coiffeur m.

bare adjective nu; (tree) dénudé; **with his b. hands** à mains nues.

barefoot adverb nu-pieds.

barely adverb (scarcely) à peine.

bargain
1 noun (deal) marché m; a b. (cheap buy) une occasion; b. price prix m exceptionnel.
2 verb négocier.

bargain for verb to b. for something s'attendre à quelque chose.

barge noun péniche f.

barge in verb (enter) faire irruption; (interrupt) interrompre.

bark
1 noun (of tree) écorce f.
2 verb (of dog) aboyer.

barking noun aboiements mpl.

barley noun orge f.

barmaid noun serveuse f de bar.

barman noun barman m.

barmy adjective Familiar dingue.

barn noun (for crops) grange f.

barometer noun baromètre m.

barracks plural noun caserne f.

barrage noun barrage m.

barrel noun (cask) tonneau m; (of oil) baril m; (of gun) canon m.

barren adjective stérile.

barricade
1 noun barricade f.
2 verb barricader.

barrier noun barrière f; (**ticket**) b. portillon m.

barrister noun avocat m.

base
1 noun base f; (of cliff, column) pied m; (of lamp) socle m.
2 verb baser.

baseball noun base-ball m.

basement noun sous-sol m.

bash
1 noun (bang) coup m; **to have a b.** (try) essayer.
2 verb (hit) cogner.

bash up verb to b. somebody up tabasser quelqu'un.

basic
1 adjective essentiel, de base; (elementary) élémentaire; (pay) de base.
2 noun **the basics** l'essentiel m.

basically adverb au fond.

basin noun bassin m; (sink) lavabo m.

basis noun (of agreement etc) bases fpl; **on the b. of** d'après; **on that b.** dans ces conditions; **on a weekly b.** chaque semaine.

bask verb se chauffer.

basket noun panier m; (for bread, laundry, litter) corbeille f.

bat
1 noun (animal) chauve-souris f; Cricket batte f; Table Tennis ra-

quette *f*; **off my own b.** de ma propre initiative.
2 *verb* **she didn't b. an eyelid** elle n'a pas sourcillé.

batch *noun* (*of people*) groupe *m*; (*of letters*) paquet *m*; (*of papers*) liasse *f*.

bath
1 *noun* bain *m*; (*tub*) baignoire *f*; **to have** *or* **take a b.** prendre un bain.
2 *verb* baigner.

bathe
1 *verb* (*wound*) baigner.
2 *verb* (*of person*) se baigner.
3 *noun* bain *m* (de mer).

bathing costume *or* **suit** *noun* maillot *m* de bain.

bathrobe *noun* robe *f* de chambre.

bathroom *noun* salle *f* de bain(s); (*toilet*) toilettes *fpl*.

bathtub *noun* baignoire *f*.

batter
1 *noun* pâte *f* à frire.
2 *verb* (*baby*) martyriser.

batter down *verb* défoncer.

battered *adjective* (*car*) cabossé.

battery *noun* batterie *f*; (*in radio, appliance*) pile *f*.

battle
1 *noun* bataille *f*; (*struggle*) lutte *f*.
2 *verb* se battre.

battleship *noun* cuirassé *m*.

bawl (out) *verb* beugler; **to b. somebody out** *Familiar* engueuler quelqu'un.

bay *noun* (*part of coastline*) baie *f*; (*for loading*) aire *f*.

BC *abbreviation* (*before Christ*) avant Jésus-Christ.

be *verb* être; **she's a doctor** elle est médecin; **it's 3 (o'clock)** il est trois heures.
▌ avoir; **to be hot/right/lucky** avoir chaud/raison/de la chance; **he's 20** il a 20 ans; **to be 2 metres high** avoir 2 mètres de haut.
▌ (*health*) aller; **how are you?** comment vas-tu?
▌ (*go, come*) **I've been to see her** je suis allé *or* j'ai été la voir; **he's (already) been** il est (déjà) venu.
▌ (*weather, calculations*) faire; **it's fine** il fait beau; **2 and 2 are 4** 2 et 2 font 4.
▌ (*cost*) faire; **how much is it?** ça fait combien?
▌ (*auxiliary*) **I am/was doing** je fais/faisais; **he was killed** il a été tué; **I've been waiting (for) two hours** j'attends depuis deux heures; **isn't it?, aren't you?** *etc* n'est-ce pas?, non?
▌ (+ *infinitive*) **he is to come** (*must*) il doit venir.
▌ **there is** *or* **are** il y a; (*pointing*) voilà; **here is** *or* **are** voici.

beach *noun* plage *f*.

beacon *noun* balise *f*.

bead *noun* perle *f*; (*of sweat*) goutte *f*; **(string of) beads** collier *m*.

beak *noun* bec *m*.

beaker *noun* gobelet *m*.

beam *noun* (*of wood*) poutre *f*; (*of light*) rayon *m*; (*of headlight*) faisceau *m*.

beaming *adjective* (*radiant*) radieux.

bean *noun* haricot *m*; (*of coffee*) grain *m*; **(broad) b.** fève *f*.

beansprouts *plural noun* germes *mpl* de soja.

bear [1] *noun* (*animal*) ours *m*.

bear [2] *verb*
1 (*carry, show*) porter; (*endure*)

supporter; (*responsibility*) assumer; **to b. in mind** tenir compte de.

2 to b. left/right tourner à gauche/droite.

bearable *adjective* supportable.

beard *noun* barbe *f.*

bearded *adjective* barbu.

bearing *noun* (*relevance*) relation *f* (**on** avec); **to get one's bearings** s'orienter.

bear out *verb* **to b. something out** corroborer quelque chose.

beast *noun* bête *f*; (*person*) brute *f.*

beastly *adjective* Familiar (*bad*) vilain.

beat
1 *noun* (*of heart, drum*) battement *m*; (*of policeman*) ronde *f.*
2 *verb* battre.

beat down *verb*
1 (*door*) défoncer.
2 (*of rain*) tomber à verse; (*of sun*) taper.

beating *noun* (*blows, defeat*) raclée *f.*

beat off *verb* **to b. somebody off** repousser quelqu'un.

beat up *verb* **to b. somebody up** tabasser quelqu'un.

beautiful *adjective* (très) beau (*f* belle).

beauty *noun* (*quality, woman*) beauté *f.*

beauty spot *noun* (*on skin*) grain *m* de beauté; (*in countryside*) endroit *m* pittoresque.

beaver *noun* castor *m.*

because *conjunction* parce que; **b. of** à cause de.

become *verb* devenir; **to b. a painter** devenir peintre; **what has b. of her?** qu'est-elle devenue?

bed *noun* lit *m*; **to go to b.** (aller) se coucher; **in b.** couché; **to get out of b.** se lever; **b. and breakfast** chambre *f* avec petit déjeuner.

bedclothes *plural noun* couvertures *fpl* et draps *mpl.*

bedroom *noun* chambre *f* à coucher.

bedside *noun* chevet *m*; **b. lamp/book** lampe *f*/livre *m* de chevet.

bedsitter *noun* chambre *f* meublée.

bedtime *noun* heure *f* du coucher.

bee *noun* abeille *f.*

beech *noun* (*tree, wood*) hêtre *m.*

beef *noun* bœuf *m.*

beefburger *noun* hamburger *m.*

beehive *noun* ruche *f.*

been *past participle of* be.

beer *noun* bière *f*; **b. glass** chope *f.*

beetle *noun* scarabée *m*; (*any beetle-shaped insect*) bestiole *f.*

beetroot *noun* betterave *f* (potagère).

before
1 *adverb* avant; (*already*) déjà; (*in front*) devant; **the day b.** la veille.
2 *preposition* (*time*) avant; (*place*) devant; **the year b. last** il y a deux ans.
3 *conjunction* avant que (+ *ne* + *subjunctive*), avant de (+ *infinitive*); **b. he goes** avant qu'il (ne) parte; **b. going** avant de partir.

beg *verb* **to b. (for)** solliciter; (*bread, money*) mendier; **to b. somebody to do** supplier quelqu'un de faire.

beggar *noun* mendiant, -ante *m*

or f.

begin *verb* commencer (**with** par, **by doing** par faire); (*campaign*) lancer; **to b. doing** *or* **to do** commencer *or* se mettre à faire; **to b. with** (*first*) d'abord.

beginner *noun* débutant, -ante *m or f.*

beginning *noun* commencement *m*, début *m.*

begrudge *verb* envier (**some-body something** quelque chose à quelqu'un); **to b. doing some-thing** faire quelque chose à contrecœur.

behalf *noun* **on b. of** pour.

behave *verb* se conduire; (*of machine*) fonctionner; **to b. (one-self)** se tenir bien; (*of child*) être sage.

behaviour *noun* conduite *f.*

behind
1 *preposition* derrière; (*in making progress*) en retard sur.
2 *adverb* derrière; (*late*) en retard.
3 *noun* (*buttocks*) *Familiar* derrière *m.*

beige *adjective & noun* beige (*m*).

belch
1 *verb* faire un renvoi.
2 *noun* renvoi *m.*

Belgian *adjective & noun* belge (*m or f*).

Belgium *noun* la Belgique *f.*

belief *noun* croyance *f* (**in** en); (*trust*) foi *f*; (*opinion*) opinion *f.*

believable *adjective* crédible.

believe *verb* croire (**in some-thing** à quelque chose, **in God** en Dieu); **I b. so** je crois que oui; **to b. in doing** croire qu'il faut faire.

believer *noun* (*religious*) croyant, -ante *m or f.*

belittle *verb* dénigrer.

bell *noun* cloche *f*; (*small*) clo-chette *f*; (*in phone*) sonnerie *f*; (*on door, bicycle*) sonnette *f.*

belly *noun* ventre *m*; **b. button** *Familiar* nombril *m.*

bellyache *noun Familiar* mal *m* au ventre.

belong *verb* appartenir (**to** à); **to b. to** (*club*) être membre de.

belongings *plural noun* affaires *fpl.*

below
1 *preposition* au-dessous de.
2 *adverb* en dessous.

belt *noun* ceinture *f*; (*in machine*) courroie *f.*

belt (along) *verb* (*rush*) *Familiar* filer à toute allure.

bench *noun* (*seat*) banc *m*; (*work table*) établi *m.*

bend
1 *noun* courbe *f*; (*in river*) coude *m*; (*in road*) virage *m*; (*of arm, knee*) pli *m.*
2 *verb* (*leg, arm, wire*) plier; (*head*) baisser.
3 (*of branch*) plier; (*of road*) tour-ner.

bend (down) *verb* se courber.

bend (over) *verb* se pencher.

beneath
1 *preposition* au-dessous de.
2 *adverb* (au-)dessous.

beneficial *adjective* bénéfique.

benefit
1 *noun* avantage *m*; (*money*) allo-cation *f*; **child b.** allocations fa-miliales; **for your (own) b.** pour vous.
2 *verb* (*be good for*) faire du bien à; (*be useful to*) profiter à.
3 *verb* **you'll b. from it** ça vous fera du bien.

bent *adjective* tordu; **b. on doing** résolu à faire.

bereavement *noun* deuil *m*.

berk *noun Familiar* andouille *f*.

berry *noun* baie *f*.

berserk *adjective* **to go b.** devenir fou *or* folle.

berth *noun* (*in ship, train*) couchette *f*.

beside *preposition* à côté de; **that's b. the point** ça n'a rien à voir.

besides
  1 *preposition* en plus de; (*except*) excepté.
  2 *adverb* de plus; (*moreover*) d'ailleurs.

best
  1 *adjective* meilleur (**in** de); **the b. part of** (*most*) la plus grande partie de.
  2 *noun* **the b. (one)** le meilleur, la meilleure; **at b.** au mieux; **to do one's b.** faire de son mieux; **to make the b. of** s'accommoder de.
  3 *adverb* (**the**) **b.** (*to play, sing etc*) le mieux; **the b. loved** le plus aimé.

best man *noun* (*at wedding*) témoin *m*.

best-seller *noun* best-seller *m*.

bet
  1 *noun* pari *m*.
  2 *verb* parier (**on** sur, **that** que).

betray *verb* trahir.

betrayal *noun* trahison *f*.

better
  1 *adjective* meilleur (**than** que); **she's (much) b.** (*in health*) elle va (bien) mieux; **that's b.** c'est mieux; **to get b.** (*recover*) se remettre; (*improve*) s'améliorer; **it's b. to go** il vaut mieux partir.
  2 *adverb* mieux; **I had b. go** il

vaut mieux que je parte.
  3 *verb* **to b. oneself** améliorer sa condition.

betting *noun* pari(s) *m*(*pl*).

betting shop *or* **office** *noun* PMU *m*.

between
  1 *preposition* entre; **in b. something and something/two things** entre quelque chose et quelque chose/deux choses.
  2 *adverb* **in b.** au milieu; (*time*) dans l'intervalle.

beware *verb* **to b. of** se méfier de; **b.!** méfiez-vous!

bewilder *verb* dérouter.

beyond
  1 *preposition* au-delà de; (*reach, doubt*) hors de; **b. my means** au-dessus de mes moyens; **it's b. me** ça me dépasse.
  2 *adverb* au-delà.

bias *noun* penchant *m* (**towards** pour); (*prejudice*) préjugé *m*.

bias(s)ed *adjective* partial; **to be b. against** avoir des préjugés contre.

bib *noun* (*baby's*) bavoir *m*.

bible *noun* bible *f*; **the B.** la Bible.

bicycle *noun* bicyclette *f*.

bid
  1 *verb* (*money*) offrir.
  2 *verb* (*of person*) faire une offre (**for** pour).
  3 *noun* (*at auction*) offre *f*; (*for doing a job*) soumission *f*.

big *adjective* grand, gros (*f* grosse); (*in age, generous*) grand; (*in bulk, amount*) gros; **b. deal!** *Familiar* (bon) et alors!

bighead *noun Familiar* (*conceited*) prétentieux, -euse *m or f*; (*boasting*) vantard, -arde *m or f*.

bigshot *noun Familiar* gros bonnet *m*.

bike *noun Familiar* vélo *m*.

bikini *noun* deux-pièces *invariable m*; **b. briefs** mini-slip *m*.

bile *noun* bile *f*.

bilingual *adjective* bilingue.

bill
  1 *noun* (*invoice*) facture *f*, note *f*; (*in restaurant*) addition *f*; (*in hotel*) note *f*; (*proposed law*) projet *m* de loi.
  2 *verb* **to b. somebody** envoyer la facture à quelqu'un.

billboard *noun* panneau *m* d'affichage.

billiards *plural noun* (*jeu m de*) billard *m*.

billion *noun* milliard *m*.

bin *noun* boîte *f*; (*for litter*) poubelle *f*.

bind
  1 *verb* lier; (*book*) relier.
  2 *noun* (*bore*) *Familiar* plaie *f*.

binder *noun* (*for papers*) classeur *m*.

binding *noun* (*of book*) reliure *f*.

bingo *noun* loto *m*.

binoculars *plural noun* jumelles *fpl*.

biological *adjective* biologique.

biology *noun* biologie *f*.

birch *noun* (*silver*) **b.** (*tree*) bouleau *m*.

bird *noun* oiseau *m*; (*fowl*) volaille *f*; **b.'s-eye view** vue *f* d'ensemble.

biro ® *noun* bic ® *m*.

birth *noun* naissance *f*; **to give b. to** donner naissance à.

birth certificate *noun* acte *m* de naissance.

birthday *noun* anniversaire *m*; **happy b.!** bon anniversaire!

biscuit *noun* biscuit *m*.

bishop *noun* évêque *m*.

bit *noun* morceau *m*; **a b.** (*a little*) un peu; **quite a b.** (*very*) très; (*a lot*) beaucoup; **not a b.** pas du tout; **b. by b.** petit à petit.

bite
  1 *noun* (*wound*) morsure *f*; (*from insect*) piqûre *f*; **a b. to eat** un morceau à manger.
  2 *verb* mordre; **to b. one's nails** se ronger les ongles.

bitter
  1 *adjective* amer; (*cold, wind*) glacial; (*conflict*) violent.
  2 *noun* bière *f* (pression).

bitterness *noun* amertume *f*; (*of conflict*) violence *f*.

bizarre *adjective* bizarre.

black
  1 *adjective* noir; **b. eye** œil *m* poché; **to give somebody a b. eye** pocher l'œil à quelqu'un; **b. and blue** (*bruised*) couvert de bleus.
  2 *noun* (*colour*) noir *m*; (*person*) Noir, -e *m or f*.

blackberry *noun* mûre *f*.

blackbird *noun* merle *m*.

blackboard *noun* tableau *m* (noir); **on the b.** au tableau.

blackcurrant *noun* cassis *m*.

blacklist
  1 *noun* liste *f* noire.
  2 *verb* mettre sur la liste noire.

blackmail
  1 *noun* chantage *m*.
  2 *verb* faire chanter.

blackmailer *noun* maître chanteur *m*.

black out *verb* (*faint*) s'évanouir.

blackout *noun* panne *f* d'électricité; (*fainting fit*) syncope *f*.

bladder *noun* vessie *f*.

blade *noun* lame *f*; (*of grass*) brin *m*.

blame
  1 *verb* accuser; **to b. somebody for something** reprocher quelque chose à quelqu'un; **you're to b.** c'est ta faute.
  2 *noun* faute *f*.

blameless *adjective* irréprochable.

bland *adjective* (*food*) fade.

blank
  1 *adjective* (*paper, page*) blanc (*f* blanche); (*cheque*) en blanc.
  2 *adjective & noun* **b. (space)** blanc *m*.

blanket *noun* couverture *f*.

blare (out) *verb* (*of radio*) beugler; (*of music*) retentir.

blast
  1 *noun* explosion *f*; (*air from explosion*) souffle *m*.
  2 *interjection* Familiar zut!

blasted *adjective* Familiar fichu.

blast-off *noun* (*of spacecraft*) mise *f* à feu.

blaze
  1 *noun* (*fire*) flamme *f*; (*large*) incendie *m*.
  2 *verb* (*of fire*) flamber; (*of sun*) flamboyer.

blazer *noun* blazer *m*.

blazing *adjective* en feu; (*sun*) brûlant.

bleach *noun* eau *f* de Javel.

bleak *adjective* morne.

bleed *verb* saigner.

bleep
  1 *noun* bip *m*.
  2 *verb* appeler au bip(-bip).

bleeper *noun* bip(-bip) *m*.

blemish *noun* défaut *m*; (*on reputation*) tache *f*.

blend
  1 *noun* mélange *m*.
  2 *verb* (*things*) mélanger.
  3 *verb* (*of things*) se mélanger.

blender *noun* (*for food*) mixer *m*.

bless *verb* bénir; **b. you!** (*sneezing*) à vos souhaits!

blessing *noun* bénédiction *f*; (*benefit*) bienfait *m*.

blew *past participle of* **blow**[1].

blind
  1 *adjective* aveugle; **b. person** aveugle *m or f*.
  2 *noun* (*on window*) store *m*; **the b.** les aveugles *mpl*.

blindfold
  1 *noun* bandeau *m*.
  2 *verb* bander les yeux à.

blindly *adverb* aveuglément.

blindness *noun* cécité *f*.

blink
  1 *verb* (*of person*) cligner des yeux; (*of eyes*) cligner.
  2 *noun* clignement *m*.

bliss *noun* félicité *f*.

blister *noun* (*on skin*) ampoule *f*.

blizzard *noun* tempête *f* de neige.

bloat *verb* gonfler.

blob *noun* goutte *f*.

block
  1 *noun* (*of stone*) bloc *m*; (*of buildings*) pâté *m* (de maisons); **b. of flats** immeuble *m*.
  2 *verb* (*obstruct*) bloquer.

blockage *noun* obstruction *f*.

block off *verb* (*road*) barrer.

block up *verb* (*pipe, hole*) bloquer.

bloke *noun* Familiar type *m*.

blond *adjective & noun* blond (*m*).

blonde *adjective & noun* blonde (*f*).

blood *noun* sang *m*; **b. donor** donneur, -euse *m or f* de sang; **b. group** groupe *m* sanguin; **b. pressure** tension *f* (artérielle); **to have high b. pressure** avoir de la tension.

bloodshed *noun* effusion *f* de sang.

bloodshot *adjective* (*eye*) injecté de sang.

bloody
1 *adjective* sanglant; *Familiar* sacré.
2 *adverb Familiar* (*very*) vachement.

bloom
1 *noun* fleur *f*; **in b.** en fleur(s).
2 *verb* fleurir.

blossom
1 *noun* fleur(s) *f(pl)*.
2 *verb* fleurir.

blot *noun* tache *f*.

blotchy *adjective* couvert de taches.

blotting paper *noun* buvard *m*.

blouse *noun* chemisier *m*.

blow[1] *verb*
1 (*of wind*) (*boat*) pousser; (*rain*) chasser; (*of person*) (*smoke*) souffler; (*bubbles*) faire; (*trumpet*) souffler dans; **to b. one's nose** se moucher; **to b. a whistle** siffler.
2 (*of wind, person*) souffler.

blow[2] *noun* (*with fist, tool etc*) coup *m*.

blow away *verb*
1 (*of wind*) (*thing*) emporter.
2 (*of thing*) s'envoler.

blow down *verb*
1 (*tree, chimney*) faire tomber.
2 (*of tree, chimney*) tomber.

blow-dry *noun* brushing *m*.

blow off *verb*
1 (*hat etc*) emporter.

2 (*of hat*) s'envoler.

blow out *verb* (*candle*) souffler.

blow over *verb*
1 (*fence*) faire tomber.
2 (*of fence*) tomber.

blowtorch *noun* chalumeau *m*.

blow up *verb*
1 (*building*) faire sauter; (*pump up*) gonfler.
2 (*of building*) exploser.

blowy *adjective* **it's b.** *Familiar* il y a du vent.

blue
1 *adjective* bleu.
2 *noun* bleu *m*.

blueberry *noun* airelle *f*.

bluff
1 *verb* bluffer.
2 *noun* bluff *m*.

blunder
1 *noun* (*mistake*) bévue *f*.
2 *verb* faire une bévue.

blunt *adjective* (*edge*) émoussé; (*person, speech*) franc (*f* franche), brusque.

blur
1 *noun* tache *f* floue.
2 *verb* rendre flou.

blurred *adjective* flou.

blush *verb* rougir (**with** de).

blustery *adjective* (*weather*) de grand vent.

board[1]
1 *noun* (*piece of wood*) planche *f*; (*for notices*) tableau *m*; (*cardboard*) carton *m*; **b. (of directors)** conseil *m* d'administration; **on b.** (*ship, aircraft*) à bord (de).
2 *verb* monter à bord de; (*bus, train*) monter dans.

board[2] *noun* (*food*) pension *f*; **b. and lodging** (chambre *f* avec) pension *f*.

boarder *noun* pensionnaire *m or*

f.

boarding *noun* (*of passengers*) embarquement *m.*

boarding house *noun* pension *f* (de famille).

boarding school *noun* pensionnat *m.*

boast *verb* se vanter (**about, of** de).

boat *noun* bateau *m;* (*small*) canot *m.*

bobby *noun Familiar* flic *m.*

bodily *adjective* (*need*) physique.

body *noun* corps *m;* (*institution*) organisme *m.*

bodyguard *noun* garde *m* du corps.

bodywork *noun* carrosserie *f.*

bogged down *adjective* to get b. down s'enliser.

bogus *adjective* faux (*f* fausse).

boil¹ *noun* (*pimple*) furoncle *m.*

boil²
   1 *noun* to come to the b. bouillir.
   2 *verb* bouillir.

boil (up) *verb* faire bouillir.

boiled *adjective* bouilli; (*potato*) à l'eau; b. egg œuf *m* à la coque.

boiler *noun* chaudière *f.*

boiling *adjective* b. (hot) bouillant; it's b. (hot) (*weather*) il fait une chaleur infernale.

boil over *verb* déborder.

bold *adjective* hardi.

boldness *noun* hardiesse *f.*

bolt
   1 *noun* (*on door*) verrou *m;* (*for nut*) boulon *m.*
   2 *verb* (*door*) fermer au verrou.
   3 *verb* (*dash*) se précipiter.

bomb
   1 *noun* bombe *f.*
   2 *verb* bombarder.

bomber *noun* (*aircraft*) bombardier *m.*

bombing *noun* bombardement *m.*

bond *noun* (*link*) lien *m;* (*investment certificate*) bon *m.*

bone *noun* os *m;* (*of fish*) arête *f.*

bonfire *noun* (*celebration*) feu *m* de joie; (*for dead leaves*) feu *m* (de jardin).

bonnet *noun* (*hat*) bonnet *m;* (*of car*) capot *m.*

bonus *noun* prime *f.*

bony *adjective* (*thin*) osseux; (*fish*) plein d'arêtes.

boo
   1 *verb* siffler.
   2 *noun* boos sifflets *mpl.*

booby-trap *verb* piéger.

book¹ *noun* livre *m;* (*of tickets*) carnet *m;* (**exercise**) b. cahier *m;* **books** (*accounts*) comptes *mpl.*

book² *verb* réserver; **fully booked** (*hotel, concert*) complet.

book up *verb* we're booked up nous sommes complets.

bookcase *noun* bibliothèque *f.*

booking *noun* réservation *f.*

booking office *noun* bureau *m* de location.

bookkeeper *noun* comptable *m* or *f.*

bookkeeping *noun* comptabilité *f.*

booklet *noun* brochure *f.*

bookmaker *noun* bookmaker *m.*

bookseller *noun* libraire *m* or *f.*

bookshelf *noun* rayon *m.*

bookshop *noun* librairie *f.*

boom *noun* (*economic*) boom *m.*

boost
   1 *verb* (*increase*) augmenter;

(*product*) faire de la réclame pour; (*economy*) stimuler.
2 *noun* to give a b. to = to **boost**.

boot *noun* (*shoe*) botte *f*; (*of car*) coffre *m*; **(ankle) b.** bottillon *m*; to get the b. *Familiar* être mis à la porte.

booth *noun* (*for phone*) cabine *f*.

boot out *verb* mettre à la porte.

booze *Familiar*
1 *noun* alcool *m*.
2 *verb* boire (beaucoup).

border *noun* (*of country*) frontière *f*; (*edge*) bord *m*.

border (on) *verb* (*country*) toucher à.

borderline case *noun* cas *m* limite.

bore
1 *verb* ennuyer; to be bored s'ennuyer.
2 *noun* (*person*) raseur, -euse *m or f*; (*thing*) ennui *m*.

boredom *noun* ennui *m*.

boring *adjective* ennuyeux.

born *adjective* né; to be b. naître; he was b. il est né.

borrow *verb* emprunter (**from** à).

Bosnia *noun* la Bosnie *f*.

Bosnian *adjective & noun* bosniaque (*m or f*).

boss *noun* patron, -onne *m or f*.

boss around or **about** *verb* to b. somebody around or about commander quelqu'un.

bossy *adjective Familiar* autoritaire.

botch (up) *verb* (*spoil*) bâcler.

both
1 *adjective* les deux.
2 *pronoun* tous or toutes (les) deux; b. of us nous deux.

3 *adverb* (*at the same time*) à la fois; b. you and I vous et moi.

bother
1 *verb* (*annoy*, *worry*) ennuyer; (*disturb*) déranger; (*pester*) importuner; to b. doing or to do se donner la peine de faire; I can't be bothered! je n'en ai pas envie!
2 *noun* (*trouble*) ennui *m*; (*effort*) peine *f*; (*inconvenience*) dérangement *m*.

bother about *verb* (*worry about*) se préoccuper de.

bottle *noun* bouteille *f*; (*small*) flacon *m*; (*for baby*) biberon *m*; **(hot-water) b.** bouillotte *f*.

bottle opener *noun* ouvre-bouteilles *invariable m*.

bottom
1 *noun* (*of sea*, *box*) fond *m*; (*of page*, *hill*) bas *m*; (*buttocks*) *Familiar* derrière *m*; to be at the b. of the class être le dernier de la classe.
2 *adjective* (*part*, *shelf*) du bas; b. floor rez-de-chaussée *m*.

boulder *noun* rocher *m*.

bounce
1 *verb* (*of ball*) rebondir; (*of cheque*) *Familiar* être sans provision.
2 *verb* (*ball*) faire rebondir.
3 *noun* (re)bond *m*.

bound *adjective* b. to do (*obliged*) obligé de faire; (*certain*) sûr de faire; it's b. to happen/snow/*etc* ça arrivera/il neigera/*etc* sûrement; b. for en route pour.

boundary *noun* limite *f*.

bounds *plural noun* out of b. (*place*) interdit.

bouquet *noun* (*of flowers*) bouquet *m*.

boutique *noun* boutique *f* (de

mode).

bow¹ *noun* (*weapon*) arc *m*; (*knot*) nœud *m*.

bow²
1 *noun* (*with knees bent*) révérence *f*; (*nod*) salut *m*.
2 *verb* s'incliner (**to** devant); (*nod*) incliner la tête (**to** devant).

bowels *plural noun* intestins *mpl*.

bowl *noun* (*for food*) bol *m*; (*for sugar*) sucrier *m*; (*for salad*) saladier *m*; (*for fruit*) coupe *f*.

bowler (hat) *noun* (chapeau *m*) melon *m*.

bowling *noun* (*tenpin*) b. bowling *m*; **b. alley** bowling.

bowls *plural noun* (*game*) boules *fpl*.

bow tie *noun* nœud *m* papillon.

box
1 *noun* boîte *f*; (*large*) caisse *f*.
2 *verb* Boxing boxer.

boxer *noun* boxeur *m*.

box in *verb* (*enclose*) enfermer.

boxing *noun* boxe *f*; **b. ring** ring *m*.

Boxing Day *noun* le lendemain de Noël.

box office *noun* bureau *m* de location.

boy *noun* garçon *m*; **English b.** jeune Anglais *m*; **oh b.!** mon Dieu!

boycott
1 *verb* boycotter.
2 *noun* boycottage *m*.

boyfriend *noun* petit ami *m*.

bra *noun* soutien-gorge *m*.

bracelet *noun* bracelet *m*.

braces *plural noun* (*trouser straps*) bretelles *fpl*.

bracket *noun* (*round sign*) parenthèse *f*; (*square sign*) crochet *m*.

brag *verb* se vanter (**about, of** de).

bragging *noun* vantardise *f*.

brain *noun* cerveau *m*; **to have brains** avoir de l'intelligence.

brainwash *verb* faire un lavage de cerveau à.

brainy *adjective* Familiar intelligent.

brake
1 *noun* frein *m*; **b. light** stop.
2 *verb* freiner.

branch *noun* branche *f*; (*of road*) embranchement *m*; (*of store, office*) succursale *f*.

branch off *verb* bifurquer.

branch out *verb* (*of firm, person*) étendre ses activités (**into** à).

brand *noun* marque *f*.

brand-new *adjective* tout neuf (*f* toute neuve).

brandy *noun* cognac *m*.

brass *noun* cuivre *m*.

brave *adjective* courageux, brave.

bravery *noun* courage *m*.

brawl *noun* bagarre *f*.

brawny *adjective* musclé.

Brazil *noun* le Brésil *m*.

Brazilian *adjective & noun* brésilien, -ienne (*m or f*).

bread *invariable noun* pain *m*; **loaf of b.** pain *m*; (*slice or piece of*) **b. and butter** tartine *f*.

breadbin *noun* boîte *f* à pain.

breadcrumb *noun* miette *f* (de pain); **breadcrumbs** (*in cooking*) chapelure *f*.

breadth *noun* largeur *f*.

breadwinner *noun* soutien *m* de famille.

break
1 *verb* (*object*) casser; (*into pieces*) briser; (*silence, spell*)

rompre; (*strike, heart, ice*) briser; (*sporting record*) battre; (*law*) violer; (*one's word, promise*) manquer à; (*journey*) interrompre; (*news*) révéler (**to** à).

2 *verb* (se) casser; se briser; se rompre; (*of news*) éclater; (*stop work*) faire la pause.

3 *noun* cassure *f*; (*in bone*) fracture *f*; (*with person, group*) rupture *f*; (*in journey*) interruption *f*; (*rest*) repos *m*; (*in activity, for tea etc*) pause *f*; (*in school*) récréation *f*; **a lucky b.** une chance.

breakable *adjective* fragile.

break away *verb* se détacher.

break down *verb*
1 (*door*) enfoncer.
2 (*of vehicle, machine*) tomber en panne; (*of talks*) échouer; (*collapse*) (*of person*) s'effondrer.

breakdown *noun* panne *f*; (*in talks*) rupture *f*; (*nervous*) dépression *f*.

breakfast *noun* petit déjeuner *m*.

break in *verb*
1 (*of burglar*) entrer par effraction.
2 (*door*) enfoncer.

break-in *noun* cambriolage *m*.

break into *verb* (*house*) cambrioler; (*safe*) forcer.

break loose *verb* s'échapper.

break off *verb*
1 (*piece*) casser; (*relations*) rompre.
2 (*become detached*) se casser; (*stop*) s'arrêter.

break out *verb* (*of war, fire*) éclater; (*escape*) s'échapper.

breakthrough *noun* percée *f*, découverte *f*.

break up *verb*
1 mettre en morceaux; (*fight*) mettre fin à.

2 (*of group*) se disperser; (*of couple*) rompre; (*from school*) partir en vacances; **to b. up with somebody** quitter quelqu'un.

breakup *noun* (*in marriage*) rupture *f*.

breast *noun* sein *m*; (*of chicken*) blanc *m*.

breastfeed *verb* allaiter.

breaststroke *noun* brasse *f*.

breath *noun* haleine *f*, souffle *m*; **out of b.** (tout) essoufflé.

breathalyser ® *noun* alcotest ® *m*.

breathe *verb* respirer; **to b. in** aspirer; **to b. out** expirer.

breathing *noun* respiration *f*; **b. space** moment *m* de repos.

breathtaking *adjective* sensationnel.

breed
1 *verb* (*animals*) élever.
2 *verb* (*of animals*) se reproduire.
3 *noun* race *f*.

breeder *noun* éleveur, -euse *m or f*.

breeze *noun* brise *f*.

breezy *adjective* (*weather*) frais (*f* fraîche).

brew *verb* (*of storm*) se préparer; (*of tea*) infuser; **something is brewing** il se prépare quelque chose.

brewery *noun* brasserie *f*.

bribe
1 *noun* pot-de-vin *m*.
2 *verb* acheter.

brick *noun* brique *f*; (*child's*) cube *m*.

bricklayer *noun* maçon *m*.

bride *noun* mariée *f*; **the b. and groom** les mariés *mpl*.

bridegroom *noun* marié *m*.

bridesmaid *noun* demoiselle *f*

d'honneur.

bridge *noun* pont *m*.

brief
1 *adjective* bref (*f* brève).
2 *verb* (*inform*) mettre au courant (on de).
3 *noun* briefs (*underpants*) slip *m*.

briefcase *noun* serviette *f*.

briefing *noun* instructions *fpl*.

briefly *adverb* brièvement.

bright
1 *adjective* brillant; (*weather*, *room*) clair; (*clever*) intelligent; (*idea*) génial.
2 *adverb* b. and early de bonne heure.

brighten (up) *verb*
1 (*room*) égayer.
2 (*of weather*) s'éclaircir.

brightly *adverb* avec éclat.

brightness *noun* éclat *m*.

brilliance *noun* éclat *m*; (*of person*) grande intelligence *f*.

brilliant *adjective* (*light*) éclatant; (*clever*) brillant.

bring *verb* (*person*, *vehicle*) amener; (*thing*) apporter; (*to cause*) amener; to b. to an end mettre fin à; to b. to mind rappeler.

bring about *verb* provoquer.

bring along *verb* (*object*) emporter; (*person*) emmener.

bring back *verb* (*person*) ramener; (*thing*) rapporter; (*memories*) rappeler.

bring down *verb* descendre; (*overthrow*) faire tomber; (*reduce*) réduire.

bring in *verb* rentrer; (*person*) faire entrer; (*introduce*) introduire.

bring out *verb* sortir; (*person*) faire sortir; (*meaning*) faire res-

sortir; (*book*) publier; (*product*) lancer.

bring round *or* **to** *verb* to b. somebody round *or* to ranimer quelqu'un.

bring together *verb* (*reconcile*) réconcilier.

bring up *verb* monter; (*child*) élever; (*subject*) mentionner.

brink *noun* bord *m*.

brisk *adjective* vif (*f* vive).

briskly *adverb* (*to walk*) vite.

bristle *noun* poil *m*.

British *adjective* britannique; the B. les Britanniques *mpl*.

British Isles *plural noun* îles *fpl* Britanniques.

Briton *noun* Britannique *m or f*.

brittle *adjective* fragile.

broad *adjective* (*wide*) large; (*outline*) général; in b. daylight en plein jour.

broadcast
1 *verb* diffuser, retransmettre.
2 *noun* émission *f*.

broccoli *noun* brocoli *m*.

brochure *noun* brochure *f*.

broke *adjective* *Familiar* fauché.

broken *past participle of* **break**.

broken-down *adjective* (*machine*) déglingué.

bronchitis *noun* bronchite *f*.

bronze *noun* bronze *m*.

brooch *noun* broche *f*.

brood
1 *noun* couvée *f*.
2 *verb* méditer tristement (**over** sur).

broody *adjective* maussade.

brook *noun* ruisseau *m*.

broom *noun* balai *m*.

broomstick *noun* manche *m* à balai.

brother *noun* frère *m.*

brother-in-law *noun* beau-frère *m.*

brought *see* bring.

brown
1 *adjective* brun; (*reddish*) marron *invariable*; (*hair*) châtain; (*tanned*) bronzé.
2 *noun* brun *m*; marron *m.*

browse *verb* (*in bookshop*) feuilleter des livres.

bruise
1 *verb* to b. one's knee/*etc* se faire un bleu au genou/*etc.*
2 *noun* bleu *m*, contusion *f.*

bruised *adjective* couvert de bleus.

brunch *noun* brunch *m.*

brunette *noun* brunette *f.*

brush
1 *noun* brosse *f.*
2 *verb* (*teeth, hair*) brosser.

brush aside *verb* écarter.

brush away or **off** *verb* enlever.

brush up (on) *verb* (*language*) se remettre à.

brutal *adjective* brutal.

brutality *noun* brutalité *f.*

brute *noun* brute *f.*

BSc *abbreviation* = Bachelor of Science.

bubble
1 *noun* bulle *f.*
2 *verb* bouillonner.

bubble over *verb* déborder.

buck *noun* Familiar dollar *m.*

bucket *noun* seau *m.*

buckle
1 *noun* boucle *f.*
2 *verb* (*fasten*) boucler; to b. one's shoes fermer la bouche de ses chaussures.
3 *verb* (*of wheel*) se voiler.

buck up *verb* Familiar
1 (*person*) remonter le moral à.
2 (*become livelier*) reprendre du poil de la bête.

bud
1 *noun* (*of tree*) bourgeon *m*; (*of flower*) bouton *m.*
2 *verb* bourgeonner; pousser des boutons.

Buddhist *adjective & noun* bouddhiste (*m or f*).

budge *verb* bouger.

budgerigar *noun* perruche *f.*

budget *noun* budget *m.*

budget for *verb* inscrire au budget.

buffalo *noun* buffle *m*; (*American*) b. bison *m.*

buffet *noun* (*table, meal*) buffet *m.*

bug [1] *noun* punaise *f*; (*any insect*) bestiole *f*; (*germ*) microbe *m*, virus *m*; (*in machine*) défaut *m*; (*in computer program*) erreur *f*; (*listening device*) micro *m* clandestin.

bug [2] *verb* Familiar embêter.

buggy *noun* (**baby**) b. (*folding*) poussette *f.*

bugle *noun* clairon *m.*

build
1 *noun* (*of person*) carrure *f.*
2 *verb* construire; (*house*) construire, bâtir.

builder *noun* maçon *m*; (*contractor*) entrepreneur *m.*

building *noun* bâtiment *m*; (*flats, offices*) immeuble *m.*

building society *noun* = société *f* de crédit immobilier.

build up *verb*
1 (*increase*) augmenter; (*collection*) constituer; (*business*) monter; (*speed*) prendre.

2 (*of tension, pressure*) augmenter.

built-in *adjective* (*cupboard*) encastré; (*part of machine*) incorporé.

built-up area *noun* agglomération *f*.

bulb *noun* (*of plant*) oignon *m*; (*of lamp*) ampoule *f*.

Bulgaria *noun* la Bulgarie *f*.

Bulgarian *adjective & noun* bulgare (*m or f*).

bulge *noun* renflement *m*.

bulge (out) *verb* se renfler.

bulging *adjective* renflé.

bulk *invariable noun* grosseur *f*; **the b. of** (*most*) la majeure partie de.

bulky *adjective* gros (*f* grosse).

bull *noun* taureau *m*.

bulldog *noun* bouledogue *m*.

bulldozer *noun* bulldozer *m*.

bullet *noun* balle *f*.

bulletin *noun* bulletin *m*.

bulletproof *adjective* (*jacket*) pare-balles *invariable*; (*car*) blindé.

bullfight *noun* corrida *f*.

bully
1 *noun* (grosse) brute *f*.
2 *verb* brutaliser.

bum *noun Familiar* (*loafer*) clochard, -arde *m or f*; (*good-for-nothing*) propre *m or f* à rien; (*buttocks*) derrière *m*.

bumblebee *noun* bourdon *m*.

bump
1 *verb* (*of car*) heurter; **to b. one's head/knee** se cogner la tête/le genou.
2 *noun* (*impact*) choc *m*; (*jerk*) cahot *m*; (*on road, body*) bosse *f*.

bumper *noun* pare-chocs *invari-*

able m.

bump into *verb* se cogner contre; (*of car*) rentrer dans; (*meet*) tomber sur.

bumpy *adjective* (*road*) cahoteux; (*journey*) agité.

bun *noun* (*cake*) petit pain *m* au lait.

bunch *noun* (*of flowers*) bouquet *m*; (*of keys*) trousseau *m*; (*of people*) bande *f*; **b. of grapes** grappe *f* de raisin.

bundle
1 *noun* paquet *m*; (*of papers*) liasse *f*.
2 *verb* (*put*) fourrer; (*push*) pousser (**into** dans).

bungalow *noun* pavillon *m*.

bung up *verb* (*stop up*) boucher.

bunk *noun* couchette *f*; **b. beds** lits *mpl* superposés.

bunny *noun Familiar* lapin *m*.

buoy *noun* bouée *f*.

burden
1 *noun* fardeau *m*.
2 *verb* accabler (**with** de).

bureaucracy *noun* bureaucratie *f*.

burger *noun* hamburger *m*.

burglar *noun* cambrioleur, -euse *m or f*.

burglar alarm *noun* alarme *f* antivol.

burglary *noun* cambriolage *m*.

burgle *verb* cambrioler.

burial *noun* enterrement *m*.

burn
1 *noun* brûlure *f*.
2 *verb* brûler; **burnt alive** brûlé vif (*f* brûlée vive).

burn down *verb*
1 (*building*) détruire par le feu.
2 (*of building*) être détruit par le feu.

burner *noun* (*of stove*) brûleur *m*.

burning *adjective* en feu; (*fire, light*) allumé.

burp
1 *noun* rot *m*.
2 *verb* roter.

burst
1 *noun* (*of laughter*) éclat *m*; (*of thunder*) coup *m*.
2 *verb* (*with force*) éclater; (*of bubble, balloon, boil, tyre*) crever.

bursting *adjective* (*full*) plein à craquer.

burst into *verb* (*room*) faire irruption dans; **to b. into tears** fondre en larmes.

burst out *verb* **to b. out laughing** éclater de rire.

bury *verb* enterrer; (*hide*) enfouir; (*plunge, absorb*) plonger.

bus *noun* (auto)bus *m*; (*long-distance*) (auto)car *m*.

bush *noun* buisson *m*.

bushy *adjective* broussailleux.

business
1 *noun* affaires *fpl*, commerce *m*; (*shop*) commerce *m*; (*task, concern, matter*) affaire *f*; **on b.** pour affaires; **it's your b. to …** c'est à vous de … ; **that's none of your b.!, mind your own b!** ça ne vous regarde pas!.
2 *adjective* commercial; (*meeting, trip*) d'affaires; **b. hours** heures *fpl* de travail; **b. card** carte *f* de visite.

businessman *noun* homme *m* d'affaires.

businesswoman *noun* femme *f* d'affaires.

bus shelter *noun* abribus ® *m*.

bus station *noun* gare *f* routière.

bus stop *noun* arrêt *m* d'auto-

bus.

bust
1 *noun* (*sculpture*) buste *m*; (*woman's breasts*) poitrine *f*.
2 *adjective* **to go b.** (*bankrupt*) faire faillite.

bustle
1 *verb* s'affairer.
2 *noun* activité *f*.

bustling *adjective* animé.

busy *adjective* occupé (**doing** à faire); (*active*) actif; (*day*) chargé; (*street*) animé; **to be b. doing** (*in the process of*) être en train de faire.

busybody *noun* **to be a b.** faire la mouche du coche.

but
1 *conjunction* mais.
2 *preposition* (*except*) sauf; **b. for that/him** sans cela / lui.
3 *adverb* (*only*) seulement.

butcher *noun* boucher *m*; **b.'s shop** boucherie *f*.

butler *noun* maître *m* d'hôtel.

butt *noun* (*of cigarette*) mégot *m*; (*buttocks*) *Familiar* derrière *m*.

butter
1 *noun* beurre *m*.
2 *verb* beurrer.

buttercup *noun* bouton-d'or *m*.

butterfly *noun* papillon *m*.

butt in *verb* interrompre.

buttock *noun* fesse *f*.

button *noun* bouton *m*; (*of phone*) touche *f*.

button (up) *verb* boutonner.

buttonhole *noun* boutonnière *f*.

buy
1 *verb* acheter (**from somebody** à quelqu'un, **for somebody** à *or* pour quelqu'un).
2 *noun* **a good b.** une bonne affaire.

buyer *noun* acheteur, -euse *m or f*.

buzz
1 *verb* bourdonner.
2 *noun* bourdonnement *m*.

buzz off *verb Familiar* décamper.

by
1 *preposition* (*agent, manner*) par; **hit**/*etc* **by** frappé/*etc* par; **surrounded**/*etc* **by** entouré/*etc* de; **by doing** en faisant; **by sea** par mer; **by car** en voiture; **by bicycle** à bicyclette; **by day** de jour; **by oneself** tout seul.
▪ (*next to*) à côté de; (*near*) près de; **by the lake** au bord du lac.
▪ (*before in time*) avant; **by**

Monday avant lundi; **by now** à cette heure-ci.
▪ (*amount*) à; **by the kilo** au kilo; **paid by the hour** payé à l'heure.
2 *adverb* **close by** tout près; **to go by, pass by** passer; **by and large** en gros.

bye(-bye)! *interjection Familiar* salut!

by-election *noun* élection *f* partielle.

bypass
1 *noun* déviation *f* (routière).
2 *verb* contourner.

bystander *noun* spectateur, -trice *m or f*.

C

cab *noun* taxi *m*.

cabbage *noun* chou *m* (*plural* choux).

cabin *noun* (*on ship*) cabine *f*; (*hut*) cabane *f*.

cabinet[1] *noun* armoire *f*; (*for display*) vitrine *f*; (**filing**) **c.** classeur *m* (de bureau).

cabinet[2] *noun* (*government ministers*) gouvernement *m*; **c. meeting** conseil *m* des ministres.

cable *noun* câble *m*; **c. television** la télévision par câble.

cable car *noun* téléphérique *m*; (*on tracks*) funiculaire *m*.

cactus *noun* cactus *m*.

café *noun* café(-restaurant) *m*.

cafeteria *noun* cafétéria *f*.

caffeine *noun* caféine *f*.

cage *noun* cage *f*.

cake *noun* gâteau *m*.

calculate *verb* calculer.

calculation *noun* calcul *m*.

calculator *noun* calculatrice *f*.

calendar *noun* calendrier *m*.

calf *noun* (*animal*) veau *m*; (*part of leg*) mollet *m*.

call
1 *noun* appel *m*; (*shout*) cri *m*; (*visit*) visite *f*; (**telephone**) **c.** communication *f*; **to make a c.** (*phone*) téléphoner (**to** à).
2 *verb* (*person*) appeler; (*shout*) crier; (*attention*) attirer (**to** sur); **he's called David** il s'appelle David; **to c. a meeting** convoquer une assemblée; **to c. somebody a liar**/*etc* qualifier quelqu'un de menteur/*etc*.
3 *verb* (*of person*) appeler; (*cry*

out) crier; (*visit*) passer.

call back *verb* rappeler.

call by *verb* (*visit*) passer.

caller *noun* visiteur, -euse *m or f*; (*on phone*) correspondant, -ante *m or f*.

call for *verb* (*require*) demander; (*summon*) appeler; (*collect*) passer prendre.

call in *verb*
1 (*into room etc*) faire venir *or* entrer.
2 (*visit*) passer (**on** chez).

call off *verb* (*cancel*) annuler.

call on *verb* (*visit*) passer voir; **to c. on somebody to do** inviter quelqu'un à faire; (*urge*) presser quelqu'un de faire.

call out *verb*
1 (*words*) crier; (*doctor*) appeler.
2 (*of person*) crier; **to c. out for** demander à haute voix.

call round *verb* (*visit*) passer.

call up *verb* (*phone*) appeler.

calm
1 *adjective* calme; **keep c.!** du calme!
2 *noun* calme *m*.
3 *verb* calmer.

calm down *verb*
1 (*of person*) se calmer.
2 (*person*) calmer.

calmly *adverb* calmement.

calorie *noun* calorie *f*.

camcorder *noun* caméscope ® *m*.

came *see* **come**.

camel *noun* chameau *m*.

camera *noun* appareil photo *m*; (**TV** *or* **film**) **c.** caméra *f*.

camp *noun* camp *m*; **c. bed** lit *m* de camp.

camp (out) *verb* camper.

campaign *noun* campagne *f*.

camper *noun* campeur, -euse *m or f*; (*vehicle*) camping-car *m*.

campfire *noun* feu *m* de camp.

camping *noun* camping *m*; **c. site** camping *m*.

campsite *noun* camping *m*.

can [1] *auxiliary verb* (*past tense* **could**) pouvoir; (*know how to*) savoir; **he couldn't help me** il ne pouvait pas m'aider; **she c. swim** elle sait nager; **you could be wrong** (*possibility*) tu as peut-être tort; **he can't be old** (*probability*) il ne doit pas être vieux; **c. I come in?** puis-je entrer?

can [2] *noun* (*for food*) boîte *f*.

Canada *noun* le Canada *m*.

Canadian *adjective & noun* canadien, -ienne (*m or f*).

canal *noun* canal *m*.

canary *noun* canari *m*.

cancel *verb* (*flight, appointment etc*) annuler; (*goods, taxi*) décommander; (*train*) supprimer; **to c. a ticket** (*punch*) composter un billet.

cancellation *noun* annulation *f*; (*of train*) suppression *f*.

cancer *noun* cancer *m*.

candid *adjective* franc (*f* franche).

candidate *noun* candidat, -ate *m or f*.

candle *noun* bougie *f*; (*in church*) cierge *m*.

candlestick *noun* bougeoir *m*; (*tall*) chandelier *m*.

cane
   1 *noun* (*stick*) canne *f*; (*for pun-*

ishing) baguette *f*.
   2 *verb* (*punish*) fouetter.

cannabis *noun* (*drug*) cannabis *m*.

canned *adjective* en boîte; **c. food** conserves *fpl*.

cannibal *noun* cannibale *m or f*.

canoe
   1 *noun* canoë *m*.
   2 *verb* **to go canoeing** faire du canoë.

can-opener *noun* ouvre-boîtes *invariable m*.

canopy *noun* (*hood of pram*) capote *f*; (*small roof*) auvent *m*.

cantaloup(e) *noun* (*melon*) cantaloup *m*.

canteen *noun* (*place*) cantine *f*.

canvas *noun* toile *f*.

canyon *noun* canyon *m*.

cap *noun* (*hat*) casquette *f*; (*for shower*) bonnet *m*; (*of soldier*) képi *m*; (*of bottle, tube*) bouchon *m*; (*of milk or beer bottle*) capsule *f*; (*of pen*) capuchon *m*; (*of child's gun*) amorce *f*.

capability *noun* capacité *f*.

capable *adjective* (*person*) capable (**of something** de quelque chose, **of doing** de faire).

capacity *noun* (*of container*) capacité *f*; (*ability*) aptitude *f*; **in my c. as** en ma qualité de.

cape *noun* (*cloak*) cape *f*; (*of cyclist*) pèlerine *f*.

capital *noun* (*money*) capital *m*; **c. (city)** capitale *f*; **c. (letter)** majuscule *f*.

capsize *verb* chavirer.

capsule *noun* capsule *f*.

captain *noun* capitaine *m*.

capture *verb* (*person, town*) prendre.

car *noun* voiture *f*, auto *f*; (*train*

carriage) wagon *m*; **c. radio** autoradio *m*.

caramel *noun* caramel *m*.

caravan *noun* caravane *f*; (*horse-drawn*) roulotte *f*; **c. site** camping *m* pour caravanes.

carbon *noun* carbone *m*; **c. copy** double *m* (au carbone).

carbon paper *noun* (papier *m*) carbone *m*.

carburettor *noun* carburateur *m*.

card *noun* carte *f*; (*cardboard*) carton *m*; (**index**) **c.** fiche *f*; **to play cards** jouer aux cartes.

cardboard *noun* carton *m*.

cardigan *noun* gilet *m*.

cardinal *adjective* (*number, point*) cardinal.

card index *noun* fichier *m*.

care

1 *verb* (*like*) aimer; **would you c. to try?** aimeriez-vous essayer?; **I don't c.** ça m'est égal; **who cares?** qu'est-ce que ça fait?
2 *noun* (*attention*) soin(s) *m(pl)*; (*protection*) garde *f*; (*anxiety*) souci *m*; **to take c. not to do** faire attention à ne pas faire; **to take c. to do** veiller à faire; **to take c. of** s'occuper de; (*sick person*) prendre soin de; **to take c. of oneself** (*manage*) se débrouiller; (*keep healthy*) faire bien attention à soi.

care about *verb* se soucier de; (*person*) avoir de la sympathie pour.

career *noun* carrière *f*.

care for *verb* (*drink etc*) avoir envie de; **to c. for somebody** s'occuper de quelqu'un; (*sick person*) soigner quelqu'un; (*like*) avoir de la sympathie pour quelqu'un; **I don't c. for it** je n'aime pas ça.

carefree *adjective* insouciant.

careful *adjective* (*exact, thorough*) soigneux (**about** de); (*cautious*) prudent; **to be c. of** *or* **with** faire attention à.

carefully *adverb* avec soin; (*cautiously*) prudemment.

careless *adjective* négligent; (*absent-minded*) étourdi.

caretaker *noun* gardien, -ienne *m or f*.

car ferry *noun* ferry-boat *m*.

cargo *noun* cargaison *f*.

Caribbean (the) *noun* la Caraïbe *f*.

caring *adjective* (*loving*) aimant; (*understanding*) très humain.

carnation *noun* œillet *m*.

carnival *noun* carnaval *m* (*plural* -als).

carol *noun* chant *m* (de Noël).

carp *noun* (*fish*) carpe *f*.

car park *noun* parking *m*.

carpenter *noun* charpentier *m*; (*for light woodwork*) menuisier *m*.

carpentry *noun* charpenterie *f*; menuiserie *f*.

carpet *noun* tapis *m*; (*fitted*) moquette *f*.

carpet sweeper *noun* balai *m* mécanique.

carriage *noun* (*of train, horse-drawn*) voiture *f*.

carriageway *noun* (*of road*) chaussée *f*.

carrier (bag) *noun* sac *m* (en plastique).

carrot *noun* carotte *f*.

carry *verb* porter; (*goods*) transporter; (*sell*) stocker; (*in calculation*) retenir.

carry away *verb* emporter; **to**

get carried away (*excited*) s'emballer.

carry back *verb* rapporter; (*person*) ramener.

carrycot *noun* porte-bébé *m*.

carry off *verb* emporter; (*prize*) remporter; **to c. it off** réussir.

carry on *verb* continuer (**doing à** faire).

carry out *verb* (*plan, order, promise*) exécuter; (*repair, reform*) effectuer; (*duty*) accomplir; (*meal*) emporter.

carry through *verb* (*plan*) mener à bonne fin.

cart *noun* (*vehicle*) charrette *f*.

cart (around) *verb Familiar* trimbal(l)er.

cart away *verb* emporter.

carton (*box*) carton *m*; (*of milk etc*) brique *f*; (*cigarettes*) cartouche *f*; (*cream*) pot *m*.

cartoon *noun* dessin *m* (humoristique); (*film*) dessin *m* animé; (**strip**) **c.** bande *f* dessinée.

cartridge *noun* cartouche *f*.

carve *verb* tailler (**out of dans**); (*initials etc*) graver.

carve (up) *verb* (*meat*) découper.

car wash *noun* (*machine*) = station de lavage automatique pour automobiles.

case [1] *noun* (*instance, in hospital*) cas *m*; (*in court*) affaire *f*; **in any c.** en tout cas; **in c. it rains** pour le cas où il pleuvrait; **in c. of** en cas de; (**just**) **in c.** à tout hasard.

case [2] *noun* (*bag*) valise *f*; (*crate*) caisse *f*; (*for pen, glasses, camera, cigarettes*) étui *m*; (*for jewels*) coffret *m*.

cash
  1 *noun* (*argent m*) liquide *m*; **to**

pay (in) c. payer en espèces.
  2 *verb* **to c. a cheque** encaisser un chèque; (*of bank*) payer un chèque.

cash desk *noun* caisse *f*.

cashier *noun* caissier, -ière *m or f*.

cash machine *noun* distributeur *m* de billets.

cash price *noun* prix *m* (au) comptant.

cash register *noun* caisse *f* enregistreuse.

casino *noun* casino *m*.

casserole *noun* cocotte *f*; (*stew*) ragoût *m* en cocotte.

cassette *noun* (*audio, video*) cassette *f*; (*film*) cartouche *f*.

cassette player *noun* lecteur *m* de cassettes.

cassette recorder *noun* magnétophone *m* à cassettes.

cast [1] *noun* (*actors*) acteurs *mpl*; (*list of actors*) distribution *f*; (*for broken bone*) plâtre *m*.

cast [2] *verb* jeter; (*light, shadow*) projeter; **to c. a vote** voter; **to c. doubt on something** faire planer un doute sur quelque chose.

caster sugar *noun* sucre *m* en poudre.

castle *noun* château *m*; *Chess* tour *f*.

castor *noun* (*wheel*) roulette *f*.

casual *adjective* (*remark*) fait en passant; (*stroll*) sans but; (*offhand*) désinvolte; (*worker*) temporaire; (*work*) irrégulier; **c. clothes** vêtements *mpl* sport.

casualty *noun* (*dead*) mort *m*, morte *f*; (*wounded*) blessé, -ée *m or f*; **c. (department)** (*of hospital*) (service *m* des) urgences *fpl*.

cat *noun* chat *m*; (*female*) chatte *f*; **c. food** pâtée *f*.

catalogue *noun* catalogue *m.*

catapult *noun* lance-pierres *invariable m.*

catastrophe *noun* catastrophe *f.*

catch
 1 *verb* (*ball, thief, illness, train etc*) attraper; (*grab, surprise*) prendre; (*understand*) saisir; (*attention*) attirer; (*on nail etc*) accrocher (**on** à); (*finger etc*) se prendre (**in** dans); **to c. fire** prendre feu; **to c. one's breath** (*rest*) reprendre haleine.
 2 *verb* **her skirt (got) caught in the door** sa jupe s'est prise dans la porte.
 3 *noun* (*trick*) piège *m;* (*on door*) loquet *m.*

catching *adjective* contagieux.

catch on *verb* (*become popular*) prendre; (*understand*) saisir.

catch out *verb* **to c. somebody out** prendre quelqu'un en défaut.

catch up *verb*
 1 **to c. somebody up** rattraper quelqu'un.
 2 **to c. up with somebody** rattraper quelqu'un; **to c. up with one's work** se mettre à jour dans son travail.

category *noun* catégorie *f.*

cater for *or* **to** *verb* (*need, taste*) satisfaire.

caterpillar *noun* chenille *f.*

cathedral *noun* cathédrale *f.*

Catholic *adjective* & *noun* catholique (*m or f*).

cauliflower *noun* chou-fleur *m.*

cause
 1 *noun* cause *f.*
 2 *verb* causer; **to c. something to move/etc** faire bouger/*etc* quelque chose.

caution *noun* (*care*) prudence *f;* (*warning*) avertissement *m.*

cautious *adjective* prudent.

cautiously *adverb* prudemment.

cave *noun* caverne *f.*

cave in *verb* (*fall in*) s'effondrer.

cavity *noun* cavité *f.*

CD *abbreviation* (*compact disc*) CD *m.*

cease *verb* cesser (**doing** de faire).

cease-fire *noun* cessez-le-feu *invariable m.*

ceiling *noun* plafond *m.*

celebrate *verb*
 1 (*event*) fêter; (*mass*) célébrer.
 2 (*of person*) faire la fête.

celebration *noun* fête *f.*

celebrity *noun* (*fame, person*) célébrité *f.*

celery *noun* céleri *m.*

cell *noun* cellule *f.*

cellar *noun* cave *f.*

cellophane ® *noun* cellophane ® *f.*

cement
 1 *noun* ciment *m;* **c. mixer** bétonnière *f.*
 2 *verb* cimenter.

cemetery *noun* cimetière *m.*

cent *noun* (*coin*) cent *m.*

centigrade *adjective* centigrade.

centimetre *noun* centimètre *m.*

centipede *noun* mille-pattes *invariable m.*

central *adjective* central.

centre *noun* centre *m.*

century *noun* siècle *m.*

ceramic *adjective* en céramique.

cereal *noun* céréale *f.*

ceremony *noun* cérémonie *f.*

certain *adjective* (*sure, particular*) certain; **she's c. to come** c'est certain qu'elle viendra; **I'm**

not c. what to do je ne sais pas très bien ce qu'il faut faire; **to be c. of something/that** être certain de quelque chose/que; **to make c. of** (*fact*) s'assurer de; (*seat etc*) s'assurer.

certainly *adverb* certainement; (*yes*) bien sûr.

certainty *noun* certitude *f*.

certificate *noun* certificat *m*; (*from university*) diplôme *m*.

certify *verb* (*confirm*) certifier.

chain *noun* (*of events, mountains*) chaîne *f*.

chain (up) *verb* (*dog*) mettre à l'attache.

chain saw *noun* tronçonneuse *f*.

chain store *noun* magasin *m* à succursales multiples.

chair *noun* chaise *f*; (*armchair*) fauteuil *m*.

chair lift *noun* télésiège *m*.

chairman *noun* président, -ente *m or f*.

chalet *noun* chalet *m*.

chalk
1 *noun* craie *f*.
2 *verb* écrire à la craie.

challenge
1 *noun* défi *m*; (*task*) challenge *m*, gageure *f*.
2 *verb* défier (**somebody to do** quelqu'un de faire); (*dispute*) contester.

challenging *adjective* (*job*) exigeant.

chamber *noun* c. of commerce chambre *f* de commerce.

champagne *noun* champagne *m*.

champion *noun* champion, -onne *m or f*.

championship *noun* championnat *m*.

chance
1 *noun* (*luck*) hasard *m*; (*possibility*) chances *fpl*; (*opportunity*) occasion *f*; **by c.** par hasard.
2 *verb* **to c. doing** prendre le risque de faire; **to c. it** risquer le coup.

chandelier *noun* lustre *m*.

change
1 *noun* changement *m*; (*money*) monnaie *f*; **for a c.** pour changer; **it makes a c. from** ça change de; **a c. of clothes** des vêtements de rechange.
2 *verb* (*thing*) changer; (*exchange*) échanger (**for** contre); (*money*) changer; **to c. trains/one's skirt**/*etc* changer de train/de jupe/*etc*; **to c. gear/the subject** changer de vitesse/sujet.
3 *verb* (*of person, thing*) changer; (*change clothes*) se changer.

changeable *adjective* changeant.

change over *verb* passer (**from** de, **to** à).

changeover *noun* passage *m* (**from** de, **to** à).

changing room *noun* vestiaire *m*.

channel *noun* (*on television*) chaîne *f*; (*for inquiry etc*) voie *f*; **the C.** la Manche; **to go through the normal channels** passer par la voie normale.

chant *verb*
1 (*slogan*) scander.
2 (*of demonstrators*) scander des slogans.

chaos *noun* chaos *m*.

chaotic *adjective* sens dessus dessous.

chap *noun* (*fellow*) *Familiar* type *m*.

chapel *noun* chapelle *f*.

chapped *adjective* gercé.

chapter *noun* chapitre *m*.

char *verb* carboniser; (*scorch*) brûler légèrement.

character *noun* caractère *m*; (*in book, film*) personnage *m*; (*strange person*) numéro *m*.

characteristic *adjective & noun* caractéristique (*f*).

charge[1]
1 *noun* (*cost*) prix *m*; **charges** (*expenses*) frais *mpl*; **there's a c. (for it)** c'est payant; **free of c.** gratuit.
2 *verb* (*amount*) demander (**for** pour); (*person*) faire payer.

charge[2]
1 *noun* (*in court*) accusation *f*; (*care*) garde *f*; **to take c. of** prendre en charge; **to be in c. of** (*child*) avoir la garde de; (*office*) être responsable de; **the person in c.** le *or* la responsable.
2 *verb* (*battery, soldiers*) charger; (*accuse*) accuser (**with** de).
3 *verb* (*rush*) se précipiter.

charity *noun* (*society*) association *f* caritative; **to give to c.** faire la charité.

charm
1 *noun* charme *m*; (*trinket*) amulette *f*.
2 *verb* charmer.

charming *adjective* charmant.

chart *noun* (*map*) carte *f*; (*graph*) graphique *m*; (*pop*) **charts** hit-parade *m*.

chartered accountant *noun* expert-comptable *m*.

charter flight *noun* charter *m*.

chase
1 *noun* poursuite *f*.
2 *verb* poursuivre; **to c. after somebody/something** courir après quelqu'un/quelque chose;

to c. somebody away chasser quelqu'un.

chasm *noun* abîme *m*, gouffre *m*.

chassis *noun* (*of car*) châssis *m*.

chat
1 *noun* petite conversation *f*; **to have a c.** bavarder.
2 *verb* causer.

chatter
1 *verb* (*of person*) bavarder; **his teeth are chattering** il claque des dents.
2 *noun* bavardage *m*.

chatterbox *noun* bavard, -arde *m or f*.

chatty *adjective* bavard.

chat up *verb* Familiar **to c. somebody up** baratiner quelqu'un.

chauffeur *noun* chauffeur *m*.

cheap
1 *adjective* bon marché *invariable*; (*rate*) réduit; (*worthless*) sans valeur; **cheaper** meilleur marché.
2 *adverb* (*to buy*) (à) bon marché.

cheaply *adverb* (à) bon marché.

cheat
1 *verb* (*person*) tromper; **to c. somebody out of something** escroquer quelque chose à quelqu'un.
2 *verb* (*at games etc*) tricher.
3 *noun* tricheur, -euse *m or f*; (*crook*) escroc *m*.

check[1]
1 *verb* (*examine*) vérifier; (*inspect*) contrôler; (*stop*) arrêter.
2 *noun* vérification *f*; (*inspection*) contrôle *m*; *Chess* échec *m*.

check[2] *adjective* à carreaux; **c. (pattern)** carreaux *mpl*.

check-in *noun* enregistrement *m* (des bagages).

check in *verb*
1 (*luggage*) enregistrer.
2 (*at hotel*) signer le registre; (*arrive*) arriver; (*at airport*) se présenter (à l'enregistrement).

checkmate *noun Chess* échec et mat *m*.

check off *verb* (*names on list etc*) cocher.

check on *verb* vérifier.

checkout *noun* (*in supermarket*) caisse *f*.

check out *verb*
1 (*person*) se renseigner sur; (*information*) vérifier.
2 (*at hotel*) régler sa note.

checkup *noun* bilan *m* de santé.

check up *verb* vérifier.

cheddar *noun* cheddar *m*.

cheek *noun* joue *f*; (*impudence*) *Familiar* culot *m*.

cheeky *adjective Familiar* effronté.

cheer
1 *noun* cheers acclamations *fpl*; cheers! *Familiar* à votre santé!
2 *verb* (*person*) acclamer.
3 *verb* (*of person*) pousser des acclamations.

cheerful *adjective* gai (*f* gaie).

cheering *noun* acclamations *fpl*.

cheerio! *interjection* salut!

cheer up *verb*
1 (*person*) donner du courage à.
2 *verb* (*of person*) reprendre courage; c. up! (du) courage!

cheese *noun* fromage *m*.

cheeseburger *noun* cheeseburger *m*.

cheesecake *noun* tarte *f* au fromage blanc.

chef *noun* (*cook*) chef *m*.

chemical
1 *adjective* chimique.

2 *noun* produit *m* chimique.

chemist *noun* pharmacien, -ienne *m* or *f*; (*scientist*) chimiste *m* or *f*; c.'s shop pharmacie *f*.

chemistry *noun* chimie *f*.

cheque *noun* chèque *m*.

chequebook *noun* carnet *m* de chèques.

cherry *noun* cerise *f*.

cherry brandy *noun* cherry *m*.

chess *noun* échecs *mpl*.

chessboard *noun* échiquier *m*.

chest *noun* (*part of body*) poitrine *f*; (*box*) coffre *m*; c. of drawers commode *f*.

chestnut *noun* châtaigne *f*.

chew *verb* mâcher, mastiquer.

chewing gum *noun* chewing-gum *m*.

chick *noun* poussin *m*.

chicken
1 *noun* poulet *m*.
2 *adjective* (*cowardly*) *Familiar* froussard.

chicken out *verb Familiar* se dégonfler.

chickenpox *noun* varicelle *f*.

chickpea *noun* pois *m* chiche.

chicory *noun* (*for salad*) endive *f*.

chief
1 *noun* chef *m*; in c. en chef.
2 *adjective* principal.

chiefly *adverb* principalement.

chilblain *noun* engelure *f*.

child *noun* enfant *m* or *f*.

childcare *noun* (*for working parents*) crèches *fpl* et garderies *fpl*.

childhood *noun* enfance *f*.

childish *adjective* puéril.

child minder *noun* nourrice *f*, assistante *f* maternelle.

chill
1 *noun* froid *m*; (*illness*) refroidis-

sement *m*; **to catch a c.** prendre froid.

2 *verb* (*wine, melon*) faire rafraîchir; (*meat*) réfrigérer.

chilled *adjective* frais (*f* fraîche).

chilli *noun* piment *m* (de Cayenne).

chilly *adjective* froid; **it's c.** il fait (un peu) froid.

chime *verb* (*of clock*) sonner.

chimney *noun* cheminée *f*.

chimneypot *noun* tuyau *m* de cheminée.

chimpanzee *noun* chimpanzé *m*.

chin *noun* menton *m*.

China *noun* la Chine *f*.

china
  1 *invariable noun* porcelaine *f*.
  2 *adjective* en porcelaine.

Chinese
  1 *adjective & invariable noun* chinois, -oise (*m or f*).
  2 *noun* (*language*) chinois *m*.

chip
  1 *verb* (*cup etc*) ébrécher; (*paint*) écailler.
  2 *noun* (*break*) ébréchure *f*; (*microchip*) puce *f*; (*counter*) jeton *m*; **chips** (*French fries*) frites *fpl*.

chipboard *noun* aggloméré *m*.

chiropodist *noun* pédicure *m or f*.

chisel *noun* ciseau *m*.

chives *plural noun* ciboulette *f*.

choc-ice *noun* (*ice cream*) = esquimau ® *m*.

chock-a-block *adjective Familiar* archiplein.

chocolate
  1 *noun* chocolat *m*; **milk c.** chocolat au lait; **plain c.** chocolat à croquer.
  2 *adjective* (*cake*) au chocolat.

choice *noun* choix *m*.

choir *noun* chœur *m*.

choke *verb*
  1 (*person*) étrangler; (*clog*) boucher.
  2 (*of person*) s'étrangler (**on** avec).

cholesterol *noun* cholestérol *m*.

choose *verb* choisir; **to c. to do** (*decide*) juger bon de faire.

choos(e)y *adjective Familiar* difficile.

chop
  1 *noun* (*of lamb, pork*) côtelette *f*.
  2 *verb* couper (à la hache); (*food*) hacher.

chop down *verb* (*tree*) abattre.

chop off *verb* couper.

chopper *noun* hachoir *m*.

chopsticks *noun* baguettes *fpl*.

chop up *verb* couper en morceaux.

chord *noun* (*in music*) accord *m*.

chore *noun* travail *m* (routinier); (*unpleasant*) corvée *f*; **chores** travaux *mpl* du ménage.

chorus *noun* (*of song*) refrain *m*.

christen *verb* baptiser.

christening *noun* baptême *m*.

Christian *adjective & noun* chrétien, -ienne (*m or f*); **C. name** prénom *m*.

Christmas
  1 *noun* Noël *m*; **Merry** or **Happy C.** Joyeux Noël; **Father C.** le père Noël; **C. Eve** la veille de Noël.
  2 *adjective* (*tree etc*) de Noël.

chrome *noun* chrome *m*.

chrysanthemum *noun* chrysanthème *m*.

chubby *adjective* potelé.

chuck *verb* (*throw*) *Familiar* jeter.

chuck away or **out** *verb* (*old*

clothes etc) *Familiar* balancer.

chuck in *or* **up** *verb* (*job etc*) *Familiar* laisser tomber.

chum *noun Familiar* copain *m*, copine *f*.

chunk *noun* (gros) morceau *m*.

church *noun* église *f*.

chute *noun* (*for refuse*) vide-ordures *invariable m*; (*in pool*) toboggan *m*.

cider *noun* cidre *m*.

cigar *noun* cigare *m*.

cigarette *noun* cigarette *f*; **c. end** mégot *m*; **c. lighter** briquet *m*.

cine-camera *noun* caméra *f*.

cinema *noun* cinéma *m*.

cinnamon *noun* cannelle *f*.

circle
1 *noun* cercle *m*; **circles** (*political etc*) milieux *mpl*.
2 *verb* (*move in a circle around*) tourner autour de; (*word*) encercler.
3 *verb* (*of aircraft etc*) décrire des cercles.

circuit *noun* (*electrical path, in sport etc*) circuit *m*.

circular
1 *adjective* circulaire.
2 *noun* (*letter*) circulaire *f*; (*advertisement*) prospectus *m*.

circulate *verb*
1 (*of blood etc*) circuler.
2 (*pass round*) faire circuler.

circulation *noun* (*of newspaper*) tirage *m*.

circumference *noun* circonférence *f*.

circumstance *noun* circonstance *f*; **in** *or* **under no circumstances** en aucun cas.

circus *noun* cirque *m*.

CIS *abbreviation* (*Commonwealth of Independent States*) la CEI *f*.

citizen *noun* citoyen, -enne *m or f*; (*of town*) habitant, -ante *m or f*.

city *noun* (grande) ville *f*; **c. centre** centre-ville *invariable m*.

civil *adjective* civil.

civilian *adjective* & *noun* civil, -ile (*m or f*).

civilization *noun* civilisation *f*.

civil servant *noun* fonctionnaire *m or f*.

civil service *noun* fonction *f* publique.

claim
1 *verb* réclamer; **to c. that** prétendre que.
2 *noun* (*demand*) revendication *f*; (*statement*) affirmation *f*; (*right*) droit *m* (**to** à); **(insurance) c.** demande *f* d'indemnité.

clam *noun* (*shellfish*) palourde *f*.

clamp *noun* **(wheel) c.** sabot *m* (de Denver).

clap *verb* applaudir; **to c. (one's hands)** battre des mains.

clapping *noun* applaudissements *mpl*.

clarinet *noun* clarinette *f*.

clash
1 *verb* (*of plates*) s'entrechoquer; (*of interests*) se heurter; (*of colours*) jurer (**with** avec); (*of people*) s'affronter; (*coincide*) tomber en même temps (**with** que).
2 *noun* (*noise*) choc *m*; (*of interests*) conflit *m*.

clasp
1 *verb* serrer.
2 *noun* (*fastener*) fermoir *m*; (*of belt*) boucle *f*.

class
1 *noun* classe *f*; (*lesson*) cours *m*.
2 *verb* classer.

classic
1 *adjective* classique.
2 *noun* (*work etc*) classique *m*.

classical *adjective* classique.

classmate *noun* camarade *m or f* de classe.

classroom *noun* (salle *f* de) classe *f*.

clause *noun* (*in sentence*) proposition *f*.

claw *noun* griffe *f*; (*of lobster*) pince *f*.

clay *noun* argile *f*.

clean
1 *adjective* (*not dirty*) propre; (*clear-cut*) net (*f* nette).
2 *adverb* (*utterly*) complètement; (*to break, cut*) net.
3 *noun* to give something a c. nettoyer quelque chose.
4 *verb* (*thing, room*) nettoyer; (*wash*) laver; (*wipe*) essuyer; to c. one's teeth se brosser les dents.
5 *verb* (*of person*) faire le ménage.

cleaner *noun* femme *f* de ménage; (**dry**) **c.** teinturier, -ière *m or f*.

cleaning *noun* nettoyage *m*; (*housework*) ménage *m*.

cleaning woman *noun* femme *f* de ménage.

cleanly *adverb* (*to break*) net.

clean out *verb* (*room etc*) nettoyer; (*empty*) vider.

cleanser *noun* démaquillant *m*.

clean up *verb* nettoyer.

clear
1 *adjective* (*sky, outline, sound, thought etc*) clair; (*glass*) transparent; (*road*) libre; (*profit*) net; (*obvious*) évident, clair; to be c. of (*free of*) être libre de; to make oneself c. se faire comprendre.
2 *adverb* to keep *or* steer c. of se tenir à l'écart de; to get c. of

s'éloigner de.
3 *verb* (*path, table*) débarrasser; (*fence*) franchir; (*accused person*) disculper; (*cheque*) faire passer (sur un compte); (*through customs*) dédouaner; to c. one's throat s'éclaircir la gorge.
4 *verb* (*of weather*) s'éclaircir; (*of fog*) se dissiper.

clearance *noun* (*sale*) soldes *mpl*; (*space*) dégagement *m*.

clear away *verb* (*remove*) enlever.

clear-cut *adjective* net (*f* nette).

clearly *adverb* clairement; (*obviously*) évidemment.

clear off *verb* (*go*) *Familiar* filer.

clear out *verb* vider; (*clean*) nettoyer; (*remove*) enlever.

clear up *verb*
1 (*mystery*) éclaircir.
2 (*tidy*) ranger.

clearway *noun* route *f* à stationnement interdit.

clementine *noun* clémentine *f*.

clench *verb* (*fist*) serrer.

clerical *adjective* (*job*) d'employé; (*work*) de bureau.

clerk *noun* employé, -ée *m or f* (de bureau).

clever *adjective* intelligent; (*smart*) astucieux; (*skilful*) habile (**at something** à quelque chose, **at doing** à faire); (*machine, book etc*) ingénieux; **c. at** (*English etc*) fort en.

click
1 *noun* déclic *m*.
2 *verb* (*of machine etc*) faire un déclic.

client *noun* client, -ente *m or f*.

cliff *noun* falaise *f*.

climate *noun* climat *m*.

climax *noun* point *m* culminant.

climb (over) verb (wall) escalader.

climb (up) verb monter; (hill, mountain) gravir; (tree, ladder) monter à.

climb down verb descendre (**from** de); (in argument) revenir sur sa décision.

climber noun (mountaineer) alpiniste m or f.

cling verb se cramponner; (stick) adhérer (**to** à).

clingfilm noun film m plastique.

clinic noun (private) clinique f; (health centre) centre m médical.

clip
1 verb couper; (hedge) tailler; (ticket) poinçonner; (attach) attacher.
2 noun (for paper) trombone m; (for hair) barrette f.

clip on verb attacher (**to** à).

clippers plural noun (for hair) tondeuse f; (for nails) coupe-ongles invariable m.

cloak noun (grande) cape f.

cloakroom noun vestiaire m; (lavatory) toilettes fpl.

clock noun horloge f; (small) pendule f; **round the c.** vingt-quatre heures sur vingt-quatre.

clockwise adverb dans le sens des aiguilles d'une montre.

close [1]
1 adjective (place, relative etc) proche (**to** de); (collaboration, connection) étroit; (friend) intime; (atmosphere) lourd.
2 adverb **c. (by)** (tout) près; **c. to** près de; **c. behind** juste derrière.

close [2]
1 noun (end) fin f.
2 verb (door, shop etc) fermer; (road) barrer; (deal) conclure.
3 verb (of door) se fermer; (of shop) fermer.

close down verb (for good) fermer (définitivement).

close in verb approcher.

closely adverb (to follow, guard) de près; (to listen) attentivement.

close up verb fermer.

closing time noun heure f de fermeture.

clot
1 noun (of blood) caillot m.
2 verb se coaguler.

cloth noun tissu m; (for dusting) chiffon m; (for dishes) torchon m; (tablecloth) nappe f.

clothes plural noun vêtements mpl; **to put one's c. on** s'habiller.

clothes brush noun brosse f à habits.

clothes line noun corde f à linge.

clothes peg noun pince f à linge.

clothes shop noun magasin m d'habillement.

clothing noun vêtements mpl; **an article of c.** un vêtement.

cloud noun nuage m.

cloud over verb (of sky) se couvrir.

cloudy adjective (weather) couvert.

clove noun **c. of garlic** gousse f d'ail.

clown noun clown m.

club noun (society, stick for golf) club m; **clubs** (at cards) trèfle m.

clue noun indice m; (of crossword) définition f; **I don't have a c.** Familiar je n'en ai pas la moindre idée.

clumsy adjective maladroit; (tool) peu commode.

clutch
  1 *verb* (*hold*) serrer; (*grasp*) saisir.
  2 *noun* (*in vehicle*) embrayage *m*;
  (*pedal*) pédale *f* d'embrayage.

clutter up *verb* (*room etc*) encombrer (**with** de).

cm *abbreviation* (*centimetre*) cm.

Co *abbreviation* (*company*) Cie.

coach
  1 *noun* (*train carriage*) voiture *f*;
  (*bus*) autocar *m*.
  2 *verb* (*pupil*) donner des leçons
  (particulières) à.

coal *noun* charbon *m*.

coalmine *noun* mine *f* de charbon.

coarse *adjective* (*person, fabric*)
grossier.

coast *noun* côte *f*.

coat
  1 *noun* manteau *m*; (*jacket*) veste
  f; (*of animal*) pelage *m*; (*of paint*)
  couche *f*.
  2 *verb* couvrir (**with** de).

coathanger *noun* cintre *m*.

coating *noun* couche *f*.

cob *noun* **corn on the c.** épi *m* de
maïs.

cobbled *adjective* pavé.

cobweb *noun* toile *f* d'araignée.

cocaine *noun* cocaïne *f*.

cock *noun* (*fowl*) coq *m*.

cockle *noun* (*shellfish*) coque *f*.

cockpit *noun* poste *m* de pilotage.

cockroach *noun* cafard *m*.

cocktail *noun* cocktail *m*; (*fruit*)
c. macédoine *f* (de fruits); **prawn**
c. crevettes *fpl* à la mayonnaise.

cocktail party *noun* cocktail *m*.

cocoa *noun* cacao *m*.

coconut *noun* noix *f* de coco.

cod *noun* morue *f*.

code *noun* code *m*.

cod-liver oil *noun* huile *f* de foie
de morue.

co-educational *adjective*
(*school etc*) mixte.

coffee *noun* café *m*; **white c.** café
m au lait.

coffee bar *noun* café *m*.

coffee break *noun* pause-café *f*.

coffeepot *noun* cafetière *f*.

coffee table *noun* table *f* basse.

coffin *noun* cercueil *m*.

cognac *noun* cognac *m*.

coil
  1 *noun* (*of wire, rope*) rouleau *m*.
  2 *verb* enrouler.

coin
  1 *noun* pièce *f* (de monnaie).
  2 *verb* (*phrase, word*) inventer.

coincide *verb* coïncider (**with**
avec).

coincidence *noun* coïncidence *f*.

coke ® *noun* (*Coca-Cola* ®)
coca ® *m*.

colander *noun* passoire *f*.

cold
  1 *noun* froid *m*; (*illness*) rhume
  m; **to catch c.** prendre froid.
  2 *adjective* froid; **to be** or **feel c.**
  avoir froid; **my hands are c.** j'ai
  froid aux mains; **it's c.** (*of weather*) il fait froid; **to get c.** (*of
  weather*) se refroidir; (*of food*)
  refroidir.

coldness *noun* froideur *f*.

coleslaw *noun* salade *f* de chou
cru.

collaborate *verb* collaborer (**on**
à).

collaboration *noun* collaboration *f*.

collapse
  1 *verb* (*of person, building*) s'effondrer.
  2 *noun* effondrement *m*.

collar *noun* col *m*; (*of dog*) collier *m*.

collarbone *noun* clavicule *f*.

colleague *noun* collègue *m or f*.

collect *verb*
1 (*pick up*) ramasser; (*gather*) rassembler; (*taxes*) percevoir; (*rent*) encaisser; (*stamps etc*) collectionner; (*fetch*) (*passer*) prendre; **to c. (money)** (*in street, church*) quêter.
2 (*of dust*) s'accumuler.

collection *noun* (*group of objects*) collection *f*; (*of poems etc*) recueil *m*; (*of money in church etc*) quête *f*; (*of mail*) levée *f*.

collector *noun* (*of stamps etc*) collectionneur, -euse *m or f*.

college *noun* université *f*; (*within university*) collège *m*.

collide *verb* entrer en collision (**with** avec).

collision *noun* collision *f*.

colloquial *adjective* familier.

cologne *noun* eau *f* de Cologne.

colon *noun* Grammar deux-points *invariable m*.

colonel *noun* colonel *m*.

colony *noun* colonie *f*.

colour
1 *noun* couleur *f*.
2 *adjective* (*photo, TV set*) en couleurs.
3 *verb* colorer.

colour (in) *verb* (*drawing*) colorier.

coloured *adjective* (*person, pencil*) de couleur.

colourful *adjective* coloré; (*person*) pittoresque.

colouring book *noun* album *m* de coloriages.

column *noun* colonne *f*; (*newspaper feature*) chronique *f*.

coma *noun* coma *m*; **in a c.** dans le coma.

comb
1 *noun* peigne *m*.
2 *verb* **to c. one's hair** se peigner.

combination *noun* combinaison *f*.

combine *verb*
1 (*thing*) joindre (**with** à); **our combined efforts achieved a result** en joignant nos efforts, nous avons obtenu un résultat.
2 (*of people, thing*) s'unir.

come *verb* venir (**from** de, **to** à); **to c. first** (*in race*) arriver premier; (*in exam*) être le premier; **to c. close to doing** faillir faire; **to c. for something/somebody** venir chercher quelque chose/quelqu'un.

come about *verb* (*happen*) se faire, arriver.

come across *verb* (*thing, person*) tomber sur.

come along *verb* venir (**with** avec); (*progress*) avancer; **c. along!** allons!

come apart *verb* (*of two objects*) se séparer.

come away *verb* (*leave, come off*) partir.

come back *verb* revenir; (*return home*) rentrer.

come by *verb* obtenir; (*find*) trouver.

comedian *noun* (*acteur m*) comique *m*, actrice *f* comique.

come down *verb* descendre; (*of rain, price*) tomber.

comedy *noun* comédie *f*.

come forward (*volunteer*) se présenter; **to c. forward with something** offrir quelque chose.

come in verb entrer; (*of tide*) monter; (*of train*) arriver.

come into verb (*room etc*) entrer dans; (*money*) hériter de.

come off verb
1 (*of button etc*) se détacher; (*succeed*) réussir.
2 (*fall from*) tomber de; (*get down from*) descendre de.

come on verb (*progress*) avancer; **c. on!** allez!

come out verb sortir; (*of sun, book*) paraître; (*of stain*) partir; **to c. out (on strike)** se mettre en grève.

come over verb
1 (*visit*) venir.
2 (*of feeling*) saisir.

come round verb (*visit*) venir; (*of date*) revenir; (*regain consciousness*) revenir à soi.

come through verb
1 (*survive*) s'en tirer.
2 (*crisis etc*) se tirer indemne de.

come to verb (*regain consciousness*) revenir à soi; (*amount to*) revenir à; (*decision*) parvenir à.

come under verb (*heading*) être classé sous; (*influence*) tomber sous.

come up verb (*rise*) monter; (*of plant*) sortir; (*of question, job*) se présenter.

come up against verb (*wall, problem*) se heurter à.

come up to verb (*reach*) arriver jusqu'à.

come up with verb (*idea, money*) trouver.

comfort
1 noun confort m; (*consolation*) réconfort m.
2 verb consoler.

comfortable adjective (*chair etc*) confortable; (*rich*) aisé; **he's c.** (*in chair etc*) il est à l'aise; **make yourself c.** mets-toi à l'aise.

comic
1 adjective comique.
2 noun (*magazine*) bande f dessinée.

comic strip noun bande f dessinée.

comings plural noun **c. and goings** allées fpl et venues.

comma noun virgule f.

command
1 verb (*order*) commander (**somebody to do** à quelqu'un de faire); (*ship etc*) commander.
2 noun (*order*) ordre m; (*mastery*) maîtrise f (**of** de); **to be in c. (of)** (*army etc*) commander; (*situation*) être maître (de).

commemorate verb commémorer.

commence verb commencer (**doing** à faire).

comment noun commentaire m.

commentary noun commentaire m; (*live*) **c.** reportage m.

commentator noun reporter m.

comment on verb (*event etc*) commenter.

commerce noun commerce m.

commercial
1 adjective commercial.
2 noun **commercial(s)** (*on television*) publicité f.

commission noun (*fee, group*) commission f.

commit verb (*crime*) commettre; **to c. suicide** se suicider.

commitment noun (*promise*) engagement m.

committee noun comité m.

commodity noun produit m.

common
1 *adjective (shared, frequent etc)* commun; **in c.** *(shared)* en commun (with avec); **in c. with** *(like)* comme.
2 *noun* House of Commons Chambre *f* des Communes.

commonly *adverb (generally)* en général.

Common Market *noun* Marché *m* commun.

commonplace *adjective* banal (*mpl* banals).

common room *noun* salle *f* commune.

commonsense *noun* sens *m* commun.

commotion *noun* agitation *f*.

communal *adjective (bathroom etc)* commun.

communicate *verb* communiquer.

communication *noun* communication *f*.

communion *noun* communion *f*.

community *noun* communauté *f*.

community centre *noun* centre *m* socio-culturel.

commute *verb* faire la navette (**to work** pour se rendre à son travail).

commuter *noun* banlieusard, -arde *m or f*.

commuting *noun* trajets *mpl* journaliers.

compact
1 *adjective* compact.
2 *noun (for powder)* poudrier *m*.

compact disc *noun* disque *m* compact.

companion *noun* compagnon *m*.

company *noun (being with others, firm)* compagnie *f*; *(guests)* invités, -ées (*mpl or fpl*); **to keep somebody c.** tenir compagnie à quelqu'un.

comparatively *adverb* relativement.

compare *verb* comparer (**with, to** à); **compared to** *or* **with** en comparaison de.

comparison *noun* comparaison *f* (**with** avec).

compartment *noun* compartiment *m*.

compass *noun (for direction)* boussole *f*; *(on ship)* compas *m*; **(pair of) compasses** compas *m*.

compatible *adjective* compatible.

compel *verb* forcer, contraindre (**to do** à faire).

compensate *verb*
1 **to c. somebody** dédommager quelqu'un (**for** de).
2 **to c. for something** compenser quelque chose.

compensation *noun* dédommagement *m*.

compère *noun* animateur, -trice *m or f*.

compete *verb (take part)* concourir (**in** à, **for** pour); **to c. (with somebody)** rivaliser (avec quelqu'un); *(in business)* faire concurrence (à quelqu'un).

competent *adjective* compétent (**to do** pour faire).

competently *adverb* avec compétence.

competition *noun (rivalry)* compétition *f*; **a c.** *(contest)* un concours; *(in sport)* une compétition.

competitive *adjective (price etc)* compétitif; *(person)* aimant la compétition.

competitor *noun* concurrent, -ente *m or f*.

compile *verb* (*list*) dresser.

complain *verb* se plaindre (**of, about** de; **that** que).

complaint plainte *f*; (*in shop etc*) réclamation *f*; (*illness*) maladie *f*.

complete
1 *adjective* (*total*) complet; (*finished*) achevé; **a c. idiot** un parfait imbécile.
2 *verb* compléter; (*finish*) achever; (*form*) remplir.

completely *adverb* complètement.

complex
1 *adjective* complexe.
2 *noun* (*feeling, buildings*) complexe *m*.

complexion *noun* teint *m*.

complicate *verb* compliquer.

complicated *adjective* compliqué.

complication *noun* complication *f*.

compliment *noun* compliment *m*.

comply *verb* obéir (**with** à).

compose *verb* composer; **to c. oneself** se calmer.

composed *adjective* calme.

composer *noun* compositeur, -trice *m or f*.

composition *noun* (*essay*) rédaction *f*.

compound *noun* (*substance, word*) composé *m*.

comprehensive *adjective* complet; (*insurance*) tous risques; **c. (school)** = collège *m* d'enseignement secondaire.

comprise *verb* comprendre.

compromise *noun* compromis *m*.

compulsive *adjective* (*smoker etc*) invétéré; **c. liar** mythomane *m or f*.

compulsory *adjective* obligatoire.

computer *noun* ordinateur *m*; **c. operator** opérateur, -trice *m or f* sur ordinateur; **c. science** informatique *f*.

computerized *adjective* informatisé.

con *verb* (*deceive*) *Familiar* escroquer.

conceal *verb* dissimuler (**from somebody** à quelqu'un); (*plan*) tenir secret.

conceited *adjective* vaniteux.

conceivable *adjective* concevable.

concentrate *verb*
1 **to c. one's efforts on something** concentrer ses efforts sur quelque chose.
2 (*of person*) se concentrer (**on** sur); **to c. on doing** s'appliquer à faire.

concentration *noun* concentration *f*.

concern
1 *verb* concerner; **to be concerned with/about** s'occuper de/s'inquiéter de.
2 *noun* (*matter*) affaire *f*; (*anxiety*) inquiétude *f*; **his c. for** son souci de; (*business*) **c.** entreprise *f*.

concerned *adjective* (*anxious*) inquiet.

concerning *preposition* en ce qui concerne.

concert *noun* concert *m*.

concise *adjective* concis.

conclude *verb*
1 (*speech, book, treaty*) conclure; **to c. that** conclure que.

2 (*come to an end*) se terminer (with par); (*of speaker*) conclure.

conclusion *noun* conclusion *f*.

concrete
  1 *noun* béton *m*.
  2 *adjective* en béton; (*real*) concret.

condemn *verb* condamner (**to** à).

condensation *noun* (*mist*) buée *f*.

condition *noun* condition *f*; **on c. that one does** à condition de faire, à condition que l'on fasse.

conditioner *noun* (*hair*) **c.** après-shampooing *m*.

condom *noun* préservatif *m*.

conduct
  1 *noun* conduite *f*.
  2 *verb* conduire; (*orchestra*) diriger.

conducted tour *noun* excursion *f* accompagnée.

conductor *noun* (*of orchestra*) chef *m* d'orchestre; (*on bus*) receveur, -euse *m or f*.

cone *noun* cône *m*; (*of ice cream*) cornet *m*.

conference *noun* conférence *f*; (*scientific etc*) congrès *m*.

confess *verb*
  1 (*crime, mistake*) avouer (**that** que).
  2 **to c.** (**to**) avouer.

confession *noun* aveu(x) *m(pl)*.

confetti *noun* confettis *mpl*.

confidence *noun* (*trust*) confiance *f*; (**self-**)**c.** confiance *f* en soi; **in c.** en confidence.

confident *adjective* sûr; (**self-**)**c.** sûr de soi.

confidential *adjective* confidentiel.

confidently *adverb* avec confiance.

confine *verb* limiter (**to** à); **to c. oneself to doing** se limiter à faire.

confined *adjective* (*space*) réduit; **c. to bed** cloué au lit.

confirm *verb* confirmer (**that** que).

confirmation *noun* confirmation *f*.

confirmed *adjective* (*bachelor*) endurci.

confiscate *verb* confisquer (**from somebody** à quelqu'un).

conflict
  1 *noun* conflit *m*.
  2 *verb* être en contradiction (**with** avec).

conflicting *adjective* (*views etc*) contradictoires; (*dates*) incompatibles.

conform *verb* (*of person*) se conformer (**to** à).

confront *verb* (*problems, danger*) faire face à; **to c. somebody** (*be face to face with*) se trouver en face de quelqu'un; (*oppose*) s'opposer à quelqu'un.

confuse *verb* (*make unsure*) embrouiller; **to c. with** (*mistake for*) confondre avec.

confused *adjective* (*situation*) confus; **to be c.** (*of person*) s'y perdre; **to get c.** s'embrouiller.

confusing *adjective* déroutant.

confusion *noun* confusion *f*.

congested *adjective* (*street*) encombré.

congestion *noun* (*traffic*) encombrement(s) *m(pl)*.

congratulate *verb* féliciter (**somebody on something** quelqu'un de quelque chose).

congratulations *plural noun* félicitations *fpl* (on pour).

congregate *verb* se rassembler.

congress *noun* congrès *m*; **C.** (*American political body*) le Congrès.

Congressman *noun* (*in America*) membre *m* du Congrès.

conjugate *verb* (*verb*) conjuguer.

conjugation *noun* conjugaison *f*.

conjunction *noun* Grammar conjonction *f*.

conjurer *noun* prestidigitateur, -trice *m or f*.

conjuring trick *noun* tour *m* de prestidigitation.

con man *noun* Familiar escroc *m*.

connect *verb*
1 (*pipes, wires, circuits*) relier (**with, to** à); (*telephone etc*) brancher; **to c. somebody with somebody** (*by phone*) mettre quelqu'un en communication avec quelqu'un.
2 **to c. with** (*of train, bus*) assurer la correspondance avec.

connected *adjective* (*facts*) liés; **to be c. with** (*have dealings with, relate to*) être lié à.

connection *noun* (*link*) rapport *m* (**with** avec); (*train*) correspondance *f*; (*phone call*) communication *f*; **connections** (*contacts*) relations *fpl*; **in c. with** à propos de.

conquer *verb* (*country*) conquérir; (*enemy, habit*) vaincre.

conscience *noun* conscience *f*.

conscientious *adjective* consciencieux.

conscious *adjective* (*awake*) conscient; **c. of something** (*aware*) conscient de quelque

chose; **to be c. of doing** avoir conscience de faire.

consent
1 *verb* consentir (**to** à).
2 *noun* consentement *m*.

consequence *noun* (*result*) conséquence *f*.

consequently *adverb* par conséquent.

conservation *noun* économies *fpl* d'énergie; (*of nature*) protection *f* de l'environnement.

Conservative *adjective* & *noun* conservateur, -trice (*m or f*).

conservatory *noun* (*room*) véranda *f*.

conserve *verb* **to c. energy** faire des économies d'énergie.

consider *verb* considérer (**that** que); (*take into account*) tenir compte de; **to c. doing** envisager de faire.

considerable *adjective* (*large*) considérable; (*much*) beaucoup de.

considerate *adjective* plein d'égards (**to** pour).

consideration *noun* considération *f*; **to take into c.** prendre en considération.

considering *preposition* compte tenu de.

consignment *noun* (*goods*) arrivage *m*.

consist *verb* consister (**of** en, **in** dans, **in doing** à faire).

consistent *adjective* (*unchanging*) constant; (*ideas*) logique; **c. with** compatible avec.

consistently *adverb* (*always*) constamment.

consolation *noun* consolation *f*; **c. prize** lot *m* de consolation.

console [1] *verb* consoler.

console[2] *noun* (*control desk*) console *f*.

consonant *noun* consonne *f*.

conspicuous *adjective* visible; (*striking*) remarquable.

constable *noun* (**police**) c. agent *m* (de police).

constant *adjective* (*frequent*) incessant; (*unchanging*) constant.

constantly *adverb* constamment.

constipated *adjective* constipé.

constitution *noun* constitution *f*.

construct *verb* construire.

construction *noun* construction *f*; under c. en construction.

consul *noun* consul *m*.

consulate *noun* consulat *m*.

consult *verb*
1 (*person*) consulter.
2 to c. with discuter avec.

consultancy (firm) *noun* cabinet *m* conseils.

consultant *noun* (*doctor*) spécialiste *m or f*; (*financial*, *legal*) consultant, -e *m or f*.

consultation *noun* consultation *f*.

consume *verb* (*food*, *supplies*) consommer.

consumer *noun* consommateur, -trice *m or f*.

consumption *noun* consommation *f* (of de).

contact
1 *noun* contact *m*; (*person*) contact *m*, relation *f*; in c. with en contact avec.
2 *verb* contacter.

contact lenses *noun* lentilles *fpl* or verres *mpl* de contact.

contagious *adjective* contagieux.

contain *verb* contenir.

container *noun* récipient *m*; (*for goods*) conteneur *m*.

contemporary *adjective & noun* contemporain, -aine (*m or f*).

contempt *noun* mépris *m*.

contend with *verb* (*problem*) faire face à; (*person*) avoir affaire à.

content[1] *adjective* satisfait (**with** de).

content[2] *noun* (*of text etc*) contenu *m*; **contents** (*of container*) contenu *m*; (**table of**) **contents** (*of book*) table *f* des matières.

contented *adjective* satisfait.

contest *noun* concours *m*; (*fight*) lutte *f*.

contestant *noun* concurrent, -ente *m or f*; (*in fight*) adversaire *m or f*.

context *noun* contexte *m*.

continent *noun* continent *m*; the C. l'Europe *f* (continentale).

continental *adjective* (*European*) européen; c. **breakfast** petit déjeuner *m* à la française.

continual *adjective* continuel.

continually *adverb* continuellement.

continue *verb* continuer (**to do** or **doing** à or de faire); **to c. (with)** (*work etc*) poursuivre; (*resume*) reprendre.

continuous *adjective* continu; c. **performance** (*at cinema*) spectacle *m* permanent.

continuously *adverb* sans interruption.

contraceptive *adjective & noun* contraceptif (*m*).

contract *noun* contrat *m*.

contradict *verb* contredire.

contradiction *noun* contradiction *f*.

contrary
1 *adverb* c. to contrairement à.
2 *noun* on the c. au contraire.

contrast *noun* contraste *m*; in c. to par opposition à.

contrasting *adjective* (*colours, opinions*) opposés.

contribute *verb*
1 (*money*) donner (**to** à); (*article*) écrire (**to** pour).
2 to c. to contribuer à; (*publication*) collaborer à.

contribution *noun* contribution *f*; (*to fund etc*) cotisation(s) *f(pl)*.

contrive *verb* to c. to do trouver moyen de faire.

contrived *adjective* artificiel.

control
1 *verb* (*organization*) diriger; (*traffic*) régler; (*prices, quality, situation, emotion*) contrôler; to c. oneself se contrôler.
2 *noun* autorité *f* (**over** sur); (*over prices, quality*) contrôle *m*; **controls** (*of train etc*) commandes *fpl*; (*of TV set etc*) boutons *mpl*; **everything is under c.** tout est en ordre; **in c. of** maître de; **to lose c. of** perdre le contrôle de.

control tower *noun* tour *f* de contrôle.

convalesce *verb* être en convalescence.

convalescence *noun* convalescence *f*.

convalescent home *noun* maison *f* de convalescence.

convenience *noun* commodité *f*; **c. foods** plats *mpl* tout préparés; **(public) conveniences** toilettes *fpl*.

convenient *adjective* commode; (*well-situated*) bien situé (**for the shops**/*etc* par rapport aux maga-

sins/*etc*); (*moment*) convenable; **to be c. (for)** (*suit*) convenir (à).

convent *noun* couvent *m*.

conversation *noun* conversation *f*.

converse *verb* s'entretenir (**with** avec).

convert *verb* convertir (**into** en, **to** à); (*building*) aménager (**into** en).

convertible *noun* (*car*) (voiture *f*) décapotable *f*.

convey *verb* (*goods, people*) transporter; (*sound, message*) transmettre; (*idea*) communiquer.

conveyor belt *noun* tapis *m* roulant.

convict *verb* déclarer coupable.

conviction *noun* (*for crime*) condamnation *f*; (*belief*) conviction *f*.

convince *verb* convaincre (**of** de).

convincing *adjective* convaincant.

convoy *noun* (*cars*) convoi *m*.

cook
1 *verb* (*food*) (faire) cuire.
2 *verb* (*of food*) cuire; (*of person*) faire la cuisine.
3 *noun* cuisinier, -ière *m or f*.

cookbook *noun* livre *m* de cuisine.

cooker *noun* (*stove*) cuisinière *f*.

cookery *noun* cuisine *f*.

cookie *noun* biscuit *m*.

cooking *noun* cuisine *f*.

cooking apple *noun* pomme *f* à cuire.

cool
1 *adjective* (*weather, place, drink etc*) frais (*f* fraîche); (*manner*) calme; (*unfriendly*) froid; **to keep**

something c. tenir quelque chose au frais.

2 *noun* (*of evening*) fraîcheur *f*; **to lose one's c.** perdre son sang-froid.

cool (down) *verb*

1 (*of angry person*) se calmer; (*of hot liquid*) refroidir.

2 (*of weather*) se rafraîchir; (*of liquid*) refroidir.

cooler *noun* (*for food*) glacière *f*.

cool-headed *adjective* calme.

coolness *noun* fraîcheur *f*; (*unfriendliness*) froideur *f*.

cool off *verb* (*refresh oneself*) se rafraîchir.

co-operate *verb* coopérer (**in** à, **with** avec).

co-operation *noun* coopération *f*.

coop up *verb* (*person*) enfermer.

cop *noun* *Familiar* flic *m*.

cope *verb* **to c. with** s'occuper de; (*problem*) faire face à; (**to be able**) **to c.** (*savoir*) se débrouiller.

copper *noun* (*metal*) cuivre *m*.

copy

1 *noun* copie *f*; (*of book, magazine etc*) exemplaire *m*.

2 *verb* copier.

copy out *or* **down** *verb* (*letter etc*) (re)copier.

cord *noun* cordon *m*; (*electrical*) fil *m* électrique.

cordial *noun* (*fruit*) c. sirop *m*.

cordon off *verb* (*of police etc*) interdire l'accès de.

corduroy *noun* velours *m* côtelé; **corduroys** pantalon *m* en velours côtelé.

core *noun* (*of apple*) trognon *m*.

cork *noun* liège *m*; (*for bottle*) bouchon *m*.

cork (up) *verb* (*bottle*) boucher.

corkscrew *noun* tire-bouchon *m*.

corn *noun* (*wheat*) blé *m*; (*maize*) maïs *m*; (*on foot*) cor *m*.

corned beef *noun* corned-beef *m*.

corner

1 *noun* coin *m*; (*bend in road*) virage *m*; *Football* corner *m*.

2 *verb* (*person in corridor etc*) coincer; (*market*) monopoliser.

cornet *noun* (*ice cream*) c. cornet *m*.

cornflakes *plural noun* céréales *fpl*.

corny *adjective* (*joke*) rebattu.

coronary *noun* infarctus *m*.

corporal *noun* caporal(-chef) *m*.

corpse *noun* cadavre *m*.

correct

1 *adjective* exact; (*proper*) correct; **he's c.** (*right*) il a raison.

2 *verb* corriger.

correction *noun* correction *f*.

correctly *adverb* correctement.

correspond *verb* correspondre (**to, with** à); (*by letter*) correspondre (**with** avec).

correspondence *noun* correspondance *f*; **c. course** cours *m* par correspondance.

corresponding *adjective* (*matching*) correspondant.

corridor *noun* couloir *m*.

corrugated *adjective* **c. iron** tôle *f* ondulée.

corrupt *adjective* corrompu.

cosmetic *noun* produit *m* de beauté.

cosmonaut *noun* cosmonaute *m* *or f*.

cost

1 *verb* coûter; **how much does it**

c.? ça coûte combien?

2 *noun* prix *m*; **at all costs** à tout prix.

costly *adjective* coûteux.

costume *noun* costume *m*; (*woman's suit*) tailleur *m*; (*swimming*) **c.** maillot *m* (de bain).

costume jewellery *noun* bijoux *mpl* fantaisie.

cosy *adjective* douillet; **make yourself c.** mets-toi à l'aise.

cot *noun* lit *m* d'enfant.

cottage *noun* petite maison *f* de campagne; (**thatched**) **c.** chaumière *f*.

cottage cheese *noun* fromage *m* blanc (maigre).

cotton *noun* coton *m*; (*yarn*) fil *m* (de coton); **c. wool** coton *m* hydrophile.

couch *noun* canapé *m*.

couchette *noun* (*on train*) couchette *f*.

cough
1 *noun* toux *f*; **c. mixture** sirop *m* contre la toux.
2 *verb* tousser.

cough up *verb*
1 (*blood*) cracher.
2 (*pay*) *Familiar* casquer.

could *see* **can**[1].

council *noun* conseil *m*; (**town**) **c.** conseil municipal, municipalité *f*; **c. house** maison *f* louée à la municipalité.

councillor *noun* (**town**) **c.** conseiller *m* municipal.

count[1]
1 *verb* compter.
2 *noun* **he's lost c. of the books he has** il ne sait plus combien il a de livres.

count[2] *noun* (*title*) comte *m*.

countdown *noun* compte *m* à rebours.

counter *noun* (*in shop, bar etc*) comptoir *m*; (*in bank etc*) guichet *m*; (*in games*) jeton *m*.

counter- *prefix* contre-.

counterattack *noun* contre-attaque *f*.

counterfoil *noun* souche *f*.

count in *verb* inclure.

count on *verb* **to c. on somebody/something** (*rely on*) compter sur quelqu'un/quelque chose; **to c. on doing** compter faire.

count out *verb* exclure; (*money*) compter.

country *noun* pays *m*; (*regarded with affection*) patrie *f*; (*opposed to town*) campagne *f*; **c. house** maison *f* de campagne.

countryside *noun* campagne *f*.

county *noun* comté *m*;.

couple *noun* (*of people*) couple *m*; **a c. of** deux ou trois; (*adjective few*) quelques.

coupon *noun* (*voucher*) bon *m*.

courage *noun* courage *m*.

courageous *adjective* courageux.

courgette *noun* courgette *f*.

courier *noun* (*for tourists*) guide *m*; (*messenger*) messager *m*.

course
1 *noun* (*duration, movement*) cours *m*; (*of ship*) route *f*; **c.** (**of action**) ligne *f* de conduite; (*option*) parti *m*; **in the c. of** au cours de.
▮ (*lessons*) cours *m*; **c. of lectures** série *f* de conférences.
▮ **c. of treatment** traitement *m*.
▮ (*of meal*) plat *m*; **first c.** entrée *f*.
▮ (*golf*) **c.** terrain *m* (de golf).
2 *adverb* **of c.!** bien sûr!; **of c.**

not! bien sûr que non!

court noun (of king etc, for trials) cour f; (tennis) c. court m (de tennis); to take somebody to c. poursuivre quelqu'un en justice.

courteous adjective poli.

courtroom noun salle f du tribunal.

courtyard noun cour f.

cousin noun cousin, -ine m or f.

cover
1 noun (lid) couvercle m; (of book) couverture f; (for furniture etc) housse f; the covers (on bed) les couvertures fpl et les draps mpl; to take c. se mettre à l'abri.
2 verb couvrir (with de); (insure) assurer.

cover charge noun (in restaurant) couvert m.

covering noun (wrapping) enveloppe f; (layer) couche f.

covering letter noun lettre f jointe (à un document).

cover over verb (floor etc) recouvrir.

cover up verb
1 (put cover on) recouvrir; (truth, tracks) dissimuler; (scandal) étouffer; to c. oneself up se couvrir.
2 to cover up for somebody cacher la vérité pour protéger quelqu'un.

cow noun vache f.

coward noun lâche m or f.

cowardice noun lâcheté f.

cowardly adjective lâche.

cowboy noun cow-boy m.

crab noun crabe m.

crack
1 noun fente f; (in glass, china, bone) fêlure f; (noise) craquement m; (of whip) claquement m; (joke)

Familiar plaisanterie f.
2 verb (glass, ice) fêler; (nut) casser; (whip) faire claquer; (joke) lancer.
3 verb (of glass, ice) se fêler; (of branch, wood) craquer; to get cracking (get to work) Familiar s'y mettre.

cracker noun (biscuit) biscuit m (salé); Christmas c. diablotin m.

crackpot noun Familiar cinglé, -ée m or f.

crack up verb (mentally) Familiar craquer.

cradle noun berceau m.

craft noun (skill) art m; (job) métier m (manuel).

craftsman noun artisan m.

crafty adjective astucieux.

cram verb
1 to c. into (force) fourrer dans; to c. with (fill) bourrer de.
2 to c. into (of people) s'entasser dans; to c. (for an exam) bachoter.

cramp noun (muscle pain) crampe f (in à).

cramped adjective à l'étroit.

crane noun (machine) grue f.

crash
1 noun accident m; (of firm) faillite f; (noise) fracas m.
2 interjection (of fallen object) patatras!
3 verb (car) avoir un accident avec; to c. one's car into faire rentrer sa voiture dans.
4 verb (of car, plane) s'écraser; to c. into rentrer dans.

crash course/diet noun cours m/régime m intensif.

crash down verb (fall) tomber; (break) se casser.

crash helmet noun casque m (anti-choc).

crash-land *verb* atterrir en catastrophe.

crash landing *noun* atterrissage *m* en catastrophe.

crate *noun* caisse *f*.

craving *noun* désir *m* (for de).

crawl
1 *verb* ramper; (*of child*) marcher à quatre pattes; (*of vehicle*) avancer au pas; **to be crawling with** grouiller de.
2 *noun* (*swimming stroke*) crawl *m*.

crayon *noun* crayon *m* de couleur.

craze *noun* manie *f* (for de).

crazy *adjective* fou (*f* folle); **c. about somebody/something** fou de quelqu'un / quelque chose.

creak *verb* (*of hinge*) grincer.

cream *noun* crème *f*; **c. cake** gâteau *m* à la crème.

cream cheese *noun* fromage *m* blanc.

creamy *adjective* crémeux.

crease
1 *verb* (*fabric*) froisser.
2 *verb* (*of fabric*) se froisser.
3 *noun* pli *m*.

create *verb* créer; (*impression, noise*) faire.

creation *noun* création *f*.

creative *adjective* créatif.

creature *noun* animal *m*; (*person*) créature *f*.

crèche *noun* (*nursery*) crèche *f*.

credible *adjective* croyable; (*politician etc*) crédible.

credit
1 *noun* (*financial*) crédit *m*; (*recognition*) mérite *m*; (*from university*) unité *f* de valeur; **to be a c. to** faire honneur à; **on c.** à crédit; **in c.** (*account*) créditeur.

2 *verb* (*of bank*) créditer (**somebody with something** quelqu'un de quelque chose).

credit card *noun* carte *f* de crédit.

credit facilities *noun* facilités *fpl* de paiement.

creditworthy *adjective* solvable.

creep *verb* ramper; (*silently*) se glisser; (*slowly*) avancer lentement.

creepy *adjective* (*causing fear*) *Familiar* terrifiant.

cremate *verb* incinérer.

cremation *noun* crémation *f*.

crematorium *noun* crématorium *m*.

crêpe paper *noun* papier *m* crêpon.

cress *noun* cresson *m*.

crest *noun* (*of wave etc*) crête *f*; (*of hill*) sommet *m*.

crew *noun* (*of ship, plane*) équipage *m*.

crew cut *noun* coupe *f* en brosse *f*.

crib *noun* (*list of answers*) antisèche *f*.

cricket *noun* (*game*) cricket *m*; (*insect*) grillon *m*.

crime *noun* crime *m*; (*less serious*) délit *m*; (*criminal practice*) criminalité *f*.

criminal *adjective* & *noun* criminel, -elle (*m or f*).

cripple *noun* (*disabled person*) infirme *m or f*.

crisis *noun* crise *f*.

crisp
1 *adjective* (*biscuit*) croustillant; (*apple*) croquant.
2 *plural noun* (**potato**) **crisps** chips *fpl*.

crispbread *noun* pain *m* suédois.

critic *noun* critique *m*.

critical *adjective* critique.

critically *adverb* (*ill*) gravement.

criticism *noun* critique *f*.

criticize *verb* critiquer.

Croat *adjective & noun* croate (*m or f*).

Croatia *noun* la Croatie *f*.

crochet
1 *verb* (*shawl etc*) faire au crochet.
2 *verb* (*of person*) faire du crochet.
3 *noun* (travail *m* au) crochet *m*.

crockery *noun* vaisselle *f*.

crocodile *noun* crocodile *m*.

crocus *noun* crocus *m*.

crook *noun* (*thief*) escroc *m*.

crooked *adjective* (*stick*) courbé; (*path*) tortueux; (*hat, picture*) de travers.

crop *noun* (*harvest*) récolte *f*; (*produce*) culture *f*.

crop up *verb* se présenter.

croquet *noun* croquet *m*.

cross[1]
1 *noun* croix *f*; **a c. between** (*animal*) un croisement entre *or* de.
2 *verb* (*street, room etc*) traverser; (*barrier*) franchir; (*legs*) croiser; (*cheque*) barrer.
3 *verb* (*of paths*) se croiser.

cross[2] *adjective* (*angry*) fâché (**with** contre).

cross-country race *noun* cross(-country) *m*.

cross-eyed *adjective* qui louche.

crossing *noun* (*by ship*) traversée *f*; (*pedestrian*) **c.** passage *m* clouté.

cross off *or* **out** *verb* (*word, name etc*) rayer.

cross over *verb* traverser.

cross-reference *noun* renvoi *m*.

crossroads *noun* carrefour *m*.

cross-section *noun* coupe *f* transversale; (*sample*) échantillon *m*.

crossword (puzzle) *noun* mots *mpl* croisés.

crouch (down) *verb* s'accroupir.

crow *noun* corbeau *m*.

crowbar *noun* levier *m*.

crowd *noun* foule *f*; (*particular group*) bande *f*.

crowded *adjective* plein (**with** de).

crowd into *verb* (*of people*) s'entasser dans.

crowd round *verb* **to c. round somebody/something** se presser autour de quelqu'un/quelque chose.

crown *noun* couronne *f*.

crucial *adjective* crucial.

crude *adjective* (*manners, language*) grossier; (*work*) rudimentaire.

cruel *adjective* cruel.

cruelty *noun* cruauté *f*; **an act of c.** une cruauté.

cruet (stand) *noun* salière *f*, poivrière *f* et huilier *m*.

cruise
1 *verb* (*of ship*) croiser; (*of car*) rouler; (*of plane*) voler; (*of tourists*) faire une croisière.
2 *noun* croisière *f*.

crumb *noun* miette *f*.

crumble *verb*
1 (*bread*) émietter.
2 (*of stone*) s'effriter; (*of bread*) s'émietter; (*become ruined*) tomber en ruine.

crumbly *adjective* friable.

crummy *adjective Familiar* moche.

crumpet *noun* petite crêpe *f* grillée (*servie beurrée*).

crumple *verb* froisser.

crunch *verb* (*food*) croquer.

crunchy *adjective* (*apple etc*) croquant; (*bread, biscuit*) croustillant.

crush
1 *noun* (*crowd*) cohue *f*; (*rush*) bousculade *f*.
2 *verb* écraser; (*clothes*) froisser; (*cram*) entasser (**into** dans).

crust *noun* croûte *f*.

crusty *adjective* (*bread*) croustillant.

crutch *noun* béquille *f*.

cry
1 *noun* (*shout*) cri *m*; **to have a c.** *Familiar* pleurer.
2 *verb* pleurer; (*shout*) pousser un cri; **to c. over somebody/something** pleurer quelqu'un/sur quelque chose.

crying *noun* (*weeping*) pleurs *mpl*.

cry off *verb* abandonner.

cry out *verb*
1 (*of person*) pousser un cri; (*exclaim*) s'écrier; **to c. out for something** demander quelque chose (à grands cris); **to be crying out for something** avoir grand besoin de quelque chose.
2 (*warning etc*) crier.

crystal *noun* cristal *m*.

cub *noun* (*scout*) louveteau *m*.

Cuba *noun* Cuba *m or f*.

Cuban *adjective & noun* cubain, -aine (*m or f*).

cube *noun* cube *m*; (*of meat*) dé *m*.

cubic *adjective* (*metre etc*) cube.

cubicle *noun* (*for changing*) cabine *f*; (*in hospital*) box *m*.

cuckoo *noun* (*bird*) coucou *m*.

cucumber *noun* concombre *m*.

cuddle
1 *verb* (*hug*) serrer; (*caress*) câliner.
2 *verb* (*of people*) se serrer.
3 *noun* caresse *f*.

cuddle up *verb* se serrer (**to** contre).

cuddly *adjective* câlin; (*toy*) doux (*f* douce).

cue *noun* (*in theatre*) réplique *f*; (*signal*) signal *m*.

cuff *noun* (*of shirt*) poignet *m*.

cuff link *noun* bouton *m* de manchette.

cul-de-sac *noun* impasse *f*.

culprit *noun* coupable *m or f*.

cultivate *verb* cultiver.

cultivated *adjective* cultivé.

cultural *adjective* culturel.

culture *noun* culture *f*.

cultured *adjective* cultivé.

cumbersome *adjective* encombrant.

cunning
1 *adjective* astucieux.
2 *noun* astuce *f*.

cup *noun* tasse *f*; (*prize*) coupe *f*.

cupboard *noun* armoire *f*; (*built-in*) placard *m*.

cupful *noun* tasse *f*.

curable *adjective* guérissable.

curd cheese *noun* fromage *m* blanc (maigre).

cure
1 *verb* guérir (**of** de).
2 *noun* remède *m* (**for** contre); **rest c.** cure *f* de repos.

curiosity *noun* curiosité *f*.

curious *adjective* (*odd*) curieux;

(*inquisitive*) curieux (**about** de).

curl
1 *verb* (*hair*) boucler.
2 *noun* boucle *f*.

curler *noun* bigoudi *m*.

curl (oneself) up *verb* se pelotonner.

curly *adjective* (*hair*) bouclé.

currant *noun* (*dried grape*) raisin *m* de Corinthe.

currency *noun* monnaie *f*; (*foreign*) devises *fpl* (étrangères).

current
1 *adjective* actuel; (*opinion*) courant; (*year*) courant.
2 *noun* (*of river, electricity*) courant *m*.

current affairs *noun* questions *fpl* d'actualité.

currently *adverb* actuellement.

curriculum *noun* programme *m* (scolaire).

curry *noun* curry *m*.

curse *verb* (*swear*) jurer.

cursor *noun* (*of computer*) curseur *m*.

curtain *noun* rideau *m*.

curts(e)y
1 *noun* révérence *f*.
2 *verb* faire une révérence.

curve
1 *noun* courbe *f*; (*in road*) virage *m*.
2 *verb* se courber; (*of road*) faire une courbe.

cushion *noun* coussin *m*.

custard *noun* crème *f* anglaise; (*when set*) crème *f* renversée.

custom *noun* coutume *f*; (*customers*) clientèle *f*.

customer *noun* client, -ente *m or f*.

customs *plural noun* (**the**) **c.** la douane; **c. (duties)** droits *mpl* de douane; **c. officer** douanier *m*.

cut
1 *noun* (*mark*) coupure *f*; (*stroke*) coup *m*; (*of clothes, hair*) coupe *f*; (*in salary, prices etc*) réduction *f*; (*of meat*) morceau *m*.
2 *verb* couper; (*glass, tree*) tailler; (*salary etc*) réduire; **to c. open** ouvrir.

cut away *verb* (*remove*) enlever.

cutback *noun* réduction *f*.

cut back (on) *verb* réduire.

cut down *verb* (*tree*) abattre.

cut down (on) *verb* réduire.

cute *adjective* Familiar (*pretty*) mignon (*f* mignonne).

cut into *verb* (*cake*) entamer.

cutlery *noun* couverts *mpl*.

cutlet *noun* côtelette *f*.

cut off *verb* couper; (*isolate*) isoler.

cut out *verb*
1 (*of engine*) caler.
2 (*article*) découper; (*remove*) enlever; **to c. out drinking** s'arrêter de boire; **c. it out!** Familiar ça suffit!; **c. out to be a doctor**/*etc* fait pour être médecin/*etc*.

cutout *noun* (*figure*) découpage *m*.

cut-price *adjective* à prix réduit.

cutting *noun* (*newspaper article*) coupure *f*.

cut up *verb* couper en morceaux.

cv *abbreviation* curriculum (vitae) *m invariable*.

cycle
1 *noun* (*bicycle*) bicyclette *f*; (*series, period*) cycle *m*.
2 *verb* aller à bicyclette (**to** à).

cycle path *or* **track** *noun* piste *f* cyclable.

cycling *noun* cyclisme *m*.

cyclist *noun* cycliste *m or f*.

cylinder noun cylindre m.

cymbal noun cymbale f.

Cypriot adjective & noun chypriote, cypriote (m or f).

Cyprus noun Chypre m or f.

Czech adjective & noun tchèque (m or f); the C. Republic la République tchèque.

Czechoslovakia noun la Tchécoslovaquie f.

D

dab *verb* (*wound*) tamponner; to d. something on something appliquer quelque chose sur quelque chose.

Dacron ® *noun* tergal ® *m*.

daddy *noun* Familiar papa *m*.

daffodil *noun* jonquille *f*.

daft *adjective* Familiar idiot, bête.

daily
  1 *adjective* quotidien; d. (paper) quotidien *m*.
  2 *adverb* quotidiennement.

dairy *adjective* (*product*) laitier.

daisy *noun* pâquerette *f*.

dam *noun* barrage *m*.

damage
  1 *noun* dégâts *mpl*; (*harm*) préjudice *m*.
  2 *verb* (*spoil*) abîmer; (*harm*) nuire à.

damn Familiar
  1 *interjection* d. (it)! zut!; d. him! qu'il aille au diable!
  2 *adjective* (*awful*) fichu.
  3 *adverb* (*very*) vachement.

damp
  1 *adjective* humide.
  2 *noun* humidité *f*.

damp(en) *verb* humecter.

dampness *noun* humidité *f*.

dance
  1 *noun* danse *f*; (*social event*) bal *m* (*plural* bals).
  2 *verb* danser.

dance hall *noun* salle *f* de danse.

dancer *noun* danseur, -euse *m* or *f*.

dandelion *noun* pissenlit *m*.

dandruff *noun* pellicules *fpl*.

Dane *noun* Danois, -oise *m or f*.

danger *noun* danger *m* (to pour); in d. en danger; to be in d. of falling/*etc* risquer de tomber/*etc*.

dangerous *adjective* dangereux (to pour).

Danish
  1 *adjective* danois.
  2 *noun* (*language*) danois *m*.

dare *verb* oser (do faire); to d. somebody to do défier quelqu'un de faire.

daring *adjective* audacieux.

dark
  1 *adjective* obscur, noir; (*colour, eyes*) foncé; (*skin, hair*) brun; it's d. il fait nuit or noir; d. glasses lunettes *fpl* noires.
  2 *noun* noir *m*, obscurité *f*.

dark-haired *adjective* aux cheveux bruns.

darkness *noun* obscurité *f*.

dark-skinned *adjective* brun.

darling *noun* (my) d. (mon) chéri, (ma) chérie.

dart *noun* fléchette *f*; darts (*game*) fléchettes *fpl*.

dartboard *noun* cible *f*.

dash
  1 *verb* se précipiter.
  2 *noun* (*stroke*) trait *m*.

dash away or **off** *verb* partir en vitesse.

dashboard *noun* (of car) tableau *m* de bord.

data *plural noun* données *fpl*.

data processing *noun* informatique *f*.

date [1]
1 *noun* (*time*) date *f*; (*meeting*) Familiar rendez-vous *invariable* *m*; (*person*) Familiar copain *m*, copine *f*; **up to d.** moderne; (*information*) à jour; (*well-informed*) au courant (**on** de); **out of d.** (*old-fashioned*) démodé; (*expired*) périmé.
2 *verb* (*letter etc*) dater; (*girl, boy*) Familiar sortir avec.

date [2] *noun* (*fruit*) datte *f*.

date stamp *noun* (tampon *m*) dateur *m*; (*mark*) cachet *m*.

daughter *noun* fille *f*.

daughter-in-law *noun* (*plural* **daughters-in-law**) belle-fille *f*.

dawdle *verb* traîner.

dawn *noun* aube *f*.

day *noun* jour *m*; (*whole day long*) journée *f*; **all d. (long)** toute la journée; **the following** *or* **next d.** le lendemain; **the d. before** la veille; **the d. before yesterday** avant-hier; **the d. after tomorrow** après-demain.

daylight *noun* (lumière *f* du) jour *m*.

day return *noun* (*on train*) aller et retour *m*.

daytime *noun* journée *f*, jour *m*.

dead
1 *adjective* mort.
2 *adverb* (*completely*) absolument; (*very*) très.

dead end *noun* impasse *f*.

deadline *noun* date *f* limite; (*hour*) heure *f* limite.

deaf *adjective* sourd; **d. and dumb** sourd-muet (*f* sourde-muette).

deafness *noun* surdité *f*.

deal [1] *noun* **a good** *or* **great d.** (*a lot*) beaucoup (**of** de).

deal [2]
1 *noun* (*in business*) marché *m*, affaire *f*; **it's a d.** d'accord.
2 *verb* (*trade*) traiter (**with somebody** avec quelqu'un); **to d. in** faire le commerce de; **to d. with** s'occuper de; (*concern*) traiter de.

deal (out) *verb* (*cards*) donner.

dealer *noun* marchand, -ande *m or f* (**in** de); (*agent*) dépositaire *m or f*; (*for cars*) concessionnaire *m or f*.

dealings *plural noun* relations *fpl* (**with** avec); (*in business*) transactions *fpl*.

dealt *see* **deal** [2].

dear
1 *adjective* (*loved, expensive*) cher; **D. Sir** (*in letter*) Monsieur; **oh d.!** oh là là!
2 *noun* **(my) d.** (*darling*) (mon) chéri, (ma) chérie; (*friend*) mon cher, ma chère.

death *noun* mort *f*.

death certificate *noun* acte *m* de décès.

debate
1 *verb* discuter.
2 *noun* débat *m*, discussion *f*.

debit
1 *noun* débit *m*; **in d.** (*account*) débiteur.
2 *verb* débiter (**somebody with something** quelqu'un de quelque chose).

debt *noun* dette *f*; **to be in d.** avoir des dettes.

decade *noun* décennie *f*.

decaffeinated *adjective* décaféiné.

decay *noun* (*of tooth*) carie(s) *f(pl)*.

deceive *verb* tromper.

December *noun* décembre *m*.

decent *adjective* (*respectable*) convenable, décent; (*good*) Familiar bon (*f* bonne); (*kind*) Familiar gentil.

decide *verb*
1 (*question etc*) décider; to d. to do décider de faire; to d. that décider que.
2 (*make decisions*) décider (on de); (*make up one's mind*) se décider (on doing à faire); (*choose*) se décider (on pour).

decimal
1 *adjective* d. point virgule *f*.
2 *noun* décimale *f*.

decision *noun* décision *f*.

decisive *adjective* décisif; (*victory*) net (*f* nette).

deck *noun* (*of ship*) pont *m*.

deckchair *noun* chaise *f* longue.

declare *verb* déclarer (that que); (*verdict, result*) proclamer.

decline *verb* (*become less*) (*of popularity etc*) être en baisse.

decorate *verb* (*cake, house, soldier*) décorer (with de); (*hat, skirt etc*) orner (with de); (*paint etc*) peindre (et tapisser).

decoration *noun* décoration *f*.

decorative *adjective* décoratif.

decorator *noun* peintre *m* décorateur; (**interior**) d. décorateur, -trice *m or f*.

decrease
1 *verb* diminuer.
2 *noun* diminution *f* (in de).

dedicated *adjective* (*teacher etc*) consciencieux.

deduct *verb* déduire (from de); (*from wage, account*) prélever (from sur).

deduction *noun* déduction *f*.

deed *noun* action *f*, acte *m*; (*document*) acte *m* (notarié).

deep *adjective* profond; (*voice*) grave; to be six metres/*etc* d. avoir six mètres/*etc* de profondeur; the d. end (*in pool*) le grand bain.

deep-freeze
1 *verb* surgeler.
2 *noun* congélateur *m*.

deer *invariable noun* cerf *m*.

defeat
1 *verb* battre.
2 *noun* défaite *f*.

defect *noun* défaut *m*.

defective *adjective* défectueux.

defence *noun* défense *f*.

defend *verb* défendre.

defendant *noun* (*accused*) prévenu, -ue *m or f*.

defiant *adjective* (*tone, attitude*) de défi; (*person*) rebelle.

deficiency *noun* manque *m*; (*of vitamins etc*) carence *f*.

deficient *adjective* insuffisant; to be d. in manquer de.

deficit *noun* déficit *m*.

define *verb* définir.

definite *adjective* (*date, plan*) précis; (*reply, improvement*) net (*f* nette); (*order, offer*) ferme; (*certain*) certain; d. **article** Grammar article *m* défini.

definitely *adverb* certainement; (*considerably*) nettement; (*to say*) catégoriquement.

definition *noun* définition *f*.

deformed *adjective* (*body*) difforme.

defrost *verb* (*fridge*) dégivrer; (*food*) décongeler.

defy *verb* défier; to d. somebody to do défier quelqu'un de faire.

degenerate *verb* dégénérer (into en).

degree *noun* (*angle, temperature*)

degré *m*; (*from university*) diplôme *m*; (*Bachelor's*) licence *f*; (*Master's*) maîtrise *f*; (*PhD*) doctorat *m*; **to such a d.** à tel point (**that** que).

de-ice *verb* (*car window etc*) dégivrer.

de-icer *noun* (*substance*) dégivreur *m*.

dejected *adjective* abattu.

delay
1 *verb* (*meeting, trip etc*) retarder; (*payment*) différer.
2 *verb* (*be slow*) tarder (**doing** à faire); (*linger*) s'attarder.
3 *noun* retard *m*; (*waiting period*) délai *m*; **without d.** sans tarder.

delegate
1 *verb* déléguer (**to** à).
2 *noun* délégué, -ée *m or f*.

delegation *noun* délégation *f*.

delete *verb* supprimer; (*cross out*) rayer.

deliberate *adjective* (*intentional*) intentionnel.

deliberately *adverb* (*intentionally*) exprès.

delicacy *noun* (*food*) mets *m* délicat.

delicate *adjective* délicat.

delicatessen *noun* traiteur *m* et épicerie *f* fine.

delicious *adjective* délicieux.

delight
1 *noun* délice *m*; **to take d. in something/in doing** se délecter de quelque chose/à faire.
2 *verb* (*person*) réjouir.
3 *verb* **to d. in doing** se délecter à faire.

delighted *adjective* ravi (**with something** de quelque chose, **to do** de faire, **that** que).

delightful *adjective* charmant;

(*meal*) délicieux.

delinquent *noun* délinquant, -ante *m or f*.

deliver *verb* (*goods etc*) livrer; (*letters*) distribuer; (*hand over*) remettre (**to** à); (*speech*) prononcer; (*warning*) lancer.

delivery *noun* livraison *f*; (*of letters*) distribution *f*; (*handing over*) remise *f*; (*birth*) accouchement *m*.

delude *verb* tromper; **to d. oneself** se faire des illusions.

de luxe *adjective* de luxe.

demand
1 *verb* exiger (**something from somebody** quelque chose de quelqu'un); (*rights, more pay*) revendiquer; **to d. that** exiger que.
2 *noun* exigence *f*; (*claim*) revendication *f*; (*for goods*) demande *f*; **in great d.** très demandé.

demanding *adjective* exigeant.

demerara (sugar) *noun* sucre *m* roux.

democracy *noun* démocratie *f*.

democratic *adjective* démocratique; (*person*) démocrate.

demolish *verb* démolir.

demolition *noun* démolition *f*.

demonstrate *verb*
1 (*show*) démontrer; (*machine*) faire une démonstration de.
2 (*protest*) manifester.

demonstration *noun* démonstration *f*; (*protest*) manifestation *f*.

demonstrative *adjective* & *noun Grammar* démonstratif (*m*).

demonstrator *noun* (*protester*) manifestant, -ante *m or f*.

demoralize *verb* démoraliser.

den *noun* tanière *f*.

denial *noun* (*of rumour*) démenti

m.

denim *noun* (toile *f* de) coton *m*; denims (*jeans*) (blue-)jean *m*.

Denmark *noun* le Danemark *m*.

denounce *verb* (*person, injustice etc*) dénoncer (**to** à).

dense *adjective* dense; (*stupid*) *Familiar* bête.

dent
1 *noun* (*in car etc*) bosse *f*.
2 *verb* cabosser.

dental *adjective* dentaire.

dentist *noun* dentiste *m or f*.

dentures *plural noun* dentier *m*.

deny *verb* nier (**doing** avoir fait, **that** que); (*rumour*) démentir; **to d. somebody something** refuser quelque chose à quelqu'un.

deodorant *noun* déodorant *m*.

depart *verb* partir; (*deviate*) s'écarter (**from** de).

department *noun* département *m*; (*in office*) service *m*; (*in shop*) rayon *m*.

department store *noun* grand magasin *m*.

departure *noun* départ *m*; **a d. from** (*rule*) un écart par rapport à.

depend *verb* dépendre (**on, upon** de); **to d. (up)on** (*rely on*) compter sur (**for something** pour quelque chose).

dependable *adjective* sûr.

dependant *noun* personne *f* à charge.

depict *verb* (*describe*) dépeindre; (*in pictures*) représenter.

deplorable *adjective* déplorable.

deplore *verb* déplorer.

deposit
1 *verb* déposer.
2 *noun* dépôt *m*; (*part payment*) acompte *m*; (*against damage*) caution *f*; (*on bottle*) consigne *f*.

depot *noun* dépôt *m*.

depress *verb* (*discourage*) déprimer.

depressed *adjective* déprimé; **to get d.** se décourager.

depression *noun* dépression *f*.

deprive *verb* priver (**of** de).

deprived *adjective* (*childhood*) malheureux; (*area*) défavorisé.

depth *noun* profondeur *f*.

deputy *noun* (*replacement*) remplaçant, -ante *m or f*; (*assistant*) adjoint, -ointe *m or f*.

derailment *noun* déraillement *m*.

derelict *adjective* abandonné.

derive *verb* **to d. something from something** (*pleasure etc*) tirer quelque chose de quelque chose; **to be derived from** (*of word etc*) dériver de.

descend *verb*
1 **to d. from** descendre de; **to d. upon** (*of tourists*) envahir.
2 (*stairs*) descendre.

descendant *noun* descendant, -ante *m or f*.

descent *noun* (*of aircraft etc*) descente *f*.

describe *verb* décrire.

description *noun* description *f*; (*on passport*) signalement *m*; **of every d.** de toutes sortes.

desert[1] *noun* désert *m*; **d. island** île *f* déserte.

desert[2] *verb* abandonner.

deserted *adjective* (*place*) désert.

deserve *verb* mériter (**to do** de faire).

design
1 *verb* (*car etc*) dessiner; **designed to do/for somebody**

conçu pour faire / pour quelqu'un; **well designed** bien conçu.
2 noun (pattern) motif m; (sketch) plan m, dessin m; (type of dress or car) modèle m.

designer noun dessinateur, -trice m or f.

designer clothes plural noun vêtements mpl griffés.

desirable adjective désirable.

desire
1 noun désir m; **I've no d. to** je n'ai aucune envie de.
2 verb désirer (**to do** faire).

desk noun (in school) table f; (in office) bureau m; (in shop) caisse f; (reception) d. réception f.

despair
1 noun désespoir m; **to be in d.** être au désespoir.
2 verb désespérer (**of somebody** de quelqu'un, **of doing** de faire).

despatch = dispatch.

desperate adjective désespéré; **to be d. for** avoir désespérément besoin de; (cigarette) mourir d'envie de fumer.

despicable adjective méprisable.

despise verb mépriser.

despite preposition malgré.

dessert noun dessert m.

dessertspoon noun cuillère f à dessert.

destination noun destination f.

destitute adjective indigent.

destroy verb détruire.

destruction noun destruction f.

destructive adjective destructeur.

detach verb détacher (**from** de).

detachable adjective (lining) amovible.

detached house noun maison f individuelle.

detail noun détail m; **in d.** en détail.

detailed adjective détaillé.

detain verb retenir; (prisoner) détenir.

detect verb (find) découvrir; (see, hear) distinguer.

detective noun inspecteur m de police; (private) détective m; **d. film/novel** film m / roman m policier.

detector noun détecteur m.

detention noun (school punishment) retenue f.

deter verb **to d. somebody** dissuader quelqu'un (**from doing** de faire).

detergent noun détergent m.

deteriorate verb se détériorer.

deterioration noun détérioration f.

determination noun (intention) ferme intention f.

determine verb déterminer; (price) fixer.

determined adjective déterminé; **d. to do** or **on doing** décidé à faire.

deterrent noun **to be a d.** être dissuasif.

detest verb détester (**doing** faire).

detour noun détour m.

develop verb
1 (muscles, idea) développer; (area, land) mettre en valeur; (habit, illness) contracter.
2 (grow) se développer; **to d. into** devenir.

development noun développement m; **housing d.** lotissement m; (large) grand ensemble m; **a (new) d.** (in situation) un fait nouveau.

deviate *verb* dévier (**from** de).

device *noun* dispositif *m*; **left to one's own devices** livré à soi-même.

devil *noun* diable *m*; **what/where/why the d.?** que/où/pourquoi diable?

devise *verb* (*plan*) mettre au point; (*invent*) inventer.

devote *verb* consacrer (**to** à).

devoted *adjective* dévoué (**to** à).

devotion *noun* dévouement *m* (**to somebody** à quelqu'un).

dew *noun* rosée *f*.

diabetes *noun* diabète *m*.

diabetic *noun* diabétique *m or f*.

diagnosis *noun* diagnostic *m*.

diagonal
    1 *adjective* diagonal.
    2 *noun* **d. (line)** diagonale *f*.

diagonally *adverb* en diagonale.

diagram *noun* schéma *m*.

dial
    1 *noun* cadran *m*.
    2 *verb* (*phone number*) faire; (*person*) appeler.

dialect *noun* dialecte *m*.

dialling code *noun* indicatif *m*.

dialling tone *noun* tonalité *f*.

dialogue *noun* dialogue *m*.

diameter *noun* diamètre *m*.

diamond *noun* diamant *m*; (*shape*) losange *m*; *Baseball* terrain *m*; **diamond(s)** (*at cards*) carreau *m*; **d. necklace** rivière *f* de diamants.

diarrh(o)ea *noun* diarrhée *f*.

diary *noun* (*calendar*) agenda *m*; (*private*) journal *m* (intime).

dice
    1 *invariable noun* dé *m*.
    2 *verb* (*food*) couper en dés.

dictate *verb* dicter (**to** à).

dictation *noun* dictée *f*.

dictionary *noun* dictionnaire *m*.

did *see* do[1].

die *verb* mourir (**of, from** de); **to be dying to do** mourir d'envie de faire; **to be dying for something** avoir une envie folle de quelque chose.

die away *verb* (*of noise*) mourir.

die down *verb* (*of storm*) se calmer.

die out *verb* (*of custom*) mourir.

diesel *adjective* & *noun* **d. (engine)** (moteur *m*) diesel *m*; **d. (oil)** gazole *m*.

diet
    1 *noun* (*for slimming*) régime *m*; (*usual food*) alimentation *f*; **to go on a d.** faire un régime.
    2 *verb* suivre un régime.

differ *verb* différer (**from** de); (*disagree*) ne pas être d'accord (**from** avec).

difference *noun* différence *f* (**in** de); **d. (of opinion)** différend *m*; **it makes no d.** ça n'a pas d'importance; **it makes no d. to me** ça m'est égal.

different *adjective* différent (**from** de); (*another*) autre; (*various*) divers.

differently *adverb* autrement (**from** que).

difficult *adjective* difficile (**to do** à faire); **it's d. for us to** il nous est difficile de.

difficulty *noun* difficulté *f*; **to have d. doing** avoir du mal à faire.

dig *verb*
    1 (*ground*) bêcher; (*hole*) creuser; **to d. something into** (*push*) enfoncer quelque chose dans.
    2 (*make a hole*) creuser.

digest *verb* digérer.

digestion *noun* digestion *f.*

digger *noun* (*machine*) pelleteuse *f.*

digit *noun* (*number*) chiffre *m.*

digital *adjective* numérique.

dig out *verb* (*from ground*) déterrer; (*accident victim*) dégager; (*find*) dénicher.

dig up *verb* (*from ground*) déterrer; (*weed*) arracher; (*earth*) retourner; (*street*) creuser des trous dans.

dilapidated *adjective* délabré.

dilute *verb* diluer.

dim
1 *adjective* (*light*) faible; (*room*) sombre; (*memory, outline*) vague; (*person*) stupide.
2 *verb* (*light*) baisser.

dimension *noun* dimension *f.*

din *noun* vacarme *m.*

dine *verb* dîner (**on** de).

dine out *verb* dîner en ville.

diner *noun* dîneur, -euse *m or f*; (*train carriage*) wagon-restaurant *m.*

dinghy *noun* petit canot *m*; (**rubber**) **d.** canot *m* pneumatique.

dingy *adjective* (*room etc*) minable; (*colour*) terne.

dining car *noun* wagon-restaurant *m.*

dining room *noun* salle *f* à manger.

dinner *noun* dîner *m*; (*lunch*) déjeuner *m*; **to have d.** dîner.

dinner jacket *noun* smoking *m.*

dinner party *noun* dîner *m* (à la maison).

dinner service *or* **set** *noun* service *m* de table.

dinosaur *noun* dinosaure *m.*

dip
1 *verb* plonger; **to d. one's headlights** se mettre en codes; **to d. into** (*pocket, savings*) puiser dans.
2 *noun* (*in road*) descente *f*; **to go for a d.** (*swim*) faire trempette.

diphthong *noun* diphtongue *f.*

diploma *noun* diplôme *m.*

dipped headlights *plural noun* (*of vehicle*) codes *mpl.*

direct
1 *adjective* direct.
2 *adverb* directement.
3 *verb* diriger; (*remark*) adresser (**to** à); **to d. somebody to** (*place*) indiquer à quelqu'un le chemin de.

direction *noun* direction *f*; **directions (for use)** mode *m* d'emploi; **in the opposite d.** en sens inverse.

directly
1 *adverb* directement; (*at once*) tout de suite.
2 *conjunction* aussitôt que (+ *indicative*).

director *noun* directeur, -trice *m or f*; (*board member in firm*) administrateur, -trice *m or f*; (*of film*) metteur *m* en scène.

directory *noun* (*telephone*) **d.** annuaire *m* (téléphonique).

directory inquiries *noun* renseignements *mpl.*

dirt *noun* saleté *f*; (*earth*) terre *f*; **d. cheap** *Familiar* très bon marché.

dirty
1 *adjective* sale; (*job*) salissant; (*word*) grossier; **to get d.** se salir; **to get something d.** salir quelque chose; **a d. joke** une histoire cochonne.
2 *verb* salir.

dis - *prefix* dé-, dés-.

disability *noun* infirmité *f*.

disabled
  1 *adjective* handicapé.
  2 *noun* the d. les handicapés *mpl*.

disadvantage *noun* désavantage *m*.

disagree *verb* ne pas être d'accord (**with** avec); **to d. with somebody** (*of food etc*) ne pas réussir à quelqu'un.

disagreeable *adjective* désagréable.

disagreement *noun* désaccord *m*; (*quarrel*) différend *m*.

disappear *verb* disparaître.

disappearance *noun* disparition *f*.

disappoint *verb* décevoir; **I'm disappointed with it** ça m'a déçu.

disappointing *adjective* décevant.

disappointment *noun* déception *f*.

disapproval *noun* désapprobation *f*.

disapprove *verb* **to d. of somebody/something** désapprouver quelqu'un/quelque chose; **I d.** je suis contre.

disarm *verb* désarmer.

disaster *noun* désastre *m*.

disastrous *adjective* désastreux.

disc *noun* disque *m*; **identity d.** plaque *f* d'identité.

discard *verb* se débarrasser de.

discharge *verb* (*patient, employee*) renvoyer; (*soldier*) libérer.

discipline
  1 *noun* discipline *f*.
  2 *verb* discipliner; (*punish*) punir.

disc jockey *noun* disc-jockey *m*.

disclose *verb* révéler.

disco *noun* boîte *f*.

discomfort *noun* douleur *f*; **I get d. from my wrist** mon poignet me gêne.

disconnect *verb* détacher; (*unplug*) débrancher; (*wires*) déconnecter; (*gas, telephone*) couper.

discontented *adjective* mécontent.

discontinued *adjective* (*article*) qui ne se fait plus.

discotheque *noun* (*club*) discothèque *f*.

discount *noun* (*on article*) remise *f*, réduction *f*; **at a d.** à prix réduit.

discount store *noun* solderie *f*.

discourage *verb* décourager; **to get discouraged** se décourager.

discover *verb* découvrir (**that** que).

discovery *noun* découverte *f*.

discreet *adjective* discret.

discriminate *verb* **to d. against** faire de la discrimination contre.

discrimination *noun* (*against somebody*) discrimination *f*.

discuss *verb* discuter de; (*price*) débattre.

discussion *noun* discussion *f*.

disease *noun* maladie *f*.

disembark *verb* débarquer.

disfigured *adjective* défiguré.

disgrace
  1 *noun* (*shame*) honte *f* (**to** à).
  2 *verb* déshonorer.

disgraceful *adjective* honteux.

disguise
  1 *verb* déguiser (**as** en).
  2 *noun* déguisement *m*; **in d.** déguisé.

disgust
1 *noun* dégoût *m* (**for, at, with** de); **in d.** dégoûté.
2 *verb* dégoûter.

disgusted *adjective* dégoûté (**at, by, with** par); **d. with somebody** (*annoyed*) fâché contre quelqu'un.

disgusting *adjective* dégoûtant.

dish *noun* (*container, food*) plat *m*; **the dishes** la vaisselle.

dishcloth *noun* (*for washing*) lavette *f*; (*for drying*) torchon *m*.

dishevelled *adjective* hirsute.

dishonest *adjective* malhonnête.

dish out *or* **up** *verb* (*food*) servir.

dishwasher *noun* (*machine*) lave-vaisselle *invariable m*.

disillusioned *adjective* déçu (**with** de, par).

disincentive *noun* mesure *f* dissuasive.

disinfect *verb* désinfecter.

disinfectant *noun* désinfectant *m*.

disk *noun* (*of computer*) disque *m*.

dislike
1 *verb* ne pas aimer (**doing** faire).
2 *noun* aversion *f* (**for, of** pour); **to take a d. to somebody/ something** prendre quelqu'un/ quelque chose en grippe.

dislocate *verb* (*limb*) démettre.

dismal *adjective* morne.

dismantle *verb* (*machine*) démonter.

dismay *verb* consterner.

dismiss *verb* (*from job*) renvoyer (**from** de).

dismissal *noun* renvoi *m*.

disobedience *noun* désobéissance *f*.

disobedient *adjective* désobéissant.

disobey *verb* désobéir à.

disorder (*confusion*) désordre *m*; (*illness*) troubles *mpl*.

disorganized *adjective* désorganisé.

dispatch *verb* expédier; (*troops, messenger*) envoyer.

dispel *verb* dissiper.

dispenser (*device*) distributeur *m*; **cash d.** distributeur *m* de billets.

disperse *verb* (*of crowd*) se disperser.

display
1 *verb* montrer; (*notice, electronic data*) afficher; (*painting, goods*) exposer; (*courage etc*) faire preuve de.
2 *noun* (*in shop*) étalage *m*; (*of data*) affichage *m*; **on d.** exposé.

displeased *adjective* mécontent (**with** de).

disposable *adjective* (*plate etc*) à jeter, jetable.

disposal *noun* **at the d. of** à la disposition de.

dispose *verb* **to d. of** (*get rid of*) se débarrasser de; (*sell*) vendre.

dispute
1 *noun* (*quarrel*) dispute *f*; (*industrial*) conflit *m*.
2 *verb* contester.

disqualify *verb* rendre inapte (**from** à); (*in sport*) disqualifier; **to d. somebody from driving** retirer son permis à quelqu'un.

disregard *verb* ne tenir aucun compte de.

disrupt *verb* (*traffic, class etc*) perturber; (*plan, books etc*) déranger.

disruption *noun* perturbation *f*;

(*of plan etc*) dérangement *m*.

disruptive *adjective* (*child*) turbulent.

dissatisfaction *noun* mécontentement *m*.

dissatisfied *adjective* mécontent (with de).

dissolve *verb* dissoudre.

dissuade *verb* dissuader (**from doing** de faire).

distance *noun* distance *f*; **in the d.** au loin; **from a d.** de loin; **it's within walking d.** on peut y aller à pied; **to keep one's d.** garder ses distances.

distant *adjective* éloigné; (*reserved*) distant.

distaste *noun* aversion *f* (**for** pour).

distasteful *adjective* désagréable.

distinct *adjective* (*voice, light*) distinct; (*difference, improvement*) net (*f* nette); (*different*) distinct (**from** de).

distinction *noun* distinction *f*; (*in university exam*) mention *f* très bien.

distinctive *adjective* distinctif.

distinctly *adverb* distinctement; (*definitely*) sensiblement.

distinguish *verb* distinguer (**from** de, **between** entre).

distinguished *adjective* distingué.

distort *verb* déformer.

distract *verb* distraire (**from** de).

distraction *noun* distraction *f*.

distress *noun* (*pain*) douleur *f*; (*anguish*) détresse *f*; **in d.** (*ship*) en détresse.

distressing *adjective* affligeant.

distribute *verb* distribuer; (*spread evenly*) répartir.

distribution *noun* distribution *f*.

distributor *noun* (*in car*) distributeur *m*; (*of goods*) concessionnaire *m or f*.

district *noun* région *f*; (*of town*) quartier *m*; **postal d.** division *f* postale.

distrust *verb* se méfier de.

disturb *verb* (*sleep*) troubler; (*papers, belongings*) déranger; **to d. somebody** (*bother*) déranger quelqu'un; (*worry*) troubler quelqu'un.

disturbance *noun* (*noise*) tapage *m*; **disturbances** (*riots*) troubles *mpl*.

disturbing *adjective* (*worrying*) inquiétant.

ditch *noun* fossé *m*.

ditto *adverb* idem.

divan *noun* divan *m*.

dive
1 *verb* plonger; (*rush*) se précipiter.
2 *noun* (*of swimmer, goalkeeper*) plongeon *m*; (*of aircraft*) piqué *m*.

diver *noun* plongeur, -euse *m or f*.

diversion *noun* (*on road*) déviation *f*; (*distraction*) diversion *f*.

divert *verb* (*traffic*) dévier; (*aircraft*) dérouter.

divide *verb* diviser (**into** en); (*share out*) partager; (*separate*) séparer (**from** de).

divide off *verb* **to d. something off** séparer quelque chose (**from something** de quelque chose).

divide up *verb* **to d. something up** (*share out*) partager quelque chose.

diving *noun* plongée *f* sousmarine.

diving board *noun* plongeoir *m*.

division *noun* division *f*.

divorce
1 *noun* divorce *m*.
2 *verb* (*husband*, *wife*) divorcer
d'avec.

divorced *adjective* divorcé (**from**
d'avec); **to get d.** divorcer.

DIY *abbreviation* (*do-it-yourself*)
bricolage *m*.

dizziness *noun* vertige *m*.

dizzy *adjective* **to be** *or* **feel d.**
avoir le vertige; **to make some-
body (feel) d.** donner le vertige
à quelqu'un.

DJ *abbreviation* = disc jockey.

do¹
1 *auxiliary verb* **do you know?**
savez-vous?, est-ce que vous sa-
vez?; **I do not** *or* **don't see** je ne
vois pas; **he DID say so** (*emphasis*) il l'a bien dit; **do stay** reste
donc; **you know him, don't
you?** tu le connais, n'est-ce pas?;
neither do I moi non plus; **so do
I** moi aussi.
2 *verb* faire; **what does she do?**
qu'est-ce qu'elle fait?; **what have
you done (with)…?** qu'as-tu fait
(de)…?; **well done** (*congratulations*) bravo!; (*steak*) bien cuit;
**to do somebody out of some-
thing** escroquer quelque chose à
quelqu'un; **he's done for** *Familiar* il est fichu.
3 *verb* (*get along*) aller; (*suit*)
faire l'affaire; (*be enough*) suffire;
(*finish*) finir; **how do you do?**
(*introduction*) enchanté; (*greeting*) bonjour; **he did well** *or* **right
to leave** il a bien fait de partir;
do as I do fais comme moi; **to
have to do with** (*relate to*) avoir
à voir avec; (*concern*) concerner.

do² *noun* (*party*) *Familiar* fête *f*.

do away with *verb* supprimer.

dock
1 *noun* (*for ship*) dock *m*.
2 *verb* (*at quayside*) se mettre à
quai.

docker *noun* docker *m*.

dockyard *noun* chantier *m* naval.

doctor *noun* médecin *m*, docteur
m; (*academic*) docteur *m*.

doctorate *noun* doctorat *m*.

document *noun* document *m*.

documentary *noun* (*film*) documentaire *m*.

dodge *verb*
1 (*blow*) esquiver; (*pursuer*)
échapper à; (*tax*) éviter de payer.
2 to d. through (*crowd*) se faufiler dans.

dodgems *plural noun* autos *fpl*
tamponneuses.

does *see* do¹.

dog *noun* chien *m*; (*female*)
chienne *f*; **d. food** pâtée *f*.

doggy bag *noun* (*in restaurant*)
petit sac *m* pour emporter les
restes.

doing *noun* **that's your d.** c'est
toi qui as fait ça.

do-it-yourself
1 *noun* bricolage *m*.
2 *adjective* (*store*, *book*) de bricolage.

dole *noun Familiar* **d. (money)**
allocation *f* de chômage; **to go
on the d.** s'inscrire au chômage.

doll *noun* poupée *f*.

dollar *noun* dollar *m*.

doll's house *noun* maison *f* de
poupée.

dolphin *noun* dauphin *m*.

dome *noun* dôme *m*.

domestic *adjective* domestique;
(*trade*, *flight*) intérieur.

domestic science *noun* arts
mpl ménagers.

dominant *adjective* dominant; (*person*) dominateur.

dominate *verb* dominer.

domino *noun* domino *m*; dominoes (*game*) dominos *mpl*.

donate *verb* faire don de; (*blood*) donner.

donation *noun* don *m*.

done *see* do[1].

donkey *noun* âne *m*.

door *noun* porte *f*; out of doors dehors.

doorbell *noun* sonnette *f*.

doorknob *noun* poignée *f* de porte.

doorknocker *noun* marteau *m*.

doorman *noun* (*of hotel*) portier *m*.

doormat *noun* paillasson *m*.

doorstep *noun* seuil *m*.

doorstop(per) *noun* butoir *m* (de porte).

doorway *noun* in the d. dans l'encadrement de la porte.

dope *noun* (*drugs*) *Familiar* drogue *f*.

dormitory *noun* dortoir *m*.

dosage *noun* (*amount*) dose *f*.

dose *noun* dose *f*.

dot *noun* point *m*.

dotted line *noun* pointillé *m*.

double
 1 *adjective* double; a d. bed un grand lit; a d. room une chambre pour deux personnes.
 2 *adverb* (*twice*) deux fois, le double; (*to fold*) en deux.
 3 *noun* double *m*.
 4 *verb* doubler.

double back *verb* (*of person*) revenir en arrière.

double-breasted *adjective* (*jacket*) croisé.

double-decker (bus) *noun* autobus *m* à impériale.

double-glazing *noun* double vitrage *m*.

double up *verb* (*with pain, laughter*) être plié en deux.

doubt
 1 *noun* doute *m*; no d. (*probably*) sans doute.
 2 *verb* douter de; to d. whether or that or if douter que (+ *subjunctive*).

doubtful *adjective* to be d. (about something) avoir des doutes (sur quelque chose); it's d. whether or that or if ce n'est pas sûr que (+ *subjunctive*).

dough *noun* pâte *f*; (*money*) *Familiar* fric *m*.

doughnut *noun* beignet *m* (rond).

do up *verb* (*coat*) boutonner; (*zip, button*) fermer; (*house*) refaire; (*goods*) emballer.

dove *noun* colombe *f*.

do with *verb* I could do with that j'en ai bien besoin.

do without *verb* se passer de.

down
 1 *adverb* en bas; (*to the ground*) par terre; to come or go d. descendre; d. there or here en bas; d. with flu grippé; to feel d. avoir le cafard.
 2 *preposition* (*at bottom of*) en bas de; (*from top to bottom of*) du haut en bas de; (*along*) le long de; to go d. (*hill, street, stairs*) descendre.

down-and-out *noun* clochard, -arde *m* or *f*.

downhill *adverb* to go d. descendre; (*of sick person, business*) aller de plus en plus mal.

down payment *noun* acompte *m*.

downpour *noun* averse *f*.

downright
  1 *adjective* (*rogue etc*) véritable; (*refusal*) catégorique.
  2 *adverb* (*rude etc*) franchement.

downstairs
  1 *adjective* (*room*, *neighbours*) d'en bas.
  2 *adverb* en bas; **to come** *or* **go d.** descendre l'escalier.

downtown *adverb* en ville; **d. Chicago** le centre de Chicago.

downward(s) *adverb* vers le bas.

doze
  1 *noun* petit somme *m*.
  2 *verb* sommeiller.

dozen *noun* douzaine *f*; **a d.** (*books etc*) une douzaine de.

doze off *verb* s'assoupir.

Dr *abbreviation* (*Doctor*) Docteur.

drab *adjective* terne; (*weather*) gris.

drag *verb* traîner; **to d. somebody/something along** traîner quelqu'un/quelque chose; **to d. somebody away from somebody/something** arracher quelqu'un à quelqu'un/quelque chose.

drag on *or* **out** *verb* (*last a long time*) se prolonger.

dragon *noun* dragon *m*.

drain
  1 *noun* (*sewer*) égout *m*; (*outside house*) puisard *m*; (*in street*) bouche *f* d'égout.
  2 *verb* (*tank*) vider; (*vegetables*) égoutter.

drain (off) *verb*
  1 (*liquid*) faire écouler.
  2 (*of liquid*) s'écouler.

drainer *noun* (*board*) paillasse *f*; (*rack*, *basket*) égouttoir *m*.

draining board *noun* paillasse *f*.

drainpipe *noun* tuyau *m* d'évacuation.

drama *noun* (*event*) drame *m*; (*dramatic art*) théâtre *m*.

dramatic *adjective* dramatique; (*very great*, *striking*) spectaculaire.

dramatically *adverb* (*to change etc*) de façon spectaculaire.

drank *see* drink.

drastic *adjective* radical.

drastically *adverb* radicalement.

draught *noun* courant *m* d'air; **draughts** (*game*) dames *fpl*.

draught beer *noun* bière *f* pression.

draughtboard *noun* damier *m*.

draughty *adjective* (*room*) plein de courants d'air.

draw¹
  1 *noun* (*in sport*) match *m* nul.
  2 *verb* (*pull*) tirer; (*money from bank*) retirer (**from** de); (*attract*) attirer.
  3 *verb* (*in sport*) faire match nul.

draw² *verb*
  1 dessiner; (*circle*) tracer.
  2 **to d. near** s'approcher (**to** de); (*of time*) approcher (**to** de).

drawback *noun* inconvénient *m*.

drawer *noun* tiroir *m*.

draw in *verb* (*of train*) arriver (en gare).

drawing *noun* dessin *m*.

drawing pin *noun* punaise *f*.

drawing room *noun* salon *m*.

drawn
  1 *see* **draw**¹, ².
  2 *adjective* **d. match** *or* **game** match *m* nul.

draw on *verb* (*savings*) puiser dans.

draw out *verb* (*money*) retirer.

draw up *verb*
1 (*chair*) approcher; (*list, plan*) dresser.
2 (*of vehicle*) s'arrêter.

dread
1 *verb* (*exam etc*) appréhender; to d. doing appréhender de faire.
2 *noun* crainte *f*.

dreadful *adjective* épouvantable; (*child*) insupportable.

dreadfully *adverb* terriblement; to be d. sorry regretter infiniment.

dream
1 *verb* (*have dreams*) rêver (**of** de, **of doing** de faire).
2 *verb* to d. that rêver que.
3 *noun* rêve *m*; to have a d. faire un rêve; to have a d. about rêver de; a d. house/*etc* une maison/*etc* de rêve.

dream up *verb* to d. something up imaginer quelque chose.

dreamt *see* dream.

dreary *adjective* (*gloomy*) morne; (*boring*) ennuyeux.

drench *verb* tremper; to get drenched se faire tremper.

dress
1 *noun* (*woman's*) robe *f*; (*style of dressing*) tenue *f*.
2 *verb* (*person*) habiller; (*wound*) panser; to get dressed s'habiller.

dressing *noun* (*for wound*) pansement *m*; (*seasoning*) assaisonnement *m*.

dressing gown *noun* robe *f* de chambre.

dressing table *noun* coiffeuse *f*.

dressmaker *noun* couturière *f*.

dress up *verb* (*smartly*) bien s'habiller; (*in disguise*) se déguiser (**as** en).

drew *see* draw[1,2].

dribble *verb*
1 (*of baby*) baver.
2 Football dribbler.

dried *adjective* (*fruit*) sec (*f* sèche); (*flowers*) séché.

drier = dryer.

drift *verb* (*of boat*) aller à la dérive.

drill
1 *noun* (*tool*) perceuse *f*; (*bit*) mèche *f*; (*pneumatic*) marteau *m* piqueur; (*dentist's*) roulette *f*.
2 *verb* (*hole*) percer.

drink
1 *noun* boisson *f*; (*glass of something*) verre *m*; to give somebody a d. donner (quelque chose) à boire à quelqu'un.
2 *verb* boire (**out of** dans); to d. to somebody boire à la santé de quelqu'un.

drinkable *adjective* potable; (*not unpleasant*) buvable.

drink down *verb* to d. something down boire quelque chose.

drinking water *noun* eau *f* potable.

drink up *verb*
1 (*liquid*) boire.
2 (*finish one's glass*) finir son verre.

drip
1 *verb* (*of liquid*) dégouliner; (*of tap*) fuir.
2 *noun* goutte *f*; (*fool*) Familiar nouille *f*.

drip-dry *adjective* (*shirt etc*) qui ne se repasse pas.

dripping *adjective* & *adverb* d. (wet) dégoulinant.

drive
1 *noun* promenade *f* en voiture;

(*energy*) énergie *f*; (*road to house*) allée *f*; **an hour's d.** une heure de voiture; **left-hand d.** (véhicule *m* à) conduite *f* à gauche.

2 *verb* (*vehicle, passenger*) conduire; (*machine*) actionner; (*chase away*) chasser; **to d. somebody to do** pousser quelqu'un à faire; **to d. somebody mad** *or* **crazy** rendre quelqu'un fou.

3 *verb* (*drive a car*) conduire; (*go by car*) rouler; **to d. on the left** rouler à gauche; **to d. to** aller (en voiture) à.

drive along *verb* (*in car*) rouler.

drive away *verb*
1 (*chase*) chasser.
2 (*leave*) partir (en voiture).

drive back *verb*
1 (*enemy*) repousser; (*passenger*) ramener (en voiture).
2 (*come back*) revenir (en voiture).

drive in *verb* (*nail*) enfoncer.

drivel *noun* idioties *fpl*.

drive off *verb* partir (en voiture).

drive on *verb* (*in car*) continuer.

drive out *verb* **to d. somebody/ something out** (*chase away*) chasser quelqu'un/quelque chose.

driven *see* drive.

driver *noun* conducteur, -trice *m or f*; (*train or engine*) **d.** mécanicien *m*; **she's a good d.** elle conduit bien.

drive up *verb* arriver (en voiture).

driving *noun* conduite *f*.

driving lesson *noun* leçon *f* de conduite.

driving licence *noun* permis *m* de conduire.

driving school *noun* auto-école *f*.

driving test *noun* examen *m* du permis de conduire.

drizzle
1 *noun* bruine *f*.
2 *verb* bruiner.

droop *verb* (*of flower*) se faner.

drop
1 *noun* (*of liquid*) goutte *f*; (*fall*) baisse *f* (**in** de).
2 *verb* (*object*) laisser tomber; (*price, voice*) baisser; (*passenger, goods*) déposer; (*put*) mettre; (*leave out*) omettre; **to d. a line** to écrire un petit mot à.
3 *verb* (*fall*) tomber; (*of price*) baisser.

drop back *or* **behind** *verb* rester en arrière.

drop in *verb* passer (**on somebody** chez quelqu'un).

drop off *verb*
1 (*fall asleep*) s'endormir; (*fall off*) tomber; (*of sales*) diminuer.
2 (*passenger*) déposer.

drop out *verb* (*withdraw*) se retirer.

drought *noun* sécheresse *f*.

drove *see* drive.

drown *verb*
1 (*die*) se noyer.
2 (*person, animal*) noyer; **to d. oneself** se noyer.

drowsy *adjective* **to be** *or* **feel d.** avoir sommeil.

drug
1 *noun* médicament *m*; (*narcotic*) stupéfiant *m*; **drugs** (*narcotics in general*) la drogue; **to be on drugs, take drugs** se droguer.
2 *verb* droguer.

drug addict *noun* drogué, -ée *m or f*.

drum *noun* tambour *m*; (*for oil*) bidon *m*; **the drums** (*of orchestra* *etc*) la batterie.

drummer *noun* (joueur, -euse *m or f* de) tambour *m*; (*in pop or jazz group*) batteur *m*.

drumstick *noun* baguette *f* (de tambour).

drunk
1 *see* drink.
2 *adjective* ivre; **to get d.** s'enivrer.
3 *noun* ivrogne *m or f*.

drunkard *noun* ivrogne *m or f*.

drunken *adjective* (*driver*) ivre; **d. driving** conduite *f* en état d'ivresse.

dry
1 *adjective* sec (*f* sèche); (*well, river*) à sec; (*day*) sans pluie; (*book*) aride; **to keep something d.** tenir quelque chose au sec; **to feel** *or* **be d.** (*thirsty*) avoir soif.
2 *verb* sécher; (*by wiping*) essuyer.

dry-clean *verb* nettoyer à sec.

dry-cleaner *noun* teinturier, -ière *m or f*.

dryer *noun* séchoir *m*; (*on stand*) casque *m*.

dry off *verb* sécher.

dry up *verb* sécher; (*dry the dishes*) essuyer la vaisselle.

dual *adjective* double.

dual carriageway *noun* route *f* à deux voies.

dub *verb* (*film*) doubler.

dubious *adjective* douteux; **I'm d. about going** je me demande si je dois y aller.

duchess *noun* duchesse *f*.

duck
1 *noun* canard *m*.
2 *verb* se baisser (vivement).

due *adjective* (*money*) dû (*f* due) (**to** à); (*rent, bill*) à payer; **to fall**

d. échoir; he's d. (*to arrive*) il doit arriver; **in d. course** en temps utile; (*finally*) à la longue; **d. to** dû à; (*because of*) à cause de.

duel *noun* duel *m*.

duffel *or* **duffle coat** *noun* duffel-coat *m*.

dug *see* dig.

duke *noun* duc *m*.

dull *adjective* (*boring*) ennuyeux; (*colour*) terne; (*weather*) maussade; (*sound, ache*) sourd.

dullness *noun* (*of life, town*) monotonie *f*.

dumb *adjective* muet (*f* muette); (*stupid*) idiot.

dummy *noun* (*of baby*) sucette *f*; (*for clothes*) mannequin *m*.

dump
1 *verb* (*rubbish*) déposer.
2 *noun* (*dull town*) *Familiar* trou *m*; (*rubbish*) **d.** tas *m* d'ordures; (*place*) dépôt *m* d'ordures; (*room*) dépotoir *m*.

dump truck *noun* camion *m* à benne basculante.

dungarees *plural noun* (*of child, workman*) salopette *f*.

duplicate
1 *noun* double *m*; **in d.** en deux exemplaires.
2 *adjective* **a d. copy** un double.

durable *adjective* (*material*) résistant.

duration *noun* durée *f*.

during *preposition* pendant.

dusk *noun* crépuscule *m*.

dust
1 *noun* poussière *f*.
2 *verb* (*furniture etc*) épousseter.
3 *verb* faire la poussière.

dustbin *noun* poubelle *f*.

dustcart *noun* camion-benne *m*.

dust cover *noun* (*for furniture*) housse *f*; (*for book*) jaquette *f*.

duster *noun* chiffon *m* (à poussière).

dustman *noun* éboueur *m*.

dusty *adjective* poussiéreux.

Dutch
1 *adjective* hollandais.
2 *noun* (*language*) hollandais *m*.

Dutchman *noun* Hollandais *m*; the D. les Hollandais *mpl*.

Dutchwoman *noun* Hollandaise *f*.

duty *noun* devoir *m*; (*tax*) droit *m*; **duties** (*responsibilities*) fonctions *fpl*; **on d.** (*policeman, teacher*) de service; (*doctor*) de garde; **off d.** libre.

duty-free *adjective* (*goods, shop*) hors-taxe *invariable*.

duvet *noun* couette *f*.

dwarf *noun* nain *m*, naine *f*.

dye
1 *noun* teinture *f*.
2 *verb* teindre; **to d. green** teindre en vert.

dynamic *adjective* dynamique.

dynamite *noun* dynamite *f*.

dynamo *noun* dynamo *f*.

dyslexic *adjective & noun* dyslexique (*m or f*).

E

each
  1 *adjective* chaque.
  2 *pronoun*; **e. (one)** chacun, -une; **e. other** l'un(e) l'autre, *plural* les un(e)s les autres; **e. of us** chacun, -une d'entre nous.

eager *adjective* impatient (**to do** de faire); (*enthusiastic*) plein d'enthousiasme; **to be e. to do** (*want*) tenir (beaucoup) à faire.

eagerly *adverb* avec enthousiasme; (*to await*) avec impatience.

eagerness *noun* impatience *f* (**to do** de faire).

eagle *noun* aigle *m*.

ear *noun* oreille *f*.

earache *noun* mal *m* d'oreille; **to have e.** avoir mal à l'oreille.

early
  1 *adjective* (*first*) premier; (*age*) jeune; **it's e.** (*on clock*) il est tôt; (*referring to meeting*) c'est tôt; **it's too e. to get up** il est trop tôt pour se lever; **to be e.** (*ahead of time*) être en avance; **to have an e. meal/night** manger/se coucher de bonne heure; **in e. summer** au début de l'été.
  2 *adverb* tôt, de bonne heure; (*ahead of time*) en avance; **as e. as possible** le plus tôt possible; **earlier (on)** plus tôt.

earn *verb* gagner; (*interest*) rapporter.

earnings *plural noun* (*wages*) rémunération *fpl*.

earphones *plural noun* casque *m*.

earplug *noun* boule *f* Quiès ®.

earring *noun* boucle *f* d'oreille.

earth *noun* (*world, ground*) terre *f*; **where/what on e.?** où/que diable?

earthquake *noun* tremblement *m* de terre.

ease
  1 *noun* facilité *f*; **with e.** facilement; **(ill) at e.** (mal) à l'aise.
  2 *verb* (*pain*) soulager; (*mind*) calmer.

ease (off *or* **up)** *verb* (*become less*) diminuer; (*of pain*) se calmer; (*not work so hard*) se relâcher.

easel *noun* chevalet *m*.

ease off *verb* **to e. something off** enlever quelque chose doucement.

easily *adverb* facilement; **e. the best/etc** de loin le meilleur/etc.

east
  1 *noun* est *m*; **(to the) e. of** à l'est de.
  2 *adjective* (*coast*) est *invariable*; (*wind*) d'est.
  3 *adverb* à l'est.

eastbound *adjective* en direction de l'est.

Easter *noun* Pâques *m or fpl*; **Happy E.!** joyeuses Pâques!

eastern *adjective* (*coast*) est *invariable*; **E. Europe** l'Europe *f* de l'Est.

eastward(s) *adverb* vers l'est.

easy
  1 *adjective* facile; (*life*) tranquille; **it's e. to do** c'est facile à faire.
  2 *adverb* doucement; **go e. on** (*sugar etc*) vas-y doucement avec; (*person*) ne sois pas trop dur avec; **take it e.** calme-toi; (*rest*)

repose-toi; (*work less*) ne te fatigue pas.

easy chair *noun* fauteuil *m.*

easygoing *adjective* (*carefree*) insouciant; (*easy to get on with*) facile à vivre.

eat *verb* manger; (*meal*) prendre.

eaten *see* eat.

eater *noun* big e. gros mangeur *m*, grosse mangeuse *f.*

eating apple *noun* pomme *f* à couteau.

eat out *verb* manger au restaurant.

eat up *verb* to e. something up (*finish*) finir quelque chose.

eau de Cologne *noun* eau *f* de Cologne.

EC *abbreviation* (*European Community*) CEE *f.*

eccentric *adjective* & *noun* excentrique (*m or f*).

echo
1 *noun* écho *m.*
2 *verb* the explosion/*etc* echoed l'écho de l'explosion/*etc* se répercuta.

economic *adjective* économique; (*profitable*) rentable.

economical *adjective* économique.

economize *verb* économiser (on sur).

economy *noun* économie *f.*

economy class *noun* (*on aircraft*) classe *f* touriste.

edge *noun* bord *m*; (*of forest*) lisière *f*; (*of town*) abords *mpl*; (*of page*) marge *f*; (*of knife*) tranchant *m*; on e. énervé; (*nerves*) tendu.

edge forward *verb* avancer doucement.

edible *adjective* comestible; (*not unpleasant*) mangeable.

edit *verb* (*newspaper*) diriger; (*article*) mettre au point; (*film*) monter; (*text*) éditer; (*compile*) rédiger.

edition *noun* édition *f.*

editor *noun* (*of newspaper*) rédacteur *m* en chef; (*compiler*) rédacteur, -trice *m or f.*

editorial *noun* e. staff rédaction *f.*

educate *verb* éduquer; (*pupil, mind*) former.

educated *adjective* (**well-**)e. instruit.

education *noun* éducation *f*; (*teaching, training*) formation *f.*

educational *adjective* (*establishment*) d'enseignement; (*game*) éducatif.

EEC *abbreviation* (*European Economic Community*) CEE *f.*

eel *noun* anguille *f.*

effect *noun* effet *m* (on sur); to put into e. mettre en application; to come into e., take e. (*of law*) entrer en vigueur; to take e. (*of drug*) agir; to have an e. (*of medicine*) faire de l'effet.

effective *adjective* (*efficient*) efficace; (*striking*) frappant.

effectively *adverb* efficacement; (*in fact*) effectivement.

efficiency *noun* efficacité *f*; (*of machine*) performances *fpl.*

efficient *adjective* efficace; (*machine*) performant.

efficiently *adverb* efficacement; to work e. (*of machine*) bien fonctionner.

effort *noun* effort *m*; to make an e. faire un effort (to pour); it isn't worth the e. ça ne *or* n'en vaut pas la peine.

e.g. *abbreviation* par exemple.

egg *noun* œuf *m*.

eggcup *noun* coquetier *m*.

egg timer *noun* sablier *m*.

Egypt *noun* l'Égypte *f*.

Egyptian *adjective & noun* égyptien, -ienne (*m or f*).

eh? *interjection Familiar* hein?

eiderdown *noun* édredon *m*.

eight *adjective & noun* huit (*m*).

eighteen *adjective & noun* dix-huit (*m*).

eighth *adjective & noun* huitième (*m or f*).

eighty *adjective & noun* quatre-vingts (*m*); e.-one quatre-vingt-un.

either
1 *adjective & pronoun* (*one or other*) l'un(e) ou l'autre; (*with negative*) ni l'un(e) ni l'autre; (*each*) chaque; **on e. side** de chaque côté.
2 *adverb* **she can't swim e.** elle ne sait pas nager non plus; **I don't e.** moi non plus.
3 *conjunction* **e. ... or** ou (bien) ... ou (bien); (*with negative*) ni ... ni.

elastic *adjective & noun* élastique (*m*).

elastic band *noun* élastique *m*.

elbow
1 *noun* coude *m*.
2 *verb* **to e. one's way** se frayer un chemin (à coups de coude) (**through** à travers).

elder *adjective & noun* (*of two people*) aîné, -ée (*m or f*).

elderly *adjective* âgé.

eldest *adjective & noun* aîné, -ée (*m or f*); **his** *or* **her e. brother** l'aîné de ses frères.

elect *verb* élire (**to** à).

election
1 *noun* élection *f*; **general e.** élections *fpl* législatives.
2 *adjective* (*campaign*) électoral; (*day*, *results*) du scrutin.

electric(al) *adjective* électrique.

electric blanket *noun* couverture *f* chauffante.

electrician *noun* électricien *m*.

electricity *noun* électricité *f*.

electrocute *verb* électrocuter.

electronic *adjective* électronique.

elegance *noun* élégance *f*.

elegant *adjective* élégant.

elegantly *adverb* avec élégance.

element *noun* élément *m*; (*of heater*) résistance *f*.

elementary *adjective* élémentaire.

elephant *noun* éléphant *m*.

elevator *noun* ascenseur *m*.

eleven *adjective & noun* onze (*m*).

eleventh *adjective & noun* onzième (*m or f*).

eligible *adjective* (*for post*) admissible (**for** à); **to be e. for** (*entitled to*) avoir droit à.

eliminate *verb* supprimer; (*applicant*, *possibility*) éliminer.

else *adverb* d'autre; **everybody e.** tous les autres; **somebody/nobody/nothing e.** quelqu'un/personne/rien d'autre; **something e.** autre chose; **anything e.?** autre chose?; (*in shop*) ce sera tout?; **somewhere e.** ailleurs; **how e.?** de quelle autre façon?; **or e.** ou bien.

elsewhere *adverb* ailleurs.

elude *verb* (*of word*, *name*) échapper à.

e-mail
1 *noun* courrier *m* électronique.
2 *verb* envoyer un courrier électronique à.

embark *verb* (s')embarquer.

embark on *verb* (*start*) commencer.

embarrass *verb* embarrasser.

embarrassing *adjective* embarrassant.

embarrassment *noun* embarras *m*.

embassy *noun* ambassade *f*.

emblem *noun* emblème *m*.

embrace
1 *verb* (*somebody*) étreindre.
2 *verb* (*of two people*) s'étreindre.
3 *noun* étreinte *f*.

embroider *verb* (*cloth*) broder.

embroidery *noun* broderie *f*.

emerald *noun* émeraude *f*.

emerge *verb* apparaître (**from** de); (*from hole*) sortir; (*of truth, from water*) émerger.

emergency
1 *noun* urgence *f*; **in an e.** en cas d'urgence.
2 *adjective* (*measure*) d'urgence; (*exit, brake*) de secours; **e. landing** atterrissage *m* forcé.

emigrate *verb* émigrer.

emotion *noun* (*strength of feeling*) émotion *f*; (*joy, love etc*) sentiment *m*.

emotional *adjective* (*person, reaction*) émotif; (*story*) émouvant.

emperor *noun* empereur *m*.

emphasis *noun* (*in word or phrase*) accent *m*; **to lay** *or* **put e. on** mettre l'accent sur.

emphasize *verb* souligner (**that** que).

empire *noun* empire *m*.

employ *verb* employer.

employee *noun* employé, -ée *m or f*.

employer *noun* patron, -onne *m or f*.

employment *noun* emploi *m*; **place of e.** lieu *m* de travail.

employment agency *noun* bureau *m* de placement.

empty
1 *adjective* vide; (*threat, promise*) vain; **to return e.-handed** revenir les mains vides.
2 *verb* (*of building, tank etc*) se vider.

empty (out) *verb* (*box, liquid etc*) vider; (*vehicle*) décharger; (*objects in box etc*) sortir (**from** de).

emulsion *noun* (*paint*) peinture *f* acrylique.

enable *verb* **to e. somebody to do** permettre à quelqu'un de faire.

enamel
1 *noun* émail *m* (*plural* émaux).
2 *adjective* en émail.

enchanting *adjective* charmant, enchanteur (*f* enchanteresse).

enclose *verb* (*send with letter*) joindre (**in, with** à); (*fence off*) clôturer.

enclosed *adjective* (*space*) clos; (*receipt etc*) ci-joint.

enclosure *noun* (*in letter*) pièce *f* jointe; (*place*) enceinte *f*.

encounter
1 *verb* rencontrer.
2 *noun* rencontre *f*.

encourage *verb* encourager (**to do** à faire).

encouragement *noun* encouragement *m*.

encyclopaedia *noun* encyclopédie *f*.

end

1 noun (of street, room etc) bout m; (of meeting, month, book etc) fin f; (purpose) fin f, but m; **at an e.** (discussion etc) fini; (patience) à bout; **in the e.** à la fin; **to come to an e.** prendre fin; **to put an e. to, bring to an e.** mettre fin à; **no e. of** Familiar beaucoup de; **for days on e.** pendant des jours et des jours.

2 verb finir (**with** par); (rumour) mettre fin à; **to e. in failure** se solder par un échec.

endanger verb mettre en danger.

ending noun fin f; (of word) terminaison f.

endive noun (curly) chicorée f; (smooth) endive f.

endless adjective interminable.

endorse verb (cheque) endosser; (action) approuver.

endorsement noun (on driving licence) contravention f.

end up verb **to e. up doing** finir par faire; **to e. up in** (London etc) se retrouver à; **he ended up in prison/a doctor** il a fini en prison/par devenir médecin.

endurance noun endurance f.

endure verb supporter (**doing** de faire).

enemy noun & adjective ennemi, -ie (m or f).

energetic adjective énergique.

energy

1 noun énergie f.

2 adjective (resources etc) énergétique; (crisis) de l'énergie.

enforce verb (law) faire respecter.

engaged adjective (person, toilet, phone) occupé; **e. (to be married)** fiancé; **to get e.** se fiancer.

engagement noun (to marry) fiançailles fpl; (meeting) rendez-vous invariable m; **e. ring** bague f de fiançailles.

engine noun (of vehicle) moteur m; (of train) locomotive f.

engineer noun ingénieur m; (repairer) dépanneur, -euse m or f.

engineering noun ingénierie f.

England noun l'Angleterre f.

English

1 adjective anglais; (teacher) d'anglais; **the E. Channel** la Manche.

2 noun (language) anglais m; **the E.** les Anglais mpl.

Englishman noun Anglais m.

English-speaking adjective anglophone.

Englishwoman noun Anglaise f.

engrave verb graver.

engraving noun gravure f.

enjoy verb aimer (**doing** faire); (meal) apprécier; **to e. the evening** passer une bonne soirée; **to e. oneself** s'amuser; **to e. being in London** se plaire à Londres.

enjoyable adjective agréable.

enjoyment noun plaisir m.

enlarge verb agrandir.

enlighten verb éclairer (**somebody on** or **about something** quelqu'un sur quelque chose).

enormous adjective énorme.

enormously adverb (very much) énormément; (very) extrêmement.

enough

1 adjective & noun assez (de); **e. time/cups/etc** assez de temps/de tasses/etc; **to have e. to live on** avoir de quoi vivre; **e. to drink** assez à boire; **to have had e. of** en avoir assez de; **that's e.** ça suffit.

2 *adverb* assez; **big/good/***etc* e. assez grand/bon/*etc* (**to** pour).

enquire = inquire.

enquiry = inquiry.

enrol *verb* s'inscrire (**in, for** à).

enrolment *noun* inscription *f*.

ensure *verb* assurer; **to e. that** s'assurer que.

entail *verb* supposer.

enter
1 *verb* (*room, vehicle etc*) entrer dans; (*university*) s'inscrire à; (*write down*) inscrire (**in** dans); **to e. somebody for** (*exam*) présenter quelqu'un à; **to e. something in** (*competition*) présenter quelque chose à; **it didn't e. my head** *or* **mind** ça ne m'est pas venu à l'esprit.
2 *verb* (*go in*) entrer.

enter for *verb* (*race, exam*) s'inscrire pour.

enter into *verb* (*career*) entrer dans; (*agreement*) conclure; **to e. into a conversation** entrer en conversation.

enterprise *noun* (*undertaking, firm*) entreprise *f*; (*spirit*) initiative *f*.

enterprising *adjective* plein d'initiative.

entertain *verb*
1 (*amuse*) amuser; (*guest*) recevoir.
2 (*receive guests*) recevoir.

entertainer *noun* artiste *m or f*.

entertaining *adjective* amusant.

entertainment *noun* amusement *m*; (*show*) spectacle *m*.

enthusiasm *noun* enthousiasme *m*.

enthusiast *noun* enthousiaste *m*

or f; **jazz/***etc* e. passionné, -ée *m or f* de jazz/*etc*.

enthusiastic *adjective* enthousiaste; (*golfer etc*) passionné; **to be e. about** (*hobby*) être passionné de; (*gift*) être emballé par; **to get e.** s'emballer (**about** pour).

enthusiastically *adverb* avec enthousiasme.

entire *adjective* entier.

entirely *adverb* tout à fait.

entitle *verb* **to e. somebody to do** donner à quelqu'un le droit de faire; **to e. somebody to something** donner à quelqu'un (le) droit à quelque chose.

entitled *adjective* **to be e. to do** avoir le droit de faire; **to be e. to something** avoir droit à quelque chose.

entrance *noun* entrée *f* (**to** de); (*to university*) admission *f* (**to** à); **e. exam** examen *m* d'entrée.

entrant *noun* (*in race*) concurrent, -ente *m or f*; (*for exam*) candidat, -ate *m or f*.

entry *noun* (*way in, action*) entrée *f*; (*bookkeeping item*) écriture *f*; (*dictionary term*) entrée *f*; (*in competition*) objet *m* (*or* œuvre *f or* projet *m*) soumis au jury; **'no e.'** 'entrée interdite'; (*road sign*) 'sens interdit'.

entry form *noun* feuille *f* d'inscription.

envelope *noun* enveloppe *f*.

envious *adjective* envieux (**of something** de quelque chose); **e. of somebody** jaloux de quelqu'un.

environment *noun* milieu *m*; (*natural*) environnement *m*.

environmental *adjective* du milieu; de l'environnement.

envy
 1 *noun* envie *f*.
 2 *verb* envier (somebody something quelque chose à quelqu'un).

epidemic *noun* épidémie *f*.

episode *noun* épisode *m*.

equal
 1 *adjective* égal (to à); to be e.
 to (*number*) égaler; she's e. to
 (*task*) elle est à la hauteur de.
 2 *noun* (*person*) égal, -ale *m or f*.

equality *noun* égalité *f*.

equalize *verb* (*score*) égaliser.

equally *adverb* également; (*to
 divide*) en parts égales.

equation *noun* équation *f*.

equator *noun* équateur *m*.

equip *verb* équiper (with de);
 (well-)equipped with pourvu
 de; (well-)equipped to do compétent pour faire.

equipment *noun* équipement *m*.

equivalent *adjective & noun*
 équivalent (*m*).

erase *verb* effacer.

eraser *noun* (*rubber for pencil
 marks*) gomme *f*.

erect
 1 *adjective* (*upright*) (bien) droit.
 2 *verb* construire; (*statue etc*) éri-
 ger; (*scaffolding, tent*) monter.

errand *noun* commission *f*.

erratic *adjective* (*service, machine
 etc*) capricieux; (*person*) luna-
 tique.

error *noun* erreur *f*; to do something in e. faire quelque chose
 par erreur.

escalator *noun* escalier *m* roulant.

escape
 1 *verb* (*run away*) s'échapper; to
 e. from (*person*) échapper à;

(*place*) s'échapper de.
 2 *verb* (*death*) échapper à; (*punishment*) éviter; that name escapes me ce nom m'échappe.
 3 *noun* (*of gas*) fuite *f*; (*of person*)
 évasion *f*.

escort
 1 *noun* (*soldiers etc*) escorte *f*.
 2 *verb* escorter.

Eskimo *noun* Esquimau, -aude *m
 or f*.

especially *adverb* (tout) spécialement; e. as d'autant plus que.

espresso *noun* express *invariable
 m*.

essay *noun* (*at school*) rédaction
 f; (*at university*) dissertation *f*.

essential *adjective* essentiel.

essentially *adverb* essentiellement.

establish *verb* établir.

establishment *noun* (*institution, firm*) établissement *m*.

estate *noun* (*land*) terre(s) *f(pl)*;
 housing e. lotissement *m*;
 (*workers'*) cité *f* (ouvrière);
 industrial e. zone *f* industrielle.

estate agent *noun* agent *m* immobilier.

estate car *noun* break *m*.

estimate
 1 *verb* estimer (that que).
 2 *noun* évaluation *f*; (*price for
 work to be done*) devis *m*.

Estonia *noun* l'Estonie *f*.

Estonian *adjective & noun* estonien, -ienne (*m or f*).

etiquette *noun* étiquette *f*.

Euro- *prefix* euro-.

Euro, euro *noun* (*European
 currency*) euro *m*.

Europe *noun* l'Europe *f*.

European *adjective & noun*
 européen, -éenne (*m or f*).

evacuate verb évacuer.

evade verb éviter; (pursuer, tax) échapper à; (question) éluder; (law) contourner.

evaluate verb évaluer (at à).

evaporated milk noun lait m concentré.

eve noun on the e. of à la veille de.

even
1 adjective (flat) uni; (equal) égal; (regular) régulier; (number) pair; **to get e. with somebody** se venger de quelqu'un; **we're e.** nous sommes quittes; (in score) nous sommes à égalité; **to break e.** (financially) s'y retrouver.
2 adverb même; **e. better/more** encore mieux/plus; **e. if** or **though** même si; **e. so** quand même.

evening noun soir m; (whole evening, event) soirée f; **in the e.** le soir; **at seven in the e.** à sept heures du soir; **every Tuesday e.** tous les mardis soir; **all e. (long)** toute la soirée.

evening dress noun tenue f de soirée; (of woman) robe f du soir.

evenly adverb de manière égale; (regularly) régulièrement.

even out or **up** verb to e. something out or up égaliser quelque chose.

event noun événement m; (in sport) épreuve f; **in the e. of death** en cas de décès; **in any e.** en tout cas.

eventual adjective final.

eventually adverb finalement; (some day or other) un jour ou l'autre.

ever adverb jamais; **more than e.** plus que jamais; **nothing e.** jamais rien; **hardly e.** presque ja-

mais; **the first e.** le tout premier; **e. since** (that event etc) depuis; **e. since then** depuis lors; **for e.** pour toujours; (continually) sans cesse; **e. so happy/etc** vraiment heureux/etc; **it's e. such a pity** c'est vraiment dommage; **why e. not?** mais pourquoi pas?

every adjective chaque; **e. one** chacun, -une; **e. single one** tous or toutes (sans exception); **e. other day** tous les deux jours; **e. so often, e. now and then** de temps en temps.

everybody pronoun tout le monde; **e. in turn** chacun or chacune à son tour.

everyday adjective (life) de tous les jours; (ordinary) banal (mpl banals); **in e. use** d'usage courant.

everyone = everybody.

everything pronoun tout; **e. I have** tout ce que j'ai.

everywhere adverb partout; **e. she goes** où qu'elle aille.

evidence noun preuve(s) f(pl); (given by witness etc) témoignage m; **e. of** (wear etc) des signes mpl de.

evident adjective évident (**that** que).

evidently adverb évidemment; (apparently) apparemment.

evil
1 adjective (influence, person) malfaisant; (deed, system) mauvais.
2 noun mal m.

ewe noun brebis f.

ex- prefix ex-; **ex-wife** ex-femme f.

exact adjective exact; **to be e. about something** préciser quelque chose.

exactly *adverb* exactement.

exaggerate *verb* exagérer.

exaggeration *noun* exagération *f*.

exam *noun* examen *m*.

examination *noun* (*in school etc*) examen *m*; (*of passport*) contrôle *m*; **class e.** devoir *m* sur table.

examine *verb* examiner; (*accounts, luggage*) vérifier; (*passport*) contrôler; (*candidate*) interroger.

examiner *noun* examinateur, -trice *m or f*.

example *noun* exemple *m*; **for e.** par exemple; **to set an e.** donner l'exemple (**to** à).

exceed *verb* dépasser.

excel *verb* **to e. in something** être excellent en quelque chose.

excellent *adjective* excellent.

except *preposition* sauf, excepté; **e. for** à part; **e. that** sauf que.

exception *noun* exception *f*; **with the e. of** à l'exception de.

exceptional *adjective* exceptionnel.

exceptionally *adverb* exceptionnellement.

excerpt *noun* extrait *m*.

excess
1 *noun* excès *m*; (*surplus*) excédent *m*.
2 *adjective* **e. fare** supplément *m* (de billet); **e. luggage** *or* **baggage** excédent *m* de bagages.

excessive *adjective* excessif.

excessively *adverb* (*too, too much*) excessivement; (*very*) extrêmement.

exchange
1 *verb* échanger (**for** contre).
2 *noun* échange *m*; (*of foreign currencies*) change *m*; (**telephone**) **e. central** *m* (téléphonique); **in e.** en échange (**for** de).

excite *verb* (*enthuse*) passionner.

excited *adjective* (*happy*) surexcité; (*nervous*) énervé; **to get e.** (*nervous, enthusiastic*) s'exciter; **she's e. about her new car** elle est toute contente d'avoir une nouvelle voiture.

excitement *noun* agitation *f*; (*emotion*) vive émotion *f*.

exciting *adjective* (*book etc*) passionnant.

exclaim *verb* s'exclamer (**that** que).

exclamation mark *noun* point *m* d'exclamation.

exclude *verb* exclure (**from** de).

exclusive *adjective* exclusif; (*club*) fermé; **e. of wine**/*etc* vin/*etc* non compris.

excursion *noun* excursion *f*.

excuse
1 *verb* excuser (**somebody for doing** quelqu'un d'avoir fait, quelqu'un de faire); (*exempt*) dispenser (**from** de).
2 *noun* excuse *f*.

ex-directory *adjective* sur liste rouge.

execute *verb* (*criminal*) exécuter.

execution *noun* exécution *f*.

executive
1 *adjective* (*job*) de cadre; (*car*) de direction.
2 *noun* (*person*) cadre *m*; **senior e.** cadre *m* supérieur; **junior e.** jeune cadre *m*; **sales e.** cadre *m* commercial.

exempt
1 *adjective* dispensé (**from** de).
2 *verb* dispenser (**from** de).

exemption *noun* dispense *f*.

exercise
1 *noun* exercice *m*.
2 *verb* (*muscles*, *rights*) exercer; (*dog*, *horse*) promener; (*tact*, *judgment*) faire preuve de.
3 *verb* (*do sport*) faire de l'exercice.

exercise book *noun* cahier *m*.

exert *verb* exercer; **to e. oneself** (*physically*) se dépenser; **don't e. yourself!** ne te fatigue pas!

exertion *noun* effort *m*.

exhaust
1 *verb* épuiser; **to become exhausted** s'épuiser.
2 *noun* **e. (pipe)** tuyau *m* d'échappement.

exhausting *adjective* épuisant.

exhibit
1 *verb* (*put on display*) exposer.
2 *noun* objet *m* exposé.

exhibition *noun* exposition *f*.

exhibitor *noun* exposant, -ante *m or f*.

exist *verb* exister; (*live*) vivre (**on** de).

existence *noun* existence *f*; **to be in e.** exister.

existing *adjective* (*situation*) actuel.

exit *noun* sortie *f*.

exorbitant *adjective* exorbitant.

expand *verb*
1 (*trade*, *ideas*) développer; (*production*) augmenter; (*gas*, *metal*) dilater.
2 (*grow*) se développer; (*of production*) augmenter; (*of gas*, *metal*) se dilater.

expanse *noun* étendue *f*.

expansion *noun* (*of trade etc*) développement *m*.

expect *verb* s'attendre à; (*think*) penser (**that** que); (*suppose*) sup-poser (**that** que); (*await*) attendre; **to e. something from somebody/something** attendre quelque chose de quelqu'un/quelque chose; **to e. to do** compter faire; **to e. that** s'attendre à ce que (+ *subjunctive*); **I e. you to come** (*want*) je compte sur votre présence; **it was expected** c'était prévu; **she's expecting (a baby)** elle attend un bébé.

expectation *noun* attente *f*.

expedition *noun* expédition *f*.

expel *verb* (*from school*) renvoyer.

expenditure *noun* (*money*) dépenses *fpl*.

expense *noun* frais *mpl*; **business expenses** frais *mpl* généraux; **at somebody's e.** (*doing somebody no good*) aux dépens de quelqu'un.

expensive *adjective* cher.

experience
1 *noun* expérience *f*; **he's had e. of driving** il a déjà conduit.
2 *verb* connaître; (*difficulty*) éprouver.

experienced *adjective* expérimenté; **to be e. in** s'y connaître en.

experiment
1 *noun* expérience *f*.
2 *verb* faire une expérience *or* des expériences.

expert *noun* expert *m* (**on, in** en); **e. advice** les conseils d'un expert.

expertise *noun* compétence *f* (**in** en).

expire *verb* expirer.

expired *adjective* (*ticket, passport etc*) périmé.

expiry date *noun* date *f* d'expiration.

explain *verb* expliquer (**to** à, **that** que).

explain away *verb* **to e. something away** justifier quelque chose.

explanation *noun* explication *f.*

explode *verb* exploser.

exploit
1 *verb* exploiter.
2 *noun* exploit *m.*

exploration *noun* exploration *f.*

explore *verb* explorer; (*causes etc*) examiner.

explorer *noun* explorateur, -trice *m or f.*

explosion *noun* explosion *f.*

explosive *noun* explosif *m.*

export
1 *noun* exportation *f.*
2 *verb* exporter (**to** vers, **from** de).

expose *verb* exposer (**to** à); (*plot etc*) révéler; (*crook etc*) démasquer.

express
1 *verb* exprimer; **to e. oneself** s'exprimer.
2 *adjective* (*letter, delivery*) exprès *invariable*; (*train*) rapide.
3 *adverb* (*to send*) par exprès.
4 *noun* (*train*) rapide *m.*

expression *noun* (*phrase, look*) expression *f.*

expresso *noun* express *invariable m.*

extend *verb*
1 (*arm*) étendre; (*line, visit*) prolonger (**by** de); (*house*) agrandir; (*time limit*) reculer.
2 (*in space*) s'étendre (**to** jusqu'à); (*in time*) se prolonger.

extension *noun* (*for table*) rallonge *f.*; (*to building*) agrandissement(s) *m(pl)*; (*of phone*) appareil *m* supplémentaire; (*of office phone*) poste *m*; **e. (cable** *or* **lead)** rallonge *f.*

extensive *adjective* étendu; (*repairs, damage*) important.

extensively *adverb* (*very much*) énormément, considérablement.

extent *noun* (*scope*) étendue *f*; (*size*) importance *f*; **to a large/ certain e.** dans une large/certaine mesure; **to such an e. that** à tel point que.

exterior *adjective & noun* extérieur (*m*).

external *adjective* extérieur; **for e. use** (*medicine*) à usage externe.

extinguisher *noun* (**fire**) **e.** extincteur *m.*

extra
1 *adjective* supplémentaire; **one e. glass** un verre de *or* en plus; **to be e.** (*spare*) être en trop; (*cost more*) être en supplément; **e. charge** *or* **portion** supplément *m.*
2 *adverb* **to pay e.** payer un supplément; **wine costs** *or* **is 3 francs e.** il y a un supplément de 3F pour le vin.
3 *noun* (*perk*) à-côté *m*; **extras** (*expenses*) frais *mpl* supplémentaires.

extra - *prefix* extra-.

extract
1 *verb* extraire (**from** de).
2 *noun* extrait *m.*

extra-curricular *adjective* extra-scolaire.

extraordinary *adjective* extra-ordinaire.

extra-special *adjective* (*occasion*) très spécial.

extravagant *adjective* (*wasteful with money*) dépensier.

extreme
1 *adjective* extrême; (*danger, poverty*) très grand.
2 *noun* extrême *m*.

extremely *adverb* extrêmement.

eye *noun* œil *m* (*plural* yeux); to keep an e. on surveiller; to lay *or* set eyes on voir; to take one's eyes off somebody/something quitter quelqu'un/quelque chose des yeux.

eyebrow *noun* sourcil *m*.

eyelash *noun* cil *m*.

eyelid *noun* paupière *f*.

eyeliner *noun* eye-liner *m*.

eye shadow *noun* fard *m* à paupières.

eyesight *noun* vue *f*.

F

fabulous *adjective* (*wonderful*)
Familiar formidable.

face

   1 *noun* (*of person*) visage *m*, figure *f*; (*of clock*) cadran *m*; **f.
down** face contre terre; (*thing*)
tourné à l'envers; **f. to f.** face à
face; **to make** *or* **pull faces** faire
des grimaces.

   2 *verb* (*danger, problem etc*) faire
face à; (*accept*) accepter; (*look in
the face*) regarder bien en face;
(*be opposite*) être en face de; (*of
window*) donner sur; **faced with**
(*problem*) confronté à; **he can't
f. leaving** il n'a pas le courage de
partir.

   3 *verb* (*of house*) être orienté
(**north**/*etc* au nord/*etc*); (*be
turned*) être tourné (**towards**
vers).

facecloth *noun* gant *m* de toilette.

face up to *verb* (*danger, problem*) faire face à; (*fact*) accepter.

facilities *plural noun* (*for sports,
cooking etc*) équipements *mpl*;
(*in harbour, airport*) installations
fpl.

fact *noun* fait *m*; **as a matter of
f., in f.** en fait.

factor *noun* facteur *m*.

factory *noun* usine *f*.

fade *verb* (*of flower*) se faner; (*of
light*) baisser; (*of colour*) passer;
(*of fabric*) se décolorer.

fade (away) *verb* (*of sound*)
s'affaiblir.

fag *noun* (*cigarette*) *Familiar*
clope *m* or *f*.

fail

   1 *verb* (*to be unsuccessful*)
échouer; (*of business*) faire faillite; (*of health, sight*) baisser; (*of
brakes*) lâcher; **to f. in an exam**
échouer à un examen.

   2 *verb* (*exam*) rater, échouer à;
(*candidate*) refuser, recaler; **to f.
to do** (*forget*) manquer de faire;
(*not be able*) ne pas arriver à faire.

   3 *noun* **without f.** à coup sûr.

failed *adjective* (*artist, poet*)
manqué.

failing

   1 *noun* défaut *m*.

   2 *preposition* **f. that** à défaut.

failure *noun* échec *m*; (*of business*) faillite *f*; (*person*) raté, -ée
m or f; **f. to do** incapacité *f* à
faire.

faint

   1 *adjective* faible; (*colour*) pâle; **I
haven't got the faintest idea** je
n'en ai pas la moindre idée; **to
feel f.** se sentir mal.

   2 *verb* s'évanouir.

faintly *adverb* faiblement;
(*slightly*) légèrement.

fair [1] *noun* foire *f*; (*for charity*)
fête *f*; (*funfair*) fête *f* foraine.

fair [2] *adjective* (*just*) juste; (*game,
fight*) loyal; (*rather good*) passable; (*weather*) beau; (*price*) raisonnable; **f. enough!** très bien!; **a
f. amount (of)** pas mal (de).

fair [3] *adjective* (*hair, person*)
blond.

fair copy *noun* copie *f* au propre.

fair-haired *adjective* blond.

fairly *adverb* (*to treat*) équitable-
ment; (*rather*) assez.

fairness *noun* justice *f*; (*of
person*) impartialité *f*.

fair play *noun* fair-play *invariable m.*

fair-sized *adjective* assez grand.

fairy *noun* fée *f*; f. **tale** *or* **story** conte *m* de fées.

faith *noun* foi *f*; **to have f. in somebody** avoir confiance en quelqu'un.

faithful *adjective* fidèle (**to** à).

faithfully *adverb* **yours f.** (*in letter*) veuillez agréer l'expression de mes salutations distinguées.

fake
1 *noun* faux *m*; (*person*) imposteur *m*.
2 *verb* (*document etc*) falsifier.
3 *verb* (*pretend*) faire semblant.
4 *adjective* faux (*f* fausse).

fall
1 *noun* chute *f*; (*in price etc*) baisse *f* (**in** de).
2 *verb* tomber; **to f. off** *or* **out of** *or* **down something** tomber de quelque chose; **to f. over** (*chair*) tomber en butant contre; (*balcony*) tomber de; **to f. ill** tomber malade.

fall apart *verb* (*of machine*) tomber en morceaux; (*of group*) se désagréger.

fall back on *verb* (*as last resort*) se rabattre sur.

fall behind *verb* rester en arrière; (*in work, payments*) prendre du retard.

fall down *verb* tomber; (*of building*) s'effondrer.

fallen *see* fall.

fall for *verb* tomber amoureux de; (*trick*) se laisser prendre à.

fall in *verb* (*collapse*) s'écrouler.

fall off *verb* (*come off*) se détacher; (*of numbers*) diminuer.

fall out *verb* (*quarrel*) se brouiller

(**with** avec).

fall over *verb* tomber; (*of table, vase*) se renverser.

fall through *verb* (*of plan*) tomber à l'eau.

false *adjective* faux (*f* fausse).

fame *noun* renommée *f*.

familiar *adjective* familier (**to** à); **f. with somebody** (*too friendly*) familier avec quelqu'un; **to be f. with** (*know*) connaître.

familiarity *noun* familiarité *f* (**with** avec).

familiarize *verb* **to f. oneself with** se familiariser avec.

family *noun* famille *f*.

famous *adjective* célèbre (**for** pour).

fan[1] *noun* (*held in hand*) éventail *m*; (*mechanical*) ventilateur *m*.

fan[2] *noun* (*of person*) fan *m or f*; (*of team etc*) supporter *m*; **to be a jazz/sports f.** être passionné de jazz/de sport.

fancy
1 *noun* **I took a f. to it, it took my f.** j'en ai eu envie.
2 *adjective* (*hat, button etc*) fantaisie *invariable*.
3 *verb* (*want*) avoir envie de; **f. (that)!** ça alors!

fancy dress *noun* déguisement *m*; **f. ball** bal *m* masqué.

fan heater *noun* radiateur *m* soufflant.

fantastic *adjective* fantastique.

far
1 *adverb* (*distance*) loin; **f. bigger/etc** beaucoup plus grand/*etc* (**than** que); **how f. is it to ... ?** combien y a-t-il d'ici à ... ?; **so f.** (*time*) jusqu'ici; **as f. as** (*place*) jusqu'à; **as f. as I know** autant que je sache; **as f. as I'm con-**

cerned en ce qui me concerne; **f. from doing** loin de faire; **f. away** or **off** au loin; **by f.** de loin.
2 adjective (side, end) autre.

faraway adjective lointain.

farce noun farce f.

fare noun (price) prix m du billet.

farewell interjection adieu.

far-fetched adjective tiré par les cheveux.

farm
1 noun ferme f.
2 adjective (worker, produce) agricole; **f. land** terres fpl cultivées.
3 verb cultiver.

farmer noun fermier, -ière m or f.

farmhouse noun ferme f.

farming noun agriculture f.

farmyard noun basse-cour f, cour f de ferme.

far-off adjective lointain.

farther adverb plus loin; **to get f. away** s'éloigner.

farthest
1 adjective le plus éloigné.
2 adverb le plus loin.

fascinate verb fasciner.

fascination noun fascination f.

fashion noun (style in clothes) mode f; (manner) façon f; **in f.** à la mode; **out of f.** démodé.

fashionable adjective à la mode; (place) chic invariable.

fashion show noun défilé m de mode.

fast
1 adjective rapide; **to be f.** (of clock) avancer (**by** de).
2 adverb (quickly) vite; **f. asleep** profondément endormi.

fasten verb attacher (**to** à); (door, window) fermer (bien).

fasten down or **up** verb to **f.**

something **down** or **up** attacher quelque chose.

fastener noun (clip) attache f; (of garment) fermeture f; (of bag) fermoir m; (hook) agrafe f.

fat
1 noun graisse f; (on meat) gras m.
2 adjective gras (f grasse); (cheek, salary) gros (f grosse); **to get f.** grossir.

fatal adjective mortel; (mistake etc) fatal (mpl fatals).

fate noun destin m, sort m.

father noun père m.

father-in-law noun beau-père m.

fatigue noun fatigue f.

fattening adjective (food) qui fait grossir.

fatty adjective (food) gras (f grasse).

faucet noun (tap) robinet m.

fault noun faute f; (defect) défaut m; (mistake) erreur f; **it's your f.** c'est ta faute; **to find f. (with)** critiquer.

faulty adjective défectueux.

favour
1 noun (act of kindness) service m; **to do somebody a f.** rendre service à quelqu'un; **to be in f. of** (support) être pour; (prefer) préférer.
2 verb (encourage) favoriser; (prefer) préférer.

favourable adjective favorable (**to** à).

favourite adjective & noun favori, -ite (m or f).

fax
1 noun (machine) télécopieur m, fax m; (message) télécopie f, fax m.

2 *verb* (*message*) faxer; **to f. somebody** envoyer une télécopie *or* un fax à quelqu'un.

fear
  1 *noun* crainte *f*, peur *f*; **for f. of doing** de peur de faire.
  2 *verb* craindre.

fearless *adjective* intrépide.

feast *noun* festin *m*.

feat *noun* exploit *m*.

feather *noun* plume *f*.

feature *noun* (*of face, person*) trait *m*; (*of thing, place*) caractéristique *f*.

February *noun* février *m*.

fed *see* feed.

fed up *adjective* **to be f. up** *Familiar* en avoir marre (**with** de).

fee *noun* prix *m*; **fee(s)** (*professional*) honoraires *mpl*; (*for registration*) droits *mpl*; **school** *or* **tuition fees** frais *mpl* de scolarité.

feeble *adjective* faible.

feed *verb* donner à manger à; (*breast-feed*) allaiter; (*bottle-feed*) donner le biberon à.

feedback *noun* réaction(s) *f(pl)*.

feel
  1 *noun* toucher *m*; (*feeling*) sensation *f*.
  2 *verb* (*be aware of*) sentir; (*experience*) éprouver; (*touch*) tâter; **to f. that** avoir l'impression que.
  3 *verb* (*tired, old etc*) se sentir; **I f. hot/sleepy/***etc* j'ai chaud/sommeil/*etc*; **she feels better** elle va mieux; **to f. like something** (*want*) avoir envie de quelque chose; **to f. up to doing something** (*well enough*) se sentir assez bien pour faire quelque chose; (*good enough*) se sentir de taille à faire quelque chose.

feel about *verb* tâtonner; (*in pocket etc*) fouiller.

feeling *noun* sentiment *m*; (*physical*) sensation *f*.

feet *see* foot.

fell *see* fall.

fellow *noun* (*man*) type *m*.

felt ¹ *see* feel.

felt ² *noun* feutre *m*.

felt-tip (pen) *noun* (*crayon m*) feutre *m*.

female
  1 *adjective* (*voice etc*) féminin; (*animal*) femelle; **f. student** étudiante *f*.
  2 *noun* femme *f*; (*animal*) femelle *f*.

feminine *adjective* féminin.

fence
  1 *noun* barrière *f*; (*in race*) obstacle *m*.
  2 *verb* (*with sword*) faire de l'escrime.

fence (in) *verb* (*land*) clôturer.

fencing *noun* (*sport*) escrime *f*.

fend *verb* **to f. for oneself** se débrouiller.

fern *noun* fougère *f*.

ferocious *adjective* féroce.

ferry *noun* ferry-boat *m*; (*small, for river*) bac *m*.

fertile *adjective* (*land*) fertile.

fertilizer *noun* engrais *m*.

festival *noun* festival *m* (*plural* -als).

festivities *plural noun* festivités *fpl*.

fetch ¹ *verb* (*bring*) amener; (*object*) apporter; **to (go and) f.** aller chercher.

fetch ² *verb* (*be sold for*) rapporter.

fetch in *verb* **to f. something in** rentrer quelque chose.

fetch out *verb* to f. something out sortir quelque chose.

fête *noun* fête *f*.

fever *noun* fièvre *f*; to have a f. avoir de la fièvre.

feverish *adjective* fiévreux.

few *adjective & pronoun* peu (de); f. towns/*etc* peu de villes/*etc*; a f. towns/*etc* quelques villes/*etc*; f. of them peu d'entre eux; a f. quelques-un(e)s (of de); a f. of us quelques-uns d'entre nous; quite a f., a good f. bon nombre (de); a f. more books/*etc* encore quelques livres/*etc*; every f. days tous les trois ou quatre jours.

fewer *adjective*
  1 moins de (than que).
  2 *pronoun* moins (than que).

fiancé(e) *noun* fiancé, -ée *m or f*.

fibre *noun* fibre *f*.

fiction *noun* (works of) f. romans *mpl*.

fiddle *noun* (dishonest act) Familiar combine *f*.

fiddle (about) with *verb* (pen etc) tripoter; (cars etc) bricoler.

fidget (about) *verb* gigoter.

field *noun* champ *m*; (for sport) terrain *m*.

fierce *adjective* féroce.

fifteen *adjective & noun* quinze (*m*).

fifteenth *adjective & noun* quinzième (*m or f*).

fifth *adjective & noun* cinquième (*m or f*).

fiftieth *adjective & noun* cinquantième (*m or f*).

fifty *adjective & noun* cinquante (*m*).

fig *noun* figue *f*.

fight
  1 *noun* bagarre *f*; *Boxing* combat

m; (struggle) lutte *f*; (quarrel) dispute *f*.
  2 *verb* (exchange blows) se battre (against contre, with avec); (struggle) lutter (for pour); (quarrel) se disputer.
  3 *verb* (somebody) se battre avec; (boxer) se battre contre.

fight back *verb* se défendre.

fighter *noun* (determined person) battant, -ante *m or f*.

fight off *verb* (attacker) repousser.

fight over *verb* to f. over something se disputer quelque chose.

figure [1] *noun* (numeral) chiffre *m*; (price) prix *m*; (of woman) ligne *f*; (diagram, important person) figure *f*.

figure [2] *verb* to f. that (guess) penser que.

figure on *verb* to f. on doing compter faire.

figure out *verb* arriver à comprendre; (problem) résoudre.

file *noun* (tool) lime *f*; (folder, information) dossier *m*; (computer data) fichier *m*; in single f. en file.

file (away) *verb* (document) classer.

file (down) *verb* limer.

file in/out *verb* entrer/sortir à la queue leu leu.

filing cabinet *noun* classeur *m*.

Filipino *adjective & noun* philippin, -ine (*m or f*).

fill *verb*
  1 (container, room) remplir (with de); (tooth) plomber.
  2 (become full) se remplir.

fillet *noun* filet *m*.

fill in *verb* (form, hole) remplir.

filling
1 *adjective* (*meal*) nourrissant.
2 *noun* (*in tooth*) plombage *m*; (*in food*) garniture *f*.

fill out *verb* (*form*) remplir.

fill up *verb*
1 (*container, form*) remplir.
2 (*become full*) se remplir; (*with petrol*) faire le plein.

film
1 *noun* film *m*; (*for camera*) pellicule *f*.
2 *verb* filmer.

film star *noun* vedette *f* (de cinéma).

filter *noun* filtre *m*; **f.-tipped cigarette** cigarette *f* (à bout) filtre.

filth *noun* saleté *f*.

filthy *adjective* sale.

fin *noun* (*of fish*) nageoire *f*.

final
1 *adjective* (*last*) dernier.
2 *noun* (*match*) finale *f*.

finalize *verb* mettre au point; (*date*) fixer.

finally *adverb* enfin.

finance
1 *noun* finance *f*.
2 *verb* financer.

financial *adjective* financier.

find
1 *noun* trouvaille *f*.
2 *verb* trouver; (*lost person, thing*) retrouver.

find out *verb*
1 (*secret etc*) découvrir; (*person*) démasquer.
2 (*inquire*) se renseigner (**about** sur); **to f. out about something** (*discover*) découvrir quelque chose.

fine¹
1 *noun* amende *f*; (*for driving offence*) contravention *f*.

2 *verb* **to f. somebody (£10/etc)** infliger une amende (de dix livres/*etc*) à quelqu'un.

fine²
1 *adjective* (*thin, not coarse*) fin; (*very good*) excellent; (*weather*) beau; **it's fine** (*weather*) il fait beau; **he's f.** (*healthy*) il va bien.
2 *adverb* (*well*) très bien.

finger *noun* doigt *m*; **little f.** petit doigt *m*; **f. mark** trace *f* de doigt.

fingernail *noun* ongle *m*.

fingerprint *noun* empreinte *f* (digitale).

fingertip *noun* bout *m* du doigt.

finish
1 *noun* fin *f*; (*of race*) arrivée *f*.
2 *verb* finir; **to f. doing** finir de faire; **to have finished with** ne plus avoir besoin de; (*situation, person*) en avoir fini avec.

finish off *verb* finir.

finish up *verb*
1 finir.
2 **to f. up in** se retrouver à; **to f. up doing** finir par faire.

Finland *noun* la Finlande *f*.

Finn *noun* Finlandais, -aise *m or f*.

Finnish *adjective* finlandais.

fir *noun* sapin *m*.

fire¹ *noun* feu *m*; (*accidental*) incendie *m*; (*electric*) radiateur *m*; **on f.** en feu; **(there's a) f.!** au feu!

fire² *verb*
1 **to f. a gun** tirer un coup de fusil *or* de revolver; **to f. somebody** (*dismiss*) renvoyer quelqu'un.
2 tirer (**at** sur).

fire alarm *noun* sirène *f* d'incendie.

fire brigade *noun* pompiers *mpl*.

firecracker *noun* pétard *m*.

fire engine *noun* voiture *f* de

pompiers.

fire escape *noun* escalier *m* de secours.

fireman *noun* pompier *m*.

fireplace *noun* cheminée *f*.

fire station *noun* caserne *f* de pompiers.

firewood *noun* bois *m* de chauffage.

firework *noun* fusée *f*; (*firecracker*) pétard *m*; **f. display** feu *m* d'artifice.

firm
1 *noun* entreprise *f*.
2 *adjective* ferme.

firmly *adverb* fermement.

first
1 *adjective* premier.
2 *adverb* (*firstly*) premièrement; (*for the first time*) pour la première fois; (**at**) **f.** d'abord.
3 *noun* premier, -ière *m or f*; **f. (gear)** (*of vehicle*) première *f*.

first aid *noun* premiers secours *mpl*.

first-class
1 *adjective* excellent; (*ticket, seat*) de première; (*mail*) ordinaire.
2 *adverb* (*to travel*) en première.

firstly *adverb* premièrement.

fish
1 *invariable noun* poisson *m*.
2 *verb* pêcher.

fisherman *noun* pêcheur *m*.

fish fingers *plural noun* bâtonnets *mpl* de poisson pané.

fishing *noun* pêche *f*; **to go f.** aller à la pêche.

fishing rod *noun* canne *f* à pêche.

fishmonger *noun* poissonnier, -ière *m or f*.

fish shop *noun* poissonnerie *f*.

fist *noun* poing *m*.

fit¹ *adjective* en bonne santé; (*in good shape*) en forme; (*suitable*) propre (**for** à, **to do** à faire); (*worthy*) digne (**for** de, **to do** de faire); (*able*) apte (**for** à, **to do** à faire); **f. to eat** bon à manger; **to keep f.** se maintenir en forme.

fit² *verb*
1 (*of clothes*) aller (bien) à.
2 **this shirt fits well** cette chemise me va.

fit³ *noun* (*attack*) accès *m*.

fit (in) *verb*
1 (*object*) faire entrer; **to f. somebody in** (*find time to see*) caser quelqu'un.
2 **to f. in something** (*go in*) aller dans quelque chose; **he doesn't f. in** il n'est pas à sa place.

fit (on) *verb* **to f. something (on) to something** (*put*) poser quelque chose sur quelque chose; (*fix*) fixer quelque chose à quelque chose.

fitness *noun* (*health*) santé *f*.

fit (out) with *verb* **to f. something (out) with something** (*house etc*) équiper quelque chose de quelque chose.

fitted carpet *noun* moquette *f*.

fitting room *noun* cabine *f* d'essayage.

five *adjective & noun* cinq (*m*).

fiver *noun* Familiar billet *m* de cinq livres.

fix *verb* (*make firm, decide*) fixer; (*mend*) réparer; (*deal with*) arranger; (*prepare, cook*) préparer.

fix (on) *verb* (*lid etc*) mettre en place.

fix up *verb* (*trip etc*) arranger; **to f. somebody up with a job/etc** procurer un travail/*etc* à quelqu'un.

fizzy *adjective* pétillant.

flag *noun* drapeau *m*; (*on ship*) pavillon *m*.

flake *noun* (*of snow*) flocon *m*; (*of soap*) paillette *f*.

flake (off) *verb* (*of paint*) s'écailler.

flame *noun* flamme *f*; **to burst into f., go up in flames** prendre feu.

flammable *adjective* inflammable.

flan *noun* tarte *f*.

flannel *noun* (*face*) f. gant *m* de toilette.

flap
  1 *verb* (*of wings etc*) battre.
  2 *verb* **to f. its wings** battre des ailes.
  3 *noun* (*of pocket etc*) rabat *m*.

flare up *verb* (*of fire*) prendre; (*of violence*) éclater.

flash
  1 *noun* (*of light*) éclat *m*; (*for camera*) flash *m*.
  2 *verb* (*shine*) briller; (*on and off*) clignoter.
  3 *verb* (*light*) projeter; (*aim*) diriger (**on, at** sur); **to f. one's headlights** faire un appel de phares.

flashlight *noun* (*torch*) lampe *f* électrique.

flask *noun* thermos ® *invariable m or f*.

flat[1]
  1 *adjective* plat; (*tyre, battery*) à plat; (*beer*) éventé; (*rate, fare*) fixe; **to put something (down) f.** mettre quelque chose à plat; **f. (on one's face)** à plat ventre.
  2 *adverb* **f. out** (*work*) d'arrachepied; (*run*) à toute vitesse.
  3 *noun* (*puncture*) crevaison *f*.

flat[2] *noun* (*rooms*) appartement *m*.

flatly *adverb* (*to deny, refuse*) catégoriquement.

flatten (out) *verb* aplatir.

flatter *verb* flatter.

flavour *noun* goût *m*; (*of ice cream etc*) parfum *m*.

flavouring *noun* (*in cake etc*) parfum *m*.

flaw *noun* défaut *m*.

flea *noun* puce *f*.

flea market *noun* marché *m* aux puces.

fled *see* flee.

flee *verb*
  1 (*run away*) s'enfuir.
  2 (*place*) s'enfuir de.

fleet *noun* (*of ships*) flotte *f*.

Flemish
  1 *adjective* flamand.
  2 *noun* (*language*) flamand *m*.

flesh *noun* chair *f*.

flew *see* fly.

flex
  1 *verb* (*limb*) fléchir.
  2 *noun* (*wire*) fil *m* (souple); (*for telephone*) cordon *m*.

flexible *adjective* souple.

flick *noun* (*with finger*) chiquenaude *f*.

flick off *verb* enlever (d'une chiquenaude).

flick through *verb* (*pages*) feuilleter.

flies *plural noun* (*on trousers*) braguette *f*.

flight *noun* (*of bird, aircraft*) vol *m*; (*escape*) fuite *f*; **f. of stairs** escalier *m*.

flimsy *adjective* (*light*) (trop) léger; (*thin*) (trop) mince.

fling *verb* lancer.

flint *noun* (*for lighter*) pierre *f*.

flip-flops *plural noun* tongs *fpl*.

flipper noun (of diver) palme f.

flip through verb (book) feuilleter.

float
1 noun (on fishing line) bouchon m; (for swimming, on net) flotteur m.
2 verb flotter (on sur).

flock
1 noun (of sheep) troupeau m; (of birds) volée f.
2 verb venir en foule.

flood
1 noun inondation f; (of letters, tears) flot m.
2 verb (field, house etc) inonder.
3 verb (of river) déborder.

flood in verb (of tourists etc) affluer.

flood into verb (of tourists etc) envahir.

floodlight noun projecteur m.

floor noun (ground) sol m; (wooden etc in building) plancher m; (storey) étage m; **on the f.** par terre; **on the first f.** au premier étage.

floorboard noun planche f.

flop
1 verb (of play etc) faire un four.
2 noun four m.

floppy adjective (soft) mou (f molle).

floppy disk noun disquette f.

florist noun fleuriste m or f.

floss noun (dental) **f.** fil m dentaire.

flour noun farine f.

flow
1 verb couler; (of electric current, information) circuler; (of traffic) s'écouler.
2 noun (of river) courant m; (of current, information) circulation f.

flow chart noun organigramme m.

flower
1 noun fleur f; **in f.** en fleur(s).
2 verb fleurir.

flower bed noun parterre m.

flower shop noun fleuriste m.

flown see **fly**.

flu noun grippe f.

fluent adjective **he's f. in Russian, his Russian is f.** il parle couramment le russe.

fluently adverb (speak a language) couramment.

fluff noun (of material) peluche(s) f(pl); (on floor) moutons mpl.

fluid adjective & noun fluide (m).

flung see **fling**.

fluorescent adjective fluorescent.

flush verb **to f. the toilet** tirer la chasse (d'eau).

flute noun flûte f.

flutter verb (of bird) voltiger; (of flag) flotter.

fly [1] (insect) mouche f.

fly [2] verb
1 (of plane, bird) voler; (of passenger) aller en avion; (of time) passer vite; (of flag) flotter.
2 (plane) piloter; (airline) voyager avec.

fly [3] noun (opening) braguette f.

fly across or **over** verb (country etc) survoler.

fly away or **off** verb s'envoler.

flying noun vol m; (air travel) l'avion m; **f. saucer** soucoupe f volante.

flyover noun toboggan ® m.

foam noun écume f; (on beer) mousse f; **f. rubber** caoutchouc *m* mousse; **f. mattress**/*etc* matelas *m*/*etc* mousse.

focus
1 *noun* (*of attention*) centre *m*; **in f.** au point.
2 *verb* (*image*) mettre au point.

fog *noun* brouillard *m*.

foggy *adjective* **it's f.** il y a du brouillard; **f. weather** brouillard *m*.

foil *noun* (*for cooking*) papier *m* alu(minium).

fold
1 *noun* (*in paper etc*) pli *m*.
2 *verb* plier; (*wrap*) envelopper (**in** dans); **to f. one's arms** croiser les bras.

folder *noun* (*file*) chemise *f*.

folding *adjective* (*chair etc*) pliant.

folk
1 *plural noun* gens *mpl*.
2 *adjective* (*dance etc*) folklorique; **f. music** (musique *f*) folk *m*.

follow *verb* suivre; (*career*) poursuivre; **followed by** suivi de.

follow around *verb* **to f. somebody around** suivre quelqu'un partout.

follower *noun* partisan *m*.

following
1 *adjective* suivant.
2 *preposition* à la suite de.

follow on *verb* (*come after*) suivre.

follow through *verb* (*plan etc*) poursuivre jusqu'au bout.

follow up *verb* (*idea, story*) creuser; (*clue*) suivre.

fond *adjective* **to be (very) f. of** aimer (beaucoup).

food *noun* nourriture *f*; (*particular substance*) aliment *m*; (*for cats, dogs*) pâtée *f*.

fool
1 *noun* imbécile *m or f*; **to play the f.** faire l'imbécile.
2 *verb* (*trick*) rouler.

fool (about or **around)** *verb* faire l'imbécile; (*waste time*) perdre son temps.

foolish *adjective* bête.

foolishly *adverb* bêtement.

foot *noun* pied *m*; (*of animal*) patte *f*; (*measure*) pied *m*; **at the f. of** (*page, stairs*) au bas de; **on f.** à pied.

football *noun* (*game*) football *m*; (*ball*) ballon *m*.

footballer *noun* joueur, -euse *m or f* de football.

footbridge *noun* passerelle *f*.

footpath *noun* sentier *m*.

footprint *noun* empreinte *f*, trace *f* de pas.

footstep *noun* pas *m*.

for *preposition* pour; (*in exchange for*) contre; (*for a distance of*) pendant; **what's it f.?** ça sert à quoi?; **the road f.** London la route de Londres; **he was away f. a month** il a été absent pendant un mois; **he won't be back f. a month** il ne sera pas de retour avant un mois; **he's been here/I haven't seen him f. a month** il est ici/je ne l'ai pas vu depuis un mois; **it's f. you to say** c'est à toi de dire; **f. that to be done** pour que ça soit fait.

forbade *see* forbid.

forbid *verb* interdire (**somebody to do** à quelqu'un de faire); **she is forbidden to leave** il lui est interdit de partir.

forbidden *see* forbid.

force
1 *noun* force *f*; **the (armed) forces** les forces armées.

2 *verb* forcer (to do à faire); (*door*) forcer; **forced to do** obligé *or* forcé de faire; **to f. one's way into** entrer de force dans.

forecast
1 *verb* prévoir.
2 *noun* prévision *f*; (*of weather*) prévisions *fpl*.

forehead *noun* front *m*.

foreign *adjective* étranger; (*trade*) extérieur; (*travel*) à l'étranger.

foreigner *noun* étranger, -ère *m or f*.

foreman *noun* (*worker*) contre-maître *m*.

foremost *adjective* principal.

forerunner *noun* précurseur *m*.

foresee *verb* prévoir.

forest *noun* forêt *f*.

forever *adverb* pour toujours; (*continually*) sans cesse.

forgave *see* forgive.

forge *verb* (*signature, money*) contrefaire; (*document*) falsifier.

forge ahead *verb* (*progress*) aller de l'avant.

forgery *noun* faux *m*.

forget *verb* oublier (**to do de** faire).

forget about *verb* oublier.

forgetful *adjective* **he's f.** il n'a pas de mémoire.

forgive *verb* pardonner (**somebody something** quelque chose à quelqu'un).

forgiven *see* forgive.

forgot , forgotten *see* forget.

fork
1 *noun* (*for eating*) fourchette *f*; (*for garden*) fourche *f*; (*in road*) bifurcation *f*.
2 *verb* (*of road*) bifurquer.

fork out *verb* (*money*) *Familiar* allonger.

form
1 *noun* forme *f*; (*document*) formulaire *m*; (*in school*) classe *f*; **on f., in good f.** en (pleine) forme.
2 *verb* (*group, basis etc*) former; (*habit*) contracter; (*opinion*) se former; **to f. part of** faire partie de.
3 *verb* (*appear*) se former.

formal *adjective* (*person, tone etc*) cérémonieux; (*official*) officiel; **f. dress** tenue *f* de soirée.

formality *noun* formalité *f*.

formation *noun* formation *f*.

former
1 *adjective* (*previous*) ancien; (*of two*) premier.
2 *pronoun* **the f.** celui-là *m*, celle-là *f*.

formerly *adverb* autrefois.

formula *noun* formule *f*; (*baby food*) lait *m* maternisé.

fort *noun* fort *m*.

fortieth *adjective & noun* quarantième (*m or f*).

fortnight *noun* quinze jours *mpl*.

fortress *noun* forteresse *f*.

fortunate *adjective* (*choice etc*) heureux; **to be f.** (*of person*) avoir de la chance; **it's f. that** c'est heureux que (+ *subjunctive*).

fortunately *adverb* heureusement.

fortune *noun* fortune *f*; **to make one's f.** faire fortune; **to have the good f. to do** avoir la chance de faire.

forty *adjective & noun* quarante (*m*).

forward
1 *adverb* **forward(s)** en avant; **to**

go f. avancer.

2 *verb* (*letter*) faire suivre; (*goods*) expédier.

fought *see* **fight**.

foul

1 *adjective* (*smell, taste*) infect; (*language*) grossier.

2 *noun* Football faute *f*.

found[1] *see* **find**.

found[2] *verb* (*town etc*) fonder.

fountain *noun* fontaine *f*.

fountain pen *noun* stylo-plume *m*.

four *adjective* & *noun* quatre (*m*).

fourteen *adjective* & *noun* quatorze (*m*).

fourth *adjective* & *noun* quatrième (*m or f*).

fowl *noun* volaille *f*.

fox *noun* renard *m*.

foyer *noun* (*in theatre*) foyer *m*.

fraction *noun* fraction *f*.

fracture

1 *noun* fracture *f*.

2 *verb* **to f. one's leg**/*etc* se fracturer la jambe/*etc*.

fragile *adjective* fragile.

fragment *noun* fragment *m*.

fragrance *noun* parfum *m*.

frail *adjective* fragile.

frame

1 *noun* (*of picture, bicycle*) cadre *m*; (*of window*) châssis *m*; **f. of mind** humeur *f*.

2 *verb* (*picture*) encadrer.

framework *noun* structure *f*.

franc *noun* franc *m*.

France *noun* la France *f*.

frank *adjective* franc (*f* franche).

frankly *adverb* franchement.

frankness *noun* franchise *f*.

frantic *adjective* (*activity*) frénétique; (*rush*) effréné; (*person*)

hors de soi.

frantically *adverb* comme un fou *or* une folle.

fraud *noun* (*crime*) fraude *f*; (*person*) imposteur *m*.

fray *verb* (*of garment*) s'effilocher.

freckle *noun* tache *f* de rousseur.

freckled *adjective* couvert de taches de rousseur.

free

1 *adjective* libre; **f. (of charge)** gratuit; **to get f.** se libérer; **f. to do** libre de faire; **f. of** (*pain etc*) débarrassé de.

2 *adverb* **f. (of charge)** gratuitement.

3 *verb* (*prisoner*) libérer; (*trapped person*) dégager.

freedom *noun* liberté *f*; **f. from** (*worry*) absence *f* de.

Freefone® *noun* = numéro *m* vert.

free kick *noun* Football coup *m* franc.

freely *adverb* librement; (*to give*) libéralement.

free-range egg *noun* œuf *m* de ferme.

freeze *verb*

1 geler.

2 (*food*) congeler; (*prices*) bloquer.

freezer *noun* congélateur *m*; (*in fridge*) freezer *m*.

freeze up *or* **over** *verb* geler; (*of window*) se givrer.

freezing *adjective* (*weather*) glacial; (*hands, person*) gelé; **it's f. on gèle**.

French

1 *adjective* français; (*teacher*) de français; (*embassy*) de France.

2 *noun* (*language*) français *m*;

the F. les *Français mpl.*

French fries *plural noun* frites *fpl.*

Frenchman *noun* Français *m.*

French-speaking *adjective* francophone.

Frenchwoman *noun* Française *f.*

frequent *adjective* fréquent; **f. visitor** habitué, -ée *m or f* (**to** de).

frequently *adverb* fréquemment.

fresh *adjective* frais (*f* fraîche); (*new*) nouveau (*f* nouvelle); **to get some f. air** prendre l'air.

freshen up *verb* (*have a wash*) faire un brin de toilette.

fret *verb* (*worry*) se faire du souci.

Friday *noun* vendredi *m;* **Good F.** Vendredi Saint.

fridge *noun* frigo *m.*

fried
1 *see* **fry.**
2 *adjective* (*fish*) frit; **f. egg** œuf *m* sur le plat.

friend *noun* ami, -ie *m or f;* (*from school, work*) camarade *m or f;* **to be friends with somebody** être ami avec quelqu'un.

friendly *adjective* aimable (**to** avec); **to be f. with** être ami avec.

friendship *noun* amitié *f.*

fright *noun* peur *f;* **to have a f.** avoir peur; **to give somebody a f.** faire peur à quelqu'un.

frighten *verb* effrayer.

frighten away *or* **off** *verb* (*animal, person*) faire fuir.

frightened *adjective* effrayé; **to be f.** avoir peur (**of** de, **to do** de faire).

frightening *adjective* effrayant.

frill *noun* (*on dress etc*) volant *m.*

fringe *noun* (*of hair*) frange *f.*

fro *adverb* **to go to and f.** aller et venir.

frock *noun* (*dress*) robe *f.*

frog *noun* grenouille *f.*

from *preposition* de; **where are you f.?** d'où êtes-vous?; **a train f.** un train en provenance de.
▪ (*time onwards*) à partir de, dès; **f. today (on), as f. today** à partir d'aujourd'hui, dès aujourd'hui.
▪ (*numbers, prices onwards*) à partir de.
▪ (*away from*) à; **to take/borrow f.** prendre/emprunter à.
▪ (*out of*) dans; sur; **to take f.** (*box*) prendre dans; (*table*) prendre sur; **to drink f. a cup/the bottle** boire dans une tasse/à la bouteille.
▪ (*according to*) d'après.
▪ (*cause*) par; **f. habit**/*etc* par habitude/*etc.*
▪ (*on behalf of*) de la part de; **tell her f. me** dis-lui de ma part.

front
1 *noun* (*of garment, building*) devant *m;* (*of boat, car*) avant *m;* (*of book*) début *m;* **in f. (of)** devant; **in f.** (*ahead*) en avant; (*in race*) en tête; **in the f.** (*in vehicle*) à l'avant.
2 *adjective* (*tooth*) de devant; (*part, wheel, car seat*) avant *invariable;* (*row, page*) premier; **f. door** porte *f* d'entrée.

frost *noun* gel *m;* (*on window*) givre *m.*

frostbite *noun* gelure *f.*

frost up *verb* (*of window etc*) se givrer.

frosty *adjective* (*window*) givré; **it's f.** il gèle.

froth *noun* mousse *f.*

frown *verb* froncer les sourcils.

froze *see* **freeze**.

frozen

1 *past participle of* **freeze**.

2 *adjective* (*vegetables etc*) sur-gelé; **f. food** surgelés *mpl*.

fruit *noun* fruit *m*; (**some**) **f.** (*one item*) un fruit; (*more than one*) des fruits; **f. drink** boisson *f* aux fruits; **f. salad** salade *f* de fruits; **f. tree** arbre *m* fruitier.

fruitcake *noun* cake *m*.

fruit machine *noun* machine *f* à sous.

frustrated *adjective* frustré.

frustrating *adjective* irritant.

fry *verb*

1 faire frire.

2 frire.

frying pan *noun* poêle *f* (à frire).

fudge *noun* (*sweet*) caramel *m* mou.

fuel *noun* combustible *m*; (*for vehicle*) carburant *m*.

fugitive *noun* fugitif, -ive *m or f*.

fulfil *verb* (*ambition*) réaliser; (*condition*) remplir; (*desire*) satis-faire.

fulfilling *adjective* satisfaisant.

full

1 *adjective* plein (**of** de); (*bus, theatre etc*) complet; (*life, day*) rempli; **the f. price** le prix fort; **to pay f. fare** payer plein tarif; **to be f. (up)** (*of person*) n'avoir plus faim; (*of hotel*) être complet; **f. name** (*on form*) nom et pré-nom.

2 *noun* **in f.** (*to read, write etc*) en entier.

full-scale, **full-sized** *adjective* (*model*) grandeur nature *invari-able*.

full stop *noun* point *m*.

full-time *adjective & adverb* à plein temps.

fully *adverb* entièrement.

fumes *plural noun* vapeurs *fpl*; (*from car exhaust*) gaz *mpl*.

fun *noun* amusement *m*; **to be (good) f.** être très amusant; **to have (some) f.** s'amuser; **to make f. of** se moquer de; **for f.** pour le plaisir.

function *noun* fonction *f*; (*meet-ing*) réunion *f*.

fund

1 *noun* (*for pension etc*) caisse *f*; **funds** (*money resources*) fonds *mpl*.

2 *verb* fournir des fonds à.

funeral *noun* enterrement *m*.

funfair *noun* fête *f* foraine.

funnel *noun* (*of ship*) cheminée *f*; (*for pouring*) entonnoir *m*.

funny *adjective* drôle; (*strange*) bizarre; **a f. idea** une drôle d'idée; **to feel f.** ne pas se sentir très bien.

fur *noun* fourrure *f*.

furious *adjective* furieux (**with, at** contre).

furnish *verb* (*room*) meubler.

furniture *noun* meubles *mpl*; **a piece of f.** un meuble.

further

1 *adverb* = **farther**; (*more*) da-vantage.

2 *adjective* supplémentaire; **f. de-tails** de plus amples détails; **a f. case/etc** un autre cas/*etc*.

further education *noun* en-seignement *m* post-scolaire.

furthermore *adverb* en outre.

furthest *adjective & adverb* = **farthest**.

fury *noun* fureur *f*.

fuse
  1 *verb* **the lights** *etc* **have fused**
les plombs ont sauté.
  2 *noun* (*wire*) fusible *m*; (*of bomb*)
amorce *f*.

fuss
  1 *noun* chichis *mpl*; **what a f.!**
quelle histoire!; **to make a f. of**
être aux petits soins pour.
  2 *verb* faire des chichis.

fuss about *verb* s'agiter.

fuss over *verb* **to f. over some-**
body être aux petits soins pour
quelqu'un.

fussy *adjective* tatillon; (*difficult*)
difficile (**about** pour ce qui est
de).

future
  1 *noun* avenir *m*; *Grammar* futur
m; **in f.** à l'avenir; **in the f.** (*one
day*) un jour.
  2 *adjective* futur; (*date*) ultérieur.

fuzzy *adjective* (*picture, idea*)
flou.

G

gadget *noun* gadget *m*.

Gaelic *adjective & noun* gaélique (*m*).

gag
1 *noun* (*over mouth*) bâillon *m*; (*joke*) gag *m*.
2 *verb* (*victim*) bâillonner.
3 *verb* (*choke*) s'étouffer (**on** avec).

gaiety *noun* gaieté *f*.

gaily *adverb* gaiement.

gain
1 *verb* (*obtain*) gagner; (*experience*) acquérir; **to g. speed/weight** prendre de la vitesse / du poids.
2 *noun* (*increase*) augmentation *f* (**in** de); (*profit*) bénéfice *m*.

gain on *verb* (*catch up with*) rattraper.

gala *noun* gala *m*; **swimming g.** concours *m* de natation.

galaxy *noun* galaxie *f*.

gale *noun* grand vent *m*.

gallant *adjective* (*chivalrous*) galant.

gallery *noun* galerie *f*; (*for public*) tribune *f*; **art g.** (*private*) galerie *f* d'art; (*public*) musée *m* d'art.

gallivant (about) *verb Familiar* vadrouiller.

gallon *noun* gallon *m*.

gallop
1 *verb* galoper.
2 *noun* galop *m*.

gamble
1 *verb* jouer (**on** sur, **with** avec).
2 *noun* coup *m* risqué.

gamble (away) *verb* (*lose*) perdre (au jeu).

gambler *noun* joueur, -euse *m or f*.

gambling *noun* jeu *m*.

game *noun* jeu *m*; (*of football, cricket etc*) match *m*; (*of tennis, chess, cards*) partie *f*; **to have a g. of** faire un match de; faire une partie de; **games** (*in school*) le sport.

gammon *noun* jambon *m* fumé.

gang *noun* (*of children, criminals*) bande *f*; (*of workers*) équipe *f*.

gangster *noun* gangster *m*.

gang up on *verb* se mettre à plusieurs contre.

gangway *noun* passage *m*; (*in train*) couloir *m*; (*in bus, cinema*) allée *f*; (*to ship, aircraft*) passerelle *f*.

gaol = jail.

gap *noun* (*empty space*) trou; (*in time*) intervalle *m*; (*in knowledge*) lacune *f*; **the g. between** (*difference*) l'écart *m* entre.

gape *verb* rester bouche bée.

gape at *verb* regarder bouche bée.

garage *noun* garage *m*.

garden
1 *noun* jardin *m*; **the gardens** (*park*) le parc.
2 *verb* jardiner.

gardener *noun* jardinier, -ière *m or f*.

gardening *noun* jardinage *m*.

gargle *verb* se gargariser.

garland *noun* guirlande *f*.

garlic *noun* ail *m*.

garment *noun* vêtement *m*.

gas
1 *noun* gaz *invariable m*; **g.**

mask/meter/*etc* masque *m*/ compteur *m*/*etc* à gaz; **g. fire** *or* **heater** appareil *m* de chauffage à gaz; **g. heating** chauffage *m* au gaz; **g. stove** cuisinière *f* à gaz; (*portable*) réchaud *m* à gaz.
2 *verb* (*poison*) asphyxier.

gash
1 *noun* entaille *f*.
2 *verb* entailler.

gasman *noun* employé *m* du gaz.

gasp
1 *verb* **to g.** (**for breath**) haleter.
2 *noun* halètement *m*.

gassy *adjective* (*drink*) gazeux.

gasworks *plural noun* usine *f* à gaz.

gate *noun* (*at level crossing, field etc*) barrière *f*; (*metal*) grille *f*; (*of castle, in airport*) porte *f*; (*at stadium*) entrée *f*.

gatecrash *verb* s'inviter.

gather
1 *verb* (*people, objects*) rassembler; (*pick up*) ramasser; (*information*) recueillir; **I g. that …** je crois comprendre que … ; **to g. speed** prendre de la vitesse.
2 *verb* (*of people*) se rassembler.

gathering *noun* (*group*) réunion *f*.

gather round *verb* s'approcher.

gaudy *adjective* voyant.

gauge
1 *noun* (*instrument*) jauge *f*.
2 *verb* (*estimate*) évaluer.

gaunt *adjective* décharné.

gauze *noun* gaze *f*.

gave *see* **give**.

gay
1 *adjective* homo(sexuel); (*cheerful*) gai (*f* gaie).
2 *noun* homo(sexuel) *m*.

gaze
1 *noun* regard *m* (fixe).
2 *verb* regarder.

gaze at *verb* regarder (fixement).

GB *abbreviation* (*Great Britain*) Grande-Bretagne *f*.

GCSE *abbreviation* (*General Certificate of Secondary Education*) = épreuve *f* de brevet.

gear
1 *noun* équipement *m*; (*belongings*) affaires *fpl*; (*clothes*) *Familiar* vêtements *mpl*; (*speed in vehicle*) vitesse *f*; **in g.** en prise; **not in g.** au point mort.
2 *verb* adapter (**to** à).

gearbox *noun* boîte *f* de vitesses.

gear up *verb* **geared up to do** prêt à faire; **to g. oneself up for** se préparer pour.

geese *see* **goose**.

gel *noun* gel *m*.

gem *noun* pierre *f* précieuse.

gen *noun* (*information*) *Familiar* tuyaux *mpl*.

gender *noun* *Grammar* genre *m*.

general
1 *adjective* général; **in g.** en général; **the g. public** le (grand) public; **for g. use** à l'usage du public.
2 *noun* (*in army*) général *m*.

generally *adverb* généralement.

generation *noun* génération *f*.

generator *noun* groupe *m* électrogène.

generosity *noun* générosité *f*.

generous *adjective* généreux; (*helping*) copieux.

generously *adverb* généreusement.

genius *noun* (*ability, person*) génie *m*.

gentle *adjective* (*person, slope etc*) doux (*f* douce); (*touch*) léger; (*exercise, speed*) modéré.

gentleman *noun* monsieur *m*.

gentleness *noun* douceur *f*.

gently *adverb* doucement.

gents *plural noun* **the g.** *Familiar* les toilettes *fpl* pour hommes.

genuine *adjective* véritable, authentique; (*sincere*) sincère.

genuinely *adverb* véritablement, sincèrement.

geographical *adjective* géographique.

geography *noun* géographie *f*.

geometric(al) *adjective* géométrique.

geometry *noun* géométrie *f*.

germ *noun* (*causing disease*) microbe *m*.

German
1 *adjective* allemand.
2 *noun* (*person*) Allemand, -ande *m* or *f*; (*language*) allemand *m*.

German measles *noun* rubéole *f*.

German shepherd *noun* (*dog*) berger *m* allemand.

gesture *noun* geste *m*.

Germany *noun* l'Allemagne *f*; East/West G. l'Allemagne de l'Est/l'Ouest.

get *verb*
1 (*obtain*) obtenir; (*find*) trouver; (*buy*) acheter; (*receive*) recevoir; (*catch*) attraper; (*bus, train*) prendre; (*seize*) saisir; (*fetch*) aller chercher; (*put*) mettre; (*derive*) tirer (**from** de); (*understand*) comprendre; (*prepare*) préparer; (*hit with fist, stick etc*) atteindre; (*reputation*) se faire; **I have got** j'ai; **to g. something to somebody** faire parvenir

quelque chose à quelqu'un; **to g. somebody to hospital**/*etc* amener quelqu'un à l'hôpital/*etc*; **to g. somebody to do something** faire faire quelque chose à quelqu'un; **to g. something built** faire construire quelque chose.
2 (*go*) aller; (*arrive*) arriver (**to** à); (*become*) devenir; **to g. caught**/*etc* se faire prendre/*etc*; **to g. washed** se laver; **where have you got to?** où en es-tu?; **you've got to stay** (*must*) tu dois rester; **to g. working** se mettre à travailler.

get about *or* **(a)round** *verb* se déplacer.

get across *verb* (*road*) traverser; (*message*) communiquer.

get along *verb* (*manage*) se débrouiller; (*be on good terms*) s'entendre (**with** avec).

get at *verb* (*reach*) parvenir à.

get away *verb* (*leave*) partir; (*escape*) s'échapper.

get back *verb*
1 (*recover*) récupérer; (*replace*) remettre.
2 (*return*) revenir; (*move back*) reculer.

get by *verb* passer; (*manage*) se débrouiller.

get down *verb* descendre.

get in *verb*
1 (*washing etc*) rentrer; (*call for*) faire venir.
2 (*enter*) entrer; (*come home*) rentrer; (*enter vehicle or train*) monter; (*of plane, train*) arriver.

get in(to) *verb* entrer dans; (*vehicle, train*) monter dans; **to g. in(to) bed** se mettre au lit.

get off *verb*
1 (*leave*) partir; (*from vehicle or train*) descendre (**from** de); (*in*

court) être acquitté.
2 *(remove)* enlever; *(send)* expédier; **to g. off a chair** se lever d'une chaise; **to g. off a bus** descendre d'un bus.

get on *verb*
1 *(shoes, clothes)* mettre; *(bus, train)* monter dans.
2 *(progress)* marcher; *(manage)* se débrouiller; *(succeed)* réussir; *(enter bus or train)* monter; *(be on good terms)* s'entendre (**with** avec); **how are you getting on?** comment ça va?; **to g. on to somebody** *(on phone)* contacter quelqu'un; **to g. on with** *(task)* continuer.

get out *verb*
1 sortir; *(from vehicle or train)* descendre (**of** de); **to g. out of** *(danger)* se tirer de; *(habit)* perdre.
2 *(remove)* enlever; *(bring out)* *(something)* sortir; *(somebody)* faire sortir.

get over *verb*
1 *(road)* traverser; *(obstacle)* surmonter; *(fence)* franchir; *(illness)* se débrouiller; *(cross)* traverser; *(visit)* passer.

get round *verb (visit)* passer; **to g. round to doing** en venir à faire.

get through *verb*
1 passer; *(finish)* finir; **to g. through to somebody** *(on phone)* contacter quelqu'un.
2 *(gap)* passer par; *(meal)* venir à bout de; *(exam)* être reçu à.

get-together *noun* réunion *f.*

get up *verb*
1 *(rise)* se lever (**from** de); **to g. up to something** *or* **to mischief** faire des bêtises.
2 *(bring up)* monter; *(wake up)* réveiller.

ghastly *adjective* affreux.

gherkin *noun* cornichon *m.*

ghetto *noun* ghetto *m.*

ghost *noun* fantôme *m.*

giant
1 *noun* géant, -e *m or f.*
2 *adjective (tree, packet)* géant.

giddy *adjective* **to be** *or* **feel g.** avoir le vertige; **to make g.** donner le vertige à.

gift *noun* cadeau *m*; *(talent)* don *m.*

gifted *adjective* doué.

gift voucher *or* **token** *noun* chèque-cadeau *m.*

gigantic *adjective* gigantesque.

giggle *verb* rire (bêtement).

gills *plural noun (of fish)* ouïes *fpl.*

gimmick *noun* truc *m.*

gin *noun (drink)* gin *m.*

ginger *adjective (hair)* roux (*f* rousse).

giraffe *noun* girafe *f.*

girl *noun* (jeune) fille *f*; *(daughter)* fille *f*; **English g.** jeune Anglaise *f.*

girlfriend *noun* amie *f*; *(of boy)* petite amie *f.*

girl guide *noun* éclaireuse *f.*

give *verb* donner (**to** à); *(support)* apporter; *(smile)* faire; *(sigh)* pousser; *(look)* jeter.

give away *verb (free of charge)* donner; *(prizes)* distribuer; *(betray)* trahir.

give back *verb (return)* rendre.

given *see* give.

give in *verb*
1 *(surrender)* céder (**to** à).
2 *(hand in)* remettre.

give out *verb (hand out)* distribuer.

give over *verb (devote)* consacrer (to à).

give up verb abandonner; (seat) céder (to à); (prisoner) livrer (to à); to g. up smoking arrêter de fumer.

give way verb (of branch, person etc) céder (to à); (in vehicle) céder la priorité (to à).

glad adjective content (of, about de).

gladly adverb volontiers.

glamorous adjective séduisant.

glamour noun (charm) enchantement m; (splendour) éclat m.

glance
1 noun coup m d'œil.
2 verb jeter un coup d'œil (at à, sur).

gland noun glande f.

glaring adjective (light) éblouissant; (injustice) flagrant.

glass noun verre m; (mirror) miroir m; a pane of g. une vitre.

glasses plural noun (for eyes) lunettes fpl.

glee noun joie f.

glen noun vallon m.

glide verb glisser; (of aircraft, bird) planer.

gliding noun (sport) vol m à voile.

glimmer noun (of hope) lueur f.

glimpse noun aperçu m; to catch or get a g. of entrevoir.

glittering adjective scintillant.

globe noun globe m.

gloom noun (sadness) tristesse f.

gloomy adjective triste; (pessimistic) pessimiste.

glorified adjective it's a glorified barn/etc ce n'est guère plus qu'une grange/etc.

glorious adjective glorieux;

(splendid) magnifique.

glory noun gloire f.

gloss noun (shine) brillant m; g. paint peinture f brillante.

glossy adjective brillant; (magazine) de luxe.

glove noun gant m.

glove compartment noun (in car) vide-poches invariable m.

glow verb (of sky, fire) rougeoyer.

glue
1 noun colle f.
2 verb coller (to, on à); with eyes glued to les yeux fixés sur.

glum adjective triste.

glut noun (of oil etc) surplus m.

glutton noun glouton, -onne m or f.

gnat noun (insect) cousin m.

gnaw verb ronger.

go [1] verb aller (to à, from de); (depart) partir, s'en aller; (disappear) disparaître, partir; (function) marcher; (become) devenir; (of fuse, bulb) sauter; (of material) s'user; to go well/badly (of event) se passer bien/mal; she's going to do (is about to, intends to) elle va faire; it's all gone il n'y en a plus; to go and get aller chercher; to go riding/on a trip/etc faire du cheval/un voyage/etc; to let go of lâcher; to go to a doctor/etc aller voir un médecin/etc; two hours/etc to go encore deux heures/etc.

go [2] noun (attempt) coup m; to have a go at (doing) something essayer (de faire) quelque chose; at one go d'un seul coup; on the go actif.

go about or (a)round verb
1 se déplacer; (of news) circuler.

2 to know how to go about it savoir s'y prendre.

go across *verb* (*cross*) traverser.

go after *verb* (*chase*) poursuivre; (*seek*) (re)chercher.

go ahead *verb* avancer; (*continue*) continuer; (*start*) commencer; **go ahead!** allez-y!; **to go ahead with** (*plan etc*) poursuivre.

go-ahead *noun* **to get the g.** avoir le feu vert.

goal *noun* but *m*.

goalkeeper *noun* gardien *m* de but.

go along *verb* aller; **to go along with** (*agree*) être d'accord avec.

goat *noun* chèvre *f*.

go away *verb* partir, s'en aller.

go back *verb* retourner; (*in time*) remonter; (*step back*) reculer; **to go back on** (*promise*) revenir sur.

go-between *noun* intermédiaire *m or f*.

god *noun* dieu *m*; **G.** Dieu *m*.

goddaughter *noun* filleule *f*.

godfather *noun* parrain *m*.

godmother *noun* marraine *f*.

go down *verb*
1 descendre; (*fall down*) tomber; (*of ship*) couler; (*of sun*) se coucher; (*of price etc*) baisser.
2 to go down the stairs/street descendre l'escalier/la rue.

godsend *noun* **to be a g.** tomber à pic.

godson *noun* filleul *m*.

goes *see* go[1].

go for *verb* (*fetch*) aller chercher.

goggles *plural noun* lunettes *fpl*.

go in *verb*
1 (r)entrer; (*of sun*) se cacher.

2 to go in a room/*etc* entrer dans une pièce/*etc*.

go in for *verb* (*exam*) se présenter à.

going
1 *noun* (*conditions*) conditions *fpl*; **it's hard** *or* **heavy g.** c'est difficile.
2 *adjective* **the g. price** le prix pratiqué (**for** pour).

goings-on *plural noun* activités *fpl*.

go into *verb* (*room etc*) entrer dans.

gold *noun or m*; **g. watch**/*etc* montre/*etc* en or.

golden *adjective* (*in colour*) doré; (*rule*) d'or.

goldfish *noun* poisson *m* rouge.

goldmine *noun* mine *f* d'or.

gold-plated *adjective* plaqué or.

golf *noun* golf *m*.

golfer *noun* golfeur, -euse *m or f*.

gone *see* go[1].

good
1 *adjective* bon (*f* bonne); (*kind*) gentil; (*weather*) beau (*f* belle); (*well-behaved*) sage; **very g.!** (*all right*) très bien!; **to feel g.** se sentir bien; **g. at French**/*etc* (*at school*) bon en français/*etc*; **to be g. with** (*children*) savoir s'y prendre avec; **it's a g. thing (that)** ... heureusement que ... ; **a g. many, a g. deal (of)** beaucoup (de); **g. morning** bonjour; (*on leaving*) au revoir; **g. evening** bonsoir; **g. night** bonsoir; (*going to bed*) bonne nuit.
2 *noun* (*advantage*, *virtue*) bien *m*; **for her own g.** pour son bien; **it's no g. crying**/*etc* ça ne sert à rien de pleurer/*etc*; **that's no g.** (*worthless*) ça ne vaut rien; (*bad*) ça ne va pas; **what's the g.?** à

quoi bon?; **for g.** pour de bon.

goodbye *interjection* au revoir.

good-looking *adjective* beau (*f* belle).

goods *plural noun* marchandises *fpl*, articles *mpl*.

goodwill *noun* bonne volonté *f*.

go off *verb* (*leave*) partir; (*go bad*) se gâter; (*of alarm*) se déclencher.

go on *verb* continuer (**doing** à faire); (*happen*) se passer; (*last*) durer.

goose *noun* oie *f*.

gooseberry *noun* groseille *f* à maquereau.

goose pimples *or* **bumps** *plural noun* chair *f* de poule.

go out *verb* sortir; (*of light, fire*) s'éteindre.

go over *verb*
1 aller (to à); **to go over to somebody('s)** faire un saut chez quelqu'un.
2 (*check*) examiner; (*in one's mind*) repasser.

gorge *noun* (*ravine*) gorge *f*.

gorgeous *adjective* magnifique.

gorilla *noun* gorille *m*.

go round *verb*
1 (*turn*) tourner; **to be enough to go round** suffire.
2 (*corner*) tourner; (*world*) faire le tour de.

Gospel *noun* Évangile *m*.

gossip *noun* (*talk*) bavardage(s) *m(pl)*; (*person*) commère *f*.

got *see* get.

go through *verb*
1 passer.
2 (*suffer*) subir; (*check*) examiner; (*search*) fouiller; (*spend*) dépenser; (*wear out*) user.

go under *verb* (*of ship, firm*)

couler.

go up *verb*
1 monter.
2 **to go up the stairs/street** monter l'escalier/la rue.

gourmet *noun* gourmet *m*.

govern *verb* (*rule*) gouverner; (*city*) administrer; (*influence*) déterminer.

government *noun* gouvernement *m*; (*local*) administration *f*.

governor *noun* gouverneur *m*; (*of school*) administrateur, -trice *m or f*.

go without *verb* se passer de.

gown *noun* (*of woman*) robe *f*.

GP *abbreviation* (*general practitioner*) généraliste *m*.

grab *verb* **to g. (hold of)** saisir; **to g. something from somebody** arracher quelque chose à quelqu'un.

grace *noun* (*charm*) grâce *f*.

graceful *adjective* gracieux.

grade
1 *noun* catégorie *f*; (*in exam etc*) note *f*.
2 *verb* (*classify*) classer; (*school paper*) noter.

gradual *adjective* progressif.

gradually *adverb* progressivement.

graduate
1 *verb* obtenir son diplôme.
2 *noun* diplômé, -ée *m or f*.

graduation *noun* remise *f* des diplômes.

graffiti *plural noun* graffiti *mpl*.

graft
1 *noun* greffe *f*.
2 *verb* greffer.

grain *noun* (*seed*) grain *m*; (*cereal*) céréales *fpl*.

gram(me) *noun* gramme *m*.

grammar *noun* grammaire *f.*

grammar school *noun* lycée *m.*

grammatical *adjective* grammatical.

grand *adjective* (*splendid*) magnifique.

grand(d)ad *noun Familiar* papi *m.*

grandchildren *plural noun* petits-enfants *mpl.*

granddaughter *noun* petite-fille *f.*

grandfather *noun* grand-père *m.*

grandma *noun Familiar* mamie *f.*

grandmother *noun* grand-mère *f.*

grandparents *plural noun* grands-parents *mpl.*

grandson *noun* petit-fils *m.*

granny *noun Familiar* mamie *f.*

grant
1 *verb* accorder (to à); (*request*) accéder à; **to take something for granted** considérer quelque chose comme acquis; **I take it for granted that** je présume que.
2 *noun* subvention *f*; (*for study*) bourse *f.*

grape *noun* grain *m* de raisin; **grapes** le raisin, les raisins *mpl*; **to eat (some) grapes** manger du raisin *or* des raisins.

grapefruit *noun* pamplemousse *m.*

graph *noun* courbe *f*; **g. paper** papier *m* millimétré.

grasp
1 *verb* (*seize, understand*) saisir.
2 *noun* (*hold*) prise *f*; (*understanding*) compréhension *f.*

grass *noun* herbe *f*; (*lawn*) gazon *m.*

grasshopper *noun* sauterelle *f.*

grate
1 *noun* (*for fireplace*) grille *f* de foyer.
2 *verb* (*cheese etc*) râper.

grateful *adjective* reconnaissant (to à, for de); **I'm g. (to you) for your help** je vous suis reconnaissant de votre aide.

grater *noun* râpe *f.*

gratifying *adjective* satisfaisant.

gratitude *noun* reconnaissance *f*, gratitude *f* (for pour).

grave [1] *noun* tombe *f.*

grave [2] *adjective* (*serious*) grave.

gravel *noun* gravier *m.*

graveyard *noun* cimetière *m.*

gravity *noun* (*force*) pesanteur *f.*

gravy *noun* jus *m* de viande.

graze
1 *verb* (*of cattle*) paître.
2 *verb* (*skin*) écorcher.
3 *noun* (*wound*) écorchure *f.*

grease
1 *noun* graisse *f.*
2 *verb* graisser.

greaseproof (paper) *noun* papier *m* sulfurisé.

greasy *adjective* plein de graisse; (*hair*) gras (*f* grasse).

great *adjective* grand; (*excellent*) *Familiar* magnifique; **a g. deal (of), a g. many** beaucoup (de); **the greatest team**/etc (*best*) la meilleure équipe/etc.

Great Britain *noun* la Grande-Bretagne *f.*

great-grandfather *noun* arrière-grand-père *m.*

great-grandmother *noun* arrière-grand-mère *f.*

greatly *adverb* (*much*) beaucoup; (*very*) très.

Greece *noun* la Grèce *f.*

greed *noun* avidité *f*; (*for food*) gourmandise *f*.

greedy *adjective* avide; (*for food*) gourmand.

Greek
  1 *adjective* grec (*f* grecque).
  2 *noun* Grec *m*, Grecque *f*; (*language*) grec *m*.

green
  1 *adjective* vert; **to turn** *or* **go g.** verdir.
  2 *noun* (*colour*) vert *m*; (*lawn*) pelouse *f*; **greens** légumes *mpl* verts.

greengrocer *noun* marchand, -ande *m or f* de légumes.

greenhouse *noun* serre *f*.

greet *verb* saluer.

greeting *noun* salutation *f*; **greetings** (*for birthday, festival*) vœux *mpl*.

grenade *noun* (*bomb*) grenade *f*.

grew *see* grow.

grey *adjective* gris; **to be going g.** grisonner.

greyhound *noun* lévrier *m*.

grief *noun* chagrin *m*.

grieve *verb* **to g. for somebody** pleurer quelqu'un.

grill
  1 *noun* (*utensil*) gril *m*; (*dish*) grillade *f*.
  2 *verb* griller.

grim *adjective* (*face, future*) sombre; (*bad*) *Familiar* affreux.

grime *noun* crasse *f*.

grimy *adjective* crasseux.

grin
  1 *verb* avoir un large sourire.
  2 *noun* large sourire *m*.

grind *verb* moudre; **to g. one's teeth** grincer des dents.

grinder *noun* **coffee g.** moulin *m* à café.

grip
  1 *verb* saisir; (*hold*) tenir serré.
  2 *noun* (*hold*) prise *f*; (*with hand*) poigne *f*; **in the g. of** en proie à.

gripping *adjective* prenant.

groan
  1 *verb* gémir.
  2 *noun* gémissement *m*.

grocer *noun* épicier, -ière *m or f*; **g.'s shop** épicerie *f*.

grocery *noun* (*shop*) épicerie *f*; **groceries** (*food*) épicerie *f*.

groin *noun* aine *f*.

groom *noun* (*bridegroom*) marié *m*.

groove *noun* (*slot*) rainure *f*.

grope about *verb* tâtonner.

grope for *verb* chercher à tâtons.

gross *adjective* (*income etc*) brut.

grossly *adverb* (*very*) extrêmement.

grotty *adjective Familiar* (*ugly*) moche; (*of poor quality*) nul (*f* nulle).

ground [1] *see* grind.

ground [2] *noun* terre *f*, sol *m*; (*for camping, football etc*) terrain *m*; **grounds** (*reasons*) raisons *fpl*; (*gardens*) parc *m*; **on the g.** (*lying, sitting*) par terre.

ground floor *noun* rez-de-chaussée *invariable m*.

groundwork *noun* préparation *f*.

group *noun* groupe *m*.

group (together) *verb* (se) grouper.

grow *verb*
  1 (*of person*) grandir; (*of plant, hair*) pousser; (*increase*) augmenter, grandir; (*of firm, town*) se développer.
  2 (*plant, crops*) cultiver; (*beard*)

laisser pousser.

grow into *verb* devenir.

growl *verb* grogner.

grown
1 *past participle of* **grow**.
2 *adjective* (*man, woman*) adulte.

grown-up *noun* grande personne *f*.

grow out of *verb* (*clothes*) devenir trop grand pour; (*habit*) perdre.

growth *noun* croissance *f*; (*increase*) augmentation *f* (**in** de); (*lump*) grosseur *f*.

grow up *verb* devenir adulte.

grub *noun* (*food*) *Familiar* bouffe *f*.

grubby *adjective* sale.

grudge *noun* rancune *f*; **to have a g. against** garder rancune à.

gruelling *adjective* éprouvant.

gruesome *adjective* horrible.

grumble *verb* râler, grogner (**about, at** contre).

grumpy *adjective* grincheux.

grunt
1 *verb* grogner.
2 *noun* grognement *m*.

guarantee
1 *noun* garantie *f*.
2 *verb* garantir (**against** contre, **somebody that** à quelqu'un que).

guard
1 *noun* (*vigilance, soldiers*) garde *f*; (*individual person*) garde *m*; (*on train*) chef *m* de train; **to keep a g. on** surveiller; **under g.** sous surveillance; **on one's g.** sur ses gardes; **on g. (duty)** de garde; **to stand g.** monter la garde.
2 *verb* protéger; (*watch over*) surveiller.

guess
1 *noun* conjecture *f*; (*intuition*) intuition *f*; **to make a g.** (essayer de) deviner.
2 *verb* deviner (**that** que); (*length, number*) estimer; (*suppose*) supposer.

guesswork *noun* hypothèse *f*; **by g.** au jugé.

guest *noun* invité, -ée *m or f*; (*in hotel*) client, -ente *m or f*; (*at meal*) convive *m or f*.

guesthouse *noun* pension *f* de famille.

guidance *noun* conseils *mpl*.

guide
1 *noun* guide *m*; **g. (book)** guide *m*.
2 *verb* guider; **guided tour** visite *f* guidée.

guidelines *plural noun* indications *fpl*.

guilt *noun* culpabilité *f*.

guilty *adjective* coupable; **g. person** coupable *m or f*.

guinea pig *noun* cobaye *m*.

guitar *noun* guitare *f*.

guitarist *noun* guitariste *m or f*.

gulf *noun* (*in sea*) golfe *m*; **a g. between** un abîme entre.

gull *noun* (*bird*) mouette *f*.

gulp *noun* (*of drink*) gorgée *f*.

gulp down *verb* avaler (vite).

gum [1] *noun* (*around teeth*) gencive *f*.

gum [2]
1 *noun* (*for chewing*) chewing-gum *m*; (*glue*) colle *f*.
2 *verb* coller.

gun *noun* pistolet *m*; (*rifle*) fusil *m*; (*firing shells*) canon *m*.

gun down *verb* abattre.

gunfire *noun* coups *mpl* de feu.

gunman *noun* bandit *m* armé.

gunpoint *noun* at g. sous la menace d'une arme.

gunpowder *noun* poudre *f* à canon.

gunshot *noun* coup *m* de feu.

gush (out) *verb* jaillir (of de).

gust *noun* g. (of wind) rafale *f* (de vent).

guts *plural noun Familiar* (insides) ventre *m*.

gutter *noun* (on roof) gouttière *f*; (in street) caniveau *m*.

guy *noun Familiar* type *m*.

gym *noun* gym *f*; (at school) gymnase *m*; (health club) club *m* de gym.

gymnasium *noun* gymnase *m*.

gymnastics *noun* gymnastique *f*.

gynaecologist *noun* gynécologue *m or f*.

H

habit *noun* habitude *f*; **to be in/ get into the h. of doing** avoir/ prendre l'habitude de faire.

hack *verb* (*cut*) tailler.

had *see* **have**.

haddock *noun* (*fish*) aiglefin *m*; **smoked h.** haddock *m*.

haemorrhage *noun* hémorragie *f*.

hag *noun* (**old**) **h.** (vieille) sorcière *f*.

haggle *verb* marchander; **to h. over the price** marchander.

hail
1 *noun* grêle *f*.
2 *verb* grêler; **it's hailing** il grêle.

hailstone *noun* grêlon *m*.

hair *noun* (*on head*) cheveux *mpl*; (*on body, of animal*) poils *mpl*; **a h.** (*on head*) un cheveu; (*on body, of animal*) un poil.

hairbrush *noun* brosse *f* à cheveux.

haircut *noun* coupe *f* de cheveux; **to have a h.** se faire couper les cheveux.

hairdo *noun Familiar* coiffure *f*.

hairdresser *noun* coiffeur, -euse *m or f*.

hair dryer *noun* sèche-cheveux *invariable m*.

-haired *suffix* **long-/red-h.** aux cheveux longs/roux.

hairgrip *noun* pince *f* à cheveux.

hairpin *noun* épingle *f* à cheveux.

hair-raising *adjective* effrayant.

hair spray *noun* laque *f*.

hairstyle *noun* coiffure *f*.

hairy *adjective* (*person, animal, body*) poilu.

half
1 *noun* moitié *f*; **h. (of) the apple/etc** la moitié de la pomme/ *etc*; **ten and a h.** dix et demi; **ten and a h. weeks** dix semaines et demie; **to cut in h.** couper en deux.
2 *adjective* demi; **h. a day, a h.-day** une demi-journée; **h. a dozen, a h.-dozen** une demi-douzaine; **at h. price** à moitié prix.
3 *adverb* (*full etc*) à demi, à moitié; **h. past one** une heure et demie.

half-hour *noun* demi-heure *f*.

half-term *noun* petites vacances *fpl*.

half-time *noun* (*in game*) mi-temps *f*.

halfway *adverb* à mi-chemin (*between* entre); **to fill/etc h.** remplir/*etc* à moitié.

halibut *noun* flétan *m*.

hall *noun* salle *f*; (*house entrance*) entrée *f*; (*of hotel*) hall *m*; **halls of residence** cité *f* universitaire; **lecture h.** amphithéâtre *m*.

hallo! = **hello**.

Hallowe'en *noun* la veille de la Toussaint.

hallstand *noun* portemanteau *m*.

hallway *noun* entrée *f*.

halt *noun* halte *f*; **to call a h. to** mettre fin à.

halve *verb* (*time, expense*) réduire de moitié.

ham *noun* jambon *m*; **h. and eggs** œufs *mpl* au jambon.

hamburger *noun* hamburger *m*.

hammer
1 *noun* marteau *m*.
2 *verb* (*nail*) enfoncer (**into** dans).

hammering *noun* (*defeat*) Familiar raclée *f*.

hammock *noun* hamac *m*.

hamper
1 *verb* gêner.
2 *noun* panier *m*.

hamster *noun* hamster *m*.

hand [1] *noun* main *f*; (*of clock*) aiguille *f*; *Cards* jeu *m*; **to hold in one's h.** tenir à la main; **to give somebody a (helping) h.** donner un coup de main à quelqu'un; **by h.** (*to make, sew etc*) à la main; **at** *or* **to h.** sous la main; **on h.** disponible; **out of h.** (*situation*) incontrôlable.

hand [2] *verb* (*give*) donner (**to** à).

handbag *noun* sac *m* à main.

handbook *noun* manuel *m*; (*guide*) guide *m*.

handbrake *noun* frein *m* à main.

handcuff *verb* passer les menottes à.

handcuffs *plural noun* menottes *fpl*.

handful *noun* (*group*) poignée *f*.

handicap
1 *noun* handicap *m*.
2 *verb* handicaper; **to be handicapped** (*after an accident etc*) rester handicapé.

handicapped *adjective* handicapé.

hand in *verb* remettre.

handkerchief *noun* mouchoir *m*.

handle
1 *noun* (*of door*) poignée *f*; (*of knife*) manche *m*; (*of bucket*) anse *f*; (*of saucepan*) queue *f*.
2 *verb* (*manipulate*) manier; (*touch*) toucher à; (*vehicle*) manœuvrer; (*deal with*) s'occuper de.

handlebars *plural noun* guidon *m*.

hand luggage *noun* bagages *mpl* à main.

handmade *adjective* fait à la main.

hand out *verb* distribuer.

handout *noun* (*leaflet*) prospectus *m*; (*money*) aumône *f*.

hand over *verb* remettre.

handrail *noun* rampe *f*.

hand round *verb* (*cakes*) passer.

handshake *noun* poignée *f* de main.

handsome *adjective* beau (*f* belle); (*profit*) considérable.

handwriting *noun* écriture *f*.

handy *adjective* commode, pratique; (*skilful*) habile (**at doing** à faire); (*within reach*) sous la main; (*place*) accessible.

handyman *noun* bricoleur *m*.

hang [1]
1 *verb* (*coat, picture etc*) suspendre (**on, from** à); (*let dangle*) laisser pendre (**from, out of** de).
2 *verb* (*of picture etc*) pendre; (*of fog*) flotter.
3 *noun* **to get the h. of something** *Familiar* arriver à comprendre quelque chose.

hang [2] *verb* (*criminal*) pendre (**for** pour).

hang about *verb* traîner; (*wait*) attendre.

hangar *noun* hangar *m*.

hang down *verb* pendre.

hanger *noun* (*coat*) h. cintre *m*.

hang-glider *noun* deltaplane *m*.

hang on *verb* résister; (*wait*) attendre; to h. on to ne pas lâcher; (keep) garder.

hang out verb
1 (washing) étendre; (flag) arborer.
2 (of tongue, shirt) pendre.

hangover noun gueule f de bois.

hang up verb
1 (picture) accrocher.
2 (on phone) raccrocher.

hangup noun complexe m.

happen verb arriver, se passer; to h. to somebody/something arriver à quelqu'un/quelque chose; I h. to know il se trouve que je le sais; do you h. to have … ? est-ce que, par hasard, vous auriez … ?

happening noun événement m.

happily adverb joyeusement; (contentedly) tranquillement; (fortunately) heureusement.

happiness noun bonheur m.

happy adjective heureux (to do de faire, about something de quelque chose); I'm not h. about it ça ne me plaît pas beaucoup; H. New Year! bonne année!

harass verb harceler.

harbour noun port m.

hard
1 adjective (not soft, severe, difficult) dur; h. worker travailleur, -euse m or f acharné(e); h. on somebody dur avec quelqu'un; h. of hearing malentendant.
2 adverb (to work, hit) dur; (to pull) fort; (to rain) à verse; to think h. bien réfléchir.

hard-boiled adjective (egg) dur.

hard core noun (group) noyau m dur.

harden verb durcir; to become hardened to s'endurcir à.

hardly adverb à peine; h. anyone presque personne; h. ever presque jamais.

hardness noun dureté f.

hard up adjective (broke) Familiar fauché.

hardware invariable noun quincaillerie f; (of computer) matériel m.

hardwearing adjective résistant.

hard-working adjective travailleur.

hare noun lièvre m.

harm
1 noun (hurt) mal m; (wrong) tort m.
2 verb (physically) faire du mal à; (health, interests etc) nuire à.

harmful adjective nuisible.

harmless adjective inoffensif.

harmonica noun harmonica m.

harmonious adjective harmonieux.

harmony noun harmonie f.

harness noun (for horse, baby) harnais m.

harp noun harpe f.

harp on about verb Familiar ne pas s'arrêter de parler de.

harsh adjective dur, sévère; (taste) âpre; (sound) désagréable.

harshly adverb durement.

harshness noun dureté f.

harvest
1 noun moisson f; (of fruit) récolte f.
2 verb moissonner; récolter.

has see have.

hassle noun Familiar (trouble) histoires fpl; (bother) mal m, peine f.

haste noun hâte f.

hasten *verb* se hâter (to do de faire).

hastily *adverb* à la hâte.

hasty *adjective* précipité; (*visit*) rapide.

hat *noun* chapeau *m*; (*of child*) bonnet *m*; (*cap*) casquette *f*.

hatch
1 *verb* (*of chick, egg*) éclore.
2 *noun* (*in kitchen wall*) passe-plats *m invariable*.

hatchback *noun* (*three-door*) trois-portes *invariable f*; (*five-door*) cinq-portes *invariable f*.

hate *verb* détester, haïr; to h. doing *or* to do détester faire.

hateful *adjective* haïssable.

hatred *noun* haine *f*.

haul *verb* (*pull*) tirer.

haunted *adjective* hanté.

have
1 *verb* avoir; (*meal, shower etc*) prendre; to h. a walk/dream faire une promenade/un rêve; will you h....? (*cake, tea etc*) est-ce que tu veux…?; to let somebody h. something donner quelque chose à quelqu'un; you've had it! *Familiar* tu es fichu!
2 *auxiliary verb* avoir; (*with monter, sortir etc & reflexive verbs*) être; to h. decided/been avoir décidé/été; to h. gone être allé; to h. cut oneself s'être coupé; I've got to go, I h. to go je dois partir, je suis obligé de partir; to h. something done faire faire quelque chose; he's had his suitcase brought up il a fait monter sa valise; haven't I?, hasn't she? *etc* n'est-ce pas?; no I haven't! non!; yes I h.! oui!; (*after negative question*) si!

havoc *noun* ravages *mpl*.

hawk *noun* faucon *m*.

hay *noun* foin *m*.

hay fever *noun* rhume *m* des foins.

haystack *noun* meule *f* de foin.

hazard *noun* risque *m*.

haze *noun* brume *f*.

hazelnut *noun* noisette *f*.

hazy *adjective* (*weather*) brumeux; (*photo, idea*) flou; I'm h. about my plans je ne suis pas sûr de mes projets.

he *pronoun* il; (*stressed*) lui; he's a happy man c'est un homme heureux.

head
1 *noun* (*of person, hammer etc*) tête *f*; (*leader*) chef *m*; it didn't enter my h. ça ne m'est pas venu à l'esprit; heads or tails? pile ou face?; per h., a h. (*each*) par personne.
2 *adjective* (*salesperson etc*) principal; h. waiter maître *m* d'hôtel.
3 *verb* (*group, firm*) être à la tête de; (*list*) être en tête de.

headache *noun* mal *m* de tête; to have a h. avoir mal à la tête.

head for *verb* (*place*) se diriger vers; (*ruin*) aller à.

heading *noun* (*of chapter etc*) titre *m*; (*of subject*) rubrique *f*.

headlight *noun* phare *m*.

headline *noun* (*of newspaper*) manchette *f*; the headlines les titres *mpl*.

headmaster *noun* directeur *m*.

headmistress *noun* directrice *f*.

headphones *plural noun* casque *m* (à écouteurs).

headquarters *plural noun* siège *m* (central); (*military*) quartier *m* général.

headway *noun* progrès *mpl*.

heal *verb* (*of wound*) (se) cicatriser; (*of bruise*) disparaître; (*of bone*) se ressouder.

health *noun* santé *f*; the (National) H. Service = la Sécurité Sociale.

health food *noun* aliments *mpl* biologiques; h. food shop magasin *m* diététique.

healthy *adjective* (*person*) en bonne santé; (*food, attitude etc*) sain.

heap
1 *noun* tas *m*; heaps of (*money, people*) *Familiar* des tas de.
2 *verb* entasser; to h. something on somebody (*praise*) couvrir quelqu'un de quelque chose; (*insults*) abreuver quelqu'un de quelque chose.

hear *verb* entendre; (*listen to*) écouter; (*learn*) apprendre (that que); have you heard from Jason? est-ce que tu as eu des nouvelles de Jason?; I've heard of or about him j'ai entendu parler de lui.

heard *see* hear.

hearing *noun* (*sense*) ouïe *f*.

hearing aid *noun* appareil *m* auditif.

hearse *noun* corbillard *m*.

heart *noun* cœur *m*; heart(s) *Cards* cœur *m*; (off) by h. par cœur.

heart attack *noun* crise *f* cardiaque.

heartbeat *noun* battement *m* de cœur.

heartbreaking *adjective* navrant.

heartening *adjective* encourageant.

hearty *adjective* (*appetite*) gros (*f* grosse).

heat *noun* chaleur *f*; (*heating*) chauffage *m*.

heat (up) *verb* chauffer.

heater *noun* radiateur *m*.

heath *noun* lande *f*.

heather *noun* bruyère *f*.

heating *noun* chauffage *m*.

heat wave *noun* vague *f* de chaleur.

heave *verb*
1 (*lift*) soulever; (*pull*) tirer; (*sigh*) pousser.
2 (*feel sick*) avoir des haut-le-cœur.

heaven *noun* ciel *m*; h. knows when Dieu sait quand.

heavily *adverb* lourdement; (*to smoke, drink*) beaucoup; to rain h. pleuvoir à verse.

heavy *adjective* lourd; (*rain*) fort; (*traffic*) dense; (*smoker, drinker*) grand.

Hebrew *noun* hébreu *m*.

hectic *adjective* fiévreux; (*period*) très agité.

hedge *noun* haie *f*.

hedgehog *noun* hérisson *m*.

heel *noun* talon *m*.

heel bar *noun* talon-minute *m*.

hefty *adjective* gros (*f* grosse).

height *noun* hauteur *f*; (*of person*) taille *f*; (*of success etc*) sommet *m*; at the h. of (*summer*) au cœur de.

heir *noun* héritier *m*.

heiress *noun* héritière *f*.

held *see* hold.

helicopter *noun* hélicoptère *m*.

hell *noun* enfer *m*; a h. of a lot (of) (*very many, very much*) *Familiar* énormément (de); h.! *Familiar* zut!

hello! *interjection* bonjour!; (*an-*

swering phone) allô!; (*surprise*) tiens!

helm *noun* (*of boat*) barre *f*.

helmet *noun* casque *m*.

help
1 *noun* aide *f*, secours *m*; (*cleaning woman*) femme *f* de ménage; (*workers*) employés *mpl*, employées *fpl*; **h.!** au secours!
2 *verb* aider (**do, to do** à faire); **to h. oneself** (**to**) se servir (de); **I can't h. laughing**/*etc* je ne peux m'empêcher de rire/*etc*.

helper *noun* assistant, -ante *m or f*.

helpful *adjective* utile; (*person*) serviable.

helping *noun* (*serving*) portion *f*.

helpless *adjective* (*powerless*) impuissant; (*disabled*) impotent.

help out *verb* aider.

hem *noun* ourlet *m*.

hemmed in *adjective* enfermé; (*surrounded*) cerné.

hemorrhage *noun* hémorragie *f*.

hen *noun* poule *f*.

hepatitis *noun* hépatite *f*.

her
1 *pronoun* la, l'; (*after preposition*, '*qu*', '*c'est*') elle; (**to**) **h.** lui; **I see h.** je la vois; **I give** (**to**) **h.** je lui donne.
2 *possessive adjective* son, sa, *plural* ses.

herb *noun* herbe *f*; **herbs** (*in cooking*) fines herbes *fpl*.

herd *noun* troupeau *m*.

here *adverb* ici; **h. is, h. are** voici; **h. she is** la voici; **summer is h.** l'été est là; **h.!** (*calling attention*) holà!, **h.** (**you are**)! (*take this*) tenez!

hermit *noun* solitaire *m or f*.

hero *noun* héros *m*.

heroic *adjective* héroïque.

heroin *noun* (*drug*) héroïne *f*.

heroine *noun* héroïne *f*.

herring *noun* hareng *m*.

hers *possessive pronoun* le sien, la sienne, *plural* les sien(ne)s; **this hat is h.** ce chapeau est à elle *or* est le sien.

herself *pronoun* elle-même; (*reflexive*) se, s'; (*after preposition*) elle.

hesitant *adjective* hésitant.

hesitate *verb* hésiter (**over, about** sur; **to do** à faire).

hesitation *noun* hésitation *f*.

het up *adjective* énervé.

hey! *interjection* hé!

hi! *interjection Familiar* salut!

hiccups *plural noun* **to have** (**the**) **h.** avoir le hoquet.

hid *see* **hide**.

hide [1] *verb*
1 cacher (**from** à).
2 se cacher (**from** de).

hide [2] *noun* (*skin*) peau *f*.

hide-and-seek *noun* cache-cache *invariable m*.

hideous *adjective* horrible.

hideously *adverb* horriblement.

hide-out *noun* cachette *f*.

hiding *noun* **a good h.** (*thrashing*) une bonne raclée.

hiding place *noun* cachette *f*.

hi-fi *noun* hi-fi *invariable f*.

high
1 *adjective* haut; (*speed*) grand; (*price, number*) élevé; (*on drugs*) *Familiar* défoncé; **h. fever** forte fièvre *f*; **to be five metres h.** avoir cinq mètres de haut.
2 *adverb* **h.** (**up**) (*to fly, throw etc*) haut.

3 *noun* **an all-time h.** un nouveau record.

high-chair *noun* chaise *f* haute.

high-class *adjective* (*service*) de premier ordre; (*building*) de luxe.

higher *adjective* supérieur (**than** à).

highlands *plural noun* régions *fpl* montagneuses.

highlight
1 *noun* (*of visit*, *day*) point *m* culminant; (*of show*) clou *m*.
2 *verb* souligner.

highly *adverb* (*very*) très; (*to recommend*) chaudement; **h. paid** très bien payé.

high-pitched *adjective* (*sound*) aigu, -uë.

high-rise *adjective* **h.building** tour *f*.

highroad *noun* grand-route *f*.

high school *noun* = collège *m* d'enseignement secondaire.

high-speed *adjective* ultra-rapide; **h. train** rapide *m*.

high street *noun* grand-rue *f*.

highway *noun f*; **public h.** voie *f* publique; **H. Code** Code *m* de la route.

hijack
1 *verb* (*aircraft*) détourner.
2 *noun* détournement *m*.

hijacker *noun* pirate *m* de l'air.

hike
1 *noun* excursion *f* à pied.
2 *verb* marcher à pied.

hiker *noun* excursionniste *m or f*.

hilarious *adjective* désopilant.

hill *noun* colline *f*.

hillside *noun* **on the h.** à flanc de colline.

hilly *adjective* accidenté.

him *pronoun* le, l'; (*after preposi-*

tion, '*than*', '*it is*') lui; (**to**) **h.** lui; **I see h.** je le vois; **I give (to) h.** je lui donne.

himself *pronoun* lui-même; (*reflexive*) se, s'; (*after preposition*) lui.

hinder *verb* gêner.

Hindu *adjective & noun* hindou, -oue (*m or f*).

hinge *noun* charnière *f*.

hint
1 *noun* allusion *f*; (*sign*) indication *f*; **hints** (*advice*) conseils *mpl*.
2 *verb* laisser entendre (**that** que).

hint at *verb* faire allusion à.

hip *noun* hanche *f*.

hippopotamus *noun* hippopotame *m*.

hire
1 *verb* (*vehicle etc*) louer; (*worker*) engager.
2 *noun* location *f*; **for h.** à louer.

hire out *verb* donner en location, louer.

hire purchase *noun* vente *f* à crédit.

his
1 *possessive adjective* son, sa, *plural* ses.
2 *possessive pronoun* le sien, la sienne, *plural* les sien(ne)s; **this hat is h.** ce chapeau est à lui *or* est le sien.

hiss
1 *verb* siffler.
2 *noun* sifflement *m*.

historic(al) *adjective* historique.

history *noun* histoire *f*.

hit
1 *verb* (*beat etc*) frapper; (*bump into*) heurter; (*reach*) atteindre; (*affect*) toucher.

2 *noun* (*blow*) coup *m*; (*play, film*) succès *m*; **h. (song)** chanson *f* à succès.

hit-and-run driver *noun* chauffard *m*.

hitch
1 *noun* (*snag*) problème *m*.
2 *verb* **to h. (a ride)** *Familiar* faire de l'auto-stop (**to** jusqu'à).

hitchhike *verb* faire de l'auto-stop (**to** jusqu'à).

hitchhiker *noun* auto-stoppeur, -euse *m or f*.

hitchhiking *noun* auto-stop *m*.

hit (up)on *verb* (*find*) tomber sur.

hit out (at) *verb Familiar* attaquer.

hive *noun* ruche *f*.

hoard *verb* amasser.

hoarding *noun* panneau *m* d'affichage.

hoarse *adjective* enroué.

hoax *noun* canular *m*.

hobby *noun* passe-temps *invariable m*.

hockey *noun* hockey *m*; **ice h.** hockey sur glace.

hold
1 *noun* (*grip*) prise *f*; (*of ship*) cale *f*; (*of aircraft*) soute *f*; **to get h. of** saisir; (*contact*) joindre; (*find*) trouver.
2 *verb* tenir; (*breath, interest, attention*) retenir; (*post*) occuper; (*record*) détenir; (*possess*) posséder; (*contain*) contenir; **to h. hands** se tenir par la main; **h. the line!** (*on phone*) ne quittez pas!; **to be held** (*of event*) avoir lieu.

holdall *noun* fourre-tout *invariable m*.

hold back *verb* (*crowd*) contenir;

(*hide*) cacher.

hold down *verb* (*price*) maintenir bas; (*job*) garder.

holder *noun* (*of passport*) titulaire *m or f*; (*of record*) détenteur, -trice *m or f*; (*device*) support *m*.

hold on *verb* attendre; (*stand firm*) tenir bon; **h. on!** (*on phone*) ne quittez pas! **h. on (tight)!** tenez bon!

hold onto *verb* (*cling to*) tenir bien; (*keep*) garder.

hold out *verb*
1 (*opportunity*) offrir; (*arm*) étendre.
2 (*not give in*) résister; (*last*) durer.

hold up *verb* lever; (*support*) soutenir; (*delay*) retarder; (*bank*) attaquer.

holdup *noun* (*attack*) hold-up *invariable m*; (*traffic jam*) bouchon *m*.

hole *noun* trou *m*.

holiday *noun* (*from work, school etc*) vacances *fpl*; **a h.** (*day off*) un congé; **a (public or bank) h.**, un jour férié; **on h.** en vacances.

holidaymaker *noun* vacancier, -ière *m or f*.

Holland *noun* la Hollande *f*.

hollow *adjective* creux.

holy *adjective* saint; (*water*) bénit.

home
1 *noun* maison *f*; (*country*) pays *m* (natal); **at h.** à la maison, chez soi; **to make oneself at h.** se mettre à l'aise; **a good h.** une bonne famille; **(old people's) h.** maison *f* de retraite; **h. life/cooking/**etc la vie/cuisine/*etc* familiale.
2 *adverb* à la maison, chez soi; **to go** or **come (back) h.** rentrer; **to be h.** être rentré.

home help *noun* aide *f* ménagère.

homeless *adjective* sans abri.

homemade *adjective* (fait à la) maison *invariable*.

homesick *adjective* to be h. avoir envie de rentrer chez soi.

home town *noun* ville *f* natale.

homework *noun* devoir(s) *m(pl)*.

homosexual *adjective & noun* homosexuel, -elle (*m or f*).

honest *adjective* honnête; (*frank*) franc (*f* franche) (**with** avec).

honesty *noun* honnêteté *f*; franchise *f*.

honey *noun* miel *m*; (*person*) *Familiar* chéri, -ie *m or f*.

honeymoon *noun* lune *f* de miel; (*trip*) voyage *m* de noces.

Hong Kong *noun* Hong Kong *m or f*.

honk *verb* (*in vehicle*) klaxonner.

honour
1 *noun* honneur *m*; **in h. of** l'honneur de; **honours degree** = licence *f*.
2 *verb* honorer (**with** de).

honourable *adjective* honorable.

hood *noun* capuchon *m*; (*mask of robber*) cagoule *f*; (*car or pram roof*) capote *f*.

hoof *noun* sabot *m*.

hook *noun* crochet *m*; (*on clothes*) agrafe *f*; *Fishing* hameçon *m*; **off the h.** (*phone*) décroché.

hooked *adjective* (*nose, object*) recourbé; **h. on** (*drugs, chess etc*) *Familiar* accro de.

hook (on or up) *verb* accrocher (**to** à).

hooligan *noun* vandale *m*.

hoop *noun* cerceau *m*.

hoot *verb* (*in vehicle*) klaxonner.

hooter *noun* klaxon ® *m*.

hoover ®
1 *noun* aspirateur *m*.
2 *verb* passer l'aspirateur dans.

hop
1 *verb* sauter (à cloche-pied); (*of bird*) sautiller; **h. in!** (*in car*) montez!
2 *noun* saut *m*.

hope
1 *noun* espoir *m*.
2 *verb* espérer (**to do** faire, **that** que); **I h. so** j'espère que oui.

hope for *verb* espérer.

hopeful *adjective* optimiste; (*promising*) prometteur; **to be h. that** avoir bon espoir que.

hopefully *adverb* (*one hopes*) on espère (que).

hopeless *adjective* désespéré; (*useless*) nul.

hopelessly *adverb* (*extremely*) complètement.

hops *plural noun* houblon *m*.

hopscotch *noun* marelle *f*.

horizon *noun* horizon *m*; **on the h.** à l'horizon.

horizontal *adjective* horizontal.

horn *noun* (*of animal*) corne *f*; (*on vehicle*) klaxon ® *m*.

horrible *adjective* horrible.

horribly *adverb* horriblement.

horrific *adjective* horrible.

horrify *verb* horrifier.

horror *noun* horreur *f*.

horse *noun* cheval *m*; **h. chestnut** marron *m* (d'Inde).

horseback *noun* **on h.** à cheval.

horseracing *noun* courses *fpl*.

horseshoe *noun* fer *m* à cheval.

hose *noun* tuyau *m*.

hosepipe *noun* tuyau *m*.

hospitable *adjective* accueillant.

hospital *noun* hôpital *m*; **in h.**, à l'hôpital.

hospitality *noun* hospitalité *f*.

hospitalize *verb* hospitaliser.

host *noun* hôte *m*; (*of TV show*) présentateur, -trice *m or f*.

hostage *noun* otage *m*; **to take somebody h.** prendre quelqu'un en otage.

hostel *noun* foyer *m*; **youth h.** auberge *f* de jeunesse.

hostess *noun* hôtesse *f*.

hostile *adjective* hostile (**to, towards** à).

hostility *noun* hostilité *f* (**to, towards** envers).

hot *adjective* chaud; (*spice*) fort; **to be** *or* **feel h.** avoir chaud; **it's h.** (*of weather*) il fait chaud.

hot dog *noun* hot-dog *m*.

hotel *noun* hôtel *m*.

hound *verb* (*pursue*) traquer.

hour *noun* heure *f*; **half an h.** une demi-heure; **a quarter of an h.** un quart d'heure.

hourly
 1 *adjective* (*pay*) horaire; **an h. bus**/*etc* un bus/*etc* toutes les heures.
 2 *adverb* toutes les heures.

house [1] *noun* maison *f*; (*audience in theatre*) salle *f*.

house [2] *verb* loger; (*of building*) abriter.

household *noun* famille *f*.

housekeeping *noun* ménage *m*.

housewarming *noun* **to have a h. (party)** pendre la crémaillère.

housewife *noun* femme *f* au foyer.

housework *noun* (travaux *mpl* du) ménage *m*.

housing *noun* logement *m*; (*houses*) logements *mpl*.

hovel *noun* taudis *m*.

hover *verb* (*of bird etc*) planer.

hovercraft *noun* aéroglisseur *m*.

how *adverb* comment; **h. kind!** comme c'est gentil!; **h. do you do?** bonjour; **h. long/high is?** quelle est la longueur/hauteur de?; **h. much?, h. many?** combien?; **h. much time**/*etc*? combien de temps/*etc*?; **h. many apples**/*etc*? combien de pommes/*etc*?; **h. about some coffee?** du café?

however
 1 *adverb* **h. big he may be** quelque grand qu'il soit; **h. she may do it** de quelque manière qu'elle le fasse.
 2 *conjunction* cependant.

howl
 1 *verb* hurler.
 2 *noun* hurlement *m*.

HP *abbreviation* = **hire purchase**.

HQ *abbreviation* = **headquarters**.

hubcap *noun* enjoliveur *m*.

huddle *verb* se blottir.

hug
 1 *verb* serrer (dans ses bras).
 2 *noun* **to give somebody a h.** serrer quelqu'un (dans ses bras).

huge *adjective* énorme.

hull *noun* (*of ship*) coque *f*.

hullo! = **hello**.

hum *verb* (*of insect*) bourdonner; (*of person*) fredonner.

human *adjective* humain; **h. being** être *m* humain.

humanity *noun* humanité *f*.

humble *adjective* humble.

humid *adjective* humide.

humidity *noun* humidité *f*.

humiliate *verb* humilier.

humiliation *noun* humiliation *f.*

humorous *adjective* (*book etc*) humoristique; (*person*) plein d'humour.

humour *noun* (*fun*) humour *m.*

hump *noun* (*lump*) bosse *f.*

hunch *noun Familiar* intuition *f.*

hundred *adjective & noun* cent (*m*); **a h. pages** cent pages; **hundreds of** des centaines de.

hundredth *adjective & noun* centième (*m or f*).

hung *see* **hang**[1,2].

Hungarian *adjective & noun* hongrois, -oise (*m or f*).

Hungary *noun* la Hongrie *f.*

hunger *noun* faim *f.*

hungry *adjective* **to be** *or* **feel h.** avoir faim; **to make h.** donner faim à.

hunt

1 *noun* (*of animal*) chasse *f;* (*of person*) recherche *f* (**for** de).

2 *verb* (*animals*) chasser; (*pursue*) poursuivre; (*seek*) chercher; **to h. for something** chercher quelque chose.

hunt down *verb* traquer.

hunter *noun* chasseur *m.*

hunting *noun* chasse *f.*

hurdle *noun* (*fence*) haie *f;* (*problem*) obstacle *m.*

hurl *verb* lancer.

hurray! *interjection* hourra!

hurricane *noun* ouragan *m.*

hurry

1 *noun* hâte *f;* **in a h.** à la hâte; **to be in a h.** être pressé.

2 *verb* (*rush*) se dépêcher (**to do** de faire); **to h. towards** se précipiter vers.

3 *verb* (*person*) bousculer; **to h. one's meal** manger à toute vitesse.

hurry up *verb* se dépêcher.

hurt

1 *verb* (*physically*) faire du mal à; (*emotionally*) faire de la peine à; (*reputation etc*) nuire à; **to h. somebody's feelings** blesser quelqu'un.

2 *verb* (*of arm, leg etc*) faire mal.

3 *noun* mal *m.*

husband *noun* mari *m.*

hush *noun* silence *m.*

hustle

1 *verb* (*shove*) bousculer.

2 *noun* **h. and bustle** tourbillon *m.*

hut *noun* cabane *f.*

hygiene *noun* hygiène *f.*

hygienic *adjective* hygiénique.

hymn *noun* cantique *m.*

hypermarket *noun* hypermarché *m.*

hyphen *noun* trait *m* d'union.

hyphenated *adjective* (*word*) à trait d'union.

hypocrisy *noun* hypocrisie *f.*

hypocrite *noun* hypocrite *m or f.*

hysterical *adjective* (*upset*) qui a une crise de nerfs; (*funny*) *Familiar* désopilant.

hysterically *adverb* (*to cry*) sans pouvoir s'arrêter.

I

I *pronoun* je, j'; (*stressed*) moi.

ice *noun* glace *f*; (*on road*) verglas *m*.

iceberg *noun* iceberg *m*.

ice-cold *adjective* glacial; (*drink*) glacé.

ice cream *noun* glace *f*.

ice cube *noun* glaçon *m*.

ice-skating *noun* patinage *m* (sur glace).

icicle *noun* glaçon *m*.

icing *noun* (*on cake*) glaçage *m*.

icy *adjective* glacé; (*weather*) glacial; (*road*) verglacé.

ID *noun* pièce *f* d'identité.

idea *noun* idée *f*; **I have an i. that** j'ai l'impression que.

ideal
  1 *adjective* idéal (*mpl* -aux *or* -als).
  2 *noun* idéal *m* (*plural* -aux *or* -als).

ideally *adverb* idéalement; **i. we should stay** l'idéal serait que nous restions.

identical *adjective* identique (**to, with** à).

identification *noun* (*document*) pièce *f* d'identité.

identify *verb* identifier; **to i. (oneself) with** s'identifier avec.

identity *noun* identité *f*.

idiom *noun* expression *f* idiomatique.

idiot *noun* idiot, -ote *m or f*.

idiotic *adjective* idiot.

idle *adjective* (*unoccupied*) inactif; (*lazy*) paresseux.

idler *noun* paresseux, -euse *m or f*.

idol *noun* idole *f*.

idolize *verb* (*adore*) traiter comme une idole.

i.e. *abbreviation* c'est-à-dire.

if *conjunction* si; **if he comes** s'il vient; **even if** même si; **if only I were rich** si seulement j'étais riche.

igloo *noun* igloo *m*.

ignorance *noun* ignorance *f* (**of** de).

ignorant *adjective* ignorant (**of** de).

ignore *verb* (*thing*) ne prêter aucune attention à; (*person*) faire semblant de ne pas reconnaître.

ill
  1 *adjective* malade; **to be in i. health** être en mauvaise santé; **i. effects** effets *mpl* néfastes.
  2 *noun* **ills** maux *mpl*.

illegal *adjective* illégal.

illegible *adjective* illisible.

illiterate *adjective* illettré.

illness *noun* maladie *f*.

ill-treat *verb* maltraiter.

illusion *noun* illusion *f* (**about** sur).

illustrate *verb* illustrer (**with** de).

illustration *noun* illustration *f*.

image *noun* image *f*; (**public**) **i.** (*of firm*) image *f* de marque.

imaginary *adjective* imaginaire.

imagination *noun* imagination *f*.

imagine *verb* (s')imaginer (**that** que).

imitate *verb* imiter.

imitation *noun* imitation *f*; **i. jewellery** bijoux *mpl* fantaisie.

immaculate *adjective* impeccable.

immature *adjective* (*person*) qui manque de maturité.

immediate *adjective* immédiat.

immediately
1 *adverb* (*at once*) tout de suite, immédiatement.
2 *conjunction* dès que.

immense *adjective* immense.

immensely *adverb* extraordinairement.

immigrant *noun* & *adjective* immigré, -ée (*m or f*).

immigration *noun* immigration *f*.

immortal *adjective* immortel.

immune *adjective* (*naturally*) immunisé (to contre); (*vaccinated*) vacciné.

immunize *verb* vacciner (against contre).

impact *noun* effet (on sur).

impatience *noun* impatience *f*.

impatient *adjective* impatient (to do de faire).

impatiently *adverb* avec impatience.

imperative *noun* Grammar impératif *m*.

impersonate *verb* se faire passer pour; (*on TV etc*) imiter.

impersonator *noun* (*on TV etc*) imitateur, -trice *m or f*.

impertinent *adjective* impertinent (to envers).

impetus *noun* impulsion *f*.

implement [1] *noun* (*tool*) instrument *m*; (*utensil*) ustensile *m*.

implement [2] *verb* mettre en œuvre.

implication *noun* conséquence *f*; (*impact*) portée *f*.

imply *verb* laisser entendre (that

que); (*assume*) impliquer.

impolite *adjective* impoli.

import
1 *verb* importer (from de).
2 *noun* importation *f*.

importance *noun* importance *f*; of no i. sans importance.

important *adjective* important.

importer *noun* importateur, -trice *m or f*.

impose *verb*
1 (*force*) imposer (on à); (*fine*) infliger (on à).
2 (*cause trouble*) déranger; to i. on somebody déranger quelqu'un.

imposing *adjective* (*building*) impressionnant.

imposition *noun* (*inconvenience*) dérangement *m*.

impossibility *noun* impossibilité *f*.

impossible *adjective* impossible (to do à faire); it is i. (for us) to do it il (nous) est impossible de le faire.

impostor *noun* imposteur *m*.

impractical *adjective* peu réaliste.

impress *verb* impressionner.

impression *noun* impression *f*.

impressive *adjective* impressionnant.

imprison *verb* emprisonner.

improbable *adjective* peu probable.

improper *adjective* indécent.

improve *verb*
1 (*make better*) améliorer.
2 (*get better*) s'améliorer; (*of business*) reprendre.

improvement *noun* amélioration *f*.

improve on *verb* faire mieux

que.

improvise *verb* improviser.

impudent *adjective* impudent.

impulse *noun* impulsion *f*; **on i.** sur un coup de tête.

impulsive *adjective* impulsif.

impulsively *adverb* de manière impulsive.

impurity *noun* impureté *f*.

in
1 *preposition* dans; **in the box/ etc** dans la boîte/*etc*; **in an hour('s time)** dans une heure.
▪ à; **in school** à l'école; **in Paris** à Paris; **in Portugal** au Portugal; **in ink** à l'encre.
▪ en; **in summer/May/French** en été/mai/français; **in Spain** en Espagne; **in an hour** (*within that period*) en une heure; **in doing** en faisant.
▪ de; **in a soft voice** d'une voix douce; **the best in** le meilleur de.
▪ **in the morning** le matin; **one in ten** un sur dix.
2 *adverb* **to be in** (*home*) être là, être à la maison; (*of train*) être arrivé; (*in fashion*) être en vogue.

in- *prefix* in-.

inability *noun* incapacité *f* (**to do** de faire).

inaccessible *adjective* inaccessible.

inaccuracy *noun* (*error*) inexactitude *f*.

inaccurate *adjective* inexact.

inadequacy *noun* insuffisance *f*.

inadequate *adjective* insuffisant; (*person*) pas à la hauteur.

inappropriate *adjective* peu approprié.

inaugurate *verb* (*building*) inaugurer.

inauguration *noun* inaugura-

tion *f*.

incapable *adjective* incapable (**of doing** de faire).

incense *verb* mettre en colère.

incentive *noun* encouragement *m*, motivation *f*.

inch *noun* pouce *m*.

incident *noun* incident *m*; (*in film etc*) épisode *m*.

incidently *adverb* (*by the way*) à propos.

incite *verb* inciter (**to do** à faire).

incitement *noun* incitation *f*.

inclination *noun* (*desire*) envie *f* (**to do** de faire).

incline *verb* (*bend*) incliner; **to be inclined to do** (*feel a wish to*) avoir bien envie de faire; (*tend to*) avoir tendance à faire.

include *verb* (*contain*) comprendre; **to be included** être compris; (*on list*) être inclus.

including *preposition* y compris; **i. service** service *m* compris; **up to and i. Monday** jusqu'à lundi inclus.

inclusive *adjective* inclus; **to be i. of** comprendre.

income *noun* revenu *m* (**from** de); **private i.** rentes *fpl*.

income tax *noun* impôt *m* sur le revenu.

incompatible *adjective* incompatible (**with** avec).

incompetent *adjective* incompétent.

incomplete *adjective* incomplet.

inconceivable *adjective* inconcevable.

inconsiderate *adjective* (*remark*) irréfléchi; (*person*) pas très gentil (**towards** avec).

inconsistency *noun* incohérence *f*.

inconsistent *adjective* en contradiction (**with** avec).

inconspicuous *adjective* peu en évidence.

inconvenience
1 *noun* (*bother*) dérangement *m*; (*disadvantage*) inconvénient *m*.
2 *verb* déranger, gêner.

inconvenient *adjective* (*moment, situation etc*) gênant; (*house*) mal situé; **it's i. (for me) to** ça me dérange de.

incorporate *verb* incorporer; (*have a quality*) comprendre.

incorrect *adjective* inexact; **you're i.** vous avez tort.

increase
1 *verb* augmenter; (*of effort, noise*) s'intensifier.
2 *noun* augmentation *f* (**in, of** de); intensification *f*; **on the i.** en hausse.

increasing *adjective* croissant.

increasingly *adverb* de plus en plus.

incredible *adjective* incroyable.

incredibly *adverb* incroyablement.

incubator *noun* (*for baby, eggs*) couveuse *f*.

incur *verb* (*expenses*) faire; (*loss*) subir.

incurable *adjective* incurable.

indecent *adjective* (*obscene*) indécent.

indecisive *adjective* indécis.

indeed *adverb* en effet; **very good/etc i.** vraiment très bon/etc; **yes i.!** bien sûr!; **thank you very much i.!** merci infiniment!

indefinite *adjective* indéfini.

indefinitely *adverb* indéfiniment.

independence *noun* indépendance *f*.

independent *adjective* indépendant (**of** de).

independently *adverb* de façon indépendante; **i. of** indépendamment de.

index
1 *noun* (*in book*) index *m*; (*in library*) catalogue *m*.
2 *verb* (*classify*) classer.

index card *noun* fiche *f*.

index finger *noun* index *m*.

index-linked *adjective* indexé (**to** sur).

India *noun* l'Inde *f*.

Indian *adjective* & *noun* indien, -ienne (*m or f*).

indicate *verb* indiquer (**that** que); **I was indicating right** (*in vehicle*) j'avais mis mon clignotant droit.

indication *noun* (*sign*) indice *m*, indication *f*.

indicator *noun* (*instrument*) indicateur *m*; (*in vehicle*) clignotant *m*.

indifference *noun* indifférence *f* (**to** à).

indifferent *adjective* indifférent (**to** à).

indigestion *noun* problèmes *mpl* de digestion; (**an attack of) i.** une indigestion.

indignant *adjective* indigné (**at** de).

indignation *noun* indignation *f*.

indirect *adjective* indirect.

indirectly *adverb* indirectement.

indiscreet *adjective* indiscret.

indiscriminate *adjective* (*random*) fait/donné *etc* au hasard.

indiscriminately *adverb* (*at random*) au hasard.

indistinguishable *adjective* indifférenciable (**from** de).

individual
1 *adjective* individuel; (*specific*) particulier.
2 *noun* (*person*) individu *m*.

individually *adverb* (*separately*) individuellement.

Indonesia *noun* l'Indonésie *f*.

Indonesian *adjective & noun* indonésien, -ienne (*m or f*).

indoor *adjective* (*games, shoes etc*) d'intérieur; (*swimming pool*) couvert.

indoors *adverb* à l'intérieur.

induce *verb* persuader (**to do** de faire); (*cause*) provoquer.

indulge *verb* (*somebody's wishes*) satisfaire; (*child etc*) gâter; **to i. in something** (*as a treat*) s'offrir quelque chose.

indulgent *adjective* indulgent (**to** envers).

industrial *adjective* industriel; (*conflict*) du travail; **i. action** mouvement *m* revendicatif; **i. estate** zone *f* industrielle.

industry *noun* industrie *f*.

inedible *adjective* immangeable.

ineffective *adjective* (*measure*) inefficace.

inefficiency *noun* inefficacité *f*.

inefficient *adjective* (*person, measure*) inefficace.

inept *adjective* (*unskilled*) peu habile (**at** à); (*incompetent*) incapable.

inequality *noun* inégalité *f*.

inevitable *adjective* inévitable.

inevitably *adverb* inévitablement.

inexcusable *adjective* inexcusable.

inexpensive *adjective* bon marché *invariable*.

inexperience *noun* inexpérience *f*.

inexperienced *adjective* inexpérimenté.

inexplicable *adjective* inexplicable.

infallible *adjective* infaillible.

infamous *adjective* (*evil*) infâme.

infancy *noun* petite enfance *f*.

infant *noun* petit(e) enfant *m or f*; (*baby*) nourrisson *m*.

infantry *noun* infanterie *f*.

infant school *noun* = cours *m* préparatoire.

infatuated *adjective* amoureux (**with** de).

infatuation *noun* engouement *m* (**for, with** pour).

infect *verb* infecter; **to get infected** s'infecter.

infection *noun* infection *f*.

infectious *adjective* contagieux.

inferior *adjective* inférieur (**to** à); (*goods, work*) de qualité inférieure.

inferiority *noun* infériorité *f*.

infernal *adjective* infernal.

infest *verb* infester (**with** de).

infinite *adjective* infini.

infinitely *adverb* infiniment.

infinitive *noun* Grammar infinitif *m*.

infinity *noun* infini *m*.

infirm *adjective* infirme.

inflamed *adjective* (*throat etc*) enflammé.

inflammation *noun* inflammation *f*.

inflate *verb* gonfler.

inflation *noun* inflation *f*.

inflexible *adjective* inflexible.

inflict verb (wound) occasionner (on à); to i. pain on somebody faire souffrir quelqu'un.

influence
 1 noun influence f; under the i. (of drink) en état d'ébriété.
 2 verb influencer.

influential adjective to be i. avoir une grande influence.

influenza noun grippe f.

influx noun flot m.

info noun Familiar renseignements mpl (on sur).

inform verb informer (of de, that que).

informal adjective simple, décontracté; (expression) familier; (meeting) non-officiel.

informally adverb sans cérémonie; (to dress) simplement; (to discuss) à titre non-officiel.

information noun renseignements mpl (about, on sur); a piece of i. un renseignement.

informative adjective instructif.

inform on verb dénoncer.

infuriate verb exaspérer.

infuriating adjective exaspérant.

ingenious adjective ingénieux.

ingratitude noun ingratitude f.

ingredient noun ingrédient m.

inhabit verb habiter.

inhabitant noun habitant, -ante m or f.

inhale verb aspirer.

inherit verb hériter (de).

inheritance noun héritage m.

inhibit verb (hinder) gêner; to be inhibited avoir des inhibitions.

inhibition noun inhibition f.

inhospitable adjective peu accueillant, inhospitalier.

inhuman adjective inhumain.

initial
 1 adjective premier.
 2 noun initials initiales fpl; (signature) paraphe m.
 3 verb parapher.

initially adverb au début.

inject verb injecter (into à).

injection noun injection f, piqûre f.

injure verb (physically) blesser, faire du mal à.

injured
 1 adjective blessé.
 2 noun the i. les blessés mpl.

injury noun blessure f; (fracture) fracture f; (sprain) foulure f.

injustice noun injustice f.

ink noun encre f.

inkling noun (petite) idée f.

inland
 1 adjective intérieur.
 2 adverb à l'intérieur.

Inland Revenue noun service m des impôts.

in-laws plural noun belle-famille f.

inmate noun (of prison) détenu, -ue m or f.

inn noun auberge f.

inner adjective intérieur; the i. city les quartiers du centre-ville.

inner tube noun (of tyre) chambre f à air.

innkeeper noun aubergiste m or f.

innocence noun innocence f.

innocent adjective innocent.

inoculate verb vacciner (against contre).

inoculation noun vaccination f.

input noun (computer operation) entrée f; (data) données fpl.

inquire *verb* se renseigner (**about** sur).

inquire into *verb* faire une enquête sur.

inquiry *noun* demande *f* de renseignements; (*investigation*) enquête *f*.

inquisitive *adjective* curieux.

insane *adjective* fou (*f* folle).

insanity *noun* folie *f*.

inscription *noun* inscription *f*; (*in book*) dédicace *f*.

insect *noun* insecte *m*.

insecticide *noun* insecticide *m*.

insecure *adjective* (*not securely fixed*) mal fixé; (*uncertain*) incertain; (*person*) qui manque d'assurance.

insensitive *adjective* insensible (**to** à).

insensitivity *noun* insensibilité *f*.

insert *verb* introduire, insérer (**in**, **into** dans).

inside
1 *adverb* dedans, à l'intérieur.
2 *preposition* à l'intérieur de.
3 *noun* dedans *m*, intérieur *m*; **on the i.** à l'intérieur (**of** de); **i. out** (*socks etc*) à l'envers.
4 *adjective* intérieur; **the i. lane** la voie de gauche.

insight *noun* (*into question*) aperçu *m* (**into** de).

insignificant *adjective* insignifiant.

insincere *adjective* peu sincère.

insist *verb*
1 insister (**on doing** pour faire).
2 (*order*) insister (**that** pour que + *subjunctive*); (*declare*) affirmer (**that** que).

insistence *noun* insistance *f*; **her i. on seeing me** l'insistance

qu'elle met à vouloir me voir.

insistent *adjective* **to be i.** insister (**that** pour que + *subjunctive*).

insist on *verb* (*demand*) exiger; (*assert*) affirmer.

insolence *noun* insolence *f*.

insolent *adjective* insolent.

insomnia *noun* insomnie *f*.

inspect *verb* inspecter; (*tickets*) contrôler.

inspection *noun* inspection *f*; (*of tickets*) contrôle *m*.

inspector *noun* inspecteur, -trice *m or f*; (*on train*) contrôleur, -euse *m or f*.

inspiration *noun* inspiration *f*.

inspire *verb* inspirer (**somebody with something** quelque chose à quelqu'un).

install *verb* installer.

instalment *noun* (*of money*) acompte *m*; (*of serial*) épisode *m*.

instance *noun* (*example*) cas *m*; **for i.** par exemple.

instant
1 *adjective* immédiat; **i. coffee** café *m* soluble.
2 (*moment*) instant *m*.

instantly *adverb* immédiatement.

instead *adverb* plutôt; **i. of (doing) something** au lieu de (faire) quelque chose; **i. of somebody** à la place de quelqu'un; **i. (of him or her)** à sa place.

instinct *noun* instinct *m*.

instinctive *adjective* instinctif.

instinctively *adverb* instinctivement.

institution *noun* institution *f*.

instruct *verb* (*teach*) enseigner (**somebody in something** quelque chose à quelqu'un); **to i. somebody to do** (*order*) charger quelqu'un de faire.

instructions *plural noun (for use)* mode *m* d'emploi; *(orders)* instructions *fpl*.

instructive *adjective* instructif.

instructor *noun (for skiing etc)* moniteur, -trice *m or f*; **driving i.** moniteur, -trice *m or f* d'auto-école.

instrument *noun* instrument *m*.

insufficient *adjective* insuffisant.

insulate *verb (against cold and electrically)* isoler; **insulating tape** chatterton *m*.

insulation *noun (material)* isolant *m*.

insult
1 *verb* insulter.
2 *noun* insulte *f* (to à).

insurance *noun* assurance *f*; **i. company** compagnie *f* d'assurances.

insure *verb* assurer (**against** contre).

intact *adjective* intact.

intellect *noun* intelligence *f*.

intellectual *adjective & noun* intellectuel, -elle *(m or f)*.

intelligence *noun* intelligence *f*.

intelligent *adjective* intelligent.

intelligible *adjective* compréhensible.

intend *verb (gift etc)* destiner (**for** à); **to be intended to do/for somebody** être destiné à faire/à quelqu'un; **to i. to do** avoir l'intention de faire.

intense *adjective* intense; *(interest)* vif *(f* vive).

intensify *verb* s'intensifier.

intensity *noun* intensité *f*.

intensive *adjective* intensif; **in i. care** en réanimation.

intent *adjective* **i. on doing** résolu à faire.

intention *noun* intention *f* (**of doing** de faire).

intentional *adjective* **it wasn't i.** ce n'était pas fait exprès.

intentionally *adverb* exprès.

intercept *verb* intercepter.

interchange *noun (on road)* échangeur *m*.

interchangeable *adjective* interchangeable.

intercom *noun* interphone *m*.

interconnected *adjective (facts etc)* liés.

interest
1 *noun* intérêt *m*; *(money)* intérêts *mpl*; **to take an i. in** s'intéresser à; **to be of i. to somebody** intéresser quelqu'un.
2 *verb* intéresser.

interested *adjective* intéressé; **to be i. in something/somebody** s'intéresser à quelque chose/quelqu'un; **I'm i. in doing** ça m'intéresse de faire.

interesting *adjective* intéressant.

interfere *verb* se mêler des affaires d'autrui.

interfere in *verb* s'ingérer dans.

interference *noun* ingérence *f*; *(on radio)* parasites *mpl*.

interfere with *verb (upset)* déranger.

interior
1 *adjective* intérieur.
2 *noun* intérieur *m*.

interjection *noun* interjection *f*.

interlude *noun (on TV)* interlude *m*; *(in theatre)* entracte *m*.

intermediary *noun* intermédiaire *m or f*.

intermediate *adjective* intermédiaire; (*course*) de niveau moyen.

internal *adjective* interne; (*flight*) intérieur.

international *adjective* international.

interpret *verb* interpréter.

interpreter *noun* interprète *m or f.*

interrogate *verb* interroger.

interrogation *noun* (*by police*) interrogatoire *m.*

interrogative *adjective & noun* Grammar interrogatif (*m*).

interrupt *verb* interrompre.

interruption *noun* interruption *f.*

intersect *verb*
1 couper.
2 s'entrecouper.

intersection *noun* (*of roads, lines*) intersection *f.*

interval *noun* intervalle *m*; (*in theatre*) entracte *m.*

intervene *verb* (*of person*) intervenir; (*of event*) survenir.

intervention *noun* intervention *f.*

interview
1 *noun* entrevue *f* (**with** avec); (*on TV etc*) interview *f.*
2 *verb* avoir une entrevue avec; (*on TV etc*) interviewer.

interviewer *noun* (*on TV etc*) interviewer *m.*

intimate *adjective* intime.

intimidate *verb* intimider.

into *preposition* dans; **to put i.** mettre dans.
■ en; **to translate i.** traduire en; **i. pieces** en morceaux.
■ **to be i. jazz**/*etc Familiar* être branché jazz/*etc.*

intolerable *adjective* intolérable (**that** que + *subjunctive*).

intoxicate *verb* enivrer.

intoxicated *adjective* ivre.

intransitive *adjective* Grammar intransitif.

intricate *adjective* complexe.

introduce *verb* (*bring in*) introduire (**into** dans); (*programme*) présenter; **to i. somebody to somebody** présenter quelqu'un à quelqu'un.

introduction *noun* introduction *f*; (*of person to person*) présentation *f*; **i. to** (*initiation*) premier contact avec.

intrude *verb* déranger (**on somebody** quelqu'un).

intruder *noun* intrus, -use *m or f.*

intrusion *noun* (*bother*) dérangement *m.*

intuition *noun* intuition *f.*

inundated *adjective* submergé (**with work/letters**/*etc* de travail/lettres/*etc*).

invade *verb* envahir.

invader *noun* envahisseur, -euse *m or f.*

invalid [1] *noun* malade *m or f*; (*through injury*) infirme *m or f.*

invalid [2] *adjective* (*ticket etc*) non valable.

invaluable *adjective* inestimable.

invariably *adverb* (*always*) toujours.

invent *verb* inventer.

invention *noun* invention *f.*

inventor *noun* inventeur, -trice *m or f.*

inventory *noun* inventaire *m.*

inverted commas *plural noun* guillemets *mpl.*

invest *verb* (*money*) placer, investir (**in** dans).

investigate *verb* examiner; (*crime*) enquêter sur.

investigation *noun* examen *m*; (*inquiry by journalist, police etc*) enquête *f* (*of, into* sur).

investigator *noun* enquêteur, -euse *m or f*.

invest in *verb* placer son argent dans; (*firm*) investir dans.

investment *noun* investissement *m*, placement *m*.

investor *noun* (*in shares*) actionnaire *m or f*; (*saver*) épargnant, -ante *m or f*.

invigorating *adjective* stimulant.

invisible *adjective* invisible.

invitation *noun* invitation *f*.

invite *verb* inviter (**to do** à faire); (*ask for*) demander; (*give occasion for*) provoquer.

inviting *adjective* engageant.

invoice
  1 *noun* facture *f*.
  2 *verb* facturer.

involve *verb* (*include*) mêler (**in** à); (*entail*) entraîner; **the job involves ...** le poste nécessite ...

involved *adjective* (*concerned*) concerné; (*committed*) engagé (**in** dans); (*complicated*) compliqué; (*at stake*) en jeu; **the person i.** la personne en question; **i. with somebody** mêlé aux affaires de quelqu'un.

involvement *noun* participation *f* (**in** à); (*commitment*) engagement *m*; (*emotional*) liaison *f*.

inward(s) *adverb* vers l'intérieur.

IOU *abbreviation* (*I owe you*) reconnaissance *f* de dette.

IQ *abbreviation* (*intelligence quotient*) QI *invariable m*.

Iran *noun* l'Iran *m*.

Iranian *adjective & noun* iranien, -ienne (*m or f*).

Iraq *noun* l'Irak *m*.

Iraqi *adjective & noun* irakien, -ienne, iraquien, -ienne (*m or f*).

Ireland *noun* l'Irlande *f*.

iris *noun* (*plant, of eye*) iris *m*.

Irish *adjective* irlandais; **the I.** les Irlandais *mpl*.

Irishman *noun* Irlandais *m*.

Irishwoman *noun* Irlandaise *f*.

iron
  1 *noun* fer *m*; (*for clothes*) fer *m* (à repasser).
  2 *verb* (*clothes*) repasser.

ironic(al) *adjective* ironique.

ironing *noun* repassage *m*.

ironing board *noun* planche *f* à repasser.

ironmonger *noun* quincaillier, -ière *m or f*.

irony *noun* ironie *f*.

irrational *adjective* (*person*) peu rationnel.

irregular *adjective* irrégulier.

irrelevance *noun* manque *m* de rapport.

irrelevant *adjective* sans rapport (**to** avec); **that's i.** ça n'a rien à voir.

irresistible *adjective* irrésistible.

irrespective of *preposition* sans tenir compte de.

irrigate *verb* irriguer.

irritable *adjective* irritable.

irritate *verb* (*annoy, inflame*) irriter.

irritating *adjective* irritant.

irritation *noun* irritation *f*.

is *see* be.

Islamic *adjective* islamique.

island *noun* île *f.*

isolate *verb* isoler (**from** de).

isolated *adjective* isolé.

isolation *noun* isolement *m;* **in i.** isolément.

Israel *noun* Israël *m.*

Israeli *adjective & noun* israélien, -ienne (*m or f*).

issue
1 *verb* publier; (*tickets*) distribuer; (*passport*) délivrer; (*order*) donner; (*warning*) lancer; (*supply*) fournir (**with** de, **to** à).
2 *noun* (*matter*) question *f;* (*newspaper*) numéro *m.*

it *pronoun* (*subject*) il, elle; (*object*) le, la, l'; **(to) it** (*indirect object*) lui; **it bites** il/elle mord; **I've done it** je l'ai fait.
▪ (*impersonal*) il; **it's snowing** il neige.
▪ (*non specific*) ce, cela, ça; **who is it?** qui est-ce?; **it was Paul who ...** c'est Paul qui ...
▪ **of it, from it, about it** en; **in it, to it, at it** y; **on it** dessus;

under it dessous.

Italian
1 *adjective & noun* italien, -ienne (*m or f*).
2 *noun* (*language*) italien *m.*

italics *plural noun* italique *m.*

Italy *noun* l'Italie *f.*

itch
1 *noun* démangeaison(s) *f(pl).*
2 *verb* démanger; **his arm itches** son bras le démange.

itching *noun* démangeaison(s) *f(pl).*

itchy *adjective* **an i. hand** une main qui démange.

item *noun* (*object*) article *m;* (*matter*) question *f;* **(news) i.** information *f.*

its *possessive adjective* son, sa, *plural* ses.

itself *pronoun* lui-même, elle-même; (*reflexive*) se, s'.

ivory *noun* ivoire *m.*

ivy *noun* lierre *m.*

J

jab
  1 *verb* enfoncer (**into** dans); (*prick*) piquer (**with something** du bout de quelque chose).
  2 *noun* (*injection*) piqûre *f*.
jack *noun* (*for car*) cric *m*; *Cards* valet *m*; **j. of all trades** homme *m* à tout faire.
jacket *noun* veste *f*; (*man's suit*) veston *m*; (*bulletproof*) gilet *m*; **j. potato** pomme *f* de terre en robe des champs.
jacuzzi *noun* jacousi *m*.
jagged *adjective* déchiqueté.
jaguar *noun* jaguar *m*.
jail
  1 *noun* prison *f*.
  2 *verb* emprisonner.
jam [1] *noun* confiture *f*.
jam [2] *verb*
  1 (*squeeze, make stuck*) coincer; (*street etc*) encombrer; **to j. something into** (*ram*) entasser quelque chose dans.
  2 (*get stuck*) se coincer.
jam into *verb* (*of crowd*) s'entasser dans.
Jamaica *noun* la Jamaïque *f*.
jamjar *noun* pot *m* à confiture.
jammed *adjective* (*machine etc*) coincé, bloqué; (*street etc*) encombré.
jam-packed *adjective* bourré de monde.
January *noun* janvier *m*.
Japan *noun* le Japon *m*.
Japanese
  1 *adjective & noun* japonais, -aise (*m or f*).
  2 *noun* (*language*) japonais *m*.
jar *noun* pot *m*; (*glass*) bocal *m*.

jaundice *noun* jaunisse *f*.
javelin *noun* javelot *m*.
jaw *noun* mâchoire *f*.
jazz *noun* jazz *m*.
jealous *adjective* jaloux (*f* -ouse) (**of** de).
jealousy *noun* jalousie *f*.
jeans *plural noun* (**pair of**) **j.** (blue-)jean *m*.
jeep ® *noun* jeep ® *f*.
jeer (at) *verb* railler; (*boo*) huer.
jeering *noun* (*of crowd*) huées *fpl*.
jeers *plural noun* huées *fpl*.
jelly *noun* gelée *f*.
jeopardize *verb* mettre en danger.
jeopardy *noun* danger *m*.
jerk
  1 *verb* donner une secousse à.
  2 *noun* secousse *f*; (*person*) *Familiar* crétin, -ine *m or f*.
jersey *noun* (*garment*) maillot *m*.
jet *noun* (*plane*) avion *m* à réaction.
jet lag *noun* fatigue *f* (due au décalage horaire).
jet-lagged *adjective* qui souffre du décalage horaire.
jetty *noun* jetée *f*.
Jew *noun* (*man*) Juif *m*; (*woman*) Juive *f*.
jewel *noun* bijou *m* (*plural* -oux); (*in watch*) rubis *m*.
jeweller *noun* bijoutier, -ière *m or f*.
jewellery *noun* bijoux *mpl*.
Jewish *adjective* juif.
jigsaw *noun* **j. (puzzle)** puzzle *m*.

jingle verb (of keys) tinter.

jittery adjective to be j. Familiar avoir la frousse.

job noun (task) travail m; (post) poste m; to have a (hard) j. doing or to do Familiar avoir du mal à faire; it's a good j. (that) Familiar heureusement que.

jobcentre noun = agence f nationale pour l'emploi, ANPE f.

jobless adjective au chômage.

jockey noun jockey m.

jog
 1 noun (shake) secousse f.
 2 verb (push) pousser; (memory) rafraîchir.
 3 verb (run) faire du jogging.

join [1]
 1 verb (put together) joindre; (wires, pipes) raccorder; (words, towns) relier; to j. somebody (catch up with, meet) rejoindre quelqu'un; (go with) se joindre à quelqu'un (in doing pour faire).
 2 verb (of roads etc) se rejoindre; (of objects) se joindre.
 3 noun raccord m.

join [2] verb (club, party) s'inscrire à; (firm, army) entrer dans.

join in verb prendre part; to join in something prendre part à quelque chose.

joint
 1 noun (in body) articulation f; (meat) rôti m.
 2 adjective (account) joint; (effort) conjugué.

joke
 1 noun plaisanterie f; (trick) tour m.
 2 verb plaisanter (about sur).

joker noun plaisantin m; Cards joker m.

jolly
 1 adjective gai (f gaie).

 2 adverb (very) Familiar rudement.

jolt verb secouer.

jostle verb
 1 (push) bousculer.
 2 (push each other) se bousculer.

jot down verb noter.

journalist noun journaliste m or f.

journey noun voyage m; (distance) trajet m.

joy noun joie f.

joyful adjective joyeux.

joystick noun manche m à balai.

judge
 1 noun juge m.
 2 verb juger.

judg(e)ment noun jugement m.

judo noun judo m.

jug noun cruche f; (for milk) pot m; (for wine) pichet m.

juggernaut noun (truck) poids m lourd.

juggle verb jongler (with avec).

juggler noun jongleur, -euse m or f.

juice noun jus m.

juicy adjective (fruit) juteux.

July noun juillet m.

jumble (up) verb mélanger.

jumble sale noun vente f de charité.

jumbo adjective géant.

jumbo jet noun gros-porteur m.

jump
 1 noun saut; (start) sursaut m; (increase) hausse f.
 2 verb sauter; (start) sursauter; to j. off something sauter de quelque chose.
 3 verb to j. the queue passer avant son tour.

jumper noun pull(-over) m.

jump in *or* **on** *verb* (*train, vehicle*) monter dans.

jumpy *adjective* nerveux.

junction *noun* carrefour *m*.

June *noun* juin *m*.

jungle *noun* jungle *f*.

junior
  1 *adjective* (*younger*) plus jeune; (*in rank*) subalterne; (*doctor*) jeune.
  2 *noun* cadet, -ette *m or f*; (*in school*) petit(e) élève *m or f*.

junior school *noun* école *f* primaire.

junk *noun* bric-à-brac *invariable m*; (*metal*) ferraille *f*; (*goods*) camelote *f*; (*waste*) ordures *fpl*.

jury *noun* jury *m*.

just *adverb* (*exactly, only*) juste; **she has/had j. left** elle vient/venait de partir; **he'll (only) j. catch the bus** il aura son bus de justesse; **he j. missed it** il l'a manqué de peu; **j. as big/***etc* tout aussi grand/*etc* (**as** que); **j. over ten** un peu plus de dix; **j. one** un(e) seul(e); **j. about** à peu près; (*almost*) presque; **j. about to do** sur le point de faire.

justice *noun* justice *f*.

justify *verb* justifier; **to be justified in doing** être fondé à faire.

jut out *verb* faire saillie.

kangaroo *noun* kangourou *m*.

karate *noun* karaté *m*.

kebab *noun* brochette *f*.

keen *adjective* (*eager*) plein d'enthousiasme; (*interest*) vif (*f* vive); **k. eyesight** vue *f* perçante; **he's k. on sport, he's a k. sportsman** c'est un passionné de sport; **to be k. to do** *or* **on doing** (*want*) tenir (beaucoup) à faire; **to be k. on doing** (*like*) aimer (beaucoup) faire.

keep
   1 *verb* garder; (*shop, car*) avoir; (*diary, promise*) tenir; (*family*) entretenir; (*rule*) respecter; (*delay*) retenir; **to k. doing** continuer à faire; **to k. somebody waiting/working** faire attendre/travailler quelqu'un; **to k. somebody in/out** empêcher quelqu'un de sortir/d'entrer.
   2 *verb* (*remain*) rester; (*of food*) se garder; **to k. going** continuer; **to k. (to the) left** tenir la gauche.
   3 *noun* **to pay for one's k.** payer le gîte et le couvert.

keep away *verb*
   1 (*person*) éloigner (**from** de).
   2 (*stay away*) ne pas s'approcher (**from** de).

keep back *verb*
   1 (*crowd*) contenir; (*delay*) retenir; (*hide*) cacher (**from** à).
   2 (*stay away*) ne pas s'approcher (**from** de).

keep down *verb* (*restrict*) limiter; (*price*) maintenir bas.

keeper *noun* (*in park, zoo*) gardien, -ienne *m or f*.

keep from *verb* (*hide*) cacher à; **to k. somebody from doing** (*prevent*) empêcher quelqu'un de faire.

keep off *verb* (*not go near*) ne pas s'approcher; **the rain kept off** il n'a pas plu.

keep on *verb* (*hat, employee*) garder; **to k. on doing** continuer à faire.

keep up *verb* continuer (**doing something** à faire quelque chose); **to k. up (with somebody)** (*follow*) suivre (quelqu'un).

kennel *noun* niche *f*.

Kenya *noun* le Kenya *m*.

Kenyan *adjective & noun* kenyan, -ane (*m or f*).

kept *see* keep.

kerb *noun* bord *m* du trottoir.

ketchup *noun* ketchup *m*.

kettle *noun* bouilloire *f*; **the k. is boiling** l'eau bout.

key
   1 *noun* clef *f*; (*of piano, typewriter, computer*) touche *f*.
   2 *adjective* (*industry, post etc*) clef (*invariable f*).

keyboard *noun* clavier *m*.

key ring *noun* porte-clefs *invariable m*.

kick
   1 *noun* coup *m* de pied.
   2 *verb* (*ball, person etc*) donner un coup de pied à.
   3 *verb* (*of person*) donner des coups de pied.

kick down *or* **in** *verb* (*door etc*) démolir à coups de pied.

kick-off *noun* Football coup *m* d'envoi.

kick out *verb* (*throw out*) Famil-

iar flanquer dehors.

kid

  1 *noun* (*child*) *Familiar* gosse *m* or *f*.

  2 *verb* (*joke, tease*) *Familiar* blaguer.

kidnap *verb* kidnapper.

kidnapper *noun* ravisseur, -euse *m* or *f*.

kidney *noun* rein *m*; (*as food*) rognon *m*.

kill *verb* tuer.

killer *noun* tueur, -euse *m* or *f*.

kilo *noun* kilo *m*.

kilogram(me) *noun* kilogramme *m*.

kilometre *noun* kilomètre *m*.

kind [1] *noun* (*sort*) sorte *f*, genre *m*, espèce *f* (of de); **all kinds of toutes sortes de; what k. of drink**/*etc* **is it?** qu'est-ce que c'est comme boisson/*etc*?; **k. of worried**/*etc* plutôt inquiet (*f* inquiète)/*etc*.

kind [2] *adjective* (*pleasant*) gentil (to avec).

kindergarten *noun* jardin *m* d'enfants.

kindness *noun* gentillesse *f*.

king *noun* roi *m*.

kingdom *noun* royaume *m*.

kiosk *noun* kiosque *m*; (telephone) **k.** cabine *f* (téléphonique).

kiss

  1 *noun* baiser *m*.

  2 *verb* (*person*) embrasser; **to k. somebody's hand** baiser la main de quelqu'un.

  3 *verb* (*of persons*) s'embrasser.

kit *noun* équipement *m*; (*set of articles*) trousse *f*; (*belongings*) affaires *fpl*; (do-it-yourself) **k.** kit *m*; **tool k.** trousse *f* à outils.

kitchen *noun* cuisine *f*.

kite *noun* (*toy*) cerf-volant *m*.

kitten *noun* chaton *m*.

knack *noun* **to have a** or **the k. of doing** avoir le don de faire.

knee *noun* genou *m* (plural -oux).

kneel (down) *verb* s'agenouiller; **to be kneeling (down)** être à genoux.

knelt *see* **kneel**.

knew *see* **know**.

knickers *plural noun* slip *m*; (*longer*) culotte *f*.

knife *noun* couteau *m*; (*penknife*) canif *m*.

knight *noun* chevalier *m*; *Chess* cavalier *m*.

knit *verb* tricoter.

knitting *noun* (*activity, material*) tricot *m*; **k. needle** aiguille *f* à tricoter.

knob *noun* (*on door*) poignée *f*; (*on radio*) bouton *m*.

knock

  1 *verb* frapper; (*collide with*) heurter; **to k. one's head on something** se cogner la tête contre quelque chose.

  2 *noun* coup *m*; **there's a k. at the door** quelqu'un frappe; **I heard a k.** j'ai entendu frapper.

knock against or **into** *verb* (*bump into*) heurter.

knock down *verb* (*vase, pedestrian etc*) renverser; (*house, wall etc*) abattre.

knocker *noun* (*on door*) marteau *m*.

knock in *verb* (*nail*) enfoncer.

knock off *verb* (*person, object*) faire tomber (**from** de).

knock out *verb* (*make unconscious*) assommer; *Boxing* mettre K.-O.; (*beat in competition*) éliminer.

knock over verb (pedestrian, vase etc) renverser.

knot

1 noun nœud m.

2 verb nouer.

know verb (facts, language etc) savoir; (person, place etc) connaître; (recognize) reconnaître (**by** à); **to k. that** savoir que; **to k. how to do** savoir faire; **I'll let you k.** je te le ferai savoir; **to k. (a lot) about** (person, event) en savoir long sur; (cars, sewing etc) s'y connaître en; **to get to k. somebody** faire la connaissance de quelqu'un; **I wouldn't k.** je n'en sais rien; **I k. about that** je suis au courant; **do you k. of a good dentist/etc?** connais-tu un bon dentiste/etc?

know-how noun savoir-faire invariable m.

knowledge noun connaissance f (**of** de); (learning) connaissances fpl.

known adjective connu; **well k.** (bien) connu (**that** que); **she is k. to be** on sait qu'elle est.

knuckle noun articulation f (du doigt).

Koran noun **the K.** le Coran m.

Korea noun la Corée f; **North/ South K.** la Corée du Nord/ Sud.

Korean adjective & noun coréen, -enne (m or f); **North/South K.** nord-/sud-coréenne, -enne.

Kuwait noun le Koweït m.

Kuwaiti adjective & noun koweïtien, -ienne (m or f).

lab noun Familiar labo m.

label
1 noun étiquette f.
2 verb (goods) étiqueter.

laboratory noun laboratoire m.

labour
1 noun (work) travail m; (workers) main-d'œuvre f; L. (political party) les travaillistes mpl; in l. en train d'accoucher.
2 adjective (market, situation) du travail.

labourer noun manœuvre m; (on farm) ouvrier m agricole.

lace noun (cloth) dentelle f; (of shoe) lacet m.

lace (up) verb (shoe) lacer.

lack
1 noun manque m.
2 verb manquer de.
3 verb to be lacking manquer (in de).

lad noun gamin m.

ladder noun échelle f.

ladle noun louche f.

lady noun dame f; a young l. une jeune fille; (married) une jeune femme; l. doctor femme f médecin; the ladies' room, the ladies les toilettes fpl pour dames.

ladybird noun coccinelle f.

lager noun bière f blonde.

laid see lay.

lain see lie 1.

lake noun lac m.

lamb noun agneau m.

lame adjective to be l. boiter.

lamp noun lampe f.

lamppost noun réverbère m.

lampshade noun abat-jour invariable m.

land
1 noun terre f; (country) pays m; (plot of) l. terrain m.
2 verb (of aircraft) atterrir; (of passengers) débarquer.
3 verb (aircraft) poser.

landing noun (of aircraft) atterrissage m; (at top of stairs) palier m.

landlady noun propriétaire f; (of pub) patronne f.

landlord noun propriétaire m; (of pub) patron m.

landscape noun paysage m.

landslide noun éboulement m.

lane noun (in country) chemin m; (in town) ruelle f; (division of road) voie f.

language
1 noun (English etc) langue f; (means of expression, style) langage m.
2 adjective (laboratory) de langues; (teacher, studies) de langue(s).

lantern noun lanterne f.

lap noun (of person) genoux mpl; (in race) tour m (de piste).

lapel noun (of coat etc) revers m.

larder noun (storeroom) garde-manger invariable m.

large adjective grand; (in volume) gros (f grosse).

largely adverb en grande mesure.

lark noun (bird) alouette f; (joke) Familiar rigolade f.

laser noun laser m.

last [1]
1 adjective dernier; l. but one avant-dernier.

2 *adverb* (*lastly*) en dernier lieu; (*on the last occasion*) (pour) la dernière fois; **to leave l.** sortir en dernier.

3 *noun* (*person, object*) dernier, -ière *m or f*; **the l. of the beer**/*etc* le reste de la bière/*etc*; **at (long) l.** enfin.

last² *verb* durer; (*endure*) tenir.

lastly *adverb* en dernier lieu, enfin.

latch *noun* loquet *m*; **the door is on the l.** la porte n'est pas fermée à clef.

late
  1 *adjective* (*not on time*) en retard (**for** à); (*meal, hour*) tardif; **he's an hour l.** il a une heure de retard; **it's l.** il est tard; **at a later date** à une date ultérieure; **at the latest** au plus tard; **of l.** dernièrement.
  2 *adverb* (*in the day, season etc*) tard; (*not on time*) en retard; **it's getting l.** il se fait tard; **later (on)** plus tard.

latecomer *noun* retardataire *m or f*.

lately *adverb* dernièrement.

Latin
  1 *adjective* latin.
  2 *noun* (*language*) latin *m*.

latter
  1 *adjective* (*last-named*) dernier; (*second*) deuxième.
  2 *noun* dernier, -ière *m or f*; second, -onde *m or f*.

laugh
  1 *noun* rire *m*.
  2 *verb* rire (**at, about** de).

laughter *noun* rire(s) *m(pl)*.

launch
  1 *verb* (*rocket, fashion*) lancer.
  2 *noun* lancement *m*.

launderette *noun* laverie *f* auto-

matique.

laundry *noun* (*place*) blanchisserie *f*; (*clothes*) linge *m*.

lavatory *noun* cabinets *mpl*.

law *noun* loi *f*; (*study, profession*) droit *m*; **court of l., l. court** cour *f* de justice.

lawn *noun* pelouse *f*, gazon *m*; **l. mower** tondeuse *f* (à gazon).

lawsuit *noun* procès *m*.

lawyer *noun* avocat *m*; (*for wills, sales*) notaire *m*.

lay
  1 *past tense of* lie¹.
  2 *verb* (*put down*) poser; (*table*) mettre; (*blanket*) étendre (**over** sur); (*trap*) tendre; (*egg*) pondre.

layabout *noun Familiar* fainéant, -ante *m or f*.

lay-by *noun* aire *f* de stationnement.

lay down *verb* (*put down*) poser.

layer *noun* couche *f*.

lay off *verb* (*worker*) licencier.

lay on *verb* installer; (*supply*) fournir.

lay out *verb* (*garden*) dessiner; (*display*) disposer.

layout *noun* disposition *f*.

lazy *adjective* paresseux.

lead¹
  1 *verb* (*conduct*) mener, conduire (**to** à); (*team, government etc*) diriger; (*life*) mener; **to l. somebody in/out**/*etc* faire entrer/sortir/*etc* qn; **to l. somebody to do** amener quelqu'un à faire.
  2 *verb* (*of street, door etc*) mener (**to** à); (*in race*) être en tête; (*in match*) mener; (*go ahead*) aller devant.
  3 *noun* (*distance or time ahead*) avance *f* (**over** sur); (*example*) exemple *m*; (*leash*) laisse *f*; (*elec-*

tric wire) fil *m*; **to be in the l.** (*in race*) être en tête; (*in match*) mener.

lead² *noun* (*metal*) plomb *m*; (*of pencil*) mine *f*.

lead away *or* **off** *verb* emmener.

leader *noun* chef *m*; (*of country, party*) dirigeant, -ante *m or f*.

leading *adjective* (*main*) principal.

lead to *verb* (*result in*) aboutir à; (*cause*) causer.

lead up to *verb* (*of street etc*) conduire à; (*precede*) précéder.

leaf *noun* feuille *f*; (*of book*) feuillet *m*.

leaflet *noun* prospectus *m*; (*containing instructions*) notice *f*.

leaf through *verb* (*book*) feuilleter.

leak
  1 *noun* (*of gas etc*) fuite *f*.
  2 *verb* (*of liquid, pipe etc*) fuir.

lean *verb*
  1 (*of object*) pencher; (*of person*) se pencher; **to l. against/on something** (*of person*) s'appuyer contre/sur quelque chose.
  2 (*rest*) appuyer (**against** contre); **to l. one's head on/out of something** pencher la tête sur/par quelque chose.

lean forward *verb* (*of person*) se pencher (en avant).

lean over *verb* (*of person*) se pencher; (*of object*) pencher.

leant *see* **lean.**

leap
  1 *noun* bond *m*.
  2 *verb* bondir.

leapt *see* **leap.**

leap year *noun* année *f* bissextile.

learn *verb* apprendre (**that** que); **to l. (how) to do** apprendre à faire; **to l. about** (*study*) étudier; (*hear about*) apprendre.

learner *noun* débutant, -ante *m or f*.

learning *noun* (*of language*) apprentissage *m* (**of** de).

learnt *see* **learn.**

leash *noun* laisse *f*.

least
  1 *adjective* **the l.** (*smallest amount of*) le moins de; (*slightest*) le *or* la moindre.
  2 *noun* **the l.** le moins; **at l.** du moins; (*with quantity*) au moins.
  3 *adverb* (*to work etc*) le moins; (*with adjective*) le *or* la moins.

leather *noun* cuir *m*.

leave
  1 *noun* (*holiday*) congé *m*.
  2 *verb* laisser; (*go away from*) quitter; **to be left** (*over*) rester; **there's no bread**/*etc* **left** il ne reste plus de pain/*etc*; **to l. go (of)** (*release*) lâcher.
  3 *verb* (*go away*) partir (**from** de, **for** pour).

leave behind *verb* (*not take*) laisser; (*in race, at school*) distancer.

leave on *verb* (*hat, gloves*) garder.

leave out *verb* (*forget to put*) oublier (de mettre); (*word, line*) sauter; (*exclude*) exclure.

Lebanese *adjective & noun* libanais, -aise (*m or f*).

Lebanon (the) *noun* le Liban *m*.

lecture
  1 *noun* (*public speech*) conférence *f*; (*as part of series at university*) cours *m*.
  2 *verb* faire une conférence *or* un cours.

lecturer *noun* conférencier, -ière *m or f*; (*at university*) professeur *m*.

led *see* **lead**[1].

leek *noun* poireau *m*.

left[1] *see* **leave**.

left[2]
  1 *adjective* (*side, hand etc*) gauche.
  2 *adverb* à gauche.
  3 *noun* gauche *f*; **on** *or* **to the l.** à gauche (*of de*).

left-hand *adjective* à *or* de gauche; **on the l. side** à gauche (*of de*).

left-handed *adjective* (*person*) gaucher.

left luggage office *noun* consigne *f*.

leftovers *plural noun* restes *mpl*.

leg *noun* jambe *f*; (*of dog etc*) patte *f*; (*of table*) pied *m*; **l.** (*of chicken*) cuisse *f* (de poulet); **l. of lamb** gigot *m* (d'agneau).

legal *adjective* légal.

legend *noun* légende *f*.

legible *adjective* lisible.

leisure *noun* **l.** (**time**) loisirs *mpl*; **l. activities** loisirs *mpl*.

lemon *noun* citron *m*; **l. drink** citronnade *f*; **l. tea** thé *m* au citron.

lemonade *noun* limonade *f*.

lend *verb* prêter (**to** à); (*colour, charm etc*) donner (**to** à).

length *noun* longueur *f*; (*of rope etc*) morceau *m*; (*duration*) durée *f*; **l. of time** temps *m*.

lengthen *verb* allonger; (*in time*) prolonger.

lenient *adjective* indulgent (**to** envers).

lens *noun* lentille *f*; (*in spectacles*) verre *m*; (*of camera*) objectif *m*.

lent *see* **lend**.

lentil *noun* lentille *f*.

leopard *noun* léopard *m*.

leotard *noun* justaucorps *m*.

less
  1 *adjective & noun* moins (**de**) (**than** que); **l. time**/*etc* moins de temps/*etc*; **l. than a kilo/ten** (*with quantity, number*) moins d'un kilo/de dix.
  2 *adverb* moins (**than** que); **l.** (**often**) moins souvent; **l. and l.** de moins en moins; **one l.** un(e) de moins.
  3 *preposition* moins.

lesson *noun* leçon *f*.

let *verb* (*allow*) laisser (**somebody do** quelqu'un faire); **to l. somebody have something** donner quelque chose à quelqu'un; **l. us** *or* **l.'s eat**/*etc* mangeons/*etc*; **l.'s go for a stroll** allons nous promener; **l. him come** qu'il vienne.

let (out) *verb* (*room etc*) louer.

let down *verb* (*lower*) baisser; **to l. somebody down** (*disappoint*) décevoir quelqu'un.

letdown *noun* déception *f*.

let in *verb* (*person*) faire entrer; (*noise, light*) laisser entrer.

let off *verb* (*firework, gun*) faire partir; **to l. somebody off** (*not punish*) ne pas punir quelqu'un; **to l. somebody off doing** dispenser quelqu'un de faire.

let out *verb* (*person*) laisser sortir; (*cry, secret*) laisser échapper.

letter *noun* lettre *f*.

letterbox *noun* boîte *f* aux *or* à lettres.

lettuce *noun* laitue *f*.

let up *verb* (*of rain etc*) s'arrêter.

level
  1 *noun* niveau *m*; (*rate*) taux *m*.
  2 *adjective* (*surface*) plat; (*object*

on surface) d'aplomb; (*equal in score*) à égalité (**with** avec); (*in height*) au même niveau (**with** que).

level crossing *noun* passage *m* à niveau.

lever *noun* levier *m*.

liable *adjective* **to be l. to do** être capable *or* susceptible de faire.

liar *noun* menteur, -euse *m or f*.

liberty *noun* liberté *f*; **at l. to do** libre de faire.

librarian *noun* bibliothécaire *m or f*.

library *noun* bibliothèque *f*.

Libya *noun* la Libye *f*.

Libyan *adjective & noun* libyenne, -enne (*m or f*).

lice *plural noun* poux *mpl*.

licence *noun* (*document*) permis *m*; **l. plate/number** plaque *f*/numéro *m* d'immatriculation.

lick *verb* lécher.

lid *noun* (*of box etc*) couvercle *m*.

lie [1] *verb* (*in flat position*) s'allonger; (*remain*) rester; (*be*) être; **to be lying** (*on the grass etc*) être allongé.

lie [2]
1 *verb* (*tell lies*) mentir.
2 *noun* mensonge *m*.

lie about *or* **around** *verb* (*of objects, person*) traîner.

lie down *verb* s'allonger; **lying down** allongé.

life *noun* vie *f*; **to come to l.** s'animer.

lifebelt *noun* ceinture *f* de sauvetage.

lifeboat *noun* canot *m* de sauvetage.

lifeguard *noun* maître nageur *m* (sauveteur).

life insurance *noun* assurance-vie *f*.

life jacket *noun* gilet *m* de sauvetage.

lifetime *noun* **in my l.** de mon vivant.

lift
1 *verb* lever.
2 *noun* (*elevator*) ascenseur *m*; **to give somebody a l.** emmener quelqu'un (en voiture) (**to** à).

lift down *or* **off** *verb* (*take down*) descendre (**from** de).

lift out *verb* (*take out*) sortir (**of** de).

lift up *verb* (*arm, object*) lever.

light [1] *noun* lumière *f*; (*on vehicle*) feu *m*; (*vehicle headlight*) phare *m*; **do you have a l.?** (*for cigarette*) est-ce que vous avez du feu?; **to set l. to** mettre le feu à.

light [2] *verb* (*match, fire, gas*) allumer.

light [3] *adjective* (*not dark*) clair; **a l. green jacket** une veste vert clair.

light [4] *adjective* (*in weight, quantity etc*) léger; **to travel l.** voyager avec peu de bagages.

light (up) *verb* (*room*) éclairer; (*cigarette*) allumer.

light bulb *noun* ampoule *f* (électrique).

lighter *noun* (*for cigarettes*) briquet *m*; (*for cooker*) allume-gaz *invariable m*.

lighthouse *noun* phare *m*.

lighting *noun* (*lights*) éclairage *m*.

lightning *noun* (*charge*) foudre *f*; (*flash of*) **l.** éclair *m*.

like [1]
1 *preposition* comme; **l. this** comme ça; **what's he l.?** com-

ment est-il?; **to be** or **look l.** ressembler à; **what was the book l.?** comment as-tu trouvé le livre? **2** conjunction (*as*) *Familiar* comme; **do l. I do** fais comme moi.

like² verb aimer (bien) (**to do, doing** faire); **she likes it here** elle se plaît ici; **to l. something best** aimer mieux quelque chose; **I'd l. to come** je voudrais (bien) or j'aimerais (bien) venir; **I'd l. a kilo of apples** je voudrais un kilo de pommes; **would you l. an apple?** voulez-vous une pomme?; **if you l.** si vous voulez.

likeable adjective sympathique.

likelihood noun **there's isn't much l. that** il y a peu de chances que (+ subjunctive).

likely **1** adjective probable; (*excuse*) vraisemblable; **it's l. (that) she'll come, she's l. to come** il est probable qu'elle viendra. **2** adverb **very l.** très probablement; **not l.!** pas question!

likewise adverb de même.

liking noun **a l. for** (*person*) de la sympathie pour; (*thing*) du goût pour.

lily noun lis m.

limb noun membre m.

lime noun (*fruit*) citron m vert.

limit **1** noun limite f (**to** à). **2** verb limiter (**to** à).

limp **1** verb (*of person*) boiter. **2** noun **to have a l.** boiter.

line¹ **1** noun ligne f; (*of poem*) vers m; (*wrinkle*) ride f; (*track*) voie f; (*rope*) corde f; (*row*) rangée f; (*of vehicles, people*) file f; **on the l.**

(*phone*) au bout du fil; **to drop a l.** (*send a letter*) envoyer un mot (**to** à). **2** verb **to l. the street** (*of trees*) border la rue; (*of people*) faire la haie le long de la rue.

line² verb (*clothes*) doubler.

linen noun (*sheets etc*) linge m.

liner noun (**ocean**) **l.** paquebot m; (**dust**)**bin l.** sac m poubelle.

line up verb (*children, objects*) aligner; (*arrange*) organiser.

lining noun (*of clothes*) doublure f.

link **1** verb (*connect*) relier; (*relate*) lier (**to** à). **2** noun lien m; (*of chain*) maillon m; (*by road, rail*) liaison f.

link up verb (*of firms etc*) s'associer; (*of roads*) se rejoindre.

lino noun lino m.

lion noun lion m.

lip noun lèvre f.

lipstick noun bâton m de rouge; (*substance*) rouge m (à lèvres).

liqueur noun liqueur f.

liquid noun & adjective liquide (m).

liquorice noun réglisse f.

list **1** noun liste f. **2** verb faire la liste de; (*names*) mettre sur la liste, inscrire; (*name one by one*) énumérer.

listen (to) verb écouter.

listener noun (*to radio*) auditeur, -trice m or f.

listen (out) for verb guetter (le bruit or les cris etc de).

lit see **light²**.

literary adjective littéraire.

literature noun littérature f; (*pamphlets etc*) documentation f.

litre *noun* litre *m*.

litter *noun* (*rubbish*) détritus *m*; (*papers*) papiers *mpl*; (*young animals*) portée *f*.

litter bin *noun* boîte *f* à ordures.

little
1 *adjective* (*small*) petit.
2 *adjective & noun* (*not much*) peu (de); **l. time**/*etc* peu de temps/*etc*; **she eats l.** elle mange peu; **as l. as possible** le moins possible; **a l. money**/*etc* (*some*) un peu d'argent/*etc*.
3 *adverb* **a l. heavy**/*etc* un peu lourd/*etc*; **to work**/*etc* **a l.** travailler/*etc* un peu; **l. by l.** peu à peu.

live [1] *verb*
1 vivre; (*reside*) habiter, vivre.
2 (*life*) mener.

live [2]
1 *adjective* (*electric wire*) sous tension; (*switch*) mal isolé.
2 *adjective & adverb* (*broadcast*) en direct.

lively *adjective* (*person, style, interest, mind*) vif (*f* vive); (*discussion*) animé.

live off *or* **on** *verb* (*eat*) vivre de.

liver *noun* foie *m*.

live through *verb* (*experience*) vivre; (*survive*) survivre à.

living
1 *adjective* (*alive*) vivant.
2 *noun* vie *f*; **to make** *or* **earn a** *or* **one's l.** gagner sa vie; **the cost of l.** le coût de la vie.

living room *noun* salle *f* de séjour.

lizard *noun* lézard *m*.

load
1 *noun* charge *f*; (*weight*) poids *m*; **a l. of, loads of** (*people, money etc*) *Familiar* un tas de.
2 *verb* (*truck, gun etc*) charger

(with de).

load up *verb* (*car, ship etc*) charger (**with** de).

loaf *noun* pain *m*; **French l.** baguette *f*.

loan
1 *noun* (*money lent*) prêt *m*; (*money borrowed*) emprunt *m*.
2 *verb* (*lend*) prêter (**to** à).

lobby *noun* (*of hotel*) hall *m*.

lobster *noun* homard *m*.

local *adjective* local.

locally *adverb* dans le coin.

locate *verb* (*find*) trouver, repérer; **to be located** être situé.

location *noun* (*site*) emplacement *m*.

lock
1 *verb* (*door etc*) fermer à clef.
2 *noun* (*on door etc*) serrure *f*; (*on canal*) écluse *f*; (*of hair*) mèche *f*.

lock away *verb* (*prisoner, jewels etc*) enfermer.

locker *noun* (*for luggage*) casier *m* de consigne automatique; (*for clothes*) vestiaire *m* (métallique).

locket *noun* (*jewel*) médaillon *m*.

lock in *verb* enfermer; **to l. somebody in something** enfermer quelqu'un dans quelque chose.

lock out *verb* (*accidentally*) enfermer dehors.

lock up *verb*
1 (*house etc*) fermer à clef; (*prisoner, jewels etc*) enfermer.
2 (*close house etc*) fermer à clef.

lodger *noun* (*room and meals*) pensionnaire *m or f*; (*room only*) locataire *m or f*.

lodgings *plural noun* (*flat*) logement *m*; (*room*) chambre *f*; **in lodgings** en meublé.

loft *noun* (*attic*) grenier *m*.

log *noun* (*tree trunk*) tronc *m* d'arbre; (*for fire*) bûche *f*.

logical *adjective* logique.

lollipop , *Familiar* **lolly** *noun*
sucette *f*; (*ice*) esquimau *m*.

London *noun* Londres *m or f*.

loneliness *noun* solitude *f*.

lonely *adjective* solitaire.

long
  1 *adjective* long (*f* longue); **to be
ten metres l.** avoir dix mètres de
long; **to be six weeks l.** durer six
semaines; **a l. time** longtemps.
  2 *adverb* longtemps; **has he been
here l.?** il y a longtemps qu'il est
ici?; **how l. ago?** il y a combien
de temps?; **before l.** sous peu;
she no longer swims elle ne nage
plus; **I won't be l.** je n'en ai pas
pour longtemps; **all summer l.**
tout l'été; **as l. as, so l. as** (*provided that*) pourvu que (+ *subjunctive*).

long-distance *adjective* (*phone
call*) interurbain; (*flight*) long-
courrier.

long-term *adjective* à long
terme.

loo *noun* (*toilet*) *Familiar* toilettes
fpl, cabinets *mpl*.

look
  1 *noun* regard *m*; (*appearance*)
air *m*; **to have a l. (at)** jeter un
coup d'œil (à); **to have a l. (for)**
chercher; **to have a l. (a)round**
regarder; (*walk*) faire un tour; **let
me have a l.** fais voir.
  2 *verb* regarder; **to l. tired**/*etc*
sembler *or* avoir l'air fatigué/*etc*;
you l. like *or* **as if you're tired**
on dirait que tu es fatigué; **to l.
well** *or* **good** (*of person*) avoir
bonne mine; **you l. good in that
hat**/*etc* ce chapeau/*etc* te va très
bien.

look after *verb* (*deal with*) s'occuper de; (*sick person*) soigner;
(*keep safely*) garder (**for somebody** pour quelqu'un); **to l. after
oneself** (*keep healthy*) faire bien
attention à soi; (*manage*) se débrouiller.

look around *verb*
  1 (*museum, house etc*) visiter.
  2 regarder; (*walk round*) faire un
tour.

look at *verb* regarder.

look down *verb* baisser les yeux;
(*from a height*) regarder en bas.

look for *verb* chercher.

look forward to *verb* (*event*)
attendre avec impatience; **to l.
forward to doing** avoir hâte de
faire.

look into *verb* examiner; (*find
out about*) se renseigner sur.

look (out) on to *verb* (*of window etc*) donner sur.

look out *verb* (*be careful*) faire
attention (**for** à).

lookout *noun* (*high place*) observatoire *m*; **to be on the l.** faire le
guet; **to be on the l. for** guetter.

look over *or* **through** *verb*
examiner; (*briefly*) parcourir;
(*region, town*) parcourir.

look round *verb*
  1 (*museum, house etc*) visiter.
  2 (*walk round*) faire un tour;
(*look back*) se retourner.

look up *verb*
  1 lever les yeux; (*into the air*) regarder en l'air; (*improve*) s'améliorer.
  2 (*word*) chercher.

loose
  1 *adjective* (*screw, belt, knot*) des-
serré; (*tooth*) branlant; (*page*) détaché; (*clothes*) flottant; (*tea etc*)
au poids; (*having escaped*) (*animal*) échappé; (*prisoner*) évadé; **l.**

change petite monnaie *f*; **to set**
or turn l. (*dog etc*) lâcher.
2 *noun* **on the l.** (*prisoner*) évadé;
(*animal*) échappé.

loosen *verb* (*knot, belt, screw*)
desserrer.

lord *noun* seigneur *m*; (*title*) lord
m.

lorry *noun* camion *m*.

lorry driver *noun* camionneur
m; **long-distance l. driver** routier *m*.

lose *verb* perdre; **to get lost** (*of*
person) se perdre; **the ticket**/*etc*
got lost on a perdu le billet/*etc*;
to l. to somebody être battu par
quelqu'un.

loser *noun* (*in contest etc*) perdant, -ante *m or f*; (*unsuccessful*
person) *Familiar* raté, -ée *m or f*.

loss *noun* perte *f*.

lost *adjective* perdu.

lost property *noun* objets *mpl*
trouvés.

lot *noun* **the l.** (*everything*) (le)
tout; **a l. of, lots of** beaucoup de;
a l. beaucoup; **quite a l.** pas mal
(**of** de); **such a l.** tellement (**of**
de); **what a l. of flowers/water/**
etc! regarde toutes ces fleurs/
toute cette eau/*etc*!

lotion *noun* lotion *f*.

lottery *noun* loterie *f*.

loud
1 *adjective* (*voice, music*) fort;
(*noise, cry*) grand; **the radio/TV**
is too l. le son de la radio/télé
est trop fort.
2 *adverb* (*to shout etc*) fort; **out l.**
tout haut.

loudly *adverb* (*to speak etc*) fort.

loudspeaker *noun* haut-parleur
m; (*for speaking to crowd*) porte-
voix *invariable m*.

lounge *noun* salon *m*.

lousy *adjective* (*food, weather*
etc) *Familiar* infect.

love
1 *noun* amour *m*; **in l.** amoureux
(**with** de); **they're in l.** ils s'aiment.
2 *verb* aimer (beaucoup) (**to do,**
doing faire).

lovely *adjective* agréable; (*excel-*
lent) excellent; (*pretty*) joli;
(*charming*) charmant; (*kind*) gentil; **l. and warm**/*etc* bien chaud/
etc.

lover *noun* **a l. of music**/*etc* un
amateur de musique/*etc*.

loving *adjective* affectueux.

low
1 *adjective* bas (*f* basse); (*speed,*
income, intelligence) faible;
(*opinion, quality*) mauvais; **to**
feel l. être déprimé; **in a l. voice**
à voix basse; **lower** inférieur.
2 *adverb* bas; **to turn (down) l.**
mettre plus bas.

lower *verb* baisser; (*by rope*) descendre.

low-fat *adjective* (*milk*) écrémé;
(*cheese*) allégé.

loyal *adjective* fidèle (**to** à), loyal
(**to** envers).

lozenge *noun* (*tablet*) pastille *f*.

LP *noun* 33 tours *invariable m*.

luck *noun* (*chance*) chance *f*; **bad**
l. malchance *f*.

luckily *adverb* heureusement.

lucky *adjective* (*person*) chanceux; (*guess, event*) heureux; **to**
be l. avoir de la chance (**to do** de
faire); **it's l. that** c'est une chance
que; **l. charm** porte-bonheur *in-*
variable m; **l. number**/*etc* chiffre
m/*etc* porte-bonheur.

ludicrous *adjective* ridicule.

luggage *noun* bagages *mpl*.

lukewarm *adjective* tiède.

lullaby *noun* berceuse *f*.

luminous *adjective* (*colour etc*) fluorescent.

lump *noun* morceau *m*; (*bump*) bosse *f*; (*swelling*) grosseur *f*.

lump sum *noun* somme *f* forfaitaire.

lunatic *noun* fou *m*, folle *f*.

lunch *noun* déjeuner *m*; **to have l.** déjeuner; **l. break, l. hour, l.**

time heure *f* du déjeuner.

luncheon voucher *noun* chèque-déjeuner *m*.

lung *noun* poumon *m*.

Luxemb(o)urg *noun* le Luxembourg *m*.

Luxemburger *noun* Luxembourgeois, -oise *m* or *f*.

luxurious *adjective* luxueux.

luxury

  1 *noun* luxe *m*.

  2 *adjective* (*goods etc*) de luxe.

M

MA *abbreviation* = Master of Arts.

mac *noun* (*raincoat*) imper *m*.

macaroni *plural noun* macaroni(s) *mpl*.

machine *noun* machine *f*.

machinegun *noun* (*heavy*) mitrailleuse *f*; (*portable*) mitraillette *f*.

machinery *noun* machines *fpl*; (*works*) mécanisme *m*.

mackerel *noun* maquereau *m*.

mackintosh *noun* imperméable *m*.

mad *adjective* fou (*f* folle); **m. (at)** (*angry*) furieux (contre); **m. about** (*person*) fou de; (*films etc*) passionné de; **like m.** comme un fou *or* une folle.

madam *noun* madame *f*; (*unmarried*) mademoiselle *f*.

made *see* make.

madman *noun* fou *m*.

madness *noun* folie *f*.

magazine *noun* magazine *m*, revue *f*.

maggot *noun* ver *m*.

magic
1 *noun* magie *f*.
2 *adjective* (*wand etc*) magique.

magical *adjective* magique.

magician *noun* magicien, -ienne *m or f*.

magistrate *noun* magistrat *m*.

magnet *noun* aimant *m*.

magnificent *adjective* magnifique.

magnifying glass *noun* loupe *f*.

mahogany *noun* acajou *m*.

maid *noun* (*servant*) bonne *f*.

mail
1 *noun* (*system*) poste *f*; (*letters*) courrier *m*.
2 *adjective* (*bag etc*) postal.
3 *verb* (*letter*) poster.

main [1] *adjective* principal; **the m. thing is to** l'essentiel est de; **m. road** grand-route *f*.

main [2] *noun* water/gas m. conduite *f* d'eau/de gaz; **the mains** (*electricity*) le secteur.

mainly *adverb* surtout.

maintain *verb* (*vehicle etc*) entretenir; (*law and order*) faire respecter; **to m. that** affirmer que.

maisonette *noun* duplex *m*.

maize *noun* maïs *m*.

majesty *noun* **Your M.** Votre Majesté.

major
1 *adjective* majeur; **a m. road** une grande route.
2 *noun* (*officer*) commandant *m*.

majorette *noun* majorette *f*.

majority *noun* majorité *f* (**of** de); **the m. of people** la plupart des gens.

make
1 *verb* faire; (*tool, vehicle etc*) fabriquer; (*decision*) prendre; (*friends, salary*) se faire; (*destination*) arriver à; **to m. happy**/*etc* rendre heureux/*etc*; **to m. somebody do something** faire faire quelque chose à quelqu'un; **to m. do** (*manage*) se débrouiller (**with** avec); **to m. do with** (*be satisfied with*) se contenter de; **to m. it** arriver; (*succeed*) réussir; **what do you m. of it?** qu'en penses-tu?

2 *noun* (*brand*) marque *f*.

make for *verb* aller vers.

make good *verb* (*loss*) compenser; (*damage*) réparer.

make off *verb* (*run away*) se sauver.

make out *verb*
1 (*see*) distinguer; (*understand*) comprendre; (*write*) faire (*chèque, liste*); (*claim*) prétendre (**that** que).
2 (*manage*) se débrouiller.

maker *noun* (*of product*) fabricant, -ante *m or f*.

make up *verb*
1 (*story*) inventer; (*collection, list*) faire; (*form*) former; (*loss*) compenser; (*quantity*) compléter; (*quarrel*) régler; (*one's face*) maquiller.
2 to m. (it) up (*of friends*) se réconcilier.

make-up *noun* (*for face*) maquillage *m*.

make up for *verb* (*loss, damage*) compenser; (*lost time, mistake*) rattraper.

malaria *noun* malaria *f*.

Malaysia *noun* la Malaisie *f*.

Malaysian *adjective & noun* malais, -aise (*m or f*).

male
1 *adjective* mâle; (*clothes, sex*) masculin.
2 *noun* mâle *m*.

malice *noun* méchanceté *f*.

malicious *adjective* malveillant.

mall *noun* (**shopping**) **m.** galerie *f* marchande.

mammal *noun* mammifère *m*.

man *noun* homme *m*.

manage *verb*
1 (*run*) diriger; (*handle*) manier; **to m. to do** (*succeed*) réussir à

faire; (*by being smart*) se débrouiller pour faire; **I'll m. it** j'y arriverai.
2 (*succeed*) y arriver; (*make do*) se débrouiller (**with** avec); **to m. without something** se passer de quelque chose.

management *noun* (*running, managers*) direction *f*.

manager *noun* directeur *m*; (*of shop, café*) gérant *m*.

manageress *noun* directrice *f*; (*of shop, café*) gérante *f*.

managing director *noun* PDG *m*.

mane *noun* crinière *f*.

maniac *noun* fou *m*, folle *f*.

man-made *adjective* artificiel.

manner *noun* (*way*) manière *f*; (*behaviour*) attitude *f*; **manners** (*social habits*) manières *fpl*; **to have no manners** être mal élevé.

manoeuvre
1 *noun* manœuvre *f*.
2 *verb* manœuvrer.

mantelpiece *noun* (*shelf*) cheminée *f*.

manual
1 *adjective* manuel.
2 *noun* (*book*) manuel *m*.

manufacture
1 *verb* fabriquer.
2 *noun* fabrication *f*.

manufacturer *noun* fabricant, -ante *m or f*.

manure *noun* fumier *m*.

many *adjective & noun* beaucoup (de); **m. things** beaucoup de choses; **I don't have m.** je n'en ai pas beaucoup; **m. came** beaucoup sont venus; (**a good** *or* **great**) **m. of** un (très) grand nombre de; **m. times** bien des fois; **as m. books**/*etc* **as** autant de livres/*etc* que.

map *noun* (*of country, region*) carte *f*; (*of town etc*) plan *m*.

marathon *noun* marathon *m*.

marble *noun* marbre *m*; (*toy*) bille *f*.

March *noun* mars *m*.

march
  1 *noun* marche *f*.
  2 *verb* (*of soldiers*) défiler.

mare *noun* jument *f*.

margarine *noun* margarine *f*.

margin *noun* (*of page*) marge *f*.

mark
  1 *noun* (*symbol*) marque *f*; (*stain, trace*) trace *f*; (*token, sign*) signe *m*; (*for school exercise etc*) note *f*; (*target*) but *m*.
  2 *verb* marquer; (*exam etc*) corriger.

marker *noun* (*pen*) marqueur *m*.

market *noun* marché *m*.

marketing *noun* marketing *m*.

mark off *verb* (*area*) délimiter.

marmalade *noun* confiture *f* d'oranges.

marriage *noun* mariage *m*.

married *adjective* marié; **to get m.** se marier.

marrow *noun* (*of bone*) moelle *f*; (*vegetable*) courge *f*.

marry *verb*
  1 épouser, se marier avec; (*of priest etc*) marier.
  2 (*get married*) se marier.

marsh *noun* marais *m*.

Martian *noun* & *adjective* martien, -ienne (*m or f*).

marvellous *adjective* merveilleux.

marzipan *noun* pâte *f* d'amandes.

mascara *noun* mascara *m*.

mascot *noun* mascotte *f*.

masculine *adjective* masculin.

mashed potatoes *noun* purée *f* (de pommes de terre).

mask *noun* masque *m*.

mass [1]
  1 *noun* (*quantity*) masse *f*; **a m. of** (*many*) une multitude de; (*pile*) un tas de; **masses of** des masses de.
  2 *adjective* (*protests, departure*) en masse.

mass [2] *noun* (*church service*) messe *f*.

massacre
  1 *noun* massacre *m*.
  2 *verb* massacrer.

massage
  1 *noun* massage *m*.
  2 *verb* masser.

masseur *noun* masseur *m*.

masseuse *noun* masseuse *f*.

massive *adjective* (*huge*) énorme.

mast *noun* (*of ship*) mât *m*.

master
  1 *noun* maître *m*; (*in secondary school*) professeur *m*; **M. of Arts/Science** (*person*) Maître *m* ès lettres/sciences.
  2 *verb* (*control*) maîtriser; (*subject, situation*) dominer; **she has mastered Latin** elle possède le latin.

masterpiece *noun* chef-d'œuvre *m*.

mat *noun* tapis *m*; (*of straw*) natte *f*; (*at door*) paillasson *m*; **(place) m.** set *m* (de table).

match [1] *noun* (*stick*) allumette *f*.

match [2]
  1 *noun* (*game*) match *m*; (*equal*) égal, -ale *m or f*; **to be a good m.** (*of colours, people etc*) être bien

assortis.

2 verb (of clothes, etc) être assorti avec; **to be well-matched** être bien assortis.

3 verb (of two things) être assortis.

match (up) verb (socks etc) assortir.

match (up to) verb égaler; (somebody's hopes or expectations) répondre à.

matchbox noun boîte f d'allumettes.

matching adjective (dress etc) assorti.

matchstick noun allumette f.

mate noun (friend) camarade m or f.

material noun matière f; (cloth) tissu m; **material(s)** (equipment) matériel m; **building materials** matériaux mpl de construction.

maternal adjective maternel.

maternity hospital noun maternité f.

mathematical adjective mathématique.

mathematics noun mathématiques fpl.

maths noun maths fpl.

matinée noun (in theatre) matinée f.

matt adjective (paint, paper) mat.

matter

1 noun matière f; (subject, affair) affaire f; **no m.!** peu importe!; **what's the m.?** qu'est-ce qu'il y a?; **what's the m. with you?** qu'est-ce que tu as?; **there's something the m.** il y a quelque chose qui ne va pas; **there's something the m. with my leg** j'ai quelque chose à la jambe.

2 verb importer (to à); **it doesn't m. if/who/etc** peu importe si/

qui/etc; **it doesn't m.!** ça ne fait rien!

mattress noun matelas m.

mature adjective mûr; (cheese) fait.

maximum adjective & noun maximum (m).

May noun mai m.

may auxiliary verb (possibility) pouvoir; **he m. come** il peut arriver; **he might come** il pourrait arriver; **I m.** or **might have forgotten it** je l'ai peut-être oublié; **we m.** or **might as well go** nous ferions aussi bien de partir.

∎ (permission) pouvoir; **m. I stay?** puis-je rester?; **m. I?** vous permettez?; **you m. go** tu peux partir.

∎ (wish) **m. you be happy** (que tu) sois heureux.

maybe adverb peut-être.

mayonnaise noun mayonnaise f.

mayor noun maire m.

maze noun labyrinthe m.

me pronoun me, m'; (after preposition, 'than', 'it is') moi; **(to) me** me, m'; **she knows me** elle me connaît; **he gives (to) me** il me donne.

meadow noun pré m.

meal noun repas m.

mean [1] verb (signify) vouloir dire; (intend) destiner (for à); (result in) entraîner; **to m. to do** avoir l'intention de faire; **I m. it** je suis sérieux; **to m. something to somebody** avoir de l'importance pour quelqu'un; **I didn't m. to!** je ne l'ai pas fait exprès!

mean [2] adjective (with money etc) avare; (nasty) méchant.

meaning noun sens m.

meaningless *adjective* qui n'a pas de sens.

meanness *noun* avarice *f*; (*nastiness*) méchanceté *f*.

means
1 *noun* (*method*) moyen *m* (to do, of doing de faire); **by m. of** (*stick etc*) au moyen de; (*work etc*) à force de; **by all m.!** très certainement!; **by no m.** nullement.
2 *plural noun* (*wealth*) moyens *mpl*.

meant *see* mean².

meantime *adverb* (**in the**) **m.** entre-temps.

meanwhile *adverb* entre-temps.

measles *noun* rougeole *f*.

measure
1 *noun* (*action, amount*) mesure *f*.
2 *verb* mesurer.

measurement *noun* (*of chest etc*) tour *m*; **measurements** mesures *fpl*.

measure up *verb* (*plank etc*) mesurer.

measure up to *verb* (*task*) être à la hauteur de.

meat *noun* viande *f*.

mechanic *noun* mécanicien, -ienne *m or f*.

mechanical *adjective* mécanique.

mechanism *noun* mécanisme *m*.

medal *noun* médaille *f*.

medallist *noun* **to be a gold m.** être médaille d'or.

media *plural noun* **the (mass) m.** les médias *mpl*.

mediaeval *adjective* médiéval.

medical *adjective* médical; (*school, studies*) de médecine; (*student*) en médecine.

medication *noun* médicaments *mpl*.

medicine *noun* médicament *m*; (*science*) médecine *f*.

medicine cabinet *or* **chest** *noun* (armoire *f* à) pharmacie *f*.

medieval *adjective* médiéval.

Mediterranean
1 *adjective* méditerranéen.
2 *noun* **the M.** la Méditerranée.

medium *adjective* moyen.

medium-sized *adjective* moyen.

meet *verb*
1 (*person, team*) rencontrer; (*person by arrangement*) retrouver; (*pass in street etc*) croiser; (*fetch*) (aller *or* venir) chercher; (*wait for*) attendre; (*be introduced to*) faire la connaissance de.
2 (*of people, teams*) se rencontrer; (*of people by arrangement*) se retrouver; (*be introduced*) se connaître; (*of club etc*) se réunir.

meeting *noun* réunion *f*; (*large*) assemblée *f*; (*between two people*) rencontre *f*; (*arranged*) rendez-vous *invariable m*.

meet up *verb* (*of people*) se rencontrer; (*by arrangement*) se retrouver; **to m. up with somebody** rencontrer / retrouver quelqu'un.

meet with *verb* (*accident*) avoir; (*difficulty*) rencontrer.

melody *noun* mélodie *f*.

melon *noun* melon *m*.

melt *verb*
1 (*of ice etc*) fondre.
2 (*butter*) faire fondre.

member *noun* membre *m*.

memo *noun* note *f*.

memory *noun* mémoire *f*; (*recollection*) souvenir *m*; **in m. of** à la mémoire de.

men *see* man.

mend verb réparer; (clothes) raccommoder.

mental adjective mental.

mentally adverb he's m. handicapped c'est un handicapé mental; she's m. ill c'est une malade mentale.

mention
1 verb mentionner; not to m ... sans parler de ... ; don't m. it! il n'y a pas de quoi!
2 noun mention f.

menu noun menu m.

mercy noun pitié f; at the m. of à la merci de.

mere adjective simple; she's a m. child ce n'est qu'une enfant.

merely adverb (tout) simplement.

merge verb (blend) se mêler (with à); (of roads) se (re)joindre; (of firms) fusionner.

merger noun fusion f.

merry adjective gai (f gaie); (drunk) éméché.

merry-go-round noun (at funfair) manège m.

mesh noun (of net) maille f.

mess noun (confusion) désordre m; (dirt) saleté f; in a m. sens dessus dessous; (trouble) dans le pétrin.

mess about verb (have fun) s'amuser; (play the fool) faire l'idiot; to m. about with something (fiddle with) s'amuser avec quelque chose.

message noun message m.

messenger noun messager m; (in office, hotel) coursier, -ière m or f.

mess up verb (spoil) gâcher; (dirty) salir; (room) mettre sens dessus dessous.

messy adjective (untidy) en désordre; (dirty) sale.

met see meet.

metal noun métal m; m. ladder/ etc échelle f/ etc métallique.

meter noun (device) compteur m; (parking) m. parcmètre m.

method noun méthode f.

methodical adjective méthodique.

metre noun mètre m.

metric adjective métrique.

Mexican adjective & noun mexicain, -aine (m or f).

Mexico noun le Mexique m.

miaow verb (of cat) miauler.

mice see mouse.

micro- prefix micro-.

microchip noun puce f.

microphone noun micro m.

microscope noun microscope m.

microwave (oven) noun four m à micro-ondes.

mid adjective (in) m.-June (à) la mi-juin; in m. air en plein ciel.

midday noun midi m.

middle
1 noun milieu m; (waist) taille f; (right) in the m. of au (beau) milieu de; in the m. of saying/ etc en train de dire/ etc.
2 adjective du milieu; (class) moyen; (name) deuxième.

middle-aged adjective d'un certain âge.

middle-class adjective bourgeois.

midnight noun minuit f.

midst noun in the m. of au milieu de.

midwife noun sage-femme f.

might see may.

mild adjective doux (f douce);

(*beer*, *punishment*) léger; (*medicine*, *illness*) bénin (*f* bénigne).

mile *noun* mile *m*.

mileage *noun* = kilométrage *m*.

military *adjective* militaire.

milk
1 *noun* lait *m*.
2 *adjective* (*chocolate*) au lait; (*bottle*) à lait.
3 *verb* (*cow*) traire.

milkman *noun* laitier *m*.

milk shake *noun* milk-shake *m*.

mill *noun* moulin *m*; (*factory*) usine *f*.

millimetre *noun* millimètre *m*.

million *noun* million *m*; **a m. men**/*etc* un million d'hommes/*etc*.

millionaire *noun* millionnaire *m* or *f*.

mime *verb* mimer.

mimic *verb* imiter.

mince(meat) *noun* hachis *m* (de viande).

mincer *noun* hachoir *m*.

mind
1 *noun* esprit *m*; (*sanity*) raison *f*; (*memory*) mémoire *f*; **to change one's m.** changer d'avis; **to make up one's m.** se décider; **to be on somebody's m.** préoccuper quelqu'un; **to have in m.** (*person*, *plan*) avoir en vue.
2 *verb* faire attention à; (*look after*) garder; (*noise etc*) être gêné par; **do you m. if?** (*I smoke*) ça vous gêne si?; (*I leave*) ça ne vous fait rien si?; **I don't m.** ça m'est égal; **I wouldn't m. a cup of tea** j'aimerais bien une tasse de thé; **never m.!** ça ne fait rien!; (*don't worry*) ne vous en faites pas!; **m. (out)!** attention!

minder *noun* **child m.** nourrice *f*.

mine [1] *possessive pronoun* le mien, la mienne, *plural* les mien(ne)s; **this hat is m.** ce chapeau est à moi *or* est le mien.

mine [2] *noun* (*for coal etc*, *explosive*) mine *f*.

miner *noun* mineur *m*.

mineral *adjective* & *noun* minéral (*m*).

mini *prefix* mini-.

miniature *adjective* (*train etc*) miniature *invariable*; **in m.** en miniature.

minibus *noun* minibus *m*.

minicab *noun* (radio-)taxi *m*.

minimum *adjective* & *noun* minimum (*m*).

minister *noun* (*politician*, *priest*) ministre *m*.

ministry *noun* ministère *m*.

minor *adjective* (*detail*, *operation*) petit.

minority *noun* minorité *f*.

mint *noun* (*herb*) menthe *f*; (*sweet*) bonbon *m* à la menthe; **m. tea**/*etc* thé *m*/*etc* à la menthe.

minus *preposition* moins; (*without*) sans.

minute [1] *noun* minute *f*.

minute [2] *adjective* (*tiny*) minuscule.

miracle *noun* miracle *m*.

miraculous *adjective* miraculeux.

mirror *noun* miroir *m*, glace *f*; (*in vehicle*) rétroviseur *m*.

misbehave *verb* se conduire mal.

miscellaneous *adjective* divers.

mischief *noun* espièglerie *f*; (*malice*) méchanceté *f*; **to get into m.** faire des bêtises.

mischievous *adjective* espiègle;

(*malicious*) méchant.

miser *noun* avare *m or f*.

miserable *adjective* (*wretched*) misérable; (*unhappy*) malheureux.

miserly *adjective* avare.

misery *noun* souffrances *fpl*; (*sadness*) tristesse *f*.

misfortune *noun* malheur *m*.

mishap *noun* contretemps *m*.

mislay *verb* égarer.

mislead *verb* tromper.

misleading *adjective* trompeur.

miss[1] *verb* manquer; (*not see*) ne pas voir; (*not understand*) ne pas comprendre; **he misses Paris/her** Paris/elle lui manque.

miss[2] *noun* (*woman*) mademoiselle *f*; **Miss Brown** Mademoiselle *or* Mlle Brown.

missile *noun* (*rocket*) missile *m*; (*object thrown*) projectile *m*.

missing *adjective* absent; (*after disaster*) disparu; (*object*) manquant; **there are two cups m.** il manque deux tasses.

mission *noun* mission *f*.

miss out *verb*
1 (*leave out*) sauter.
2 **to m. out on something** rater quelque chose.

miss out on *verb* (*opportunity etc*) rater.

mist *noun* (*fog*) brume *f*; (*on glass*) buée *f*.

mistake
1 *noun* erreur *f*, faute *f*; **to make a m.** se tromper; **by m.** par erreur.
2 *verb* (*meaning etc*) se tromper sur; **to m. the date/etc** se tromper de date/etc; **to m. somebody/something for** prendre quelqu'un/quelque chose pour;

you're **mistaken** tu te trompes.

mistaken *see* **mistake**.

mistakenly *adverb* par erreur.

mistook *see* **mistake**.

mistress *noun* maîtresse *f*; (*in secondary school*) professeur *m*.

mistrust
1 *noun* méfiance *f*.
2 *verb* se méfier de.

misty *adjective* brumeux.

misunderstand *verb* mal comprendre.

misunderstanding *noun* malentendu *m*.

mitten *noun* (*glove*) moufle *f*.

mix *verb*
1 mélanger, mêler.
2 se mêler; **she doesn't m.** elle n'est pas sociable; **to m. with somebody** fréquenter quelqu'un.

mixed *adjective* (*school*) mixte; (*chocolates etc*) assortis.

mixer *noun* (*electric, for cooking*) mixe(u)r *m*.

mixture *noun* mélange *m*.

mix-up *noun* confusion *f*.

mix up *verb* (*ingredients, papers etc*) mélanger; (*person*) embrouiller; **he mixed the dates up** il a confondu les dates.

moan *verb* (*groan*) gémir; (*complain*) se plaindre (**to** à, **about** de, **that** que).

mob
1 *noun* foule *f*.
2 *verb* assiéger.

mobile *adjective* mobile.

model
1 *noun* (*example etc*) modèle *m*; (*fashion*) **m.** mannequin *m*; (*scale*) **m.** modèle *m* (réduit).
2 *adjective* miniature.

moderate *adjective* modéré.

moderation noun modération f.

modern adjective moderne; **m. languages** langues fpl vivantes.

modernize verb moderniser.

modest adjective modeste.

modesty noun modestie f.

modification noun modification f.

modify verb modifier.

moist adjective humide; (sticky) moite.

moisture noun humidité f; (on glass) buée f.

mole noun (on skin) grain m de beauté; (animal) taupe f.

moment noun moment m; **the m. she leaves** dès qu'elle partira.

Monday noun lundi m.

money noun argent m.

moneybox noun tirelire f.

money order noun mandat m.

monk noun moine m.

monkey noun singe m.

monopolize verb monopoliser.

monotonous adjective monotone.

monotony noun monotonie f.

monster noun monstre m.

month noun mois m.

monthly
1 adjective mensuel.
2 adverb mensuellement.

monument noun monument m.

moo verb meugler.

mood noun (of person) humeur f; Grammar mode m; **in a good/ bad m.** de bonne/mauvaise humeur; **to be in the m. to do** être d'humeur à faire.

moody adjective (bad-tempered) de mauvaise humeur.

moon noun lune f.

moonlight noun clair m de lune.

moor noun lande f.

mop
1 noun balai m (à laver).
2 verb (floor etc) essuyer.

moped noun mobylette ® f.

mop up verb (liquid) éponger.

moral noun (of story) morale f.

morale noun moral m.

more
1 adjective & noun plus (de) (than que); (other) d'autres; **m. cars/ etc** plus de voitures/etc; **he has m. (than you)** il en a plus (que toi); **a few m. months** encore quelques mois; **(some) m. tea/ etc** encore du thé/etc; **m. than a kilo/ten** (with quantity, number) plus d'un kilo/de dix; **many m., much m.** beaucoup plus (de).
2 adverb plus (than que); **m. and m.** de plus en plus; **m. or less** plus ou moins; **she doesn't have any m.** elle n'en a plus.

moreover adverb de plus.

morning noun matin m; (duration of morning) matinée f; **in the m.** le matin; (tomorrow) demain matin; **at seven in the m.** à sept heures du matin; **every Tuesday m.** tous les mardis matin.

Moroccan adjective & noun marocain, -aine (m or f).

Morocco noun le Maroc m.

mortal adjective & noun mortel, -elle (m or f).

mortgage noun prêt-logement m.

Moslem adjective & noun musulman, -ane (m or f).

mosque noun mosquée f.

mosquito noun moustique m.

moss noun mousse f.

most

1 *adjective & noun* the m. le plus (de); **I have (the) m. books** j'ai le plus de livres; **I have (the) m.** j'en ai le plus; **m. (of the) books**/*etc* la plupart des livres/*etc*; **m. of the cake**/*etc* la plus grande partie du gâteau/*etc*; **at (the very) m.** tout au plus.

2 *adverb* (le) plus; (*very*) très; **the m. beautiful** le plus beau, la plus belle (**in, of** de); **to talk (the) m.** parler le plus; **m. of all** surtout.

mostly *adverb* surtout.

motel *noun* motel *m*.

moth *noun* papillon *m* de nuit; (*in clothes*) mite *f*.

mother *noun* mère *f*; **M.'s Day** la fête des Mères.

mother-in-law *noun* belle-mère *f*.

motion

1 *noun* (*of arm etc*) mouvement *m*.

2 *verb* **to m. (to) somebody to do** faire signe à quelqu'un de faire.

motivated *adjective* motivé.

motive *noun* motif *m* (**for** de).

motor *noun* (*engine*) moteur *m*.

motorbike *noun* moto *f*.

motor boat *noun* canot *m* automobile.

motorcar *noun* automobile *f*.

motorcycle *noun* moto *f*.

motorcyclist *noun* motocycliste *m* or *f*.

motorist *noun* automobiliste *m* or *f*.

motorway *noun* autoroute *f*.

mould

1 *noun* (*shape*) moule *m*; (*growth*) moisissure *f*.

2 *verb* (*clay etc*) mouler.

mouldy *adjective* moisi; **to go m.** moisir.

mount

1 *noun* (*frame for photo*) cadre *m*.

2 *verb* (*horse, photo*) monter.

3 *verb* (*get on horse*) se mettre en selle.

mountain *noun* montagne *f*; **m. bike** VTT *invariable m*.

mountaineer *noun* alpiniste *m* or *f*.

mountaineering *noun* alpinisme *m*.

mountainous *adjective* montagneux.

mount up *verb* (*add up*) chiffrer (**to** à); (*accumulate*) s'accumuler.

mourn *verb* **to m. (for) somebody, m. the loss of somebody** pleurer (la perte de) quelqu'un; **she's mourning** elle est en deuil.

mourning *noun* deuil *m*; **in m.** en deuil.

mouse *noun* souris *f*.

mousse *noun* mousse *f*.

moustache *noun* moustache *f*.

mouth *noun* bouche *f*; (*of dog, lion etc*) gueule *f*; (*of river*) embouchure *f*.

mouthorgan *noun* harmonica *m*.

mouthwash *noun* bain *m* de bouche.

move

1 *noun* mouvement *m*; (*change of house*) déménagement *m*; (*in game*) coup *m*, (*one's turn*) tour *m*; (*act*) démarche *f*; **to make a m.** (*leave*) se préparer à partir.

2 *verb* (*thing etc*) bouger; (*put*) mettre; (*transport*) transporter; (*piece in game*) jouer; **to m. somebody** (*emotionally*) émouvoir quelqu'un; (*transfer in job*) muter quelqu'un; **to m. house** déménager.

3 verb (go) aller (**to** à); (out of house) déménager; (change seats) changer de place; (play) jouer; **to m. to a new house**/etc aller habiter une nouvelle maison/etc; **to m. into a house** emménager dans une maison.

move about verb se déplacer; (fidget) remuer.

move along verb avancer.

move away verb s'éloigner; (move house) déménager.

move back verb
1 (chair etc) reculer; (to its position) remettre.
2 (step backwards) reculer; (return) retourner.

move forward verb avancer.

move in verb (into house) emménager.

movement noun (action, group etc) mouvement m.

move off verb (go away) s'éloigner; (of vehicle) démarrer.

move on verb avancer; **move on!** circulez!

move out verb (out of house) déménager.

move over verb
1 (thing) pousser.
2 (of person) se pousser.

move up verb (on seats etc) se pousser.

movie noun film m.

movie camera noun caméra f.

moving adjective en mouvement; (touching) émouvant.

mow verb **to m. the lawn** tondre le gazon.

mower noun (lawn) m. tondeuse f (à gazon).

MP abbreviation (Member of Parliament) député m.

Mr abbreviation **Mr Brown** Monsieur Brown.

Mrs abbreviation **Mrs Brown** Madame or Mme Brown.

Ms abbreviation **Ms Brown** Madame or Mme Brown.

MSc abbreviation = **Master of Science.**

much
1 adjective & noun beaucoup (de); **not m. time**/etc pas beaucoup de temps/etc; **I don't have m.** je n'en ai pas beaucoup; **as m. as** autant que; **as m. wine**/etc as autant de vin/etc que; **twice as m.** deux fois plus (de).
2 adverb **very m.** beaucoup; **not (very) m.** pas beaucoup.

mud noun boue f.

muddle noun (mix-up) confusion f; (mess) désordre m; **in a m.** (person) désorienté; (mind, ideas) embrouillé.

muddle (up) verb (person, facts) embrouiller; (papers) mélanger.

muddy adjective (water, road) boueux; (hands etc) couvert de boue.

muesli noun muesli m.

muffin noun = petite brioche f.

mug [1] noun (cup) grande tasse f; (beer) m. chope f.

mug verb (in street) agresser, attaquer.

mugger noun agresseur m.

mule noun (male) mulet m; (female) mule f.

multiple adjective & noun multiple (m).

multiplication noun multiplication f.

multiply verb multiplier.

mum noun Familiar maman f.

mumble *verb* marmotter.

mummy *noun Familiar* maman *f*.

mumps *noun* oreillons *mpl*.

murder
  1 *noun* meurtre *m*, assassinat *m*.
  2 *verb* tuer, assassiner.

murderer *noun* meurtrier, -ière *m or f*, assassin *m*.

murmur *verb* murmurer.

muscle *noun* muscle *m*.

muscular *adjective* (*pain*) musculaire; (*arm, person*) musclé.

museum *noun* musée *m*.

mushroom *noun* champignon *m*.

music *noun* musique *f*.

musical
  1 *adjective* musical; (*instrument*) de musique; **to be m.** être musicien.
  2 *noun* comédie *f* musicale.

musician *noun* musicien, -ienne *m or f*.

Muslim *adjective & noun* musul-man, -ane (*m or f*).

mussel *noun* moule *f*.

must *auxiliary verb* (*necessity*) devoir; **you m. obey** tu dois obéir, il faut que tu obéisses.
  ▮ (*certainty*) devoir; **she m. be clever** elle doit être intelligente; **I m. have seen it** j'ai dû le voir.

mustard *noun* moutarde *f*.

musty *adjective* **to smell m.** sentir le moisi.

mutter *verb* marmonner.

mutton *noun* (*meat*) mouton *m*.

mutual *adjective* (*help etc*) mutuel; (*friend*) commun.

muzzle *noun* (*for animal*) muselière *f*.

my *possessive adjective* mon, ma, *plural* mes.

myself *pronoun* moi-même; (*reflexive*) me, m'; (*after preposition*) moi.

mysterious *adjective* mystérieux.

mystery *noun* mystère *m*.

N

nail *noun* (*of finger, toe*) ongle *m*; (*metal*) clou *m*.

nail (down) *verb* clouer.

nail file/polish *noun* lime *f*/vernis *m* à ongles.

naïve *adjective* naïf.

naked *adjective* nu.

name
1 *noun* nom *m*; (*reputation*) réputation *f*; my n. is … je m'appelle … ; first n. prénom *m*; last n. nom *m* de famille.
2 *verb* nommer; (*date, price*) fixer; he was named after il a reçu le nom de.

nanny *noun* nurse *f*; (*grandmother*) *Familiar* mamie *f*.

nap *noun* (*sleep*) petit somme *m*; to have *or* take a n. faire un petit somme.

napkin *noun* (*at table*) serviette *f*.

nappy *noun* (*for baby*) couche *f*.

narrow *adjective* étroit.

narrow (down) *verb* (*choice etc*) limiter.

narrowly *adverb* he n. escaped being killed/*etc* il a failli être tué/*etc*.

nastily *adverb* (*to behave*) méchamment; (*to rain*) horriblement.

nasty *adjective* mauvais; (*spiteful*) méchant (to(wards) avec).

nation *noun* nation *f*.

national *adjective* national.

nationality *noun* nationalité *f*.

native
1 *adjective* (*country*) natal (*mpl* -als); to be an English n. speaker parler l'anglais comme langue maternelle.
2 *noun* to be a n. of être originaire de.

natural *adjective* naturel; (*actor etc*) né.

naturally *adverb* (*as normal, of course*) naturellement; (*to behave etc*) avec naturel.

nature *noun* (*natural world, character*) nature *f*.

nature study *noun* sciences *fpl* naturelles.

naughty *adjective* (*child*) vilain.

naval *adjective* naval (*mpl* -als); (*officer*) de marine.

navel *noun* nombril *m*.

navigate *verb*
1 naviguer.
2 (*boat*) diriger.

navigation *noun* navigation *f*.

navy
1 *noun* marine *f*.
2 *adjective* n. (blue) bleu marine *inv*.

near
1 *adverb* près; quite n. tout près; n. to près de; to come n. to being killed/*etc* faillir être tué/*etc*; n. enough (*more or less*) plus ou moins.
2 *preposition* n. (to) près de; n. (to) the end vers la fin; to come n. somebody s'approcher de quelqu'un.
3 *adjective* proche; in the n. future dans un avenir proche.

nearby
1 *adverb* tout près.
2 *adjective* proche.

nearly *adverb* presque; she (very) n. fell elle a failli tomber; not n.

as **clever**/*etc* as loin d'être aussi intelligent/*etc* que.

neat *adjective* (*clothes, work*) soigné; (*room*) bien rangé.

neatly *adverb* avec soin.

necessarily *adverb* not n. pas forcément.

necessary *adjective* nécessaire (to do de faire); to do what's n. faire le nécessaire.

necessity *noun* nécessité *f.*

neck *noun* cou *m*; (*of dress, horse*) encolure *f.*

necklace *noun* collier *m.*

nectarine *noun* nectarine *f.*

need
   1 *noun* besoin *m*; to be in n. of avoir besoin de; there's no n. (for you) to do tu n'as pas besoin de faire; if n. be si besoin est.
   2 *verb* avoir besoin de; her hair needs cutting elle a besoin d'une coupe de cheveux; n. he wait? a-t-il besoin d'attendre?; I needn't have rushed ce n'était pas la peine que je me dépêche.

needle *noun* aiguille *f*; (*of record player*) saphir *m.*

needlessly *adverb* inutilement.

needlework *noun* couture *f*; (*object*) ouvrage *m.*

negative
   1 *adjective* négatif.
   2 *noun* (*of photo*) négatif *m*; *Grammar* forme *f* négative.

neglect *verb* (*person, work, duty etc*) négliger; (*garden, car*) ne pas s'occuper de.

neglected *adjective* (*appearance*) négligé; (*garden, house*) mal tenu; to feel n. sentir qu'on vous néglige.

negligence *noun* négligence *f.*

negligent *adjective* négligent.

negotiate *verb* (*discuss*) négocier.

negotiation *noun* négociation *f.*

neigh *verb* (*of horse*) hennir.

neighbour *noun* voisin, -ine *m* or *f.*

neighbourhood *noun* quartier *m*; (*neighbours*) voisinage *m.*

neighbouring *adjective* voisin.

neither
   1 *adverb* n. ... nor ni ... ni; he n. sings nor dances il ne chante ni ne danse.
   2 *conjunction* (*not either*) n. shall I go je n'y irai pas non plus; n. do I, n. can I *etc* (ni) moi non plus.
   3 *adjective* n. boy (came) aucun des deux garçons (n'est venu).
   4 *pronoun* n. (of them) ni l'un(e) ni l'autre.

neon *adjective* (*lighting etc*) au néon.

nephew *noun* neveu *m.*

nerve *noun* nerf *m*; (*courage*) courage *m* (to do de faire); (*calm*) sang-froid *m*; (*cheek*) culot *m* (to do de faire); you get on my nerves tu me tapes sur les nerfs.

nervous *adjective* (*tense*) nerveux; (*worried*) inquiet (about de); (*uneasy*) mal à l'aise; to be or feel n. (*before exam etc*) avoir le trac.

nest *noun* nid *m.*

net
   1 *noun* filet *m.*
   2 *adjective* (*profit, weight etc*) net (*f* nette).

netting *noun* (*wire*) n. grillage *m.*

nettle *noun* ortie *f.*

network *noun* réseau *m.*

neutral
1 *adjective* neutre.
2 *noun* in n. (gear) au point
mort.

never *adverb* (ne …) jamais; **she
n.** lies elle ne ment jamais; **n.
again** plus jamais.

never-ending *adjective* interminable.

nevertheless *adverb* néanmoins.

new *adjective* nouveau (*f* nouvelle); (*brand-new*) neuf (*f* neuve);
a n. glass/*etc* (*different*) un autre
verre/*etc*; **what's n.?** *Familiar*
quoi de neuf?; **a n.-born baby**
un nouveau-né.

newcomer *noun* nouveau-venu
m, nouvelle-venue *f*.

newly *adverb* (*recently*) nouvelle-
ment.

news *noun* nouvelle(s) *f*(*pl*); (*in
the media*) informations *fpl*;
sports n. (*newspaper column*)
chronique *f* sportive; **a piece of
n.**, **some n.** une nouvelle; (*in the
media*) une information.

newsagent *noun* marchand,
-ande *m or f* de journaux.

news flash *noun* flash *m*.

newsletter *noun* bulletin *m*.

newspaper *noun* journal *m*.

New Zealand *noun* la Nouvelle-
Zélande *f*.

New Zealander *noun* Néo-
Zélandais, -aise *m or f*.

next
1 *adjective* prochain; (*room,
house*) d'à-côté; (*following*) suivant; **n. month** (*in the future*) le
mois prochain; **the n. day** le lendemain; **the n. morning** le lendemain matin; **(by) this time n.
week** d'ici (à) la semaine prochaine; **to live n. door** habiter à

côté (**to** de); **n.-door neighbour**
voisin *m* d'à-côté.
2 *noun* suivant, -ante *m or f*.
3 *adverb* (*afterwards*) ensuite;
(*now*) maintenant; **when you
come in. n.** la prochaine fois que tu
viendras.
4 *preposition* **n. to** (*beside*) à côté
de.

NHS *abbreviation* (*National
Health Service*) = la Sécurité
Sociale.

nib *noun* (*of pen*) plume *f*.

nibble *verb* (*eat*) grignoter; (*bite*)
mordiller.

nice *adjective* (*pleasant*) agréable;
(*pretty*) joli; (*kind*) gentil (**to**
avec); **it's n. here** c'est bien ici;
n. and easy/*etc* (*very*) bien
facile/*etc*.

nicely *adverb* agréablement;
(*kindly*) gentiment.

nickname *noun* surnom *m*.

niece *noun* nièce *f*.

Nigeria *noun* le Nigeria *m*.

Nigerian *adjective & noun* nigérian, -ane (*m or f*).

night *noun* nuit *f*; (*evening*) soir
m; **last n.** (*evening*) hier soir;
(*night*) la nuit dernière; **to have
an early/late n.** se coucher tôt/
tard; **to have a good night('s
sleep)** bien dormir.

nightclub *noun* boîte *f* de nuit.

nightdress, **nightgown**, *Familiar* **nightie** *noun* chemise *f*
de nuit.

nightingale *noun* rossignol *m*.

nightmare *noun* cauchemar *m*.

nighttime *noun* nuit *f*.

night watchman *noun* veilleur
m de nuit.

nil *noun* zéro *m*.

nine *adjective & noun* neuf (*m*).

nineteen *adjective & noun* dix-neuf (*m*).

ninetieth *adjective & noun* quatre-vingt-dixième (*m or f*).

ninety *adjective & noun* quatre-vingt-dix (*m*).

ninth *adjective & noun* neuvième (*m or f*).

nip *verb* pincer.

nip in/out *verb* (*dash*) *Familiar* entrer/sortir un instant.

nipple *noun* bout *m* de sein.

nip round *verb Familiar* to n. round to somebody faire un saut chez quelqu'un.

nitrogen *noun* azote *m*.

no
1 *adverb & noun* non (*invariable m*); no more than ten/*etc* pas plus de dix/*etc*; no more time/ *etc* plus de temps/etc.
2 *adjective* aucun(e); pas de; I have no idea je n'ai aucune idée; no child came aucun enfant n'est venu; I have no time/*etc* je n'ai pas de temps/*etc*; of no importance/*etc* sans importance/*etc*; 'no smoking' 'défense de fumer'; no way! *Familiar* pas question!; no one = nobody.

noble *adjective* noble.

nobody *pronoun* (ne …) personne; n. came personne n'est venu.

nod
1 *verb* to n. (one's head) faire un signe de tête.
2 *noun* signe *m* de tête.

nod off *verb* s'assoupir.

noise *noun* bruit *m*; (*of bell, drum*) son *m*; to make a n. faire du bruit.

noisily *adverb* bruyamment.

noisy *adjective* bruyant.

nominate *verb* (*appoint*) nommer.

non- *prefix* non-.

none *pronoun* aucun(e) *m or f*; (*in filling out a form*) néant; she has n. (at all) elle n'en a pas (du tout); n. (at all) came pas un(e) seul(e) n'est venu(e); n. of the cake/*etc* pas une seule partie du gâteau/*etc*; n. of the trees/*etc* aucun des arbres/*etc*.

nonetheless *adverb* néanmoins.

non-existent *adjective* inexistant.

non-fiction *noun* (*in library*) ouvrages *mpl* généraux.

nonsense *noun* absurdités *fpl*; that's n. c'est absurde.

non-smoker *noun* non-fumeur, -euse *m or f*.

non-stick *adjective* (*pan*) antiadhésif.

non-stop
1 *adjective* sans arrêt; (*train, flight*) direct.
2 *adverb* sans arrêt; (*to fly*) sans escale.

noodles *plural noun* nouilles *fpl*; (*in soup*) vermicelle(s) *m(pl)*.

noon *noun* midi *m*; at n. à midi.

nor *conjunction* ni; neither you n. me ni toi ni moi; she neither drinks n. smokes elle ne fume ni ne boit; n. do I, n. can I *etc* (ni) moi non plus.

normal
1 *adjective* normal.
2 *noun* above/below n. audessus/au-dessous de la normale.

normally *adverb* normalement.

north
1 *noun* nord *m*; (to the) n. of au nord de.
2 *adjective* (*coast*) nord *invariable*.

3 *adverb* au nord.

North American *adjective & noun* nord-américain, -aine (*m or f*).

northbound *adjective* en direction du nord.

north-east
1 *noun* nord-est *m*.
2 *adjective* nord-est *invariable*.

northern *adjective* (*coast*) nord *invariable*; (*town*) du nord.

northerner *noun* habitant, -ante *m or f* du Nord.

northward(s) *adverb* vers le nord.

north-west
1 *noun* nord-ouest *m*.
2 *adjective* nord-ouest *invariable*.

Norway *noun* la Norvège *f*.

Norwegian *adjective & noun* norvégien, -ienne (*m or f*).

nose *noun* nez *m*; her n. is bleeding elle saigne du nez.

nosebleed *noun* saignement *m* de nez.

nostril *noun* (*of person*) narine *f*; (*of horse*) naseau *m*.

nos(e)y *adjective* indiscret.

not *adverb* (ne ...) pas; he's n. there, he isn't there il n'est pas là; n. yet pas encore; why n.? pourquoi pas?; n. one reply/*etc* pas une seule réponse/*etc*; n. at all pas du tout; (*after 'thank you'*) je vous en prie.
▮ non; I think/hope n. je pense/j'espère que non; isn't she?, don't you? *etc* non?

note
1 *noun* (*comment, musical etc*) note *f*; (*banknote*) billet *m*; (*message*) petit mot *m*; to make a n. of prendre note de.
2 *verb* noter.

notebook *noun* carnet *m*; (*for school*) cahier *m*.

note down *verb* (*word etc*) noter.

notepad *noun* bloc-notes *m*.

notepaper *noun* papier *m* à lettres.

nothing *pronoun* (ne ...) rien; he knows n. il ne sait rien; n. to eat/*etc* rien à manger/*etc*; n. big/*etc* rien de grand/*etc*; n. much pas grand-chose; I've got n. to do with it je n'y suis pour rien; to come to n. (*of efforts etc*) ne rien donner; for n. (*in vain, free of charge*) pour rien; to have n. on être tout nu.

notice
1 *noun* avis *m*; (*sign*) pancarte *f*; (*poster*) affiche *f*; to give (in) one's n. donner sa démission; to give somebody (advance) n. avertir quelqu'un (of de); to take n. faire attention (of à); until further n. jusqu'à nouvel ordre.
2 *verb* remarquer (that que).

noticeable *adjective* visible.

notice board *noun* tableau *m* d'affichage.

notification *noun* avis *m*.

notify *verb* avertir (somebody of something quelqu'un de quelque chose).

notion *noun* idée *f*.

nought *noun* zéro *m*.

noun *noun* nom *m*.

nourishing *adjective* nourrissant.

novel
1 *noun* roman *m*.
2 *adjective* nouveau (*f* nouvelle).

novelist *noun* romancier, -ière *m or f*.

November *noun* novembre *m*.

now

1 *adverb* maintenant; **just n., right n.** en ce moment; **I saw her just n.** je l'ai vue à l'instant; **for n.** pour le moment; **from n. on** désormais; **before n.** avant; **n. and then** de temps à autre; **n. (then)!** bon!; (*telling somebody off*) allons!

2 *conjunction* **n. (that)** maintenant que.

nowadays *adverb* aujourd'hui.

nowhere *adverb* nulle part; **n. near the house** loin de la maison; **n. near enough** loin d'être assez.

nozzle *noun* (*hose*) jet *m*.

nuclear *adjective* nucléaire.

nude *noun* **in the n.** (tout) nu (*f* toute nue).

nudge

1 *verb* pousser du coude.

2 *noun* coup *m* de coude.

nuisance *noun* embêtement *m*; (*person*) peste *f*; **that's a n.** c'est embêtant.

numb *adjective* (*hand etc*) engourdi.

number

1 *noun* nombre *m*; (*of page, house, telephone etc*) numéro *m*;

a n. of un certain nombre de.

2 *verb* (*page etc*) numéroter.

number plate *noun* plaque *f* d'immatriculation.

numeral *noun* chiffre *m*.

numerous *adjective* nombreux.

nun *noun* religieuse *f*.

nurse

1 *noun* infirmière *f*; **(male) n.** infirmier *m*.

2 *verb* (*look after*) soigner.

nursery *noun* chambre *f* d'enfants; (*for plants*) pépinière *f*; **(day) n.** (*school*) crèche *f*, garderie *f*.

nursery rhyme *noun* chanson *f* enfantine.

nursery school *noun* école *f* maternelle.

nut¹ *noun* (*walnut*) noix *f*; (*hazelnut*) noisette *f*; (*peanut*) cacah(o)uète *f*.

nut² *noun* (*for bolt*) écrou *m*.

nutcracker(s) *noun* casse-noix *invariable m*.

nylon

1 *noun* nylon *m*; **nylons** bas *mpl* nylon.

2 *adjective* (*shirt etc*) en nylon.

oak *noun* chêne *m*.

OAP *abbreviation* (*old age pensioner*) retraité, -ée *m or f*.

oar *noun* aviron *m*.

oats *plural noun* avoine *f*; (*porridge*) o. flocons *mpl* d'avoine.

obedience *noun* obéissance *f* (to à).

obedient *adjective* obéissant.

obey *verb*
1 (*person*) obéir à; **to be obeyed** être obéi.
2 obéir.

object [1] *noun* (*thing, aim*) objet *m*; *Grammar* complément *m* (d'objet).

object [2] *verb* **to o. to something/somebody** désapprouver quelque chose/quelqu'un; **I o. to you(r) doing that** je ne suis pas d'accord pour que tu fasses ça.

objection *noun* objection *f*.

objective *noun* (*aim*) objectif *m*.

obligation *noun* obligation *f*.

oblige *verb* (*compel*) contraindre (**somebody to do** quelqu'un à faire); (*help*) rendre service à.

obliging *adjective* serviable.

oblique *adjective* oblique.

obscene *adjective* obscène.

observant *adjective* observateur.

observation *noun* observation *f*.

observe *verb* observer; (*say*) remarquer (**that** que).

obstacle *noun* obstacle *m*.

obstinate *adjective* (*person, resistance*) obstiné.

obstruct *verb* (*block*) boucher;

(*hinder*) gêner.

obtain *verb* obtenir.

obtainable *adjective* disponible.

obvious *adjective* évident (**that** que).

obviously *adverb* évidemment.

occasion *noun* (*time, opportunity*) occasion *f*; (*event, ceremony*) événement *m*.

occasional *adjective* (*odd*) qu'on fait, voit *etc* de temps en temps; **she drinks the o. whisky** elle boit un whisky de temps en temps.

occasionally *adverb* de temps en temps.

occupant *noun* occupant, -ante *m or f*.

occupation *noun* (*job*) profession *f*, métier *m*; (*pastime, of house, land*) occupation *f*.

occupy *verb* occuper; **to keep oneself occupied** s'occuper (**doing** à faire).

occur *verb* (*happen*) avoir lieu; (*be found*) se rencontrer; **it occurs to me that …** il me vient à l'esprit que …

occurrence *noun* (*event*) événement *m*.

ocean *noun* océan *m*.

o'clock *adverb* (**it's**) **three o'c./** *etc* (il est) trois heures/*etc*.

October *noun* octobre *m*.

octopus *noun* pieuvre *f*.

odd *adjective* (*strange*) bizarre.
▪ (*number*) impair.
▪ (*left over*) **I have an o. penny** il me reste un penny; **a few o. stamps** quelques timbres (qui restent); **the o. man out** l'excep-

tion *f*; **sixty o.** soixante et quelques; **an o. glove**/*etc* un gant/
etc dépareillé.

■ **o. jobs** menus travaux *mpl*; **o.
job man** homme *m* à tout faire.

oddly *adverb* bizarrement.

odds *plural noun* (*in betting*) cote
f; (*chances*) chances *fpl*; **at o.** en
désaccord (**with** avec); **o. and
ends** des petites choses.

odour *noun* odeur *f*.

of *preposition* de, d' (de + le = du,
de + les = des); **she has a lot of
it** *or* **of them** elle en a beaucoup;
a friend of his un ami à lui; **there
are ten of us** nous sommes dix;
that's nice of you c'est gentil de
ta part.

off
1 *adverb* (*gone away*) parti; (*light,
radio etc*) éteint; (*tap*) fermé;
(*detached*) détaché; (*removed*)
enlevé; (*cancelled*) annulé; (*not
fit to eat or drink*) mauvais; (*milk,
meat*) tourné; **2 km o.** à 2 km
(d'ici *or* de là); **to be** *or* **go o.**
(*leave*) partir; **a day o.** un jour
de congé; **time o.** du temps libre;
5% o. une réduction de 5%;
hands o.! pas touche!; **to be
better o.** être mieux.
2 *preposition* (*from*) de; (*distant*)
éloigné de; **to get o. the bus**/*etc*
descendre du bus/*etc*; **to take
something o. the table**/*etc*
prendre quelque chose sur la
table/*etc*; **o. Dover** au large de
Douvres.

off-colour *adjective* (*ill*) patraque.

offence *noun* (*crime*) délit *m*; **to
take o.** s'offenser (**at** de).

offend *verb* froisser; **to be
offended** (**at**) se froisser (**de**).

offensive *adjective* choquant;
(*smell*) repoussant; **to be o. to**

somebody se montrer blessant
envers quelqu'un.

offer
1 *noun* offre *f*; **on (special) o.** (*in
shop*) en promotion.
2 *verb* offrir (**to do** de faire).

offhand
1 *adjective* désinvolte.
2 *adverb* (*to say, know etc*)
comme ça.

office *noun* (*room*) bureau *m*;
(*post*) fonction *f*; **head o.** siège *m*
central; **o. block** immeuble *m* de
bureaux.

officer *noun* (*in the army etc*)
officier *m*; (*police*) **o.** agent *m*
(de police).

official
1 *adjective* officiel.
2 *noun* (*civil servant*) fonctionnaire *m or f*.

officially *adverb* officiellement.

off-licence *noun* magasin *m* de
vins et spiritueux.

often *adverb* souvent; **how o.?**
combien de fois?; **how o. do they
run?** (*train etc*) il y en a tous les
combien?; **every so o.** de temps
en temps.

oh! *interjection* oh!, ah!; **oh yes!**
mais oui!; **oh yes?** ah oui?

oil
1 *noun* huile *f*; (*extracted from
ground*) pétrole *m*; (*fuel*) mazout
m; **o. change** vidange *f*.
2 *verb* (*machine*) graisser.

oilcan *noun* burette *f*.

ointment *noun* pommade *f*.

OK , okay = all right.

old *adjective* vieux (*f* vieille); (*former*) ancien; **how o. is he?** quel
âge a-t-il?; **he's ten years o.** il a
dix ans; **he's older than me** il est
plus âgé que moi; **an older son**
un fils aîné; **the oldest son** le fils

aîné; **o. man** vieillard *m*; **o. woman** vieille femme *f*; **to get** *or* **grow old(er)** vieillir; **o. age** vieillesse *f*.

old-fashioned *adjective* démodé; (*person*) rétro *invariable*.

olive *noun* olive *f*; **o. oil** huile *f* d'olive.

Olympic *adjective* (*games etc*) olympique.

omelet(te) *noun* omelette *f*; **cheese**/*etc* **o.** omelette au fromage/*etc*.

on
1 *preposition* (*position*) sur; **to put on (to)** mettre sur.
■ (*about*) sur; **to speak on** parler de.
■ (*manner, means*) **on foot** à pied; **on the train**/*etc* dans le train/*etc*; **to be on** (*course*) suivre; (*salary*) toucher; (*team*) être membre de; **to keep** *or* **stay on** (*path etc*) suivre.
■ (*time*) **on Monday** lundi; **on Mondays** le lundi; **on May 3rd** le 3 mai.
■ (+ *present participle*) en; **on seeing this** en voyant ceci.
2 *adverb* (*ahead*) en avant; (*in progress*) en cours; (*lid, brake*) mis (*f* mise); (*light, radio*) allumé; (*gas, tap*) ouvert; **on (and on)** sans cesse; **to play**/*etc* **on** continuer à jouer/*etc*; **what's on?** (*television*) qu'y a-t-il à la télé?; (*cinema etc*) qu'est-ce qu'on joue?; **from then on** à partir de là.

once
1 *adverb* une fois; (*formerly*) autrefois; **o. a month** une fois par mois; **o. again, o. more** encore une fois; **at o.** tout de suite; **all at o.** tout à coup; (*at the same time*) à la fois.

2 *conjunction* une fois que.

one
1 *adjective* un, une; **o. man** un homme; **o. woman** une femme; **page o.** la page un; **twenty-o.** vingt-et-un.
■ (*only*) seul; **my o. (and only) aim** mon seul (et unique) but.
■ (*same*) même; **in the o. bus** dans le même bus.
2 *pronoun* un, une; **do you want o.?** en veux-tu (un)?; **o. of them** l'un d'eux, l'une d'elles; **a big**/*etc* **o.** un grand/*etc*; **that o.** celui-là, celle-là; **the o. who** *or* **which** celui *or* celle qui; **another o.** un(e) autre.
■ (*impersonal*) on; **o. knows** on sait; **it helps o.** ça nous *or* vous aide; **one's family** sa famille.

oneself *pronoun* soi-même; (*reflexive*) se, s'.

one-way *adjective* (*street*) à sens unique; (*ticket*) simple.

onion *noun* oignon *m*.

onlooker *noun* spectateur, -trice *m or f*.

only
1 *adjective* seul; **the o. one** le seul, la seule; **an o. son** un fils unique.
2 *adverb* seulement, ne … que; **I o. have ten** je n'en ai que dix, j'en ai dix seulement; **not o.** non seulement; **I have o. just seen it** je viens tout juste de le voir; **o. he knows** lui seul le sait.
3 *conjunction* (*but*) *Familiar* seulement.

onto = on to.

onward(s) *adverb* en avant; **from that time o.** à partir de là.

opaque *adjective* opaque.

open
1 *adjective* ouvert; (*ticket*) open

inv; **wide o.** grand ouvert.
2 *noun* **in the o.** en plein air.
3 *verb* (*box, door etc*) ouvrir.
4 *verb* (*of flower, door, eyes etc*)
s'ouvrir.

open-air *adjective* (*pool, market etc*) en plein air.

opening *noun* ouverture *f*;
(*career prospect*) débouché *m*.

openly *adverb* ouvertement.

openness *noun* franchise *f*.

open out *verb*
1 (*paper, map*) ouvrir.
2 (*of flower*) s'ouvrir; (*widen*)
s'élargir.

open up *verb*
1 (*shop etc*) ouvrir.
2 (*of flower*) s'ouvrir; (*open the door*) ouvrir.

opera *noun* opéra *m*.

operate *verb*
1 (*of surgeon*) opérer (**on some-body** quelqu'un, **for** de); (*of machine etc*) fonctionner; (*proceed*) opérer.
2 (*machine*) faire fonctionner;
(*business*) gérer.

operation *noun* opération *f*;
(*working*) fonctionnement *m*.

operator *noun* (*on phone*)
standardiste *m or f*.

opinion *noun* opinion *f*, avis *m*;
in my o. à mon avis.

opponent *noun* adversaire *m or f*.

opportunity *noun* occasion *f* (**to do** de faire); **opportunities**
(*prospects*) perspectives *fpl*.

oppose *verb* s'opposer à.

opposed *adjective* opposé (**to** à).

opposing *adjective* (*characters, viewpoints*) opposé; (*team*)
adverse.

opposite
1 *adjective* (*direction, opinion etc*) opposé; (*house*) d'en face.
2 *adverb* (*to sit etc*) en face.
3 *preposition* **o. (to)** en face de.
4 *noun* **the o.** le contraire.

opposition *noun* opposition *f*
(**to** à).

opt *verb* **to o. for something**
décider pour quelque chose.

optician *noun* opticien, -ienne *m or f*.

optimist *noun* **to be an o.** être
optimiste.

optimistic *adjective* optimiste.

option *noun* (*choice*) choix *m*.

optional *adjective* facultatif.

or *conjunction* ou; **he doesn't
drink or smoke** il ne boit ni ne
fume.

oral
1 *adjective* oral.
2 *noun* (*exam*) oral *m*.

orange
1 *noun* (*fruit*) orange *f*; **o. juice**
jus *m* d'orange.
2 *adjective & noun* (*colour*)
orange (*invariable m*).

orangeade *noun* orangeade *f*.

orbit *noun* orbite *f*.

orchard *noun* verger *m*.

orchestra *noun* orchestre *m*.

ordeal *noun* épreuve *f*.

order
1 *noun* (*command, arrangement*)
ordre *m*; (*purchase*) commande *f*;
in o. (*passport etc*) en règle; **in o.
to do** pour faire; **in o. that** pour
que (+ *subjunctive*); **out of o.**
(*machine*) en panne; (*telephone*)
en dérangement.
2 *verb* ordonner (**somebody to
do** à quelqu'un de faire); (*meal,
goods etc*) commander; (*taxi*)

appeler.

3 verb (in café etc) commander.

order around verb commander.

ordinary adjective (usual, commonplace) ordinaire; (average) moyen; **it's out of the o.** ça sort de l'ordinaire.

ore noun minerai m.

organ noun (in body) organe m; (instrument) orgue m.

organic adjective (vegetables etc) biologique.

organization noun organisation f.

organize verb organiser.

organizer noun organisateur, -trice m or f.

oriental adjective oriental.

origin noun origine f.

original

1 adjective original; (first) premier.

2 noun (document, painting) original m.

originality noun originalité f.

originally adverb (at first) au départ.

ornament noun (on dress etc) ornement m; (vase etc) bibelot m.

orphan noun orphelin, -ine m or f.

orphanage noun orphelinat m.

ostrich noun autruche f.

other

1 adjective autre; **o. doctors** d'autres médecins; **the o. one** l'autre m or f.

2 pronoun **the o.** l'autre m or f; (some) **others** d'autres; **some do, others don't** les uns le font, les autres ne le font pas.

3 adverb **o. than** autrement que.

otherwise adverb autrement.

ouch! interjection aïe!

ought auxiliary verb (obligation, desirability) devoir; **you o. to leave** tu devrais partir; **I o. to have done it** j'aurais dû le faire; **he said he o. to stay** il a dit qu'il devait rester.

I (probability) devoir; **it o. to be ready** ça devrait être prêt.

ounce noun once f.

our possessive adjective notre, plural nos.

ours pronoun le nôtre, la nôtre, plural les nôtres; **this book is o.** ce livre est à nous or est le nôtre.

ourselves pronoun nous-mêmes; (reflexive & after preposition) nous.

out

1 adverb (outside) dehors; (not at home etc) sorti; (light, fire) éteint; (news, secret) connu; (book) publié; (eliminated from game) éliminé; **to be** or **go o. a lot** sortir beaucoup; **to have a day o.** sortir pour la journée; **the tide's o.** la marée est basse; **o. there** là-bas.

2 preposition **o. of** en dehors de; (danger, water) hors de; (without) sans; **o. of pity**/etc par pitié/etc; **o. of the window** par la fenêtre; **to drink/take/copy o. of something** boire/prendre/copier dans quelque chose; **made o. of** (wood etc) fait en; **to make something o. of a box**/etc faire quelque chose avec une boîte/etc; **she's o. of town** elle n'est pas en ville; **four o. of five** quatre sur cinq; **to feel o. of place** ne pas se sentir intégré.

outbreak noun (of war) début m; (of violence) éruption f.

outburst noun (of anger, joy) explosion f.

outcome noun résultat m.

outdated adjective démodé.

outdo verb surpasser (**in** en).

outdoor adjective (*pool, market*) en plein air; **o. clothes** tenue f pour sortir.

outdoors adverb dehors.

outer adjective extérieur.

outer space noun l'espace m (cosmique).

outfit noun (*clothes*) costume m; (*for woman*) toilette f; (*toy*) panoplie f; **ski o.** tenue f de ski.

outing noun sortie f, excursion f.

outlet noun (*market for goods*) débouché m.

outline noun (*shape*) contour m.

outlook noun (*for future*) perspective(s) f(pl); (*point of view*) perspective f (**on** sur).

outnumber verb être plus nombreux que.

out-of-date adjective (*expired*) périmé; (*old-fashioned*) démodé.

out-of-doors adverb dehors.

output noun rendement m; (*computer data*) données fpl de sortie.

outrage
1 noun scandale m; (*anger*) indignation f.
2 verb **outraged by something** indigné de quelque chose.

outrageous adjective (*shocking*) scandaleux.

outright adverb (*to say, tell*) franchement.

outside
1 adverb (au) dehors; **to go o.** sortir.
2 preposition en dehors de.
3 noun extérieur m.
4 adjective extérieur; **the o. lane** la voie de droite.

outskirts plural noun banlieue f.

outstanding adjective remarquable; (*problem*) non réglé; (*debt*) impayé.

outward adjective (*sign, appearance*) extérieur; **o. journey** or **trip** aller m.

outward(s) adverb vers l'extérieur.

oval adjective & noun ovale (m).

oven noun four m; **o. glove** gant m isolant.

over
1 preposition (*on*) sur; (*above*) au-dessus de; (*on the other side of*) de l'autre côté de; **to jump/ look/etc o. something** sauter/ regarder/etc par-dessus quelque chose; **o. it** (*on*) dessus; (*above*) au-dessus; (*to jump etc*) par-dessus; **to criticize/etc o. something** (*about*) critiquer/etc à propos de quelque chose; **o. the phone** au téléphone; **o. the holidays** pendant les vacances; **o. ten days** (*more than*) plus de dix jours; **men o. sixty** les hommes de plus de soixante ans; **all o. Spain** dans toute l'Espagne; **all o. the carpet** partout sur le tapis.
2 adverb (*above*) (par-)dessus; **o. here** ici; **o. there** là-bas; **to come** or **go o.** (*visit*) passer; **to ask o.** inviter (à venir); **all o.** (*everywhere*) partout; **it's (all) o.** (*finished*) c'est fini; **a kilo or o.** un kilo ou plus; **I have ten o.** il m'en reste dix; **o. and o. (again)** à plusieurs reprises; **o. pleased**/etc trop content/etc.

overall adjective (*length etc*) total.

overalls plural noun bleus mpl de travail.

overboard adverb à la mer.

overcame see overcome.

overcharge verb **to o. somebody for something** faire payer

quelque chose trop cher à quelqu'un.

overcoat noun pardessus m.

overcome verb (problem)
surmonter.

overdid see overdo.

overdo verb to o. it ne pas y aller
doucement; don't o. it! vas-y
doucement!

overdone
1 past participle of overcome.
2 adjective (food) trop cuit.

overdraft noun découvert m.

overdue adjective (train etc) en
retard.

overeat verb manger trop.

overexcited adjective surexcité.

overflow verb (of river, bath etc)
déborder.

overhead adverb au-dessus.

overhear verb surprendre.

overheat verb (of engine)
chauffer.

overjoyed adjective fou (f folle)
de joie.

overlap verb se chevaucher.

overleaf adverb au verso.

overload verb surcharger.

overlook verb ne pas remarquer;
(forget) oublier; (ignore) passer
sur; (of window etc) donner sur.

overnight
1 adverb (pendant) la nuit; (suddenly) du jour au lendemain; to
stay o. passer la nuit.
2 adjective (train) de nuit; o. stay
séjour m d'une nuit.

overrated adjective surfait.

overseas
1 adverb (abroad) à l'étranger.
2 adjective (visitor etc) étranger;
(trade) extérieur.

oversight noun oubli m.

oversleep verb ne pas se réveiller
à temps.

overspend verb dépenser trop.

overtake verb dépasser.

overtime
1 noun heures fpl supplémentaires.
2 adverb to work o. faire des
heures supplémentaires.

overtook see overtake.

overturn verb (of car, boat) se
retourner.

overweight adjective to be o.
(of person) avoir des kilos en
trop.

overwhelm verb accabler; overwhelmed with (work, offers)
submergé de.

overwork
1 noun surmenage m.
2 verb se surmener.

owe verb (money etc) devoir (to
à).

owing to preposition à cause de.

owl noun hibou m (plural -oux).

own
1 adjective propre; my o. house
ma propre maison.
2 pronoun it's my (very) o. c'est
à moi; her o. money son propre
argent; a house of his o. une
maison à lui; (all) on one's o.
tout seul; to get one's o. back se
venger.
3 verb posséder; who owns this
ball/etc? à qui appartient cette
balle/etc?

owner noun propriétaire m or f.

own up verb avouer (to something quelque chose).

ox noun bœuf m.

oxygen noun oxygène m.

oyster noun huître f.

P

pa *noun Familiar* papa *m*.

pace *noun* pas *m*.

Pacific
  1 *adjective* pacifique.
  2 *noun* the P. le Pacifique.

pack
  1 *noun* paquet *m*; (*rucksack*) sac *m* (à dos); (*of wolves*) meute *f*; (*of cards*) jeu *m*; (*of lies*) tissu *m*.
  2 *verb* (*fill*) remplir (**with** de); (*suitcase*) faire; (*object into box etc*) emballer; (*object into suitcase*) mettre dans sa valise.

pack (down) *verb* (*crush*) tasser.

package *noun* paquet *m*; (*computer programs*) progiciel *m*.

package tour *noun* voyage *m* organisé.

packaging *noun* emballage *m*.

pack away *verb* (*tidy away*) ranger.

packed *adjective* (*bus etc*) bourré.

packed lunch *noun* casse-croûte invariable *m*.

packet *noun* paquet *m*.

pack in *verb Familiar* laisser tomber.

packing *noun* emballage *m*.

pack into *verb*
  1 (*cram*) entasser dans.
  2 (*crowd into*) s'entasser dans.

pack up *verb*
  1 (*put into box*) emballer; (*give up*) *Familiar* laisser tomber.
  2 *Familiar* (*stop*) s'arrêter; (*of machine*) tomber en panne.

pad *noun* (*of cloth etc*) tampon *m*; (*for writing etc*) bloc *m*.

padded *adjective* (*armchair*) capitonné; (*jacket*) matelassé.

paddle
  1 *noun* (*pole*) pagaie *f*.
  2 *verb* (*dip one's feet*) se mouiller les pieds.
  3 *verb* to p. a canoe pagayer.

paddling pool *noun* (*small, inflatable*) piscine *f* gonflable.

padlock *noun* cadenas *m*; (*on bicycle*) antivol *m*.

page *noun* (*of book etc*) page *f*; p. (**boy**) (*in hotel*) groom.

pain *noun* douleur *f*; (*grief*) peine *f*; **pains** (*efforts*) efforts *mpl*; **to be in p.** souffrir; **to take (great) pains to do** se donner du mal à faire.

painful *adjective* douloureux.

pain-killer *noun* calmant *m*; **on painkillers** sous calmants.

paint
  1 *noun* peinture *f*; **paints** (*in box, tube*) couleurs *fpl*.
  2 *verb* peindre; **to p. something blue/etc** peindre quelque chose en bleu/etc.

paintbrush *noun* pinceau *m*.

painter *noun* peintre *m*.

painting *noun* (*activity, picture*) peinture *f*.

paint stripper *noun* décapant *m*.

pair *noun* (*two*) paire *f*; (*man and woman*) couple *m*.

Pakistan *noun* le Pakistan *m*.

Pakistani *adjective & noun* pakistanais, -aise (*m or f*).

pal *noun Familiar* copain *m*, copine *f*.

palace *noun* palais *m*.

palate *noun* (*in mouth*) palais *m.*
pale *adjective* pâle.
palette *noun* (*of artist*) palette *f.*
palm *noun* (*of hand*) paume *f*; **p.** (**tree**) palmier *m*; **p.** (**leaf**) palme *f.*
pamphlet *noun* brochure *f.*
pan *noun* casserole *f*; (*for frying*) poêle *f.*
pancake *noun* crêpe *f.*
pane *noun* vitre *f.*
panel *noun* (*of door etc*) panneau *m*; (*of judges*) jury *m*; (*of experts*) groupe *m*; (**control**) **p.** console *f.*
panic
 1 *noun* panique *f.*
 2 *verb* s'affoler.
pant *verb* haleter.
panties *plural noun* (*female*) slip *m*; (*longer*) culotte *f.*
pantomime *noun* spectacle *m* de Noël.
pantry *noun* (*larder*) garde-manger *invariable m.*
pants *plural noun* (*male*) slip *m*; (*long*) caleçon *m.*
paper
 1 *noun* papier *m*; (*newspaper*) journal *m*; (*wallpaper*) papier *m* peint; (*exam*) épreuve *f* (écrite); **brown p.** papier *m* d'emballage; **to put down on p.** mettre par écrit.
 2 *adjective* (*bag, towel etc*) en papier; (*cup, plate*) en carton.
paperback *noun* livre *m* de poche.
paper clip *noun* trombone *m.*
paper knife *noun* coupe-papier *invariable m.*
parachute *noun* parachute *f.*
parade *noun* (*procession*) défilé *m*; (*street*) avenue *f.*
paradise *noun* paradis *m.*

paraffin *noun* pétrole *m* (lampant).
paragraph *noun* paragraphe *m*; '**new p.**' 'à la ligne'.
parakeet *noun* perruche *f.*
parallel *adjective* parallèle (**with**, **to** à).
paralyse *verb* paralyser.
parasite *noun* parasite *m.*
parasol *noun* (*over table, on beach*) parasol *m.*
parcel *noun* colis *m*, paquet *m.*
pardon
 1 *noun* **I beg your p.** je vous demande pardon; (*not hearing*) je vous demande pardon?; **p.?** (*not hearing*) pardon?, comment?; **p. (me)!** (*sorry*) pardon!
 2 *verb* pardonner (**somebody for something** quelque chose à quelqu'un).
parent *noun* père *m*, mère *f*; **one's parents** ses parents *mpl.*
parish *noun* paroisse *f*; (*civil*) commune *f.*
Paris *noun* Paris *m or f.*
Parisian *adjective & noun* parisien, -ienne (*m or f*).
park
 1 *noun* parc *m.*
 2 *verb* (*vehicle*) garer.
 3 *verb* (*driver*) se garer; (*remain parked*) stationner.
parking *noun* stationnement *m*; '**no p.**' 'défense de stationner'.
parking light *noun* veilleuse *f.*
parking meter *noun* parcmètre *m.*
parking place *or* **space** *noun* place *f* de parking.
parking ticket *noun* contravention *f.*
parliament *noun* parlement *m.*
parrot *noun* perroquet *m.*

parsley noun persil m.

parsnip noun panais m.

part
1 noun partie f; (of machine) pièce f; (of serial) épisode m; (role) rôle m; **to take p.** participer (in à); **in p.** en partie; **for the most p.** dans l'ensemble; **to be a p. of something** faire partie de quelque chose; **in these parts** dans ces parages.
2 adverb (partly) en partie.
3 verb (of friends etc) se quitter; (of married couple) se séparer; **to p. with something** se défaire de quelque chose.

part exchange noun reprise f; **to take something in p.** reprendre quelque chose.

partial adjective partiel; **to be p. to something** (fond of) Familiar avoir un faible pour quelque chose.

participant noun participant, -ante m or f.

participate verb participer (in à).

participation noun participation f.

participle noun Grammar participe m.

particular
1 adjective particulier; (fussy) difficile (about sur); (showing care) méticuleux; **in p.** en particulier.
2 plural noun **particulars** détails mpl; **somebody's particulars** les coordonnées fpl de quelqu'un.

particularly adverb particulièrement.

parting noun (in hair) raie f.

partition noun (in room) cloison f.

partly adverb en partie.

partner noun partenaire m or f;
(in business) associé, -ée m or f;
(dancing) **p.** cavalier, -ière m or f.

partnership noun association f.

partridge noun perdrix f.

part-time adjective & adverb à temps partiel.

party noun (formal) réception f; (with friends) soirée f; (for birthday) fête f; (group) groupe m; (political) parti m.

pass
1 noun (entry permit) laissez-passer invariable m; (over mountains) col m; Football etc passe f; **to get a p.** (in exam) être reçu (in French/etc en français/etc).
2 verb passer (to à, through par); (overtake) dépasser; (in exam) être reçu (in French/etc en français/etc).
3 verb (go past) passer devant; (vehicle) dépasser; (exam) être reçu à; **to p. somebody** (in street) croiser quelqu'un; **to p. something to somebody** passer quelque chose à quelqu'un.

passable adjective (not bad) passable; (road) praticable.

passage noun (of text etc) passage m; (corridor) couloir m.

passageway noun (corridor) couloir m.

pass away verb (die) mourir.

passbook noun livret m de caisse d'épargne.

pass by verb passer (à côté); (building etc) passer devant; **to p. by somebody** (in street) croiser quelqu'un.

passenger noun passager, -ère m or f; (on train) voyageur, -euse m or f.

passer-by noun passant, -ante m or f.

passion *noun* passion *f*.

passionate *adjective* passionné.

passive
1 *adjective* passif.
2 *noun* Grammar passif *m*.

pass mark *noun* (*in exam*) moyenne *f*.

pass off *verb*
1 (*happen*) se passer.
2 to p. oneself off as se faire passer pour.

pass on *verb* (*message etc*) transmettre (**to** à).

pass out *verb* (*faint*) s'évanouir.

pass over *verb* to p. over something passer sur quelque chose.

passport *noun* passeport *m*.

pass round *verb* (*cakes etc*) faire passer.

pass through *verb* passer.

pass up *verb* (*chance*) laisser passer.

past
1 *noun* passé *m*; in the p. (*formerly*) dans le temps.
2 *adjective* (*gone by*) passé; (*former*) ancien; these p. months ces derniers mois; in the p. tense au passé.
3 *preposition* (*in front of*) devant; (*after*) après; (*further than*) plus loin que; p. four o'clock quatre heures passées.
4 *adverb* devant; to go p. passer.

pasta *noun* pâtes *fpl*.

paste
1 *noun* (*of meat*) pâté *m*; (*of fish*) beurre *m*; (*glue*) colle *f*.
2 *verb* coller.

pasteurized *adjective* (*milk*) pasteurisé.

pastille *noun* pastille *f*.

pastime *noun* passe-temps *m invariable*.

pastry *noun* pâte *f*; (*cake*) pâtisserie *f*.

pasture *noun* pâturage *m*.

pat *verb* (*cheek etc*) tapoter; (*animal*) caresser.

patch *noun* (*for clothes*) pièce *f*; (*over eye*) bandeau *m*; (*of colour*) tache *f*; cabbage p. carré *m* de choux; bad p. mauvaise période *f*.

patch (up) *verb* (*clothing*) rapiécer.

path *noun* sentier *m*; (*in park*) allée *f*.

pathetic *adjective* (*results etc*) lamentable.

pathway *noun* sentier *m*.

patience *noun* patience *f*; to lose p. perdre patience (**with** somebody avec quelqu'un).

patient
1 *adjective* patient.
2 *noun* malade *m or f*; (*on doctor's or dentist's list*) patient, -ente *m or f*.

patiently *adverb* patiemment.

patio *noun* patio *m*.

patriotic *adjective* patriotique; (*person*) patriote.

patrol
1 *noun* patrouille *f*.
2 *verb* patrouiller dans.

pattern *noun* dessin *m*; (*paper model for garment*) patron *m*.

pause
1 *noun* pause *f*; (*in conversation*) silence *m*.
2 *verb* faire une pause; (*hesitate*) hésiter.

paved *adjective* pavé.

pavement *noun* trottoir *m*.

pavilion *noun* pavillon *m*.

paving stone *noun* pavé *m*.

paw *noun* patte *f*.

pawn *noun Chess* pion *m*.

pay
  1 *noun* salaire *m*; (*of workman, soldier*) paie *f*; **p. slip** bulletin *m* de paie.
  2 *verb* payer; (*deposit*) verser; (*compliment, visit*) faire (**to** à); (*of investment*) rapporter; **to p. somebody to do** *or* **for doing** payer quelqu'un pour faire; **to p. (somebody) for something** payer quelque chose à (quelqu'un); **to p. money into one's account** verser de l'argent sur son compte; **he paid a lot (of money) for that vase** il a payé ce vase très cher.

payable *adjective* payable; **a cheque p. to** un chèque à l'ordre de.

pay back *verb* (*person, loan*) rembourser.

pay cheque *noun* chèque *m* de règlement de salaire.

pay in *verb* (*cheque*) verser (**to one's account** sur son compte).

payment *noun* paiement *m*; (*of deposit*) versement *m*.

pay off *verb* (*debt, person*) rembourser.

pay out *verb* (*spend*) dépenser.

payphone *noun* téléphone *m* public.

pay up *verb* payer.

PE *abbreviation* (*physical education*) EPS *f*.

pea *noun* pois *m*; **peas, garden** *or* **green peas** petits pois *mpl*; **p. soup** soupe *f* aux pois.

peace *noun* paix *f*; **p. of mind** tranquillité *f* d'esprit; **in p.** en paix; **to have (some) p. and quiet** avoir la paix.

peaceful *adjective* paisible; (*demonstration*) pacifique.

peach *noun* pêche *f*.

peacock *noun* paon *m*.

peak
  1 *noun* (*mountain top*) sommet *m*; (*mountain*) pic *m*; **to be at its p.** être à son maximum.
  2 *adjective* (*hours, period*) de pointe.

peaky *adjective Familiar* (*ill*) patraque.

peanut *noun* cacah(o)uète *f*.

pear *noun* poire *f*; **p. tree** poirier *m*.

pearl *noun* perle *f*.

pebble *noun* caillou *m* (*plural* -oux); (*on beach*) galet *m*.

pecan *noun* noix *f* de pécan.

peck *verb* **to p. (at)** (*of bird*) (*bread*) picorer; (*person*) donner un coup de bec à.

peckish *adjective* **to be p.** *Familiar* avoir un petit creux.

peculiar *adjective* bizarre; (*special*) particulier (**to** à).

peculiarity *noun* (*feature*) particularité *f*.

pedal
  1 *noun* pédale *f*.
  2 *verb* pédaler.

pedal boat *noun* pédalo *m*.

pedestrian *noun* piéton *m*; **p. crossing** passage *m* pour piétons; **p. street** rue *f* piétonne.

peek *noun* **to have a p.** jeter un petit coup d'œil (**at** à).

peel
  1 *noun* épluchure(s) *f*(*pl*); **a piece of p., some p.** une épluchure.
  2 *verb* (*apple, potato etc*) éplucher.
  3 *verb* (*of sunburnt skin*) peler; (*of paint*) s'écailler.

peeler *noun* (*potato*) **p.** éplucheur *m*.

peel off *verb (label etc)* décoller.

peep
  1 *noun* coup *m* d'œil (furtif).
  2 *verb* to p. (at) regarder furtivement.

peer *verb* to p. (at) regarder attentivement.

peg *noun (for tent)* piquet *m*; *(for clothes)* pince *f* (à linge); *(for coat, hat)* patère *f*.

pen *noun (fountain, ballpoint)* stylo *m*; *(enclosure)* parc *m*.

penalty *noun (prison sentence)* peine *f*; *(fine)* amende *f*; Football penalty *m*.

pence *see* penny.

pencil *noun* crayon *m*; in p. au crayon.

pencil case *noun* trousse *f*.

pencil in *verb (note down)* noter provisoirement.

pencil sharpener *noun* taille-crayon(s) *invariable m*.

penetrate *verb (substance)* pénétrer; *(forest)* pénétrer dans.

pen friend *noun* correspondant, -ante *m or f*.

penguin *noun* manchot *m*.

penicillin *noun* pénicilline *f*.

peninsula *noun* presqu'île *f*.

penknife *noun* canif *m*.

penniless *adjective* sans le sou.

penny *noun* penny *m*; not a p.! pas un sou!

pension *noun* pension *f*; *(retirement)* p. retraite *f*.

pensioner *noun (old age)* p. retraité, -ée *m or f*.

people
  1 *plural noun* gens *mpl*; *(specific persons)* personnes *fpl*; the p. *(citizens)* le peuple; old p. les personnes *fpl* âgées; old people's home hospice *m* de vieillards; *(private)* maison *f* de retraite; English p. les Anglais *mpl*.
  2 *noun (nation)* peuple *m*.

pepper *noun* poivre *m*; *(vegetable)* poivron *m*.

peppermint *noun (flavour)* menthe *f*; *(sweet)* bonbon *m* à la menthe.

per *preposition* par; p. annum par an; p. person par personne; p. cent pour cent; 50 pence p. kilo 50 pence le kilo.

percentage *noun* pourcentage *m*.

perch
  1 *noun (for bird)* perchoir *m*.
  2 *verb (of bird, person)* se percher.

percolater *noun* cafetière *f*; *(in café etc)* percolateur *m*.

perfect
  1 *adjective* parfait.
  2 *adjective & noun* Grammar p. (tense) parfait *m*.
  3 *verb (technique)* mettre au point; *(one's French etc)* parfaire ses connaissances en.

perfection *noun* perfection *f*.

perfectly *adverb* parfaitement.

perform *verb*
  1 *(task, miracle)* accomplir; *(one's duty)* remplir; *(surgical operation)* pratiquer (on sur); *(play, piece of music)* jouer.
  2 *(act, play)* jouer; *(sing)* chanter; *(dance)* danser; *(of machine)* fonctionner.

performance *noun (in theatre)* représentation *f*; *(in cinema, concert hall)* séance *f*; *(of actor, musician)* interprétation *f*; *(of athlete, machine)* performance *f*.

performer *noun (entertainer)* artiste *m or f*.

perfume *noun* parfum *m*.

perhaps *adverb* peut-être; **p. not** peut-être que non.

peril *noun* péril *m*.

period *noun* période *f*; *(historical)* époque *f*; *(lesson)* leçon *f*; **(monthly) period(s)** *(of woman)* règles *fpl*.

periodical *noun* périodique *m*.

perk *noun* *(in job)* avantage *m* en nature.

perk up *verb* *(become livelier)* reprendre du poil de la bête.

perm
  1 *noun* permanente *f*.
  2 *verb* **to have one's hair permed** se faire faire une permanente.

permanent *adjective* permanent; *(address)* fixe.

permanently *adverb* à titre permanent.

permission *noun f* **(to do** de faire); **to ask p.** demander la permission.

permit
  1 *verb* permettre **(somebody to do** à quelqu'un de faire).
  2 *noun* permis *m*; *(entrance pass)* laissez-passer *invariable m*.

perpendicular *adjective* perpendiculaire **(to** à).

persecute *verb* persécuter.

persecution *noun* persécution *f*.

perseverance *noun* persévérance *f*.

persevere *verb* persévérer **(in** dans).

persist *verb* persister **(in doing** à faire, **in something** dans quelque chose).

persistent *adjective* *(person)* obstiné; *(noise etc)* continuel.

person *noun* personne *f*; **in p.** en personne.

personal *adjective* personnel; *(application)* en personne; *(friend)* intime; *(life)* privé; *(indiscreet)* indiscret.

personality *noun* personnalité *f*.

personally *adverb* personnellement; *(in person)* en personne.

personnel *noun* personnel *m*.

persuade *verb* persuader **(somebody to do** quelqu'un de faire).

persuasion *noun* persuasion *f*.

pessimist *noun* **to be a p.** être pessimiste.

pessimistic *adjective* pessimiste.

pest *noun* animal *m* or insecte *m* nuisible; *(person)* casse-pieds *invariable m*.

pester *verb* harceler **(with questions** de questions); **to p. somebody to do something/for something** harceler quelqu'un pour qu'il fasse quelque chose/jusqu'à ce qu'il donne quelque chose.

pet
  1 *noun* animal *m* (domestique); *(favourite person)* chouchou, -oute *m or f*.
  2 *adjective* *(dog, cat etc)* domestique; *(favourite)* favori (*f* -ite).

petal *noun* pétale *m*.

petition *noun* *(signatures)* pétition *f*.

petrol *noun* essence *f*.

petrol station *noun* station-service *f*.

petticoat *noun* jupon *m*.

petty *adjective* *(minor)* petit; *(mean)* mesquin; **p. cash** petite caisse *f*.

pharmacist *noun* pharmacien, -ienne *m or f*.

pharmacy *noun* pharmacie *f*.

phase *noun* phase *f*.

phase in *verb* to p. something in introduire quelque chose progressivement.

phase out *verb* to p. something out supprimer quelque chose progressivement.

PhD *abbreviation* (*university degree*) doctorat *m*.

pheasant *noun* faisan *m*.

phenomenal *adjective* phénoménal.

phenomenon *noun* phénomène *m*.

Philippines (the) *plural noun* les Philippines *fpl*.

philosopher *noun* philosophe *m* or *f*.

philosophical *adjective* philosophique; (*resigned*) philosophe.

philosophy *noun* philosophie *f*.

phlegm *noun* (*in throat*) glaires *fpl*.

phone *noun* téléphone *m*; on the p. au téléphone; (*at other end*) au bout du fil.

phone (up) *verb*
1 (*person*) téléphoner à.
2 (*of person*) téléphoner.

phone back *verb* rappeler.

phone book *noun* annuaire *m*.

phone booth or **box** *noun* cabine *f* téléphonique.

phone call *noun* coup *m* de fil; to make a p. call téléphoner (to à).

phonecard *noun* télécarte ® *f*.

phone number *noun* numéro *m* de téléphone.

phonetic *adjective* phonétique.

photo *noun* photo *f*; to take a p. of prendre une photo de; to have one's p. taken se faire prendre en photo.

photocopier *noun* photocopieuse *f*.

photocopy
1 *noun* photocopie *f*.
2 *verb* photocopier.

photograph *noun* photographie *f*.

photographer *noun* photographe *m* or *f*.

photographic *adjective* photographique.

photography *noun* photographie *f*.

phrase *noun* expression *f*; (*idiom*) locution *f*.

phrasebook *noun* manuel *m* de conversation.

physical *adjective* physique; p. (**examination**) visite *f* médicale; *f* physique.

physics *noun* physique *f*.

pianist *noun* pianiste *m* or *f*.

piano *noun* piano *m*.

pick
1 *noun* to take one's p. faire son choix.
2 *verb* choisir; (*flower, fruit*) cueillir; (*hole*) faire (in dans); to p. one's nose mettre les doigts dans le nez.

pick(axe) *noun* pioche *f*.

pickled *adjective* (*onion etc*) au vinaigre.

pickles *plural noun* pickles *mpl*.

pick off *verb* enlever.

pick on *verb* s'en prendre à.

pick out *verb* choisir; (*identify*) reconnaître.

pickpocket *noun* pickpocket *m*.

pick up *verb*
1 (*object*) ramasser; (*fallen person or chair*) relever; (*person into air, weight*) soulever; (*cold*) attraper; (*habit, accent, speed*) prendre; (*fetch*) (*passer*) prendre; (*find*) trouver; (*learn*) apprendre.

2 (*improve*) s'améliorer; (*of business*) reprendre; (*of patient*) aller mieux.

picnic *noun* pique-nique *m*.

picture
1 *noun* image *f*; (*painting*) tableau *m*; (*photo*) photo *f*; (*film*) film *m*; **the pictures** *Familiar* le cinéma.
2 *verb* (*imagine*) s'imaginer (**that** que).

picture frame *noun* cadre *m*.

picturesque *adjective* pittoresque.

pie *noun* (*open*) tarte *f*; (*with pastry on top*) tourte *f*; **meat p.** pâté *m* en croûte.

piece *noun* morceau *m*; (*of fabric, machine, in game*) pièce *f*; (*coin*) pièce *f*; **in pieces** en morceaux; **to take to pieces** (*machine*) démonter; **a p. of news/etc** une nouvelle/*etc*; **in one p.** intact; (*person*) indemne.

pier *noun* jetée *f*.

pierce *verb* percer.

piercing *adjective* (*cry, cold*) perçant.

pig *noun* cochon *m*.

pigeon *noun* pigeon *m*.

pigeonhole *noun* casier *m*.

piggyback *noun* **to give somebody a p.** porter quelqu'un sur son dos.

pigtail *noun* (*hair*) natte *f*.

pilchard *noun* pilchard *m*.

pile
1 *noun* tas *m*; (*neatly arranged*) pile *f*; **piles of** *Familiar* beaucoup de.
2 *verb* entasser; (*neatly*) empiler.

pile into *verb* (*crowd into*) s'entasser dans.

piles *plural noun* (*illness*) hémorroïdes *fpl*.

pile up *verb*
1 (*things*) entasser; (*neatly*) empiler.
2 (*of things, problems*) s'accumuler.

pileup *noun* (*on road*) carambolage *m*.

pill *noun* pilule *f*; **to be on the p.** prendre la pilule.

pillar *noun* pilier *m*.

pillar-box *noun* boîte *f* aux *or* à lettres.

pillow *noun* oreiller *m*.

pillowcase *noun* taie *f* d'oreiller.

pilot *noun* pilote *m*.

pimple *noun* bouton *m*.

pin *noun* épingle *f*; (*drawing pin*) punaise *f*.

pin (on) *verb* épingler (**to** sur, à); (*to wall*) punaiser (**to, on** à).

pinafore *noun* (*apron*) tablier *m*.

pinball *noun* flipper *m*; **p. machine** flipper *m*.

pincers *plural noun* (*tool*) tenailles *fpl*.

pinch
1 *noun* (*of salt*) pincée *f*; **to give somebody a p.** pincer quelqu'un.
2 *verb* pincer; (*steal*) *Familiar* piquer (**from** à).

pincushion *noun* pelote *f* (à épingles).

pine *noun* pin *m*.

pineapple *noun* ananas *m*.

pink *adjective* & *noun* (*colour*) rose (*m*).

pinkie *noun* petit doigt *m*.

pint *noun* pinte *f* (= 0,57 litre); **a p. of beer** = un demi.

pin up *verb* (*on wall*) punaiser (**on** à); (*notice*) afficher.

pip *noun* (*of fruit*) pépin *m*.

pipe noun tuyau m; (of smoker) pipe f; **to smoke a p.** fumer la pipe.

pirate noun pirate m.

pistachio noun pistache f.

pistol noun pistolet m.

pit noun (hole) trou m; (coalmine) mine f; (quarry) carrière f.

pitch
1 noun Football etc terrain m.
2 verb (tent) dresser; (ball) lancer.

pitch-black , pitch-dark adjective noir comme dans un four.

pity
1 noun pitié f; (what) a p.! (quel) dommage!; it's a p. c'est dommage (that que (+ subjunctive), to do de faire).
2 verb plaindre.

pizza noun pizza f.

placard noun (notice) affiche f.

place
1 noun endroit m, lieu m; (house) maison f; (seat, position, rank) place f; **in the first p.** en premier lieu; **to take p.** avoir lieu; **p. of work** lieu m de travail; **market p.** place f du marché; **at my p., to my p.** (house) chez moi; **all over the p.** partout; **to take the p. of** remplacer; **in p. of** à la place de.
2 verb placer; (order) passer (with somebody à quelqu'un); **to p. somebody** (identify) remettre quelqu'un.

place mat noun set m (de table).

place setting noun couvert m.

plague
1 noun peste f; (nuisance) plaie f.
2 verb harceler (with de).

plaice noun carrelet m.

plain [1] adjective (clear) clair; (simple) simple; (madness) pur; (without pattern) uni; (woman, man) sans beauté; **to make it p. to somebody that** faire comprendre à quelqu'un que.

plain [2] noun plaine f.

plainly adverb clairement; (frankly) franchement.

plait
1 noun tresse f.
2 verb tresser.

plan
1 noun projet m; (economic, of house etc) plan m; **according to p.** comme prévu.
2 verb (foresee) prévoir; (organize) organiser; (design) concevoir; **to p. to do** or **on doing** avoir l'intention de faire; **to p. for the future** faire des projets d'avenir; **as planned** comme prévu.

plane noun (aircraft) avion m; (tool) rabot m.

planet noun planète f.

plane tree noun platane m.

plank noun planche f.

plant
1 noun plante f; (factory) usine f; **house p.** plante verte.
2 verb (flower etc) planter.

plaster noun plâtre m; (sticking) p. sparadrap m; **in p.** dans le plâtre.

plaster cast noun (for broken arm etc) plâtre m.

plastic
1 adjective (object) en plastique.
2 noun plastique m.

plasticine ® noun pâte f à modeler.

plastic surgery noun chirurgie f esthétique.

plate noun (dish) assiette f; (metal sheet) plaque f.

platform noun (at train station)

quai *m*; (*on bus etc*) plate-forme *f*; (*for speaker etc*) estrade *f*.

play
1 *noun* (*in theatre*) pièce *f* (de théâtre).
2 *verb* (*part, tune etc*) jouer; (*game*) jouer à; (*instrument*) jouer de; (*team*) jouer contre; (*record, compact disc*) passer; **to p. a part in doing/in something** contribuer à faire/à quelque chose.
3 *verb* (*of child*) jouer (**at** à); (*of tape recorder etc*) marcher; **what are you playing at?** *Familiar* à quoi tu joues?

play about or **around** *verb* jouer.

play back *verb* (*tape*) réécouter.

play down *verb* minimiser.

player *noun* (*in game, of instrument*) joueur, -euse *m or f*; **cassette/CD p.** lecteur *m* de cassettes/CD.

playground *noun* (*in school*) cour *f* de récréation; (*with swings etc*) terrain *m* de jeux.

playgroup = **playschool**.

playing card *noun* carte *f* à jouer.

playing field *noun* terrain *m* de jeux.

playpen *noun* parc *m* (pour enfants).

playschool *noun* garderie *f*.

playtime *noun* récréation *f*.

pleasant *adjective* agréable.

pleasantly *adverb* agréablement.

please
1 *adverb* s'il vous plaît, s'il te plaît.
2 *verb* **to p. somebody** faire plaisir à quelqu'un; **do as you p.** fais comme tu veux; **to be eager to p.** vouloir plaire.

pleased *adjective* content (**with** de, **that** que (+ *subjunctive*), **to do** de faire); **p. to meet you!** enchanté!

pleasing *adjective* agréable.

pleasure *noun* plaisir *m*.

pleat *noun* (*in skirt*) pli *m*.

pleated *adjective* plissé.

plentiful *adjective* abondant.

plenty *pronoun* **p. of** beaucoup de; **that's p.** (*of food*) merci, j'en ai assez.

pliers *plural noun* pince(s) *f(pl)*.

plimsoll *noun* (chaussure *f* de) tennis *m*.

plot
1 *noun* complot *m* (**against** contre); **p.** (*of land*) terrain *m*.
2 *verb* comploter (**to do** de faire).

plot (out) *verb* (*route*) déterminer.

plough
1 *noun* charrue *f*.
2 *verb* (*field*) labourer.

pluck *verb* (*fowl*) plumer; (*flower*) cueillir.

plug *noun* (*of cotton wool*) tampon *m*; (*for sink, bath*) bonde *f*; (*electrical*) fiche *f*, prise *f* (mâle); (*socket*) prise *f* de courant; **(wall) p.** (*for screw*) cheville *f*.

plug (up) *verb* boucher.

plug in *verb* (*radio etc*) brancher.

plum *noun* prune *f*.

plumber *noun* plombier *m*.

plumbing *noun* plomberie *f*.

plump *adjective* potelé.

plunge *verb* plonger (**into** dans); (*fall*) tomber (**from** de).

plural
1 *adjective* (*form*) pluriel; (*noun*) au pluriel.
2 *noun* pluriel *m*; **in the p.** au

pluriel.

plus

1 *preposition* plus; two p. two deux plus deux.

2 *adjective* twenty p. vingt et quelques.

p.m. *adverb* de l'après-midi; (*evening*) du soir.

pneumatic drill *noun* marteau *m* piqueur.

poach *verb* (*egg*) pocher.

PO Box *noun* boîte *f* postale.

pocket *noun* poche *f*; p. money/ *etc* argent *m*/*etc* de poche.

pocketful *noun* a p. of une pleine poche de.

poem *noun* poème *m*.

poet *noun* poète *m*.

poetic *adjective* poétique.

poetry *noun* poésie *f*.

point

1 *noun* (*position, score etc*) point *m*; (*decimal*) virgule *f*; (*meaning*) sens *m*; (*of knife etc*) pointe *f*; (*power*) p. prise *f* (de courant); points (*for train*) aiguillage *m*; p. of view point *m* de vue; at this p. (*in time*) en ce moment; what's the p.? à quoi bon? (*of waiting*/*etc* attendre/*etc*); there's no p. (in) staying/*etc* ça ne sert à rien de rester/*etc*.

2 *verb* (*aim*) pointer (at sur); to p. one's finger (at) montrer du doigt.

point (at *or* to) *verb* (*with finger*) montrer du doigt.

pointed *adjective* pointu.

pointless *adjective* inutile.

point out *verb* (*show*) indiquer; (*mention*) signaler (that que).

point to *verb* (*indicate*) indiquer.

poison

1 *noun* poison *m*; (*of snake*) venin *m*.

2 *verb* empoisonner.

poisonous *adjective* toxique; (*snake*) venimeux; (*plant*) vénéneux.

poke *verb* pousser (*du doigt etc*); (*fire*) tisonner; to p. something into something fourrer quelque chose dans quelque chose; to p. one's head out of the window passer la tête par la fenêtre.

poke about *or* **around in** *verb* (*drawer etc*) fouiner dans.

poker *noun* (*for fire*) tisonnier *m*.

Poland *noun* la Pologne *f*.

polar bear *noun* ours *m* blanc.

Pole *noun* Polonais, -aise *m or f*.

pole *noun* (*rod*) perche *f*; (*fixed*) poteau *m*; North/South P. pôle Nord/Sud.

police *plural noun* police *f*.

police car *noun* voiture *f* de police.

police force *noun* police *f*.

policeman *noun* agent *m* de police.

policewoman *noun* femme *f* agent de police .

policy *noun* (*plan etc*) politique *f*; (*insurance*) p. police *f* (d'assurance).

polio *noun* polio *f*.

Polish

1 *adjective* polonais.

2 *noun* (*language*) polonais *m*.

polish

1 *verb* cirer; (*metal*) astiquer; (*rough surface*) polir.

2 *noun* (*for shoes*) cirage *m*; (*for floor etc*) cire *f*; (*shine*) vernis *m*; to give something a p. faire briller quelque chose.

polish off *verb* (*food etc*) *Familiar* liquider.

polish up *verb* (*one's French etc*) travailler.

polite *adjective* poli (**to, with** avec).

politely *adverb* poliment.

politeness *noun* politesse *f*.

political *adjective* politique.

politician *noun* homme *m* or femme *f* politique.

politics *noun* politique *f*.

poll *noun* (*voting*) scrutin *m*; **to go to the polls** aller aux urnes; (*opinion*) **p.** sondage *m* (d'opinion).

pollen *noun* pollen *m*.

polling station *noun* bureau *m* de vote.

pollute *verb* polluer.

pollution *noun* pollution *f*.

polo neck *noun* (*sweater*) col *m* roulé.

polyester
1 *noun* polyester *m*.
2 *adjective* (*shirt etc*) en polyester.

polytechnic *noun* établissement *m* d'enseignement supérieur.

polythene *adjective* **p. bag** sac *m* en plastique.

pomegranate *noun* (*fruit*) grenade *f*.

pond *noun* étang *m*; (*artificial*) bassin *m*.

pony *noun* poney *m*.

ponytail *noun* (*hair*) queue *f* de cheval.

poodle *noun* caniche *m*.

pool *noun* (*puddle*) flaque *f*; (*for swimming*) piscine *f*; (*billiards*) billard *m* américain.

pooped *adjective* (*tired*) *Familiar* vanné.

poor
1 *adjective* pauvre; (*bad*) mauvais; (*weak*) faible.
2 *noun* **the p.** les pauvres *mpl*.

poorly *adverb* (*badly*) mal.

pop [1] *verb*
1 (*burst*) crever.
2 (*put*) *Familiar* mettre.

pop [2]
1 *noun* (*music*) pop *m*; (*drink*) soda *m*.
2 *adjective* (*concert etc*) pop *invariable*.

popcorn *noun* pop-corn *m*.

pope *noun* pape *m*.

pop in/out *verb* entrer/sortir un instant.

pop over or **round** *verb* faire un saut (**to** chez).

poppy *noun* coquelicot *m*.

popular *adjective* populaire; (*fashionable*) à la mode; **to be p. with** plaire beaucoup à.

populated *adjective* **highly/sparsely/etc p.** très/peu/*etc* peuplé; **p. by** peuplé de.

population *noun* population *f*.

porch *noun* porche *m*; (*veranda*) véranda *f*.

pork *noun* (*meat*) porc *m*.

porridge *noun* porridge *m*.

port *noun* (*harbour*) port *m*.

portable *adjective* portable, portatif.

porter *noun* (*for luggage*) porteur *m*.

porthole *noun* hublot *m*.

portion *noun* (*share*) portion *f*; (*of train, book etc*) partie *f*.

portrait *noun* portrait *m*.

Portugal *noun* le Portugal *m*.

Portuguese
1 *adjective* & *invariable noun*

portugais, -aise (*m or f*).
2 *noun* (*language*) portugais *m*.
pose
1 *noun* (*of model*) pose *f*.
2 *verb* poser (**for** pour).
posh *adjective Familiar* (*smart*) chic *invariable*.
position *noun* position *f*; (*job, circumstances*) situation *f*; **in a p. to do** en mesure de faire.
positive *adjective* positif; (*progress, change*) réel; (*answer*) affirmatif; (*sure*) certain (**of** de, **that** que).
possess *verb* posséder.
possessions *plural noun* biens *mpl*.
possessive *adjective & noun Grammar* possessif (*m*).
possibility *noun* possibilité *f*.
possible *adjective* possible; **it is p. (for us) to do it** il (nous) est possible de le faire; **it is p. that** il est possible que (+ *subjunctive*); **as far as p.** autant que possible; **if p.** si possible; **as much or as many as p.** le plus possible.
possibly *adverb* (*perhaps*) peut-être; **if you p. can** si cela t'est possible; **to do all one p. can** faire tout son possible.
post¹
1 *noun* (*system*) poste *f*; (*letters*) courrier *m*; **by p.** par la poste; **to miss the p.** manquer la levée.
2 *verb* (*put in postbox*) poster; (*send*) envoyer.
post² *noun* (*job, place*) poste *m*.
post³ *noun* (*pole*) poteau *m*; (*of door*) montant *m*; **winning p.** poteau *m* d'arrivée.
post (up) *verb* (*notice etc*) afficher.
postage *noun* tarif *m* (postal) (**to** pour).

postage stamp *noun* timbre-poste *m*.
postal *adjective* (*services etc*) postal; **p. order** mandat *m* postal.
postbox *noun* boîte *f* aux *or* à lettres.
postcard *noun* carte *f* postale.
postcode *noun* code *m* postal.
poster *noun* affiche *f*; (*for decoration*) poster *m*.
postgraduate *noun* étudiant, -ante *m or f* de troisième cycle.
postman *noun* facteur *m*.
postmark *noun* cachet *m* de la poste.
post office *noun* (bureau *m* de) poste *f*.
postpone *verb* remettre (**for** de, **until** à).
postponement *noun* remise *f*.
pot *noun* pot *m*; (*for cooking*) marmite *f*; (*drug*) *Familiar* hasch *m*; **pots and pans** casseroles *fpl*.
potato *noun* pomme *f* de terre.
potential
1 *adjective* (*client, sales*) éventuel.
2 *noun* **to have p.** avoir de l'avenir.
potter *noun* potier *m*.
pottery *noun* (*article*) poterie *f*; (*objects*) poteries *fpl*; **a piece of p.** une poterie.
potty *noun* pot *m* (de bébé).
pouch *noun* petit sac *m*; (*of kangaroo*) poche *f*.
pouf(fe) *noun* (*seat*) pouf *m*.
poultry *noun* volaille *f*.
pounce *verb* sauter (**on** sur).
pound *noun* (*weight*) livre *f* (= 453,6 grammes); (*money*) livre *f* (sterling); (*for cars, dogs*) fourrière *f*.

pour *verb* (*liquid*) verser; **to p. money into something** investir beaucoup d'argent dans quelque chose.

pour (down) *verb* se déverser; **it's pouring (down)** il pleut à verse.

pour away or **off** *verb* (*liquid*) vider.

pour in *verb*
1 (*liquid*) verser.
2 (*of water, rain*) entrer à flots; (*of people*) affluer.

pour out *verb*
1 (*liquid*) verser; (*cup etc*) vider.
2 (*of liquid*) couler à flots; (*of people*) sortir en masse.

poverty *noun* pauvreté *f*.

powder
1 *noun* poudre *f*.
2 *verb* **to p. one's face** se poudrer.

powdered *adjective* (*milk, eggs*) en poudre.

power *noun* (*ability, authority*) pouvoir *m*; (*strength, nation*) puissance *f*; (*energy*) énergie *f*; (*current*) courant *m*; **in p.** au pouvoir; **p. cut** coupure *f* de courant.

powerful *adjective* puissant.

power station *noun* centrale *f* (électrique).

practical *adjective* pratique.

practical joke *noun* farce *f*.

practically *adverb* (*almost*) pratiquement.

practice *noun* (*exercise, way of proceeding*) pratique *f*; (*habit*) habitude *f*; (*sports training*) entraînement *m*; (*rehearsal*) répétition *f*; **to be out of p.** avoir perdu la pratique.

practise *verb*
1 (*sport, art etc*) pratiquer; (*medicine, law*) exercer; (*flute, piano*

etc) s'exercer à; (*language*) s'exercer à parler (**on** avec).
2 (*of musician*) s'exercer; (*of sportsman*) s'entraîner; (*of doctor, lawyer*) exercer.

praise
1 *verb* louer (**for something** de quelque chose); **to p. somebody for doing** louer quelqu'un d'avoir fait.
2 *noun* louange(s) *f(pl)*.

pram *noun* landau *m* (*plural* -aus).

prank *noun* (*trick*) farce *f*.

prawn *noun* crevette *f* (rose).

pray *verb*
1 prier; **to p. for good weather/ a miracle** prier pour qu'il fasse beau/pour qu'il y ait un miracle.
2 **to p. that** prier pour que (+ *subjunctive*).

prayer *noun* prière *f*.

precaution *noun* précaution *f* (**of doing** de faire); **as a p.** par précaution.

precede *verb* précéder.

preceding *adjective* précédent.

precious *adjective* précieux.

precise *adjective* précis; (*person*) minutieux.

precocious *adjective* (*child*) précoce.

predecessor *noun* prédécesseur *m*.

predicament *noun* situation *f* fâcheuse.

predict *verb* prédire.

predictable *adjective* prévisible.

prediction *noun* prédiction *f*.

preface *noun* préface *f*.

prefer *verb* préférer (**to** à); **to p. to do** préférer faire.

preferable *adjective* préférable (**to** à).

preferably *adverb* de préférence.

preference *noun* préférence *f* (for pour).

prefix *noun* préfixe *m*.

pregnancy *noun* grossesse *f*.

pregnant *adjective* (*woman*) enceinte; **five months p.** enceinte de cinq mois.

prehistoric *adjective* préhistorique.

prejudice *noun* préjugé *m*; **to be full of p.** être plein de préjugés.

preliminary *adjective* préliminaire.

premises *plural noun* locaux *mpl*; **on the p.** sur les lieux.

premium *noun* (*insurance*) **p.** prime *f* (d'assurance).

preparation *noun* préparation *f*; **preparations** préparatifs *mpl* (for de).

prepare *verb*
1 préparer (**something for** quelque chose pour, **somebody for** quelqu'un à); **to p. to do** se préparer à faire.
2 **to p. for** (*journey*, *occasion*) faire des préparatifs pour; (*exam*) préparer.

prepared *adjective* (*ready*) prêt (**to do** à faire); **to be p. for something** (*expect*) s'attendre à quelque chose.

preposition *noun* Grammar préposition *f*.

prep school *noun* école *f* primaire privée.

prescribe *verb* (*of doctor*) prescrire.

prescription *noun* (*for medicine*) ordonnance *f*.

presence *noun* présence *f*; **in the p. of** en présence de.

present [1]
1 *adjective* (*not absent*) présent (**at** à, **in** dans); (*year*, *state*, *job*, *house etc*) actuel.
2 *noun* (*gift*) cadeau *m*; **present** (**tense**) présent *m*; **at p.** à présent.

present [2] *verb* présenter (**to** à); **to p. somebody with** (*gift*) offrir à quelqu'un; (*prize*) remettre à quelqu'un.

presentation *noun* présentation *f*; (*of prize*) remise *f*.

presently *adverb* (*soon*) tout à l'heure; (*now*) à présent.

preservation *noun* conservation *f*.

preservative *noun* conservateur *m*.

preserve
1 *verb* (*keep*) conserver.
2 *noun* (*jam*) confiture *f*.

presidency *noun* présidence *f*.

president *noun* président, -ente *m or f*.

presidential *adjective* présidentiel.

press [1]
1 *noun* (*newspapers*, *machine*) presse *f*.
2 *adjective* (*conference etc*) de presse.

press [2] *verb*
1 (*button etc*) appuyer sur; (*tube*, *lemon*) presser; (*clothes*) repasser; **to p. somebody to do** (*urge*) presser quelqu'un de faire.
2 (*with finger*) appuyer (**on** sur); (*of weight*) faire pression (**on** sur).

press down *verb* (*button etc*) appuyer sur.

press on *verb* (*carry on*) continuer (**with something** quelque chose).

pressure *noun* pression *f*; **the p. of work** le surmenage; **under p.** (*worker, to work*) sous pression.

pressure cooker *noun* cocotte-minute ® *f*.

presume *verb* présumer (**that** que).

pretend *verb* (*make believe*) faire semblant (**to do** de faire, **that** que).

pretext *noun* prétexte *m*; **on the p. of/that** sous prétexte de/que.

pretty
1 *adjective* joli.
2 *adverb* (*rather, quite*) assez; **p. well, p. much** (*almost*) pratiquement.

prevent *verb* empêcher (**from doing** de faire).

prevention *noun* prévention *f*.

previous *adjective* précédent; (*experience*) préalable; **p. to** avant.

previously *adverb* avant.

prey *noun* proie *f*; **bird of p.** rapace *m*.

price *noun* prix *m*.

price list *noun* tarif *m*.

prick *verb* piquer (**with** avec); (*burst*) crever.

prickly *adjective* (*plant, beard*) piquant.

pride
1 *noun* (*satisfaction*) fierté *f*; (*exaggerated*) orgueil *m*; (*self-respect*) amour-propre *m*; **to take p. in** être fier de; (*look after*) prendre soin de.
2 *verb* **to p. oneself on something/on doing** s'enorgueillir de quelque chose/de faire.

priest *noun* prêtre *m*.

primarily *adverb* essentiellement.

primary school *noun* école *f* pri-maire.

Prime Minister *noun* Premier ministre *m*.

prime number *noun* nombre *m* premier.

primitive *adjective* primitif.

primrose *noun* primevère *f*.

prince *noun* prince *m*.

princess *noun* princesse *f*.

principal *noun* (*of school*) direc-teur, -trice *m or f*; (*of university*) président, -ente *m or f*.

print
1 *noun* (*of finger, foot etc*) em-preinte *f*; (*letters*) caractères *mpl*; (*engraving*) gravure *f*; (*photo*) épreuve *f*; **out of p.** épuisé.
2 *verb* (*book etc*) imprimer; (*photo*) tirer; (*write*) écrire en caractères d'imprimerie; **print-ing works** imprimerie *f*.

printer *noun* (*of computer*) impri-mante *f*.

print out *verb* (*of computer*) imprimer.

print-out *noun* (*of computer*) sortie *f* sur imprimante.

prior *adjective* précédent; (*experi-ence*) préalable.

priority *noun* priorité *f* (**over** sur).

prison *noun* prison *f*; **in p.** en prison.

prisoner *noun* prisonnier, -ière *m or f*; **to take somebody p.** faire quelqu'un prisonnier.

privacy *noun* intimité *f*.

private
1 *adjective* privé; (*lesson, car, secretary*) particulier; (*report*) confidentiel; (*dinner etc*) intime.
2 *noun* (*soldier*) (simple) soldat *m*; **in p.** en privé; (*to have dinner etc*) dans l'intimité.

privately *adverb* en privé; *(to have dinner etc)* dans l'intimité.

prize *noun* prix *m*; *(in lottery)* lot *m*.

prizegiving *noun* distribution *f* des prix.

prize-winner *noun* lauréat, -ate *m or f*; *(in lottery)* gagnant, -ante *m or f*.

probable *adjective* probable **(that** que); *(convincing)* vraisemblable.

probably *adverb* probablement.

problem *noun* problème *m*; **no p.!** *Familiar* pas de problème!; **to have a p. doing** avoir du mal à faire.

proceed *verb (go)* avancer; *(act)* procéder; *(continue)* continuer.

process *noun (method)* procédé *m* **(for doing** pour faire); *(chemical, economic etc)* processus *m*; **in the p. of doing** en train de faire.

processed cheese *noun* = fromage *m* fondu.

procession *noun* cortège *m*.

produce
1 *verb (manufacture, cause etc)* produire; *(bring out)* sortir; *(passport)* présenter.
2 *noun* produits *mpl*.

producer *noun (of goods, film)* producteur, -trice *m or f*.

product *noun* produit *m*.

production *noun* production *f*; *(of play)* mise *f* en scène.

profession *noun* profession *f*.

professional
1 *adjective* professionnel; *(piece of work)* de professionnel.
2 *noun* professionnel, -elle *m or f*.

professor *noun* professeur *m* (d'université).

profit
1 *noun* profit *m*, bénéfice *m*; **to sell at a p.** vendre à profit.
2 *verb* **to p. by** or **from something** tirer profit de quelque chose.

profitable *adjective* rentable.

program
1 *noun (of computer)* programme *m*.
2 *verb* programmer.

programme *noun* programme *m*; *(broadcast)* emission *f*.

progress
1 *noun* progrès *m(pl)*; **to make p.** faire des progrès; *(when driving etc)* bien avancer; **in p.** en cours.
2 *verb* progresser; *(of story, meeting)* se dérouler.

prohibit *verb* interdire **(somebody from doing** à quelqu'un de faire).

project *noun* projet *m* **(for something** pour quelque chose); *(at school)* étude *f*.

projector *noun (for films etc)* projecteur *m*.

prolong *verb* prolonger.

promenade *noun (at seaside)* promenade *f*.

prominent *adjective (person)* important.

promise
1 *noun* promesse *f*; **to show p.** être prometteur.
2 *verb* promettre **(somebody something, something to somebody** quelque chose à quelqu'un; **to do** de faire; **that** que).
3 *verb* **I p.!** je te le promets!; **p.?** promis?

promising *adjective (situation)* prometteur *(f* -euse).

promote *verb* **to p. somebody** *(in job etc)* donner de l'avancement à quelqu'un.

promotion noun (of person) avancement m.

prompt
1 adjective (speedy) rapide.
2 adverb at 8 o'clock p. à 8 heures pile.

prone adjective p. to (illnesses, accidents) prédisposé à.

pronoun noun pronom m.

pronounce verb prononcer.

pronunciation noun prononciation f.

proof noun (evidence) preuve(s) f(pl).

propeller noun hélice f.

proper adjective (suitable, respectable) convenable; (downright) véritable; (noun, meaning) propre; the p. address/method/etc (correct) la bonne adresse/méthode/etc.

properly adverb comme il faut, convenablement.

property noun (building, possessions) propriété f.

proportion noun (ratio) proportion f; (portion) partie f; proportions (size) dimensions fpl.

proposal noun proposition f; (of marriage) demande f(en mariage).

propose
1 verb (suggest) proposer (to à, that que (+ subjunctive)).
2 verb faire une demande (en mariage) (to à).

props plural noun (in theatre) accessoires mpl.

prop up verb (ladder etc) appuyer (against contre); (one's head) caler; (wall) étayer.

prose noun prose f.

prospect noun (outlook, possibility) perspective f (of de); (future) prospects perspectives fpl d'avenir.

prosperous adjective riche.

protect verb protéger (from de, against contre).

protection noun protection f.

protective adjective (clothes etc) de protection.

protest
1 noun protestation f (against contre).
2 verb protester (against contre); (of students etc) contester.

Protestant adjective & noun protestant, -ante (m or f).

protester noun (student etc) contestataire m or f.

protractor noun (for measuring) rapporteur m.

proud adjective fier (of de, to do de faire); (superior to others) orgueilleux.

proudly adverb fièrement; orgueilleusement.

prove verb
1 (demonstrate) prouver (that que).
2 to p. difficult/etc s'avérer difficile/etc.

proverb noun proverbe m.

provide verb (supply) fournir (somebody with something quelque chose à quelqu'un); to p. somebody with something (equip) pourvoir quelqu'un de quelque chose.

provided , providing conjunction p. (that) pourvu que (+ subjunctive).

provide for verb to p. for somebody pourvoir aux besoins de quelqu'un; (somebody's future) assurer l'avenir de quelqu'un.

province noun province f; the provinces la province.

provincial adjective provincial.

provoke verb (annoy) agacer.

prowl (around) verb rôder.

prowler noun rôdeur, -euse m or f.

prune
1 noun pruneau m.
2 verb (tree, bush) tailler.

pruning shears noun sécateur m.

psychiatrist noun psychiatre m or f.

psychological adjective psychologique.

psychologist noun psychologue m or f.

pub noun pub m.

public
1 adjective public (f -ique); (library, swimming pool) municipal.
2 noun public m; in p. en public.

publication noun publication f.

publicity noun publicité f.

publish verb publier; (book, author) éditer.

publisher noun éditeur, -trice m or f.

publishing noun (profession) édition f.

pudding noun pudding m; Christmas p. pudding m; rice p. riz m au lait.

puddle noun flaque f (d'eau).

puff
1 noun (of smoke, wind) bouffée f.
2 verb (of person) souffler.

puff at verb (cigar etc) tirer sur.

pull
1 noun to give something a p. tirer quelque chose.
2 verb tirer (at, on sur); (trigger) appuyer sur; (muscle) se claquer;

to p. apart or to bits mettre en pièces; to p. a face faire la moue.

pull along verb traîner (to jusqu'à).

pull away verb
1 (move) éloigner; (snatch) arracher (from à).
2 (in vehicle) démarrer; to p. away from s'éloigner de.

pull back verb
1 (of person) se retirer.
2 tirer; (curtains) ouvrir.

pull down verb baisser; (knock down) faire tomber; (demolish) démolir.

pull in verb
1 (into room etc) faire entrer (de force); (crowd) attirer.
2 (of train, bus) arriver; (of vehicle, driver) se ranger (sur le côté).

pull off verb (remove) enlever.

pull on verb (boots etc) mettre.

pull out verb
1 (tooth, hair) arracher; (cork, pin) enlever; (from pocket etc) tirer, sortir (from de).
2 (move out in vehicle) déboîter; (withdraw) se retirer (from, of de).

pull over verb
1 traîner (to jusqu'à); (knock down) faire tomber.
2 (in vehicle) se ranger (sur le côté).

pullover noun pull(-over) m.

pull through verb s'en tirer.

pull up verb
1 (socks, sleeve, collar, blind) remonter, relever; (plant, tree) arracher.
2 (in vehicle) s'arrêter.

pulse noun pouls m.

pump
1 noun pompe f; (air) p. (in service station) gonfleur m.

2 *verb* pomper.

pumpkin *noun* potiron *m*.

pump up *verb* (*mattress etc*) gonfler.

punch[1]
1 *noun* (*blow*) coup *m* de poing.
2 *verb* donner un coup de poing à.

punch[2]
1 *noun* (*for paper*) perforeuse *f*.
2 *verb* (*ticket*) poinçonner; (*with date*) composter; **to p. a hole in something** faire un trou dans quelque chose.

punctual *adjective* (*on time*) à l'heure; (*regularly*) ponctuel.

punctuation *noun* ponctuation *f*.

puncture
1 *noun* (*in tyre*) crevaison *f*; **to have a p.** crever.
2 *verb* (*burst*) crever.

punish *verb* punir (**for something** de quelque chose, **for doing** pour avoir fait).

punishment *noun* punition *f*.

pupil *noun* élève *m* or *f*; (*of eye*) pupille *f*.

puppet *noun* marionnette *f*.

pup(py) *noun* (*dog*) chiot *m*.

purchase
1 *noun* achat *m*.
2 *verb* acheter (**from somebody** à quelqu'un, **for somebody** à *or* pour quelqu'un).

pure *adjective* pur.

purely *adverb* (*only*) strictement.

purple
1 *adjective* violet (*f* -ette).
2 *noun* violet *m*.

purpose *noun* (*aim*) but *m*; **for this p.** dans ce but; **on p.** exprès.

purposely *adverb* exprès.

purse *noun* (*for coins*) porte-monnaie *invariable m*.

pursue *verb* (*inquiry*, *aim etc*) poursuivre.

push
1 *noun* **to give somebody/something a p.** pousser quelqu'un/quelque chose.
2 *verb* pousser (**to, as far as** jusqu'à); **to p. something into/between** enfoncer quelque chose dans/entre; **to p. somebody into doing** pousser quelqu'un à faire.

push (down) *verb* (*button*) appuyer sur; (*lever*) abaisser.

push about *or* **around** *verb* (*bully*) marcher sur les pieds à.

push aside *verb* écarter.

push away *or* **back** *verb* repousser.

push-button *noun* bouton *m*; (*of phone*) touche *f*; **p. phone** téléphone *m* à touches.

pushchair *noun* poussette *f*.

pushed *adjective* **to be p.** (*for time*) être très bousculé.

push in *verb* (*in queue*) resquiller.

push on *verb* continuer (**with something** quelque chose).

push over *verb* renverser.

push through *verb* **to p. one's way through** (*a crowd*) se frayer un chemin (à travers une foule).

push up *verb* (*lever*, *sleeve*, *collar*) relever; (*increase*) augmenter.

puss *noun* (*cat*) minou *m*.

put *verb* mettre; (*money*) placer (**into** dans); (*question*) poser (**to** à); (*say*) dire.

put across *verb* (*message etc*) communiquer (**to** à).

put aside *verb* (*money*, *object*) mettre de côté.

put away verb (*book, car etc*) ranger; (*criminal*) mettre en prison.

put back verb (*replace, postpone*) remettre; (*telephone receiver*) raccrocher; (*clock, date*) retarder.

put by verb (*money*) mettre de côté.

put down verb (*on floor etc*) poser; (*passenger*) déposer; (*deposit*) verser; (*write down*) inscrire.

put forward verb (*clock, meeting*) avancer; (*candidate*) proposer (*for* à).

put in verb (*something into box etc*) mettre dedans; (*insert*) introduire; (*add*) ajouter; (*install*) installer; (*application*) faire.

put off verb renvoyer (à plus tard); (*gas, radio*) fermer; **to p. somebody off** dissuader quelqu'un (**doing** de faire); (*disgust*) dégoûter quelqu'un (**something** de quelque chose); **to p. somebody off doing** (*disgust*) ôter à quelqu'un l'envie de faire.

put on verb (*clothes etc*) mettre; (*weight*) prendre; (*gas, radio*) mettre; (*record, cassette*) passer; (*clock*) avancer.

put out verb (*take outside*) sortir; (*arm, leg*) étendre; (*hand*) tendre; (*tongue*) tirer; (*gas, light*) éteindre; (*bother*) déranger.

put through verb **to p. somebody through** (*on phone*) passer quelqu'un (**to** à).

put together verb mettre ensemble; (*assemble*) assembler; (*compose*) composer.

putty noun mastic m (*pour vitres*).

put up verb
1 (*stay*) descendre (**at a hotel** à un hôtel).
2 (*lift*) lever; (*window*) remonter; (*tent, statue, ladder*) dresser; (*building*) construire; (*umbrella*) ouvrir; (*picture*) mettre; (*price*) augmenter; (*candidate*) proposer (**for** à); (*guest*) loger.

put up with verb **to p. up with something/somebody** supporter quelque chose/quelqu'un.

puzzle
1 noun mystère m; (*jigsaw*) puzzle m.
2 verb laisser perplexe.

puzzled adjective perplexe.

puzzling adjective curieux.

pyjamas plural noun pyjama m; **a pair of p.** un pyjama.

pylon noun pylône m.

pyramid noun pyramide f.

Q

qualification *noun* diplôme *m*; qualifications (*skills*) qualités *fpl* nécessaires (**for** pour, **to do** pour faire).

qualified *adjective* (*able*) qualifié (**to do** pour faire); (*teacher etc*) diplômé.

qualify *verb* obtenir son diplôme (**as a doctor**/*etc* de médecin/*etc*); (*in sport*) se qualifier (**for** pour).

quality *noun* qualité *f*.

quantity *noun* quantité *f*.

quarrel
  1 *noun* dispute *f*; **to pick a q.** chercher des histoires (**with somebody** à quelqu'un).
  2 *verb* se disputer (**with somebody** avec quelqu'un).

quarrelling *noun* disputes *fpl*.

quarry *noun* (*to extract stone etc*) carrière *f*.

quart *noun* litre *m* (= 1,14 litres).

quarter [1] *noun* quart *m*; (*of fruit*) quartier *m*; **to divide something into quarters** diviser quelque chose en quatre; **q. (of a) pound** quart *m* de livre; **a q. past nine** neuf heures et quart *or* un quart; **a q. to nine** neuf heures moins le quart.

quarter [2] *noun* (*district*) quartier *m*.

quartz *adjective* (*watch etc*) à quartz.

quay *noun* quai *m*, débarcadère *m*.

Quebec *noun* le Québec *m*.

queen *noun* reine *f*; *Chess Cards* dame *f*.

queer *adjective* (*odd*) bizarre; (*ill*)

Familiar patraque.

quench *verb* **to q. one's thirst** se désaltérer.

query *noun* (*question*) question *f*.

question
  1 *noun* question *f*; **it's out of the q.** il n'en est pas question.
  2 *verb* interroger (**about** sur); (*doubt*) mettre en question.

question mark *noun* point *m* d'interrogation.

questionnaire *noun* questionnaire *m*.

queue *noun* queue *f*; (*of cars*) file *f*; **to form a q.** faire la queue.

queue (up) *verb* faire la queue.

quibble *verb* ergoter (**over** sur).

quiche *noun* quiche *f*.

quick
  1 *adjective* rapide; **be q.!** fais vite!; **to have a q. meal**/*etc* manger/*etc* en vitesse.
  2 *adverb* vite.

quickly *adverb* vite.

quiet *adjective* (*silent, peaceful*) tranquille; (*machine, vehicle*) silencieux; (*voice, sound*) doux (*f* douce); **to be** *or* **keep q.** (*shut up*) se taire; (*make no noise*) ne pas faire de bruit; **q.!** silence!; **to keep q. about something** ne pas parler de quelque chose.

quietly *adverb* tranquillement; (*not loudly*) doucement; (*silently*) silencieusement.

quilt *noun* édredon *m*; (**continental**) **q.** (*duvet*) couette *f*.

quit *verb*
  1 (*person, place*) quitter; **to q. doing** arrêter de faire.
  2 (*give up*) abandonner; (*resign*)

démissionner.

quite *adverb* (*entirely*) tout à fait; (*really*) vraiment; (*rather*) assez; q. a lot pas mal (of de).

quiz *noun* q. (programme) jeu (-concours) *m*.

quotation *noun* citation *f*; (*estimate*) devis *m*.

quotation marks *plural noun*

guillemets *mpl*; in q. marks entre guillemets.

quote
1 *verb* (*author, passage*) citer; (*reference*) rappeler; (*price*) indiquer.
2 *verb* to q. from citer.
3 *noun* citation *f*; (*estimate*) devis *m*.

R

rabbi *noun* rabbin *m*.

rabbit *noun* lapin *m*.

rabies *noun* rage *f*.

race [1]
  1 *noun* (*contest*) course *f*.
  2 *verb* (*horse*) faire courir; **to r. (against** *or* **with) somebody** faire une course avec quelqu'un.
  3 *verb* (*run*) courir.

race [2] *noun* (*group*) race *f*.

racecourse *noun* champ *m* de courses.

racehorse *noun* cheval *m* de course.

racial *adjective* racial.

racialism , racism *noun* racisme *m*.

racing *noun* courses *fpl*.

racing car *noun* voiture *f* de course.

racing driver *noun* coureur *m* automobile.

racist *adjective* & *noun* raciste (*m or f*).

rack *noun* (*for bottles, letters etc*) casier *m*; (*for drying dishes*) égouttoir *m*; **(luggage) r.** (*on bus, train*) filet *m* à bagages.

racket *noun* (*for tennis*) raquette *f*; (*din*) vacarme *m*.

radar *noun* radar *m*.

radiator *noun* radiateur *m*.

radio *noun* radio *f*; **on** *or* **over the r.** à la radio; **r. set** poste *m* de radio.

radioactive *adjective* radioactif.

radish *noun* radis *m*.

radius *noun* (*of circle*) rayon *m*.

raffle *noun* tombola *f*.

raft *noun* (*boat*) radeau *m*.

rag *noun* (*old clothing*) haillon *m*; (*for dusting etc*) chiffon *m*; **in rags** (*clothes*) en loques; (*person*) en haillons.

rage *noun* rage *f*; **to fly into a r.** se mettre en rage.

ragged *adjective* (*clothes*) en loques; (*person*) en haillons.

raid
  1 *noun* (*military*) raid *m*; (*by police*) descente *f*; (*by thieves*) hold-up *invariable m*; **air r.** raid *m* aérien.
  2 *verb* faire un raid *or* une descente *or* un hold-up dans.

rail *noun* (*for train*) rail *m*; (*rod on balcony*) balustrade *f*; (*on stairs*) rampe *f*; (*curtain rod*) tringle *f*; **(towel) r.** porte-serviettes *invariable m*; **by r.** (*to travel*) par le train; (*to send*) par chemin de fer.

railing *noun* (*of balcony*) balustrade *f*; **railings** (*fence*) grille *f*.

railway
  1 *noun* chemin *m* de fer; (*track*) voie *f* ferrée.
  2 *adjective* (*ticket*) de chemin de fer; **r. line** ligne *f* de chemin de fer; (*track*) voie *f* ferrée.

railway station *noun* gare *f*.

rain
  1 *noun* pluie *f*; **in the r.** sous la pluie.
  2 *verb* pleuvoir; **it's raining** il pleut.

rainbow *noun* arc-en-ciel *m*.

raincoat *noun* imperméable *m*.

rainy *adjective* pluvieux.

raise *verb* (*lift*) lever; (*child, family, voice*) élever; (*salary, price*) augmenter; (*question*) soulever;

to r. **money** réunir des fonds.

raisin noun raisin m sec.

rake
1 noun râteau m.
2 verb (garden) ratisser.

rake (up) verb (leaves) ratisser.

rally noun (political) rassemblement m.

rally round verb to r. around somebody venir en aide (à quelqu'un).

ram
1 noun (animal) bélier m.
2 verb (vehicle) emboutir; to r. something into something enfoncer quelque chose dans quelque chose.

ramble noun randonnée f.

ramp noun (slope for wheelchair etc) rampe f (d'accès).

ran see run.

ranch noun ranch m.

random
1 noun at r. au hasard.
2 adjective (choice) (fait) au hasard; (sample) prélevé au hasard; r. **check** (by police) contrôle-surprise m.

rang see ring ².

range
1 noun (of gun, voice etc) portée f; (of singer's voice) étendue f; (of colours, prices, products) gamme f; (of sizes) choix m; (of mountains) chaîne f.
2 verb (vary) varier (from de, to à).

rank noun rang m.

ransom noun (money) rançon f.

rape
1 verb violer.
2 noun viol m.

rapid adjective rapide.

rapidly adverb rapidement.

rapist noun violeur m.

rare adjective rare; (meat) saignant.

rarely adverb rarement.

rascal noun coquin, -ine m or f.

rash
1 noun éruption f.
2 adjective irréfléchi.

rashly adverb sans réfléchir.

raspberry noun framboise f; r. **jam** confiture f de framboise.

rat noun rat m.

rate
1 noun (level) taux m; (speed) vitesse f; (price) tarif m; at the r. of à une vitesse de; (amount) à raison de; at this r. (slow speed) à ce train-là; at any r. en tout cas.
2 verb évaluer (at à); (regard) considérer (as comme); (deserve) mériter.

rather adverb (preferably, quite) plutôt; I'd r. stay j'aimerais mieux rester (than que); r. than leave/etc plutôt que de partir/etc.

ratio noun proportion f.

ration
1 noun ration f; rations (food) vivres mpl.
2 verb rationner.

rational adjective (person) raisonnable.

rationing noun rationnement m.

rattle
1 noun (baby's toy) hochet m; (of sports fan) crécelle f.
2 verb (of chains, keys) cliqueter; (of window) trembler.
3 verb (shake) secouer.

ravenous adjective I'm r. j'ai une faim de loup.

raw adjective (vegetable etc) cru;

(*skin*) écorché; r. **material**
matière *f* première.

ray *noun* (*of light, sun*) rayon *m*.

razor *noun* rasoir *m*.

re - *prefix* ré-, re-, r-.

re *preposition* concernant; re your
letter suite à votre lettre.

reach
  1 *verb* (*place, distant object, aim*)
atteindre; (*gain access to*) accéder
à; (*of letter*) parvenir à; (*contact*)
joindre; (*conclusion*) arriver à; **to
r. something for somebody, to
r. somebody something** attraper quelque chose à quelqu'un.
  2 *verb* (*of forest, property*)
s'étendre (**to** jusqu'à); (*with arm*)
(é)tendre le bras (**for** pour prendre).
  3 *noun* portée *f*; **within r. of** à
portée de; (*near*) à proximité de;
within (easy) r. (*object*) à portée
de main.

reach out *verb* (é)tendre le bras
(**for** pour prendre).

react *verb* réagir (**against** contre,
to à).

reaction *noun* réaction *f*.

reactor *noun* réacteur *m* (*nucléaire*).

read *verb* lire; (*meter*) relever; (*of
instrument*) indiquer; **to r. to
somebody** faire la lecture à quelqu'un; **to r. about somebody/
something** lire quelque chose
sur quelqu'un / quelque chose.

read back *verb* **to r. something
back** relire quelque chose.

reader *noun* lecteur, -trice *m or f*;
(*book*) livre *m* de lecture.

readily *adverb* (*willingly*) volontiers; (*easily*) facilement.

reading *noun* lecture *f*; (*of meter*)
relevé *m*; (*by instrument*) indication *f*.

read out *verb* **to r. something
out** lire quelque chose (à haute
voix).

read over *verb* **to r. something
over** relire quelque chose.

read through *verb* **to r. something through** lire rapidement
quelque chose.

read up on *verb* **to r. up on
something** étudier quelque
chose.

ready *adjective* prêt (**to do** à
faire, **for something** à *or* pour
quelque chose); **to get some-
thing/somebody r.** préparer
quelque chose / quelqu'un; **to get
r.** se préparer (**for something** à
or pour quelque chose, **to do** à
faire); **r. cash** argent *m* liquide.

ready-cooked *adjective* tout
cuit.

ready-made *adjective* tout fait;
r. clothes prêt-à-porter *invariable m*.

real *adjective* vrai (*f* vraie); (*life,
world*) réel.

realistic *adjective* réaliste.

reality *noun* réalité *f*.

realize *verb* (*know*) se rendre
compte de; (*understand*) comprendre (**that** que).

really *adverb* vraiment.

rear
  1 *noun* (*back part*) arrière *m*; **in**
or **at the r.** à l'arrière.
  2 *adjective* arrière *invariable*, de
derrière.
  3 *verb* (*family, animals*) élever.

rear (up) *verb* (*of horse*) se
cabrer.

rearrange *verb* (*hair, room*) réar-
ranger; (*plans*) changer.

reason
  1 *noun* raison *f*; **the r. for/
why ...** la raison de / pour la-

quelle … ; for no r. sans raison.
2 *verb* raisonner; **to r. with somebody** raisonner quelqu'un.

reasonable *adjective* raisonnable.

reasonably *adverb* (*fairly, rather*) assez.

reasoning *noun* raisonnement *m*.

reassure *verb* rassurer.

reassuring *adjective* rassurant.

rebel
1 *noun* rebelle *m or f*; (*against parents etc*) révolté, -ée *m or f*.
2 *verb* se revolter (**against** contre).

rebellion *noun* révolte *f*.

rebound
1 *verb* (*of ball*) rebondir; (*of stone*) ricocher.
2 *noun* rebond *m*; ricochet *m*.

rebuild *verb* reconstruire.

recall *verb* (*remember*) se rappeler (**that** que, **doing** avoir fait); **to r. something to somebody** rappeler quelque chose à quelqu'un.

receipt *noun* (*for payment, object left etc*) reçu *m* (**for** de); **on r. of** dès réception de.

receive *verb* recevoir.

receiver *noun* (*of phone*) combiné *m*; **to pick up the r.** (*of phone*) décrocher.

recent *adjective* récent; **in r. months** ces mois-ci.

recently *adverb* récemment.

reception *noun* (*party, of radio etc*) réception *f*; **r. (desk)** réception *f*, accueil *m*.

receptionist *noun* secrétaire *m or f*, réceptionniste *m or f*.

recharge *verb* (*battery*) recharger.

recipe *noun* recette *f* (**for** de).

recite *verb* (*poem*) réciter; (*list*) énumérer.

reckless *adjective* (*rash*) imprudent.

reckon *verb* (*calculate*) calculer; (*think*) *Familiar* penser (**that** que).

reckon on *verb* **to r. on something/somebody** (*rely on*) compter sur quelque chose/quelqu'un; **to r. on doing** compter faire.

reckon with *verb* **to r. with something/somebody** (*take into account*) compter avec quelque chose/quelqu'un.

reclaim *verb* (*luggage at airport*) récupérer.

recognize *verb* reconnaître (**by** à).

recollect *verb* se souvenir de; **to r. that** se souvenir que.

recollection *noun* souvenir *m*.

recommend *verb* recommander (**to** à, **for** pour); **to r. somebody to do** recommander à quelqu'un de faire.

recommendation *noun* recommandation *f*.

record
1 *noun* (*disc*) disque *m*; (*best performance*) record *m*; (*register*) registre *m*; (*mention*) mention *f*; (*background*) antécédents *mpl*; (**public**) **records** archives *fpl*; **to keep a r. of** noter.
2 *adjective* (*time, number etc*) record *invariable*.
3 *verb* (*on tape, in register*) enregistrer; (*in diary*) noter.

recorder *noun* flûte *f* à bec; (**tape**) **r.** magnétophone *m*; (**video**) **r.** magnétoscope *m*.

recording *noun* enregistrement *m*.

record player *noun* électrophone m.

recover verb
1 (get back) retrouver.
2 (from illness etc) se remettre (from de); (of economy) se redresser.

recruit noun recrue f.

rectangle noun rectangle m.

rectangular adjective rectangulaire.

recycle verb recycler.

red
1 adjective rouge; (hair) roux (f rousse); to turn or go r. rougir; r. light (traffic light) feu m rouge.
2 noun (colour) rouge m; in the r. (firm, account) dans le rouge, en déficit.

red-handed adjective caught r. pris en flagrant délit.

redhead noun roux m, rousse f.

red-hot adjective brûlant.

redirect verb (mail) faire suivre.

redo verb (exercise, house etc) refaire.

reduce verb réduire (to à, by de); at a reduced price (ticket, goods) à prix réduit.

reduction noun réduction f (in de).

redundancy noun licenciement m.

redundant adjective to make somebody r. licencier quelqu'un.

reed noun (plant) roseau m.

reef noun récif m.

reel noun (of thread, film) bobine f; (film itself) bande f.

refectory noun réfectoire m.

refer verb
1 to r. to (mention) faire allusion à; (speak of) parler de; (apply to) s'appliquer à.
2 to r. something to somebody soumettre quelque chose à quelqu'un.

referee
1 noun Football Boxing arbitre m.
2 verb arbitrer.

reference noun (in book, for job) référence f; (mention) mention f (to de); with r. to concernant; r. book ouvrage m de référence.

refill
1 verb remplir (à nouveau); (lighter, pen) recharger.
2 noun recharge f; a r. (drink) un autre verre.

reflect verb (light etc) refléter; to be reflected se refléter.

reflection noun (image) reflet m.

reflex noun réflexe m.

reform noun réforme f.

refrain verb s'abstenir (from doing de faire).

refresh verb (of bath, drink) rafraîchir; (of sleep, rest) délasser.

refresher course noun cours m de recyclage.

refreshing adjective (drink) rafraîchissant.

refreshments plural noun (drinks) rafraîchissements mpl; (snacks) petites choses fpl à grignoter.

refrigerate verb (food) conserver au frais.

refrigerator noun réfrigérateur m.

refuge noun refuge m; to take r. se réfugier.

refugee noun réfugié, -ée m or f.

refund
1 verb rembourser.
2 noun remboursement m.

refusal noun refus m.

refuse *verb* refuser (**somebody something** quelque chose à quelqu'un, **to do** de faire).

regain *verb* (*lost ground*) regagner; (*health, strength*) retrouver.

regard
1 *verb* considérer; **as regards** en ce qui concerne.
2 *noun* considération *f* (**for** pour); **to have (a) high r. for somebody** estimer quelqu'un; **to give one's regards to somebody** transmettre son meilleur souvenir à quelqu'un.

regarding *preposition* en ce qui concerne.

regardless
1 *adjective* **r. of** sans tenir compte de.
2 *adverb* (*all the same*) quand même.

regiment *noun* régiment *m*.

region *noun* région *f*; **in the r. of £50/etc** (*about*) dans les 50 livres/*etc*.

regional *adjective* régional.

register
1 *noun* registre *m*; (*in school*) cahier *m* d'appel; **to take the r.** faire l'appel.
2 *verb* (*birth etc*) déclarer; **registered letter** lettre recommandée; **to send by registered post** envoyer en recommandé.
3 *verb* (*enrol*) s'inscrire (**for a course** à un cours); (*in hotel*) signer le registre.

registration *noun* (*enrolment*) inscription *f*; **r. (number)** (*of vehicle*) numéro *m* d'immatriculation.

regret
1 *verb* regretter (**doing, to do** de faire; **that** que (+ *subjunctive*)).

2 *noun* regret *m*.

regular *adjective* (*steady*) régulier; (*surface*) uni; (*usual*) habituel; (*price, size*) normal; (*listener*) fidèle.

regularly *adverb* régulièrement.

regulations *plural noun* (*rules*) règlement *m*.

rehearsal *noun* répétition *f*.

rehearse *verb* répéter.

reign
1 *noun* règne *m*; **in the r. of** sous le règne de.
2 *verb* régner (**over** sur).

reindeer *invariable noun* renne *m*.

reinforce *verb* renforcer (**with** de).

reinforcements *plural noun* (*troops*) renforts *mpl*.

reins *plural noun* (*for horse*) rênes *fpl*; (*for baby*) bretelles *fpl* de sécurité (avec laisse).

reject *verb* rejeter.

rejection *noun* rejet *m*; (*of candidate*) refus *m*.

rejoice *verb* (*celebrate*) faire la fête; (*be delighted*) se réjouir (**over** *or* **at something** de quelque chose).

related *adjective* (*linked*) lié (**to** à); **to be r. to somebody** (*by family*) être parent de quelqu'un.

relate to *verb* (*apply to*) se rapporter à.

relation *noun* (*relative*) parent, -ente *m or f*; (*relationship*) rapport *m*; **international relations** relations *fpl* internationales.

relationship *noun* (*in family*) lien(s) *m(pl)* de parenté; (*relations*) relations *fpl*; (*connection*) rapport *m*.

relative
1 *noun* (*person*) parent, -ente *m* or *f*.
2 *adjective* relatif; (*qualities etc of two or more people*) respectif.

relatively *adverb* relativement.

relax *verb*
1 (*person*) détendre; (*grip, pressure*) relâcher.
2 (*become calmer*) se détendre; r.! (*calm down*) du calme!

relaxation *noun* (*rest*) détente *f*.

relaxed *adjective* décontracté.

release
1 *verb* (*free*) libérer (**from** de); (*bomb*) lâcher; (*brake*) desserrer; (*film, record*) sortir; (*trapped person*) dégager.
2 *noun* (*of prisoner*) libération *f*; (*of film etc*) sortie *f*; **press r.** communiqué *m* de presse.

relevant *adjective* pertinent (**to** à); (*useful*) utile; **that's not r.** ça n'a rien à voir.

reliability *noun* fiabilité *f*; (*of person*) sérieux *m*.

reliable *adjective* fiable; (*person*) sérieux.

relief *noun* (*from pain etc*) soulagement *m* (**from** à); (*help*) secours *m*; (*in geography etc*) relief *m*.

relieve *verb* (*pain, person etc*) soulager; (*take over from*) relayer.

religion *noun* religion *f*.

religious *adjective* religieux.

relish *noun* (*seasoning*) assaisonnement *m*.

reload *verb* (*gun, camera*) recharger.

reluctance *noun* manque *m* d'enthousiasme (**to do** à faire).

reluctant *adjective* peu enthousiaste (**to do** pour faire).

reluctantly *adverb* sans enthousiasme.

rely (up)on *verb* (*count on*) compter sur; (*be dependent on*) dépendre de.

remain *verb* rester.

remaining *adjective* qui reste(nt).

remark
1 *noun* remarque *f*.
2 *verb* (faire) remarquer (**that** que).
3 *verb* **to r. on something** faire des remarques sur quelque chose.

remarkable *adjective* remarquable (**for** par).

remarkably *adverb* remarquablement.

remedial *adjective* **r. class** cours *m* de rattrapage.

remember *verb*
1 (*event, date etc*) se souvenir de, se rappeler; **to r. that/doing** se rappeler que/d'avoir fait; **to r. to do** penser à faire.
2 se souvenir, se rappeler.

remind *verb* rappeler (**somebody of something** quelque chose à quelqu'un, **somebody that** à quelqu'un que); **to r. somebody to do** faire penser à quelqu'un à faire.

reminder *noun* (*of event & letter*) rappel *m*; **to give somebody a r. to do** faire penser à quelqu'un à faire.

remorse *noun* remords *m(pl)*.

remote *adjective* (*far-off*) lointain; (*isolated*) isolé; (*slight*) petit.

remote control *noun* télécommande *f*.

removal *noun* enlèvement *m*; suppression *f*.

removal man *noun* déménageur

m.

removal van *noun* camion *m* de déménagement.

remove *verb* (*clothes, stain etc*) enlever (**from somebody** à quelqu'un, **from something** de quelque chose); (*obstacle, word*) supprimer.

renew *verb* renouveler; (*resume*) reprendre; (*library book*) renouveler le prêt de.

rent
1 *noun* (*for house etc*) loyer *m*.
2 *verb* louer.

rental *noun* (*of television*) (prix *m* de) location *f*; (*of telephone*) abonnement *m*.

rent out *verb* louer.

reorganize *verb* (*firm etc*) réorganiser.

repair
1 *verb* réparer.
2 *noun* réparation *f*; **in bad r.** en mauvais état.

repairman *noun* réparateur *m*, dépanneur *m*.

repay *verb* (*pay back*) rembourser; (*reward*) récompenser (**for** de).

repayment *noun* remboursement *m*; récompense *f*.

repeat
1 *verb* répéter (**that** que); (*promise, threat*) réitérer; (*class*) redoubler; **to r. oneself** se répéter.
2 *noun* (*on TV, radio*) rediffusion *f*.

repeated *adjective* (*attempts etc*) répétés.

repeatedly *adverb* à maintes reprises, de nombreuses fois.

repel *verb* repousser.

repetition *noun* répétition *f*.

repetitive *adjective* répétitif.

replace *verb* (*take the place of*) remplacer (**by, with** par); (*put back*) remettre; (*telephone receiver*) raccrocher.

replacement *noun* (*person*) remplaçant, -ante *m or f*; (*machine part*) pièce *f* de rechange.

replica *noun* copie *f* exacte.

reply
1 *verb* répondre (**to** à, **that** que).
2 *noun* réponse *f*.

report
1 *noun* (*account*) rapport *m*; (*of meeting*) compte rendu *m*; (*in media*) reportage *m*; (*of pupil*) bulletin *m*; (*rumour*) rumeur *f*.
2 *verb* rapporter; (*announce*) annoncer (**that** que); (*notify*) signaler (**to** à); (*inform on*) dénoncer (**to** à).
3 *verb* faire un rapport; (*of journalist*) faire un reportage (**on** sur); (*go*) se présenter (**to** à, **to somebody** chez quelqu'un).

report card *noun* bulletin *m* (scolaire).

reported *adjective* (*speech*) indirect.

reporter *noun* reporter *m*.

represent *verb* représenter.

representative *noun* représentant, -ante *m or f*.

reptile *noun* reptile *m*.

republic *noun* république *f*.

reputable *adjective* de bonne réputation.

reputation *noun* réputation *f*; **to have a r. for being** avoir la réputation d'être.

request
1 *noun* demande *f* (**for** de).
2 *verb* demander (**something from somebody** quelque chose à quelqu'un, **somebody to do** à quelqu'un de faire).

require verb (of thing) demander; (of person) avoir besoin de; **if required** s'il le faut.

required adjective **the r. qualities/etc** les qualités/etc qu'il faut.

rescue
1 verb (save) sauver; (set free) délivrer (from de).
2 noun sauvetage m (of de); (help) secours mpl; **to go to somebody's r.** aller au secours de quelqu'un.

research
1 noun recherches fpl (on, into sur).
2 verb faire des recherches.

researcher noun chercheur, -euse m or f.

resemblance noun ressemblance f (to avec).

resemble verb ressembler à.

reservation noun (booking) réservation f; (doubt) réserve f.

reserve
1 verb réserver; (right) se réserver.
2 noun **r. (player)** remplaçant, -ante m or f; **nature r.** réserve f naturelle; **in r.** en réserve.

reserved adjective (person, place) réservé.

reserve tank noun réservoir m de secours.

residence noun (home) résidence f; (of students) foyer m.

resident
1 noun habitant, -ante m or f; (of hotel) pensionnaire m or f.
2 adjective **to be r. in London** résider à Londres.

residential adjective (district) résidentiel.

resign verb
1 **to r. oneself to sth/to doing** se résigner à qch/à faire.
2 démissionner; **to r. from one's job** démissionner.

resignation noun (from job) démission f.

resist verb
1 (attack etc) résister à; **to r. doing something** se retenir de faire quelque chose; **she can't r. cakes** elle ne peut pas résister devant des gâteaux.
2 résister.

resistance noun résistance f (to à).

resit verb (exam) repasser.

resort[1]
1 verb **to r. to doing** en venir à faire; **to r. to something** avoir recours à quelque chose.
2 noun **as a last r.** en dernier ressort.

resort[2] noun (holiday) **r. station** f de vacances; **seaside r.** station f balnéaire; **ski r.** station de ski.

resources plural noun (wealth, means) ressources fpl.

respect
1 noun respect m (for pour, de); **with r. to** en ce qui concerne.
2 verb respecter.

respectable adjective (honourable, quite good) respectable; (clothes, behaviour) convenable.

respond verb répondre (to à); **to r. to treatment** bien réagir au traitement.

response noun réponse f.

responsibility noun responsabilité f.

responsible adjective responsable (for de, to somebody devant quelqu'un); (job) à responsabilités.

rest[1]
1 noun repos m; (support) support

m; **to have** *or* **take a r.** se reposer. **2** *verb* (*relax*) se reposer; **to be resting on something** (*of hand etc*) être posé sur quelque chose. **3** *verb* (*lean*) appuyer (**on** sur, **against** contre).

rest [2] *noun* (*remaining part*) reste *m* (**of** de); **the r.** (*others*) les autres *mpl or fpl*; **the r. of the men**/*etc* les autres hommes/*etc*.

restaurant *noun* restaurant *m*.

restful *adjective* reposant.

restless *adjective* agité.

restore *verb* (*give back*) rendre (**to** à); (*building etc*) restaurer.

restrict *verb* restreindre (**to** à).

restricted *adjective* restreint.

restriction *noun* restriction *f*.

result *noun* résultat *m*; **as a r. of** par suite de.

resume *verb* reprendre.

retail
1 *adjective* (*price, shop*) de détail. **2** *adverb* (*to sell*) au détail.

retailer *noun* détaillant, -ante *m or f*.

retain *verb* (*freshness etc*) conserver.

retire *verb* (*from work*) prendre sa retraite; (*withdraw*) se retirer (**from** de, **to** à); (*go to bed*) aller se coucher.

retired *adjective* (*no longer working*) retraité.

retirement *noun* retraite *f*.

return
1 *verb* (*come back*) revenir; (*go back*) retourner; (*go back home*) rentrer.
2 *verb* (*give back*) rendre; (*put back*) remettre; (*send back*) renvoyer.
3 *noun* retour *m*; (*on investment*) rendement *m*; **r. (ticket)** (billet

m) aller et retour *m*; **tax r.** déclaration *f* de revenus; **in r.** en échange (**for** de).
4 *adjective* (*flight etc*) (de) retour; **r. game** revanche *f*.

returnable *adjective* (*bottle*) consigné.

reveal *verb* (*make known*) révéler (**that** que).

revenge *noun* vengeance *f*; **to get one's r.** se venger (**on somebody** de quelqu'un, **for something** de quelque chose); **in r.** pour se venger.

reverse
1 *adjective* (*order*) inverse.
2 *noun* contraire *m*; **in r. (gear)** en marche arrière.
3 *verb* **to r. the charges** (*when telephoning*) téléphoner en PCV.
4 *verb* **to r. (the car)** faire marche arrière; **to r. in/out** rentrer/sortir en marche arrière.

review
1 *verb* (*book*) faire la critique de.
2 *noun* critique *f*.

revise *verb* réviser (**for** pour).

revision *noun* révision *f*.

revive *verb* (*unconscious person*) ranimer.

revolt *noun* révolte *f*.

revolting *adjective* dégoûtant.

revolution *noun* révolution *f*.

revolutionary *adjective & noun* révolutionnaire (*m or f*).

revolve *verb* tourner (**around** autour de).

revolver *noun* revolver *m*.

revolving door(s) *noun* (*porte f* à) tambour *m*.

reward
1 *noun* récompense *f* (**for** de, pour).
2 *verb* récompenser (**somebody**

for something quelqu'un de *or* pour quelque chose).

rewind *verb*
1 (*tape*) rembobiner.
2 (*of tape*) se rembobiner.

rheumatism *noun* rhumatisme *m*; **to have r.** avoir des rhumatismes.

rhinoceros *noun* rhinocéros *m*.

rhubarb *noun* rhubarbe *f*.

rhyme
1 *noun* rime *f*; (*poem*) vers *mpl*.
2 *verb* rimer (**with** avec).

rhythm *noun* rythme *m*.

rhythmical *adjective* rythmé.

rib *noun* (*in body*) côte *f*.

ribbon *noun* ruban *m*.

rice *noun* riz *m*.

rich
1 *adjective* riche.
2 *noun* **the r.** les riches *mpl*.

riches *plural noun* richesses *fpl*.

rid *adjective* **to get r. of** se débarrasser de.

riddle *noun* (*puzzle*) énigme *f*.

ride
1 *noun* (*on bicycle, by car, on horse etc*) promenade *f*; (*distance*) trajet *m*; **to go for a (car) r.** faire une promenade (en voiture); **to give somebody a r.** (*in car*) emmener quelqu'un en voiture.
2 *verb* aller (à bicyclette, à moto, à cheval *etc*) (**to** à); **to r., go riding** (*on horse*) monter (à cheval).
3 *verb* (*horse*) monter; (*distance*) faire (à cheval *etc*); **to r. a horse** *or* **horses** monter à cheval; **I was riding (on) a bicycle** j'étais à bicyclette; **to r. a bicycle to** aller à bicyclette à.

rider *noun* (*on horse*) cavalier, -ière *m or f*.

ridiculous *adjective* ridicule.

riding *noun* (*horse*) **r.** équitation *f*.

rifle *noun* fusil *m*.

rig *noun* (*oil*) **r.** derrick *m*; (*at sea*) plate-forme *f* pétrolière.

right [1]
1 *adjective* (*correct*) bon (*f* bonne); (*fair*) juste; (*angle*) droit; **to be r.** (*of person*) avoir raison (**to do** de faire); **the r. choice/ time** le bon choix/moment; **it's the r. time** (*accurate*) c'est l'heure exacte; **the clock's r.** la pendule est à l'heure; **it's not r. to steal** ce n'est pas bien de voler; **to put r.** (*error*) corriger; **r.!** bien!; **that's r.** c'est ça.
2 *adverb* (*straight*) (tout) droit; (*completely*) tout à fait; (*correctly*) juste; (*well*) bien; **she did r.** elle a bien fait; **r. round** tout autour (**something** de quelque chose); **r. here** ici même; **r. away, r. now** tout de suite.
3 *noun* **r. and wrong** le bien et le mal.

right [2]
1 *adjective* (*hand, side etc*) droit.
2 *adverb* à droite.
3 *noun* droite *f*; **on** *or* **to the r.** à droite (**of** de).

right [3] *noun* (*claim*) droit *m* (**to do** de faire); **to have a r. to something** avoir droit à quelque chose.

right-hand *adjective* à *or* de droite; **on the r. side** à droite (**of** de).

right-handed *adjective* (*person*) droitier.

rightly *adverb* à juste titre.

rigid *adjective* rigide.

rim *noun* (*of cup etc*) bord *m*.

rind *noun* (*of cheese*) croûte *f*.

ring [1] *noun* (*on finger, curtain etc*) anneau *m*; (*with jewel*) bague *f*; (*of people, chairs*) cercle *m*; *Boxing* ring *m*; (*burner on stove*) brûleur *m*; **diamond r.** bague *f* de diamants.

ring [2]
1 *noun* (*sound*) sonnerie *f*; **there's a r.** on sonne; **to give somebody a r.** (*phone call*) passer un coup de fil à quelqu'un.
2 *verb* sonner; **to r. the (door) bell** sonner (à la porte).

ring (round) *verb* entourer (**with** de); (*item on list etc*) encadrer.

ring (up) *verb*
1 (*person*) téléphoner à.
2 (*of person*) téléphoner.

ring back *verb* (*phone*) rappeler.

ringing tone *noun* (*on phone*) sonnerie *f*.

ring off *verb* (*after phoning*) raccrocher.

ring out *verb* (*of bell*) sonner; (*of sound*) retentir.

ring road *noun* route *f* de ceinture; (*motorway*) périphérique *m*.

rinse
1 *verb* rincer; **to r. one's hands** se rincer les mains.
2 *noun* **to give something a r.** rincer quelque chose.

rinse out *verb* rincer.

riot
1 *noun* (*uprising*) émeute *f*; (*fight*) bagarre *f*.
2 *verb* faire une émeute; (*fight*) se bagarrer.

rip
1 *verb* déchirer.
2 *verb* (*of fabric*) se déchirer.
3 *noun* déchirure *f*.

ripe *adjective* mûr; (*cheese*) fait.

ripen *verb* mûrir.

rip off *verb* (*button etc*) arracher (**from** de); **to r. somebody off** *Familiar* rouler quelqu'un.

rip-off *noun Familiar* **it's a r.** c'est du vol.

rip out *verb* **to r. something out** arracher quelque chose (**from** de).

rip up *verb* **to r. something up** déchirer quelque chose.

rise
1 *verb* (*of temperature, balloon, price*) monter; (*of sun, curtain, person*) se lever; **to r. in price** augmenter de prix.
2 *noun* (*in price etc*) hausse *f* (**in** de); (*slope in ground*) montée *f*; (**pay**) **r.** augmentation *f* (**de** salaire); **to give r. to something** donner lieu à quelque chose.

risk
1 *noun* risque *m* (**of doing** de faire, **in doing** à faire); **at r.** (*person*) en danger; (*job*) menacé.
2 *verb* risquer; **she won't r. leaving** elle ne se risquera pas à partir.

risky *adjective* risqué.

rival
1 *adjective* (*firm etc*) rival.
2 *noun* rival, -ale *m or f*.
3 *verb* (*compete with*) rivaliser avec (**in** de); (*equal*) égaler (**in** en).

river *noun* rivière *f*; (*flowing into sea*) fleuve *m*.

Riviera *noun* **the (French) R.** la Côte d'Azur.

road
1 *noun* route *f* (**to** qui va à); (*small*) chemin *m*; (*in town*) rue *f*; (*roadway*) chaussée *f*; **across** or **over the r.** (*building etc*) en face; **by r.** par la route.
2 *adjective* (*map, safety*) routier;

(*accident*) de la route; **r. sign** panneau *m* (routier).

roadside *adjective & noun* **(by the) r.** au bord de la route.

roadway *noun* chaussée *f*.

roadworks *noun* travaux *mpl*.

roam *verb* parcourir; **to r. the streets** (*of child, dog etc*) traîner dans les rues.

roar
  1 *verb* (*of lion*) rugir; (*of person*) hurler.
  2 *noun* (*of lion*) rugissement *m*.

roast
  1 *verb* (*meat*) rôtir; (*coffee*) griller.
  2 *verb* (*of meat*) rôtir.
  3 *noun* (*meat*) rôti *m*.
  4 *adjective* (*chicken etc*) rôti; **r. beef** rosbif *m*.

rob *verb* (*person*) voler; (*bank*) attaquer; (*by breaking in*) cambrioler; **to r. somebody of something** voler quelque chose à quelqu'un.

robber *noun* voleur, -euse *m or f*.

robbery *noun* vol *m*.

robe *noun* (*dressing gown*) robe *f* de chambre.

robin *noun* rouge-gorge *m*.

robot *noun* robot *m*.

rock [1]
  1 *verb* (*baby, boat*) bercer.
  2 *verb* (*sway*) se balancer; (*of building*) trembler.
  3 *noun* (*music*) rock *m*.

rock [2] *noun* (*substance*) roche *f*; (*boulder, rock face*) rocher *m*; (*stone*) pierre *f*; **r. face** paroi *f* rocheuse.

rocket *noun* fusée *f*.

rocking chair *noun* fauteuil *m* à bascule.

rod *noun* (*wooden*) baguette *f*;

(*metal*) tige *f*; (*of curtain*) tringle *f*; (*for fishing*) canne *f* (à pêche).

rode *see* ride.

rogue *noun* (*dishonest*) crapule *f*; (*mischievous*) coquin, -ine *m or f*.

role *noun* rôle *m*.

roll
  1 *noun* (*of paper etc*) rouleau *m*; (*small bread loaf*) petit pain *m*; (*of drum*) roulement *m*.
  2 *verb* (*of ball etc*) rouler; (*of thunder*) gronder.
  3 *verb* (*ball*) faire rouler.

roll down *verb* (*car window etc*) baisser; (*slope*) descendre (en roulant).

roller *noun* (*for hair, painting etc*) rouleau *m*.

roller-skate
  1 *noun* patin *m* à roulettes.
  2 *verb* faire du patin à roulettes.

rolling pin *noun* rouleau *m* à pâtisserie.

roll over *verb* (*many times*) se rouler; (*once*) se retourner.

roll up *verb* (*map, cloth*) rouler; (*sleeve, trousers*) retrousser.

Roman *adjective & noun* romain, -aine (*m or f*).

Roman Catholic *adjective & noun* catholique (*m or f*).

romance *noun* (*love*) amour *m*; (*affair*) aventure *f* amoureuse.

Romania *noun* la Roumanie *f*.

Romanian *adjective & noun* roumain, -aine (*m or f*).

romantic *adjective* romantique.

roof *noun* toit *m*; (*of tunnel, cave*) plafond *m*.

roof rack *noun* (*of car*) galerie *f*.

room *noun* (*in house etc*) pièce *f*; (*bedroom*) chambre *f*; (*large, public*) salle *f*; (*space*) place *f* (**for** pour); **men's r., ladies' r.**

toilettes *fpl.*

roommate *noun* camarade *m* or *f* de chambre.

roomy *adjective* spacieux; (*clothes*) ample.

root *noun* racine *f*; (*origin*) origine *f*; **to take r.** (*of plant*) prendre racine.

root for *verb Familiar* encourager.

rope *noun* corde *f*.

rope off *verb* (*of police etc*) interdire l'accès de.

rose[1] *see* rise.

rose[2] *noun* (*flower*) rose *f*; **r. bush** rosier *m*.

rot (away) *verb* pourrir.

rota *noun* liste *f* (de service).

rotten *adjective* (*fruit, weather etc*) pourri; (*bad*) *Familiar* moche; **to feel r.** (*ill*) être mal fichu.

rough[1] *adjective* (*surface, plank*) rugueux; (*ground*) inégal; (*brutal*) brutal; (*sea*) agité.

rough[2] *adjective* (*calculation etc*) approximatif; **r. guess** approximation *f*; **r. copy, r. draft** brouillon *m*; **(some) r. paper** du (papier) brouillon; **r. book** cahier *m* de brouillon.

roughly[1] *adverb* (*not gently*) rudement; (*brutally*) brutalement.

roughly[2] *adverb* (*more or less*) à peu (de choses) près.

round[1]
1 *adverb* autour; **all r., right r.** tout autour; **to go r. to somebody('s)** passer chez quelqu'un; **to ask r.** inviter chez soi; **r. here** par ici.
2 *preposition* autour de; **r. about** (*approximately*) environ.

round[2]
1 *adjective* rond.
2 *noun* (*slice*) tranche *f*; *Boxing* round *m*; (*of drinks, visits*) tournée *f*; (*of policeman*) ronde *f*.

roundabout
1 *adjective* indirect.
2 *noun* (*at funfair*) manège *m*; (*junction*) rond-point *m* (à sens giratoire).

round off *verb* (*meal etc*) terminer (**with** par); (*figure*) arrondir.

round up *verb* (*people, animals*) rassembler.

route *noun* itinéraire *m*; (*of ship, aircraft*) route *f*; **bus r.** ligne *f* d'autobus.

routine *noun* train-train *m*.

row[1]
1 *noun* (*line*) rang *m*, rangée *f*; (*one behind another*) file *f*; **two days in a r.** deux jours de suite.
2 *verb* (*in boat*) ramer.
3 *verb* (*boat*) faire aller à la rame.

row[2]
1 *noun* (*noise*) vacarme *m*; (*quarrel*) dispute *f*.
2 *verb* se disputer (**with** avec).

rowing boat *noun* bateau *m* à rames.

royal *adjective* royal.

royalty *noun* personnages *mpl* royaux.

rub *verb* frotter; (*person*) frictionner.

rubber *noun* caoutchouc *m*; (*eraser*) gomme *f*.

rubber stamp *noun* tampon *m*.

rubbish *noun* (*waste*) ordures *fpl*; (*junk*) saletés *f*; (*nonsense*) idioties *fpl*.

rubbish bin *noun* poubelle *f*.

rubbish dump *noun* décharge *f* (publique); (*untidy place*) dépotoir *m*.

rubbishy *adjective* (*book, film*) nul; (*goods*) de mauvaise qualité.

rubble *noun* décombres *mpl*.

rub down *verb* (*person*) frictionner; (*with sandpaper*) poncer.

rub in *verb* (*cream*) faire pénétrer (en massant).

rub off *or* **out** *verb* (*mark*) effacer.

ruby *noun* rubis *m*.

rucksack *noun* sac *m* à dos.

rudder *noun* gouvernail *m*.

rude *adjective* impoli (**to** envers); (*coarse, insolent*) grossier (**to** envers); (*indecent*) obscène.

rudeness *noun* impolitesse *f*; grossièreté *f*.

rug *noun* carpette *f*.

rugby *noun* rugby *m*.

ruin
  1 *noun* ruine *f*; **in ruins** (*building*) en ruine.
  2 *verb* (*health, person etc*) ruiner; (*clothes*) abîmer.

rule
  1 *noun* règle *f*; **against the rules** contraire au règlement; **as a r.** en règle générale.
  2 *verb* (*country*) gouverner.
  3 *verb* (*of king etc*) régner (**over** sur).

rule out *verb* **to r. something out** exclure quelque chose.

ruler *noun* (*for measuring*) règle *f*; (*king, queen etc*) souverain, -aine *m* or *f*.

rum *noun* rhum *m*.

Rumania = Romania.

Rumanian = Romanian.

rumour *noun* bruit *m*, rumeur *f*.

run
  1 *noun* (*period*) période *f*; (*for skiing*) piste *f*; **to go for a r.** aller courir; (*in car*) (aller) faire un tour; **on the r.** (*prisoner*) en fuite; **in the long r.** à la longue.
  2 *verb* (*of river, nose, tap*) couler; (*of colour in washing*) déteindre; (*of play, film*) se jouer; (*function*) marcher; (*of car engine*) tourner; **to r. down/in**/*etc* descendre / entrer / *etc* en courant; **to go running** faire du jogging.
  3 *verb* (*race, risk*) courir; (*temperature, errand*) faire; (*business, country etc*) diriger; (*bath*) faire couler; **to r. a car** avoir une voiture.

run across *verb* **to r. across somebody** tomber sur quelqu'un.

run along *verb* filer.

run away *verb* s'enfuir (**from** de).

run down *verb* (*pedestrian*) renverser.

rung [1] *see* **ring** [2].

rung [2] *noun* (*of ladder*) barreau *m*.

run into *verb* (*meet*) tomber sur; (*crash into*) percuter.

runner *noun* (*athlete*) coureur *m*.

runner-up *noun* second, -onde *m* or *f*.

running
  1 *noun* (*on foot*) course *f*; (*of firm, country*) direction *f*.
  2 *adjective* **r. water** eau *f* courante; **six days**/*etc* **r.** six jours/ *etc* de suite.

runny *adjective* (*nose*) qui coule.

run off *verb* (*flee*) s'enfuir.

run out *verb* (*of stocks*) s'épuiser; (*of lease*) expirer; **to r. out of** (*time, money*) manquer de; **we've**

r. out of coffee on n'a plus de café.

run over *verb* (*kill pedestrian*) écraser; (*knock down pedestrian*) renverser.

runway *noun* piste *f* (d'envol).

rush
  1 *verb* se précipiter (**at** sur, **towards** vers); (*hurry*) se dépêcher (**to do** de faire).
  2 *verb* (*hurry*) bousculer; **to r. somebody to hospital** transporter quelqu'un d'urgence à l'hôpital; **to r. (through) something** (*job, meal etc*) faire, manger *etc* quelque chose en vitesse.
  3 *noun* ruée *f* (**for** vers); (*confu-*sion) bousculade *f*; (*hurry*) hâte *f*; **in a r.** pressé (**to do** de faire).

rush hour *noun* heure *f* d'affluence.

rush out *verb* partir en vitesse.

Russia *noun* la Russie *f*.

Russian
  1 *adjective & noun* russe (*m or f*).
  2 *noun* (*language*) russe *m*.

rust
  1 *noun* rouille *f*.
  2 *verb* rouiller.

rusty *adjective* (*metal, memory etc*) rouillé.

rye bread *noun* pain *m* de seigle.

S

sack
  1 *noun* (*bag*) sac *m*; **to get the s.** (*from one's job*) se faire virer; **to give somebody the s.** virer quelqu'un.
  2 *verb* (*dismiss*) virer.

sacrifice
  1 *noun* sacrifice *m*.
  2 *verb* sacrifier (**to** à, **for** pour).

sad *adjective* triste.

sadden *verb* attrister.

saddle *noun* selle *f*.

sadly *adverb* tristement; (*unfortunately*) malheureusement.

sadness tristesse *f*.

safe ¹ *adjective* (*person*) en sécurité; (*equipment*, *toy*, *animal*) sans danger; (*place*, *investment*, *method*) sûr; (*bridge*, *ladder*) solide; **s. (and sound)** sain et sauf (*f* saine et sauve); **it's s. to go out** on peut sortir sans danger; **s. from** à l'abri de.

safe ² *noun* (*for money etc*) coffre-fort *m*.

safely *adverb* (*without accident*) sans accident; (*without risk*) sans risque; (*in a safe place*) en lieu sûr.

safety *noun* sécurité *f*.

safety belt *noun* ceinture *f* de sécurité.

safety pin *noun* épingle *f* de sûreté.

sag *verb* (*of roof*, *ground*) s'affaisser.

said *see* **say**.

sail
  1 *verb* naviguer; (*leave*) partir; (*as sport*) faire de la voile; **to s. round the world/an island** faire le tour du monde/d'une île en bateau.
  2 *verb* (*boat*) piloter.
  3 *noun* voile *f*.

sailboard *noun* planche *f* (à voile).

sailing *noun* navigation *f*; (*sport*) voile *f*; (*departure*) départ *m*.

sailing boat *noun* voilier *m*.

sailor *noun* marin *m*.

saint *noun* saint *m*, sainte *f*.

sake *noun* **for my/your/his/*etc* s.** pour moi/toi/lui/*etc*; **(just) for the s. of eating/*etc*** simplement pour manger/*etc*.

salad *noun* salade *f*.

salad bowl *noun* saladier *m*.

salad dressing *noun* sauce *f* de salade.

salary *noun* (*professional*) traitement *m*; (*wage*) salaire *m*.

sale *noun* vente *f*; **sale(s)** (*at reduced prices*) soldes *mpl*; **to be on s.** (*cheap*) soldé; **on s.** (*available*) en vente; **I bought it in the s.** je l'ai acheté en solde; **(up) for s.** à vendre.

salesman *noun* (*in shop*) vendeur *m*; **(travelling) s.** représentant *m* (de commerce).

saleswoman *noun* vendeuse *f*; (*who travels*) représentante *f* (de commerce).

saliva *noun* salive *f*.

salmon *noun* saumon *m*.

salt
  1 *noun* sel *m*; **bath salts** sels *mpl* de bain.
  2 *verb* saler.

saltcellar *noun* salière *f*.

salty *adjective* salé.

same
1 *adjective* même; **the (very) s. house as** (exactement) la même maison que.
2 *pronoun* **the s.** le *or* la même, *plural* **les mêmes; it's all the s. to me** ça m'est égal; **all** *or* **just the s.** tout de même; **to do the s.** en faire autant.

sample
1 *noun* échantillon *m*; (*of blood*) prélèvement *m*.
2 *verb* (*wine etc*) goûter.

sand
1 *noun* sable *m*.
2 *verb* (*road*) sabler.

sandal *noun* sandale *f*.

sandcastle *noun* château *m* de sable.

sandpaper *noun* papier *m* de verre.

sandwich *noun* sandwich *m*; **cheese/etc s.** sandwich au fromage/*etc*; **s. bar** sandwicherie *f*.

sandy *adjective* (*beach*) de sable; (*road*) sablonneux.

sanitary towel *noun* serviette *f* hygiénique.

sank *see* **sink**.

Santa Claus *noun* le père Noël.

sardine *noun* sardine *f*.

sat *see* **sit**.

satchel *noun* cartable *m*.

satellite *noun* satellite *m*.

satin *noun* satin *m*.

satisfaction *noun* satisfaction *f*.

satisfactory *adjective* satisfaisant.

satisfy *verb* satisfaire; **to s. one-self that** s'assurer que; **satisfied (with)** satisfait (de).

satisfying *adjective* satisfaisant.

satsuma *noun* (*fruit*) mandarine *f*, satsuma *f*.

saturate *verb* (*soak*) tremper.

Saturday *noun* samedi *m*.

sauce *noun* sauce *f*; **tomato s.** sauce *f* tomate.

saucepan *noun* casserole *f*.

saucer *noun* soucoupe *f*.

Saudi *adjective & noun* saudien, -ienne (*m or f*).

Saudi Arabia *noun* l'Arabie Saoudite *f*.

sauna *noun* sauna *m*.

sausage *noun* saucisse *f*; (*dried, for slicing*) saucisson *m*.

save
1 *verb* (*rescue*) sauver (**from** de); (*keep*) garder; (*money, time*) économiser; (*stamps*) collection-ner; **to s. somebody from doing** empêcher quelqu'un de faire; **that will s. him** *or* **her (the bother of) going** ça lui évitera d'y aller.
2 *noun Football* arrêt *m*.

save up *verb*
1 (*money*) économiser.
2 faire des économies (**for something, to buy something** pour acheter quelque chose).

savings *plural noun* (*money*) économies *fpl*.

savings bank *noun* caisse *f* d'épargne.

saw [1]
1 *noun* scie *f*.
2 *verb* scier.

saw [2] *see* **see**.

sawdust *noun* sciure *f*.

sawn *see* **saw**.

saw off *verb* **to s. something off** scier quelque chose.

saxophone *noun* saxophone *m*.

say *verb* dire (**to** à, **that** que); (*of dial*) marquer; **to s. again** répéter; **(let's)** s. tomorrow disons demain; **that is to** s. c'est-à-dire.

saying *noun* proverbe *m*.

scab *noun* (*of wound*) croûte *f*.

scaffolding *noun* échafaudage *m*.

scald *verb* ébouillanter.

scale *noun* (*of map, wages etc*) échelle *f*; (*on fish*) écaille *f*; (*in music*) gamme *f*.

scales *plural noun* (*for weighing*) balance *f*; **(bathroom)** s. pèse-personne *m*.

scandal *noun* scandale *m*; (*gossip*) médisances *fpl*.

Scandinavian *adjective & noun* scandinave (*m or f*).

scanner *noun* scanner *m*.

scar *noun* cicatrice *f*.

scarce *adjective* rare.

scarcely *adverb* à peine.

scare *verb* faire peur à.

scarecrow *noun* épouvantail *m*.

scared *adjective* effrayé; **to be s. (stiff)** avoir (très) peur.

scarf *noun* (*long*) écharpe *f*; (*square, for women*) foulard *m*.

scarlet fever *noun* scarlatine *f*.

scary *adjective* **it's s.** ça fait peur.

scatter *verb*
1 (*crowd, clouds etc*) disperser; (*throw or dot about*) éparpiller (*papiers etc*).
2 (*of crowd*) se disperser.

scene *noun* (*setting, fuss, part of play or film*) scène *f*; (*of crime, accident*) lieu *m*; (*view*) vue *f*.

scenery *noun* paysage *m*; (*for play or film*) décor(s) *m(pl)*.

scent *noun* (*fragrance, perfume*) parfum *m*.

schedule
1 *noun* (*of work etc*) programme *m*; (*timetable*) horaire *m*; **on** s. (*on time*) à l'heure; **according to** s. comme prévu.
2 *verb* (*to plan*) prévoir; (*event*) fixer le programme de.

scheduled *adjective* (*planned*) prévu; (*service, flight*) régulier.

scheme *noun* plan *m* (**to do** pour faire); (*dishonest trick*) combine *f*.

scholarship *noun* (*grant*) bourse *f* (d'études).

school
1 *noun* école *f*; (*teaching, lessons*) classe *f*; **in** *or* **at** s. à l'école; **secondary** s. collège *m*; **public** s. école *f* privée; **summer** s. cours *mpl* d'été.
2 *adjective* (*year etc*) scolaire.

schoolboy *noun* écolier *m*.

schoolgirl *noun* écolière *f*.

schoolmate *noun* camarade *m or f* de classe.

schoolteacher *noun* (*primary*) instituteur, -trice *m or f*; (*secondary*) professeur *m*.

science *noun* science *f*; **to study** s. étudier les sciences.

science fiction *noun* science-fiction *f*.

scientific *adjective* scientifique.

scientist *noun* scientifique *m or f*.

scissors *plural noun* ciseaux *mpl*.

scold *verb* gronder (**for doing** pour avoir fait).

scone *noun* scone *m*.

scooter *noun* (*child's*) trottinette *f*; (*motorcycle*) scooter *m*.

scope *noun* (*range*) étendue *f*; (*limits*) limites *fpl*; **s. for some-thing/for doing** (*opportunity*) des possibilités *fpl* de quelque chose / de faire.

scorch *verb* roussir.

score[1]

  1 *noun* (*in sport*) score *m*; (*at cards*) marque *f*; (*music*) partition *f*.

  2 *verb* (*point, goal*) marquer.

  3 *verb* marquer un point *or* un but; (*count points*) marquer les points.

score[2] *noun* a s. (of) (*twenty*) une vingtaine (de).

scorn *noun* mépris *m*.

Scot *noun* Écossais, -aise *m or f*.

Scotch *noun* (*whisky*) scotch *m*.

Scotland *noun* l'Écosse *f*.

Scotsman *noun* Écossais *m*.

Scotswoman *noun* Écossaise *f*.

Scottish *adjective* écossais.

scoundrel *noun* vaurien *m*.

scout *noun* (*boy*) s. scout *m*.

scrambled *adjective* (*egg*) brouillé.

scrap

  1 *noun* petit morceau *m* (of de); (*of information*) fragment *m*; (*metal*) ferraille *f*; **scraps** (*food*) restes *mpl*.

  2 *verb* se débarrasser de; (*vehicle*) mettre à la ferraille; (*plan*) abandonner.

scrapbook *noun* album *m* (*pour collages etc*).

scrape

  1 *verb* racler; (*skin, knee etc*) érafler.

  2 *verb* to s. against something frotter contre quelque chose.

  3 *noun* (*on skin*) éraflure *f*.

scrape away *or* **off** *verb* (*mud etc*) racler.

scrape through *verb* (*in exam*) réussir de justesse.

scrape together *verb* (*money, people*) réunir (difficilement).

scrap metal *noun* ferraille *f*.

scrap paper *noun* (*papier m*) brouillon *m*.

scratch

  1 *noun* (*mark, injury*) éraflure *f*; **to start from s.** repartir de zéro; **she isn't up to s.** elle n'est pas à la hauteur.

  2 *verb* (*arm etc that itches*) gratter; (*skin, furniture etc*) érafler; (*one's name*) graver (**on** sur).

  3 *verb* (*relieve an itch*) se gratter.

scream

  1 *verb* crier; **to s. at somebody** crier après quelqu'un.

  2 *noun* cri *m* (perçant).

screen *noun* écran *m*; (**folding**) s. paravent *m*.

screw

  1 *noun* vis *f*.

  2 *verb* visser (**to** à).

screw down *or* **on** *verb* to s. something down or on visser quelque chose.

screwdriver *noun* tournevis *m*.

screw up *verb* (*paper*) chiffonner; (*eyes*) plisser.

scribble *verb* griffonner.

script *noun* (*of film*) scénario *m*; (*of play*) texte *m*; (*in exam*) copie *f*.

scrub *verb* nettoyer (à la brosse); (*pan*) récurer.

scrubbing brush *noun* brosse *f* dure.

scrum *noun* Rugby mêlée *f*.

scuba diving *noun* plongée *f* sous-marine.

sculptor *noun* sculpteur *m*.

sculpture *noun* (*article, object*) sculpture *f*.

sea *noun* mer *f*; (**out**) at s. en mer; by s. par mer; by *or* beside the s. au bord de la mer.

seafood *noun* fruits *mpl* de mer.

seafront *noun* bord *m* or front *m* de mer.

seagull *noun* mouette *f*.

seal
  1 *noun* (*animal*) phoque *m*; (*mark, design*) sceau *m*; (*of wax*) cachet *m* (de cire).
  2 *verb* (*document, container*) sceller; (*envelope*) cacheter; (*with putty*) boucher.

sea lion *noun* otarie *f*.

seal off *verb* (*of police etc*) interdire l'accès de.

seam *noun* (*in cloth*) couture *f*.

search
  1 *noun* recherche *f* (for de); (*of person, place*) fouille *f*; **in s. of** à la recherche de.
  2 *verb* (*person, place*) fouiller (**for** pour trouver); **to s. (through) one's papers**/*etc* **for something** chercher quelque chose dans ses papiers/*etc*; **to s. for something** chercher quelque chose.

seashell *noun* coquillage *m*.

seashore *noun* bord *m* de la mer.

seasick *adjective* **to be s.** avoir le mal de mer.

seasickness *noun* mal *m* de mer.

seaside *noun* bord *m* de la mer.

season
  1 *noun* saison *f*.
  2 *verb* (*food*) assaisonner.

seasoning *noun* assaisonnement *m*.

season ticket *noun* carte *f* d'abonnement.

seat
  1 *noun* siège *m*; (*on train, bus*) banquette *f*; (*in cinema, theatre*) fauteuil *m*; (*place*) place *f*; **to take** or **have a s.** s'asseoir.
  2 *verb* (*at table*) placer; **the room seats 50** la salle a 50 places (as-

sises); **be seated!** asseyez-vous!

seat belt *noun* ceinture *f* de sécurité.

seated *adjective* (*sitting*) assis.

seating *noun* (*seats*) places *fpl* assises.

seaweed *noun* algue(s) *f(pl)*.

second [1]
  1 *adjective* deuxième, second; **every s. week** une semaine sur deux; **in s.** (*gear*) en seconde.
  2 *adverb* **to come s.** se classer deuxième.
  3 *noun* (*person, object*) deuxième *m* or *f*, second, -onde *m* or *f*.

second [2] *noun* (*part of minute*) seconde *f*.

secondary *adjective* secondaire.

second-class *adjective* (*ticket*) de seconde (classe); (*mail*) non urgent.

secondhand *adjective & adverb* (*not new*) d'occasion.

secondly *adverb* deuxièmement.

secret *adjective & noun* secret (*m*); **in s.** en secret.

secretary *noun* secrétaire *m* or *f*.

section *noun* (*of town, book etc*) partie *f*; (*of machine, furniture*) élément *m*; (*in store*) rayon *m*; **the sports**/*etc* **s.** (*of newspaper*) la page des sports/*etc*.

secure
  1 *adjective* (*person, valuables*) en sûreté; (*place*) sûr; (*solid*) solide; (*door, window*) bien fermé.
  2 *verb* (*fasten*) attacher; (*window etc*) bien fermer.

securely *adverb* (*firmly*) solidement; (*safely*) en sûreté.

security *noun* sécurité *f*; (*for loan*) caution *f*.

sedation *noun* **under s.** sous calmants.

sedative noun calmant m.

see verb voir; **we'll s.** on verra (bien); **I saw him run(ning)** je l'ai vu courir; **s. you (later)!** à tout à l'heure!; **s. you (soon)!** à bientôt!; **to s. that** (take care that) veiller à ce que (+ subjunctive); (check) s'assurer que.

see about verb s'occuper de; (consider) songer à.

seed noun graine f; (in grape) pépin m.

seeing conjunction s. (that) vu que.

seek verb chercher (to do à faire); (ask for) demander (from à).

seem verb sembler (to do faire); **it seems that** (impression) il semble que (+ subjunctive or indicative); (rumour) il paraît que (+ indicative); **it seems to me that** il me semble que (+ indicative).

see off verb **to s. somebody off** accompagner quelqu'un (à la gare etc).

see out verb **to s. somebody out** raccompagner quelqu'un.

seesaw noun bascule f.

see to verb (deal with) s'occuper de; (mend) réparer; **to see to it that** veiller à ce que (+ subjunctive); (check) s'assurer que.

see to verb **to s. somebody to** (accompany) raccompagner quelqu'un à.

segment noun segment m; (of orange) quartier m.

seize verb saisir; (power, land) s'emparer de.

seldom adverb rarement.

select verb choisir (from parmi); (candidates, players etc) sélectionner.

selection noun sélection f.

self-assurance noun assurance f.

self-assured adjective sûr de soi.

self-confidence noun assurance f.

self-confident adjective sûr de soi.

self-conscious adjective gêné.

self-control noun maîtrise f de soi.

self-defence noun légitime défense f.

self-employed adjective qui travaille à son compte.

selfish adjective égoïste.

self-respect noun amour-propre m.

self-service noun & adjective libre-service (invariable m).

sell
1 verb vendre; **to have** or **be sold out of something** n'avoir plus de quelque chose.
2 verb (of product) se vendre.

seller noun vendeur, -euse m or f.

sellotape ® noun scotch ® m.

semester noun semestre m.

semi- prefix demi-, semi-.

semicircle noun demi-cercle m.

semicolon noun point-virgule m.

semidetached house noun maison f jumelle.

semifinal noun demi-finale f.

semolina noun semoule f.

senator noun sénateur m.

send verb envoyer (to à); **to s. somebody for something/somebody** envoyer quelqu'un chercher quelque chose/quelqu'un.

send away or **off** verb
1 envoyer (to à); (dismiss)

renvoyer.

2 to s. away or **off for something** commander quelque chose (par courrier).

send back verb renvoyer.

sender noun expéditeur, -trice m or f.

send for verb (doctor etc) faire venir; (by mail) commander (par courrier).

send in verb (form etc) envoyer; (person) faire entrer.

send on verb (letter, luggage) faire suivre.

send out verb (invitation etc) envoyer; (from room etc) faire sortir; **to s. out for** (meal) envoyer chercher.

send up verb (luggage) faire monter.

senior

1 adjective (older) plus âgé; (position, rank) supérieur.

2 noun aîné, -ée m or f; (in school) grand m, grande f; (in sport) senior m or f.

sensation noun sensation f.

sensational adjective (terrific) Familiar sensationnel.

sense

1 noun (meaning) sens m; **s. of smell** odorat m; **a s. of** (shame etc) un sentiment de; **to have a s. of humour** avoir de l'humour; **to have (good) s.** avoir du bon sens; **to have the s. to do** avoir l'intelligence de faire; **to make s.** (of story) tenir debout; **to make no s.** n'avoir aucun sens.

2 verb sentir (intuitivement) (**that** que).

senseless adjective (stupid) insensé.

sensible adjective (wise) raisonnable.

sensitive adjective sensible (**to** à); (skin) délicat; (touchy) susceptible (**about** à propos de).

sent see send.

sentence

1 noun Grammar phrase f; (punishment, in prison) peine f.

2 verb **to s. somebody to 3 years (in prison)** condamner quelqu'un à 3 ans de prison.

separate

1 adjective (distinct) séparé; (independent) indépendant; (different) différent.

2 verb séparer (**from** de).

3 verb se séparer (**from** de).

separately adverb séparément.

September noun septembre m.

sequence noun (order) ordre m; (series) succession f.

sequin noun paillette f.

Serb adjective & noun serbe (m or f).

Serbia noun la Serbie f.

sergeant noun sergent m; (in police force) brigadier m.

serial noun (story, film) feuilleton m.

series invariable noun série f.

serious adjective sérieux; (illness, mistake) grave.

seriously adverb sérieusement; (ill) gravement; **to take s.** prendre au sérieux.

servant noun (in house etc) domestique m or f.

serve verb servir (**to somebody** à quelqu'un, **somebody with something** quelque chose à quelqu'un); (of train, bus etc) desservir; **(it) serves you right!** ça t'apprendra!

serve out or **up** verb (meal etc) servir.

service
1 *noun* service *m*; (*machine or vehicle repair*) révision *f*; **s. (charge)** (*in restaurant*) service *m*.
2 *verb* (*machine, vehicle*) réviser.
service area *noun* (*on motorway*) aire *f* de service.
service station *noun* station-service *f*.
serviette *noun* serviette *f* (de table).
session *noun* séance *f*.
set
1 *noun* (*of keys, tools etc*) jeu *m*; (*of stamps, numbers*) série *f*; (*of people*) groupe *m*; (*in mathematics*) ensemble *m*; (*of books*) collection *f*; (*scenery*) décor *m*; (*hairstyle*) mise *f* en plis; *Tennis* set *m*; **chess s.** jeu *m* d'échecs.
2 *adjective* (*time, price etc*) fixe; (*book at school*) au programme; **the s. menu** le plat du jour; **s. on doing** résolu à faire; **to be s. on something** vouloir quelque chose à tout prix; **all s.** (*ready*) prêt (**to do** pour faire).
3 *verb* (*put*) mettre; (*date, limit etc*) fixer; (*record*) établir; (*mechanism, clock*) régler; (*alarm clock*) mettre (**for** pour); (*arm etc in plaster*) plâtrer; (*task*) donner (**for somebody** à quelqu'un); (*trap*) tendre; **to have one's hair s.** se faire faire une mise en plis.
4 *verb* (*of sun*) se coucher; (*of jelly*) prendre.
set (off) *verb* **to s. somebody (off) crying**/*etc* faire pleurer/*etc* quelqu'un.
set about *verb* **to s. about something/doing** (*begin*) se mettre à quelque chose/à faire.
setback *noun* revers *m*.
set down *verb* (*object*) déposer.

set off *verb*
1 (*bomb*) faire exploser; (*mechanism*) déclencher.
2 (*leave*) partir.
set out *verb*
1 (*display, explain*) exposer (**to** à); (*arrange*) disposer.
2 (*leave*) partir; **to s. out to do** entreprendre de faire.
setsquare *noun* équerre *f*.
settee *noun* canapé *m*.
setting *noun* (*surroundings*) cadre *m*.
settle *verb*
1 (*decide, arrange, pay*) régler; (*date*) fixer; **that's (all) settled** c'est décidé.
2 (*live*) s'installer.
settle down *verb* (*in chair or house*) s'installer; (*calm down*) se calmer; (*in one's lifestyle*) se ranger.
settlement *noun* (*agreement*) accord *m*.
settler *noun* colon *m*.
settle (up) with *verb* **to s. (up) with somebody** (*pay*) régler quelqu'un.
set up *verb*
1 (*tent*) dresser; (*business*) créer.
2 **to s. up in business** monter une affaire.
seven *adjective & noun* sept (*m*).
seventeen *adjective & noun* dix-sept (*m*).
seventh *adjective & noun* septième (*m or f*).
seventieth *adjective & noun* soixante-dixième (*m or f*).
seventy *adjective & noun* soixante-dix (*m*); **s.-one** soixante et onze.
several *adjective & pronoun* plusieurs (**of** d'entre).

severe *adjective* (*tone etc*) sévère; (*winter*) rigoureux; (*test*) dur.

sew *verb* coudre.

sewer *noun* égout *m*.

sewing *noun* couture *f*.

sewing machine *noun* machine *f* à coudre.

sewn *see* sew.

sew on *verb* (*button*) (re)coudre.

sew up *verb* (*tear*) (re)coudre.

sex
  1 *noun* sexe *m*; (*activity*) relations *fpl* sexuelles; **to have s. with somebody** faire l'amour avec quelqu'un.
  2 *adjective* (*education, life etc*) sexuel.

sexual *adjective* sexuel.

sexy *adjective* sexy *invariable*.

sh! *interjection* chut!

shabby *adjective* (*room etc*) minable.

shade *noun* ombre *f*; (*of colour*) ton *m*; (*of lamp*) abat-jour *invariable m*; **in the s.** à l'ombre.

shadow *noun* ombre *f*.

shady *adjective* (*place*) ombragé.

shake *verb*
  1 (*object, person*) secouer; (*bottle*) agiter; (*upset*) bouleverser; **to s. one's head** (*say no*) secouer la tête; **to s. hands with somebody** serrer la main à quelqu'un; **we shook hands** nous nous sommes serré la main.
  2 (*of voice, person, building*) trembler (**with** de).

shaken *see* shake.

shall *auxiliary verb* (*future*) **I s. come, I'll come** je viendrai; **we s. not come, we shan't come** nous ne viendrons pas.
  ∎ (*question*) **s. I open it?** veux-tu que je l'ouvre?; **s. we leave?** on

part?

shallow *adjective* (*water, river etc*) peu profond.

shame *noun* (*feeling, disgrace*) honte *f*; **it's a s.** c'est dommage (**to do** de faire); **it's a s. (that)** c'est dommage que (+ *subjunctive*); **what a s.!** (quel) dommage!

shameful *adjective* honteux.

shampoo
  1 *noun* shampooing *m*.
  2 *verb* **to s. somebody's hair** faire un shampooing à quelqu'un.

shandy *noun* panaché *m*.

shan't = shall not.

shape *noun* forme *f*; **in (good) s.** (*fit*) en (pleine) forme; **to be in good/bad s.** (*of vehicle etc*) être en bon/mauvais état; (*of business*) marcher bien/mal; **to take s.** (*of plan, book etc*) prendre forme; (*progress well*) avancer.

-shaped *suffix* **pear-s./etc** en forme de poire/*etc.*

share
  1 *noun* part *f* (**of, in** de); (*in company*) action *f*.
  2 *verb* (*meal, opinion etc*) partager (**with** avec); (*characteristic*) avoir en commun.

shareholder *noun* actionnaire *m or f*.

share in *verb* **to s. in something** avoir sa part de quelque chose.

share out *verb* **to s. something out** partager *or* répartir quelque chose (**among** entre).

shark *noun* requin *m*.

sharp
  1 *adjective* (*knife etc*) tranchant; (*pointed*) pointu; (*point, pain*) aigu (*f* -uë); (*bend*) brusque.
  2 *adverb* **five o'clock/etc s.** cinq

heures/*etc* pile.

sharpen *verb* (*knife*) aiguiser; (*pencil*) tailler.

sharply *adverb* (*suddenly*) brusquement.

shatter *verb*
1 (*glass, bone*) briser en mille morceaux.
2 (*of glass*) voler en éclats.

shattered *adjective* (*exhausted*) *Familiar* crevé.

shave
1 *verb* (*person, head*) raser; **to s. off one's beard** se raser la barbe.
2 *verb* (*of man*) se raser.
3 *noun* **to have a s.** se raser.

shaver *noun* rasoir *m* électrique.

shaving cream *noun* crème *f* à raser.

shawl *noun* châle *m*.

she *pronoun* elle; **she's a happy woman** c'est une femme heureuse.

shed[1] *noun* (*in garden*) abri *m* (de jardin); (*for goods or machines*) hangar *m*.

shed[2] *verb* (*lose*) perdre; (*tears*) répandre.

sheep *noun* mouton *m*.

sheepskin *noun* peau *f* de mouton.

sheet *noun* (*on bed*) drap *m*; (*of paper*) feuille *f*; (*of glass, ice*) plaque *f*.

shelf *noun* étagère *f*; (*in shop*) rayon *m*.

shell
1 *noun* (*of egg etc*) coquille *f*; (*of tortoise*) carapace *f*; (*seashell*) coquillage *m*; (*explosive*) obus *m*.
2 *verb* (*peas*) écosser.

shellfish *noun* (*oysters etc*) fruits *mpl* de mer.

shelter
1 *noun* abri *m*; **to take s.** se mettre à l'abri (**from** de).
2 *verb* s'abriter (**from** de).

shelving *noun* rayonnage(s) *m(pl)*.

shepherd *noun* berger *m*.

sheriff *noun American* shérif *m*.

sherry *noun* sherry *m*.

shield
1 *noun* bouclier *m*; (*screen*) écran *m*.
2 *verb* protéger (**from** de).

shift
1 *noun* (*change*) changement *m* (**of, in** de); (*period of work*) poste *m*; (*workers*) équipe *f*.
2 *verb* (*move*) bouger.

shin *noun* tibia *m*.

shine
1 *verb* (*of light, sun*) briller.
2 *verb* (*polish*) faire briller; **to s. a light** *or* **a torch on something** éclairer quelque chose.
3 *noun* (*on shoes, cloth*) brillant *m*.

shiny *adjective* brillant.

ship *noun* navire *m*, bateau *m*; **by s.** en bateau.

shipping *noun* (*traffic*) navigation *f*.

shipwreck *noun* naufrage *m*.

shipwrecked *adjective* naufragé; **to be s.** faire naufrage.

shipyard *noun* chantier *m* naval.

shirt *noun* chemise *f*; (*of woman*) chemisier *m*; (*of sportsman*) maillot *m*.

shiver
1 *verb* frissonner (**with** de).
2 *noun* frisson *m*.

shock
1 *noun* (*emotional, physical*) choc *m*; (**electric**) **s.** décharge *f* (élec-

trique); **suffering from s.** en état de choc.
2 verb (offend) choquer; (surprise) stupéfier.

shock absorber noun amortisseur m.

shocking adjective affreux; (outrageous) scandaleux.

shoe noun chaussure f, soulier m.

shoelace noun lacet m.

shoe polish noun cirage m.

shone see shine.

shook see shake.

shoot verb tirer (**at** sur); (kill) tuer (d'un coup de feu); (wound) blesser (d'un coup de feu); (execute) fusiller; (gun) tirer un coup de; (film) tourner.

shoot ahead/off verb (rush) avancer/partir à toute vitesse.

shooting noun (shots) coups mpl de feu; (murder) meurtre m.

shoot up verb (of price) monter en flèche.

shop
1 noun magasin m; (small) boutique f; **at the baker's s.** à la boulangerie, chez le boulanger.
2 verb faire ses courses (**at** chez).

shop assistant noun vendeur, -euse m or f.

shopkeeper noun commerçant, -ante m or f.

shopping noun (goods) achats mpl; **to go s.** faire des courses.

shopping bag noun sac m à provisions.

shopping centre noun (purpose-built) centre m commercial; (district) quartier m commerçant.

shop window noun vitrine f.

shore noun (of sea, lake) rivage m; (coast) côte f.

short
1 adjective court; (person, distance) petit; **a s. time** or **while** (ago) (il y a) peu de temps; **to be s. of money/time** être à court d'argent/de temps; **we're s. of ten men** il nous manque dix hommes; **to be s. for something** (of name) être l'abréviation de quelque chose.
2 adverb **to cut s.** (hair) couper court; (visit etc) raccourcir; (person) couper la parole à; **to get** or **run s.** manquer (**of** de).

shortage noun manque m.

short cut noun raccourci m.

shorten verb (dress, text etc) raccourcir.

shorthand typist noun sténodactylo f.

shortly adverb (soon) bientôt; **s. after** peu après.

shorts plural noun **(a pair of)** s. un short.

shortsighted adjective myope.

short-term adjective à court terme.

shot noun (from gun) coup m; (with camera) prise f de vues.

shotgun noun fusil m (de chasse).

should auxiliary verb (= ought to) **you s. do it** vous devriez le faire; **I s. have stayed** j'aurais dû rester; **that s. be Paul** ça doit être Paul.
▪ (= would) **I s. like to** j'aimerais bien; **it's strange she s. say no** il est étrange qu'elle dise non.
▪ (possibility) **if he s. come** s'il vient.

shoulder noun épaule f; **(hard) s.** (of motorway) bas-côté m.

shoulder bag noun sac m à bandoulière.

shout
1 *noun* cri *m*.
2 *verb* crier; **to s. to somebody to do** crier à quelqu'un de faire.

shout at *verb* **to s. at somebody** (*scold*) crier après quelqu'un.

shouting *noun* (*shouts*) cris *mpl*.

shout out *verb* crier.

shove
1 *noun* poussée *f*; **to give a s. (to)** pousser.
2 *verb* pousser; (*put*) *Familiar* fourrer.

shovel
1 *noun* pelle *f*.
2 *verb* (*snow etc*) enlever à la pelle.

show
1 *noun* (*in theatre*) spectacle *m*; (*in cinema*) séance *f*; **the Motor S.** le Salon de l'Automobile; **on s.** (*painting etc*) exposé.
2 *verb* montrer (**to** à, **that** que); (*in exhibition*) exposer; (*film*) passer; (*indicate*) indiquer; **to s. somebody to the door** reconduire quelqu'un.
3 *verb* (*be visible*) se voir; (*of film*) passer.

shower *noun* (*bath*) douche *f*; (*of rain*) averse *f*.

show in *verb* (*visitor*) faire entrer.

showing *noun* (*cinema performance*) séance *f*.

shown *see* show.

show off *verb* crâner.

show-off *noun* crâneur, -euse *m or f*.

show out *verb* (*visitor*) reconduire.

show (a)round *verb* **to s. somebody (a)round** faire visiter à quelqu'un; **to s. somebody (a)round the house** faire visiter la maison à quelqu'un.

show up *verb*
1 (*of person*) arriver.
2 (*embarrass*) mettre dans l'embarras.

shrank *see* shrink.

shrimp *noun* crevette *f* (grise).

shrink *verb* (*of clothes*) rétrécir.

shrub *noun* arbuste *m*.

shrug *verb* **to s. one's shoulders** hausser les épaules.

shrunk *see* shrink.

shudder *verb* frémir (**with** de).

shuffle *verb* (*cards*) battre.

shush! *interjection* chut!

shut *verb*
1 (*door, box etc*) fermer.
2 *verb* (*of door etc*) se fermer; (*of shop etc*) fermer.

shut down *verb* fermer.

shut in *verb* enfermer.

shut off *verb* (*gas etc*) fermer; (*engine*) arrêter; (*isolate*) isoler.

shut out *verb* (*light*) empêcher d'entrer; **to s. somebody out** (*accidentally*) enfermer quelqu'un dehors.

shutter *noun* (*on window*) volet *m*; (*of shop*) rideau *m* (métallique).

shuttle *noun* **s.** (*service*) navette *f*; **space s.** navette spatiale.

shut up *verb*
1 (*house etc*) fermer; (*person, object*) enfermer.
2 (*be quiet*) se taire.

shy *adjective* timide.

shyness *noun* timidité *f*.

sick
1 *adjective* malade; **to be s.** (*vomit*) vomir; **off s.** en congé de maladie; **to feel s.** avoir mal au cœur; **to be s. (and tired) of something/somebody** *Familiar*

en avoir marre de quelque chose/ quelqu'un.
2 *noun* the s. les malades *mpl*.

sickness *noun* maladie *f*.

sick up *verb* vomir.

side *noun* côté *m*; (*of hill, animal*) flanc *m*; (*of road, river*) bord *m*; (*team*) équipe *f*; **at** *or* **by the s.** **of** à côté de; **at** *or* **by my s.** à côté de moi, à mes côtés; **s. by s.** l'un à côté de l'autre; **to move to one s.** s'écarter; **on this s.** de ce côté; **on the other s.** de l'autre côté; **to take sides with somebody** se ranger du côté de quelqu'un; **on our s.** de notre côté.

sideboard *noun* buffet *m*.

sidelight *noun* (*of vehicle*) veilleuse *f*.

sideways *adverb* & *adjective* de côté.

sieve *noun* tamis *m*; (*for liquids*) passoire *f*.

sift *verb* (*flour etc*) tamiser.

sigh
  1 *noun* soupir *m*.
  2 *verb* soupirer.

sight *noun* vue *f*; (*thing seen*) spectacle *m*; **to lose s. of** perdre de vue; **to catch s. of** apercevoir; **by s.** de vue; **in s.** (*target etc*) en vue; **out of s.** caché; **the (tourist) sights** les attractions *fpl* touristiques.

sightseeing *noun* **to go s.** faire du tourisme.

sign
  1 *noun* signe *m*; (*notice*) panneau *m*; (*over shop, inn*) enseigne *f*; **no s. of** aucune trace de.
  2 *verb* (*with signature*) signer.

signal *noun* signal *m*; **traffic signals** feux *mpl* de circulation.

signature *noun* signature *f*.

significant *adjective* (*important,*

large) important.

significantly *adverb* sensible-ment.

sign in *verb* (*in hotel etc*) signer le registre.

sign on *or* **up** *verb* (*of soldier, worker*) s'engager; (*of student*) s'inscrire (**for** à).

signpost *noun* poteau *m* indicateur.

silence
  1 *noun* silence *m*; **in s.** en silence.
  2 *verb* faire taire.

silent *adjective* silencieux; (*film*) muet (*f* muette); **to keep s.** garder le silence (**about** sur).

silently *adverb* silencieusement.

silk *noun* soie *f*.

sill *noun* (*of window*) rebord *m*.

silly *adjective* bête; **to do something s.** faire une bêtise.

silver
  1 *noun* argent *m*; (*plates etc*) argenterie *f*.
  2 *adjective* (*spoon etc*) en argent; **s. paper** papier *m* d'argent.

silver-plated *adjective* plaqué argent.

silverware *invariable noun* argenterie *f*.

similar *adjective* semblable (**to** à).

similarity *noun* ressemblance *f* (**to** avec).

simple *adjective* simple.

simplify *verb* simplifier.

simply *adverb* (*plainly, merely*) simplement; (*absolutely*) absolument.

simultaneous *adjective* simultané.

simultaneously *adverb* simultanément.

sin *noun* péché *m*.

since
1 *preposition* depuis.
2 *conjunction* depuis que; (*because*) puisque; **s. she's been here** depuis qu'elle est ici; **it's a year s. I saw him** ça fait un an que je ne l'ai pas vu.
3 *adverb* **(ever) s.** depuis.

sincere *adjective* sincère.

sincerely *adverb* sincèrement; **yours s.** (*in letter*) veuillez croire à mes sentiments dévoués.

sincerity *noun* sincérité *f*.

sing *verb* chanter.

singer *noun* chanteur, -euse *m or f*.

single
1 *adjective* seul; (*room, bed*) pour une personne; (*unmarried*) célibataire; **not a s. book/etc** pas un seul livre/*etc*; **s. ticket** billet *m* simple; **every s. day** tous les jours sans exception.
2 *noun* (*ticket*) aller *m* (simple); (*record*) 45 tours *invariable m*.

single out *verb* choisir.

singular
1 *adjective* (*form*) singulier; (*noun*) au singulier.
2 *noun* singulier *m*; **in the s.** au singulier.

sinister *adjective* sinistre.

sink[1] *noun* (*in kitchen*) évier *m*; (*washbasin*) lavabo *m*.

sink[2] *verb* (*of ship, person etc*) couler.

sink (down) into *verb* (*mud*) s'enfoncer dans; (*armchair*) s'affaler dans.

sip *verb* boire à petites gorgées.

sir *noun* monsieur *m*; **S.** (*title*) sir.

siren *noun* (*of factory etc*) sirène *f*.

sister *noun* sœur *f*.

sister-in-law *noun* belle-sœur *f*.

sit *verb*
1 s'asseoir; **to be sitting** être assis; **she was sitting reading** elle était assise à lire.
2 (*child on chair etc*) asseoir.

sit (for) *verb* (*exam*) se présenter à.

sit around *verb* traîner; (*do nothing*) ne rien faire.

sit down *verb*
1 s'asseoir; **to be sitting down** être assis.
2 (*child etc*) asseoir.

site *noun* (*position*) emplacement *m*; (*building*) **s.** chantier *m*.

sitting room *noun* salon *m*.

situate *verb* situer; **to be situated** être situé, se situer.

situation *noun* situation *f*.

sit up (straight) *verb* s'asseoir (bien droit).

six *adjective & noun* six (*m*).

sixteen *adjective & noun* seize (*m*).

sixth *adjective & noun* sixième (*m or f*); **(lower) s. form** = classe *f* de première; **(upper) s. form** = classe *f* terminale.

sixtieth *adjective & noun* soixantième (*m or f*).

sixty *adjective & noun* soixante (*m*).

size *noun* (*of person, clothes, packet etc*) taille *f*; (*measurements*) dimensions *fpl*; (*of town, sum*) importance *f*; (*of shoes, gloves*) pointure *f*; (*of shirt*) encolure *f*; **hip/chest s.** tour *m* de hanches/de poitrine.

skate
1 *noun* patin *m*.
2 *verb* patiner.

skateboard *noun* planche *f* (à

roulettes).

skater noun patineur, -euse m or f.

skating noun patinage m; **to go s.** faire du patinage.

skating rink noun (ice-skating) patinoire f.

skeleton noun squelette m.

sketch
1 noun (drawing) croquis m; (comic play) sketch m.
2 verb faire un or des croquis.

skewer noun (for meat etc) broche f; (for kebab) brochette f.

ski
1 noun ski m.
2 verb faire du ski.

skid
1 verb déraper; **to s. into something** déraper et heurter quelque chose.
2 noun dérapage m.

skier noun skieur, -euse m or f.

skiing
1 noun ski m.
2 adjective (school, clothes, etc) de ski.

skilful adjective habile (**at doing** à faire, **at something** à quelque chose).

ski lift noun remonte-pente m.

skill noun habileté f (**at** à); (technique) technique f.

skilled worker noun ouvrier, -ière qualifié(e).

skimmed milk noun lait m écrémé.

skin noun peau f.

skin diving noun plongée f sous-marine.

skinny adjective maigre.

skip [1] verb
1 (hop about) sautiller; (with rope) sauter à la corde.

2 (miss) sauter.

skip [2] noun (container for rubbish) benne f.

skipping rope noun corde f à sauter.

skirt noun jupe f.

skittle noun quille f; **to play skittles** jouer aux quilles.

skull noun crâne m.

sky noun ciel m.

skyscraper noun gratte-ciel m invariable.

slack adjective (knot, spring) lâche; **to be s.** (of rope) avoir du mou; (in office etc) être calme.

slacken verb (rope) relâcher.

slacks plural noun pantalon m.

slam
1 verb claquer.
2 noun claquement m.

slang noun argot m.

slant
1 noun inclinaison f.
2 verb (of roof) être en pente.

slap
1 noun tape f; (on face) gifle f.
2 verb (person) donner une tape à; **to s. somebody's face** gifler quelqu'un; **to s. somebody's bottom** donner une fessée à quelqu'un.

slate noun ardoise f.

slaughter
1 verb massacrer; (animal) abattre.
2 noun massacre m; abattage m.

slave noun esclave m or f.

slave away verb trimer.

slavery noun esclavage m.

sledge noun luge f; (horse-drawn) traîneau m.

sleep
1 noun sommeil m; **to have a s., get some s.** dormir.

2 *verb* dormir; (*spend the night*) coucher; **to go** *or* **get to s.** s'endormir.

sleeper *noun* (*compartment*) couchettes *fpl*; (*train*) train *m* couchettes.

sleeping *adjective* (*asleep*) endormi.

sleeping bag *noun* sac *m* de couchage.

sleeping car *noun* wagon-lit *m*.

sleeping pill *noun* somnifère *m*.

sleepy *adjective* **to be s.** (*of person*) avoir sommeil.

sleet
1 *noun* neige *f* fondue.
2 *verb* **it's sleeting** il tombe de la neige fondue.

sleeve *noun* (*of shirt etc*) manche *f*; (*of record*) pochette *f*; **long-/short-sleeved** à manches longues/courtes.

sleigh *noun* traîneau *m*.

slept *see* sleep.

slice *noun* tranche *f*.

slice (up) *verb* couper (en tranches).

slide
1 *noun* (*in playground*) toboggan *m*; (*for hair*) barrette *f*; (*film*) diapositive *f*.
2 *verb* (*letter etc*) glisser (**into** dans); (*table, chair etc*) faire glisser.

sliding door *noun* porte *f* à glissière *or* coulissante.

slight *adjective* (*noise, mistake etc*) léger, petit; (*chance*) faible; **the slightest thing** la moindre chose; **not in the slightest** pas le moins du monde.

slightly *adverb* légèrement.

slim
1 *adjective* mince.

2 *verb* maigrir.

sling
1 *noun* (*for arm*) écharpe *f*; **in a s.** en écharpe.
2 *verb Familiar* balancer.

slip
1 *noun* (*mistake*) erreur *f*; (*woman's undergarment*) combinaison *f*; **a s. of paper** un bout de papier.
2 *verb* glisser (**to** à, **into** dans).

slip away *verb* s'esquiver.

slip in *verb* entrer furtivement.

slip into *verb* (*room etc*) se glisser dans; (*bathrobe etc*) mettre, passer.

slip off *verb* (*garment*) enlever.

slip on *verb* (*garment*) mettre.

slip out *verb* sortir furtivement; (*for a moment*) sortir (un instant).

slipper *noun* pantoufle *f*.

slippery *adjective* glissant.

slip up *verb* (*make a mistake*) gaffer.

slit *noun* (*opening*) fente *f*; (*cut*) coupure *f*.

slogan *noun* slogan *m*.

slope
1 *noun* pente *f*; (*of mountain*) versant *m*; (*for skiing*) piste *f*.
2 *verb* (*of ground, roof etc*) être en pente.

sloping *adjective* en pente.

slot *noun* (*slit*) fente *f*; (*groove*) rainure *f*.

slot machine *noun* distributeur *m* automatique; (*for gambling*) machine *f* à sous.

Slovakia *noun* la Slovaquie *f*.

Slovakian *adjective & noun* slovaque (*m or f*).

slow
1 *adjective* lent; **to be s.** (*of clock,*

watch) retarder; **to be five minutes s.** retarder de cinq minutes; **in s. motion** au ralenti.
2 *adverb* lentement.

slowcoach *noun Familiar* tortue *f.*

slow down or **up** *verb* ralentir.

slowly *adverb* lentement; (*bit by bit*) peu à peu.

slug *noun* limace *f.*

slum *noun* (*house*) taudis *m*; **the slums** les quartiers *mpl* pauvres.

slung *see* sling.

sly *adjective* rusé.

smack
1 *noun* claque *f*; gifle *f*; fessée *f.*
2 *verb* (*person*) donner une claque à; **to s. somebody's face** gifler quelqu'un; **to s. somebody('s bottom)** donner une fessée à quelqu'un.

small
1 *adjective* petit.
2 *adverb* (*to cut, chop*) menu.

smallpox *noun* petite vérole *f.*

smart *adjective* (*in appearance*) élégant; (*clever*) intelligent.

smash *verb*
1 (*break*) briser; (*shatter*) fracasser.
2 se briser.

smashing *adjective Familiar* formidable.

smash into *verb* **to s. into something** (*of vehicle*) (r)entrer dans quelque chose.

smash-up *noun* collision *f.*

smell
1 *noun* odeur *f*; (*sense of*) **s.** odorat *m.*
2 *verb* sentir; (*stink*) sentir (mauvais); (*have a smell*) avoir une odeur; **to s. of smoke**/*etc* sentir la fumée/*etc.*

smelt *see* smell.

smile
1 *noun* sourire *m.*
2 *verb* sourire (**at somebody** à quelqu'un).

smock *noun* blouse *f.*

smoke
1 *noun* fumée *f*; **to have a s.** fumer une cigarette *etc.*
2 *verb* fumer; **'no smoking'** 'défense de fumer'; **smoking compartment** compartiment *m* fumeurs.

smoker *noun* fumeur, -euse *m or f*; (*train compartment*) compartiment *m* fumeurs.

smooth *adjective* (*surface, skin etc*) lisse; (*flight*) agréable.

smooth down or **out** *verb* (*dress, hair etc*) lisser.

smuggle *verb* passer (en fraude).

smuggler *noun* contrebandier, -ière *m or f.*

smuggling *noun* contrebande *f.*

snack *noun* (*meal*) casse-croûte *invariable m*; **snacks** (*things to eat*) petites choses *fpl* à grignoter; (*sweets*) friandises *fpl*; **to eat a s.** or **snacks** grignoter.

snack bar *noun* snack(-bar) *m.*

snail *noun* escargot *m.*

snake *noun* serpent *m.*

snap *verb*
1 (*break*) casser net.
2 se casser net.

snap (fastener) *noun* bouton-pression *m.*

snap(shot) *noun* photo *f.*

snatch *verb* saisir (*d'un geste vif*); **to s. something from somebody** arracher quelque chose à quelqu'un.

sneaker *noun* (*chaussure f de*) tennis *m.*

sneer verb ricaner.

sneeze
1 verb éternuer.
2 noun éternuement m.

sniff verb to s. (at) renifler.

snip (off) verb couper.

snooker noun snooker m (sorte de jeu de billard).

snore verb ronfler.

snoring noun ronflements mpl.

snout noun museau m.

snow
1 noun neige f.
2 verb neiger; **it's snowing** il neige.

snowball noun boule f de neige.

snowdrift noun congère f.

snowflake noun flocon m de neige.

snowman noun bonhomme m de neige.

snowplough noun chasse-neige invariable m.

snowstorm noun tempête f de neige.

so
1 adverb (to such a degree) si, tellement (that que); (thus) ainsi; so that (purpose) pour que (+ subjunctive); (result) si bien que (+ indicative); **so as to do** pour faire; **I think so** je le pense; **if so** si oui; **is that so?** c'est vrai?; **so am I, so do I** etc moi aussi; **so much** (to work etc) tant (that que); **so much courage**/etc tant de courage/etc; **so many** tant; **so many books**/etc tant de livres/etc; **ten or so** environ dix; **and so on** et ainsi de suite.
2 conjunction (therefore) donc; **so what?** et alors?

soak verb
1 (drench) tremper; (washing, food) faire tremper.
2 (of washing etc) tremper.

soaked through adjective (person) trempé jusqu'aux os.

soaking adjective & adverb s. (wet) trempé.

soak up verb to s. **something up** absorber quelque chose.

soap noun savon m.

soapflakes plural noun savon m en paillettes.

soap powder noun lessive f.

soapy adjective savonneux.

sob
1 noun sanglot m.
2 verb sangloter.

sober adjective **he's s.** (not drunk) il n'est pas ivre.

soccer noun football m.

social adjective social; **s. club** club m; **s. evening** soirée f; **to have a good s. life** sortir beaucoup; **s. security** aide f sociale; **S. Security** = Sécurité f sociale; **the s. services** les services sociaux; **s. worker** assistant, -ante m or f social(e).

socialist adjective & noun socialiste (m or f).

society noun société f.

sock noun chaussette f.

socket noun (for electric plug) prise f de courant.

soda (water) noun eau f gazeuse.

sofa noun canapé m; **s. bed** canapé-lit m.

soft adjective (gentle, not stiff) doux (f douce); (butter, ground) mou (f molle); **s. drink** boisson f non alcoolisée.

softly adverb doucement.

software invariable noun logiciel m.

soil *noun* sol *m*, terre *f*.

sold *see* sell.

soldier *noun* soldat *m*.

sole *noun* (*of shoe*) semelle *f*; (*of foot*) plante *f*; (*fish*) sole *f*; **lemon s.** limande *f*.

solemn *adjective* (*formal*) solennel; (*serious*) grave.

solicitor *noun* notaire *m*.

solid
  1 *adjective* (*car, meal etc*) solide; (*wall, line*) plein; (*gold*) massif; **s. line** ligne *f* continue.
  2 *noun* solide *m*.

solution *noun* solution *f* (**to** de).

solve *verb* (*problem*) résoudre.

some
  1 *adjective* (*amount, number*) du, de la, des; **s. wine** du vin; **s. water** de l'eau; **s. dogs** des chiens; **s. pretty flowers** de jolies fleurs.
  ▮ (*unspecified*) un, une; **s. man (or other)** un homme (quelconque).
  ▮ (*a few*) quelques; (*a little*) un peu de.
  2 *pronoun* (*number*) quelques-un(e)s (**of** de).
  ▮ (*a quantity*) en; **I want s.** j'en veux.

somebody = someone.

someday *adverb* un jour.

somehow *adverb* d'une manière ou d'une autre; (*for some reason*) on ne sait pourquoi.

someone *pronoun* quelqu'un; **s. small**/*etc* quelqu'un de petit/*etc*.

someplace *adverb* quelque part.

somersault *noun* (*on the ground*) roulade *f*; (*in the air*) saut *m* périlleux.

something *pronoun* quelque chose; **s. awful**/*etc* quelque chose d'affreux/*etc*; **s. of a liar**/*etc* un

peu menteur/*etc*.

sometime *adverb* un jour.

sometimes *adverb* quelquefois.

somewhat *adverb* quelque peu.

somewhere *adverb* quelque part.

son *noun* fils *m*.

song *noun* chanson *f*.

son-in-law *noun* gendre *m*.

soon *adverb* bientôt; (*quickly*) vite; (*early*) tôt; **s. after** peu après; **as s. as she leaves** aussitôt qu'elle partira; **no sooner had he spoken than** à peine avait-il parlé que; **I'd sooner leave** je préférerais partir; **I'd just as s. leave** j'aimerais autant partir; **sooner or later** tôt ou tard.

soot *noun* suie *f*.

soothe *verb* (*pain, nerves*) calmer.

sore
  1 *adjective* (*painful*) douloureux; **she has a s. throat** elle a mal à la gorge.
  2 *noun* plaie *f*.

sorrow *noun* chagrin *m*.

sorry *adjective* **to be s.** (*regret*) être désolé (**to do** de faire); **I'm s. she can't come** je regrette qu'elle ne puisse pas venir; **I'm s. about the delay** je m'excuse pour ce retard; **s.!** pardon!; **to feel** *or* **be s. for somebody** plaindre quelqu'un.

sort¹ *noun* sorte *f*, espèce *f* (**of** de); **all sorts of** toutes sortes de; **what s. of drink**/*etc* **is it?** qu'est-ce que c'est comme boisson/*etc*?

sort² *verb* (*papers etc*) trier.

sort out *verb* (*classify, select*) trier; (*separate*) séparer (**from** de); (*tidy*) ranger; (*problem*) régler.

sought *see* seek.

soul *noun* âme *f.*

sound [1]
1 *noun* son *m*; (*noise*) bruit *m*; I
don't like the s. of it ça ne me
plaît pas du tout.
2 *verb* sonner; (*seem*) sembler; to
s. one's horn klaxonner; to s.
like sembler être; (*resemble*)
ressembler à.

sound [2]
1 *adjective* (*healthy*) sain; (*good,
reliable*) solide.
2 *adverb* s. asleep profondément
endormi.

soundproof *verb* insonoriser.

soup *noun* soupe *f*, potage *m.*

sour *adjective* aigre.

source *noun* source *f.*

south
1 *noun* sud *m*; (to the) s. of au
sud de.
2 *adjective* (*coast*) sud *invariable.*
3 *adverb* au sud.

southbound *adjective* en
direction du sud.

south-east *noun & adjective*
sud-est (*invariable m*).

southern *adjective* (*town*) du
sud; (*coast*) sud *invariable.*

southerner *noun* habitant, -ante
m or f du Sud.

southward(s) *adverb* vers le
sud.

south-west *noun & adjective*
sud-ouest (*invariable m*).

souvenir *noun* (*object*) souvenir
m.

sow *verb* (*seeds*) semer.

sown *see* sow.

space *noun* (*gap, emptiness,
atmosphere*) espace *m*; (*period*)
période *f*; (*for parking*) place *f*;

to take up s. (*room*) prendre de
la place.

space out *verb* espacer.

spaceship *noun* engin *m* spatial.

spacesuit *noun* combinaison *f*
spatiale.

spacious *adjective* spacieux.

spade *noun* bêche *f*; (*of child*)
pelle *f*; **spade(s)** *Cards* pique *m.*

spaghetti *noun* spaghetti(s) *mpl.*

Spain *noun* l'Espagne *f.*

Spaniard *noun* Espagnol, -ole *m
or f.*

Spanish
1 *adjective* espagnol.
2 *noun* (*language*) espagnol *m.*

spank
1 *verb* donner une fessée à.
2 *noun* claque *f* sur les fesses.

spanking *noun* fessée *f.*

spanner *noun* (*tool*) clef *f*
(à écrous).

spare
1 *adjective* (*extra*) de trop;
(*clothes*) de rechange; (*wheel*) de
secours; (*bed, room*) d'ami; s.
time loisirs *mpl.*
2 *noun* s. (part) pièce *f* détachée.
3 *verb* (*do without*) se passer de;
to s. somebody (*details etc*)
épargner à quelqu'un; (*time*)
accorder à quelqu'un; (*money*)
donner à quelqu'un.

spark *noun* étincelle *f.*

sparkle *verb* (*of diamond, star*)
étinceler.

sparkling *adjective* (*wine, water*)
pétillant.

spark(ing) plug *noun* bougie *f.*

sparrow *noun* moineau *m.*

spat *see* spit.

speak *verb*
1 parler (**about, of** de);
English-/French-speaking qui

parle anglais/français.

2 (*language*) parler; (*say*) dire.

speaker *noun* (*public*) orateur *m*; (*loudspeaker*) haut-parleur *m*; (*of stereo system*) enceinte *f*.

speak up *verb* parler plus fort.

spear *noun* lance *f*.

special

1 *adjective* spécial; (*care, attention*) (tout) particulier.

2 *noun* today's s. (*in restaurant*) le plat du jour.

specialist *noun* spécialiste *m or f* (in de).

speciality *noun* spécialité *f*.

specialize *verb* se spécialiser (in dans).

specially *adverb* spécialement.

species *invariable noun* espèce *f*.

specific *adjective* précis.

specimen *noun* (*example, person*) spécimen *m*.

spectacular *adjective* spectaculaire.

spectator *noun* spectateur, -trice *m or f*.

sped *see* speed.

speech *noun* (*talk, lecture*) discours *m* (on, about sur); (*power of language*) parole *f*; (*spoken language*) langage *m*.

speed

1 *noun* (*rate*) vitesse *f*; (*quickness*) rapidité *f*; s. limit limitation *f* de vitesse.

2 *verb* (*drive too fast*) aller trop vite.

speedboat *noun* vedette *f*.

speedometer *noun* compteur *m* (de vitesse).

speed up *verb*

1 accélérer; (*person*) faire aller plus vite.

2 (*of person*) aller plus vite.

spell [1] *noun* (*period*) (courte) période *f*; (*magic*) charme *m*; cold s. vague *f* de froid.

spell [2] *verb* (*write*) écrire; (*say aloud*) épeler; (*of letters*) former; how do you s. it? comment ça s'écrit?

spelling *noun* orthographe *f*.

spelt *see* spell.

spend *verb* dépenser (on pour); (*time, hour, day*) passer (on something sur quelque chose, doing à faire).

spent *see* spend.

sphere *noun* sphère *f*.

spice

1 *noun* épice *f*.

2 *verb* épicer.

spicy *adjective* (*food*) épicé.

spider *noun* araignée *f*; s.'s web toile *f* d'araignée.

spike *noun* pointe *f*.

spill *verb*

1 (*liquid*) répandre, renverser.

2 (*of liquid*) se répandre, se renverser (on, over sur).

spill out *verb*

1 (*empty*) vider (*café, verre etc*).

2 (*of coffee etc*) se renverser.

spill over *verb* déborder.

spilt *see* spill.

spin *verb* (*wheel etc*) faire tourner; (*washing*) essorer.

spin (round) *verb* (*of dancer, wheel etc*) tourner.

spinach *noun* (*food*) épinards *mpl*.

spine *noun* (*of back*) colonne *f* vertébrale.

spiral *noun* spirale *f*.

spire *noun* flèche *f*.

spirits *plural noun* (*drinks*) alcool *m*.

spit
1 *verb* cracher.
2 *noun* (*for meat*) broche *f*.

spite *noun* in s. of malgré.

spiteful *adjective* méchant.

splash
1 *verb* éclabousser (**with** de, **over** sur).
2 *noun* (*mark*) éclaboussure *f*.

splash (about) *verb* (*in river, mud*) patauger; (*in bath*) barboter.

splendid *adjective* splendide.

splinter *noun* (*in finger*) écharde *f*.

split
1 *noun* fente *f*; (*tear*) déchirure *f*.
2 *verb* (*break apart*) fendre; (*tear*) déchirer.

split (up) *verb*
1 (*group*) diviser; (*money, work*) partager (**between** entre).
2 (*of group*) se diviser (**into** en); (*because of disagreement*) se séparer.

spoil *verb* gâter; (*damage, ruin*) abîmer; (*child, dog etc*) gâter.

spoilt *see* spoil.

spoke *noun* (*of wheel*) rayon *m*.

spoke , spoken *see* speak.

spokesman *noun* porte-parole *m invariable* (**for, of** de).

sponge *noun* éponge *f*.

sponge bag *noun* trousse *f* de toilette.

sponge cake *noun* gâteau *m* de Savoie.

sponge down *verb* to s. somebody/something down laver quelqu'un/quelque chose à l'éponge.

spontaneous *adjective* spontané.

spool *noun* bobine *f*.

spoon *noun* cuillère *f*.

spoonful *noun* cuillerée *f*.

sport *noun* sport *m*; **to do s.** faire du sport; **sports club** club *m* sportif; **sports car/jacket/ground** voiture *f*/veste *f*/terrain *m* de sport.

sportsman *noun* sportif *m*.

sportswoman *noun* sportive *f*.

spot [1] *noun* (*stain, mark*) tache *f*; (*dot*) point *m*; (*pimple*) bouton *m*; (*place*) endroit *m*; **on the s.** sur place.

spot [2] *verb* (*notice*) apercevoir.

spotless *adjective* (*clean*) impeccable.

spotlight *noun* (*in theatre etc*) projecteur *m*; (*for photography*) spot *m*.

spotted *adjective* (*animal*) tacheté.

spout *noun* (*of teapot etc*) bec *m*.

sprain
1 *noun* foulure *f*.
2 *verb* to s. one's ankle/wrist se fouler la cheville/le poignet.

sprang *see* spring.

spray
1 *noun* (*can*) bombe *f*; **hair s.** laque *f* à cheveux.
2 *verb* (*liquid, surface*) vaporiser; (*plant*) arroser; (*car*) peindre à la bombe.

spread
1 *verb* (*stretch, open out*) étendre; (*legs, fingers*) écarter; (*distribute*) répandre (**over** sur); (*paint, payment, visits*) étaler; (*news, germs*) propager.
2 *verb* (*of fire*) s'étendre; (*of news, epidemic*) se propager.
3 *noun* (*paste*) pâte *f* (à tartiner); **cheese s.** fromage *m* à tartiner.

spread out *verb*
1 étendre; écarter; répandre;

étaler.

2 (*of people*) se disperser.

spring [1]

1 *noun* (*metal device*) ressort *m*.

2 *verb* (*leap*) bondir.

spring [2] *noun* (*season*) printemps *m*; **in (the) s.** au printemps.

spring [3] *noun* (*of water*) source *f*.

springboard *noun* tremplin *m*.

spring onion *noun* oignon *m* vert.

springtime *noun* printemps *m*.

sprinkle *verb* (*sand etc*) répandre (**on, over** sur); **to s. with water, s. water on** asperger d'eau; **to s. with** (*sugar, salt, flour*) saupoudrer de.

sprinkler *noun* (*in garden*) arroseur *m*.

sprout *noun* (Brussels) **s.** chou *m* (*plural* choux) de Bruxelles.

sprung *see* spring.

spun *see* spin.

spur *noun* (*of horse rider*) éperon *m*.

spurt (out) *verb* (*of liquid*) jaillir.

spy *noun* espion, -onne *m or f*.

spying *noun* espionnage *m*.

spy on *verb* espionner.

square

1 *noun* carré *m*; (*in town*) place *f*.

2 *adjective* carré; (*meal*) solide.

squash

1 *verb* (*crush*) écraser; (*squeeze*) serrer.

2 *noun* (*game*) squash *m*; **lemon/ orange s.** sirop *m* de citron/ d'orange; (*diluted*) citronnade *f*/ orangeade *f*.

squat (down) *verb* s'accroupir.

squatting *adjective* accroupi.

squeak *verb* (*of door*) grincer; (*of shoe*) craquer.

squeal

1 *verb* pousser des cris aigus.

2 *noun* cri *m* aigu.

squeeze *verb*

1 (*press*) presser; (*hand, arm*) serrer.

2 (*force oneself*) se glisser (**through/into/***etc* par/dans/ *etc*).

squeeze (out) *verb* (*juice etc*) faire sortir (**from** de).

squeeze in *verb* (*of person*) trouver un peu de place.

squeeze into *verb* **to s. something into something** faire rentrer quelque chose dans quelque chose.

squeeze up *verb* se serrer (**against** contre).

squint

1 *noun* **to have a s.** loucher.

2 *verb* loucher; (*in the sunlight etc*) plisser les yeux.

squirrel *noun* écureuil *m*.

squirt *verb*

1 (*liquid*) faire gicler.

2 (*of liquid*) gicler.

stab *verb* (*with knife*) poignarder.

stable [1] *adjective* stable.

stable [2] *noun* écurie *f*.

stack *noun* (*heap*) tas *m*; **stacks of** *Familiar* un *or* des tas de.

stack (up) *verb* entasser.

stadium *noun* stade *m*.

staff *noun* personnel *m*; (*of school*) professeurs *mpl*; (*of army*) état-major *m*; **s. room** (*of school*) salle *f* des professeurs.

stag *noun* cerf *m*.

stage [1]

1 *noun* (*platform*) scène *f*.

2 *verb* (*play*) monter.

stage [2] *noun* (*phase, of journey*) étape *f*.

stagecoach noun diligence f.

stagger verb chanceler.

stain

1 verb (to mark) tacher (with de).

2 noun tache f.

stained glass window noun vitrail m (plural vitraux).

stainless steel adjective (knife etc) en inox.

stain remover noun détachant m.

staircase noun escalier m.

stairs plural noun escalier m.

stake noun (post) pieu m.

stale adjective (bread etc) rassis (f rassie).

stalk noun (of plant) tige f.

stall

1 noun (in market) étal m (plural étals); (for newspapers, flowers) kiosque m.

2 verb (of car engine) caler.

stammer

1 verb bégayer.

2 noun to have a s. être bègue.

stamp

1 noun (for postage, instrument) timbre m; (mark) cachet m.

2 verb (document) tamponner; (letter) timbrer; **stamped addressed envelope** enveloppe f timbrée à votre adresse.

3 verb to s. (one's feet) taper des pieds.

stamp collecting noun philatélie f.

stand

1 noun (support) support m; (at exhibition) stand m; (for spectators) tribune f; **news/flower s.** kiosque m à journaux/à fleurs.

2 verb (pain, person etc) supporter; (put) mettre (debout); **to s. a chance** avoir une chance.

3 verb être or se tenir (debout); (get up) se lever; (remain) rester (debout); (be situated) se trouver.

stand about or **around** verb traîner.

standard

1 noun norme f; (level) niveau m; **standards** (morals) principes mpl; **s. of living** niveau m de vie; **up to s.** (of work etc) au niveau.

2 adjective (model, size) standard invariable.

standard lamp noun lampadaire m.

stand aside verb s'écarter.

stand back verb reculer.

stand by verb rester là (sans rien faire); (be ready) être prêt; **to s. by somebody** rester fidèle à quelqu'un.

standby adjective (ticket) sans garantie.

stand for verb (mean) signifier, représenter; (put up with) supporter.

stand in for verb remplacer.

standing adjective debout invariable.

stand out verb ressortir (against sur).

standpoint noun point m de vue.

standstill noun **to bring to a s.** immobiliser; **to come to a s.** s'immobiliser.

stand up verb

1 **to s. something up** mettre quelque chose debout; **to s. somebody up** Familiar poser un lapin à quelqu'un.

2 (of person) se lever.

stand up for verb défendre.

stand up to verb **to s. up to something** résister à quelque chose; **to s. up to somebody**

tenir tête à quelqu'un.

stank *see* **stink**.

staple
1 *noun* (*for paper etc*) agrafe *f*.
2 *verb* agrafer.

stapler *noun* agrafeuse *f*.

star
1 *noun* étoile *f*; (*person*) vedette *f*;
four-s. (*petrol*) du super.
2 *verb* (*of actor*) être la vedette
(**in** de).
3 *verb* (*of film*) avoir pour
vedette.

stare
1 *noun* regard *m* (fixe).
2 *verb* **to s. at** fixer (du regard).

start [1]
1 *noun* commencement *m*, début
m; (*of race*) départ *m*; (*lead*)
avance *f* (**on** sur); **to make a s.**
commencer.
2 *verb* commencer (**with** something par quelque chose, **by**
doing par faire); **to s. doing** *or*
to do commencer à faire; **to s.**
on something commencer
quelque chose; **starting from**
(*price etc*) à partir de.

start [2] *verb* (*jump*) sursauter.

start (off *or* **out)** *verb* partir
(**for** pour).

start (up) *verb*
1 (*engine, vehicle*) mettre en
marche; (*business*) fonder.
2 (*of engine, vehicle*) démarrer.

starter *noun* (*in vehicle*) démarreur *m*; (*course of meal*) hors-
d'œuvre *invariable m*, entrée *f*;
(*soup*) potage *m*.

startle *verb* (*make jump*) faire
sursauter.

starvation *noun* faim *f*.

starve *verb* souffrir de la faim;
(*die*) mourir de faim; **I'm star-**
ving! *Familiar* je meurs de faim!

state [1] *noun* (*condition*) état *m*; **S.**
(*nation etc*) État *m*; **the States**
Familiar les États-Unis *mpl*.

state [2] *verb* déclarer (**that** que);
(*time, date*) fixer.

statement *noun* déclaration *f*;
(**bank**) **s.** relevé *m* de compte.

statesman *noun* homme *m*
d'État.

station *noun* (*for trains*) gare *f*;
(*for the underground*) station *f*;
(**police**) **s.** commissariat *m* (de
police); **bus** *or* **coach s.** gare *f*
routière; **radio s.** station *f* de
radio; **service** *or* **petrol s.**
station-service *f*.

stationary *adjective* (*vehicle*) à
l'arrêt.

stationer's (shop) *noun*
papeterie *f*.

stationery *noun* articles *mpl* de
bureau.

stationmaster *noun* chef *m* de
gare.

statistic *noun* (*fact*) statistique *f*;
statistics les statistiques *fpl*.

statue *noun* statue *f*.

stay
1 *noun* (*visit*) séjour *m*.
2 *verb* rester; (*reside*) loger; (*visit*)
séjourner; **to s. put** ne pas
bouger.

stay away *verb* ne pas s'approcher (**from** de); **to s. away from**
(*school etc*) ne pas aller à.

stay in *verb* rester à la maison;
(*of nail, screw*) tenir.

stay out *verb* rester dehors; (*not
come home*) ne pas rentrer.

stay out of *verb* **to s. out of**
something (*not interfere in*) ne
pas se mêler de quelque chose.

stay up *verb* ne pas se coucher;
(*of fence etc*) tenir; **to s. up late**

se coucher tard.

steadily *adverb* (*gradually*) progressivement; (*regularly*) régulièrement; (*without stopping*) sans arrêt.

steady *adjective* stable; (*hand*) sûr; (*progress, speed*) régulier; **s. (on one's feet)** solide sur ses jambes.

steak *noun* steak *m*, bifteck *m*.

steal *verb* voler (**from somebody** à quelqu'un).

steam
 1 *noun* vapeur *f*; (*on glass*) buée *f*.
 2 *verb* (*food*) cuire à la vapeur.

steamroller *noun* rouleau *m* compresseur.

steel *noun* acier *m*.

steep *adjective* (*stairs, slope etc*) raide; (*hill, path*) escarpé; (*price*) excessif.

steeple *noun* clocher *m*.

steer *verb* (*vehicle, ship, person*) diriger (**towards** vers).

steering wheel *noun* volant *m*.

stem *noun* (*of plant*) tige *f*.

step
 1 *noun* pas *m*; (*of stairs*) marche *f*; (*on train, bus*) marchepied *m*; (*doorstep*) pas *m* de la porte; (*action*) mesure *f*; (**flight of**) **steps** escalier *m*; (*outdoors*) perron *m*; (**pair of**) **steps** (*ladder*) escabeau *m*.
 2 *verb* (*walk*) marcher (**on** sur).

step aside *verb* s'écarter.

step back *verb* reculer.

stepbrother *noun* demi-frère *m*.

stepdaughter *noun* belle-fille *f*.

stepfather *noun* beau-père *m*.

step forward *verb* faire un pas en avant.

step into /out of *verb* (*car etc*)

monter dans / descendre de.

stepladder *noun* escabeau *m*.

stepmother *noun* belle-mère *f*.

step over *verb* (*obstacle*) enjamber.

stepsister *noun* demi-sœur *f*.

stepson *noun* beau-fils *m*.

stereo
 1 *noun* (*record player*) chaîne *f* (stéréo *invariable*).
 2 *adjective* stéréo *invariable*.

sterilize *verb* stériliser.

stew *noun* ragoût *m*.

steward *noun* (*on plane, ship*) steward *m*.

stewardess *noun* hôtesse *f*.

stewed fruit *noun* compote *f*.

stick [1] *noun* bâton *m*; (*for walking*) canne *f*.

stick [2] *verb* coller (**to** à); (*of food in pan*) attacher (**to** dans); (*of drawer etc*) se coincer, être coincé; (*put*) *Familiar* mettre, fourrer; **to s. something into something** fourrer quelque chose dans quelque chose.

stick down *noun* (*envelope*) coller.

sticker *noun* autocollant *m*.

sticking plaster *noun* sparadrap *m*.

stick on *verb* (*stamp*) coller.

stick out *verb*
 1 (*tongue*) tirer.
 2 (*of petticoat etc*) dépasser.

stick up *verb* (*notice*) afficher.

stick up for *verb* défendre.

sticky *adjective* collant; (*label*) adhésif.

stiff *adjective* raide; (*leg etc*) ankylosé; (*brush*) dur; **to have a s. neck** avoir le torticolis; **to feel s.** être courbaturé.

stifle *verb* **it's stifling** on étouffe.

still [1] *adverb* encore, toujours; (*even*) encore; (*nevertheless*) tout de même.

still [2] *adjective* (*not moving*) immobile; (*calm*) calme; **to keep** *or* **stand s.** rester tranquille.

sting
  1 *verb* (*of insect, ointment etc*) piquer.
  2 *noun* piqûre *f*.

stink *verb* puer; **to s. of smoke/** *etc* empester la fumée/*etc*.

stink out *verb* (*room*) empester.

stir *verb* (*coffee, leaves etc*) remuer.

stirrup *noun* étrier *m*.

stitch *noun* point *m*; (*in knitting*) maille *f*; (*in wound*) point *m* de suture.

stitch (up) *verb* (*sew*) coudre; (*repair*) recoudre.

stock
  1 *noun* (*supply*) provision *f*; (*soup*) bouillon *m*; **stocks and shares** valeurs *fpl* (boursières); **in s.** en magasin, en stock; **out of s.** épuisé; **the S. Exchange** *or* **Market** la Bourse.
  2 *verb* (*sell*) vendre.

stock (up) *verb* (*shop, larder*) approvisionner.

stocking *noun* bas *m*.

stock up *verb* s'approvisionner (**with** de, en).

stole , stolen *see* **steal.**

stomach *noun* (*for digestion*) estomac *m*; (*front of body*) ventre *m*.

stomachache *noun* mal *m* de ventre; **to have a s.** avoir mal au ventre.

stone *noun* pierre *f*; (*pebble*) caillou *m* (*plural* cailloux); (*in fruit*)

noyau *m*; (*weight*) = 6,348 kg.

stood *see* **stand.**

stool *noun* tabouret *m*.

stop
  1 *noun* (*place, halt*) arrêt *m*; (*for plane, ship*) escale *f*; **bus s.** arrêt *m* d'autobus; **to put a s. to something** mettre fin à quelque chose; **s. sign** (*on road*) stop *m*.
  2 *verb* arrêter; (*end*) mettre fin à; (*prevent*) empêcher (**from doing** de faire).
  3 *verb* (*of person, vehicle*) s'arrêter; (*of pain, conversation etc*) cesser; **to s. eating/***etc* s'arrêter de manger/*etc*; **to s. snowing/***etc* cesser de neiger/*etc*.

stop by *verb* passer (**some-body's** chez quelqu'un).

stoplight *noun* (*on vehicle*) stop *m*.

stop off *or* **over** *verb* (*on journey*) s'arrêter.

stopoff , stopover *noun* halte *f*.

stopper *noun* bouchon *m*.

stop up *verb* (*sink, pipe etc*) boucher.

stopwatch *noun* chronomètre *m*.

store *noun* (*supply*) provision *f*; (*warehouse*) entrepôt *m*; (*shop*) grand magasin *m*.

store (away) *verb* (*furniture*) entreposer.

store (up) *verb* (*in warehouse etc*) stocker; (*for future use*) mettre en réserve.

storeroom *noun* (*in house*) débarras *m*; (*in office, shop*) réserve *f*.

storey *noun* étage *m*.

stork *noun* cigogne *f*.

storm *noun* tempête *f*; (*thunder-*

storm) orage *m*.

stormy *adjective* orageux.

story *noun* histoire *f*; (*newspaper article*) article *m*; (*plot*) intrigue *f*; **short s.** nouvelle *f*.

stove *noun* (*for cooking*) cuisinière *f*; (*portable*) réchaud *m*; (*for heating*) poêle *m*.

straight
  1 *adjective* droit; (*hair*) raide; (*route*) direct; (*tidy*) en ordre; (*frank*) franc (*f* franche).
  2 *adverb* (*to walk etc*) droit; (*directly*) tout droit; (*to drink whisky etc*) sec; **s. away** tout de suite; **s. ahead** *or* **on** tout droit.

straighten (up) *verb* (*tie, hair, room*) arranger.

straightforward *adjective* (*easy, clear*) simple.

strain
  1 *noun* (*tiredness*) fatigue *f*; (*mental*) tension *f* nerveuse.
  2 *verb* (*eyes*) fatiguer; (*voice*) forcer; **to s. one's back** se faire mal au dos.

strainer *noun* passoire *f*.

strange *adjective* (*odd*) étrange; (*unknown*) inconnu.

stranger *noun* (*unknown*) inconnu, -ue *m or f*; (*person from outside*) étranger, -ère *m or f*.

strangle *verb* étrangler.

strap *noun* sangle *f*, courroie *f*; (*on dress*) bretelle *f*; (*on watch*) bracelet *m*; (*on sandal*) lanière *f*.

strap (down *or* **in)** *verb* attacher (avec une courroie).

straw *noun* paille *f*; **a (drinking) s.** une paille.

strawberry
  1 *noun* fraise *f*.
  2 *adjective* (*ice cream*) à la fraise; (*jam*) de fraises; (*tart*) aux fraises.

streak *noun* (*line*) raie *f*; (*of colour*) strie *f*; (*of paint*) traînée *f*.

stream *noun* (*brook*) ruisseau *m*; (*flow*) flot *m*.

street *noun* rue *f*; **s. door** porte *f* d'entrée.

street lamp *or* **light** *noun* réverbère *m*.

street map *or* **plan** *noun* plan *m* des rues.

strength *noun* force *f*; (*health, energy*) forces *fpl*; (*of wood etc*) solidité *f*.

strengthen *verb* renforcer.

stress
  1 *noun* (*mental*) stress *m*; (*emphasis*) & *Grammar* accent *m*; **under s.** stressé.
  2 *verb* insister sur; (*word*) accentuer; **to s. that** souligner que.

stretch
  1 *verb* (*rope, neck*) tendre; (*shoe, rubber*) étirer; **to s. one's legs** se dégourdir les jambes.
  2 *verb* (*of person, elastic*) s'étirer.
  3 *noun* (*area*) étendue *f*.

stretch (out) *verb*
  1 (*arm, leg*) étendre; **to s. (out) one's arm** (*reach out*) tendre le bras (**to take** pour prendre).
  2 (*of plain etc*) s'étendre.

stretcher *noun* brancard *m*.

strict *adjective* strict.

strictly *adverb* strictement; **s. forbidden** formellement interdit.

strictness *noun* sévérité *f*.

stride *noun* (grand) pas *m*, enjambée *f*.

stridden *see* **stride** along/out.

stride along /out/*etc verb* avancer / sortir /*etc* à grands pas.

strike [1] *verb* (*hit, impress*) frapper; (*collide with*) heurter; (*match*) frotter; (*of clock*) sonner (*l'heure*); **it strikes me that** il me semble que (+ *indicative*).

strike² *noun* (*of workers*) grève *f*; **to go (out) on s.** se mettre en grève (**for** pour obtenir).

striker *noun* (*worker*) gréviste *m or f*.

striking *adjective* (*impressive*) frappant.

string *noun* ficelle *f*; (*of anorak, apron*) cordon *m*; (*of violin, racket etc*) corde *f*; (*of pearls*) collier *m*.

strip *noun* (*piece*) bande *f*; (**thin**) **s.** (*of metal etc*) lamelle *f*.

strip (off) *verb* se déshabiller.

stripe *noun* rayure *f*.

striped *adjective* rayé.

strode *see* **stride along/out**.

stroke
1 *noun* (*movement*) coup *m*; (*illness*) coup *m* de sang; (**swimming**) **s.** nage *f*; **a s. of luck** un coup de chance.
2 *verb* (*beard, cat etc*) caresser.

stroll
1 *noun* promenade *f*.
2 *verb* se promener.

strong *adjective* fort; (*shoes, chair etc*) solide.

struck *see* **strike**.

structure *noun* structure *f*; (*building*) construction *f*.

struggle
1 *noun* (*fight*) lutte *f* (**to do** pour faire); **to have a s. doing** *or* **to do** avoir du mal à faire.
2 *verb* (*fight*) lutter, se battre (**with** avec); (*move about wildly*) se débattre; **to s. to do** s'efforcer de faire.

stub *noun* (*of cigarette etc*) bout *m*; (*of ticket, cheque*) talon *m*.

stubborn *adjective* (*person*)

entêté.

stubbornness *noun* entêtement *m*.

stub out *verb* (*cigarette*) écraser.

stuck
1 *see* **stick²**.
2 *adjective* (*caught, jammed*) coincé; **I'm s.** (*unable to carry on*) je ne sais pas quoi faire *or* dire *etc*.

stud *noun* (*for collar*) bouton *m* de col; (*off football boot etc*) crampon *m*.

student
1 *noun* étudiant, -ante *m or f*; **music/etc s.** étudiant, -ante en musique/*etc*.
2 *adjective* (*life, protest*) étudiant; (*restaurant, residence*) universitaire.

studio *noun* (*of cinema etc*) studio *m*; **s. flat** studio *m*.

study
1 *noun* étude *f*; (*office*) bureau *m*.
2 *verb* étudier; **to s. to be a doctor/etc** faire des études pour devenir médecin/*etc*; **to s. for an exam** préparer un examen.

stuff
1 *noun* (*thing*) truc *m*; (*things*) trucs *mpl*; (*possessions*) affaires *fpl*; **it's good s.** c'est bon.
2 *verb* (*fill*) bourrer (**with** de); (*cushion etc*) rembourrer (**with** avec); (*put*) fourrer (**into** dans); (*chicken etc*) farcir.

stuffed (up) *adjective* (*nose*) bouché.

stuffing *noun* (*for chicken etc*) farce *f*.

stuffy *adjective* (*room etc*) mal aéré; **it smells s.** ça sent le renfermé.

stumble *verb* trébucher (**over** sur).

stump noun (of tree) souche f.

stun verb (with punch etc) étourdir.

stung see sting.

stunk see stink.

stunned adjective (amazed) stupéfait (by par).

stupid adjective stupide; **a s. thing** une stupidité; **s. fool** idiot, -ote m or f.

stupidity noun stupidité f.

sturdy adjective robuste.

stutter
1 verb bégayer.
2 noun **to have a s.** être bègue.

sty noun (for pigs) porcherie f.

style noun style m; (fashion) mode f; (design of dress etc) modèle m; (of hair) coiffure f.

stylish adjective chic invariable.

subject noun (matter) & Grammar sujet m; (at school, university) matière f; (citizen) ressortissant, -ante m or f.

subjunctive noun Grammar subjonctif m.

submarine noun sous-marin m.

subscriber noun abonné, -ée m or f.

subscribe to verb (take out subscription) s'abonner à; (be a subscriber) être abonné à.

subscription noun (to newspaper etc) abonnement m.

subside verb (of ground) s'affaisser.

substance noun substance f.

substantial adjective important; (meal) copieux.

substitute noun produit m de remplacement; (person) remplaçant, -ante m or f (for de).

subtitle noun sous-titre m.

subtle adjective subtil.

subtract verb soustraire (from de).

subtraction noun soustraction f.

suburb noun banlieue f; **the suburbs** la banlieue.

suburban adjective (train etc) de banlieue.

subway noun (underpass) passage m souterrain; (underground railway) métro m.

succeed verb réussir (in doing à faire, in something dans quelque chose).

success noun succès m, réussite f; **he was a s.** il a eu du succès; **it was a s.** c'était réussi.

successful adjective (effort etc) couronné de succès; (firm) prospère; (candidate in exam) admis; (writer, film etc) à succès; **to be s.** réussir (in dans, in an exam à un examen, in doing à faire).

successfully adverb avec succès.

such
1 adjective tel (f telle); **s. a car/etc** une telle voiture/etc; **s. happiness/etc** tant de bonheur/etc; **s. as** comme, tel que.
2 adverb (so very) si; (in comparisons) aussi; **s. a large helping** une si grosse portion; **s. a kind woman as you** une femme aussi gentille que vous.

suck verb sucer; (of baby) téter.

suck (up) verb (with straw) aspirer.

sudden adjective soudain; **all of a s.** tout à coup.

suddenly adverb subitement.

suds plural noun (soap) s. mousse f (de savon).

suede
1 noun daim m.

2 *adjective* de daim.

suffer *verb* souffrir (from de); (*loss*) subir; (*pain*) ressentir.

suffering *noun* souffrance(s) *f(pl)*.

sufficient *adjective* (*quantity*) suffisant; **s. money**/*etc* suffisamment d'argent/*etc*.

sufficiently *adverb* suffisamment.

suffix *noun* suffixe *m*.

suffocate *verb* étouffer.

sugar
  1 *noun* sucre *m*; **granulated**/ **lump s.** sucre cristallisé/en morceaux.
  2 *verb* sucrer.

sugar bowl *noun* sucrier *m*.

suggest *verb* (*propose*) suggérer, proposer (**to** à, **doing** de faire, **that** que (+ *subjunctive*)); (*imply*) suggérer.

suggestion *noun* suggestion *f*.

suicide *noun* suicide *m*; **to commit s.** se suicider.

suit [1] *noun* (*man's*) costume *m*; (*woman's*) tailleur *m*; *Cards* couleur *f*; **flying**/**diving**/**ski s.** combinaison *f* de vol/plongée/ski.

suit [2] *verb* (*be acceptable to*) convenir à; (*of dress, colour etc*) aller (bien) à; **it suits me to stay** ça m'arrange de rester; **suited to** (*job, activity*) fait pour.

suitable *adjective* qui convient (**for** à), convenable (**for** pour); (*dress, colour*) qui va (bien).

suitcase *noun* valise *f*.

suite *noun* (*rooms*) suite *f*; (*furniture*) mobilier *m*.

sulk *verb* bouder.

sultana *noun* raisin *m* sec.

sum *noun* (*amount of money, total*) somme *f*; (*calculation*) calcul *m*; **sums** le calcul.

summarize *verb* résumer.

summary *noun* résumé *m*.

summer
  1 *noun* été *m*; **in (the) s.** en été.
  2 *adjective* d'été; **s. holidays** grandes vacances *fpl*.

summertime *noun* été *m*.

sum up *verb* (*facts etc*) résumer.

sun *noun* soleil *m*; **in the s.** au soleil; **the sun is shining** il fait (du) soleil; **s. lotion**/**oil** crème *f*/ huile *f* solaire.

sunbathe *verb* prendre un bain de soleil, se faire bronzer.

sunburn *noun* coup *m* de soleil.

sunburnt *adjective* (*tanned*) bronzé; (*burnt*) brûlé par le soleil.

sundae *noun* glace *f* aux fruits.

Sunday *noun* dimanche *m*.

sunglasses *plural noun* lunettes *fpl* de soleil.

sunk *see* **sink**.

sunlamp *noun* lampe *f* à bronzer.

sunlight *noun* (*lumière f du*) soleil *m*.

sunny *adjective* (*day etc*) ensoleillé; **it's s.** il fait (du) soleil; **s. periods** *or* **intervals** éclaircies *fpl*.

sunrise *noun* lever *m* du soleil.

sunroof *noun* toit *m* ouvrant.

sunset *noun* coucher *m* du soleil.

sunshade *noun* (*over table, on beach*) parasol *m*.

sunshine *noun* soleil *m*.

sunstroke *noun* insolation *f*.

suntan *noun* bronzage *m*; **s. lotion**/**oil** crème *f*/huile *f* solaire.

suntanned *adjective* bronzé.

super *adjective Familiar* sensationnel.

superb *adjective* superbe.

superficial *adjective* superficiel.

superior *adjective* supérieur (**to** à).

superiority *noun* supériorité *f*.

supermarket *noun* supermarché *m*.

superstition *noun* superstition *f*.

superstitious *adjective* superstitieux.

supervise *verb* (*person*, *work*) surveiller; (*office*, *research*) diriger.

supervisor *noun* surveillant, -ante *m or f*; (*in office*) chef *m* de service; (*in store*) chef *m* de rayon.

supper *noun* dîner *m*, souper *m*; (*late-night*) souper *m*; **to have s.** dîner, souper.

supple *adjective* souple.

supply
  1 *verb* fournir; (*with electricity*, *gas*, *water*) alimenter (**with** en); (*equip*) équiper (**with** de); **to s. somebody with something, s. something to somebody** fournir quelque chose à quelqu'un.
  2 *noun* (*stock*) provision *f*; (*food*) **supplies** vivres *mpl*.

support
  1 *verb* (*bear weight of*, *help*, *encourage*) soutenir; (*be in favour of*) être en faveur de; (*family etc*) subvenir aux besoins de.
  2 *noun* (*help*) soutien *m*; (*object*) support *m*.

supporter *noun* partisan *m*; (*in sport*) supporter *m*.

suppose *verb* supposer (**that** que); **I'm supposed to work** *or* **be working** je suis censé travailler; **he's supposed to be rich** on le dit riche; **I s. (so)** je pense; **you're tired, I s.** vous êtes fati-gué, je suppose; **s. we go** (*suggestion*) et si nous partions; **s.** *or* **supposing you're right** supposons que tu aies raison.

sure *adjective* sûr (**of** de, **that** que); **she's s. to accept** il est sûr qu'elle acceptera; **to make s. of something** s'assurer de quelque chose; **be s. to do it!** ne manquez pas de le faire!

surely *adverb* sûrement; **s. he didn't refuse?** (*I hope*) il n'a tout de même pas refusé.

surface *noun* surface *f*; **s. area** superficie *f*; **s. mail** courrier *m* par voie(s) de surface.

surfboard *noun* planche *f* (de surf).

surfing *noun* surf *m*; **to go s.** faire du surf.

surgeon *noun* chirurgien *m*.

surgery *noun* (*doctor's office*) cabinet *m*; **to have s.** avoir une opération (**for** pour).

surname *noun* nom *m* de famille.

surprise
  1 *noun* surprise *f*; **to take somebody by s.** prendre quelqu'un au dépourvu.
  2 *adjective* (*visit etc*) inattendu.
  3 *verb* (*astonish*) étonner, surprendre.

surprised *adjective* surpris (**that** que (+ *subjunctive*), **at something** de quelque chose); **I'm s. to see you** je suis surpris de te voir.

surprising *adjective* surprenant.

surrender *verb* se rendre (**to** à).

surround *verb* entourer (**with** de); (*of army*, *police*) encercler; **surrounded by** entouré de.

surrounding *adjective* environnant.

surroundings *plural noun* environs *mpl*; (*setting*) cadre *m*.

survey *noun* enquête *f*; (*of opinion*) sondage *m*.

surveyor *noun* (*of land*) géomètre *m*.

survive *verb*
1 (*illness, accident*) survivre.
2 (*of person*) survivre à.

survivor *noun* survivant, -ante *m* or *f*.

suspect
1 *noun* suspect, -ecte *m* or *f*.
2 *verb* soupçonner (**that** que, **of something** de quelque chose, **of doing** d'avoir fait).

suspend *verb* (*postpone, dismiss*) suspendre; (*pupil*) renvoyer.

suspense *noun* (*in book etc*) suspense *m*.

suspension *noun* (*of vehicle*) suspension *f*.

suspicion *noun* soupçon *m*.

suspicious *adjective* (*person*) méfiant; (*behaviour*) suspect; **s.(-looking)** suspect; **to be s. of** se méfier de.

swallow[1] *verb* avaler.

swallow[2] *noun* hirondelle *f*.

swallow down *verb* **to s. something down** avaler quelque chose.

swam *see* **swim**.

swamp *noun* marécage *m*.

swan *noun* cygne *m*.

swap
1 *noun* échange *m*.
2 *verb* échanger (**for** contre); **to s. seats** changer de place.

swarm *noun* (*of bees etc*) essaim *m*.

sway *verb* se balancer.

swear *verb* jurer (**at** contre, **to do** de faire, **that** que).

swearword *noun* gros mot *m*.

sweat
1 *noun* sueur *f*.
2 *verb* transpirer, suer; **I'm sweating** je suis en sueur.

sweater *noun* pull *m*.

sweat shirt *noun* sweat-shirt *m*.

Swede *noun* Suédois, -oise *m* or *f*.

Sweden *noun* la Suède *f*.

Swedish
1 *adjective* suédois.
2 *noun* (*language*) suédois *m*.

sweep *verb* (*with broom*) balayer; (*chimney*) ramoner.

sweep away *verb* (*leaves etc*) balayer; (*carry off*) emporter.

sweep out *verb* (*room etc*) balayer.

sweep up *verb* balayer.

sweet
1 *adjective* (*not sour*) doux (*f* douce); (*tea, coffee etc*) sucré; (*child, house, cat*) mignon (*f* mignonne); (*kind*) aimable.
2 *noun* (*candy*) bonbon *m*; (*dessert*) dessert *m*.

sweet corn *noun* maïs *m*.

sweeten *verb* (*tea etc*) sucrer.

sweetly *adverb* (*kindly*) aimablement; (*agreeably*) agréablement.

sweet shop *noun* confiserie *f*.

swell (up) *verb* (*of hand, leg etc*) enfler; (*of wood, dough*) gonfler.

swelling *noun* enflure *f*.

swept *see* **sweep**.

swerve *verb* (*of vehicle*) faire une embardée.

swim
1 *noun* **to go for a s.** se baigner.
2 *verb* nager; (*as sport*) faire de la natation; **to go swimming** aller nager.

swimmer *noun* nageur, -euse *m* or *f*.

swimming *noun* natation *f*.

swimming costume *noun* maillot *m* de bain.

swimming pool *noun* piscine *f*.

swimming trunks *noun* slip *m* de bain.

swimsuit *noun* maillot *m* de bain.

swing
1 *noun* (*in playground etc*) balançoire *f*.
2 *verb* (*move to and fro*) se balancer.
3 *verb* (*arms etc*) balancer.

swing round *verb* (*turn*) virer; (*of person*) se retourner (vivement).

Swiss
1 *adjective* suisse.
2 *invariable noun* Suisse *m*, Suissesse *f*; the S. les Suisses *mpl*.

switch
1 *noun* (*electric*) bouton *m* (électrique).
2 *verb* (*money, employee*) transférer (**to** à); (*exchange*) échanger (**for** contre); **to s. places** *or* **seats** changer de place.

switch off *verb* (*lamp, gas etc*) éteindre; (*engine*) arrêter.

switch on *verb* (*lamp, gas etc*) mettre, allumer; (*engine*) mettre en marche.

switch over *verb* (*change TV channels*) changer de chaîne; **to s. over to something** passer à quelque chose.

Switzerland *noun* la Suisse *f*.

swollen *adjective* (*leg etc*) enflé; (*stomach*) gonflé.

swop = swap.

sword *noun* épée *f*.

swore , sworn *see* swear.

swum *see* swim.

swung *see* swing.

syllable *noun* syllabe *f*.

syllabus *noun* programme *m* (scolaire).

symbol *noun* symbole *m*.

symbolic *adjective* symbolique.

sympathetic *adjective* (*showing pity*) compatissant; (*understanding*) compréhensif.

sympathize *verb* I s. (**with you**) (*pity*) je suis désolé (pour vous); (*understanding*) je vous comprends.

sympathy *noun* (*pity*) compassion *f*; (*understanding*) compréhension *f*; (*when somebody dies*) condoléances *fpl*.

symphony *noun* symphonie *f*.

symptom *noun* symptôme *m*.

synagogue *noun* synagogue *f*.

synonym *noun* synonyme *m*.

Syria *noun* la Syrie *f*.

Syrian *adjective* & *noun* syrien, -ienne (*m or f*).

syringe *noun* seringue *f*.

syrup *noun* sirop *m*.

system *noun* système *m*; (*human body*) organisme *m*; (*order*) méthode *f*.

ta! *interjection Familiar* merci!

tab *noun* (*on garment*) étiquette *f*.

table *noun* (*furniture, list*) table *f*; **bedside t.** table *f* de nuit; **to lay** *or* **set/clear the t.** mettre/débarrasser la table.

tablecloth *noun* nappe *f*.

tablemat *noun* (*of cloth*) napperon *m*; (*hard*) dessous-de-plat *invariable m*.

tablespoon *noun* = cuillère *f* à soupe.

tablespoonful *noun* = cuillerée *f* à soupe.

tablet *noun* (*pill*) comprimé *m*.

tack *noun* (*nail*) petit clou *m*.

tackle *verb* (*problem etc*) s'attaquer à; *Rugby* plaquer; *Football* tacler.

tacky *adjective* (*in appearance*) moche; (*remark etc*) de mauvais goût.

tact *noun* tact *m*.

tactful *adjective* **to be t.** (*of person*) avoir du tact.

tactic *noun* **a t.** une tactique; **tactics** la tactique.

tag *noun* (*label*) étiquette *f*.

tail *noun* (*of animal etc*) queue *f*.

tailor *noun* tailleur *m*.

take *verb* prendre; (*prize*) remporter; (*exam*) passer; (*subtract*) soustraire (**from** de); (*tolerate*) supporter; **to t. something to somebody** (ap)porter quelque chose à quelqu'un; **to t. somebody somewhere** amener quelqu'un quelque part; **to t. somebody (out) to the theatre/etc** emmener quelqu'un au théâtre/etc; **to t. something with one**
emporter quelque chose; **to t. somebody home** ramener quelqu'un; **it takes courage/etc** il faut du courage/etc (**to do** pour faire); **I took an hour to do it** j'ai mis une heure à le faire; **to t. after somebody** ressembler à quelqu'un.

take along *verb* (*object*) emporter; (*person*) emmener.

take apart *verb* (*machine*) démonter.

take away *verb* (*thing*) emporter; (*person*) emmener; (*remove*) enlever; (*subtract*) soustraire (**from** de).

take-away
1 *adjective* (*meal*) à emporter.
2 *noun* (*shop*) restaurant *m* qui fait des plats à emporter; (*meal*) plat *m* à emporter.

take back *verb* reprendre; (*return*) rapporter; (*accompany*) ramener (**to** à).

take down *verb* (*object*) descendre; (*notes*) prendre.

take in *verb* (*chair, car etc*) rentrer; (*include*) inclure; (*understand*) comprendre; (*deceive*) *Familiar* rouler.

taken *adjective* (*seat*) pris; **to be t. ill** tomber malade.

take off *verb*
1 (*remove*) enlever; (*lead away*) emmener; (*subtract*) déduire (**from** de).
2 (*of aircraft*) décoller.

takeoff *noun* (*of aircraft*) décollage *m*.

take on *verb* (*work, staff, passenger*) prendre.

take out verb (from pocket etc) sortir; (stain) enlever; (tooth) arracher; (insurance) prendre.

take over verb (company etc) prendre la direction de; **to t. over somebody's job** remplacer quelqu'un; **to t. over (from somebody)** prendre la relève (de quelqu'un).

take round verb (thing) apporter (**to** à); (person) amener (**to** à); (visitor) faire visiter à.

take up verb (carry up) monter; (space, time) prendre; (hobby) se mettre à.

takings plural noun recette f.

tale noun (story) conte m; **to tell tales** Familiar rapporter.

talent noun talent m; **to have a t. for** avoir du talent pour.

talented adjective doué.

talk
1 noun propos mpl; (gossip) bavardage(s) m(pl); (conversation) conversation f; (lecture) exposé m (**on** sur); **talks** pourparlers mpl; **to have a t. with somebody** parler avec quelqu'un; **there's t. of** on parle de.
2 verb parler (**to** à; **with** avec; **about, of** de); **to t. nonsense** dire des bêtises; **to t. somebody into doing/out of doing** persuader quelqu'un de faire/de ne pas faire.

talkative adjective bavard.

talk over verb **to t. something over** discuter de quelque chose.

tall adjective (person) grand; (tree, house) haut; **how t. are you?** combien mesures-tu?

tambourine noun tambourin m.

tame
1 adjective (animal) apprivoisé.
2 verb apprivoiser.

tampon noun tampon m hygiénique.

tan
1 noun (suntan) bronzage m.
2 verb bronzer.

tangerine noun mandarine f.

tangled adjective enchevêtré.

tank noun (storing liquid or gas) réservoir m; (vehicle) char m; (fish) t. aquarium m.

tanker noun (oil) t. (ship) pétrolier m.

tap
1 noun (for water) robinet m; (blow) petit coup m.
2 verb (hit) frapper légèrement.

tape [1]
1 noun (of cloth, paper) ruban m; (sticky or adhesive) t. ruban m adhésif.
2 verb coller (avec du ruban adhésif).

tape [2]
1 noun (for recording) bande f; (cassette) cassette f.
2 verb enregistrer.

tape measure noun mètre m (à) ruban.

tape recorder noun magnétophone m.

tar noun goudron m.

target noun cible f; (objective) objectif m.

tarpaulin noun bâche f.

tart noun (open) tarte f; (with pastry on top) tourte f.

tartan noun écossais m; **t. tie/ jacket** cravate f/ veste f écossaise.

task noun travail m.

taste
1 noun goût m.
2 verb (eat, drink) goûter; (try) goûter à; (make out the taste of)

sentir (le goût de).
3 verb to t. of or like something avoir un goût de quelque chose; to t. delicious/etc avoir un goût délicieux / etc.

tasty adjective savoureux.

tattered adjective (clothes) en lambeaux.

tattoo
1 noun (on body) tatouage m.
2 verb tatouer.

taught see teach.

tax
1 noun taxe f, impôt m; (on income) impôts mpl.
2 verb (person) imposer; (goods) taxer.

taxable adjective imposable.

taxi noun taxi m; t. rank station f de taxis.

taxpayer noun contribuable m or f.

TB noun tuberculose f.

tea noun thé m; (snack) goûter m; to have t. prendre le thé; (snack) goûter; t. break pause-thé f; t. party thé m; t. set service m à thé.

teabag noun sachet m de thé.

teach verb
1 (subject) apprendre (somebody something quelque chose à quelqu'un, that que); (in school etc) enseigner (somebody something quelque chose à quelqu'un); to t. somebody (how) to do apprendre à quelqu'un à faire.
2 (of teacher) enseigner.

teacher noun professeur m; (in primary school) instituteur, -trice m or f.

teaching noun enseignement m; t. staff personnel m enseignant.

teacup noun tasse f à thé.

team noun équipe f.

team up verb faire équipe (with avec).

teapot noun théière f.

tear [1]
1 noun (rip) déchirure f.
2 verb déchirer.

tear [2] noun (in eye) larme f; in tears en larmes.

tear off or out verb (with force) arracher; (receipt, stamp etc) détacher.

tear up verb (letter etc) déchirer.

tease verb taquiner.

teaspoon noun petite cuillère f, cuillère f à café.

teaspoonful noun = cuillerée f à café.

teat noun (of bottle) tétine f.

teatime noun l'heure f du thé.

tea towel noun torchon m.

technical adjective technique.

technician noun technicien, -ienne m or f.

technique noun technique f.

technology noun technologie f.

teddy (bear) noun ours m (en peluche).

teenager noun adolescent, -ente m or f.

tee-shirt noun tee-shirt m.

teeth see tooth.

tele- prefix télé-.

telegram noun télégramme m.

telegraph pole noun poteau m télégraphique.

telephone
1 noun téléphone m; on the t. (speaking) au téléphone.
2 adjective (call, line etc) téléphonique; (number) de téléphone; t. booth, t. box cabine f téléphonique; t. directory annuaire m du

téléphone.

3 *verb* téléphoner.

4 *verb* to t. somebody téléphoner à quelqu'un.

telescope *noun* télescope *m*.

televise *verb* retransmettre à la télévision.

television *noun* télévision *f*; **on (the) t.** à la télévision; **t. set** téléviseur *m*.

tell *verb* dire (**somebody something** quelque chose à quelqu'un, **that** que); (*story*) raconter; (*distinguish*) distinguer (**from** de); (*know*) savoir; **to t. somebody to do** dire à quelqu'un de faire; **to t. the difference** voir la différence; **to t. of** *or* **about something/somebody** parler de quelque chose/quelqu'un.

teller *noun* (**bank**) **t.** guichetier, -ière *m or f*.

tell off *verb* to t. somebody off gronder quelqu'un.

telltale *noun* *Familiar* rapporteur, -euse *m or f*.

telly *noun* *Familiar* télé *f*.

temper *noun* to lose one's t. se mettre en colère; **in a bad t.** de mauvaise humeur.

temperature *noun* température *f*; **to have a t.** avoir de la température.

temple *noun* (*building*) temple *m*.

temporary *adjective* provisoire; (*job*) temporaire; (*secretary*) intérimaire.

tempt *verb* tenter; **tempted to do** tenté de faire.

temptation *noun* tentation *f*.

tempting *adjective* tentant.

ten *adjective* & *noun* dix (*m*).

tenant *noun* locataire *m or f*.

tend *verb* to t. to do avoir

tendance à faire.

tendency *noun* tendance *f* (**to do** à faire).

tender *adjective* (*soft, loving*) tendre; (*painful*) sensible.

tennis *noun* tennis *m*; **table t.** tennis *m* de table; **t. court** court *m* (de tennis).

tenpin bowling *noun* bowling *m*.

tense

1 *adjective* (*person, muscle, situation*) tendu.

2 *noun* (*of verb*) temps *m*.

tension *noun* tension *f*.

tent *noun* tente *f*.

tenth *adjective* & *noun* dixième (*m or f*).

term *noun* (*word*) terme *m*; (*period*) période *f*; (*of school year*) trimestre *m*; (*semester*) semestre *m*; **terms** (*conditions*) conditions *fpl*; (*prices*) prix *mpl*; **on good/ bad terms** en bons/mauvais termes (**with** avec).

terminal *noun* (**air**) **t.** aérogare *f*; (**computer**) **t.** terminal *m* (d'ordinateur).

terrace *noun* (*next to house etc*) terrasse *f*; (*houses*) maisons *fpl* en bande.

terraced house *noun* maison *f* attenante aux maisons voisines.

terrible *adjective* affreux.

terribly *adverb* (*badly, very*) affreusement.

terrific *adjective* *Familiar* (*excellent, very great*) formidable.

terrify *verb* terrifier; **to be terrified of** avoir très peur de.

terrifying *adjective* terrifiant.

territory *noun* territoire *m*.

terror *noun* terreur *f*.

terrorist *noun* & *adjective*

terroriste (*m or f*).

terrorize *verb* terroriser.

Terylene ® *noun* tergal ® *m*.

test
1 *verb* (*try*) essayer; (*product, machine*) tester; (*pupil*) interroger; (*of doctor*) examiner; (*analyse*) analyser.
2 *noun* essai *m*; (*of product*) test *m*; (*in school*) interrogation *f*, test *m*; (*by doctor*) examen *m*; (*of blood etc*) analyse *f*; **eye t.** examen *m* de la vue.

test tube *noun* éprouvette *f*.

text *noun* texte *m*.

textbook *noun* manuel *m* (scolaire).

textile *adjective & noun* textile (*m*).

Thai *adjective & noun* thaïlandais, -aise (*m or f*).

Thailand *noun* la Thaïlande *f*.

than *conjunction* que; **happier t.** plus heureux que; **more t. six** plus de six.

thank
1 *verb* remercier (**for something** de quelque chose, **for doing** d'avoir fait); **t. you!** merci!; **no, t. you!** (non) merci!
2 *noun* **thanks** remerciements *mpl*; **(many) thanks!** merci (beaucoup)!; **thanks to** (*because of*) grâce à.

thankful *adjective* reconnaissant (**for** de).

Thanksgiving (day) *noun American* jour *m* d'action de grâce(s).

that
1 *conjunction* que; **to say t.** dire que.
2 *relative pronoun* (*subject*) qui; (*object*) que; (*after preposition*) lequel, laquelle, *plural* les-

quel(le)s; **the boy t. left** le garçon qui est parti; **the book t. I read** le livre que j'ai lu; **the carpet t. I put it on** le tapis sur lequel je l'ai mis; **the house t. she told me about** la maison dont elle m'a parlé; **the day/moment t.** le jour/moment où.
3 *demonstrative adjective* (*plural* those) ce, cet (*before m noun beginning with a vowel or mute h*), cette; **t. girl** cette fille; (*as opposed to this girl*) cette fille-là; **t. one** celui-là *m*, celle-là *f*.
4 *demonstrative pronoun* (*plural* those) ça, cela; **give me t.** donne-moi ça; **t.'s right** c'est juste; **who's t.?** qui est-ce?; **t.'s the house** voilà la maison; **t. is (to say)** c'est-à-dire.
5 *adverb* (*so*) si; **not t. good** pas si bon; **it didn't cost t. much** ça n'était pas si cher que ça.

thaw
1 *noun* dégel *m*.
2 *verb* dégeler; (*of snow*) fondre; (*of food*) décongeler; **it's thawing** ça dégèle.
3 *verb* (*food*) (faire) décongeler.

the *definite article* le, l' (*before noun beginning with vowel or mute h*), la, *plural* les; **t. roof** le toit; **t. man** l'homme; **t. moon** la lune; **t. boxes** les boîtes.

theatre *noun* théâtre *m*.

theft *noun* vol *m*.

their *possessive adjective* leur, *plural* leurs.

theirs *possessive pronoun* le leur, la leur, *plural* les leurs; **this book is t.** ce livre est à eux *or* est le leur.

them *pronoun* les; (*after preposition*) eux *mpl*, elles *fpl*; **I see t.** je les vois; **I gave it to t.** je le leur ai donné; **I phoned t.** je leur ai téléphoné; **more than t.** plus qu'eux; **it's t.** c'est eux; **ten of t.** dix d'entre eux *or* elles; **all of t. came** tous sont venus, toutes sont venues; **I like all of t.** je les aime tous *or* toutes.

themselves *pronoun* eux-mêmes *mpl*, elles-mêmes *fpl*; *(reflexive)* se, s'; *(after prep etc)* eux *mpl*, elles *fpl*.

then
1 *adverb* *(at that time)* à cette époque-là; *(just a moment ago)* à ce moment-là; *(next)* ensuite; **from t.** on dès lors; **before t.** avant cela; **until t.** jusque-là.
2 *conjunction* *(therefore)* donc.

theory *noun* théorie *f*.

there *adverb* là; **(down** *or* **over) t.** là-bas; **on t.** là-dessus; **t. is, t. are** il y a; *(pointing)* voilà; **t. he is** le voilà; **that man t.** cet homme là-bas.

therefore *adverb* donc.

thermometer *noun* thermomètre *m*.

Thermos ® **(flask)** *noun* thermos ® *m or f*.

thermostat *noun* thermostat *m*.

these
1 *demonstrative adjective* *(singular* **this)** ces; **t. men** ces hommes; *(as opposed to those men)* ces hommes-ci; **t. ones** ceux-ci *mpl*, celles-ci *fpl*.
2 *demonstrative pronoun* *(singular* **this)** **t. are my friends** voici mes amis.

they *pronoun* ils *mpl*, elles *fpl*; *(stressed)* eux *mpl*, elles *fpl*.
1 *(people in general)* on; **t. say** on dit.

thick
1 *adjective* épais *(f* épaisse).
2 *adverb* *(to spread)* en couche

épaisse.

thicken *verb*
1 épaissir.
2 *(of fog etc)* s'épaissir; *(of cream etc)* épaissir.

thickly *adverb* *(to spread)* en couche épaisse.

thickness *noun* épaisseur *f*.

thief *noun* voleur, -euse *m or f*.

thigh *noun* cuisse *f*.

thimble *noun* dé *m* (à coudre).

thin
1 *adjective* *(slice, paper etc)* mince; *(person, leg)* maigre; *(soup)* peu épais *(f* peu épaisse).
2 *adverb* *(to spread)* en couche mince.

thin (down) *verb* *(paint etc)* diluer.

thing *noun* chose *f*; **one's things** *(belongings)* ses affaires *fpl*.

think *verb* penser **(about, of** à, **that** que); **to t. (carefully)** réfléchir **(about, of** à); **to t. of doing** penser à faire; **she doesn't t. much of it** ça ne lui dit pas grand-chose; **I t. so** je pense que oui; **what do you t. of him?** que penses-tu de lui?

think over *verb* **to t. something over** réfléchir à quelque chose.

think up *verb* inventer.

thinly *adverb* *(to spread)* en couche mince.

third
1 *adjective* troisième.
2 *noun* troisième *m or f*; **a t.** *(fraction)* un tiers.
3 *adverb* **to come t.** se classer troisième.

thirdly *adverb* troisièmement.

thirst *noun* soif *f*.

thirsty *adjective* **to be** *or* **feel t.** avoir soif; **to make somebody**

t. donner soif à quelqu'un.

thirteen *adjective & noun* treize (*m*).

thirteenth *adjective & noun* treizième (*m or f*).

thirtieth *adjective & noun* trentième (*m or f*).

thirty *adjective & noun* trente (*m*).

this
1 *demonstrative adjective* (*plural* these) ce, cet (*before m noun beginning with a vowel or mute h*), cette; t. **photo** cette photo; (*as opposed to that photo*) cette photo-ci; t. **one** celui-ci *m*, celle-ci *f*.
2 *demonstrative pronoun* (*plural* these) ceci; I'll take t. je prendrai ceci; t. **is** Paul voici Paul; (*on telephone*) c'est Paul à l'appareil.
3 *adverb* t. **high** (*pointing*) haut comme ceci; t. **far** jusqu'ici; I didn't think it would cost t. much je ne pensais pas que ça coûterait tant que ça.

thorn *noun* épine *f*.

thorough *adjective* (*careful*) minutieux; (*knowledge, examination*) approfondi; **to give something a t. washing**/*etc* laver/*etc* quelque chose à fond.

thoroughly *adverb* (*completely*) tout à fait; (*carefully*) avec minutie; (*to know, clean etc*) à fond.

those
1 *demonstrative adjective* (*singular* that) ces; t. **men** ces hommes; (*as opposed to these men*) ces hommes-là; t. **ones** ceux-là *mpl*, celles-là *fpl*.
2 *demonstrative pronoun* (*singular* that) t. **are my friends** voilà mes amis.

though
1 *conjunction* (**even**) t. bien que (+ *subjunctive*); **as** t. comme si.
2 *adverb* (*however*) cependant.

thought
1 *see* think.
2 *noun* pensée *f*; (**careful**) t. réflexion *f*.

thoughtful *adjective* (*considerate*) gentil (*f* gentille), attentionné.

thoughtless *adjective* (*towards others*) pas très gentil (*f* pas très gentille); (*absent-minded*) étourdi.

thousand *adjective & noun* mille *adjective & invariable m*; **a** t. **pages** mille pages; **two** t. **pages** deux mille pages; **thousands of** des milliers de.

thread
1 *noun* (*yarn*) fil *m*.
2 *verb* (*needle, beads*) enfiler.

threat *noun* menace *f*.

threaten *verb* menacer (**to do** de faire, **with something** de quelque chose).

threatening *adjective* menaçant.

three *adjective & noun* trois (*m*).

threw *see* throw.

thrill *noun* frisson *m*.

thrilled *adjective* ravi (**with something** de quelque chose, **to do** de faire).

thriller *noun* film *m or* roman *m* à suspense.

thrilling *adjective* passionnant.

thriving *adjective* prospère.

throat *noun* gorge *f*.

throne *noun* trône *m*.

through
1 *preposition* (*place*) à travers; (*window, door*) par; (*time*) pen-

dant; (*means*) par; **to go** *or* **get t.** (*forest etc*) traverser; (*hole etc*) passer par; (*wall etc*) passer à travers.

2 *adverb* à travers; **to let t.** laisser passer; **to be t.** (*finished*) avoir fini; **t. to** *or* **till** jusqu'à; **I'll put you t.** (**to him**) (*on phone*) je vous le passe.

throughout
1 *preposition* **t. the neighbourhood/etc** dans tout le quartier/etc; **t. the day/etc** pendant toute la journée/etc.
2 *adverb* (*everywhere*) partout; (*all the time*) tout le temps.

throw *verb* jeter (**to, at** à); (*party*) donner.

throw away *verb* (*unwanted object*) jeter.

thrown *see* throw.

throw out *verb* (*unwanted object*) jeter; (*expel*) mettre à la porte.

throw up *verb* (*vomit*) *Familiar* rendre.

thud *noun* bruit *m* sourd.

thug *noun* voyou *m*.

thumb *noun* pouce *m*.

thunder
1 *noun* tonnerre *m*.
2 *verb* tonner; **it's thundering** il tonne.

thunderstorm *noun* orage *m*.

Thursday *noun* jeudi *m*.

tick *noun* (*mark*) = croix *f*.

tick (off) *verb* (*on list etc*) cocher.

ticket *noun* billet *m*; (*for bus, underground, cloakroom*) ticket *m*; (*price*) **t.** étiquette *f*.

ticket collector *noun* contrôleur, -euse *m or f*.

ticket office *noun* guichet *m*.

tickle *verb* chatouiller.

ticklish *adjective* chatouilleux.

tide *noun* marée *f*.

tidily *adverb* (*to put away*) soigneusement.

tidy *adjective* (*place, toys etc*) bien rangé; (*clothes, hair*) soigné; (*person*) ordonné; (*in appearance*) soigné.

tidy (up *or* **away)** *verb* **to t. something up** *or* **away** ranger quelque chose.

tie
1 *noun* (*around neck*) cravate *f*; (*drawn match*) match *m* nul.
2 *verb* (*fasten*) attacher (**to** à); (*knot*) faire (**in** à); (*shoe*) lacer.

tie up *verb* attacher (**to** à); (*person*) ligoter.

tiger *noun* tigre *m*.

tight
1 *adjective* (*clothes fitting too closely*) (trop) étroit; (*drawer, lid*) dur; (*knot, screw*) serré; (*rope, wire*) raide.
2 *adverb* (*to hold, shut*) bien; (*to squeeze*) fort.

tighten (up) *verb* (*bolt etc*) (res)serrer.

tightly *adverb* (*to hold*) bien; (*to squeeze*) fort.

tights *plural noun* collant(s) *m(pl)*.

tile
1 *noun* (*on roof*) tuile *f*; (*on wall or floor*) carreau *m*.
2 *verb* (*wall, floor*) carreler.

till [1]
1 *preposition* jusqu'à; **t. then** jusque-là.
2 *conjunction* jusqu'à ce que (+ *subjunctive*).

till [2] *noun* caisse *f* (enregistreuse).

tilt *verb* pencher.

timber *noun* bois *m* (de construction).

time
1 *noun* temps *m*; (*point in time*) moment *m*; (*period in history*) époque *f*; (*on clock*) heure *f*; (*occasion*) fois *f*; **some/most of the t.** une partie/la plupart du temps; **all the t.** tout le temps; **in a year's t.** dans un an; **it's t. (to do)** il est temps (de faire); **to have a good t.** s'amuser; **in t.** (*to arrive*) à temps; **from t. to t.** de temps en temps; **what t. is it?** quelle heure est-il?; **on t.** à l'heure; **at the same t.** en même temps (**as** que); (*simultaneously*) à la fois; **for the t. being** pour le moment; **one at a t.** un à un. **2** *verb* (*sportsman etc*) chronométrer; (*activity*) minuter; (*choose the time of*) choisir le moment de.

timer *noun* (*device*) minuteur *m*; (*built into appliance*) programmateur *m*; (*plugged into socket*) prise *f* programmable.

timetable *noun* horaire *m*; (*in school*) emploi *m* du temps.

timid *adjective* (*afraid*) craintif; (*shy*) timide.

timing *noun* **what good t.!** quelle synchronisation!

tin *noun* (*metal*) étain *m*; (*coated steel or iron*) fer-blanc *m*; (*can*) boîte *f*.

tinfoil *noun* papier *m* (d')alu.

tinned *adjective* en boîte.

tin opener *noun* ouvre-boîtes *invariable m*.

tiny *adjective* tout petit (*f* toute petite).

tip
1 *noun* (*end*) bout *m*; (*pointed*) pointe *f*; (*money*) pourboire *m*;

(*advice*) conseil *m*; (*for rubbish*) décharge *f*.
2 *verb* (*waiter etc*) donner un pourboire à.

tip (out) *verb* (*liquid, load*) déverser (**into** dans).

tip over *verb*
1 (*object*) renverser.
2 (*of object*) se renverser.

tip up *verb*
1 (*object*) renverser.
2 (*of object*) basculer.

tipped cigarette *noun* cigarette *f* (à bout) filtre.

tiptoe *noun* **on t.** sur la pointe des pieds.

tire *verb*
1 (*person*) fatiguer.
2 (*of person*) se fatiguer.

tired *adjective* fatigué; **to be t. of something/somebody/doing** en avoir assez de quelque chose/de quelqu'un/de faire.

tiredness *noun* fatigue *f*.

tire out *verb* **to t. somebody out** épuiser quelqu'un.

tiring *adjective* fatigant.

tissue *noun* (*handkerchief etc*) mouchoir *m* en papier.

title *noun* titre *m*.

to *preposition*
▪ (*towards*) à; **to go to school** aller à l'école; **to go to France** aller en France; **to go to somebody's house** aller chez quelqu'un; **the train to Paris** le train pour Paris; **the road to London** la route de Londres.
▪ (*until*) jusqu'à; **to count to ten** compter jusqu'à dix; **it's ten to six** il est six heures moins dix.
▪ (*expressing indirect object*) **to give something to somebody** donner quelque chose à quelqu'un.

▌ (*expressing proportion*) **six votes to four** six voix contre quatre; **two goals to one** deux buts à un.

▌ (*with infinitive*) **to go** aller; **in order to remember** pour se souvenir; **to have things to do** avoir des choses à faire; **she came to help me** elle est venue m'aider; **I want him to stay** je veux qu'il reste; **she told me to do it** elle m'a dit de le faire.

▌ (*representing verb*) **I want to** je veux le faire; **I was told to** on m'a dit de le faire.

▌ (*with adjective*) **to be kind/cruel to somebody** être gentil/cruel envers quelqu'un; **to be happy to do something** être heureux de faire quelque chose; **it's easy/difficult to do** c'est facile/difficile à faire.

toad *noun* crapaud *m*.

toadstool *noun* champignon *m* (vénéneux).

toast
  1 *noun* pain *m* grillé; **piece** *or* **slice of t.** tranche *f* de pain grillé, toast *m*.
  2 *verb* (faire) griller.

toaster *noun* grille-pain *invariable m*.

tobacco *noun* tabac *m*.

tobacconist's (shop) *noun* (bureau *m* de) tabac *m*.

toboggan *noun* luge *f*.

today *adverb* aujourd'hui.

toddler *noun* enfant *m or f* (en bas âge).

toe *noun* orteil *m*.

toenail *noun* ongle *m* du pied.

toffee *noun* caramel *m* (dur).

together *adverb* ensemble; (*at the same time*) en même temps; **t. with** avec.

toilet *noun* (*room*) toilettes *fpl*; **to go to the t.** aller aux toilettes.

toilet flush *noun* chasse *f* d'eau.

toilet paper *noun* papier *m* hygiénique.

toiletries *plural noun* articles *mpl* de toilette.

toilet roll *noun* rouleau *m* de papier hygiénique.

toilet water *noun* (*perfume*) eau *f* de toilette.

token *noun* (*disc*) jeton *m*; **book t.** chèque-livre *m*; **record t.** chèque-disque *m*.

told *see* **tell**.

tolerant *adjective* tolérant (**of** à l'égard de).

tolerate *verb* tolérer.

toll *noun* (*fee*) péage *m*; **t. road/bridge** route *f*/pont *m* à péage.

tomato *noun* tomate *f*.

tomb *noun* tombeau *m*.

tomorrow *adverb* demain; **t. morning** demain matin; **the day after t.** après-demain.

ton *noun* tonne *f* (= *1016 kg*); **tons of** (*lots of*) *Familiar* des tonnes de.

tone *noun* ton *m*; (*of telephone*) tonalité *f*; **engaged t.** sonnerie *f* 'occupé'.

tongs *plural noun* **sugar t.** pince *f* à sucre.

tongue *noun* langue *f*.

tonic *noun* **t. (water)** eau *f* gazeuse (tonique); **gin and t.** gin-tonic *m*.

tonight *adverb* (*this evening*) ce soir; (*during the night*) cette nuit.

tonsil *noun* amygdale *f*.

tonsillitis *noun* **to have t.** avoir une angine.

too *adverb* trop; (*also*) aussi;

(*moreover*) en plus; **t. tired to play** trop fatigué pour jouer; **t. hard to solve** trop difficile à résoudre; **t. much, t. many** trop; **t. much salt/t. many people**/*etc* trop de sel/gens/*etc*; **one t. many** un de trop.

took *see* take.

tool *noun* outil *m*.

tooth *noun* dent *f*.

toothache *noun* mal *m* de dents; **to have a t.** avoir mal aux dents.

toothbrush *noun* brosse *f* à dents.

toothpaste *noun* dentifrice *m*.

toothpick *noun* cure-dent *m*.

top [1]
  1 *noun* (*of mountain, tower, tree*) sommet *m*; (*of wall, ladder, page, garment*) haut *m*; (*of table*) dessus *m*; (*of list*) tête *f*; (*of bottle, tube*) bouchon *m*; (*bottle cap*) capsule *f*; (*of saucepan*) couvercle *m*; (*of pen*) capuchon *m*; **to be t. of the class** être le premier de la classe; **on t. of** sur.
  2 *adjective* (*drawer, shelf*) du haut; (*step, layer*) dernier; (*in exam*) premier; (*maximum*) maximum; **on the t. floor** au dernier étage; **at t. speed** à toute vitesse.

top [2] *noun* (*spinning*) **t.** toupie *f*.

topic *noun* sujet *m*.

top up *verb* (*glass*) remplir; (*coffee, tea*) remettre.

torch *noun* (*electric*) lampe *f* électrique; (*flame*) torche *f*.

tore *see* tear[1].

torment *verb* (*annoy*) agacer.

tornado *noun* tornade *f*.

torn *see* tear[1].

tortoise *noun* tortue *f*.

tortoiseshell *noun* écaille *f*.

torture
  1 *noun* torture *f*.
  2 *verb* torturer.

toss *verb*
  1 (*throw*) jeter (**to** à); **to t. a coin** jouer à pile ou face.
  2 **let's t. up** jouons à pile ou face.

total *adjective & noun* total (*m*).

totally *adverb* totalement.

touch
  1 *noun* (*contact*) contact *m*; (*sense*) toucher *m*; **in t. with somebody** en contact avec quelqu'un; **to get in t.** se mettre en contact.
  2 *verb* toucher; (*interfere with*) toucher à.
  3 *verb* (*of lines, hands etc*) se toucher; **don't t.!** n'y *or* ne touche pas!

touch down *verb* (*of aircraft*) atterrir.

touchy *adjective* susceptible.

tough *adjective* (*meat*) dur; (*sturdy*) solide; (*strong*) fort; (*difficult, harsh*) dur.

tour
  1 *noun* (*journey*) voyage *m*; (*visit*) visite *f*; (*by artist etc*) tournée *f*.
  2 *verb* visiter.

tourism *noun* tourisme *m*.

tourist
  1 touriste *m or f*.
  2 *adjective* touristique.

tourist office *noun* syndicat *m* d'initiative.

tournament *noun* tournoi *m*.

tow *verb* (*car, boat*) remorquer; (*caravan, trailer*) tracter.

toward(s) *preposition* vers; (*of feelings*) envers; **cruel**/*etc* **t. somebody** cruel/*etc* envers quelqu'un.

towel *noun* serviette *f* (de toilette); (*for dishes*) torchon *m*.

towelling *noun* tissu-éponge *m*.

tower *noun* tour *f*.

tower block *noun* tour *f*.

town *noun* ville *f*; **in t., (in)to t.** en ville; **t. centre** centre-ville *m*.

town council *noun* conseil *m* municipal.

town hall *noun* mairie *f*.

toy
   1 *noun* jouet *m*.
   2 *adjective* (*gun*) d'enfant; (*house, car*) miniature.

toyshop *noun* magasin *m* de jouets.

trace
   1 *noun* trace *f* (**of** de).
   2 *verb* (*with tracing paper*) (dé)calquer; (*find*) retrouver.

tracing paper *noun* papier-calque *invariable m*.

track *noun* (*of animal, sports stadium etc*) piste *f*; (*of record*) plage *f*; (*for train*) voie *f*; (*path*) chemin *m*; **tracks** (*of wheels*) traces *fpl*; **on the right t.** sur la bonne voie.

tracksuit *noun* survêtement *m*.

tractor *noun* tracteur *m*.

trade
   1 *noun* commerce *m*; (*job*) métier *m*.
   2 *verb* faire du commerce (**with** avec); (*swap*) échanger (**for** contre); **to t. places** changer de place.

trade in *noun* reprise *f*.

trademark *noun* marque *f* de fabrique; (**registered**) **t.** marque déposée.

trade union *noun* syndicat *m*.

trading *noun* commerce *m*.

tradition *noun* tradition *f*.

traditional *adjective* tradition-nel.

traffic *noun* circulation *f*; (*air, sea, rail*) trafic *m*.

traffic island *noun* refuge *m*.

traffic jam *noun* embouteillage *m*.

traffic lights *plural noun* feux *mpl* (de signalisation); (*when red*) feu *m* rouge.

traffic sign *noun* panneau *m* de signalisation.

tragedy *noun* tragédie *f*.

tragic *adjective* tragique.

trail
   1 *noun* (*of smoke, blood etc*) traînée *f*.
   2 *verb* (*on the ground etc*) traîner.

trailer *noun* (*for car*) remorque *f*.

train¹ *noun* train *m*; (*underground*) rame *f*; **to go** *or* **come by t.** prendre le train; **t. set** petit train *m*.

train² *verb*
   1 (*teach*) former (**to do** à faire); (*in sport*) entraîner; (*animal, child*) dresser (**to do** à faire).
   2 (*of sportsman*) s'entraîner; **he trained as a doctor**/*etc* il est médecin/*etc* de formation.

trained *adjective* (*skilled*) qualifié; (*nurse, engineer*) diplômé.

trainer *noun* (*running shoe*) jogging *m*.

training *noun* formation *f*; (*in sport*) entraînement *m*.

traitor *noun* traître *m*.

tram *noun* tramway *m*.

tramp *noun* clochard, -arde *m or f*.

tranquillizer *noun* tranquillisant *m*.

transfer
   1 *verb* (*person, goods etc*) transférer (**to** à); **to t. the charges**

téléphoner en PCV.
2 *noun* transfert *m* (**to** à); (*image*) décalcomanie *f*.

transfusion *noun* (blood) t. transfusion *f* (sanguine).

transistor *noun* t. (radio) transistor *m*.

transitive *adjective* Grammar transitif.

translate *verb* traduire (**from** de, **into** en).

translation *noun* traduction *f*.

translator *noun* traducteur, -trice *m or f*.

transparent *adjective* transparent.

transplant *noun* greffe *f*.

transport
1 *verb* transporter.
2 *noun* transport *m* (**of** de); **means of t.** moyen *m* de transport; **public t.** les transports en commun.

trap
1 *noun* piège *m*.
2 *verb* (*animal*) prendre (au piège); (*jam*) coincer; (*cut off by snow etc*) bloquer (**by** par).

trap door *noun* trappe *f*.

trash *noun* (*nonsense*) sottises *fpl*; (*junk*) bric-à-brac *invariable m*.

travel
1 *verb* voyager.
2 *verb* (*country, distance*) parcourir.
3 *noun* **travel(s)** voyages *mpl*; **t. agent** agent *m* de voyages.

traveller *noun* voyageur, -euse *m or f*.

traveller's cheque *noun* chèque *m* de voyage.

travelling *noun* voyages *mpl*.

travelsickness *noun* (*in car*) mal *m* de la route; (*in aircraft*) mal *m* de l'air.

tray *noun* plateau *m*.

treacherous *adjective* (*road, conditions*) très dangereux.

tread *verb* marcher (**on** sur).

treasure *noun* trésor *m*.

treat
1 *verb* traiter; (*consider*) considérer (**as** comme); **to t. somebody to something** offrir quelque chose à quelqu'un.
2 *noun* (*special*) t. petit extra *m*; **to give somebody a (special) t.** donner une surprise à quelqu'un.

treatment *noun* traitement *m*.

treble *verb* tripler.

tree *noun* arbre *m*.

tremble *verb* trembler (**with** de).

trench *noun* tranchée *f*.

trial *noun* (*in court*) procès *m*; **to go** *or* **be on t.** être jugé, passer en jugement.

triangle *noun* triangle *m*.

triangular *adjective* triangulaire.

tribe *noun* tribu *f*.

trick
1 *noun* (*joke, of conjurer etc*) tour *m*; (*clever method*) astuce *f*; **to play a t. on somebody** jouer un tour à quelqu'un.
2 *verb* tromper.

trickle
1 *noun* (*of liquid*) filet *m*.
2 *verb* dégouliner.

tricky *adjective* (*problem etc*) difficile.

tricycle *noun* tricycle *m*.

trigger *noun* (*of gun*) gâchette *f*.

trim *verb* couper (un peu).

trip *noun* (*journey*) voyage *m*; (*outing*) excursion *f*.

trip (over *or* **up)** *verb* trébucher;

to t. over something trébucher contre quelque chose.

triple *verb* tripler.

trip up *verb* to t. somebody up faire trébucher quelqu'un.

triumph
1 *noun* triomphe *m* (**over** sur).
2 *verb* triompher (**over** de).

trivial *adjective* (*unimportant*) insignifiant.

trod , trodden *see* tread.

trolley *noun* (*for luggage*) chariot *m*; (*in supermarket*) caddie ® *m*; (**tea**) t. table *f* roulante.

trombone *noun* trombone *m*.

troops *plural noun* troupes *fpl*.

trophy *noun* coupe *f*, trophée *m*.

tropical *adjective* tropical.

trot
1 *noun* trot *m*.
2 *verb* trotter.

trouble
1 *noun* (*difficulty*) ennui(s) *m(pl)*; (*effort*) peine *f*; **trouble(s)** (*social unrest, illness*) troubles *mpl*; **to be in t.** avoir des ennuis; **to get into t.** s'attirer des ennuis (**with** avec); **to go to the t. of doing, take the t. to do** se donner la peine de faire.
2 *verb* (*inconvenience*) déranger; (*worry, annoy*) ennuyer.

trousers *plural noun* pantalon *m*; **a pair of t., some t.** un pantalon.

trout *noun* truite *f*.

truant *noun* **to play t.** sécher (les cours).

truck *noun* (*lorry*) camion *m*.

true *adjective* vrai (*f* vraie); (*accurate*) exact; **t. to** (*one's promise etc*) fidèle à; **to come t.** se réaliser.

trump (card) *noun* atout *m*.

trumpet *noun* trompette *f*.

trunk *noun* (*of tree, body*) tronc *m*; (*of elephant*) trompe *f*; (*case*) malle *f*; **trunks** (*for swimming*) slip *m* de bain.

trust
1 *noun* (*faith*) confiance *f* (**in** en).
2 *verb* (*person, judgment*) avoir confiance en; **to t. somebody with something, t. something to somebody** confier quelque chose à quelqu'un.

truth *noun* vérité *f*.

try
1 *verb* essayer (**to do, doing** de faire); **to t. one's luck** tenter sa chance.
2 *verb* essayer; **to t. hard** faire un gros effort.
3 *noun* (*attempt*) & *Rugby* essai *m*; **to have a t.** essayer.

try (out) *verb* (*car, method etc*) essayer; (*person*) mettre à l'essai.

try on *verb* (*clothes, shoes*) essayer.

T-shirt *noun* tee-shirt *m*.

tub *noun* (*basin*) baquet *m*; (*bath*) baignoire *f*.

tube *noun* tube *m*; (*underground railway*) métro *m*.

tuck in *verb* (*shirt, blanket*) rentrer; (*person in bed*) border.

Tuesday *noun* mardi *m*.

tuft *noun* touffe *f*.

tug *verb* tirer (**at** sur).

tug(boat) *noun* remorqueur *m*.

tuition *noun* enseignement *m*; (*lessons*) leçons *fpl*.

tulip *noun* tulipe *f*.

tumble *noun* dégringolade *f*.

tumble (down) *verb* dégringoler.

tumble drier *or* **dryer** *noun* sèche-linge *invariable m*.

tumbler noun (glass) gobelet m.

tummy noun Familiar ventre m.

tuna (fish) noun thon m.

tune
1 noun air m; in t./out of t. (instrument) accordé/désaccordé;
to sing in t./out of t. chanter juste/faux.
2 verb (instrument) accorder;
(engine) régler.

tuning noun (of engine) réglage m.

Tunisia noun la Tunisie f.

Tunisian adjective & noun tunisien, -ienne (m or f).

tunnel noun tunnel m.

turban noun turban m.

Turk noun Turc, Turque (m or f).

Turkey noun la Turquie f.

turkey noun dindon m, dinde f;
(as food) dinde f.

Turkish adjective turc (f turque).

turn
1 noun (movement, in game) tour m; (in road) tournant m; to take turns se relayer; it's your t. (to play) c'est à toi or (à) ton tour (de jouer).
2 verb tourner; (mattress, pancake) retourner; to t. something red/etc rendre quelque chose rouge/etc; she's turned twenty elle a vingt ans passés.
3 verb (of wheel etc) tourner;
(turn head or body) se (re)tourner;
(become) devenir; to t. red/etc rougir/etc.

turn around verb (of person) se retourner.

turn away verb
1 (eyes) détourner; (person) renvoyer.
2 (of person) se détourner.

turn back verb retourner.

turn down verb (gas, radio etc) baisser; (offer, person) refuser.

turning noun petite rue f; (bend in road) tournant m.

turn into verb
1 (transform) changer en.
2 (become) se changer en.

turnip noun navet m.

turn off verb (light, radio etc) éteindre; (tap) fermer; (machine) arrêter.

turn on verb (light, radio etc) allumer; (tap) ouvrir; (machine) mettre en marche.

turn out verb
1 (light) éteindre.
2 (result) se terminer; (attend, appear) se déplacer; to t. out to be s'avérer (être); it turned out that ... il s'est avéré que ...

turn over verb
1 (page) tourner.
2 (of vehicle, person) se retourner.

turn round verb
1 (head, object) tourner; (vehicle) faire faire demi-tour à.
2 (of person) se retourner.

turn up verb
1 (radio, light etc) mettre plus fort; (collar) remonter.
2 (arrive) arriver.

turnup noun (on trousers) revers m.

turtle noun tortue f de mer.

turtleneck noun (sweater) col m roulé.

tusk noun défense f.

tutor
1 noun précepteur, -trice m or f;
(at university) directeur, -trice m or f d'études.
2 verb donner des cours particuliers à.

TV noun télé f.

tweezers *plural noun* pince *f* à épiler.

twelfth *adjective & noun* douzième (*m or f*).

twelve *adjective & noun* douze (*m*).

twentieth *adjective & noun* vingtième (*m or f*).

twenty *adjective & noun* vingt (*m*).

twice *adverb* deux fois; **t. as heavy**/*etc* deux fois plus lourd/ *etc*.

twig *noun* brindille *f*.

twilight *noun* crépuscule *m*.

twin *noun* jumeau *m*, jumelle *f*; **t. brother** frère *m* jumeau; **t. sister** sœur *f* jumelle; **t. beds** lits *mpl* jumeaux.

twine *noun* (grosse) ficelle *f*.

twinkle *verb* (*of star*) scintiller.

twist
1 *verb* (*wire, arm etc*) tordre; (*roll*) enrouler (**round** autour de); (*knob*) tourner; **to t. one's ankle** se tordre la cheville.
2 *noun* (*turn*) tour *m*; (*in road*) zigzag *m*.

twist off *verb* (*lid*) dévisser.

two *adjective & noun* deux (*m*); **t.-way traffic** circulation *f* dans les deux sens.

type [1] *noun* (*sort*) genre *m*, type *m*; (*print*) caractères *mpl*.

type [2] *verb* (*write*) taper (à la machine).

typewriter *noun* machine *f* à écrire.

typewritten *adjective* dactylo-graphié.

typical *adjective* typique (**of** de); **that's t. (of him)!** c'est bien lui!

typing *noun* dactylo *f*; **t. error** faute *f* de frappe.

typist *noun* dactylo *f*.

tyre *noun* pneu *m* (*plural* pneus).

UFO *abbreviation* (*unidentified flying object*) OVNI *m*.

ugliness *noun* laideur *f*.

ugly *adjective* laid.

ulcer *noun* ulcère *m*.

umbrella *noun* parapluie *m*.

umpire *noun* arbitre *m*.

un - *prefix* in-, peu, non, sans.

unable *adjective* to be u. to do être incapable de faire; **he's u. to swim** il ne sait pas nager.

unacceptable *adjective* inacceptable.

unaccustomed to be u. to something/to doing ne pas être habitué à quelque chose/à faire.

unanimous *adjective* unanime.

unanimously *adverb* à l'unanimité.

unattractive *adjective* (*idea, appearance*) peu attrayant; (*ugly*) laid.

unavailable *adjective* (*person*) qui n'est pas disponible; (*product*) épuisé.

unavoidable *adjective* inévitable.

unavoidably *adverb* inévitablement; (*delayed*) pour une raison indépendante de sa volonté.

unaware *adjective* to be u. of something ignorer quelque chose; to be u. that ignorer que.

unawares *adverb* to catch somebody u. prendre quelqu'un au dépourvu.

unbearable *adjective* insupportable.

unbelievable *adjective* incroyable.

unbreakable *adjective* incassable.

unbutton *verb* déboutonner.

uncertain *adjective* incertain (about, of de); it's u. whether il n'est pas certain que (+ *subjunctive*); I'm u. whether to stay je ne sais pas très bien si je dois rester.

uncertainty *noun* incertitude *f*.

unchanged *adjective* inchangé.

uncle *noun* oncle *m*.

unclear *adjective* (*meaning*) qui n'est pas clair; (*result*) incertain; it's u. whether on ne sait pas très bien si.

uncomfortable *adjective* (*chair etc*) inconfortable; (*uneasy*) mal à l'aise.

uncommon *adjective* rare.

unconnected *adjective* (*facts etc*) sans rapport (with avec).

unconscious *adjective* (*person*) sans connaissance.

unconvincing *adjective* peu convaincant.

uncooperative *adjective* peu coopératif.

uncork *verb* (*bottle*) déboucher.

uncover *verb* découvrir.

undamaged *adjective* (*goods*) en bon état.

undecided *adjective* (*person*) indécis (about sur).

undeniable *adjective* incontestable.

under

1 *preposition* sous; (*less than*) moins de; (*according to*) selon; children u. nine les enfants de

moins de neuf ans; **u. the cir-cumstances** étant donné les circonstances; **u. there** là-dessous; **u. it** dessous.
2 *adverb* au-dessous.

under - *prefix* sous-.

undercharge *verb* **I under-charged him (for it)** je ne (le) lui ai pas fait payer assez.

underclothes *plural noun* sous-vêtements *mpl*.

underdone *adjective* (*steak*) saignant.

underestimate *verb* sous-estimer.

undergo *verb* subir.

undergraduate *noun* étudiant, -ante *m or f* (qui prépare la licence).

underground
1 *adjective* souterrain.
2 *noun* (*railway*) métro *m*.

underline *verb* (*word etc*) souligner.

underneath
1 *preposition* sous.
2 *adverb* (en) dessous; **the book u.** le livre d'en dessous.
3 *noun* dessous *m*.

underpants *plural noun* slip *m*; (*loose, long*) caleçon *m*.

underpass *noun* passage *m* souterrain.

understand *verb* comprendre.

understandable *adjective* compréhensible.

understanding
1 *noun* compréhension *f*; (*agree-ment*) accord *m*; (*sympathy*) entente *f*.
2 *adjective* (*person*) compréhen-sif.

understood *adjective* (*agreed*) entendu.

undertake *verb* entreprendre (**to do** de faire).

undertaker *noun* entrepreneur *m* de pompes funèbres.

undertaking *noun* (*task*) entreprise *f*.

underwater
1 *adjective* sous-marin.
2 *adverb* sous l'eau.

underwear *noun* sous-vêtements *mpl*.

undo *verb* défaire.

undone *adjective* **to come u.** (*of knot etc*) se défaire.

undoubtedly *adverb* sans aucun doute.

undress *verb*
1 (*of person*) se déshabiller.
2 (*person*) déshabiller; **to get undressed** se déshabiller.

uneasy *adjective* (*ill at ease*) mal à l'aise.

unemployed
1 *adjective* au chômage.
2 *noun* **the u.** les chômeurs *mpl*.

unemployment *noun* chômage *m*.

uneven *adjective* inégal.

uneventful *adjective* (*trip etc*) sans histoires.

unexpected *adjective* inatten-du.

unexpectedly *adverb* à l'impro-viste; (*suddenly*) subitement.

unfair *adjective* injuste (**to some-body** envers quelqu'un).

unfairly *adverb* injustement.

unfairness *noun* injustice *f*.

unfaithful *adjective* infidèle (**to** à).

unfamiliar *adjective* inconnu; **to be u. with something** ne pas connaître quelque chose.

unfashionable *adjective* (*sub-*

ject etc) démodé; (*restaurant etc*) peu chic *invariable*.

unfasten *verb* défaire.

unfavourable *adjective* défavorable.

unfinished *adjective* inachevé.

unfit *adjective* en mauvaise santé; (*in bad shape*) pas en forme; (*unsuitable*) impropre; (*for* à, *to do* à faire); (*unworthy*) indigne (**for** de, **to do** de faire); (*unable*) inapte (**for** à, **to do** à faire).

unfold *verb* déplier.

unforgettable *adjective* inoubliable.

unforgivable *adjective* impardonnable.

unfortunate *adjective* malheureux; **you were u.** tu n'as pas eu de chance.

unfortunately *adverb* malheureusement.

unfriendly *adjective* froid, peu aimable (**to** avec).

unfurnished *adjective* non meublé.

ungrateful *adjective* ingrat.

unhappiness *noun* tristesse *f*.

unhappy *adjective* (*sad*) malheureux; **u. with** *or* **about something** mécontent de quelque chose.

unharmed *adjective* (*person*) indemne.

unhealthy *adjective* (*climate etc*) malsain; (*person*) en mauvaise santé.

unhelpful *adjective* (*person*) peu serviable.

unhook *verb* (*picture, curtain*) décrocher; (*dress*) dégrafer.

unhurt *adjective* indemne.

unhygienic *adjective* pas très hygiénique.

uniform *noun* uniforme *m*.

unimportant *adjective* peu important.

uninhabited *adjective* inhabité.

uninjured *adjective* indemne.

unintentional *adjective* involontaire.

uninteresting *adjective* (*book etc*) peu intéressant.

union
  1 *noun* union *f*; (*trade union*) syndicat *m*.
  2 *adjective* syndical; **u. member** syndiqué, -ée *m or f*; **U. Jack** drapeau *m* britannique.

unique *adjective* unique.

unit *noun* unité *f*; (*of furniture etc*) élément *m*; (*team*) groupe *m*.

unite *verb*
  1 unir; (*country, party*) unifier.
  2 (*of students etc*) s'unir.

united *adjective* **the U. Kingdom** le Royaume-Uni *m*; **the U. Nations** les Nations *fpl* Unies; **the U. States (of America)** les États-Unis *mpl* (d'Amérique).

universal *adjective* universel.

universe *noun* univers *m*.

university
  1 *noun* université *f*; **at u.** à l'université.
  2 *adjective* universitaire; (*student*) d'université.

unjust *adjective* injuste.

unkind *adjective* peu gentil (*f* peu gentille) (**to somebody** avec quelqu'un).

unknown *adjective* inconnu.

unleaded *adjective* (*petrol*) sans plomb.

unless *conjunction* à moins que (+ *subjunctive*); **u. she comes** à moins qu'elle ne vienne.

unlike *preposition* **he, u. his**

father ... lui, à la différence de son père ...; **that's u. him** ça ne lui ressemble pas.

unlikely *adjective* peu probable; (*unbelievable*) incroyable; **she's u. to win** il est peu probable qu'elle gagne.

unlimited *adjective* illimité.

unload *verb* décharger.

unlock *verb* ouvrir (*avec une clef*).

unluckily *adverb* malheureusement.

unlucky *adjective* (*person*) malchanceux; (*number etc*) qui porte malheur; **you're u.** tu n'as pas de chance.

unmade *adjective* (*bed*) défait.

unmarried *adjective* célibataire.

unnecessary *adjective* inutile.

unnoticed *adjective* **to go u.** passer inaperçu.

unoccupied *adjective* (*house*) inoccupé; (*seat*) libre.

unpack *verb*
1 (*suitcase*) défaire; (*goods, belongings*) déballer.
2 (*of person*) défaire ses bagages.

unpaid *adjective* (*bill, sum*) impayé; (*work, worker*) bénévole.

unpleasant *adjective* désagréable (**to somebody** avec quelqu'un).

unplug *verb* (*appliance*) débrancher.

unpopular *adjective* peu populaire; **to be u. with somebody** ne pas plaire à quelqu'un.

unpredictable *adjective* imprévisible; (*weather*) indécis.

unprepared *adjective* **to be u. for something** (*not expect*) ne pas s'attendre à quelque chose.

unreasonable *adjective* qui n'est pas raisonnable.

unrecognizable *adjective* méconnaissable.

unrelated *adjective* (*facts etc*) sans rapport (**to** avec).

unreliable *adjective* (*person*) peu sûr; (*machine*) peu fiable.

unrest *noun* agitation *f*.

unroll *verb* dérouler.

unsafe *adjective* (*place, machine etc*) dangereux; (*person*) en danger.

unsatisfactory *adjective* peu satisfaisant.

unscrew *verb* dévisser.

unskilled worker *noun* ouvrier, -ière *m or f* non qualifié(e).

unstable *adjective* instable.

unsteadily *adverb* (*to walk*) d'un pas mal assuré.

unsteady *adjective* (*hand, step*) mal assuré; (*table, ladder etc*) instable.

unsuccessful *adjective* (*attempt etc*) vain; (*candidate*) malheureux; **to be u.** ne pas réussir (**in doing** à faire).

unsuccessfully *adverb* en vain.

unsuitable *adjective* qui ne convient pas (**for** à).

unsuited *adjective* **u. to** (*job, activity*) peu fait pour.

unsure *adjective* incertain (**of, about** de).

untangle *verb* démêler.

untidy *adjective* (*clothes, hair*) peu soigné; (*room*) en désordre; (*person*) désordonné; (*in appearance*) peu soigné.

untie *verb* (*person, hands*) détacher; (*knot, parcel*) défaire.

until
1 *preposition* jusqu'à; **u. then** jusque-là; **I didn't come u. yester-**

day je ne suis venu qu'hier; **not u. tomorrow** pas avant demain. **2** *conjunction* jusqu'à ce que + *subjunctive*; **do nothing u. I come** ne fais rien avant mon arrivée.

untrue *adjective* faux (*f* fausse).

unused *adjective* (*new*) neuf (*f* neuve).

unusual *adjective* exceptionnel; (*strange*) étrange.

unusually *adverb* exceptionnellement.

unwell *adjective* indisposé.

unwilling *adjective* **he's u. to do** il ne veut pas faire.

unwillingly *adverb* à contre-cœur.

unworthy *adjective* indigne (**of** de).

unwrap *verb* ouvrir.

unzip *verb* ouvrir (la fermeture éclair ® de).

up
1 *adverb* en haut; (*in the air*) en l'air; (*out of bed*) levé, debout; **to come** *or* **go up** monter; **prices are up** les prix ont augmenté; **up there** là-haut; **further** *or* **higher up** plus haut; **up to** (*as far as*) jusqu'à; **it's up to you to do it** c'est à toi de le faire; **that's up to you** ça dépend de toi; **what are you up to?** que fais-tu?; **to walk up and down** marcher de long en large.
2 *preposition* (*hill*) en haut de; (*tree*) dans; (*ladder*) sur; **to go up** (*hill, stairs*) monter.

uphill *adverb* **to go u.** monter.

upon *preposition* sur.

upper *adjective* supérieur.

upright *adjective* & *adverb* (*straight*) droit.

uproar *noun* vacarme *m*, tapage *m*.

upset
1 *verb* (*stomach, routine etc*) déranger; **to u. somebody** (*make sad*) peiner quelqu'un; (*offend*) vexer quelqu'un.
2 *adjective* peiné; vexé; (*stomach*) dérangé.
3 *noun* **to have a stomach u.** avoir l'estomac dérangé.

upside down *adverb* à l'envers.

upstairs
1 *adverb* en haut; **to go u.** monter (l'escalier).
2 *adjective* (*people, room*) du dessus.

up-to-date *adjective* moderne; (*information*) à jour; (*well-informed*) au courant (**on** de).

upward(s) *adverb* vers le haut; **from five francs u.** à partir de cinq francs.

urge *verb* **to u. somebody to do** conseiller vivement à quelqu'un de faire.

urgency *noun* urgence *f*.

urgent *adjective* urgent.

urgently *adverb* d'urgence.

us *pronoun* nous; **(to) us sees us** elle nous voit; **he gives (to) us** il nous donne; **all of us** nous tous; **let's** *or* **let us eat!** mangeons!

use
1 *noun* usage *m*, emploi *m*; **to make u. of something** se servir de quelque chose; **not in u.** hors d'usage; **to be of u.** être utile; **it's no u. crying**/*etc* ça ne sert à rien de pleurer/*etc*; **what's the u. of worrying**/*etc*? à quoi bon s'inquiéter/*etc*?
2 *verb* se servir de, utiliser (**as** comme; **to do, for doing** pour

faire); **it's used to do** or **for
doing** ça sert à faire; **it's used as**
ça sert de.

use (up) verb (fuel) consommer;
(supplies) épuiser; (money)
dépenser.

used
1 adjective (secondhand) d'occasion.
2 auxiliary verb I **u. to sing**/etc
avant, je chantais/etc.
3 adjective **u. to something**/**to
doing** habitué à quelque chose/à
faire; **to get u. to** s'habituer à.

useful adjective utile (**to** à); **to
come in u.** être utile.

usefulness noun utilité f.

useless adjective inutile; (person)
nul (f nulle).

user noun (of road) usager m; (of
machine, dictionary) utilisateur,
-trice m or f.

usual adjective habituel; **as u.**
comme d'habitude.

usually adverb d'habitude.

utensil noun ustensile m.

utter
1 adjective complet; (idiot)
parfait.
2 verb (cry) pousser; (word) dire.

utterly adverb complètement.

U-turn noun (in vehicle) demi-tour
m.

vacancy noun (post) poste m vacant; (room) chambre f libre.

vacant adjective (room, seat) libre.

vacation noun vacances fpl; on v. en vacances.

vaccinate verb vacciner.

vaccination noun vaccination f.

vaccine noun vaccin m.

vacuum verb (carpet) passer l'aspirateur sur; (room) passer l'aspirateur dans.

vacuum cleaner noun aspirateur m.

vacuum flask noun thermos ® m or f.

vague adjective vague; (outline) flou.

vaguely adverb vaguement.

vain adjective in v. en vain.

valid adjective (ticket etc) valable.

valley noun vallée f.

valuable
  1 adjective (object) de (grande) valeur.
  2 plural noun valuables objets mpl de valeur.

value noun valeur f; it's good v. (for money) c'est d'un bon rapport qualité/prix.

van noun camionnette f, fourgonnette f; (large) camion m.

vandal noun vandale m or f.

vandalize verb saccager.

vanilla
  1 noun vanille f.
  2 adjective (ice cream) à la vanille.

vanish verb disparaître.

varied adjective varié.

variety noun variété f; a v. of reasons/etc diverses raisons/etc; v. show spectacle m de variétés.

various adjective divers.

varnish
  1 verb vernir.
  2 noun vernis m.

vary verb varier.

vase noun vase m.

Vaseline ® noun vaseline f.

vast adjective vaste.

VAT abbreviation (value added tax) TVA f.

VCR abbreviation (video cassette recorder) magnétoscope m.

VDU abbreviation (visual display unit) écran m d'ordinateur.

veal noun (meat) veau m.

vegetable noun légume m.

vegetarian adjective & noun végétarien, -ienne (m or f).

vegetation noun végétation f.

vehicle noun véhicule m.

veil noun voile m.

vein noun (in body) veine f.

velvet
  1 noun velours m.
  2 adjective de velours.

vending machine noun distributeur m automatique.

venetian blind noun store m vénitien.

ventilation noun (in room) aération f.

verb noun verbe m.

verdict noun verdict m.

verge noun (of road) accotement m.

verse *noun* (*part of song*) couplet *m*; (*poetry*) poésie *f*; **in v.** en vers.

version *noun* version *f*.

vertical *adjective* vertical.

very
1 *adverb* très; **v. much** beaucoup; **at the v. latest** au plus tard.
2 *adjective* (*actual*) même; **his** *or* **her v. brother** son frère lui-même.

vest *noun* tricot *m* de corps; (*woman's*) chemise *f* (américaine).

vet *noun* vétérinaire *m or f*.

via *preposition* par.

vibrate *verb* vibrer.

vibration *noun* vibration *f*.

vicar *noun* pasteur *m*.

vice *noun* vice *m*; (*tool*) étau *m*.

vicious *adjective* (*spiteful*) méchant; (*violent*) brutal.

victim *noun* victime *f*; **to be the v. of** être victime de.

victory *noun* victoire *f*.

video
1 *noun* (*cassette*) cassette *f*; **v. cassette** vidéocassette *f*; **v. (recorder)** magnétoscope *m*; **on v.** sur cassette.
2 *adjective* (*game, camera etc*) vidéo *invariable*.
3 *verb* (*event*) faire une (vidéo)-cassette de.

videotape *noun* bande *f* vidéo.

Vietnam *noun* le Viêt Nam *m*.

Vietnamese *adjective & noun* vietnamien, -ienne (*m or f*).

view *noun* vue *f*; **to come into v.** apparaître; **in my v.** à mon avis; **in v. of** compte tenu de.

viewer *noun* (*person*) téléspectateur, -trice *m or f*.

viewpoint *noun* point *m* de vue.

villa *noun* villa *f*.

village *noun* village *m*.

villager *noun* villageois, -oise *m or f*.

vinegar *noun* vinaigre *m*.

vineyard *noun* vignoble *m*.

violence *noun* violence *f*.

violent *adjective* violent.

violently *adverb* violemment.

violin *noun* violon *m*.

virus *noun* virus *m*.

visa *noun* visa *m*.

visible *adjective* visible.

visit
1 *noun* visite *f*; (*stay*) séjour *m*.
2 *verb* (*place*) visiter; **to v. somebody** rendre visite à quelqu'un; (*stay with*) faire un séjour chez quelqu'un.
3 *verb* (*of person*) être de passage.

visiting hours *noun* heures *fpl* de visite.

visitor *noun* visiteur, -euse *m or f*; (*guest*) invité, -ée *m or f*.

vital *adjective* essentiel; **it's v. that** il est essentiel que (+ *subjunctive*).

vitamin *noun* vitamine *f*.

vivid *adjective* vif (*f* vive); (*description*) vivant.

vocabulary *noun* vocabulaire *m*.

vodka *noun* vodka *f*.

voice *noun* voix *f*; **at the top of one's v.** à tue-tête.

volcano *noun* volcan *m*.

volume *noun* (*book, capacity, loudness*) volume *m*.

voluntary *adjective* volontaire; (*unpaid*) bénévole.

volunteer
1 *noun* volontaire *m or f*.
2 *verb* se proposer (**for something** pour quelque chose, **to do**

pour faire).

vomit *verb* vomir.

vote

  1 *noun* vote *m*.

  2 *verb* voter; to v. Labour voter travailliste.

voter *noun* électeur, -trice *m or f*.

voucher *noun* (*for meal, gift etc*) chèque *m*.

vowel *noun* voyelle *f*.

voyage *noun* voyage *m* (par mer).

vulgar *adjective* vulgaire.

W

wad *noun* (*of banknotes etc*) liasse *f*; (*of cotton wool*) tampon *m*.

waddle *verb* se dandiner.

wade through *verb* (*mud, water etc*) patauger dans.

wafer (biscuit) *noun* gaufrette *f*.

wag *verb* (*tail*) remuer.

wage(s) (*plural*) *noun* salaire *m*.

wage earner *noun* salarié, -ée *m or f*.

wag(g)on *noun* (*of train*) wagon *m* (de marchandises).

waist *noun* taille *f*; **stripped to the w.** torse nu.

waistcoat *noun* gilet *m*.

wait
1 *noun* attente *f*.
2 *verb* attendre; **to w. for somebody/something** attendre quelqu'un/quelque chose; **w. until I've gone, w. for me to go** attends que je sois parti; **to keep somebody waiting** faire attendre quelqu'un.

wait behind *verb* rester.

waiter *noun* garçon *m* (de café); **w.!** garçon!

waiting *noun* attente *f*; **'no w.'** (*street sign*) 'arrêt interdit'.

waiting room *noun* salle *f* d'attente.

waitress *noun* serveuse *f*; **w.!** mademoiselle!

wait up *verb* veiller; **to w. up for somebody** attendre le retour de quelqu'un avant de se coucher.

wake (up) *verb*
1 (*of person*) se réveiller.
2 (*person*) réveiller.

Wales *noun* le Pays *m* de Galles.

walk
1 *noun* promenade *f*; (*shorter*) (petit) tour *m*; (*path*) allée *f*; **to go for a w.** faire une promenade; (*shorter*) faire un (petit) tour; **to take for a w.** (*child*) emmener se promener; (*baby, dog*) promener; **five minutes' w. (away)** à cinq minutes à pied.
2 *verb* marcher; (*stroll*) se promener; (*go on foot*) aller à pied.
3 *verb* (*distance*) faire à pied; (*take for a walk*) promener (*chien*).

walk away or **off** *verb* s'éloigner (**from** de).

walker *noun* (*for pleasure*) promeneur, -euse *m or f*.

walk in *verb* entrer.

walking stick *noun* canne *f*.

Walkman ® *noun* baladeur *m*.

walk out *verb* (*leave*) partir.

wall *noun* mur *m*; (*of cabin, tunnel*) paroi *f*.

wallet *noun* portefeuille *m*.

wallpaper
1 *noun* papier *m* peint.
2 *verb* tapisser.

wall-to-wall carpet(ing) *noun* moquette *f*.

walnut *noun* (*nut*) noix *f*.

walrus *noun* (*animal*) morse *m*.

wander (about or **around)** *verb* errer; (*stroll*) flâner.

want *verb* vouloir (**to do** faire); (*need*) avoir besoin de; **I w. him to go** je veux qu'il parte; **you're wanted** on vous demande.

war *noun* guerre *f*; **at w.** en guerre (**with** avec).

ward *noun* (*in hospital*) salle *f.*

warden *noun* (**traffic**) w. contractuel, -elle *m or f.*

wardrobe *noun* (*cupboard*) penderie *f.*

warehouse *noun* entrepôt *m.*

warm
1 *adjective* chaud; **to be** *or* **feel w.** avoir chaud; **it's (nice and) w.** (*of weather*) il fait (agréablement) chaud.
2 *verb* (*person, food etc*) réchauffer.

warmth *noun* chaleur *f.*

warm up *verb*
1 (*person, food etc*) réchauffer.
2 (*of person, room, engine*) se réchauffer; (*of food, water*) chauffer.

warn *verb* avertir (**that** que); **to w. somebody against something** mettre quelqu'un en garde contre quelque chose; **to w. somebody against doing** conseiller à quelqu'un de ne pas faire.

warning *noun* avertissement *m;* (*advance notice*) (pré)avis *m;* (**hazard**) **w. lights** (*of vehicle*) feux *mpl* de détresse.

warship *noun* navire *m* de guerre.

wart *noun* verrue *f.*

was *see* be.

wash
1 *noun* **to have a w.** se laver; **to give something a w.** laver quelque chose.
2 *verb* laver; **to w. one's hands** se laver les mains.
3 *verb* (*have a wash*) se laver.

washable *adjective* lavable.

wash off *or* **out** *verb*
1 (*stain*) faire partir (en lavant).
2 (*of stain*) partir (au lavage).

washbasin *noun* lavabo *m.*

washing *noun* (*act*) lavage *m;* (*clothes*) lessive *f;* **to do the w.** faire la lessive.

washing machine *noun* machine *f* à laver.

washing powder *noun* lessive *f.*

washing-up *noun* vaisselle *f;* **to do the w.** faire la vaisselle; **w. liquid** produit *m* pour la vaisselle.

wash out *verb* (*bowl etc*) laver.

wash up *verb* (*do the dishes*) faire la vaisselle.

wasp *noun* guêpe *f.*

waste
1 *noun* gaspillage *m;* (*of time*) perte *f;* (*rubbish*) déchets *mpl.*
2 *verb* (*money, food etc*) gaspiller; (*time*) perdre; (*opportunity*) gâcher.

wastebin *noun* (*in kitchen*) poubelle *f.*

waste ground *noun* (*in town*) terrain *m* vague.

waste paper *noun* vieux papiers *mpl.*

wastepaper basket *noun* corbeille *f* (à papier).

watch
1 *noun* (*small clock*) montre *f.*
2 *verb* regarder; (*be careful of*) faire attention à.

watch (out) for *verb* (*wait for*) guetter.

watch (over) *verb* (*suspect, baby etc*) surveiller.

watch out *verb* (*take care*) faire attention (**for** à); **w. out!** attention!

watchstrap *noun* bracelet *m* de montre.

water
1 *noun* eau *f;* **w. pistol** pistolet *m*

à eau.
2 *verb* (*plant etc*) arroser.

watercolour *noun* (*picture*)
aquarelle *f*; (*paint*) couleur *f* pour
aquarelle.

watercress *noun* cresson *m* (de
fontaine).

water down *verb* (*wine etc*)
couper (d'eau).

waterfall *noun* chute *f* d'eau.

watering can *noun* arrosoir *m*.

watermelon *noun* pastèque *f*.

waterproof *adjective* (*material*)
imperméable.

water skiing *noun* ski *m*
nautique.

watertight *adjective* étanche.

wave
1 *noun* (*of sea*) vague *f*; (*in hair*)
ondulation *f*; **medium/short w.**
(*on radio*) ondes *fpl* moyennes/
courtes; **long w.** grandes ondes.
2 *verb* (*with hand*) faire signe (de
la main); **to w. to somebody**
(*greet*) saluer quelqu'un de la
main.
3 *verb* (*arm, flag etc*) agiter.

wavelength *noun* longueur *f*
d'ondes.

wavy *adjective* (*hair*) ondulé.

wax
1 *noun* cire *f*.
2 *verb* cirer.

way¹
1 *noun* (*path*) chemin *m* (**to** de);
(*direction*) sens *m*; (*distance*) distance *f*; **all the w., the whole w.**
(*to talk etc*) pendant tout le chemin; **this w.** par ici; **that way**
par là; **which w.?** par où?; **to lose
one's w.** se perdre; **the w. there**
l'aller *m*; **the w. back** le retour;
the w. in l'entrée *f*; **the w. out** la
sortie; **on the w.** en route (**to**
pour); **to be** *or* **stand in some-**

body's w. être sur le chemin de
quelqu'un; **to get out of the w.**
s'écarter; **a long w. (away** *or*
off) très loin.
2 *adverb* (*behind etc*) très loin; **w.
ahead** très en avance (**of** sur).

way² *noun* (*manner*) façon *f*;
(*means*) moyen *m*; **(in) this w.** de
cette façon; **no w.!** *Familiar* pas
question!

WC *noun* w-c *mpl*.

we *pronoun* nous; **we teachers**
nous autres professeurs.

weak *adjective* faible; (*tea, coffee*)
léger.

weaken *verb*
1 (*resistance, determination etc*)
affaiblir.
2 (*of strength, influence etc*)
faiblir.

weakness *noun* faiblesse *f*;
(*fault*) point *m* faible.

wealth *noun* richesse(s) *f(pl)*.

wealthy *adjective* riche.

weapon *noun* arme *f*.

wear
1 *verb* (*have on body*) porter;
(*put on*) mettre.
2 *noun* **w. (and tear)** usure *f*.

wear off *verb* (*of colour, pain
etc*) disparaître.

wear out *verb*
1 (*clothes etc*) user; (*person*)
épuiser.
2 (*of clothes etc*) s'user.

weary *adjective* fatigué.

weasel *noun* belette *f*.

weather *noun* temps *m*; **what's
the w. like?** quel temps fait-il?;
it's nice w. il fait beau; **under
the w.** (*ill*) patraque.

weather forecast *or* **report**
noun météo *f*.

weave *verb* (*cloth*) tisser.

web *noun* (*of spider*) toile *f*.

wedding *noun* mariage *m*.

wedding ring *noun* alliance *f*.

wedge
1 *noun* (*under wheel etc*) cale *f*.
2 *verb* (*table etc*) caler.

Wednesday *noun* mercredi *m*.

weed *noun* mauvaise herbe *f*.

week *noun* semaine *f*; a w. from tomorrow, tomorrow w. demain en huit.

weekday *noun* jour *m* de semaine.

weekend *noun* week-end *m*; at *or* on *or* over the w. ce weekend.

weekly
1 *adjective* hebdomadaire.
2 *adverb* toutes les semaines.
3 *noun* (*magazine*) hebdomadaire *m*.

weep *verb* pleurer.

weigh *verb* peser.

weight *noun* poids *m*; by w. au poids; to put on w. grossir; to lose w. maigrir.

weird *adjective* (*odd*) bizarre.

welcome
1 *adjective* to be w. (*warmly received, of person*) être bien reçu; w.! bienvenue!; to make somebody (feel) w. faire bon accueil à quelqu'un; you're w.! (*after 'thank you'*) il n'y a pas de quoi!; a coffee/a break would be w. un café/une pause ne ferait pas de mal.
2 *noun* accueil *m*.
3 *verb* accueillir; (*warmly*) faire bon accueil à; I w. you! (*I say welcome to you*) je vous souhaite la bienvenue!

weld *verb* souder.

welfare *noun* to be on w. vivre des allocations.

well [1] *noun* (*for water*) puits *m*; (oil) w. puits *m* de pétrole.

well [2]
1 *adverb* bien; w. done! bravo!; as w. (*also*) aussi; as w. as aussi bien que; as w. as two cats, he has … en plus de deux chats, il a …
2 *adjective* bien *invariable*; she's w. (*healthy*) elle va bien; to get w. se remettre.
3 *interjection* eh bien!; huge, w., quite big énorme, enfin, assez grand.

well-behaved *adjective* sage.

well-informed *adjective* bien informé.

wellington (boot) *noun* botte *f* en caoutchouc.

well-known *adjective* (bien) connu.

well-mannered *adjective* bien élevé.

well-off *adjective* riche.

Welsh
1 *adjective* gallois; the W. les Gallois *mpl*.
2 *noun* (*language*) gallois *m*.

Welshman *noun* Gallois *m*.

Welshwoman *noun* Galloise *f*.

went *see* go [1].

wept *see* weep.

were *see* be.

west
1 *noun* ouest *m*; (to the) w. of à l'ouest de.
2 *adjective* (*coast*) ouest *invariable*; the W. Indies les Antilles *fpl*; W. Indian antillais, -aise.
3 *adverb* à l'ouest.

westbound *adjective* en direction de l'ouest.

western
  1 *adjective* (*coast*) ouest *invariable*; (*culture etc*) occidental.
  2 *noun* (*film*) western *m*.

westward(s) *adverb* vers l'ouest.

wet
  1 *adjective* mouillé; (*damp*, *rainy*) humide; (*day*, *month*) de pluie; '**w. paint**' 'peinture fraîche'; **to get w.** se mouiller; **to make w.** mouiller; **it's w.** (*raining*) il pleut.
  2 *verb* mouiller.

whale *noun* baleine *f*.

wharf *noun* quai *m*, débarcadère *m*.

what
  1 *adjective* quel, quelle, *plural* quel(le)s; **w. book?** quel livre?; **w. a fool!** quel idiot!
  2 *pronoun* (*in questions*) qu'est-ce qui; (*object*) (qu'est-ce) que; (*after preposition*) quoi; **w.'s happening?** qu'est-ce qui se passe?; **w. does he do?** qu'est-ce qu'il fait?, que fait-il?; **w. is it?** qu'est-ce que c'est?; **w.'s that book?** c'est quoi, ce livre?; **w.!** (*surprise*) quoi!; **w.'s it called?** comment ça s'appelle?; **w. for?** (*for what purpose?*) pour quoi faire?; (*why?*) pourquoi?; **w. about me?** et moi?; **w. about leaving?** si on partait?
  3 *pronoun* (*indirect*, *relative*) ce qui; (*object*) ce que; **I know w. will happen/w. she'll do** je sais ce qui arrivera/ce qu'elle fera; **w. I need** ce dont j'ai besoin.

whatever
  1 *adjective* **w. (the) mistake/***etc* quelle que soit l'erreur/*etc*; **no chance w.** pas la moindre chance; **nothing w.** rien du tout.
  2 *pronoun* (*no matter what*) quoi que (+ *subjunctive*); **w. you do**

quoi que tu fasses; **w. is important** tout ce qui est important; **do w. you want** fais tout ce que tu veux.

wheat *noun* blé *m*.

wheel
  1 *noun* roue *f*; **at the w.** (*driving*) au volant.
  2 *verb* pousser.

wheelbarrow *noun* brouette *f*.

wheelchair *noun* fauteuil *m* roulant.

when
  1 *adverb* quand.
  2 *conjunction* quand; **w. I finish, w. I've finished** quand j'aurai fini; **w. I saw him** *or* **w. I'd seen him, I left** après l'avoir vu, je suis parti; **the day/moment w.** le jour/moment où.

whenever *conjunction* quand; (*each time that*) chaque fois que.

where
  1 *adverb* où; **w. are you from?** d'où êtes-vous?
  2 *conjunction* (là) où; **I found it w. she'd left it** je l'ai trouvé là où elle l'avait laissé; **the place/house w.** l'endroit/la maison où.

whereabouts
  1 *adverb* où (donc).
  2 *noun* **his w.** l'endroit *m* où il est.

whereas *conjunction* alors que.

wherever *conjunction* **w. you go** partout où tu iras; **I'll go w. you like** j'irai (là) où vous voudrez.

whether *conjunction* si; **I don't know w. to leave** je ne sais pas si je dois partir; **w. she does it or not** qu'elle le fasse ou non.

which
  1 *adjective* (*in questions etc*) quel, quelle, *plural* quel(le)s; **w. hat?**

quel chapeau?; **in w. case** auquel
cas.

2 *relative pronoun* (*subject*) qui;
(*object*) que; (*after preposition*)
lequel, laquelle, *plural* lesquel(le)s; (*after clause*) ce qui; ce
que; **the house w. is old** la maison qui est vieille; **the book w. I
like** le livre que j'aime; **the table
which I put it on** la table sur laquelle je l'ai mis; **the film of w.**
le film dont; **she's ill, w. is sad**
elle est malade, ce qui est triste;
he lies, w. I don't like il ment,
ce que je n'aime pas.

3 *pronoun* **w. (one)** (*in questions*)
lequel, laquelle, *plural* lesquel(le)s; **w. (one) of us?** lequel
or laquelle d'entre nous *or* de
nous?

■ **w. (one)** (*the one that*) celui
qui, celle qui, *plural* ceux qui,
celles qui; (*object*) celui *etc* que; **I
know w. (ones) you want** je sais
ceux *or* celles que vous désirez.

whichever *adjective & pronoun*
w. book/*etc* **or w. of the books**/
etc **you buy** quel que soit le
livre/*etc* que tu achètes; **take w.
books interest you** prenez les
livres qui vous intéressent; **take
w. (one) you like** prends celui *or*
celle que tu veux; **w. (ones) remain** ceux *or* celles qui restent.

while
1 *conjunction* (*when*) pendant
que; (*although*) bien que (+ *subjunctive*); (*as long as*) tant que;
(*whereas*) tandis que; **while
eating**/*etc* en mangeant/*etc*.
2 *noun* **a w.** un moment; **all the
w.** tout le temps.

whim *noun* caprice *m*.

whine *verb* gémir.

whip
1 *noun* fouet *m*.

2 *verb* fouetter.

whirl (round) *verb* tourbillon-
ner.

whisk
1 *noun* (*for eggs etc*) fouet *m*.
2 *verb* fouetter.

whiskers *plural noun* (*of cat*)
moustaches *fpl*.

whisky *noun* whisky *m*.

whisper
1 *verb* chuchoter.
2 *noun* chuchotement *m*.

whistle
1 *noun* sifflement *m*; (*object*)
sifflet *m*; **to blow the** *or* **one's
w.** siffler.
2 *verb* siffler.

white
1 *adjective* blanc (*f* blanche); **to
go** *or* **turn w.** blanchir; **w. coffee**
café *m* au lait; **w. man** blanc *m*;
w. woman blanche *f*.
2 *noun* (*colour, of egg*) blanc *m*.

whitewash *verb* (*wall*) badigeonner.

Whitsun *noun* la Pentecôte.

whizz past *verb* passer à toute
vitesse.

who *pronoun* qui; **w. did it?** qui
(est-ce qui) a fait ça?

whoever *pronoun* qui que ce soit
qui; (*object*) qui que ce soit que;
this man, w. he is cet homme,
quel qu'il soit.

whole
1 *adjective* entier; (*intact*) intact;
the w. time tout le temps; **the w.
lot** le tout.
2 *noun* **the w. of the village**/*etc*
tout le village/*etc*; **on the w.**
dans l'ensemble.

wholemeal *adjective* (*bread*)
complet.

wholesale
1 *adjective* (*price*) de gros.

2 *adverb* (*to sell*) au prix de gros; (*in bulk*) en gros.

wholesaler *noun* grossiste *m* or *f*.

whom *pronoun* (*object*) que; (*in questions and after preposition*) qui; **of w.** dont.

whooping cough *noun* coqueluche *f*.

whose *possessive pronoun & adjective* à qui, de qui; **w. book is this?** à qui est ce livre?; **w. daughter are you?** de qui es-tu la fille?; **the woman w. book I have** la femme de qui j'ai le livre.

why
1 *adverb* pourquoi; **w. not?** pourquoi pas?
2 *conjunction* **the reason w. they …** la raison pour laquelle ils …

wick *noun* mèche *f* (*de bougie*).

wicked *adjective* (*evil*) méchant; (*mischievous*) malicieux.

wicker
1 *noun* osier *m*.
2 *adjective* (*basket etc*) en osier.

wide
1 *adjective* large; (*choice, variety*) grand; **to be three metres w.** avoir trois mètres de large.
2 *adverb* (*to open*) tout grand.

wide-awake *adjective* éveillé.

widely *adverb* (*to travel*) beaucoup.

widen *verb*
1 (*road, gap etc*) élargir.
2 (*of road, gap etc*) s'élargir.

widespread *adjective* (*très*) répandu.

widow *noun* veuve *f*.

widower *noun* veuf *m*.

width *noun* largeur *f*.

wife *noun* femme *f*.

wig *noun* perruque *f*.

wild *adjective* (*animal, flower etc*) sauvage.

wilderness *noun* région *f* sauvage.

will [1] *auxiliary verb* **he will come, he'll come** (*future tense*) il viendra; **you will not come, you won't come** tu ne viendras pas; **w. you have tea?** veux-tu prendre un thé?; **w. you be quiet!** veux-tu te taire!

will [2] *noun* volonté *f*; (*legal document*) testament *m*; **ill w.** mauvaise volonté *f*; **against one's w.** à contrecœur.

willing *adjective* (*helper, worker*) de bonne volonté; **to be w. to do** vouloir bien faire.

willingly *adverb* (*with pleasure*) volontiers; (*voluntarily*) volontairement.

willingness *noun* bonne volonté *f*; **his** or **her w. to do** son empressement *m* à faire.

willow *noun* saule *m*.

win
1 *noun* victoire *f*.
2 *verb* gagner.

wind [1] *noun* vent *m*; **to have w.** (*in stomach*) avoir des gaz.

wind [2] *verb*
1 (*roll*) enrouler (**round** autour de).
2 (*of river, road*) serpenter.

wind (up) *verb* (*clock*) remonter.

windcheater *noun* blouson *m*.

windmill *noun* moulin *m* à vent.

window *noun* fenêtre *f*; (*pane & in vehicle or train*) vitre *f*; (*in shop*) vitrine *f*; (*counter*) guichet *m*; **to go w. shopping** faire du lèche-vitrines.

window box noun jardinière f.

windowpane noun vitre f.

windowsill noun (*inside*) appui m de (la) fenêtre; (*outside*) rebord m de (la) fenêtre.

windscreen noun pare-brise *invariable* m; **w. wiper** essuie-glace m.

windsurfing noun **to go w.** faire de la planche (à voile).

windy adjective **it's w.** (*of weather*) il y a du vent.

wine noun vin m; **w. bottle** bouteille f à vin; **w. list** carte f des vins.

wineglass noun verre m à vin.

wing noun aile f.

wink

1 verb faire un clin d'œil (**at, to** à).

2 noun clin m d'œil.

winner noun gagnant, -ante m or f; (*of argument, fight*) vainqueur m.

winning

1 adjective (*number, horse etc*) gagnant; (*team*) victorieux.

2 noun **winnings** gains mpl.

winter

1 noun hiver m; **in (the) w.** en hiver.

2 adjective d'hiver.

wintertime noun hiver m.

wipe verb essuyer; **to w. one's feet/hands** s'essuyer les pieds/ les mains.

wipe away or **off** or **up** verb (*liquid*) essuyer.

wipe out verb (*clean*) essuyer.

wiper noun (*in vehicle*) essuie-glace m.

wipe up verb (*dry the dishes*) essuyer la vaisselle.

wire noun fil m.

wire mesh or **netting** noun grillage m.

wiring noun (*electrical*) installation f électrique.

wise adjective (*in knowledge*) sage; (*advisable*) prudent.

wish

1 verb souhaiter, vouloir (**to do** faire); **I w. (that) you could help me/could have helped me** je voudrais que/j'aurais voulu que vous m'aidiez; **I w. I hadn't done that** je regrette d'avoir fait ça; **if you w.** si tu veux; **I w. you a happy birthday** je vous souhaite un bon anniversaire; **I w. I could** si seulement je pouvais.

2 verb **to w. for something** souhaiter quelque chose.

3 noun (*specific*) souhait m; (*general*) désir m; **best wishes** (*on greeting card*) meilleurs vœux mpl; (*in letter*) amitiés fpl; **send him** or **her my best wishes** fais-lui mes amitiés.

witch noun sorcière f.

with preposition avec; **come w. me** viens avec moi; **w. no hat/** *etc* sans chapeau/*etc*.

▪ (*at the house etc of*) chez; **she's staying w. me** elle loge chez moi.

▪ (*cause*) de; **to jump w. joy** sauter de joie.

▪ (*instrument, means*) avec, de; **to write w. a pen** écrire avec un stylo; **to fill w.** remplir de.

▪ (*description*) à; **w. blue eyes** aux yeux bleus.

withdraw verb

1 (*money, support etc*) retirer (**from** de).

2 (*of person*) se retirer (**from** de).

wither verb (*of plant etc*) se flétrir.

within preposition (*place, box*

etc) à l'intérieur de; **w. 10 km (of)** (*less than*) à moins de 10 km (de); (*inside an area of*) dans un rayon de 10 km (de); **w. a month** (*to return etc*) avant un mois; (*to finish*) en moins d'un mois.

without *preposition* sans; **w. a tie**/*etc* sans cravate/*etc*; **w. doing** sans faire.

witness
1 *noun* (*person*) témoin *m*.
2 *verb* (*accident etc*) être (le) témoin de.

wobbly *adjective* (*table, tooth*) branlant.

woke , woken *see* **wake (up)**.

wolf *noun* loup *m*.

woman *noun* femme *f*; **w. doctor** femme *f* médecin; **w. teacher** professeur *m* femme; **women's** (*clothes etc*) féminin.

won *see* **win**.

wonder
1 *noun* (**it's**) **no w.** ce n'est pas étonnant (**that** que (+ *subjunctive*)).
2 *verb* se demander (**if** si, **why** pourquoi).
3 *verb* (*think*) réfléchir; **I was just wondering** je réfléchissais.

wonderful *adjective* merveilleux.

won't = **will not**.

wood *noun* (*material, forest*) bois *m*.

wooden *adjective* de *or* en bois.

woodwork *noun* (*school subject*) menuiserie *f*.

wool *noun* laine *f*.

woollen
1 *adjective* en laine.
2 *noun* **woollens** lainages *mpl*.

word *noun* mot *m*; (*promise*) parole *f*; **words** (*of song etc*)

paroles *fpl*; **to have a w. with somebody** parler à quelqu'un; **in other words** autrement dit.

wording *noun* termes *mpl*.

word processing *noun* traitement *m* de texte.

word processor *noun* machine *f* de traitement de texte.

wore *see* **wear**.

work
1 *noun* travail *m*; (*product, book etc*) œuvre *f*; (*building or repair work*) travaux *mpl*; **out of w.** au chômage; **a day off w.** un jour de congé; **he's off w.** il n'est pas allé travailler; **the works** (*of clock etc*) le mécanisme; **gas works** usine *f* à gaz.
2 *verb* travailler; (*of machine etc*) marcher; (*of drug*) agir.
3 *verb* (*machine*) faire marcher; **to get worked up** s'exciter.

work at *or* **on** *verb* (*improve*) travailler à *or* sur.

workbench *noun* établi *m*.

worker *noun* travailleur, -euse *m or f*; (*manual*) ouvrier, -ière *m or f*; (**office**) **w.** employé, -ée *m or f* (de bureau).

working *adjective* **w. class** classe *f* ouvrière; **in w. order** en état de marche.

workman *noun* ouvrier *m*.

work out *verb*
1 (*succeed*) marcher; (*do exercise*) s'entraîner; **it works out at 50 francs** ça fait 50 francs.
2 (*calculate*) calculer; (*problem*) résoudre; (*scheme*) préparer; (*understand*) comprendre.

workout *noun* séance *f* d'entraînement.

workshop *noun* atelier *m*.

world
1 *noun* monde *m*; **all over the w.**

dans le monde entier.
2 *adjective* (*war etc*) mondial; (*champion*, *cup*, *record*) du monde.

worm *noun* ver *m*.

worn *adjective* (*clothes etc*) usé.

worn-out *adjective* (*object*) complètement usé; (*person*) épuisé.

worry
1 *noun* souci *m*.
2 *verb* s'inquiéter (**about something** de quelque chose, **about somebody** pour quelqu'un).
3 *verb* (*person*) inquiéter; **to be worried** être inquiet (*f* inquiète).

worrying *adjective* inquiétant.

worse
1 *adjective* pire, plus mauvais (**than** que); **to get w.** se détériorer; **he's getting w.** (*in health*) il va de plus en plus mal.
2 *adverb* plus mal (**than** que); **to be w. off** s'en sortir moins bien (financièrement).

worsen *verb* empirer.

worship *verb* (*person*, *god*) adorer.

worst
1 *adjective* pire, plus mauvais.
2 *adverb* (**the**) **w.** le plus mal.
3 *noun* **the w.** (**one**) le *or* la pire, le *or* la plus mauvais(e); **at w.** au pire.

worth
1 *noun* valeur *f*; **to buy 50 pence w. of chocolates** acheter pour cinquante pence de chocolats.
2 *adjective* **to be w. something** valoir quelque chose; **how much** *or* **what is it w.?** ça vaut combien?; **the film's w. seeing** le film vaut la peine d'être vu; **it's w. (one's) while** ça (en) vaut la peine; **it's w. (while) waiting** ça vaut la peine d'attendre.

worthy *adjective* **w. of something/somebody** digne de quelque chose/quelqu'un.

would *auxiliary verb* **I w. stay, I'd stay** (*conditional tense*) je resterais; **he w. have done it** il l'aurait fait; **w. you help me, please?** voulez-vous m'aider, s'il vous plaît?; **w. you like some tea?** voulez-vous du thé?; **I w. see her every day** (*in the past*) je la voyais chaque jour.

wound
1 *verb* blesser; **the wounded** les blessés *mpl*.
2 *noun* blessure *f*.

wove, woven *see* weave.

wrap (up) *verb*
1 (*child etc*) envelopper; (*parcel*) emballer.
2 **to w. (oneself) up** (*dress warmly*) se couvrir.

wrapper *noun* (*of sweet*) papier *m*.

wrapping *noun* (*action*, *material*) emballage *m*; **w. paper** papier *m* d'emballage.

wreath *noun* couronne *f*.

wreck
1 *noun* (*ship*) épave *f*; (*sinking*) naufrage *m*; (*train etc*) train *m etc* accidenté.
2 *verb* détruire.

wrench *noun* (*tool*) clef *f*.

wrestle *verb* lutter (**with somebody** avec quelqu'un).

wrestler *noun* lutteur, -euse *m or f*; catcheur, -euse *m or f*.

wrestling *noun* (*sport*) lutte *f*; (**all-in**) **w.** catch *m*.

wring (out) *verb* (*clothes by hand*) tordre.

wrinkle *noun* (*on skin*) ride *f*.

wrist *noun* poignet *m*.

wristwatch *noun* montre *f*.

write *verb* écrire.

write away *or* **off** *or* **up for** *verb* (*details etc*) écrire pour demander.

write back *verb* répondre.

write down *verb* to w. something down noter quelque chose.

write out *verb* to w. something out écrire quelque chose; (*copy*) recopier quelque chose.

writer *noun* auteur *m* (of de); (*literary*) écrivain *m*.

writing *noun* (*handwriting*) écriture *f*; to put something (down) in w. mettre quelque chose par écrit; some w. (*on page*) quelque chose d'écrit.

writing desk *noun* secrétaire *m*.

writing pad *noun* bloc *m* de papier à lettres; (*for notes*) bloc-notes *m*.

writing paper *noun* papier *m* à lettres.

wrong

1 *adjective* (*sum*, *idea etc*) faux (*f* fausse); (*direction*, *time etc*) mauvais; (*unfair*) injuste; to be w. (*of person*) avoir tort (to do de faire); (*mistaken*) se tromper; it's w. to swear/*etc* c'est mal de jurer/*etc*; the clock's w. la pendule n'est pas à l'heure; something's w. quelque chose ne va pas; something's w. with the phone le téléphone ne marche pas bien; something's w. with her arm elle a quelque chose au bras; what's w. with you? qu'est-ce que tu as?; the w. way round *or* up à l'envers.

2 *adverb* mal; to go w. (*of plan*) mal tourner; (*of machine*) tomber en panne.

3 *noun* to be in the w. être dans son tort.

wrongly *adverb* (*incorrectly*) mal.

wrote *see* write.

X

xenophobia *noun* xénophobie *f*.
xenophobic *adjective*
   xénophobe.
Xmas *noun Familiar* Noël *m*.
X-ray
   1 *noun* (*photo*) radio(graphie) *f*;

(*beam*) rayon *m* X; **to have an
X-ray** passer une radio.
   2 *verb* radiographier.

xylophone *noun* xylophone *m*.

Y

yacht *noun* yacht *m*.

yard *noun* (*of farm, school etc*) cour *f*; (*for storage*) dépôt *m*; (*measure*) yard *m* (= *91,44 cm*).

yarn *noun* (*thread*) fil *m*.

yawn
  1 *verb* bâiller.
  2 *noun* bâillement *m*.

year *noun* an *m*, année *f*; **school/tax y.** année *f* scolaire/fiscale; **this y.** cette année; **in the y. 2020** en (l'an) 2020; **he's ten years old** il a dix ans; **New Y.** Nouvel An; **New Year's Day** le jour de l'An; **New Year's Eve** la Saint-Sylvestre.

yearly *adjective* annuel.

yeast *noun* levure *f*.

yell *noun* hurlement *m*.

yell (out) *verb* hurler.

yell at *verb* **to y. at somebody** (*scold*) crier après quelqu'un.

yellow *adjective & noun* (*colour*) jaune (*m*).

yes *adverb* oui; (*contradicting negative question*) si.

yesterday *adverb* hier; **y. morning** hier matin; **the day before y.** avant-hier.

yet
  1 *adverb* encore; (*already*) déjà; **she hasn't come (as) y.** elle n'est pas encore venue; **is he here y.?** il est arrivé?; **y. again** encore une fois; **y. another mistake** encore une erreur.
  2 *conjunction* (*nevertheless*) pourtant.

YMCA *abbreviation* (*Young Men's Christian Association*) = association chrétienne proposant hébergement et activités sportives.

yog(h)urt *noun* yaourt *m*.

yolk *noun* jaune *m* (d'œuf).

you *pronoun* (*polite form singular*) vous; (*familiar form singular*) tu; (*polite and familar form plural*) vous; (*object*) vous; te, t'; *plural* vous; (*after preposition, 'than', 'it is'*) vous; toi; *plural* vous; **(to) y.** vous; te, t'; *plural* vous; **y. are** vous êtes; tu es; **I see y.** je vous vois; je te vois; **y. teachers** vous autres professeurs; **y. idiot!** espèce d'imbécile!
  ▪ (*indefinite*) on; (*object*) vous; te, t'; *plural* vous; **y. never know** on ne sait jamais.

young
  1 *adjective* jeune; **my young(er) brother** mon (frère) cadet; **his** *or* **her youngest brother** le cadet de ses frères; **the youngest** son le cadet.
  2 *noun* (*of animals*) petits *mpl*; **the y.** (*people*) les jeunes *mpl*.

youngster *noun* jeune *m or f*.

your *possessive adjective* (*polite form singular, polite and familiar form plural*) votre, *plural* vos; (*familiar form singular*) ton, ta, *plural* tes; (*one's*) son, sa, *plural* ses.

yours *possessive pronoun* le vôtre, la vôtre, *plural* les vôtres; (*familiar form singular*) le tien, la tienne, *plural* les tien(ne)s; **this book is y.** ce livre est à vous *or* est le vôtre; ce livre est à toi *or* est le tien.

yourself *pronoun* (*polite form*) vous-même; (*familiar form*) toi-même; (*reflexive*) vous; te, t';

(*after preposition*) vous; toi.

yourselves *plural pronoun* vous-mêmes; (*reflexive & after preposition*) vous.

youth *noun* jeunesse *f*; (*young man*) jeune *m*; **y. club** maison *f* des jeunes.

Yugoslavia *noun* la Yougoslavie *f*; **the former Y.** l'ex-Yougoslavie.

YWCA *abbreviation* (*Young Women's Christian Association*) = association chrétienne proposant hébergement et activités sportives.

Z

zebra *noun* zèbre *m*.
zebra crossing *noun* passage *m* pour piétons.
zero *noun* zéro *m*.
zigzag
1 *noun* zigzag *m*.
2 *adjective* en zigzag.
3 *verb* zigzaguer.

zip (fastener) *noun* fermeture *f* éclair ®.
zip (up) *verb* fermer (avec une fermeture éclair ®).
zit *noun* (*pimple*) *Familiar* bouton *m*.
zone *noun* zone *f*.
zoo *noun* zoo *m*.